Hitler's War in the East, 1941–1945

A Critical Assessment

Rolf-Dieter Müller *and* Gerd R. Ueberschär

Translation of texts by
Bruce D. Little

A publication of the Bibliothek für Zeitgeschichte /
Library of Contemporary History, Stuttgart

Berghahn Books
Providence • Oxford

First published in 1997 by

Berghahn Books

Editorial offices:
165 Taber Avenue, Providence, RI 02906, USA
3, NewTec Place, Magdalen Road, Oxford, OX4 1RE, UK

Library of Congress Cataloging-in-Publication Data

Müller, Rolf-Dieter, 1948-
Hitler's war in the East, 1941-1945 : a critical assessment / Rolf-Dieter Müller and Gerd R. Ueberschär.
p. cm. -- (Library of contemporary history ; vol. 1)
Includes bibliographical references.
ISBN 1-57181-068-4 (alk. paper)
1. World War, 1939-1945--Campaigns--Eastern Front. 2. World War, 1939-1945--Germany. 3. World War, 1939-1945--Soviet Union. I. Ueberschär, Gerd R. II. Title. III. Series.
D764.M825 1997
940.54'21--dc20 96-44941
CIP

British Library Cataloguing in Publication Data

A catalogue record for this book is available from the British Library.

Printed in the United States on acid-free paper.

Contents

Foreword vi

Preface viii

Part A: Policy and Strategy (Rolf-Dieter Müller)

Introduction 1

Bibliography 42

1. General *42*
   a. Overview
   b. Sources
2. History of Soviet-German Relations, 1933–1939 *46*
3. The Conclusion of the Nazi-Soviet Pact *48*
4. Hitler's Program and Decision to Attack the Soviet Union, 1940–1941 *53*
5. War Policy and Strategy, 1941–1942 *55*
6. Allies and Neutrals *56*
   a. Hitler's Alliance Policy
   b. Finland
   c. Hungary
   d. Rumania
   e. Italy
   f. Japan
   g. Sweden
   h. Bulgaria
   i. Turkey
   j. Volunteer Units
7. The Search for Peace, 1942–1945 *64*
   a. Soviet-German Peace Feelers
   b. The National Committee for Free Germany and the League of German Officers
   c. The Anti-Hitler Coalition
8. The End of the Eastern Empire *69*

Part B: The Military Campaign (Gerd R. Ueberschär)

Introduction 73
Bibliography 144
1. General: 1941–1945 *144*
a. Bibliographies, Literature, and Research Reports
b. Overviews
c. Biographies
d. Sources and Contemporary Literature
e. Personal Accounts and Memoirs
2. Planning, Preparations, and Armaments for Operation Barbarossa *157*
3. The Attack and Campaign of 1941 *162*
4. The Turning Point before the Gates of Moscow as a Result of the Winter Offensive, 1941–1942 *167*
5. The War on the Northern Front, 1941–1944: Leningrad, Volkhov, and the Polar Sea Front *169*
6. The Wehrmacht Regains the Initiative: the Summer Offensive of 1942 (Sebastopol, Crimea) *173*
7. The Battles of Stalingrad and the Caucasus, 1941–1943 *174*
8. From the Don to Operation Citadel: the Battles of Charkhov and Kursk, 1943 *180*
9. The Collapse of the Eastern Front in 1944 (Operation Bagration): White Russia, the Crimea, and the Southern Front *182*
10. The Soviet Breakthrough to the Balkans and East Prussia *183*
11. The Struggle for the Vistula and Oder and in Bohemia, Moravia, Poland, Pomerania, and Silesia *186*
12. The Air War in the Eastern Theater *188*
13. The Naval War in the Eastern Theater *190*
14. The Military Use of Helper Forces and Allies by the Wehrmacht and the Red Army *193*
15. Logistics, Weapons, Intelligence, Railways, and Communications *196*
16. Daily Life of Civilians and Soldiers in the War (Home Front) *198*
17. The Struggle in Courland and on the Baltic Coast, 1945 *198*
18. The Red Army Conquers Berlin and the Fighting Ends *199*

Part C: The Ideologically Motivated War of Annihilation in the East (Gerd R. Ueberschär)

Introduction 209
Bibliography 253
1. General, Overviews, and Sources *253*
2. The Indoctrination of the Wehrmacht and Its Participation in the War of Annihilation *255*
3. The "Criminal Orders" Issued to German Forces *256*
4. The Treatment and Fate of Soviet Prisoners of War *257*
5. The Genocide of the Jews in the East *260*
6. Propaganda and Reporting for the War of Annihilation in the East *277*
7. Propaganda about Communist Class Warfare, German Prisoners of War in the USSR, and Soviet War Crimes until 1945 *277*

Part D: The Occupation (Rolf-Dieter Müller)

Introduction 283
Bibliography 315
1. General *315*
a. Bibliographies
b. Overviews
c. Sources
2. War Aims *318*
3. Military Administration *320*
4. Civilian Administration *320*
5. Individual Regions *322*
a. Reichskommissariat Ostland
b. Reichskommissariat Ukraine
c. Other Areas and Regions
6. Partisan War, Resistance, and Suppression *326*
a. General Overviews
b. Baltic States
c. Northern Russia
d. White Russia
e. Central Russia
f. Southern Russia
g. Ukraine
h. Other Areas and Regions
7. The Recruitment of "Hilfswillige" and Eastern Legions *333*
8. Economic Exploitation *334*
9. The Recruitment of "Ostarbeiter" and Their Fate *340*

Part E: The Results of the War and Coming to Terms with Them

1. The Results of the War (Rolf-Dieter Müller) 345
2. Avoiding and Coming to Terms with the Past (Gerd R. Ueberschär) 367
Bibliography: 1. The Results of the War *375*
a. Soviet Policy toward Germany and the Occupation
b. The Expulsion of the East German Population
c. The Fate and Eventual Return Home of German Prisoners of War after the End of the War
d. Reparations and Spoils of War
Bibliography: 2. Avoiding and Coming to Terms with the Past *386*
a. Eyewitness Accounts, Letters, and Documentary Stories
b. Works on Tactical Military Experience of the Soviet-German War
c. Literary Accounts of the War in Poetry and Novels
d. Coming to Terms with the Past: Apologias, Reception of Research Results, Struggles over Tradition, and the German "Historikerstreit"
Conclusion: From Historical Memories to "Bridges of Understanding" and Reconciliation (Gerd R. Ueberschär) *401*
Bibliography *404*

Foreword

The major theater of war in the Second World War was the titanic struggle on the Eastern Front between the forces of Germany and its satellites on the one hand and those of the Soviet Union on the other. It was in this struggle that the Axis powers suffered the overwhelming majority of their casualties in the conflict; it was in this fight of unprecedented ferocity that over twenty-five million Soviet citizens lost their lives. The success of the Soviet Union in this confrontation provided the regime of Josef Stalin and the Communist party with its only period of legitimacy in the eyes of the bulk of the population inside the country. It simultaneously gave the Soviet system the opportunity to add a new colonial empire in eastern and southeastern Europe to the empire its Romanov predecessors had created in prior centuries and also assured it of great power status in the postwar world. Conversely, the crushing of the German and satellite military by the Soviets contributed mightily to the victory of the Allies in the war as a whole.

Despite the centrality of the Eastern Front to the history of the Second World War, it has been extremely difficult for both specialists and other interested readers to inform themselves about this portion of the great upheaval. This has been due to much more than the language problem. Almost all of the Soviet literature on the Eastern Front was subject to ideological direction and distortion. The archives were closed not only to foreigners but, for the most part, to Soviet scholars as well. And when limited access was granted to specially approved individuals, the results still had to fit into predetermined contours.

Most of the German archives were likewise closed to private scholars until well into the 1950s, and many remained closed for years thereafter. Furthermore, those that fell into the hands of the Red Army were also not made freely accessible. And as research in the records that did become accessible in the Western world quickly showed, the vast memoir literature emanating from German military figures was often not only tendentious but in some cases essentially misleading.

With first the loosening of restrictions in Eastern Europe and then the collapse of the Soviet Union, a new era began both in openness of discussion and in access to sources. This has begun to change the confused picture, but there are still great problems. It is not only that the financial and technical problems of the archives in Eastern Europe and the former Soviet Union are excruciatingly complex and therefore impose great difficulties for scholars but that recent trends in archival access in the Russian Federation have been retrograde rather than forward looking. Much important material has been made available and many significant documents and studies have been published in the last decade, but the whole field remains an exceedingly troubled one.

It is in view of this situation that scholars and general readers will be pleased to see a book devoted to a survey of the literature on the Eastern Front. The authors have made a major effort to bring together information on this literature. By stressing ideological and political as well as more specifically military aspects, they have provided a broad coverage of the conflict, its antecedents, its course and implications, and its aftermath. What I have found stimulating in this work is that the authors are not satisfied to list works in alphabetical or chronological order but have instead created an analytical survey in which the trends over time and the differing perspectives resulting from new sources or international developments are set forth in a manner some may find opinionated but all will find challenging. No one is required to agree with all the judgments advanced – anymore than I do – but the well-informed comments offered will be a helpful starting point for everyone interested in the front where most of the Second World War was actually fought.

It is especially to be welcomed that such a work should appear in English. There has been a tendency in the English-speaking world, particularly obvious in recent commemorations of the invasion of Normandy in 1944 and victory in Europe in 1945, to focus on the American and British participation in both events. That the invasion was made possible by the need for Germany to keep the great majority of its forces on the front in the East and that victory was in large measure bought at enormous expense in Soviet lives somehow seemed to escape the attention of much of the public. Similarly, the terrible nature of the war in the East, a product of German plans and intentions, has rarely been grasped by people in the United States or Great Britain. On all such issues, this book may serve to open the eyes of anyone willing to look at the war as a whole.

Gerhard L. Weinberg, Chapel Hill, North Carolina

Preface

Any attempt to stake out the history of one of the most complicated and important theaters of the Second World War in a compact and accessible research summary, and to provide an overview of the literature, necessarily poses a number of problems. We would have liked to include countless aspects and delve into various controversies and differing points of view. Once the decision was made to examine the struggle principally from the viewpoint of the aggressor, that is, to present it as "Hitler's war in the East," the emphasis swung to one of the two main combatants. However, the other certainly could not be ignored. Historians in general have concluded that military history cannot be solely a matter of military operations; it must also deal with the numerous international, domestic, economic, and social facets of war. This means that our study could not focus all too narrowly on purely military affairs.

Although our subject matter was therefore extremely broad and far-reaching, references to the literature about the Soviet-German war had to be both highly selective and very brief for reasons of space. The thematic organization of this volume reflects the emphasis and results found in the research, both the many monographs and the overviews that have meanwhile been published.

The initial commentaries provide an introduction to each topic, an overview about problems concerning the source materials and the directions that the research is taking, and a selection of literature to assist students and researchers in their continuing efforts. The bibliography enumerates works that are relevant to the topics discussed in the individual chapters. Since many works address a number of different aspects, it was impossible to avoid repeating titles in several parts of the bibliography. For issues with extensive ramifications, however, it is still best to look through more chapters in order to gain a comprehensive view from a number of different vantage points. The search is facilitated by the list of authors and the continuous numbering of the listed works.

Both important standard works and detailed or specialized literature are included in the selection of titles, even though they were sometimes published in unusual places. Very short publications and miscellaneous works are generally not covered, nor are newspaper articles. The selection of works was not made according to any consistent, generally accepted qualitative evaluation but rather was topic-oriented, in order to afford readers at least an entrée into each particular topic. The initial works mentioned here, plus the additional information to be found in them, will enable readers to undertake further research of their own. Readers are encouraged to reach their own conclusions on the basis of the comments included here and their further reading.

The commentaries attempt to follow the main trails blazed by the research, although they also point to important blank spots and possible future developments. In this, they naturally reflect the views of the authors, who would appreciate any suggestions for possible additions or changes of emphasis. The limited volume of this book immediately choked off any hopes the authors may have cherished of being all-inclusive. As a result, readers may well feel that particular things should have been included or a different emphasis given.

This research summary was written during a time of particularly rapid change. Most of the literature that we needed to review was from the earlier period of Soviet historiography. Until the political about-face of 1990, Soviet historians were constrained to follow party instructions, i.e., to adhere to a Marxist-Leninist interpretation of history. As a result, most of their works are of no help in determining the historical truth. As a working group at the Moscow Institute of Military History stated, when it was striving toward a new understanding of the "Great Patriotic War" for a popular work on it, the "tendentious and one-sided subservience of many publications" to party instructions had often led in the past to "distorted interpretations of the military past." It is therefore fully understandable that this research review does not emphasize Soviet publications.

Nevertheless, works and memoirs written under party pressure constitute an important source on historical writing under communism. This is especially true for research into propaganda, historiography, and methodology. Despite a certain uniformity and lack of sources, works such as memoirs and accounts of personal experiences during the Second World War can still provide access to particular facts and events. Although their statements must, of course, always be checked very carefully, these works often cannot be replaced by other sources, at least for the foreseeable future.

Despite looser government rules and regulations, access to archives in the countries of the former Soviet Union will probably remain difficult for quite some time to come. A new, critical approach to history is still only beginning to emerge in these countries, and thus the older literature cannot be totally disregarded. A reliable overview of the older literature for German-speaking readers can be found in Karin Borck's bibliography *Sowjetische Forschungen (1917 bis 1991) zur Geschichte der deutsch-russischen Beziehungen von den Anfängen bis 1949* (Berlin, 1993). English-speaking readers can turn to a two-volume work by Michael Parrish: *The U.S.S.R. in World War II – An Annotated Bibliography of Books Published in the Soviet Union, 1945–1975, with an Addenda for the Years 1975–1980* (New York, London, 1981).

Historical writings from the former German Democratic Republic (GDR) were subject to many of the same constraints as those from the Soviet Union, although they are included in this bibliography in a selection despite some methodological and scholarly reservations. Historians in the GDR were not allowed to write free of ideological straitjackets or to determine for themselves what they should say. For decades they were shackled to the Soviet and Marxist-Leninist interpretation of the war and were compelled to follow it at all times. In this regard as well, former GDR historians have written self-critical studies freely admitting that their works and conclusions before 1989 were not based on an impartial, scholarly approach. In comparison with the Soviet literature, East German works are more differentiated, at least in regard to accounts of the Germans on the Eastern Front, and show greater familiarity with the sources.

It is hardly surprising that literature in German predominates on this topic. However, the authors hoped to build bridges between German and Anglo-American historiography, so that researchers from each language group could become better informed about each other's results and main points of emphasis. Readers will quickly recognize that English-speaking historians have carried out extensive research into many aspects of the war and have provided important impulses for other historians. Specialized literature in other languages also deserves recognition, for instance, works on Hitler's allies and the *Hilfstruppen*, or foreign helper troops. Here, too, we had to limit our selection, although the reader should at least be provided with an entrée that could lead to further research.

This manuscript was completed in 1994. More recent literature could be included only in exceptional cases. We would like to thank in particular the translator of the English edition, Dr. Bruce Little; members of staff at the Library of Contemporary History in Stuttgart; its director, Professor Gerhard Hirschfeld, who always took a great interest in this project and provided strong support; and Professor Gerhard L. Weinberg from Chapel Hill, North Carolina, who has written a special foreword for English-speaking readers.

Rolf-Dieter Müller and Gerd R. Ueberschär

Part A

POLICY AND STRATEGY

Introduction

What were the reasons for the German attack on the Soviet Union – thus beginning a war that Hitler so confidently unleashed on 22 June 1941, only to realize just six months later that it was already lost, although he managed to extend the conflict for almost another four years before it all finally ended with his suicide in the Chancellery bunker under the drumfire of the victorious Red Army? Hitler and his Minister of Propaganda, Joseph Goebbels, tried to convince Germans and the world at large that Operation Barbarossa was a preventive attack undertaken in order to ward off the Bolshevik menace. However, the German war aims, of which the Nazis made no secret, made it obvious to everyone, victims and aggressors alike, that the reasons for this most murderous war in world history reached back much further than the immediate political and strategic situation at the time of the attack.

The victorious powers took it upon themselves in the Nuremberg Trials to explore these reasons, to put on trial and condemn the men responsible for the war, and to make a record of the crimes committed for historians and future generations. The captured German documents were analyzed and countless witnesses questioned at these trials. What emerged was a survey that has not been discredited in the least by later corrections and amplifications and whose essence has been confirmed again and again by later historians.

The accusers and the accused at Nuremberg agreed on at least one thing: one of the most important origins of the attack on the Soviet Union stretched back to the First World War. However, the Allied powers understood this origin to be primarily Prussian militarism and megalomania, while the defendants pointed to the humiliation of Versailles, which they attempted to use in order to explain the rise of Hitler and the war.

Both sides believed that Hitler personally played an even more crucial role in the decision to attack the Soviet Union than he had in any previous decision. The Führer escaped being called to answer for his crimes, however, and so the exploration of his motives assumed only secondary importance. The other Nazi leaders clung stubbornly to their claim that it had been a preventive war, but this was never really a plausible explanation. The Allied prosecutors attempted to demonstrate the responsibility of the remaining Nazi leaders for the attack, although they were only moderately successful in doing so. It was left largely to later historians therefore to investigate in detail the reasons for the Russian campaign.

What, then, were the reasons for this attack? The variable relations between Germany and the Soviet Union in the period between 1918 and 1941 had produced moments of close cooperation – for instance, when the Kaiserreich provided assistance to the Bolsheviks in 1917–18, at the time of the Treaty of Rapallo in 1922–23, and finally during the Nazi-Soviet pact in 1939–41. All this could hardly be said to have systematically set the stage for the savage attack of 1941. The historical analysis undertaken at Nuremberg quickly fell into two main camps. For the Soviet Union and the historians cooperating with its official view, German "monopoly capitalism" had sought to dominate the world, employing Hitler as a puppet and rabble-rouser. Historians from the Western democracies, who were not bound to any particular party line, tended to ascribe ever greater importance to Hitler himself and the program he developed. The controversy generated by these different points of view was stoked by the Cold War and has dominated historical research for the last four decades.

This is probably one of the main reasons why no overview of Soviet-German relations has yet been produced. In view of the mountains of literature dealing with the actual events of the war with the Soviet Union, the lack of studies of its origins and causes is truly surprising. There is only one exception: the Nazi-Soviet pact of 23 August 1939. Disputes over the importance and meaning of this nonaggression pact began almost immediately after the war, reaching a first high-water mark during the

Nuremberg Trials. The dogged denial by the Soviets that any secret protocols to the pact existed, and the interpretations given to it by the Germans as part of their political defense at Nuremberg, created a unique situation for later historians – a veritable primer on the possibilities and limitations of research into contemporary events. We will therefore quickly outline the main features of this dispute.

The Allied prosecutors at Nuremberg wished to demonstrate that the Nazi defendants had conspired to wage a war of aggression, and it was essential that the defendants were not able to show in return that the Soviet Union itself had concluded a treaty with Hitler dividing up spheres of interest in eastern Europe. Nothing was yet known publicly about such a "fourth division of Poland," and both Berlin and Moscow had denied the rumors about a secret agreement in 1939. A public admission after the war that such an agreement did exist would have severely undermined the Soviet Union's position as a prosecutor, for it led straight to the conclusion that Stalin had encouraged Hitler's attack on Poland and quietly expected to profit from it. It was for this reason that Moscow was already insisting by the end of 1945 that the ticklish question of secret protocols should be placed on the trial's taboo list, i.e., those topics to be excluded from the proceedings at all costs. The existence of such a taboo list was not revealed until early 1991, by the Soviet writer Lev Besymenski.[1]

Since the former German foreign minister, Joachim von Ribbentrop, refused to speak at the trials, the defense attempted to bolster its claims by calling former diplomats to the witness stand. Alfred Seidl (the lawyer for Rudolf Heß, Hitler's former deputy) was particularly anxious to explore the question of the secret protocols at the trial, using a sworn deposition of the former German ambassador, Dr. Friedrich Gauß. So far as the Soviets were concerned, Gauß was a "dangerous" witness because he and Ribbentrop had been responsible for formulating the protocols during the negotiations in Moscow. He could therefore confirm their contents without producing any actual documents.

The chief Soviet prosecutor, General Rudenko, immediately recognized the explosiveness of Gauß's testimony and demanded that it be excluded. Rudenko insisted that Moscow had absolutely no knowledge of any secret agreements, and he did manage in the end to have Gauß's testimony excluded. The Soviets

1. Lev Besymenski, "Niemand kann uns überführen," *Der Spiegel,* no. 3 (1991): 104–112.

felt confident that they would not suddenly be caught red-handed in these lies because Foreign Minister Molotov had removed the Soviet copy of the treaty from his archives in early 1946, while the German copy (according to what Besymenski now claims) had apparently fallen into the hands of the Red Army and had also "disappeared."

Since the attorneys for Heß and Ribbentrop failed to produce the original treaty or a certified copy of it, the Soviets were able to discredit Gauß's affidavit as a crude "provocation" of the court. The defense succeeded eventually in producing copies of the secret protocols of 23 August and 28 September 1939, when they were leaked from somewhere in the West, but the court still refused to admit them as evidence because the copies had not been officially certified and Seidl either would not or could not reveal his sources. General Rudenko attacked the copies as worthless "forgeries," and the Allied court finally decided on 21 May 1946 not to accept them as evidence because they were of unknown origin. The Soviets therefore succeeded, temporarily at least, in casting doubt on the authenticity of the protocols.

In so doing, however, Stalin had maneuvered the Soviet Union into a corner, out of which it was unable to free itself for the next forty years. Each new document that came to light from the archives hinting at the existence of secret protocols forced Moscow to engage in more deceits and falsehoods. Even though the Soviet archives could be firmly controlled, the archives of the former German foreign office in Berlin had fallen into Western hands and provided plenty of ammunition for researchers.

Documents were soon published in English by Carroll and Epstein and translated into German by Seidl (Nos. 53, 90, 87). There is overlap, but the main purpose of Seidl's edition was, first, to prove the existence of the secret protocols and hence the expansive designs of the Soviet Union and, second, to prove that the initiative for the Nazi-Soviet pact of 1939 had actually lain with the Soviets. Consequently, the Soviets were allegedly to blame for the failure of Britain, France, and the Soviet Union to negotiate a military entente in the summer of 1939 – apparently the final opportunity to stop Hitler – and the leaders in Moscow were once again painted as unreliable and unscrupulous partners. The theory of totalitarianism equating Hitler and Stalin, communism and fascism, which gained greatest credence during the Cold War, also played a large role in this. The 1939 Nazi-Soviet pact was the strongest evidence that this theory could provide in order to conjure up new or repackaged enemies.

The Soviet government responded at once to these "unilateral" publications. The information office of the Council of Ministers of the USSR published *Falsificators of History* (No. 157), in which it accused the three Western powers of publishing phony documents. Moscow attempted to lend credibility to this charge by claiming that the former Western Allies had refused to allow the Soviets to participate in reviewing and selecting the documents for publication. The Americans were accused of calumny and falsehood, and the documents were said to be of no use in "presenting an objective view of historical events." Instead, reality was distorted in order to "spread lies about the Soviet Union." Moscow also threatened to retaliate by publishing captured secret German documents that would purportedly cast the Western powers in a poor light and give a different impression of the preparations for the Second World War and responsibility for it (No. 57). In the end, however, the Soviets proved unable to produce any new documents of this kind and had to satisfy themselves with publishing a "historical survey" from a Marxist-Leninist perspective.

Here the information office in Moscow continued its assaults on "monopoly circles" in the United States that had allegedly made capital available to Germany for rearmament and preparations for war, while Moscow was engaged in a long, steadfast struggle against the Third Reich and for the "consolidation of collective security." The Nazi-Soviet nonaggression pact of August 1939 was portrayed as a last desperate attempt to frustrate the provocative efforts of the Western powers to "incite Hitler Germany against the Soviet Union." The pact had helped the Soviet Union to shore up its defenses, not least of all by shifting its border well to the west. This had rebounded to the benefit of the Western powers themselves in their later struggle with the Soviet Union against fascism. According to the Moscow information office, the victory over Hitler was therefore largely due to Stalin's foresight and tactics. The Soviets, however, continued stubbornly to avoid any mention of the secret protocols of 23 August 1939.

Moscow's attempts to expunge any memory of this troublesome detail were aided and abetted by the Dietz Verlag in East Berlin. The same year, it published a corrected version of the Soviet brochure under a license from the Soviet military authorities and with a foreword by Otto Meier (No. 156). Here Meier, too, heaped much of the blame for the outbreak of the Second World War on monopoly capitalism in the United States. The original Soviet publication had had the particular merit, he said, of drawing attention to the political prelude to the war prior to 1939, and not just focusing on the 1939–41 period, as in the falsified American documents. The German edition of the Soviet brochure also carried two newspaper commentaries by the leading Soviet information officer in the Eastern zone, Colonel S.J. Tjulpanov, in which he remarked on the "historical rectifications" contained in the brochure. It had demonstrated that "the aggression by German imperialism was only made possible by the direct participation of monopoly capitalism in the United States, England and France in the planning and unleashing of these attacks" (No. E/84, p. 73). However, Tjulpanov recognized the danger that this attitude could invite the conclusion that it was not the National Socialists who were responsible for the war but monopoly capitalists in the West. Since he did not want to go that far, he warned explicitly that it would be "absolutely wrong" to draw any such apologetic conclusions. The struggle against German fascism and Nazi criminals remained an important task for all progressive forces.

In the West, the American publication of German documents encouraged former Nazi diplomats to begin changing their tune. In their memoirs published in the early 1950s, they praised the German foreign policy of old, which allegedly succeeded in 1939 in renewing the Bismarckian tradition of Russo-German cooperation – albeit at the price of having to recognize Soviet claims to territory and despite the fact that this cooperation failed to prevent the declaration of war on Germany by the Western powers (Nos. 3, 8, 18, 27, 28). Ultimately, however, these memoirs merely reiterated the basic justification for the attack on the Soviet Union that Hitler had employed in his address of 22 June 1941.

* * *

Not until much later did serious historians follow up on these government-sponsored publications of eyewitness accounts and documents from the archives. The archives of the victorious powers and their captured German documents were still virtually closed to historians, and source materials on the events of the summer of 1939 necessarily remained very patchy. The first serious surveys on German-Soviet negotiations were delivered by Tasca (Rossi) and Weinberg (Nos. 126, 131).

One of the first historians to investigate the delicate topic of Soviet-German relations just before the outbreak of the war was the Swiss historian Walter Hofer in 1954. His presentation and analysis of the events leading to the outbreak of the Second World War became a standard work that retained its status as such well into the 1960s (No. 169). It was reprinted many times and translated into major world languages. In this traditional study of the history of diplomacy, Hofer attempted to prove that the Nazis had unleashed the war intentionally and in full cognizance of what they were doing. His reconstruction of the various phases of Germany's expansionary policy in the spring and summer of 1939 has by and large proved itself. Hofer pointed out the crucial part played by the Hitler-Stalin pact in the decision to unleash the war, although he was unable to provide any plausible explanation of why the Führer was temporarily able to set aside his anti-Bolshevik fixation.

The search for the origins of the Soviet-German rapprochement led Hofer back to the termination of Britain's appeasement policy in March 1939. This step suddenly cast Stalin in the light of a valued partner for the Western powers, although he was extending feelers to the Germans as well. The ultimate failure of the Western powers to negotiate an alliance with the Soviet Union was due to the inordinate demands that Stalin made of them, according to Hofer. Hitler, on the other hand, was prepared to offer Stalin huge territorial concessions in order to escape from the political dead end in which he found himself, and in coming to terms with Stalin he wittingly accepted a declaration of war by the Western powers.

Hofer succeeded in providing plausible answers to a number of questions that were continually arising even later about the Nazi-Soviet pact, related both to the various stages in the rapprochement between Hitler and Stalin and to the motives of the two dictators, i.e., the course of the negotiations and the historic meaning of the secret protocols. Although Hofer still had access to only a limited number of source materials and some of his answers were fairly sketchy, he succeeded nevertheless in producing a compelling overall analysis.

When a reprint was issued in 1964, he decided to include many key original documents in response to another flood of apologetic works prompted by the publications of "revisionist" historians. Hofer vehemently attacked the revisionist assessment of the Nuremberg Trials in the appendix to his book. His ire was raised in particular by the rough-hewn historical pastiches of the American David L. Hoggan, who depicted Hitler as a victim of British intrigues on whom the war was "forced" in

1939 (No. 171). According to Hoggan, the "peace-loving" Führer had signed the treaty with Stalin only out of self-defense. Hofer accused Hoggan of trying to absolve Hitler of responsibility both for the Second World War and for enabling the Bolsheviks to surge into the heart of Europe.

At about the same time as Hoggan's works appeared, the translation of A.J.P. Taylor's book about the origins of the war met with considerable success in Germany (Nos. 197, 177). Hofer disproved the questionable assertions of this Oxford historian and exposed the contradictions in his argument. Taylor also portrayed Hitler as desiring only a peaceful and quite justified revision of the Treaty of Versailles and blamed the outbreak of the war on a series of diplomatic mistakes on the part of *all* the leading countries. In Taylor's view, Soviet foreign policy aimed at peace and security. It was only the failure of attempts to negotiate an alliance with the Western powers that prompted Stalin to cast about for alternatives. Accordingly, he interpreted Ribbentrop's telegram of 14 August 1939 as the first step toward a possible Soviet-German rapprochement. However, Taylor failed to adduce convincing evidence for this as well as for other, more controversial conclusions.

The "revisionists" in the English-speaking countries therefore found little support among German historians. The latter were more influenced by the research of the British historian Hugh R. Trevor-Roper, who shed light on Hitler's long-term ideological motives in a much discussed essay on German war aims published in 1960 (No. D/79). Trevor-Roper reaffirmed the widely accepted emphasis on Hitler himself in research into the Second World War, and though not denying German responsibility for the war, he confined it to the megalomaniacal Führer. However, his view that there was a long-term ideological plan underlying Nazi foreign policy (of which the Hitler-Stalin pact was only one expression, though probably the most clever) met with considerable skepticism. Older German historians, schooled to think in terms of great power politics, had difficulty with a more ideological interpretation. In their view, German foreign policy on the eve of the Second World War was typified by the contrast between "apolitical" foreign policy professionals in the foreign office, such as Freiherr von Weizsäcker, and the irrational, "demonic" Adolf Hitler, with his incompetent foreign minister, Joachim von Ribbentrop.

For instance, in his address upon becoming vice-chancellor of the University of Bonn in November 1959, Max Braubach claimed that the driving force behind the Führer's decision to seek a rapprochement with Stalin was simply his own desire for more power and not some grand political design – whether the greatness of Germany, or the creation of a huge Reich in Europe, or the destruction of Bolshevism (No. 146). Hitler therefore sought accomplices whenever and wherever they could be of use to him. This viewpoint tended to preclude any probing questions about German war guilt similar to the vehement "Fischer controversy" that erupted among German historians at about the same time in regard to the First World War. All the more attention was thus focused on the Soviet side.

By the early 1960s, old taboos had begun to be broken by Soviet historians as a result of "de-Stalinization." This held true as well for discussions of the Nazi-Soviet pact. However, it soon became evident that the Western approach was not the only one to this delicate topic. Even though Soviet historians at this time were often critical of Stalin, they continued to defend the pact with Hitler as a reasonable act of self-defense. According to them, Moscow made serious attempts to negotiate a military alliance with the Western powers in the summer of 1939, but the West at this time was interested only in channeling German aggression eastward. Under these circumstances, the Soviet Union was virtually compelled to accept the German offer of a nonaggression treaty. This step, in the view of the Soviet historians, averted the creation of a capitalist front and bought time for the Soviet Union to strengthen its defenses. The occupation of eastern Poland by the Red Army helped to protect the population and, in any case, recovered for the Soviet Union only those lands that had been seized by the Polish bourgeoisie in 1920. It remained taboo, however, to mention the secret protocols to the Nazi-Soviet pact (Nos. 123, 142).

Although these studies did not produce any major new insights into the Nazi-Soviet pact some twenty years after it had been signed, they made substantial contributions in various specialized areas. For some time, German translations of the works of A. Tasca (under the pseudonym of A. Rossi) and of Gerhard L. Weinberg had been available, which analyzed Soviet-German relations between the summer of 1939, when the pact was concluded, and June 1941, when Operation Barbarossa was launched. These studies were based largely on the materials collected for Nuremberg (Nos. 126, 131).

Ferdinand Friedensburg, the former Nazi economic expert and later president of the German Institute for Economic

Research, produced in 1962 an outline of Soviet-German economic cooperation under the Hitler-Stalin pact (No. 155). Here again the main emphasis was on denouncing Stalin as Hitler's all-too-willing companion-at-arms and supplier of raw materials. It was not until many years later that a more differentiated view came to be accepted of the economic relations between Germany and the Soviet Union (Nos. 143, 224).

English-speaking historians were long much further advanced in their studies of Soviet-German relations, as could be seen in such important works as those of Dallin and Reitlinger, which were also translated into German. This was true, for example, of the important publication of Hitler's previously unpublished "secret book" written in 1928 (No. 71). This work, the English edition of which is not a reliable translation, confirmed Hitler's ideological maxims and relatively firm foreign program, which played a major role in his pact with Stalin.

In Germany, the writer Philipp W. Fabry responded more quickly than university historians to the attempts of "revisionists" to reassess the Hitler-Stalin pact and the question of German war guilt. In 1962 he published a much discussed study in which he basically reiterated the views set forth by Taylor, although he improved on Taylor's inadequate use of sources and line of argument, thereby raising Taylor's work to the level of the historical discussion in Germany (No. 101).

Fabry engaged in lopsided criticism of the "aggressive" Soviet foreign policy at the time and of the extent of Stalin's initiatives leading to the Soviet-German pact in order to maximize the Soviet leader's responsibility for the war. At the same time, he minimized Hitler's role, describing him as a pragmatic politician who reacted to events and did not have any long-term, ideologically motivated plans for expansion. Fabry's study was not very convincing, however, and was subjected to sharp criticism, especially by Fritz T. Epstein and Gerhard L. Weinberg.

Fabry revisited the same topic ten years later, this time including recent advances in the historical research, providing documentation and treating a broader period (No. 102). He discussed the conflicting ideologies of the dictators and the political delusions that led them to engage in a "joint venture on borrowed time." He repeated the old, long-disproved thesis that Hitler ended the period of cooperation with a preventive war.

By the early 1960s, the careful, gradual relaxation in tensions between the Soviet Union and the Federal Republic of Germany had created a more favorable climate for the discussion of recent history. West German historians gradually shed their aversion to studying the Nazi period. At the same time, the Western allies began returning captured German documents, which made it easier to work intensively with source materials. In addition, the publication of extensive materials, such as several volumes of private war diaries by the former Chief of General Staff, Franz Halder, provided detailed accounts of the events surrounding historic decisions, especially in regard to the Soviet-German rapprochement of the summer and autumn of 1939 (No. 63).

An important step forward was taken in 1965 with the publication of Andreas Hillgruber's *Hitlers Strategie* in the years 1940–41, a book that became a standard work and still retains most of its validity (No. 19). Despite vehement criticism by some of his older colleagues, Hillgruber undertook a somewhat new interpretation of Hitler's foreign policy in this doctoral thesis. Basing his work on the numerous specialized studies that had appeared and on extensive analysis of the source materials, Hillgruber focused on Hitler's aims and accomplishments in the area of foreign policy, while highlighting the ideological component much more than Hofer had done. Hillgruber believed that Hitler had already developed a relatively firm foreign policy by the mid-1920s and that he implemented this policy after seizing power in a consistent, deliberate fashion. The chief aim of Hitler's foreign policy, imbued with notions of racial superiority, was to conquer new *Lebensraum* in the East and achieve a position of world dominance. The Nazi-Soviet pact was just one step in the accomplishment of this goal. This interpretation of Nazi foreign policy clearly differentiated Hillgruber from Fabry and the other revisionists, and his work held up well enough to be reprinted twenty years later with only minor changes.

Hillgruber devoted particular effort in his later publications to exposing Germany's role in the outbreak of the Second World War and the true significance of the Nazi-Soviet pact (Nos. 109, 167). In respect to Hitler's basic program, Hillgruber interpreted British appeasement policies, in contrast to Soviet historians, as an attempt to commit Hitler to a firm political order and not simply to deflect his aggressiveness eastward. The British felt that a strong Poland was needed because the Soviet Union was no longer a powerful bulwark after Stalin's bloody purge of the Red Army officer corps. This was also the reason, Hillgruber believed, why the Western powers rejected Stalin's demands that the Soviet Union be allowed to move its troops through Poland during the negotiations over a military alliance.

Hillgruber then compared these developments with the sudden change of course in Berlin. He claimed that Hitler had always been inclined to seek a compromise with Britain. However, at Ribbentrop's urging, the Führer began after 1938 to form a continental bloc against Britain. This postponed for a while his "grand solution," namely to carve out new German territories in the East after reaching a compromise agreement with London that would provide him with the rear cover that he needed. After April 1939, Hitler and Ribbentrop concentrated all of their foreign policy efforts on politically isolating Poland, which had been strengthened suddenly by the British guarantees, in order to conquer it in a short, limited war. As a result, a decision was made in early August "in a 180-degree tactical reversal" to seek a temporary compromise with Stalin. This Nazi-Soviet agreement would so shake the British government that it would feel forced to accept the conquest of Poland without retaliation, despite the cost to the countries of eastern Europe.

The ground had been prepared for Stalin to accept Hitler's blandishments ever since the Munich agreements. In his attempts to forestall the perceived threat of another Anglo-German understanding like that achieved at Munich, Stalin believed that a rapprochement of his own with Hitler could provide many advantages. It would go a long way toward fulfilling his own long-term goal of encouraging a great war among the "imperialist" powers that would propel the Soviet Union into a leading position in world affairs. In his famous address of 19 January 1925, Stalin expressed this hope as follows: "We will enter the fray at the end, throwing our critical weight onto the scale, a weight that should prove decisive."[2] Hillgruber believed that the initiative for the Nazi-Soviet pact clearly emanated from Germany. Stalin adopted a rather defensive posture at least in 1939 – while cherishing the hope, nevertheless, that he might be able to accomplish some of his own expansionary dreams if a long war of attrition such as the First World War were to break out between Germany and the Western powers.

Hillgruber therefore interpreted Soviet foreign policy in much the same way as German foreign policy, that is, as dependent on a particular totalitarian ideology. However, while he saw that Germany's experiences in the First World War with the

2. Stalin's speech on 19 January 1925 at the plenary meeting of the Central Committee of the Communist party of Russia, quoted by J.W. Stalin, *Werke* (East Berlin, 1952), vol. 7, 11f.

naval blockade and wars on several fronts influenced Hitler's strategic thinking, he did not see any similar influences in Stalin's case. Nevertheless, Russia had also suffered many painful lessons in the past that probably affected the approach of the new political elite in Moscow. In particular Russia had attacked Germany in 1914, in accordance with its treaty obligations to the Western powers, only to collapse and be defeated despite its impressive marshaling of forces and the many sacrifices that it made and regardless of how hard-pressed the Germans were on the Western Front. The Russian defeats on the battlefield led subsequently to a revolution. In the face of such experiences, who could possibly have ignored parallels to the situation in 1939, especially as Stalin's position was considerably worse than that of the Czar in 1914 in view of the fact that Stalin had practically decapitated his own army and that there was obviously no love lost between the Soviets and any Western powers with which they might hope to ally themselves.

On the whole, Hillgruber adopted a moderate position between, on the one hand, the extreme Communist view that the leadership in Moscow harbored absolutely no expansionist desires and, on the other, the view of Nazi apologists and revisionists that Stalin was the real warmonger. However, under the influence of the theory of totalitarianism that was on the ascendant at the time, Hillgruber tended to equate Hitler's and Stalin's foreign policy as predicated on ideologically driven expansionism, and this prevented him from perceiving other motivations.

Hillgruber developed a considerable reputation before his death in 1989 as the godfather of West German research into the war and a celebrated historian of the German state created by Bismarck. As such, he did not shy away from drawing modern-day political parallels to his historical research. The position history assumes in the tension between the politics of the present and of the past was particularly evident in his comments on the Nazi-Soviet pact.

On the occasion of the fortieth anniversary of the signing of the pact, Hillgruber, together with his younger colleague Klaus Hildebrand, developed a highly politicized and staunchly conservative interpretation of it. The subtitle of one article – "Parallels with Today?" – is indicative of this attempt to employ the Nazi-Soviet pact as proof for the theory of totalitarianism and to use it as a cautionary tale for present-day politicians (No. 108).

Hillgruber confined himself explicitly to studying the two dictators and arriving at a historical "understanding" of their similar views and decisions. Only in this way could the events be comprehended. Hillgruber wished at the same time to distance himself from "many new 'revisionist' views among West German historians about an alleged 'polycracy' in the Third Reich." Hildebrand also attacked the concept of "anti-Fascism" and related the collaboration of Hitler and Stalin to the natural affinity that existed between fascism and socialism. The Nazi-Soviet pact was not only a result, however, of the alleged similarity between the two regimes. It depended as well on the absolute rule of single dictators at the top. "The attitudes of Hitler and Stalin regarding the development and implementation of the Nazi-Soviet nonaggression pact provide 'clear evidence of the dominating, all-important role of the Leader'" (p. 56, with quotation from Karl Dietrich Erdmann, *Zeitgeschichtliche Kontroversen um Faschismus, Totalitarismus, Demokratie* [Munich, 1976]).

The Nazi-Soviet pact was therefore a product of dictatorship by autocratic leaders and of the absolute primacy of political goals. The pact also helped, in Hillgruber's view, to disprove the view that other forces played a part – for instance, the needs of the capitalist economy. This interpretation of the pact tended to support the totalitarian theory of fascism and to discredit other views, while functioning as a cautionary tale against the détente policies of the 1970s and 1980s. Hildebrand even went so far as to investigate why the appeasement policy of the Western powers had failed in the 1930s and to cast doubt on the ability of present-day democratic nations to pursue successful foreign policies when challenged by dictators.

Hillgruber and Hildebrand did not bring to light any new facts or details about the Nazi-Soviet pact, and their comments were aimed really at the political disputes raging in the academic community at the time. The 1960s and 1970s had witnessed a flood of theories about fascism that greatly influenced the discussion among contemporary historians. While some historians on the Left were eager to use their more theoretical than empirical interpretations of fascism in order to condemn capitalism in general, other historians were keen to employ the Nazi-Soviet pact (which the theoreticians of fascism were equally eager to ignore) as the cornerstone of an opposing interpretation.

East German historians did not make any original contributions to the debate, contenting themselves with following the new, harder line laid down in Moscow now that the loosening surrounding de-Stalinization began to pass. Stalin's policies in

1939–40 were again interpreted as the inescapable consequence of "imperialist" saber rattling, as an understandable attempt to parry the perfidious attempts of the Western powers to urge Nazi Germany upon the "peace-loving" Soviet Union (Nos. 12, 13). According to this view, not only Hitler and the capitalist circles behind him were responsible for the war but the Western powers as well. The origins of the war were sought in the conflicting capitalist interests and imperialist strategies, to which the "peace-loving" foreign policy of the Soviet Union stood in marked contrast. Any mention of the secret protocols to the Nazi-Soviet pact remained, of course, taboo.

The Moscow writer Lev Besymenski, whose work was published in the Federal Republic of Germany in 1968 (No. 49), provided a prime example of the Soviet line and probably played a leading role in setting it. By publishing the Soviet notes on the failed discussions surrounding a military alliance with Britain and France in the summer of 1939, he attempted to prove that the Western powers were not seriously interested in containing Hitler and therefore bore responsibility for the consequences: a rapprochement between Germany and the Soviet Union, and Hitler's attack on Poland.

The views of the Nazi-Soviet pact advanced by Hillgruber and Hildebrand were not only a reaction to the flood of left-wing theories of fascism and to the consequent undermining of Western resolve vis-à-vis the Communist world; they were also a response to the enormous surge in research into the Third Reich as a result of the increased accessibility of sources and the mounting interest in this period in Germany in the 1960s and 1970s. The monocausal interpretation of Nazism as the creation of a single individual, Adolf Hitler, was beginning to be displaced by an analysis more influenced by social history. No longer was the focus on the Führer himself but rather on the ever more clearly emerging "polycracy" in the Third Reich and on the struggle for power among various interest groups and elites. As a result of this historiographical trend, the origins and causes of the Second World War and the ideological roots of Nazi foreign policy were sought out not only in Hitler's personal biography but also in currents of nationalist and conservative thought extending back to the Wilhelmine period. This highlighted the connection between Hitler's policies and the traditional political elites.

Numerous studies of social and economic policy in the 1930s led to a reinterpretation of Hitler's celebrated about-face in the summer of 1939. A leading role was played by the British historian Timothy Mason, who attempted to demonstrate that Hitler's absurd rearmament policies had prompted a severe internal crisis by early 1939 that could be resolved only by declaring war, even at the price of an accommodation with the Nazis' mortal ideological enemy, Joseph Stalin (No. 177a).

In his very important survey of Hitler's foreign policy, Gerhard L. Weinberg confirmed Stalin's fear of German strength and his aim to involve other countries in a war against Germany. Moscow preferred to stay aside and provided a stimulus for Hitler to strike at others (Nos. 132, 133).

More and more details about Nazi decision-making and war preparations came to light, for instance, thanks to the publication of the diaries of Hitler's aide-de-camp, Major Engel (No. 74). They tended to confirm what the research had been showing. The same held true for the extensive documentation published by J.W. Brügel in Vienna in 1973 (No. 51) and for the work of Markus Wüthrich, who once again explored the negotiating stances of the Western powers in Moscow in the summer of 1939 (No. 205). The British historian Donald C. Watt focused in his presentation on exactly when Hitler and Stalin decided to open serious negotiations with one another (No. 201).

* * *

While conservative historians in Germany attempted at first to play down the "leftist," socially critical approaches, well-known popular writers once again took it upon themselves to make their own contributions to our understanding of Soviet-German relations. The journalists Friedrich A. Krummacher and Helmut Lange produced an extensive survey in a companion volume to a television series, spanning the period from the Treaty of Brest-Litovsk, imposed by Imperial Germany in 1917–18, to the Nazi attack in 1941 (No. 112). Based on new sources and original research, they pointed out a persistent trend in German foreign policy toward eastward expansion, a trend that was particularly imbued with anti-Polish attitudes. This movement reached its first climax with the signing of the notorious Treaty of Rapallo in 1922 and peaked again with the Nazi-Soviet pact. The shared hostility to Poland (which in earlier eras had brought Prussia and Russia together and then, after 1918, brought a humbled Germany together with the international pariah, the Soviet Union) flared up once again in the summer of

1939. According to Krummacher and Lange, Stalin took the initiative in this rapprochement as early as 17 April when the negotiations with the Western powers had scarcely commenced and the Soviet ambassador in Berlin began to hint that it might be possible to reach a Soviet-German understanding.

Sebastian Haffner provided an even more pointed analysis of the alliance between the two dictators and its origins in his essay "Der Teufelspakt" (No. 106). He found that this most stunning reversal in twentieth-century diplomatic history could not be satisfactorily explained by the various forces at work within the Third Reich, not to mention the economic situation alone or the foreign policy situation. According to Haffner, Hitler's ideological program was only one aspect of a German *Sonderweg* that had begun well before 1933 and that led the country to look eastward in an attempt to attain a dominant position in world politics. This interpretation was later adopted by other historians and extended further – for example, to the economic and armament policies of the Kaiserreich (No. 119). However, such claims that there was an ongoing policy of eastward expansion remained highly controversial.

More recent studies of Hitler's political program and war aims by Axel Kuhn and Jochen Thies also revealed the central role of eastward expansion (Nos. 29, 39). Thies' very important book demonstrated on the lines of Hitler's building plans and architecture that his political aims first mentioned in the book *Mein Kampf* had been the basis of his foreign policy. Hitler's ultimate goal was world domination based in his rule over Russia. Kuhn also provided a cursory summary of this interpretation in a short essay, blaming the war on Hitler's long-cherished political program and attempting to explain his prewar political and diplomatic maneuvers on this basis (No. 113). Wolfgang Wippermann's work under the heading of *"Deutscher Drang nach Osten"* was strongly oriented toward the study of ideology and Nazi concepts (No. D/82). This author, who made a name for himself in the fascism debate, explored the historical roots of German expansionism to the east and examined the reception of contemporary historical studies in the East and West. In so doing, however, Wippermann never denied the unique nature of the Nazi drive for more *Lebensraum* with its racial preconceptions.

Finally, the Swedish historian and diplomat Sven Allard provided solid information about Stalin's political intentions and the diplomatic maneuvering that preceded the Nazi attack on the Soviet Union (No. 97). He had an excellent background for this study, for he had observed the prelude to war on the spot as an envoy to the leading capitals of Europe in the 1930s. After the conflict, he deepened his knowledge of the strategy pursued by the Soviet Union as a diplomat in Eastern European capitals and in Vienna after 1954. He took an abiding interest in the extent to which Marxist-Leninist ideology shaped the foreign policy of the Soviet Union and was familiar with the leading international specialized studies.

Allard compares the various phases of Stalin's and Hitler's foreign policy. He believes that Stalin's supreme strategic goal was to prevent at any cost the demise of the only "socialist state" in the world. Stalin's assessments of Hitler varied considerably over time. Not until the murders at the time of the Röhm putsch was he convinced that Hitler had really become the absolute ruler of Germany. In Stalin's view, this increased the likelihood that war would erupt between the capitalist states and made it essential to maneuver the Soviet Union into as neutral a position as possible. Allard comes to the conclusion that Stalin decided fairly early to attempt to reach an understanding with Hitler in order to facilitate the war that he hoped would erupt between Germany and the Western powers. The continuing ticklishness of this topic in the Soviet Union was evidenced by the works of I.K. Kobljakow and Vilnis J. Sipols (the latter was published as well under license in the Federal Republic), attempting to justify the rapprochement with Hitler (Nos. 111, 194).

In the meantime, West German research into Eastern Europe had succeeded in freeing itself from the thought patterns imposed by the Third Reich and anti-Bolshevism. New approaches, which also considered the Soviet literature and, above all, the ever more voluminous source materials, reinforced the view that Soviet foreign policy in the 1930s aimed first and foremost at security. A study by Bianca Pietrow examined Soviet conceptions of the Third Reich in the 1930s, to the extent that this was possible so long as the Soviet archives were closed. In contrast to Fabry and in basic agreement with the British historian J. Haslam, for instance (No. 107), Pietrow interpreted Stalin's concept of "collective security" as a purely defensive policy at first. Not until the bloody purges of 1936–37 and the dismissal in early 1939 of Litinov, the foreign minister for many years, did Stalin change his tack and begin seeking opportunities to expand to the west. According to Pietrow, as well as her colleague Arnold Sywottek (Nos. 121, 254), Stalin became convinced that the greatest gains, both territorial and strategic, could be made through a pact with Hitler.

The *Osteuropa-Handbuch*, appearing in several volumes, reflected some of the new trends in research (No. 120). However, the third volume, devoted to Soviet foreign policy from 1917 to 1955, was still strongly influenced by Andreas Hillgruber. Here he described the Soviet-German relationship of 1939–41 as a solid "partnership," which the Soviet leadership believed would enhance its freedom to maneuver and strategic security. Hillgruber particularly emphasized the territorial and political realignment of Eastern Europe, which he interpreted primarily as a product of the secret protocols of 1939 and not of the final victory of the Allies in 1945.

Views such as these were always vehemently attacked by Soviet historians. Even the interest expressed by West German historians in examining the immediate effects of the Nazi-Soviet pact on the Baltic Germans, who were expelled and resettled in 1939–41, was viewed with considerable suspicion because of the direct reference to the secret protocols. The voluminous documentation gathered by Dietrich A. Loeber illuminated the momentous consequences for these people of the Soviet-German "partnership" in the first two years of the war (No. 76).

* * *

In response to the fortieth anniversary of the Nazi-Soviet pact, when the political and research climate had improved considerably, many detailed studies were undertaken, especially of the positions adopted by the Western powers in 1939. In the English-speaking countries, the appeasement policy of the 1930s was hotly debated (No. 134). Gottfried Niedhart added a German voice to this discussion with his penetrating analysis, drawing a well-balanced portrait of Great Britain's role in the decisions made in the summer of 1939 (Nos. 179, 180, 181). In contrast to Walter Hofer, he did not believe that British policy took a radical turn. Appeasement had been a long-term policy that Prime Minister Neville Chamberlain, at least, wished to continue pursuing even after the shift in British public opinion in March 1939.

Heinrich Bartel discussed the often underestimated role played by France, using newly available source materials (No. 139). He pointed out that France was anxious in the spring of 1939 to regain some of the ground it had lost in eastern Europe and was urging the hesitant British to reach an agreement with Moscow. While Chamberlain played for time, the French were doing all they could to remove any obstacles to an agreement.

Reinhold W. Weber then produced a new survey of the diplomatic prologue to the Nazi-Soviet pact (No. 202). On the basis of the available archival materials and numerous memoirs, he attempted a synchronous study of the negotiations between Moscow and Berlin and between Moscow and the two Western capitals, showing the mutual influences. His central conclusion was that in this web of multilateral relationships and influences, Hitler managed ultimately to impose his preferred solution: war. Weber examined all the available documents on the Nazi-Soviet pact in greater detail than ever before, although this did not produce any striking new insights.

The omnibus volumes *Sommer 1939* and *Kriegsbeginn 1939* provided a good overview of historical research at the time (Nos. 141, 181). Niedhart's volume focused primarily on the foundations of German foreign policy. The article in this volume by GDR historian Gerhart Hass hewed to the traditional views set forth by Marxist historians in the Soviet Union. Hass was unstinting in his praise of the "numerous" Soviet attempts to mitigate the threat to world peace, while failing to mention the active role that Moscow played in devising the Nazi-Soviet pact. Although most Western historians had long abandoned the view that Hitler's beliefs and decisions were solely responsible for the build-up to the Second World War and its outbreak, Niedhart's volume explained the political crisis of the summer of 1939 by pointing mainly to Hitler's program. Ludolf Herbst in particular dismissed other views – for instance, Tim Mason's argument about economic pressures (No. 163).

Wolfgang Michalka's dissertation about the foreign policy views of Joachim von Ribbentrop, Hitler's foreign minister, confirmed the belief that the Nazi regime did not have a single, monolithic foreign policy program (No. 31). Unlike Hitler, Ribbentrop did not consider Nazi ideology and anti-Bolshevism to be rigid dogma, and he aimed at pragmatic political goals. After the about-face in the summer of 1939, he encouraged the alliance with Moscow as the keystone of an anti-British policy on the Continent. The Nazi-Soviet pact therefore bore Ribbentrop's personal stamp to a large extent, although Hitler alone was responsible for making the decision to approve the treaty, as Michalka readily admits.

Hans von Herwarth also described the contradictoriness of Nazi foreign policy in his memoirs (No. 15), drawing a compelling portrait of the attempts of German diplomats in Moscow, led by Ambassador Count von der Schulenburg, to improve Soviet-German relations in the 1930s. They viewed the Nazi-Soviet pact as the crowning achievement of their work of many years – although the fruit of their labors would soon be swept aside.

The overwhelming responsibility of the Third Reich and of Adolf Hitler in particular for the outbreak of the Second World War was finally made crystal clear in the first comprehensive portrait of the entire war, *Das Deutsche Reich und der Zweite Weltkrieg*, a ten-volume work produced by the Militärgeschichtliches Forschungsamt in Freiburg (No. 151). Summarizing the Western research, it proved with massive documentary evidence that the Nazi regime had consistently prepared for war and aspired to war ever since 1933. Rearmament and war preparations were an essential part of Hitler's ideology and plan to conquer new *Lebensraum* in the East and rule over Europe, thereby propelling Germany into a position of world dominance. However, by the spring of 1939 Hitler found that he had reached a dead end because of the overheated German economy generated by the production of war matériel and as a result of his own hectic maneuvering on the international stage. His margin of maneuver was becoming extremely narrow, and only the stunning about-face of the deal with Stalin enabled him to begin the war he wanted with an attack on Poland and to regain the economic and strategic initiative he needed to carry out his plans for conquest.

In a parallel work that had already been published in the GDR, interpretations continued along the well-worn paths of Stalinist dogma (No. 151a). No new sources or insights were provided, and the Nazi-Soviet pact continued to be celebrated as a great success of Soviet diplomacy because it prevented the contradictions in the capitalist system, which were propelling it toward war, from being solved on the backs of the people of the Soviet Union. Forty years after the signing of the pact, the disagreement between historians on either side of the Iron Curtain seemed forever cast in cement – a mirror image of the political situation in Europe at the time.

In the next few years, attention turned to various details of the pact. Particular notice was paid to people who suffered direct consequences. Wolfgang Leonhard was a young Communist who emigrated from Germany to the Soviet Union and was directly affected by the concordat between the two dictators in 1939. He published the reminiscences of seventy eyewitnesses to the "shock" caused by the pact (Nos. 174, 168). This multifaceted overview portrayed a wealth of reactions, ranging from stupefaction and complete confusion to spectacular resignations from the Communist party and suicide. Leonhard shed light primarily on the effect of the abrupt about-face in Soviet policy on the Comintern and on communism as an international political force. He showed how the Nazi-Soviet pact became a turning point in the lives of an entire generation of committed Communists.

All the more noteworthy, then, were the forlorn but defiant attempts of Communist parties in Western Europe, completely taken by surprise by the pact, to explain it all away in the fall of 1939. The source materials published by Jan Foitzik about the posture adopted by the central committee of the German Communist party illustrate the apparently inescapable dilemma in which it found itself and which has plagued Communist historians ever since (No. 60).

Erwin Oberländer, a specialist in eastern European history teaching in Mainz, published a collection of essays about the effects of the pact on smaller countries that historians often tend to overlook (No. 182). The various contributions provide excellent insights into the swath of countries in eastern Europe running from Finland to Rumania that suddenly found themselves caught between the "red" hammer and the "brown" anvil. Their shock over German ruthlessness was surpassed only by their dislike for and even hatred of the Soviet Union. For this reason, many of them continued to seek salvation by aligning themselves with Germany, even though it had curtly brushed their concerns aside. The contributions in this volume also outline the present-day discussion in these countries about the Nazi-Soviet pact.

Another approach was taken by Rolf Ahmann in his doctoral thesis on the system of nonaggression treaties in the 1930s, a summary of which also appeared in Oberländer's volume (No. 136). He analyzed these treaties from the point of view of international law, concluding that they were a key element in European security policy at the time, with the exception of the Nazi-Soviet pact, which formed an anomaly in every way. It established political spheres of interest between the two signatories at the cost of other countries that were destined to be overrun, and it aimed to destroy the existing nonaggression-treaty system in eastern Europe and pave the way for war.

Ingeborg Plettenberg, on the other hand, adopted quite a different perspective, at least insofar as the Soviet Union was concerned (No. 184). Basing her work on traditional Soviet historiography, she portrayed Stalin's foreign policy in the 1930s as seeking "peaceful co-existence among states with different social orders." She then drew conclusions about the general conditions that would be necessary for a continuation of this policy in the present and about promising possibilities for future relations. This approach remains very unconvincing in view of both later political developments and the knowledge that has been gained about Stalinism itself.

* * *

The activities in 1989 surrounding the fiftieth anniversary of the outbreak of the war also failed to produce any major new insights. They did, however, provide an opportunity to reconsider and recapitulate the research – for instance, about Hitler's war aims and his ideologically determined ideas about the East, which were recurrent subjects of debate (No. 198).

The well-known contemporary historian Hermann Graml presented a new overview of the prelude to the war. He analysed international politics in the interwar years as the backdrop against which Hitler drove Europe into war in 1939 (No. 161). According to Graml, there is no doubt at all that Hitler's desire for expansion was solely responsible for the war, while Stalin clearly preferred to reach an accommodation with Germany as early as the spring of 1939.

At the same time, the *Gesellschaft für bedrohte Völker* drew attention to "the betrayed peoples between Hitler and Stalin" (No. 200). This volume is a plea for recognition and respect for emigrants and "fighters for national independence" in the former border states. It contains contributions not only from experts but also from people directly affected, including members of the Jewish and German minorities. In the introduction, Wolfgang Leonhard again recounts his personal memories of the Nazi-Soviet pact. Lev Kopelev speaks about the "fraternal enemies" Hitler and Stalin. Besides depicting the years of suffering before and during the Second World War, the volume also portrays the present situation of the peoples between eastern Finland and Bessarabia. It does not fail to mention that alongside the victims during the war were also some extremists who cooperated with Hitler and often became his henchmen in carrying out the Holocaust.

Ingeborg Fleischhauer wrote a comprehensive analysis of the negotiations leading to the conclusion of the Nazi-Soviet pact

(No. 153). Using the unpublished notes of the German ambassador Count Friedrich von der Schulenburg, she arrives at new insights and interpretations that are particularly deserving of attention. She places the German embassy in Moscow at the center of her description of what are, for the most part, well-known events and documents. More than other historians, however, she delves into the initiatives undertaken by Germany's diplomatic corps in Russia after the Munich agreement. According to Fleischhauer, these conservative, nationalist professionals of the old school hoped to design a treaty with the Soviet Union that would serve as a solid framework for German foreign policy and help thereby to rein in Hitler's expansionary dreams. Insofar as the Soviet Union was concerned, they hoped to satisfy Moscow's security interests and reinforce the status quo in eastern Europe.

However, Hitler did not embrace this defensive vision of Soviet-German rapprochement, and it was the Führer's own ambitions that shaped the final form of the treaty. For Hitler, any accommodation with the Soviets was merely a temporary tactical concession, for which he offered the bait of territorial expansion. The Soviet Union's response is best explained by its fear of encirclement and inner destabilization. The negotiations with the Western powers did not seem to hold out much promise of reinforcing Soviet security, and saddled with dilettantish military planning, Stalin finally sought security in a questionable strategy of "forward defense."

Fleischhauer points out that the logic of the Soviet position was recognized at the time by leading observers, including Winston Churchill. The Soviets did not respond positively to the German offers until 15 August 1939, and therefore no duplicity was involved, as is often alleged. Stalin simply had little choice, first because the Western powers could not provide him with much security in the event of a war that appeared to be in the offing and the brunt of which would inevitably be borne by the Soviet Union, and second because the border states in eastern Europe were, in their fear, turning more to Germany than to the Soviets.

Hitler and Stalin, according to Fleischhauer, approached one another hesitantly, brimming with distrust and groping their way to an agreement. However, a major distinction in the strategic and political thought of the two dictators needs to be emphasized: Stalin aimed above all at peace and security, primarily through recognition of the status quo, whereas Hitler was driven by a sense of unrest and a desire to go to war in order to rearrange the relationships between the great powers in Europe. In Fleischhauer's view, the German economy had reached its maximum output, after a tremendous tour de force, but now faced collapse. Meanwhile, the Soviet economy was just beginning to fall into place, after the profound structural changes of the 1930s, although it held out little hope of approaching maximum efficiency for many years.

Hitler offered Stalin a dangerous bait, and whether Stalin took it largely because of his own expansionary desires will likely remain a subject of speculation forever. However, what is known for certain about his behavior and policies would not lead one to this conclusion, for he was the quintessential practitioner of cold-blooded, pragmatic, defensive Realpolitik. According to Fleischhauer, he knew that he was playing a dangerous game when he accepted Hitler's offer, but he saw no other real choices. Thus the Soviet Union also practiced appeasement politics at the expense of others, just as the Western powers had done a year earlier at Munich. Fleischhauer also points out that the meaning of the words in the secret protocols is very unclear and open to interpretation.

With this knowledgeable and stimulating study, it became clear that fifty years after the event a general consensus had been reached among historians about one of the most controversial chapters in contemporary history. Recent publications in English-speaking countries confirm this view. In *The Unholy Alliance*, Geoffrey Roberts outlines Soviet foreign policy from 1917 to 1938, the Nazi-Soviet pact, and its consequences until 1941 (No. 186). Although he completely disregards German research, concentrating solely on Soviet and English-language publications, Roberts comes to much the same conclusion as Fleischhauer.

According to Roberts, the Soviets viewed the pact with Hitler as marking the transition to classical great power politics and a renunciation of ideology. In any case, Stalin did not really have any other choice. A comprehensive study by Anthony Read and David Fisher, *The Deadly Embrace*, takes more account of German publications (No. 185). Based on all the leading international archives and previous research, the authors emphasize traditional German expansion eastward and recount the diplomatic game played by the great powers between 1938 and 1941.

The general consensus surrounding the outbreak of the war was consecrated at an international symposium held in the German Reichstag in August 1989. Once again, the unleashing of the war and the failure of the international system were under discussion (No. 141). Particular attention was paid to Soviet contributions because Communist historiography had begun to change enormously with *glasnost*. The taboo surrounding the Nazi-Soviet pact could only be dissolved in Moscow, and this happened amazingly quickly. Former champions of the Stalinist interpretation felt compelled to make the sudden transition themselves. Lev Besymenski, probably the best-known proponent of "old thinking," no longer totally denied the existence of the secret protocols – probably in response to instructions from above and not as the result of some new insight. He was able to save face, however, by traveling to Bonn as chairman of a special commission in order to "review" the relevant documents in the Foreign Office archives, even though they had been well known for forty years.

The ultimate result surprised no one: the Soviets accepted thereafter without any reservations the Western view of the Nazi-Soviet pact. This recognition had become in the meantime a touchstone for the credibility of Gorbachev's *perestroika*. Acceptance of the Western view of the Nazi-Soviet pact was a bitter pill for Moscow to swallow because it confirmed the illegitimacy of Soviet rule over the Baltic states. Although other territorial gains from 1939 to 1940, such as eastern Finland, eastern Poland, and Bessarabia were not immediately called into question, the renewed demands of the Baltic peoples for independence proved a heavy burden for Gorbachev.

Although the facts of the Nazi-Soviet pact were no longer disputed in the Soviet Union, the interpretation of these facts still varied considerably. While some historians such as Cubarjan, Semirjaga, and Dasicev (Nos. 148, 191, 149) maintained that the pact with Hitler was a fateful error on the part of the Soviet Union, others continued to insist that Stalin had no other reasonable choice. Wolkogonow, the director of the Institute for Military History in Moscow and an energetic champion of "new thinking" in Soviet historiography, wrote a biography of Stalin but did not produce any major new insights from a Western point of view into Stalin's motives in 1939 (No. 45). The well-known British historian Walter Laqueur wrote another study of Stalin in which he described the entire recent discussion among Soviet historians and added penetrating comments on it for Western readers (Nos. 30, 135, 147).

However, there were also many opposing voices in the Soviet Union that sought to uphold the traditional views of military history on the fiftieth anniversary of the outbreak of the war.

Once again they glossed over the Nazi-Soviet pact, and they even sought to compare the secret preparations for war by "Fascist Germany" with NATO's war preparations. The supposed lesson of the past was that the Soviet Union needed to be ever alert to the threat of a surprise attack by "imperialist aggressors" (No. 235).

In the summer of 1991, the fiftieth anniversary of the German attack on the Soviet Union thus gave fresh stimulus to the voices of the Communist military establishment – until the failed putsch and the ensuing dissolution of the Soviet Union in December 1991 created fundamentally new conditions for historians in the states that emerged. Now historiography in the lands of the former Soviet Union is undergoing a complete revision, and historians are attempting to see their own way through to something approaching the results of their Western colleagues.

In the West, in the meantime, the search for a better understanding of the essence of Stalinism has begun. The Nazi-Soviet pact, as the most intensive point of contact between the two totalitarian systems, provides a particular stimulus to revisit the theory of totalitarianism and attempt now, after the exhaustive research into Nazism over the last three decades, to establish empirically more justifiable comparisons and contrasts with Stalinism. The celebrated British historian and biographer of Hitler, Alan Bullock, produced a monumental work in 1991 that set out to do just this (No. 6). Bullock distanced himself at the outset from all-too-superficial comparisons of the two dictators, as was done by some parties to the West German *Historikerstreit*. He was as much interested in the differences as in the similarities between the two systems. In comparing the two regimes, Bullock sought to illuminate the unique natures of both Nazism and Stalinism. He recounted the lives of Hitler and Stalin (they were curiously similar in many ways), providing a synchronous portrait of the times from the viewpoint of the two dictators focused on the 1930s and 1940s. Although their private lives and work methods showed many striking similarities, their thought processes and reactions were also marked by characteristic differences. Bullock's flowing account is generally based on the latest research, although in regard to the Nazi-Soviet pact he emphasizes older views of the type set forth by Hofer. His account of the war between Germany and the Soviet Union does not include any striking new insights, but it affords a stimulating survey of the most important events and the background to them.

At about the same time, the American diplomat and historian Robert Conquest published another biography of Stalin. It was the harvest of decades of research and writing about the Stalinist terror and purges (No. 7). In Conquest's view, it was Stalin's "absolute will to power" that led him to join in a pact with Hitler. Having reviewed the most recent studies in the former Soviet Union, Conquest came to the conclusion that Stalin, brutal and covetous of power, did not trust the Germans at all but believed he could outwit them in the end. Insofar as the agreements to divide Poland and annex the Baltic states are concerned, Conquest claimed that the Soviets were not primarily motivated by strategic concerns, as is often alleged in the literature, but clearly by political concerns. He considered the annexations to have been a successful step on Stalin's part that took not only German interests into account but also the likely reaction of the Western powers.

Just as conservative interpretations constantly resurface in the former Soviet Union in an attempt to evoke and vindicate the glory and splendor of the former Soviet empire, so too emerge in the West occasional works by pseudo-scientific apologists for Hitler. This holds true, for instance, for the writings of the British author David Irving, who cleaves to the old line of defense adopted at the Nuremberg Trials that seeks to exculpate Hitler and heap the main responsibility for the outbreak of the war on Stalin (No. 21). These attempts always find individual supporters here and there, especially in Germany. In this camp as well belong efforts to revive the earlier revisionism of people such as Hoggan or Taylor and to portray Hitler as a pragmatic politician who, devoid of all ideological convictions himself, was driven into the war and through to its final conclusion by the clever strategic ploys of his great adversaries Stalin and Churchill (No. 233).

The Austrian philosopher Ernst Topitsch (No. 239) has been attempting for years to win the sympathy of historians for his largely unproved theories and speculations of this ilk. Instead, sharp rebuke has been the response (No. 227). According to Topitsch, the Second World War was Stalin's war from the outset. He is the real villain of the twentieth century, while Hitler was merely the dupe of his clever ploys in 1939. Topitsch's views found some support in the book of a certain Victor Suworow, published with great media clamor in 1989 (No. 129). Behind this pseudonym hid a defector from the Soviet secret service who, writing under the protection of its British counterpart, sought to reveal that Hitler was merely a tool that Stalin attempted to use in order to initiate a Soviet-style revolution in Europe. Again here the Nazi-Soviet pact of 1939 was portrayed as a ploy to induce the "useful fool" Hitler to declare war on the Western powers. In order to support his assertion that Stalin was preparing for an assault on Western Europe and that Hitler beat him to the punch only by a matter of two weeks in 1941, the unknown author relies on a highly slanted and questionable interpretation of Soviet documents that have long been available. "Suworow" failed to produce any new documents or evidence.

The views of these obscure political authors remained marginal and found no echo among serious historical researchers, as could be seen in the omnibus volumes about policy and strategy published on the occasion of the fiftieth anniversary of the German attack on the Soviet Union. These volumes, which provided a comprehensive overview of the research as well as a myriad of specialized studies, focused primarily on international aspects and on the particular nature of the German war effort in the East (Nos. 34, 203, 225, 240).

The reactions of East German historians to the anniversary year of 1989 testify to the difficulty of freeing oneself from politically motivated and long-held caricatures of one's enemies and from the reasons that have been concocted to support them. GDR historians remained faithful to the old Soviet line until the bitter end and were still proclaiming the old shibboleths at a time when such heretical publications were making the rounds in Moscow that they had to be banned from the GDR. An omnibus volume by the best-known East German historians on the prelude to the Second World War contained the same old doctrinaire postures (No. 125). Günter Rosenfeld, one of the most knowledgeable historians in the area of Soviet-German relations, even went so far as to celebrate the pact as a great success for Soviet diplomacy.

Similarly, Heinz Kühnrich's contribution on the attitude adopted by the German Communist party at the time attempted to show the admiration that Communists around the world felt in 1939 for the Herculean efforts of the Soviet Union to avoid another world war (No. 172). There was no mention of the profound shock that Communists in many countries felt when the pact was announced. According to Kühnrich's misleading interpretation, "the statements made at the time help us to broaden our understanding of the fact that threats to peace always originate from the most reactionary imperialist forces and are aimed not only at the socialist countries but also at the vital interests of all peoples. The Soviet Union, on the other hand, has always attempted to secure the peace and continues to do so today."

When these lines were finally printed, the German Democratic Republic was on the brink of revolution. After the *Wende* in the fall of 1989, Gerhart Hass quickly issued extensive documentation on the Nazi-Soviet pact (No. 67). But this did not suffice for East German historiography to regain its credibility. The saying that "those who come too late are punished by life" apparently applies to historians as well.

* * *

Among Western historians, views of Hitler's policies between the signing of the Nazi-Soviet pact and the subsequent attack on the Soviet Union had converged quite early. The 1965 study by Andreas Hillgruber mentioned above (No. 19) set an internationally recognized standard that has remained valid to this day. In the early 1950s, a controversy erupted about the exact date of Hitler's decision to invade the Soviet Union, a debate in which Hillgruber himself participated. The controversy was triggered by the first overview of Soviet-German relations between 1939 and 1941, written by the American historian Gerhard L. Weinberg (No. 131). At the time it was quite clear that the signing of the Nazi-Soviet pact and the outbreak of war with the Western powers in September 1939 had not distracted Hitler from his ultimate goals in the East. But when exactly did he decide that the time had come to turn his energies eastward?

Weinberg decided upon 31 July 1940, when, according to the notes of Hitler's Chief of General Staff, Franz Halder, the Führer issued instructions for military preparations. Hillgruber on the other hand decided upon a later date, namely after Molotov's visit in November 1940 (No. 242). Two contrasting positions were thus staked out and much discussed in subsequent research.

The debate revolved essentially around what Hitler's real motives were for this most portentous decision of his life. Was he responding primarily to his political and ideological motivations when he turned eastward after the conquest of France toward the real goal of the war: the conquest of new *Lebensraum* in the East – as several authors have asserted (Nos. D/65–67, 240)? Or was Hitler more influenced by strategic considerations prompted by the fact that Great Britain was not showing any desire to agree to a peace treaty, despite having been evicted from the

Continent, and that the entry of the United States into the war was already beginning to look imminent?

The old arguments about a preventive war occasionally surfaced in the memoirs of German military leaders, but this official Nazi rationale for the attack on the Soviet Union was eventually rejected by later historians. It was contradicted, for instance, by the situation analyses produced by the former German military attaché in Moscow, published in 1965, or by the papers of the Secretary of State in the Foreign Office, Ernst Freiherr von Weizsäcker (Nos. 44, 62).

Although Hillgruber had still emphasized the strategic considerations in 1953, he changed his mind and put greater emphasis on the ideological considerations by the time that his monumental study of Hitler's strategy was published. Many specialized studies in the last three decades have served to confirm and further develop his compelling analysis of Hitler's strategic and political decision-making until the tide of war began to change in December 1941 as the German forces approached Moscow. In the second edition of his work, published in 1980, Hillgruber included a fine survey of these works. He himself has always taken a very clear position in this regard in his numerous other works on the history of the Second World War (No. 20).

Of particular importance to Hillgruber was the fact that Hitler did not have a "European" program and instead planned on "worldwide blitzkrieg." Expansion to the east was accordingly only one step on the path to world dominance; it was to provide a staging ground for the eventual conflict with the United States and the British Empire. According to Hillgruber, Hitler's overall strategy had already begun to focus on the United States by the summer of 1940.

In the dictator's inner circle, however, there were a variety of views about Germany's future plans. Foreign Minister Joachim von Ribbentrop hoped primarily to establish a Eurasian "continental bloc" including the Soviet Union and conducted his discussions with Molotov in November 1940 with this goal in mind (No. 31). The high command of the navy, on the other hand, wanted to concentrate the bulk of the war effort on the Mediterranean and the Near East, as well as on northwest Africa (Nos. 230, 231). Leading circles in Germany were also divided about the role that Japan should play, whether mainly as a partner in the attack on the Soviet Union or as the spearhead of an attack on the United States (No. 369). Most specialized studies of Hitler's foreign policy and alliances came to the conclusion that in the end Germany failed in 1940–41 to develop any consistent overall strategy for continuing the war. This seemed to be an ongoing structural flaw in German attempts in the twentieth century to achieve great power status, a flaw that could be traced back to the nineteenth century.

The fact that Hillgruber ultimately concluded that ideology was the main factor in Hitler's decision to invade the Soviet Union does not mean that he underestimated the strategic problems that the Führer faced. In his later works he illuminated these problems very well. However, he continued to argue convincingly against the attempts of various individuals on the periphery of historical research to ascribe Hitler's decision to invade the Soviet Union to strategic reasons alone (Nos. 237, E/2d). Hillgruber has been supported in this by virtually all recent studies of Hitler's policies and strategy in the first years of the war (Nos. 17, 36, 213).

Hillgruber could take some satisfaction that this extensive and to some extent still controversial German research finally began to be received in the English-speaking world as well. The Canadian historian Barry A. Leach (No. 221) initiated this debate in 1973, with his response to a controversy among British and American historians, many of whom still viewed Hitler as primarily a pragmatist who decided to attack the Soviet Union solely on the basis of a strategic situation that began to go awry in the summer of 1940. Grounding his work on the German and Soviet research, Leach provided an overview of the relationship between all the various ideological, economic, strategic, and operational factors that went into the decision to attack the Soviet Union. He, too, saw the concept of *Lebensraum* and the available tool of blitzkrieg as the foundations of Hitler's overall strategy. Shortly thereafter, Robert Cecil came to a similar conclusion in his depiction of Operation Barbarossa (No. 208).

In his recently published global history of the Second World War, Gerhard L. Weinberg gives Hitler's war in the East much more attention than other Western publications. His book is the best survey on the political and strategical aspects of the war, representative of modern research and a valuable guide to literature and sources (No. 42).

In the mid-1960s, the British historian Alan S. Milward had portrayed blitzkrieg as a fundamental element in German strategy. According to him, the Nazi leaders hoped to carry out their conquests in discrete steps, isolating their victims diplomatically and then eliminating them in a series of quick, one-on-one struggles. There would be breaks between the campaigns in order not to overextend the German civilian population and to allow time to accumulate the necessary stores for the next attack through exploitation of the occupied territories (No. 223).

Marxist historians largely espoused this interpretation, although they were always eager to demonstrate above all that Hitler's wartime decisions could be traced back to the influence of big capital. Despite producing worthwhile insights into the war aims of German industry, they never succeeded in demonstrating their fundamental thesis (Nos. D/24, 26). Studies of the economic aspects of the war with the Soviet Union, which were not generally undertaken until the 1980s, and of the role played by the traditional elites in the German army, economy, the churches, and the state bureaucracy shed considerable new light on the war in the East (Nos. D/468, 81). By 1983, the fourth volume of the series *Das Deutsche Reich und der Zweite Weltkrieg* had provided a balanced outline and analysis of many aspects of the German decision-making process and campaign preparations (No. 224). It offered not only a new survey of the economic facets of the war but also new insights into military decision-making and planning.

The result was a war plan that, although it possessed elements of a blitzkrieg strategy, had not consistently developed and pursued this strategy by the summer of 1940 – despite Milward's assertions to the contrary (No. D/9). Developed under the influence of particular ideological convictions and economic aspirations, as well as an extremely exaggerated view of German strengths and Soviet weaknesses, this preposterous war plan brought the Wehrmacht to the verge of collapse in just a few short months.

The various individual stations along the way are still the object of some discussion and even dispute among historians, despite the grand overview provided by Hillgruber. This is true, in particular, of the significance of the Balkan campaign in April 1941, which interrupted preparations to attack the Soviet Union for a few weeks. The older view was that Hitler felt compelled to reinforce the German position in the Balkans, because of British support for Greek resistance and spreading Soviet influence in Yugoslavia, before turning his attention to the Soviet Union. As a result, the attack had to be postponed and valuable time was lost, time that proved to be crucial as the advance on Moscow began to stall in October and November 1941. More recent studies have concluded, however, that only a little time was lost and have emphasized that the original date for the attack, 15 May, could not have been adhered to in any case because of weather conditions and delays in the delivery of armaments, among other things (Nos. 210, B/9).

* * *

The period between the beginning of the German invasion of the Soviet Union on 22 June 1941 and the turning point in the campaign in December 1941 proved to be critical, and not only for the struggle in the East, because it also saw the transition from a European war to a global war. All the great powers were compelled therefore to develop new war aims and strategies for the remainder of the war – a task that was virtually impossible for Hitler. Only a few weeks after the beginning of the war of annihilation against the Soviet Union, it became clear that this would be no blitzkrieg and that preparations would have to be made for a much longer campaign. However, this undermined all the German measures for new priorities in armaments production and all the strategic plans for the start of a world war only after "Barbarossa" was complete. These designs were thereby exposed as little more than airy illusions of the General Staff.

By the end of July 1941, Hitler's war plans had reached a dead end, exactly one year after he had made the fateful decision, standing on the heights of his success against France, to invade the Soviet Union. Despite the latent atmosphere of crisis surrounding his leadership, the need to adopt new approaches was ignored and temporary comfort was taken from expectations of fresh victories. The Führer still had some opportunity until the end of the year to adopt new political approaches and fresh strategies, but thereafter his options were closed. Hitler's decision in July 1940 to invade the Soviet Union has often been discussed by historians; only recently, however, has the July 1941 failure of his plans for "worldwide blitzkrieg" been clearly pointed out (Nos. 247; 151, vol. 4; D/9). The apparently brilliant string of military successes in the summer of 1941 cloaked the failure of Hitler's political plans. While the coalition between the United States, Great Britain, and the Soviet Union was slowly coming together, the "triple alliance" between Germany, Italy, and Japan failed to amount to much. The shortcomings in Germany's attempts to forge alliances and wage coalition wars have often been described in specialized studies (Nos. 265, 268, 403).

Japan sought, with Hitler's encouragement, to expand across the Pacific. This kept the United States preoccupied but at the same time freed the Soviets from the threat of a second front in the Far East. Forces were freed to be transferred west, and Stalin was able to bring the German offensive to a halt and inexorably turn the military situation to his advantage. The turning point in the war in December 1941 was not only militarily significant but was also of profound political importance. The Soviet Union began its ascent to the position of an acknowledged superpower alongside the United States and received strong material support from the Western Allies as a full-fledged partner in the anti-Hitler coalition.

Hitler on the other hand was left with his political plans and strategies in tatters, and there were signs that he realized that the game was up. It would be hopeless, he believed, to seek a political end to the war, as his Minister of Armaments, Fritz Todt, was recommending (No. D/9). There was no way forward and no way back. Ever since 1939 he had always been willing to gamble everything on a single roll of the dice and had intentionally burned his bridges behind him. World power or annihilation, to be or not to be, that was his creed.

Hitler's biographer Joachim C. Fest comments therefore that the Führer ensconced himself in his ideological beliefs at the outset of the war and never returned to pragmatic politics (Nos. 9, 10). The more the conduct of the war occupied his time, eventually consuming him entirely, the less able he was to go beyond day-to-day military tactics in order to ponder political and strategic options.

This inability condemned to failure all attempts of his inner circle and of the army high command to shift from a war of plunder and annihilation in the East to a politicized war that might have undermined the resistance of the Red Army and improved the military situation (Part D). Hitler also totally disregarded the advice of foreign politicians. The shift in the fortunes of war before the gates of Moscow had sown the first seeds of doubt about final victory among the allies of the Third Reich, and they began to attempt to extricate themselves from the embrace of the Führer. But all Hitler wanted were acolytes and cannon fodder for the Eastern Front. He was ready therefore to meet regularly with representatives of the satellite states, but this had little to do with political planning. Hitler himself quite accurately qualified these meetings as "hypnotic treatments" (No. 69). The effectiveness of this behavior dwindled, however, as the war dragged on, and while Hitler prepared his own ruination, his allies thrashed about seeking to find an escape from the war.

Hitler's embrace of utter ruination cut two ways, however. It was directed first of all against the Jews, the systematic genocide of whom began as soon as Hitler realized that the war was lost (Part C). Second, it was directed against Hitler's own people, whom he wished to drag into the vortex of his own ultimate destruction. His whole conduct of the war revolved thereafter around a single aim: to gain time and cling to the conquered lands as long as possible. This no longer had anything to do with rational politics and strategy.

In the summer of 1942, the successful offensive toward the Caucasus and the Volga awakened new hope and dreams of victory in the German leadership. It provided a window of opportunity before the opening of the feared "second front" in Europe. If German possessions in the East could be extended in time to encompass more essential raw materials and strategic positions, then the gathering onslaught against *Festung Europa* could be awaited with some confidence. Although Hitler's conduct of the war in 1941 has been studied often and thoroughly, most discussions of the Russian campaign end around the spring of 1942. Only recent German overviews (No. 151a, vol. 3; No. 4) have provided a deeper analysis of events, including political and economic factors and new source materials.

These studies have shown conclusively that there were no alternatives to more offensives because Germany could not support a long war unless it conquered the oil fields of the Caucasus. The "September crisis" (No. 255) in the Führer's headquarters, when he dismissed his Chief of General Staff, Franz Halder (No. 63), again fostered flight into a poorly considered "holdout" mentality, the only acceptable form of defensive warfare in Hitler's view. It was hardly any kind of strategy for regaining the initiative but simply an expression of Hitler's mounting helplessness and incompetence. The consequence of this obtuseness and failure of military leadership was the destruction of the Sixth Army at Stalingrad.

This battle is usually portrayed as the turning point in the war. This is true at least insofar as the political consequences are concerned, for the mood of the German people sank to new depths. No less serious were the psychological effects on Germany's allies, as shown in works on "cracks in the alliance" (Nos. 263, 281). There were mounting attempts to find one's own way out of the lost war in Finland, Rumania, Hungary, and Italy, which had seen a large portion of their armed forces destroyed in the East. For Germany this spelled the final loss of all strategic initiative. Thereafter there could be no more rational hope of victory or partial victory in the East. The only certainty was that Germany lacked sufficient men and materials to meet the gathering onslaught of the anti-Hitler coalition. All it could do was play for time.

While Hitler sought solace in declarations that the war effort would be intensified, all forces would be fully mobilized, and new "wonder weapons" would soon be developed, the people around him made occasional, isolated attempts to find a political solution – attempts that he at least tolerated in some instances. His only hope under the circumstances was to divide the enemy coalition and conclude separate peace treaties with individual opponents. Even Heinrich Himmler, Hitler's most blood-stained accomplice, took part in this highly secret game, which continued through various channels until the spring of 1945.

Historians have traditionally paid little attention to these final political acts and "peace feelers" extended by the Third Reich (No. 421). The source documents were too uncertain and obscure, and the tangle of secret service operations, intentional disinformation, and provocation was too complicated to unwind. Recently, however, considerable light has been shed on this subject in the systematic studies undertaken by Josef Schröder and Ingeborg Fleischhauer on the basis of the available sources, circumstantial evidence, and statements made by the people involved (Nos. 428, 415). According to these researchers, most feelers about eliminating the Eastern Front did not emanate from the Third Reich but rather from other countries, particularly Japan, Italy, and the Soviet Union. Japan attempted to mediate a separate peace between Germany and the Soviet Union in order to advance its own cause of a war directed primarily against the United States. Italy, meanwhile, hoped that a truce on the Eastern Front would enable the Axis powers to concentrate on asserting Italian hegemony in the Mediterranean, or at least on defending Italy itself, while the Soviet Union hoped that its ostensible interest in reaching a separate peace with Germany would put pressure on the Western Allies and compel them quickly to open a second front on the Continent. There is some truth to the assertion that the Cold War, which dominated the postwar era for more than four decades, began with these peace feelers.

Although even Rome and Tokyo failed to coordinate their attempts to arrange a separate peace, the ultimate responsibility remains with one man, Adolf Hitler, who refused to abandon his racially and politically motivated fixation with annihilating the Soviet Union. Not until the Red Army crossed into Germany itself was the Führer able to conceive of a separate peace with Stalin along the lines of the 1939 pact, because in his view only Stalin now had the power to enforce it. At the same time, however, Hitler realized that after all that had happened on the Eastern battlefields, both the Soviet and German peoples would have little heart for another about-face, and all thoughts of a separate peace remained idle speculation in the Führerbunker as annihilation drew ever nearer.

At the same time that occasional peace feelers were being extended, the two great contestants on the Eastern battlefields responded to the turning point of Stalingrad by heightening their political warfare. Hitler yielded to the persistent suggestions of his closest advisers and agreed to the creation of the so-called Vlasov movement (see Part D). Stalin countered with the establishment of the National Committee for Free Germany and the League of German Officers. These associations of captured German soldiers conducted strong propaganda campaigns not only in the prisoner-of-war camps but also along the front.

Hitler's concerns about the old tale of Tauroggen, where in 1813 the Prussian auxiliary forces had abandoned Napoleon's Grande Armée and concluded a separate peace with the Russians, proved to be totally unfounded. Even the "spirit of Rapallo" and the close cooperation between the Reichswehr and the Red Army in the 1920s had left little impression on German army officers. When a small group of officers finally did attempt a coup against Hitler on 20 July 1944, they looked to the Western powers for support rather than to the Soviets. The ideological aspect of the war on the Eastern Front was so firmly entrenched even in the Wehrmacht that all thoughts of reaching an understanding with the Red Army, let alone of establishing fraternal relations, were far removed. Indeed, it was in the East that ordinary German soldiers fought most bitterly to defend the old German border areas, side by side with their radical Nazi leaders (No. 532). Hillgruber's conviction that German patriots had no other possibility after 20 July 1944 than to fight on doggedly against the Red Army "in spite of Hitler," because Stalin was determined to destroy the old German Reich, prompted considerable controversy during the West German *Historikerstreit* in the mid-1980s.

The particular political coloration of the war on the Eastern Front, for which there was no counterpart in the West, hindered all attempts to reach a separate peace with the English-speaking powers. The collapse of the Eastern Front in the summer of 1944 crushed all German hopes of sufficiently stabilizing the situation in the East in order to draw off enough forces to prevent an invasion in the West. The success of Operation Overlord, the landing in Normandy, caught the German army in a vice from which it had no hope of escape. Even the promised "wonder weapons" provided little respite. On the Eastern Front, the Red Army pushed inexorably forward, despite the German "scorched earth" strategy – the intentional devastation of wide tracts of land. The anti-Hitler coalition held, contrary to all expectations in Germany and despite mounting internal tensions. Hitler responded to the repeated attempts within his inner circle to reach a political settlement with the foe with the comment: "Politics? I'm not interested in politics any more. I'm sick of it."[3]

Hitler's suicide in the Chancellery, as Berlin blazed around him, symbolized the total collapse of Germany's attempts in the twentieth century to become a great world power. In the meantime, however, German political fantasies of great empires in the East had precipitated two world wars and cost more than fifty million lives.

3. Quoted by J. Fest, "Hitlers Krieg," *Vierteljahrshefte für Zeitgeschichte* 38 (1990): 370.

Bibliography

1. General

a) Overview

1) *Die Befreiungsmission der Sowjetunion im Zweiten Weltkrieg*. Moscow, 1985
2) Bloch, Charles. *Das Dritte Reich und die Welt. Die deutsche Außenpolitik 1933–1945*. Paderborn, 1992
3) Blücher, Wipert von. *Gesandter zwischen Diktatur und Demokratie. Erinnerungen aus den Jahren 1935–1944*. Wiesbaden, 1951
4) Boog, Horst, Werner Rahn, Reinhard Stumpf, and Bernd Wegner. *Der globale Krieg. Die Ausweitung zum Weltkrieg und der Wechsel der Initiative 1941–1943*. Das Deutsche Reich und der Zweite Weltkrieg, vol. 6. Stuttgart, 1990
5) Bullock, Alan. *Hitler: A Study in Tyranny*. London, 1962
6) _____. *Hitler und Stalin. Parallele Leben*. Berlin, 1991
7) Conquest, Robert. *Stalin – Breaker of Nations*. London, 1991
8) Dirksen, Herbert von. *Moskau, Tokio, London. Erinnerungen und Betrachtungen zu zwanzig Jahren deutscher Außenpolitik 1919–1939*. Stuttgart, 1949
9) Fest, Joachim C. *Hitler*. New York, 1974
10) _____. "Hitlers Krieg." *Vierteljahrshefte für Zeitgeschichte* vol. 38 (1990): pp. 359–373
11) Funke, Manfred, ed. *Hitler, Deutschland und die Mächte. Materialien zur Außenpolitik des Dritten Reiches*. Bonner Schriften zur Politik und Zeitgeschichte, no. 12. Düsseldorf, 1976
12) *Geschichte der sowjetischen Außenpolitik 1917 bis 1945*. Edited by B.N. Ponomarev. Part 1. East Berlin, 1969
13) *Geschichte des Zweiten Weltkrieges 1939–1945*. Edited by A.A. Gretschko. Vol. 2, *Am Vorabend des Krieges*. East Berlin, 1975

14) Gruchmann, Lothar. *Der Zweite Weltkrieg. Kriegführung und Politik*. 7th edn. Munich, 1982
15) Herwarth von Bittenfeld, Hans-Heinrich. *Against Two Evils. Memoirs of a Diplomat*. New York, 1981
16) Higgins, Trumbull. *Hitler and Russia. The Third Reich in a Two-Front War, 1937–1943*. New York, 1966
17) Hildebrand, Klaus. *Deutsche Außenpolitik, 1933–1945. Kalkül oder Dogma?* 4th edn. Stuttgart, 1980
18) Hilger, Gustav. *The Incompatible Allies: A Memoir-History of German-Soviet Relations, 1918–1941*. New York, 1953
19) Hillgruber, Andreas. *Hitlers Strategie. Politik und Kriegführung 1940–1941*. 2nd edn. Frankfurt a.M., 1982
20) ____. *Der Zweite Weltkrieg 1939–1945. Kriegsziele und Strategie der Großen Mächte*. Stuttgart, 1982
21) Irving, David. *Hitler's War, 1939–1942*. London, 1983
22) Israeljan, V. L. *Diplomaticeskaja istorija Velikoj Otecestvennoj vojny 1941–1945 gg*. Edited by G.A. Alekseev, et al. Moscow, 1959
23) *Istorija mezdunarodnych otnosenij i vnesnej politiki SSSR. 1917–1960gg*. 3 vols. Moscow, 1961–1964 (German edn: East Berlin, 1963, 1965)
24) *Istorija Velikoj Otecestvennoj Vojny Sovetskogo Sojuza 1941–1945*. Edited by P. N. Pospelow, et al. Vols 1–6. Moscow 1960–1965 (German edn: East Berlin, 1962–1968)
25) *Istorija vnesnej politiki SSSR 1917–1970*. Edited by B.N. Ponomarev, A.A. Gromyko, et al. 5th edn. Moscow, 1985–1986 (English edn: *History of Soviet Foreign Policy, 1917–1955*. Moscow 1969; German edn: *Geschichte der sowjetischen Außenpolitik*. Frankfurt a.M., 1970–1971)
26) Jacobsen, Hans-Adolf. *Der Zweite Weltkrieg. Grundzüge der Politik und Strategie in Dokumenten*. Frankfurt a.M., 1965
27) Kleist, Peter. *Zwischen Hitler und Stalin 1939–1945*. Bonn, 1950
28) Kordt, Erich. *Nicht aus den Akten: Die Wilhelmstraße in Frieden und Krieg*. Stuttgart, 1950
29) Kuhn, Axel. *Hitlers außenpolitisches Programm. Entstehung und Entwicklung 1919–1933*. Stuttgart, 1970
30) Laqueur, Walter. *Stalin. Abrechnung im Zeichen von Glastnost*. Munich, 1990
31) Michalka, Wolfgang. *Ribbentrop und die deutsche Weltpolitik 1933–1940. Außenpolitische Konzeptionen und Entscheidungsprozesse im Dritten Reich*. Munich, 1980
32) *Osvoboditel'naja missija sovetskich vooruzennych sil v Evrope vo 2 mirovoj vojne. Dokumenty i materialy*. Moscow, 1985
33) Recker, Marie-Luise. *Die Außenpolitik des Dritten Reiches*. Enzyklopädie deutscher Geschichte, vol. 8. Munich, 1990
34) Schafranek, Hans, and Robert Streibel. *22. Juni 1941. Der Überfall auf die Sowjetunion*. Vienna, 1991
35) Schmidt, Paul. *Statist auf diplomatischer Bühne, 1923–1945*. Bonn, 1949
36) Schreiber, Gerhard. "Deutsche Politik und Kriegführung 1939 bis 1945." In *Deutschland 1933–1945. Neue Studien zur nationalsozialistischen Herrschaft*, edited by Karl Dietrich Bracher, Manfred Funke and Hans-Adolf Jacobsen, pp. 333–356. Bonn, 1992
37) *SSSR v bor'be protiv fasistskoj agressi 1933–1945*. 2nd edn. Moscow, 1986
38) *SSSR v Velikoj Otecestvennoj vojne. 1941–1945. Kratkaja chronika*. 2nd edn. Moscow, 1970

39) Thies, Jochen. *Architekt der Weltherrschaft. Die "Endziele" Hitlers.* Düsseldorf, 1976
40) Toland, John. *Adolf Hitler*. New York, 1976
41) *Vtoraja mirovaja Vojna*. Edited by S.L. Sokolov. Moscow, 1985.
42) Weinberg, Gerhard L. *A World at Arms. A Global History of World War II.* Cambridge, 1994
43) _____. *World in the Balance. Behind the Scenes of World War II*. The Tamber Institute Series, no. 1. Hanover, 1981
44) Weizsäcker, Ernst von. *Erinnerungen. Mein Leben*. Edited by Richard von Weizsäcker. Munich, 1950
45) Wolkogonow, Dimitri. *Stalin. Triumph und Tragödie. Ein politisches Porträt*. Düsseldorf, 1989

b) Sources

46) *Akten zur deutschen auswärtigen Politik 1918–1945*. Serie D: 1937–1941, vols VI–XIII, (2.3.1939–11.12.1941). Baden-Baden, 1956ff
47) Baynes, N.H., ed. *Hitler's Speeches, 1922–39*. 2 vols. Oxford, 1942
48) Beitzel, Robert. *Teheran, Yalta, Potsdam. The Soviet Protocols*. The Russian Series, no. 17. Hattiesburg, 1970
49) Besymenski, Lew. *Sonderakte Barbarossa. Dokumentarbericht zur Vorgeschichte des deutschen Überfalls auf die Sowjetunion – aus sowjetischer Sicht*. Reinbek, 1973
50) *Briefwechsel Stalins mit Churchill, Attlee, Roosevelt und Truman 1941–1945*. East Berlin, 1961
51) Brügel, Johann Wolfgang. *Stalin und Hitler. Pakt gegen Europa*. Vienna, 1973
52) Bundesminister des Innern, ed. *Dokumente zur Deutschlandpolitik*. 2nd series. Vol. 1, *Die Konferenz von Potsdam*. Frankfurt a.M., 1992
53) Carroll, E.M., and Fritz T. Epstein. *Das nationalsozialistische Deutschland und die Sowjetunion 1939–1941. Akten aus dem Archiv des deutschen Auswärtigen Amtes*. Washington, 1948
54) Deuerlein, Ernst. *Die Einheit Deutschlands*. Vol. 1, *Die Erörterungen und Entscheidungen der Kriegs- und Nachkriegskonferenzen 1941–1949. Darstellung, Dokumente*. 2nd edn. Frankfurt, 1961
55) _____. ed. *Potsdam 1945. Quellen zur Konferenz der "Großen Drei."* Munich, 1963
56) *Deutsch-sowjetische Geheimverbindungen. Unveröffentlichte diplomatische Depeschen zwischen Berlin und Moskau im Vorfeld des Zweiten Weltkrieges*. Edited by Karl Höffkes. Tübingen, 1988
57) *Documents and Materials Relating to the Eve of the Second World War*. 2 vols. Moscow, 1948
58) Domarus, Max. *Hitler. Reden und Proklamationen 1932–1945. Kommentiert von einem deutschen Zeitgenossen*. 2 vols. Wiesbaden, 1973
59) Fischer, Alexander von. *Teheran, Jalta, Potsdam. Die sowjetischen Protokolle von den Kriegskonferenzen der "Grossen Drei"*. Dokumente der Außenpolitik, vol. 2. Cologne, 1968
60) Foitzik, Jan. "Die Kommunistische Partei Deutschlands und der Hitler-Stalin-Pakt. Die Erklärung des Zentralkomitees vom 25. August 1939 im Wortlaut." *Vierteljahrshefte für Zeitgeschichte* vol. 37 (1989): pp. 499–514

61) *Foreign Relations of the United States. Diplomatic Papers*. Edited by the Department of State. *1943*. Vol. I, *The Conference at Cairo and Tehran*. Washington, 1961. *1945: The Conference at Malta and Yalta*. Washington, 1955. *1945: Conference of Berlin (the Potsdam Conference)*. 2 vols. Washington, 1960. *1945*. Vol. III, *European Advisory Commission, Austria, Germany*. Washington, 1968

62) *General Ernst Köstring. Der militärische Mittler zwischen dem Deutschen Reich und der Sowjetunion 1921–1941*. Edited by Hermann Teske. Profile bedeutender Soldaten, vol. 1. Frankfurt a.M., 1965

63) *Generaloberst Halder. Kriegstagebuch. Tägliche Aufzeichnungen des Chefs des Generalstabes des Heeres 1939–1942*. Edited by Hans-Adolf Jacobsen. Vols 1–3. Stuttgart, 1962–1964

64) Goebbels, Joseph. *Tagebücher 1945. Die letzten Aufzeichnungen*. Introduction by Rolf Hochhuth. Hamburg, 1977

64a) Goebbels, Joseph. *Die Tagebücher von Joseph Goebbels. Sämtliche Fragmente*. Edited by Elke Fröhlich. Part I, *Aufzeichnungen 1924–1941*. 4 vols. Munich, 1987. Part II, *Diktate 1941–1945*. 15 vols. Munich, 1993–1996

65) *God krizisa, 1938–1939: Dokumenty i materialy*. 2 vols. Moscow, 1990

66) Gromyko, A.A., et al., eds. *Sovetsko-francuzskie otnosenija vo vremja Velikoj Otecestvennoj vojny 1941–1945. Dokumenty i materialy*. 2 vols. Moscow, 1983

67) Hass, Gerhart. *23. August 1939. Der Hitler-Stalin-Pakt. Dokumentation*. Berlin, 1990

68) Hill, Leonidas E., ed. *Die Weizsäcker-Papiere 1933–1950*. Frankfurt a.M., 1974

69) Hillgruber, Andreas, ed. *Staatsmänner und Diplomaten bei Hitler. Vertrauliche Aufzeichnungen über Unterredungen mit Vertretern des Auslandes 1939–1941*. 2 vols. Frankfurt a.M., 1967

70) *Hitlers politisches Testament. Die Bormann-Diktate vom Februar und April 1945*. With an essay by Hugh R. Trevor-Roper and a postface by André Francois-Poncet. Hamburg, 1981

71) *Hitlers Zweites Buch. Ein Dokument aus dem Jahr 1928*. Introduction and commentary by Gerhard L. Weinberg. Stuttgart, 1961

72) *Die Jalta-Dokumente, vollständige deutsche Ausgabe der offiziellen Dokumente des U.S. State Departments über die Konferenz von Jalta*. Göttingen, 1957

73) Jankowski, T., and E. Weese, eds. *Documents on Polish-Soviet Relations, 1939–1945*. London, 1961

74) Kotze, Hildegard von, ed. *Heeresadjutant bei Hitler 1938–1943. Aufzeichnungen des Majors Engel*. Stuttgart, 1974

75) *Krymskaja Konferencija rukovoditelej trech sojuznych derzav – SSSR, SSA i Veliko-britanii (4–11 fevr. 1945 g.). Sbornik dok*. Moscow, 1979.

76) Loeber, Dietrich A., ed. *Diktierte Option. Die Umsiedlung der Deutsch-Balten aus Estland und Lettland 1939–1941*. Neumünster, 1972

77) Lochner, Louis P., ed. *Joseph Goebbels: Tagebücher aus den Jahren 1942–1943*. Zürich, 1948

78) Pätzold, Kurt, and Günter Rosenfeld, eds. *Sowjetstern und Hakenkreuz 1938 bis 1941. Dokumente zu den deutsch-sowjetischen Beziehungen*. Berlin, 1991

79) *Das Potsdamer Abkommen. Dokumentensammlung*. Edited by Historische Gedenkstätte des Potsdamer Abkommens Cecilienhof, Potsdam. 4th edn. East Berlin, 1984
80) *Proklamationen des Führers an das Deutsche Volk und Note des Auswärtigen Amtes an die Sowjet-Regierung nebst Anlagen*. Berlin, 1941
81) *Der Prozeß gegen die Hauptkriegsverbrecher vor dem Internationalen Militärgerichtshof Nürnberg 14. Oktober 1945–1. Oktober 1946*. 42 vols. Nuremberg, 1947–1949
82) Ribbentrop, Joachim von. *Zwischen London und Moskau: Erinnerungen und letzte Aufzeichnungen*. Stuttgart, 1955
83) Rozanov, German L. *Stalin – Gitler: Dokumental'nyi ocerk sovetsko-germanskich diplomaticeskich otnosenij 1939–1941*. Moscow, 1991
84) Rosenbusch, Michael, Horst Schützler, and Sonja Striegnitz, eds. *Schauplatz Baltikum: Szenarium einer Okkupation und Angliederung. Dokumente 1939/1940*. Berlin, 1991
85) Sanakojew, Slava P. and B.L. Zybulewski. *Teheran, Jalta, Potsdam. Dokumentensammlung*. Frankfurt a.M., 1978
86) Schumann, Wolfgang, and Ludwig Nestler, eds. *Weltherrschaft im Visier. Dokumente zu den Europa- und Weltherrschaftsplänen des deutschen Imperialismus von der Jahrhundertwende bis Mai 1945*. East Berlin, 1975
87) Seidl, Alfred, ed. *Die Beziehungen zwischen Deutschland und der Sowjetunion 1939–1941. Dokumente des AA*. Tübingen, 1949
88) *Sovetskij Sojuz na mezdunarodnych konferencijach perioda Velikoj Otecestvennoj vojny 1941–1945gg*. 6 vols. Moscow, 1978–1980
89) *Sovetsko-fracuzskie otnosenija vo vremja Velikoj Otecestvennoj voiny 1941–1945. Dokumenty i materialy*. Moscow, 1959
90) Sontag, Raymond James, and James Stuart Beddie, eds. *Nazi-Soviet Relations, 1939–1941. Documents from the Archives of the German Foreign Office*. Washington, 1948
90a) Speer, Albert. *Erinnerungen*. Frankfurt a.M., 1969
91) Taylor, Fred, ed. *The Goebbels Diaries, 1939–41*. London, 1982
92) *Teheran, Jalta, Potsdam. Sbornik dokumentov*. Edited by S.P. Sanakoev, and B.L. Cybulevskij. 2nd edn. Moscow, 1970
93) Toynbee, A.J., ed. "Relations between the U.S.S.R. and Germany from 17 April 1939 to the Conclusion of the Treaty of Non-Aggression on 23 August 1939." In *Documents on International Affairs 1939–1946*, vol. 1, pp. 370–410. London, 1951
94) *Die unheilige Allianz. Stalins Briefwechsel mit Churchill 1941–1945*. With an introduction by Manfred Rexin. Reinbek, 1964
95) Volz, Hans. *Der Kampf gegen den Osten 1941*. Berlin, 1944
96) Watts, Franklin, ed. *Voices of 1942–43. Speeches and Papers of Roosevelt, Churchill, Stalin, Chiang, Hitler and Other Leaders, Delivered during 1942*. New York, 1943

2. History of Soviet-German Relations, 1933–1939

97) Allard, Sven. *Stalin und Hitler. Die sowjetrussische Außenpolitik 1930–1941*. Bern, 1974

98) Anderle, Alfred, et al. "Zur Entwicklung der deutsch-sowjetischen Beziehungen von 1933 bis zum faschistischen Überfall auf die UdSSR." In *Auf antisowjetischem Kriegskurs*, edited by Hans Höhn et al., pp. 15–61. East Berlin, 1970

99) Basler, Werner. "Der deutsche Imperialismus und die Sowjetunion. Grundzüge der Außenpolitik Deutschlands gegenüber dem Sowjetstaat 1917–1941." In *Juni 1941*, edited by Alfred Anderle and Werner Basler, pp. 44–82. East Berlin, 1961

100) Carr, Edward H. *Berlin-Moskau. Deutschland und Rußland zwischen den beiden Weltkriegen*. Stuttgart, 1954

101) Fabry, Philipp W. *Der Hitler-Stalin-Pakt*. Darmstadt, 1962

102) _____. *Die Sowjetunion und das Dritte Reich. Eine dokumentierte Geschichte der deutsch-russischen Beziehungen von 1933 bis 1941*. Stuttgart, 1971

103) Fleischhauer, Ingeborg. *Diplomatischer Widerstand gegen "Unternehmen Barbarossa". Die Friedensbemühungen der Deutschen Botschaft Moskau 1939–1941*. Berlin, 1991

104) Fomin, V.T. *Agressija fasitskoj Germanii v Evrope 1933–1938gg*. Moscow, 1963

105) *Geschichte der sowjetischen Außenpolitik 1917–1966 in zwei Teilen*. Edited by Boris Nikolaevic Ponomarev et al. East Berlin, 1969

106) Haffner, Sebastian. *Der Teufelspakt. Fünfzig Jahre deutsch-russische Beziehungen*. Reinbek, 1968

107) Haslam, J. *The Soviet Union and the Struggle for Collective Security in Europe, 1933–1939*. London, 1984

108) Hillgruber, Andreas, and Klaus Hildebrand. *Kalkül zwischen Macht und Ideologie. Der Hitler-Stalin-Pakt: Parallelen bis heute?* Zürich, 1980

109) Hillgruber, Andreas. *Deutschlands Rolle in der Vorgeschichte der beiden Weltkriege*. Göttingen, 1967

110) Kennan, George F. *Soviet Foreign Policy, 1917–1941*. Princeton, 1960

111) Kobljakow, I.K. *Die UdSSR im Kampf für den Frieden gegen die Aggression, 1933–1941*. Moscow, 1977

112) Krummacher, F.A., and H. Lange. *Krieg und Frieden. Von Brest-Litowsk zum Unternehmen Barbarossa*. Munich, 1970

113) Kuhn, Axel. "Das nationalsozialistische Deutschland und die Sowjetunion." In *Deutschland und die Mächte. Materialien zur Außenpolitik des Dritten Reiches*, edited by Manfred Funke, pp. 639–653. Düsseldorf, 1976

114) McMurry, Dean Scott. *Deutschland und die Sowjetunion 1933–1936*. Cologne, 1979

115) McSherry, James. *Stalin, Hitler, and Europe*. Vol. 2, *The Imbalance of Power, 1939–1941*. Cleveland, 1970

116) Maximytschew, I.F. *Der Anfang vom Ende. Deutsch-sowjetische Beziehungen 1933–1939*. Cologne, 1985

117) Michalka, Wolfgang. *Ribbentrop und die deutsche Weltpolitik 1933–1940. Außenpolitische Konzeptionen und Entscheidungsprozesse im Dritten Reich*. Munich, 1980

118) Müller, Rolf-Dieter. "Die deutsche Ostpolitik 1938/39 zwischen Realismus und Weltmachtillusionen." In *Machtbewußtsein in Deutschland am Vorabend des Zweiten Weltkriegs*, edited by Franz Knipping and Klaus-Jürgen Müller, pp. 119–130. Paderborn, 1984

119) _____. *Das Tor zur Weltmacht. Die Bedeutung der Sowjetunion für die deutsche Wirtschafts- und Rüstungspolitik zwischen den Weltkriegen.* Boppard, 1984
120) *Osteuropa-Handbuch.* Begründet von Werner Markert. Vol. 3.1, *Sowjetunion. Außenpolitik 1917–1955*, edited by Dietrich Geyer. Cologne, 1972
121) Pietrow, Bianca. *Stalinismus, Sicherheit, Offensive. Das Dritte Reich in der Konzeption der sowjetischen Außenpolitik 1933–1941.* Melsungen, 1983
122) Plettenberg, Ingeborg. *Die Sowjetunion im Völkerbund 1934 bis 1939. Bündnispolitik zwischen Staaten unterschiedlicher Gesellschaftsordnung in der internationalen Organisation für Friedenssicherung: Ziele, Voraussetzungen, Möglichkeiten, Wirkungen.* Cologne, 1987
123) Rauch, Georg v. "Die deutsch-sowjetischen Beziehungen von 1917 bis 1941 im Spiegel der Geschichtsforschung." *Europa-Archiv* vol. 22 (1967): pp. 505–514
124) Richter, Oskar. "Die deutsche Ostpolitik zwischen München und Prag." Diss., Kiel, 1967
125) Rosenfeld, Günter. "Die Sowjetunion und das faschistische Deutschland am Vorabend des zweiten Weltkrieges." In *Der Weg in den Krieg*, edited by Dietrich Eichholtz and Kurt Pätzold, pp. 345–380. East Berlin, 1989
126) Rossi, Andre. *Zwei Jahre deutsch-sowjetisches Bündnis.* Cologne, 1954
127) *The Russo-German Alliance.* London, 1950
128) Sluc, S.Z. "Vnesnjaja politika fasistskoj Germanii, 1933–1939gg: Osnovnye etapy podgotovki k vojne". In *Evropa v mezdunarodnych otnosenijach, 1917–1939,* pp. 206–270. Moscow, 1979
129) Suworow, Victor [pseud.]. *Der Eisbrecher. Hitler in Stalins Kalkül.* Stuttgart, 1989
130) Volkmann, Hans-Erich. "Die Sowjetunion im ökonomischen Kalkül des Dritten Reiches 1933–1941." In *"Unternehmen Barbarossa"*, edited by Roland G. Foerster, pp. 89–107. Munich, 1993
131) Weinberg, Gerhard L. *Germany and the Soviet Union, 1939–1941.* Leiden, 1954
132) _____. *The Foreign Policy of Hitler's Germany. Diplomatic Revolution in Europe 1933–36.* Chicago, 1970
133) _____. *The Foreign Policy of Hitler's Germany. Starting World War II, 1937–1939.* Chicago, 1980

3. The Conclusion of the Nazi-Soviet Pact

134) Adamthwaite, Anthony P. *The Making of the Second World War.* London, 1977
135) Ahmann, Rolf. "Der Hitler-Stalin-Pakt. Eine Bewertung der Interpretationen sowjetischer Außenpolitik mit neuen Fragen und neuen Forschungen." In *Der Zweite Weltkrieg*, edited by Wolfgang Michalka, pp. 93–107. Munich, 1989
136) _____. *Nichtangriffspakte: Entwicklung und operative Nutzung in Europa 1922–1939. Mit einem Ausblick auf die Renaissance des Nichtangriffsvertrages nach dem Zweiten Weltkrieg.* Baden-Baden, 1988

137) Andrejewa, M., and K. Dmitrijewa. "Zu den militärischen Verhandlungen zwischen der UdSSR, Großbritannien und Frankreich im Jahre 1939." *Deutsche Außenpolitik* vol. 4, no. 5 (1959): pp. 541–546; no. 6: pp. 674–715

138) Axel, S., et al. *Der "Hitler-Stalin-Pakt" von 1939. Diskussionsbeiträge und Dokumente*. Cologne, 1979

139) Bartel, Heinrich. *Frankreich und die Sowjetunion 1938–1940. Ein Beitrag zur französischen Ostpolitik zwischen dem Münchener Abkommen und dem Ende der Dritten Republik*. Stuttgart, 1986

140) Basler, Werner. "Die britisch-französisch-sowjetischen Militärbesprechungen im August 1939." *Zeitschrift für Geschichtswissenschaft* vol. 5 (1957): pp. 18–56

141) Benz, Wolfgang, and Hermann Graml, eds. *Sommer 1939. Die Großmächte und der Europäische Krieg*. Stuttgart, 1979

142) Bereschkow, Valentin. *In diplomatischer Mission bei Hitler in Berlin 1940–1941*. Frankfurt a.M., 1967

143) Birkenfeld, Wolfgang. "Stalin als Wirtschaftspartner Hitlers (1939–1941)." *Viertelsjahrsschrift für Sozial- und Wirtschaftsgeschichte* vol. 53 (1966): pp. 477–610

144) Bisovsky, Gerhard, et al. *Der Hitler-Stalin-Pakt. Voraussetzungen, Hintergründe, Auswirkungen*. Vienna, 1990

145) Bonwetsch, Bernd. "Vom Hitler-Stalin-Pakt zum 'Unternehmen Barbarossa'. Die deutsch-russischen Beziehungen 1939–1941 in der Kontroverse." *Osteuropa* vol. 41 (1991): pp. 562–579

146) Braubach, Max. *Hitlers Weg zur Verständigung mit Rußland im Jahre 1939. Rede zum Antritt des Rektorats der Rheinischen Friedrich-Wilhelm-Universität zu Bonn am 14. November 1959*. Bonn, 1960

147) Bühl, Achim. *Der Hitler-Stalin-Pakt. Die sowjetische Debatte*. Cologne, 1989

148) Cubarjan, Aleksandr. "Die UdSSR und der Beginn des Zweiten Weltkrieges." In *1939. An der Schwelle zum Weltkrieg. Die Entfesselung des Zweiten Weltkrieges und das internationale System*, edited by Klaus Hildebrand, Jürgen Schmädecke and Klaus Zernack, pp. 277–292. Berlin, 1990

149) Dasicev, Vjaceslav. "Planungen und Fehlschläge Stalins am Vorabend des Krieges – der XVIII. Parteitag der KPdSU (B) und der sowjetisch-deutsche Nichtangriffspakt." In *1939. An der Schwelle zum Weltkrieg. Die Entfesselung des Zweiten Weltkrieges und das internationale System*, edited by Klaus Hildebrand, Jürgen Schmädecke and Klaus Zernack, pp. 303–314. Berlin, 1990

150) Deschner, Günther. *Bomben auf Baku. Angriffspläne Englands und Frankreichs auf die Sowjetunion 1940*. Erlangen, 1990

151) *Germany and the Second World War*, edited by Militärgeschichtliches Forschungsamt, Freiburg i.Br., Germany. Translated by Paul Stephen Falla et al. Vol. 1. Oxford, 1990 (German edn: *Das Deutsche Reich und der Zweite Weltkrieg*. Vol. 1, *Ursachen und Voraussetzungen der deutschen Kriegspolitik*, by Wilhelm Deist et al. Stuttgart, 1979)

151a) *Deutschland im Zweiten Weltkrieg*. Vol. 1, *Vorbereitung, Entfesselung und Verlauf des Krieges bis zum 22. Juni 1941*, edited by Gerhart Hass. East Berlin, 1974

152) Fischer, Alexander. "Die Sowjetunion und das Prinzip der kollektiven Sicherheit am Vorabend des Zweiten Weltkrieges." In *1939. An der*

Schwelle zum Weltkrieg. Die Entfesselung des Zweiten Weltkrieges und das internationale System, edited by Klaus Hildebrand, Jürgen Schmädecke and Klaus Zernack, pp. 315–320. Berlin, 1990

153) Fleischhauer, Ingeborg. *Der Pakt. Hitler, Stalin und die Initiative der deutschen Diplomatie, 1938–1939*. Berlin, 1990

154) ____. "Der deutsch-sowjetische Grenz- und Freundschaftsvertrag vom 28. September 1939. Die deutschen Aufzeichnungen über die Verhandlungen zwischen Stalin, Molotov und Ribbentrop in Moskau." *Vierteljahrshefte für Zeitgeschichte* vol. 39 (1991): pp. 447–470

155) Friedensburg, Ferdinand. "Die sowjetischen Kriegslieferungen an das Hitlerreich." *Vierteljahrshefte zur Wirtschaftsforschung* (1962): pp. 331–338

156) *Geschichtsfälscher. Aus Geheimdokumenten über die Vorgeschichte des 2. Weltkrieges*. With an introduction by Otto Meier. Berlin, 1948

157) *Geschichtsfälscher (Geschichtlicher Überblick). Der tatsächliche Verlauf der Vorbereitung und Entwicklung der Hitleraggression und des Zweiten Weltkrieges*. Published by Informationsbüro des Ministerrats der UdSSR. Berlin, 1948

158) Goldman, Stuart. "The Forgotten War: The Soviet Union and Japan, 1937–1939." Diss., Washington, DC, 1970; Ann Arbor, 1977

159) Gorlov Sergej A. "Sovetsko-germanskij dialog nakanune pakta Molotova-Ribbentropa v 1939g." *Novaja i Novejsaja Istorija* vol. 4 (1993): pp. 13–34

160) Gornig, Gilbert-Hanno. *Der Hitler-Stalin-Pakt*. Schriften zum Staats- und Völkerrecht, vol. 41. Frankfurt a.M., 1990

161) Graml, Hermann. *Europas Weg in den Krieg. Hitler und die Mächte 1939*. Quellen und Darstellungen zur Zeitgeschichte, vol. 29. Munich, 1990

162) Helmer, Karl. *Der Handelsverkehr zwischen Deutschland und der UdSSR in den Jahren 1933–1941*. Berichte des Osteuropa-Instituts an der Freien Universität Berlin, Reihe Wirtschaft, no. 13. Berlin, 1954

163) Herbst, Ludolf. "Die Mobilmachung der Wirtschaft 1938/39 als Problem des nationalsozialistischen Herrschaftssystems." In *Sommer 1939. Die Großmächte und der Europäische Krieg*, edited by Wolfgang Benz and Hermann Graml, pp. 62–106. Stuttgart, 1979

164) Hiden, John, and Thomas Lane, eds. *The Baltic and the Outbreak of the Second World War*. Cambridge, 1992

165) Hildebrand, Klaus. "Die Entfesselung des Zweiten Weltkrieges und das internationale System: Probleme und Perspektiven der Forschung." In *1939. An der Schwelle zum Weltkrieg, Die Entfesselung des Zweiten Weltkrieges und das internationale System,* edited by Klaus Hildebrand, Jürgen Schmädecke and Klaus Zernack, pp. 3–20. Berlin, 1990

166) Hildebrand, Klaus, Jürgen Schmädecke, and Klaus Zernack, eds. *1939. An der Schwelle zum Weltkrieg. Die Entfesselung des Zweiten Weltkrieges und das internationale System*. Veröffentlichungen der Historischen Kommission zu Berlin, vol. 76. Berlin, 1990

167) Hillgruber, Andreas. "Zum Kriegsbeginn im September 1939." *Österreichische Militärische Zeitschrift* no. 5 (1969): pp. 357–361

168) Bisovsky, Gerhard, Hans Schafranek, and Robert Streibel, eds. *Der Hitler-Stalin-Pakt. Voraussetzungen, Hintergründe, Auswirkungen*. Vienna, 1990

169) Hofer, Walter. *Die Entfesselung des Zweiten Weltkrieges. Eine Studie über die internationalen Beziehungen im Sommer 1939*. Frankfurt a.M., 1954; 3rd edn 1964; reprint Düsseldorf, 1984

170) ____. "1939–1989: 50 Jahre Hitler-Stalin-Pakt." In *1.9.39*, edited by Walter Leimgruber, pp. 127–149. Zürich, 1990

171) Hoggan, David L. *Der erzwungene Krieg*. 7th edn. Tübingen, 1966

172) Kühnrich, Heinz. "Der deutsch-sowjetische Nichtangriffsvertrag vom 28. August 1939 aus der zeitgenössischen Sicht der KPD." In *Der Weg in den Krieg*, edited by Dietrich Eichholtz and Kurt Pätzold, pp. 517–551

173) Laser, Kurt. "Der Rußlandausschuß der Deutschen Wirtschaft 1928–1941." *Zeitschrift für Geschichtswissenschaft* vol. 20 (1972): pp. 1382–1400

174) Leonhard, Wolfgang. *Der Schock des Hitler-Stalin-Paktes. Erinnerungen aus der Sowjetunion, Westeuropa und USA*. Freiburg, 1986; new edn Munich, 1989

175) Lorbeer, Hans-Joachim. *Westmächte gegen die Sowjetunion*. Einzelschriften zur militärischen Geschichte des Zweiten Weltkrieges, vol. 18. Freiburg, 1975

176) Manne, Robert. "The British Decision for Alliance with Russia, May 1939." *Journal of Contemporary History* no. 9 (1974): pp. 3–26

177) Martel, Gordon, ed. *The Origins of the Second World War Reconsidered. The A.J.P. Taylor Debate after Twenty-Five Years*. London, 1988

177a) Mason, Timothy W. "Innere Krise und Angriffskrieg 1938/39." In *Wirtschaft und Rüstung am Vorabend des Zweiten Weltkrieges*, edited by Friedrich Forstmeier and Hans-Erich Volkmann, pp. 158–188. Düsseldorf, 1975

178) Myllyniemi, Seppo. *Die baltische Krise 1938–1941*. Schriftenreihe der Vierteljahrshefte für Zeitgeschichte, no. 38. Stuttgart, 1979

179) Niedhart, Gottfried. "Der Bündniswert der Sowjetunion im Urteil Großbritanniens 1936–1939." *Militärgeschichtliche Mitteilungen* no. 2 (1972): pp. 55–67

180) ____. *Großbritannien und die Sowjetunion 1934–1939. Studien zur britischen Politik der Friedenssicherung zwischen den beiden Weltkriegen*. Munich, 1972

181) ____. *Kriegsbeginn 1939. Entfesselung oder Ausbruch des Zweiten Weltkriegs?* Darmstadt, 1976

182) Oberländer, Erwin, ed. *Hitler-Stalin-Pakt 1939. Das Ende Ostmitteleuropas?* Frankfurt a.M., 1989

183) Orlov, Aleksandr S. "Die sowjetisch-deutschen Beziehungen vom August 1939 bis Juni 1941." In *"Unternehmen Barbarossa"*, edited by Roland G. Foerster, pp. 55–69. Munich, 1993

184) Plettenberg, Ingeborg. *Die Sowjetunion im Völkerbund 1934 bis 1939. Bündnispolitik zwischen Staaten unterschiedlicher Gesellschaftsordnung in der internationalen Organisation für Friedenssicherung: Ziele, Voraussetzungen, Möglichkeiten, Wirkungen*. Cologne, 1987

185) Read, Anthony, and David Fisher. *The Deadly Embrace. Hitler, Stalin and the Nazi-Soviet Pact 1939–1941*. London, 1988

186) Roberts, Geoffrey. *The Unholy Alliance. Stalin's Pact with Hitler*. London, 1989

187) Rosenbusch, Michael, Horst Schützler, and Sonja Striegnitz, eds. *Schauplatz Baltikum. Szenarium einer Okkupation und Angliederung. Dokumente 1939/40*. Berlin, 1991

188) Schafranek, Hans. *Zwischen NKWD und Gestapo. Die Auslieferung deutscher und österreichischer Antifaschisten aus der Sowjetunion an Nazideutschland, 1937–1941*. Frankfurt a.M., 1990

189) Schützler, Horst. "Die politischen Verhandlungen der Sowjetunion mit Großbritannien und Frankreich im Frühjahr und Sommer 1939." *Archiv für Sozialgeschichte* vol. 2 (1962): pp. 87–166

190) Schwendemann, Heinrich. *Die wirtschaftliche Zusammenarbeit zwischen dem Deutschen Reich und der Sowjetunion 1939 bis 1941. Alternative zu Hitlers Ostprogramm?* Berlin, 1993

191) Semirjaga, Michail. "Die sowjetisch-deutschen Verträge im System der internationalen Beziehungen des Jahres 1939." In *1939. An der Schwelle zum Weltkrieg. Die Entfesselung des Zweiten Weltkrieges und das internationale System*, edited by Klaus Hildebrand, Jürgen Schmädecke and Klaus Zernack, pp. 293–302. Berlin, 1990

192) _____. *Tajny stalinskoj diplomatii 1939–1941*. Moscow, 1991

193) Sevostjanov, Pavel P. *Pered velikim ispytvaniem 1939–1941*. Moscow, 1981

194) Sipols, Vilnis J. *Die Vorgeschichte des deutsch-sowjetischen Nichtangriffsvertrages*. Cologne, 1981

195) Slutsch, Sergej. "Warum brauchte Hitler einen Nichtangriffspakt mit Stalin?" In *Zwei Wege nach Moskau. Vom Hitler-Stalin-Pakt zum "Unternehmen Barbarossa"*, edited by Bernd Wegner, pp. 69–87. Munich, 1991

196) Tarulis, Albert N. *Soviet Policy Toward the Baltic States, 1918–1944*. Notre Dame, Ind., 1959

197) Taylor, A.J.P. *The Origins of the Second World War*. London, 1961

198) Ueberschär, Gerd R. "'Der Pakt mit dem Satan, um den Teufel auszutreiben'. Der deutsch-sowjetische Nichtangriffsvertrag und Hitlers Kriegsabsicht gegen die UdSSR." In *Der Zweite Weltkrieg*, edited by Wolfgang Michalka, pp. 568–585. Munich, 1989

199) _____. *Hitler und Finnland 1939–1941. Die deutsch-finnischen Beziehungen während des Hitler-Stalin-Paktes*. Wiesbaden, 1978

200) Vollmer, Johannes, and Tilman Zülch, eds. *Aufstand der Völker. Verratene Völker zwischen Hitler und Stalin*. Göttingen, 1989

201) Watt, Donald C. "The Initiatives of the Negotations Leading to the Nazi-Soviet Pact: A Historical Problem." In *Essays in Honour of E.H. Carr*, edited by C. Abramsky. London, 1974

202) Weber, Reinhold W. *Die Entstehungsgeschichte des Hitler-Stalin-Paktes 1939*. Frankfurt, 1980

203) Wegner, Bernd, ed. *Zwei Wege nach Moskau. Vom Hitler-Stalin-Pakt zum "Unternehmen Barbarossa"*. Munich, 1991

204) Weinberg, Gerhard L. "Hitlers Entschluß zum Krieg." In *1939. An der Schwelle zum Weltkrieg. Die Entfesselung des Zweiten Weltkrieges und das internationale System*, edited by Klaus Hildebrand, Jürgen Schmädecke and Klaus Zernack, pp. 31–36. Berlin, 1990

205) Wüthrich, Markus. *Die Verhandlungen der Westmächte mit der Sowjetunion im Sommer 1939. Ein Beitrag zur west-östlichen Kontroverse um die Entfesselung des zweiten Weltkrieges*. Munich, 1967

4. Hitler's Program and Decision to Attack the Soviet Union, 1940–41

206) Brügel, Johann W. "Das sowjetische Ultimatum an Rumänien im Juni 1940." *Vierteljahrshefte für Zeitgeschichte* vol. 11 (1963): pp. 403–417
207) Cartier, Raymond. "Pourquoi Hitler voulait-il envahir l'URSS?" *Historia* no. 235 (1966): pp. 66–73
208) Cecil, Robert. *Hitler's Decision to Invade Russia, 1941*. London, 1975 (German edn: *Hitlers Griff nach Rußland*. Graz, 1977)
209) Eichler, Gerhard. "Die deutsch-sowjetischen Wirtschaftsbeziehungen vom August 1939 bis zum faschistischen Überfall im Juni 1941", Diss., Halle, 1965
210) Fanning, William J. "The German War Economy in 1941. A Study of Germany's Material and Manpower Problems in Relation to the Overall Military Effort." D. Phil. diss., Texas Christian Univ, 1983
211) Fleischhauer, Ingeborg. "'Unternehmen Barbarossa'. Die deutsche Kriegserklärung in Moskau im Licht sowjetischer Dokumente." *Osteuropa* vol. 41 (1991): pp. 517–544
212) ____. *Diplomatischer Widerstand gegen "Unternehmen Barbarossa". Die Friedensbemühungen der Deutschen Botschaft 1939–1941*. Berlin, 1991
213) Förster, Jürgen. "Hitlers Entscheidung für den Krieg gegen die Sowjetunion." In *Das Deutsche Reich und der Zweite Weltkrieg*, vol. IV, pp. 3–37. Stuttgart 1983
214) Gafencu, Grigore. *Vorspiel zum Krieg im Osten. Vom Moskauer Abkommen (21.8.1939) bis zum Ausbruch der Feinseligkeiten in Rußland (22.6.1941)*. Zürich, 1944
215) Gibbons, Robert J. "Opposition gegen 'Barbarossa' im Herbst 1940. Eine Denkschrift aus der deutschen Botschaft in Moskau." *Vierteljahrshefte für Zeitgeschichte* vol. 23 (1975): pp. 332–340
216) Gorlov, Sergej A. "Warnungen vor dem 'Unternehmen Barbarossa'. Aus den Akten der Sowjetvertretung in Berlin 1940–1941." *Osteuropa* vol. 41 (1991): pp. 545–561
217) Gorodetsky, Gabriel. *Stafford Cripps' Mission to Moscow, 1940–1942*. Cambridge, 1984
218) Kynin, G.P. "Unbekannte Aufzeichnungen von weiteren Unterredungen Schulenburgs mit Dekanosov im Mai 1941 (neue Dokumente aus dem Präsidialarchiv)." *Berliner Jahrbuch für osteuropäische Geschichte* vol. 1 (1994): pp. 197–211
219) Koch, Hannsjoachim W. "Hitler's 'Programme' and the Genesis of Operation 'Barbarossa'." *Historical Journal* vol. 26 (1983): pp. 891–919
220) Krosby, Hans P. "Petsamo in the Spotlight. A Study in Finnish-German Relations, 1940–1941", D. Phil. diss., Columbia Univ., 1967
221) Leach, Barry A. *German Strategy against Russia, 1939–1941*. Oxford, 1973
222) Liddell Hart, B.H. "Why Hitler Invaded Russia – and Failed." *Marine Corps Gazette* vol. 40, no. 12 (1956): pp. 22–26
223) Milward, Alan S. "Der Einfluß ökonomischer und nicht-ökonomischer Faktoren auf die Strategie des Blitzkrieges." In *Wirtschaft und Rüstung am Vorabend des Zweiten Weltkrieges*, edited by Friedrich Forstmeier and Hans-Erich Volkmann, pp. 189–201. Düsseldorf, 1975

224) Müller, Rolf-Dieter. "Von der Wirtschaftsallianz zum kolonialen Ausbeutungskrieg." In *Das Deutsche Reich und der Zweite Weltkrieg*, vol. 4, pp. 98–189. Stuttgart, 1983
225) Nolte, Hans-Heinrich. *Der deutsche Überfall auf die Sowjetunion 1941. Text und Dokumentation*. Hanover, 1991
226) Petrov, Vladimir. *June 22, 1941. Soviet Historians and the German Invasion*. Columbia, SC, 1968
227) Pietrow-Ennker, Bianca. "Deutschland im Juni 1941 – ein Opfer sowjetischer Aggression? Zur Kontroverse über die Präventivkriegsthese." In *Der Zweite Weltkrieg*, edited by Wolfgang Michalka, pp. 586–625. Munich, 1989
228) Rich, Norman. *Hitler's War Aims: Ideology, the Nazi State and the Course of Expansion*. New York, 1973
229) Robertson, Esmonde M. "Hitler Turns from the West to Russia, May–December 1940." In *Paths to War. New Essays on the Origins of the Second World War*, edited by Robert Boyse, pp. 367–382. London, 1989
230) Schreiber, Gerhard. "Der Mittelmeerraum in Hitlers Strategie 1940. 'Programm' und militärische Planung." *Militärgeschichtliche Mitteilungen* vol. 28 (1980): pp. 69–99
231) ____. "Das strategische Dilemma im Sommer und Herbst 1940: Alternativ- oder Interimsstrategie?" In *Das Deutsche Reich und der Zweite Weltkrieg*, vol. 3, pp. 162–277. Stuttgart, 1983
232) Schreiber, Gerhard, Bernd Stegemann, and Detlev Vogel. "Der Mittelmeerraum und Südosteuropa. Von der "non belligeranza" Italiens bis zum Kriegseintritt der Vereinigten Staaten." In *Das Deutsche Reich und der Zweite Weltkrieg*, vol. 3. Stuttgart, 1984
233) Schustereit, Hartmut. *Vabanque. Hitlers Angriff auf die Sowjetunion 1941 als Versuch, durch den Sieg im Osten den Westen zu bezwingen*. Herford, 1988
234) Slutsch, Sergej. "Der 22. Juni 1941 und die Frage nach dem Eintritt der Sowjetunion in den Zweiten Weltkrieg." In *22. Juni 1941. Der Überfall auf die Sowjetunion*, edited by Hans Schafranek and Robert Streibel, pp. 53–61. Vienna, 1991
235) Solowjow, Boris G. *Von Plan "Weiß" zu "Barbarossa": Die geheime Vorbereitung des Zweiten Weltkrieges*. Moscow, 1989
236) Sommer, Erich F. *Das Memorandum. Wie der Sowjetunion der Krieg erklärt wurde*. Munich, 1981
237) Stegemann, Bernd. "Hitlers Ziele im ersten Kriegsjahr 1939/40. Ein Beitrag zur Quellenkritik." *Militärgeschichtliche Mitteilungen* vol. 27 (1980): pp. 93–105
238) Tichvinskij, S.L. "Zakljucenie sovetsko-japonskogo pakta o nejtralitete 1941g." *Novaja i Novejsaja Istorija* (1990): pp. 21–34
239) Topitsch, Ernst. *Stalins Krieg. Die sowjetische Langzeitstrategie gegen den Westen als rationale Machtpolitik*. Munich, 1985; 3rd edn Herford, 1990
240) Ueberschär, Gerd R. "Hitlers Entschluß zum 'Lebensraum'-Krieg im Osten. Programmatisches Ziel oder militärstrategisches Kalkül?" In "*Unternehmen Barbarossa*", edited by Gerd R. Ueberschär and Wolfram Wette, pp. 83–110. Paderborn, 1984
241) Vogel, Detlef. "Der deutsche Überfall auf Jugoslawien und Griechenland vor dem Hintergrund des bevorstehenden Angriffs gegen die

Sowjetunion." In *22. Juni 1941. Der Überfall auf die Sowjetunion*, edited by Hans Schafranek and Robert Streibel, pp. 35–43. Vienna, 1991

242) Weinberg, Gerhard L. "Der deutsche Entschluß zum Angriff auf die Sowjetunion." *Vierteljahrshefte für Zeitgeschichte* vol. 1 (1953): pp. 301–318

243) ____. "Der Überfall auf die Sowjetunion im Zusammenhang mit Hitlers diplomatischen und militärischen Gesamtplanungen." In *"Unternehmen Barbarossa"*, edited by Roland G. Foerster, pp. 177–185. Munich, 1993

244) Zapantis, Andrew L. *Hitler's Balkan Campaign and the Invasion of the USSR*. East European Monograph, no. 129. Boulder, Colo., 1987

5. War Policy and Strategy, 1941–42

245) Bosl, Karl, ed. *Das Jahr 1941 in der europäischen Politik*. Munich, 1972

246) Förster, Gerhard, and Wolfgang Wünsche. "Zur militärpolitischen und strategisch-operativen Planung des Sommerfeldzuges der faschistischen Wehrmacht 1942." *Zeitschrift für Militärgeschichte* vol. 6, no. 6 (1967): pp. 660–675

247) Hillgruber, Andreas. *Der Zenit des Zweiten Weltkrieges Juli 1941*. Institut für Europäische Geschichte Mainz, Vorträge 65. Wiesbaden, 1977

248) Knjaz'kov, Anatolij. "Die sowjetische Strategie im Jahre 1942." In *Stalingrad*, edited by Jürgen Förster, pp. 39–51. Munich, 1992

249) Müller, Rolf-Dieter. "Die Mobilisierung der deutschen Wirtschaft für Hitlers Kriegführung." In *Das Deutsche Reich und der Zweite Weltkrieg*, vol. 5/1, pp. 349–692. Stuttgart, 1988

250) ____. "Das Scheitern der wirtschaftlichen 'Blitzkriegstrategie'." In *Das Deutsche Reich und der Zweite Weltkrieg*, vol. 4, pp. 936–1029. Stuttgart, 1983

251) Pron'ko, Valentin A. "Die sowjetische Strategie im Jahre 1943." In *Stalingrad*, edited by Jürgen Förster, pp. 313–326. Munich, 1992

252) Reinhardt, Klaus. *Die Wende vor Moskau. Das Scheitern der Strategie Hitlers im Winter 1941/42*. Beiträge zur Militär- und Kriegsgeschichte, vol. 13. Stuttgart, 1972

253) Schreiber, Gerhard. "Politik und Kriegführung 1941." In *Das Deutsche Reich und der Zweite Weltkrieg*, vol. 3, pp. 516–590. Stuttgart, 1984

254) Sywottek, Arnold. "Die sowjetische Kriegszielpolitik im Zweiten Weltkrieg 1941–1945. Zum Stand der historisch-politischen Analyse und Diskussion." In *"Unternehmen Barbarossa"*, edited by Gerd R. Ueberschär and Wolfram Wette, pp. 237–252. Paderborn, 1984

255) Wegner, Bernd. "Hitlers Strategie zwischen Pearl Harbour und Stalingrad." In *Das Deutsche Reich und der Zweite Weltkrieg*, vol. 6, pp. 97–126. Stuttgart, 1990

256) ____. "Hitlers zweiter Feldzug gegen die Sowjetunion. Strategische Grundlagen und historische Bedeutung." In *Der Zweite Weltkrieg*, edited by Wolfgang Michalka, pp. 652–666. Munich, 1989

257) Weinberg, Gerhard L. "Germany's Declaration of War on the United States: A New Look." In *Germany and America. Essays on Problems of International Relations and Immigrations*, edited by Hans L. Trefousse, pp. 54–70. New York, 1980

6. Allies and Neutrals

a) Hitler's Alliance Policy

258) Abbott, Peter, and Nigel Thomas. *Germany's Eastern Front Allies 1941–45*. Colour plates: Mike Chappell. Men-at-Arms Series, no. 131. London, 1982

259) Broszat, Martin. "Deutschland – Ungarn – Rumänien. Entwicklung und Grundfaktoren nationalsozialistischer Hegemonial- und Bündnispolitik, 1938–1941." *Historische Zeitschrift* vol. 206 (1968): pp. 45–96

260) Dülffer, Jost. "The Tripartite Pact of 27th September 1940. Fascist Alliance or Propaganda Trick?" *International Studies* vol. 3 (1984): pp. 1–24

261) Förster, Jürgen. "Die Entscheidungen der 'Dreierpaktstaaten'." In *Das Deutsche Reich und der Zweite Weltkrieg*, vol. 4, pp. 883–907. Stuttgart, 1983

262) _____. "Die Gewinnung von Verbündeten in Südosteuropa." In *Das Deutsche Reich und der Zweite Weltkrieg*, vol. 4, pp. 327–364. Stuttgart, 1983

263) _____. *Stalingrad. Risse im Bündnis 1942–43*. Einzelschriften zur militärischen Geschichte des 2. Weltkrieges, no. 16. Freiburg, 1975

264) Groehler, Olaf, and Wolfgang Schumann. "Zu den Bündnisbeziehungen des faschistischen Deutschlands im zweiten Weltkrieg." *Zeitschrift für Geschichtswissenschaft* vol. 28 (1980): pp. 624–639

265) Hillgruber, Andreas. "Hitler's Allies." *Military Review* vol. 41, no. 10 (1961): pp. 65–78

266) Hoppe, Hans-Joachim. "Die Balkanstaaten Rumänien, Jugoslawien, Bulgarien. Nationale Gegensätze und NS-Großraumpolitik." In *Innen- und Außenpolitik unter nationalsozialistischer Bedrohung. Determinanten internationaler Beziehungen in historischen Fallstudien*, edited by Erhard Forndran, Franz Golczewski and Dieter Riesenberger, pp. 161–175. Opladen, 1977

267) Ueberschär, Gerd R. "Die Einbeziehung Skandinaviens in die Planung 'Barbarossa'." In *Das Deutsche Reich und der Zweite Weltkrieg*, vol. 4, pp. 365–412. Stuttgart, 1983

268) _____. "Kriegführung und Politik in Nordeuropa." In *Das Deutsche Reich und der Zweite Weltkrieg*, vol. 4, pp. 810–882. Stuttgart, 1983

269) Wegner, Bernd. "Die Mobilisierung der Verbündeten." In *Das Deutsche Reich und der Zweite Weltkrieg*, vol. 6, pp. 816–839. Stuttgart, 1990

b) Finland

270) Andreen, Per G. *Finland i Brännpunkten. Mars 1940–Juni 1941*. Stockhom, 1980

271) Berry, R. Michael. *American Foreign Policy and the Finnish Exception. Ideological Preferences and Wartime Realities*. Studia Historica, no. 24. Helsinki, 1987

272) Erfurth, Waldemar. *Der Finnische Krieg 1941–1944*. 2nd edn. Wiesbaden, 1977

273) Jokipii, Mauno. "Finland's Entrance into the Continuation War." *Revue Internationale d'Histoire Militaire* no. 53 (1982): pp. 85–103

274) ____. *Jatkosodan synty. Tutkimuksia Saksan ja Suomen sotilaallisesta yhteistyöstä 1940–41*. Keuruu, 1987
275) Klink, Ernst. "Deutsch-finnische Waffenbrüderschaft, 1941–1944." *Wehrwissenschaftliche Rundschau* vol. 8 (1958): pp. 389–412
276) Korhonen, Arvi. *Barbarossaplanen och Finland*. Tammerfors, 1963
277) ____. *Barbarossa-suunnitelma ja Suomi*. Porvoo, 1961
278) Krosby, Hans P. *Finland, Germany and the Soviet Union, 1940–41: The Petsamo Dispute*. Madison, 1968
279) Lundin, Charles L. *Finland in the Second World War*. Bloomington, Ind., 1957
280) Manninen, Ohto. "Die Beziehungen zwischen den finnischen und deutschen Militärbehörden in der Ausarbeitungsphase des Barbarossaplanes." *Militärgeschichtliche Mitteilungen* vol. 26, no. 2 (1979): pp. 79–95
281) Menger, Manfred. *Deutschland und Finnland im zweiten Weltkrieg. Genesis und Scheitern einer Militärallianz*. Militärhistorische Studien, N.F., vol. 26. East Berlin, 1988
282) Mikola, K.J. *Finland's Wars During World War II, 1939–1945*. Mikkeli, 1973
283) Polvinen, Tuomo. "The Great Powers and Finland 1941–1944." *Revue Internationale d'Histoire Militaire* no. 62 (1985): pp. 133–152
284) Stein, George H., and Hans P. Krosby."Das finnische Freiwilligen-Bataillon der Waffen-SS. Eine Studie zur SS-Diplomatie und zur ausländischen Freiwilligen-Bewegung." *Vierteljahrshefte für Zeitgeschichte* vol. 14 (1966): pp. 413–453
285) Terae, Martti V. *Tienhaarassa. Syksyn 1940 tapahtumat Barbarossa-suunnitelman taustaa vasten*. Helsingissä, 1962
286) Ueberschär, Gerd R. "Guerre de coalition ou guerre séparée. Conception et structures de la stratégie germano-finlandaise dans la guerre contre l'URSS, 1941–1944." *Revue d'Histoire de la Deuxième Guerre Mondiale* vol. 30, no. 118 (1980): pp. 27–68
287) ____. *Hitler und Finnland 1939–1941. Die deutsch-finnischen Beziehungen während des Hitler-Stalin-Paktes*. Frankfurter Historische Abhandlungen, vol. 16. Wiesbaden, 1978
288) ____. "Koalitionskriegführung im Zweiten Weltkrieg. Probleme der deutsch-finnischen Waffenbrüderschaft im Kampf gegen die Sowjetunion." In *Militärgeschichte. Probleme, Thesen, Wege*, edited by Manfred Messerschmidt, Klaus A. Maier, Werner Rahn and Bruno Thoß, pp. 355–382. Stuttgart, 1982
289) Vehviläinen, Olli. "Die Einschätzung der Lage Deutschlands aus finnischer Sicht." In *Die Zukunft des Reiches: Gegner, Verbündete und Neutrale (1943–1945)*, edited by Manfred Messerschmidt and Ekkehart Guth, pp. 147–160. Herford, 1990
290) Vainu, Herbert. "Zu militärischen Aspekten der Einbeziehung Finnlands in die faschistische Aggression gegen die UdSSR." *Nordeuropa-Studien* vol. 7 (1974): pp. 59
291) Wegner, Bernd. "Hitlers Besuch in Finnland 1942 (Dokumentation)." *Vierteljahrshefte für Zeitgeschichte* vol. 41, no. 1 (1993): pp. 117–137
292) ____. "Jenseits der Waffenbrüderschaft. Die deutsch-finnischen Beziehungen im Schatten von Stalingrad." In *Stalingrad*, edited by Jürgen Förster, pp. 293–309. Munich, 1992

c) Hungary

293) Adonyi, Ferenc. *A magyar Katona a Második Világháborúban 1941–1945.* Klagenfurt, 1954

294) Adonyi-Naredy, Franz von. *Ungarns Armee im Zweiten Weltkrieg. Deutschlands letzter Verbündeter.* Neckargemünd, 1971

295) Bálvány, Andreas von. "Der Untergang der 2. ungarischen Armee am Don 1943." *Allgemeine schweizerische Militär-Zeitschrift* vol. 126, no. 12 (1960): pp. 1051–1062

296) Borsányi, Julian. *Das Rätsel des Bombenangriffs auf Kaschau 26. Juni 1941. Wie wurde Ungarn in den Zweiten Weltkrieg hineingerissen? Ein dokumentarischer Bericht.* Studia Hungarica, vol. 16. Munich, 1978

297) Borus, Josef. "Stalingrads Widerhall und Wirkung in Ungarn." In *Stalingrad*, edited by Jürgen Förster, pp. 21–228. Munich, 1992

298) Fenyo, Mario D. *Hitler, Horthy, and Hungary. German-Hungarian Relations, 1914–1944.* Yale Russian and East European Studies, no. 11. New Haven, Conn., 1972

299) Gosztonyi, Péter. *A magyar Honvédség a második világháborúban.* Rome, 1986

300) ____. "Die ungarische antifaschistische Bewegung in der Sowjetunion während des Zweiten Weltkrieges." *Militärgeschichtliche Mitteilungen* no. 11 (1972): pp. 85–107

301) Hillgruber, Andreas. "Deutschland und Ungarn 1933–1944. Ein Überblick über die politischen und militärischen Beziehungen im Rahmen der europäischen Politik." *Wehrwissenschaftliche Rundschau* vol. 9 (1959): pp. 651–676

302) Horváth, Miklós. *A 2. magyar hadsereg megsemmisülése a Donnál.* Budapest, 1959

303) Juhász, Gyula. *Hungarian Foreign Policy, 1919–1945.* Budapest, 1979

304) Miklós, Horváth. "Die Vernichtung der 2. ungarischen Armee am Don." *Österreichische Militärische Zeitschrift* no. 5 (1964): pp. 315–320

305) Nemeskürty, István. *Requiem egy hadseregért.* Budapest 1972 (German edn: *Untergang einer Armee.* East Berlin, 1976)

306) Nebelin, Manfred. *Die deutsche Ungarnpolitik 1939–1941.* Opladen, 1989

307) ____. "'Barbarossa' und Ungarn. Aus dem Kriegstagebuch des Deutschen Generals beim Oberkommando der Königlich Ungarischen Wehrmacht 1941." *Militärgeschichtliche Mitteilungen* vol. 53 (1994): pp. 101–121

308) Ranki, György. "L'occupation de la Hongrie par les allemands." *Revue d'Histoire de la Deuxième Guerre Mondiale* vol. 16, no. 62 (1966): pp. 37–52

309) Szabó, Lázló Bárfai. *Az utolsó emberig. Egy csapatparancsnok visszemlékezesei a Don menti harcokra.* Budapest, 1988

310) Tilkovszky, L. "Die Werbeaktionen der Waffen-SS in Ungarn." *Acta Historica Academiae Scientarium Hungaricae* vol. 20 (1974): pp. 37–180

311) Tóth, Sándor. "A Horthy-Hadsereg gyorshadteste a Szovjetunió elleni rablóháborúban." *Hadtörténelmi Közlemények* vol. 13, no. 2 (1966): pp. 223–257

312) ____. "Ungarns militärische Rolle im zweiten Weltkrieg. Historiographischer Überblick." In *Ostmitteleuropa im zweiten Weltkrieg*, edited by F. Glatz, pp. 79–99. Budapest, 1978

313) Vörös, János. "Das private Kriegstagebuch des Chefs des ungarischen Generalstabes vom Jahre 1944." *Wehrwissenschaftliche Rundschau* vol. 20, no. 11 (1970): pp. 634–659; no. 12, pp. 702–732

314) Wimpffen, Hans. "Die zweite ungarische Armee im Feldzug gegen die Sowjetunion. Ein Beitrag zur Koalitionskriegführung im Zweiten Weltkrieg." D. Phil. diss., Würzburg, 1968

d) Rumania

315) Ancel, Jean. "Stalingrad und Rumänien." In *Stalingrad*, edited by Jürgen Förster, pp. 189–214. Munich, 1992

316) Barbul, Gheorghe. *Mémorial Antonescu, le IIIe Homme de l'Axe*. Vol. 1. Paris, 1950

317) Constantinescu, Miron. "L'Insurrection armée du peuple roumain de 23 août 1944." In *Histoire de la Roumanie*, pp. 359–373. Roanne, 1970

318) Förster, Jürgen. "Rumäniens Weg in die deutsche Abhängigkeit. Zur Rolle der deutschen Militärmission, 1940/41." *Militärgeschichtliche Mitteilungen* no. 25 (1979): pp. 47–77

319) _____. "Zur Bündnispolitik Rumäniens vor und während des Zweiten Weltkrieges." In *Militärgeschichte. Probleme, Thesen, Wege*, edited by Manfred Messerschmidt, Klaus A. Maier, Werner Rahn and Bruno Thoß, pp. 294–310. Stuttgart, 1982

320) Gheorghe, Ion. *Rumäniens Weg zum Satellitenstaat*. Heidelberg, 1952

321) Hegemann, Margot. "Einige Dokumente zur 'Deutschen Heeresmission in Rumänien', 1940/41." *Jahrbuch für Geschichte der UdSSR und der volksdemokratischen Länder Europas* vol. 5 (1961): pp. 315–346

322) Hillgruber, Andreas. *Hitler, König Carol und Marschall Antonescu. Die deutsch-rumänischen Beziehungen 1938–1944*. 2nd edn. Wiesbaden, 1965

323) _____. "Die letzten Monate der deutsch-rumänischen Waffenbrüderschaft, 1944." *Wehrwissenschaftliche Rundschau* vol. 7, no. 7 (1957): pp. 377–397

324) Pandea, Adrian, Ion Pavelescu, and Eftimie Ardeleanu. *Romani la Stalingrad. Viziunea romaneasca asugra tragediei din Cotul Donului si Stepa Calmuca*. Bucarest, 1992

325) Zaharia, G. "La Résistance en Roumanie." In *Europäischer Widerstand im Vergleich. Die Internationale Konferenzen Amsterdam*, edited by Ger van Roon, pp. 383–399. Berlin, 1985

e) Italy

326) Bedeschi, Giulio. "Il corpo d'armata alpino sul fronto russo." *Rivista militare* no. 2 (1983): pp. 39–48

327) Benz, Wigbert. "Die Haltung des Vatikans zum 'Unternehmen Barbarossa'." In *22. Juni 1941. Der Überfall auf die Sowjetunion*, edited by Hans Schafranek and Robert Streibel, pp. 87–97. Vienna, 1991

328) Beolchini, Aldo. "La Sforzesca nella prima battaglia difensiva sul Don. Ricordi e riflessioni di un reduce." *Rivista militare* no. 1 (1983): pp. 99–120

329) Bonabello, Pietro. "L'8ª armata italiana nella 2ª battaglia difensiva del Don." *Rivista militare* no. 1 (1984): pp. 129–142
330) Budin, Giovanni B. *Dall'Isonzo al Don*. Trieste, 1985
331) Caballero, Carlos. "La 'Division Azul'." *Defensa* vol. 4, no. 37 (1981): pp. 66–75
332) Caballero Jurado, Carlos. "El ejercito italiano en la campana de Russia." *Defensa* vol. 4, no. 42 (1981): pp. 74–81
333) Castiglioni, Vittorio de. "Dal Dniester al Don." *Rivista militare* vol. 101, no. 2 (1978): pp. 74–82
334) Cavallero, Ugo. *Comando Supremo. Diario 1940–43 del Capo di S.M.G.* Bologna, 1948
335) Ciano, Galeazzo. *Diario 1937–1943*. Edited by Renzo De Felice. Milan, 1980
336) Colotti, Enzo. "L'alleanza italo-tedesca 1941–1943." In *Gli italiani sul Fronte Russo*, edited by Instituto Storico delle Resistenza in Cuneo e Provincia, pp. 3–61. Bari, 1982
337) Corradi, Egisto. *La Ritirata di Russia*, 3rd edn. Milan, 1964
338) Cruccu, Rinaldo. "Le operazioni italiane in Russia 1941–1943." In *Gli italiani sul fronte Russo*, edited by Instituto Storico delle Resistenza in Cuneo e Provincia, pp. 209–227. Bari, 1982
339) Deakin, F. W. *Die brutale Freundschaft. Hitler, Mussolini und der Untergang des italienischen Faschismus*. Cologne, 1964
340) Dotti, Stefano. *Ritirata in Russia (1942–43)*. Testimoni per la storia del "nostro tempo." Collana di memorie diari e documenti, no. 29. Bologna, 1967
341) Filatov, G. "Razgrom italjanskoj ékspedicionnoj armii na sovetsko-germanskom fronte". *Voenno-Istoriceskij Zurnal* vol. 10, no. 4 (1968): pp. 44–54
342) Förster, Jürgen. "Il ruolo dell'8ª armata dal punto di vista tedesco." In *Gli italieni sul Fronte Russo*, edited by Instituto Storico delle Resistenza in Cuneo e Provincia, pp. 229–259. Bari, 1982
343) Francesconi, Manlio. *Russia 1943*. Pordenone, 1983
344) *Fronte russo: C'ero anch'io, a cura di Giulio Bedeschi*. Vols 1, 2. Testimonianze fra cronaca e storia, nos. 119, 120. Milan, 1983
345) Gariboldo, Mario. "L'Italia in Russia: L'ARMIR." In *Cinquant'anni dopo l'entrata dell'Italia della 2ª Guerra Mondiale. Aspetti e problemi*, pp. 273–296. Rome, 1993
346) Gianbartolomei, Aldo. "L'Italia in Russia: CSIR." In *Cinquant'anni dopo l'entrata dell'Italia della 2ª Guerra Mondiale. Aspetti e problemi*, pp. 273–296. Rome, 1993
347) Inaudi, Guiseppe. "Condizioni d'impiego delle forze sul fronte russo." *Revue Internationale d'Histoire Militaire* no. 39 (1978): pp. 209–248
348) Instituto Storico della Resistenza in Cuneo e Provincia, ed. *Gli italieni sul Fronte Russo*. Bari, 1982
349) *I servizi logistici delle unità italiane al fronte russo (1941–1943)*. Edited by Constantino de Franceschi, Giorgio de Vecchi de Val Cismon, Riccardo Grazionsi and Mauro de Serriis. Rome, 1975
350) *L'8a Armata Italiana nella seconda battaglia difensiva del Don*. Edited by Stato Maggiore Esercito, Ufficio Storico. Rome, 1946
351) *Le Operazioni del C.S.I.R. el dell'ARMIR dal Giugno 1941 all'Ottobre 1942*. Edited by Stato Maggiore Esercito, Ufficio Storico. Rome, 1947

352) *Le operazioni delle unità al fronte russo (1941–1943)*. Edited by Constantino De Franceschi, Giorgio de Vecchi and Fabio Mantovani. Rome, 1977
353) Lupinacci, Pier F. *Attivita della marina in Mar Nero e sul Lago Ladoga*. La marina italiana nella seconda guerra mondiale, vol. 11. 2nd edn. Rome, 1965
354) Malaparte, Curzio. *Il Volga nasce in Europa*. 3rd edn. Rome, 1951
355) Massignani, Alessandro. *Alpini e tedeschi sul Don. Documenti e testimonianze sulla ritirata del corpo d'armata alpino e del XXIV Panzerkorps germanico in Russia nel gennaio 1943 – con il diario del "Generale tedesco presso l`8ª armata italiana"*. Novale di Valdegno, 1991
355a) Negri, Cristoforo M. *I lunghi fucili. Ricordi della guerra di Russia*. Torino, 1967
356) Ragionieri, Ernesto. "Italien und der Überfall auf die UdSSR." *Zeitschrift für Geschichtswissenschaft* vol. 9 (1961): pp. 761–808
357) Revelli, Nuto. *Mai tardi. Diario di un alpino in Russia*. Turin, 1967
358) Ricchezza, Antonio. *L'Avanzata del corpo di spedizione*. Storia illustrata di tutta la campagna di Russia, vol. 1. Milan, 1971
359) ____. *La Ritirata al sud. La ritirata al nord*. Storia illustrata di tutta la campagna di Russia, vol. 3. Milan, 1972
360) Rintelen, Enno v. *Mussolini als Bundesgenosse. Erinnerungen des deutschen Militärattachés in Rom 1936–1943*. Tübingen, 1951
361) Santoro, Giuseppe. "Le operazioni aeree sul fronte russo (luglio 1941–maggio 1943)." *Rivista Aeronautica* vol. 30, no. 6 (1954): pp. 613–637; no. 7 (1954): pp. 723–741
362) Scala, Edoardo. "La 2a battaglia del Don ed il ripiegamento delle notre unità." In *Le fanterie nella 2a Guerra mondiale*, edited by Edoardo Scala, pp. 507–523. Roma, 1956
363) ____. "La Guerra in Russia. 1.Le operazioni del C.S.I.R. 2.Le operazioni dell' A.R.M.I.R." In *Le fanterie nella 2a Guerra mondiale*, edited by Edoardo Scala, pp. 468–523. Rome, 1956
364) Schreiber, Gerhard. "Italiens Teilnahme am Krieg gegen die Sowjetunion. Motive, Fakten und Folgen." In *Stalingrad*, edited by Jürgen Förster, pp. 250–292. Munich, 1992
365) Simoni, Léonardo. *Berlin, Ambassade d'Italie*. Paris, 1947
366) Stern, Mario R. *Il Sergente nella neve. Ricordi della ritirata di Russia (1942/43)*. 2nd edn. Turin, 1962
367) Ufficio Storico dello Stato Maggiore dell'Esercito, ed. *Le Operazioni Della Unità Italiane al Fronte Russo, 1941–1943*. Rome, 1977
368) Vacca, G. *In Russia: tappa a Karkow (1942–1943)*. Bari, 1955

f) Japan

369) Hillgruber, Andreas. "Japan und der Fall 'Barbarossa'. Japanische Dokumente zu den Gesprächen Hitlers und Ribbentrops mit Botschafter Oshima vom Februar bis Juni 1941." *Wehrwissenschaftliche Rundschau* vol. 18 (1968): pp. 312–336
370) Hosoya, Chihiro. "The Japanese-Soviet Neutrality Pact." In *The Fateful Choice. Japan's Advance into Southeast Asia 1939–1941*, edited by James W. Morley, pp. 13–114. New York, 1980
371) Krebs, Gerhard. "Japan und der deutsch-sowjetische Krieg." In *Zwei Wege nach Moskau*, edited by Bernd Wegner, pp. 564–583. Munich, 1991

372) Lensen, George Alexander. *The Strange Neutrality. Soviet-Japanese Relations during the Second World War 1941–1945*. Tallahessee, Fla., 1972

373) Martin, Bernd. "Das deutsch-japanische Bündnis im Zweiten Weltkrieg." In *Deutschland – Japan in der Zwischenkriegszeit*, edited by Josef Kreiner et al., pp. 199–222. Bonn, 1990

374) ____. "The German-Japanese Alliance in the Second World War." In *The Pacific War. A Reappraisal after Fifty Years*, edited by Saki Dockrill and L. Freedman. London, 1992

375) ____. *Deutschland und Japan im Zweiten Weltkrieg. Vom Angriff auf Pearl Harbor bis zur deutschen Kapitulation*. Göttingen, 1969

376) Meskill, Johanna M. *Hitler & Japan: The Hollow Alliance*. New York, 1966

377) Morley, James W., ed. *Japan, Germany, and the USSR, 1935–1940*. New York, 1976

378) Rahn, Werner. "Japan und der Krieg in Europa." In *Das Deutsche Reich und der Zweite Weltkrieg*, vol. 6, pp. 143–170. Stuttgart, 1990

g) Sweden

379) Bindschedler, Rudolf L., et al. *Schwedische und schweizerische Neutralität im Zweiten Weltkrieg*. Basle, 1985

380) Björkman, L. *Sverige inför Operation Barbarossa. Svensk neutralitetspolitik, 1940–1941*. Stockhom, 1971

381) Böhme, Klaus-Richard. "Stalingrad und Schweden." In *Stalingrad*, edited by Jürgen Förster, pp. 375–396. Munich, 1992

382) Carlgren, Wilhelm M. *Swedish Foreign Policy during the Second World War*. London, 1977

383) ____. "Die Einschätzung der Lage Deutschlands in der zweiten Kriegshälfte aus schwedischer Sicht." In *Die Zukunft des Reiches*, edited by Manfred Messerschmidt and Ekkehart Guth, pp. 177–193. Herford, 1990

384) Gruchmann, Lothar. "Schweden im Zweiten Weltkrieg. Ergebnisse eines Stockholmer Forschungsprojekts." *Vierteljahrshefte für Zeitgeschichte* vol. 25 (1977): pp. 591–657

385) Lutzhöft, Hans-Jürgen. "Schwedische Reaktionen auf die deutsche Politik im Osten 1939–1943." *Zeitschrift für Ostforschung* vol. 29, no. 1 (1980): pp. 71–83

386) West, John M. "German-Swedish Relations, 1939–1942." Ph.D. diss., Univ. of Denver, 1976

387) Wilhelmus, Wolfgang. "Zu den Beziehungen zwischen dem faschistischen Deutschland und Schweden nach dem Überfall auf die Sowjetunion (Juni bis Dezember 1941)." *Zeitschrift für Geschichtswissenschaft* vol. 26, no. 8 (1978): pp. 687–699

388) Zetterberg, Kent. "Le transit allemand par la Suède de 1940 à 1943." *Revue d'Histoire de la Deuxième Guerre Mondiale* vol. 28, no. 109 (1978): pp. 59–80

h) Bulgaria

389) Cohen, David B. "Le pillage de l'économie bulgare par les Allemands." *Revue d'Histoire de la Deuxième Guerre Mondiale* vol. 18, no. 72 (1968): pp. 43–67

390) Hoppe, Hans-Joachim. *Bulgarien, Hitlers eigenwilliger Verbündeter. Eine Fallstudie zur nationalsozialistischen Südosteuropapolitik*. Studien zur Zeitgeschichte, vol. 15. Stuttgart, 1979
391) Miller, Marshall L. *Bulgaria during the Second World War*. Stanford, Calif., 1975
392) Semerdshiew, A., F. Christow, and S. Penkow. *Geschichte der bulgarischen Volksarmee*. East Berlin, 1977

i) Turkey

393) Deringil, Selim. *Turkish Foreign Policy during the Second World War. An "Active" Neutrality*. Cambridge, 1989
394) Glasneck, Johannes, and Inge Kircheisen. *Türkei und Afghanistan – Brennpunkte der Orientpolitik im Zweiten Weltkrieg*. East Berlin, 1968
395) Krecker, Lothar. *Deutschland und Türkei im Zweiten Weltkrieg*. Frankfurt a.M., 1964
396) Önder, Zehra. *Die türkische Außenpolitik im Zweiten Weltkrieg*. Munich, 1977
397) Schönherr, Klaus. "Die Türkei im Schatten Stalingrad. Von der 'aktiven Neutralität' zum Kriegseintritt." In *Stalingrad*, edited by Jürgen Förster, pp. 397–415. Munich, 1992

j) Volunteer Units

398) Buss, Philip H., and Andrew Mollo. *Hitler's Germanic Legions. An Illustrated History of the Western European Legions with the SS, 1941–1943*. London, 1978
399) Crespo, Alberto. *De las Memorias de un combatiente sentimental*. Madrid, 1945
400) Davey, Owen A. "La Légion des Volontaires Français contre le Bolchevisme. A Study in the Military Aspects of French Collaboration, 1941–1942", Ph.D. diss., Univ. of New Brunswick, 1969
401) ____. "The Origins of the Légion des Volontaires Français contre le Bolchevisme." *Journal of Contemporary History* vol. 6, no. 4 (1971): pp. 29–45
402) Förster, Jürgen. "'Croisade de l'Europe contre le Bolchevisme': la participation d'unités de volontaires européens à l'opération 'Barberousse', en 1941." *Revue d'Histoire de la Deuxième Guerre Mondiale* vol. 30, no. 118 (1980): pp. 1–26
403) Förster, Jürgen, and Gerd R. Ueberschär. "Freiwillige für den 'Kreuzzug Europas gegen den Bolschewismus'." In *Das Deutsche Reich und der Zweite Weltkrieg*, vol. 4, pp. 908–935. Stuttgart, 1983
404) Kleinfeld, Gerald R., and Lewis A. Tambs. *Hitler's Spanish Legion. The Blue Division in Russia*. London, 1979
405) Littlejohn, David. *Foreign Legions of the Third Reich*. Vol. 2, *Belgium, Great Britain, Holland, Italy and Spain*. San José, Calif., 1981
406) Mabire, Jean. *Division Wallonie sur la Baltique, 1944–1945*. Paris, 1989
407) Merglen, Albert. "Soldats français sous uniformes allemands 1941–1945. LVF et 'Waffen-SS' français." *Revue d'Histoire de la Deuxième Guerre Mondiale* vol. 27, no. 108 (1977): pp. 71–84

408) Neulen, Hans W. *An deutscher Seite. Internationale Freiwillige von Wehrmacht und Waffen-SS*. Munich, 1985
409) Pozarskaja, S. P. "'Golubaja divizija' na sovestko-germanskom fronte (1941–1943gg)." *Voprosy Istorii* no. 8 (1969): pp. 107–126
410) Proctor, Raymond. *Agonia de un Neutral. Las relacions hispanoalemanas durante le segunda guerra mundial y la División Azul*. Madrid, 1972
411) Schou, Soren. *De danske Ostfront-frivillige*. Copenhagen, 1981
412) Wegner, Bernd. "Auf dem Wege zur pangermanischen Armee. Dokumente zur Entstehungsgeschichte des III. ('germanischen') SS-Panzerkorps." *Militärgeschichtliche Mitteilungen* vol. 28, no. 2 (1980): pp. 101–136

7. The Search for Peace, 1942–45

a) Soviet-German Peace Feelers

413) Blasius, Rainer A. "Zweifel an Uncle Joe's Treue? Chancen eines sowjetisch-deutschen Sonderfriedens vor Casablanca im Urteil des Foreign Office." In *Der Zweite Weltkrieg*, edited by Wolfgang Michalka, pp. 155–173. Munich, 1989
414) Fischer, Alexander. *Sowjetische Deutschlandpolitik im Zweiten Weltkrieg 1941–1945*. Studien zur Zeitgeschichte, vol. 7. Stuttgart, 1975
415) Fleischhauer, Ingeborg. *Die Chance des Sonderfriedens. Deutsch-sowjetische Geheimgespräche 1941–1945*. Berlin, 1986
416) Kempner, Robert M. W. "Stalin's 'Separate Peace' in 1943." *United Nations* vol. 4 (1950): pp. 7–9,57
417) Koch, H. W. "The Spectre of a Separate Peace in the East: Russo-German 'Peace Feelers', 1942–1944." *Journal of Contemporary History* vol. 10 (1975): pp. 531–549
418) Martin, Bernd. "Deutsche Oppositions- und Widerstandskreise und die Frage eines separaten Friedensschlusses im Zweiten Weltkrieg." In *Der deutsche Widerstand, 1933–1945*, edited by Klaus-Jürgen Müller, pp. 79–107. Paderborn, 1986
419) ____. "Deutsch-sowjetische Sondierungen über einen separaten Friedensschluß im Zweiten Weltkrieg. Bericht und Dokumentation." In *Felder und Vorfelder russischer Geschichte. Studien zu Ehren von Peter Scheibert*, edited by Inge Auerbach et al., pp. 280–308. Freiburg, 1985
420) ____. "Das 'Dritte Reich' und die 'Friedens'-Frage im Zweiten Weltkrieg." In *Nationalsozialistische Außenpolitik*, edited by Wolfgang Michalka, pp. 526–549. Darmstadt, 1978
421) ____. *Friedensinitiativen und Machtpolitik im Zweiten Weltkrieg 1939–1942*. Geschichtliche Studien zur Politik und Gesellschaft, vol. 6. Düsseldorf, 1974
422) ____. "Verhandlungen über separate Friedensschlüsse 1942–1945. Ein Beitrag zur Entstehung des Kalten Krieges." *Militärgeschichtliche Mitteilungen* no. 20 (1976): pp. 95–113
423) Mastny, Vojtech. "Stalin and the Prospects of a Separate Peace in World War II." *The American Historical Review* vol. 77 (1972): pp. 1365–1388
424) Meissner, Boris. *Rußland, die Westmächte und Deutschland. Die sowjetische Deutschlandpolitik, 1943–1953*. Hamburg, 1954

425) Minuth, Karl-Heinz. "Sowjetisch-deutsche Friedenskontakte 1943." *Geschichte in Wissenschaft und Unterricht* vol. 16 (1965): pp. 38–45
426) Mourin, Maxime. *Les tentatives de paix dans la seconde guerre mondiale (1939–1945).* Paris, 1949
427) Sanders, Donald B. "Stalin Plotted a Separate Peace." *American Mercury* no. 65 (1947): pp. 519–527
428) Schröder, Josef. *Bestrebungen zur Eliminierung der Ostfront, 1941–1943.* Göttingen, 1985

b) The National Committee for Free Germany and the League of German Officers

429) Ackermann, Anton. "Das Nationalkomitee 'Freies Deutschland' – miterlebt und mitgestaltet." In *Im Kampf bewährt*, edited by Heinz Voßke, pp. 303–366. East Berlin, 1969
430) Blank, A., and B. Lëvel. *Nasa cel' - svobodnaja Germanija. Iz istorii antifasistskogo dvizenija "Svobodnaja Germanija" (1943–1945 gg.).* Moscow, 1969
431) Boehm, Eric H. "The 'Free Germans' in Soviet Psychological Warfare." In *A Psychological Warfare Casebook*, edited by William E. Dougherty and Morris Janowitz, pp. 812–821. Baltimore, 1958
432) Bungert, Heike. "Ein meisterhafter Schachzug. Das Nationalkomitee Freies Deutschland in der Beurteilung der Amerikaner, 1943–1945." In *Geheimdienstkrieg gegen Deutschland: Subversion, Propaganda und politische Planungen des amerikanischen Geheimdienstes im Zweiten Weltkrieg*, edited by Jürgen Heideking and Christof Mauch, pp. 90–121. Göttingen, 1993
433) Burzew, Michail I. "Deutsche Antifaschisten an der Seite der Roten Armee im Großen Vaterländischen Krieg der Sowjetunion. Gedanken und Erinnerungen." *Zeitschrift für Militärgeschichte* vol. 8 (1969): pp. 416–431
434) Carnes, James D. *General zwischen Hitler und Stalin. Das Schicksal des Walther v. Seydlitz.* Düsseldorf, 1980
435) *Deutsche Offiziere haben das Wort.* Stockholm, 1943,
436) Diesener, Gerald. "Die Propagandaarbeit des Nationalkomitees 'Freies Deutschland' im Jahre 1943." *Beiträge zur Geschichte der Arbeiterbewegung* vol. 30, no. 4 (1988): pp. 514–525
437) Dreeth, Dieter. "Weg und Bekenntnis des Generalfeldmarschalls Friedrich Paulus zum Nationalkomitee 'Freies Deutschland'." *Zeitschrift für Militärgeschichte* 1 (1962): pp. 95–192
438) Einsiedel, Heinrich Graf von. *Tagebuch der Versuchung, 1942–1950.* Frankfurt a.M., 1985
439) _____. *Rückkehr an die Front. Erlebnisse eines deutschen Antifaschisten.* East Berlin, 1972
440) *First Conference of German Prisoners of War, Privates and Noncommissioned Officers in the Soviet Union.* Moscow, 1941
441) Fischer, Alexander. "Die Bewegung 'Freies Deutschland' in der Sowjetunion: Widerstand hinter Stacheldraht?" In *Aufstand des Gewissens*, edited by Militärgeschichtliches Forschungsamt, pp. 439–463. Herford, 1984

442) Gosztony, Peter. "Über die Entstehung des Nationalkomitees und der nationalen Militärformationen der osteuropäischen Nationen in der Sowjetunion während des Zweiten Weltkrieges." *Militärgeschichtliche Mitteilungen* no. 2 (1973): pp. 31–56; no. 1 (1975): pp. 75–98
443) Hamacher, Gottfried. "Als Frontbeauftragter des Nationalkomitees 'Freies Deutschland' im Einsatz." *Zeitschrift für Militärgeschichte* vol. 7 (1968): pp. 355–369
444) Korfes, Otto. "Das Nationalkomitee Freies Deutschland." In *Juni 1941*, edited by A. Anderle, pp. 343–366. East Berlin, 1961
445) Kuczynski, Jürgen. *Freie Deutsche – Damals und heute*. London, 1944
446) Kügelgen, Bernt von. *Die Nacht der Entscheidung. Der Weg eines deutschen Offiziers zum Nationalkomitee Freies Deutschland*. Cologne 1984
447) Kügelgen, Bernt von, and Else von Kügelgen, eds. *Die Front war überall. Erlebnisse und Berichte vom Kampf des Nationalkomitees "Freies Deutschland"*. 2nd edn. East Berlin, 1963
448) Langhoff, Wolfgang. *Die Bewegung Freies Deutschland und ihre Ziele*. Zürich, 1945
449) Latein-Amerikanisches Komitee der Freien Deutschen, ed. *Deutsche wohin? Protokolle der Gründungsversammlung des National-Komitees Freies Deutschland und des Bundes deutscher Offiziere*. Mexiko, 1944
450) Lewenfeld, Andreas F. "The Free German Committee – a Historical Study." *The Review of Politics* 14 (1952): pp. 346–366
451) Martens, Hans. *General von Seydlitz 1942–1945. Analyse eines Konflikts*. Berlin, 1971
452) Puttkammer, Jesco von. *Irrtum und Schuld. Geschichte des Nationalkomitees 'Freies Deutschland'*. Neuwied, 1948
453) Scheurig, Bodo. *Freies Deutschland. Das Nationalkomitee und der Bund Deutscher Offiziere in der Sowjetunion 1943–1945*. Munich, 1960
454) Seydlitz, Walter von. *Stalingrad. Konflikt und Konsequenz*. Oldenburg, 1977
455) *Sie kämpften für Deutschland. Zur Geschichte des Kampfes der Bewegung "Freies Deutschland" bei der 1. Ukrainischen Front der Sowjetarmee*. East Berlin, 1959
456) *Verrat hinter Stacheldraht? Das Nationalkomitee "Freies Deutschland" und der Bund Deutscher Offiziere in der Sowjetunion 1943–1945*. Edited by Bodo Scheurig. Munich, 1965
457) Weinert, Erich. *Das Nationalkomitee "Freies Deutschland" 1943–1945. Tätigkeit und seine Auswirkung*. East Berlin, 1957
458) Wolff, Willi. *An der Seite der Roten Armee. Zum Wirken des Nationalkomitees "Freies Deutschland" an der sowjetisch-deutschen Front 1943–1945*. East Berlin, 1973

c) The Anti-Hitler Coalition

459) Bell, Philip M. H. "Großbritannien und die Schlacht von Stalingrad." In *Stalingrad*, edited by Jürgen Förster, pp. 350–372. Munich, 1992
460) Bereshkow, Valentin M. *Zeuge dramatischer Augenblicke. Dolmetscher und Diplomat im Kampf für den Frieden. Teheran, Jalta, Potsdam*. Frankfurt a.M., 1985
461) ____. *Ich war Stalins Dolmetscher. Hinter den Kulissen der politischen Weltbühne*. Munich 1991

462) Böttger, Peter. *Winston Churchill und die Zweite Front (1941–1943). Ein Aspekt der britischen Strategie im Zweiten Weltkrieg*. Europäische Hochschulschriften, R.3, vol. 172. Frankfurt a.M., 1984

463) Boog, Horst. "Die Anti-Hitler-Koalition." In *Das Deutsche Reich und der Zweite Weltkrieg*, vol. 6, pp. 3–94. Stuttgart, 1990

464) Borisov, J.V. *Sovetsko-francuzskie otnosenija (1924–1945gg.)*. Moscow, 1964

465) Buhite, Russell D. *Decisions at Yalta*. Wilmington, Del., 1986

466) Campell, Vice-Admiral Sir Ian, and Captain Macintyre. *The Kola Run. A Record of the Arctic Convoys, 1941–45*. London, 1958

467) Clemens, Diane S. *Yalta*. New York, 1970

468) Coates, W.P., and Zelda K. Coates. *A History of Anglo-Soviet Relations*. London, 1943

469) Davis, Lynn Etheridge. *The Cold War Begins. Soviet-American Conflict over Eastern Europe*. Princeton, N J, 1974

469a) Deane, James R. *The Strange Alliance*. New York, 1946

470) Elliot, Mark R. *Pawns of Yalta. Soviet Refugees and America's Role in their Repatriation*. Urbana, 1982

471) Feis, Herbert. *Churchill, Roosevelt, Stalin. The War They Waged and the Peace They Sought*. London, 1957

472) Fenno, Richard, ed. *The Yalta Conference*. Lexington, 1972

473) Fischer, Louis. *The Road to Yalta. Soviet Foreign Relations 1941–1945*. New York, 1972

474) Gaddis, J.L. *The United States and the Origins of the Cold War 1941–1947*. New York, 1972

475) Gilbert, Martin. "Winston Churchill and the Soviet Union, 1939–45." In *World War 2 and the Soviet People*, edited by John and Carol Garrard, pp. 234–260. Basingstoke, 1993

476) Görtemaker, Manfred. *Die unheilige Allianz. Die Geschichte der Entspannungspolitik 1943–1979*. Munich, 1979

477) Gorodetsky, Gabriel. "The Hess Affair and the Anglo-Soviet Relations on the Eve of 'Barbarossa'." *English Historical Review*, 101 (1986): pp. 405–420

478) _____. *Stafford Cripps Mission to Moscow, 1940–42*. Cambridge, 1984

479) Graml, Hermann. *Die Alliierten und die Teilung Deutschlands. Konflikte und Entscheidungen 1941–1948*. Frankfurt a.M., 1985

480) Griffith, Hubert. *R.A.F. in Russia*. London, 1942

481) Harriman, W. Averell. *Special Envoy to Churchill and Stalin, 1941–1946*. New York, 1975

482) Hawkes, James R. *Stalin's Diplomatic Offensive: The Politics of the Second Front, 1941–1943*. Ph.D. diss., Univ. of Illinois, 1966; Ann Arbor, Mich., 1977;

483) Herring, George C. *Aid to Russia 1941–1946. Strategy, Diplomacy, the Origins of the Cold War*. New York, 1973

484) Israeljan, V. *Jaltinskaja konferencija 1945. Uroki istorii*. Moscow, 1985

485) _____. *Antigliterovskaja koalicija (Diplomaticeskoe sotrudnicestvo SSSR, SSA i Anglii v gody vtoroj mirovoj vojny)*. Moscow, 1964

486) Jeremjew, Leonid. *USSR in World War Two. Through the Eyes of Friends and Foes*. Moscow, 1985

487) Jones, Robert Huhn. *The Roads to Russia. United States Lend-Lease to the Soviet Union*. Norman, Okla., 1969

488) Kettenacker, Lothar. "The Anglo-Soviet Alliance and the Problem of Germany, 1941–1945." *Journal of Contemporary History* 17 (1982): pp. 435–458

489) Kimball, Warren F. "Stalingrad und das Dilemma der amerikanisch-sowjetischen Beziehungen." In *Stalingrad*, edited by Jürgen Förster, pp. 327–349. Munich, 1992

490) Kitchen, Martin. *British Foreign Policy towards the Soviet Union during the Second World War*. London, 1986

491) ____. "Winston Churchill and the Soviet Union during the Second World War." *Historical Journal* 30 (1987), pp. 415–436

492) Kowalski, Hans-Günter. "Die 'European Advisory Commission' als Instrument alliierter Deutschlandplanung 1943–1945." *Vierteljahreshefte für Zeitgeschichte*, vol. 19, 1971, pp. 261–293

493) Laloy, Jean. *Wie Stalin Europa spaltete. Die Wahrheit über Jalta*. Translated by Markus Schmid. Vienna, 1990

494) Lebedeva, N.S. "Evropejskaja konsul'tativnaja kommissija i razrabotka uslovij bezogovorocnoj kapituljacii fasitskoj Germanii." *Ezegodnik Germanskoj istorii* 1979: pp. 176–208. Moscow, 1981

495) Loth, Wilfried. *Die Teilung der Welt. Geschichte des Kalten Krieges*. dtv-Weltgeschichte des 20. Jahrhunderts, vol. 12. Munich, 1980; 5th edn 1985

496) Lukas, Richard G. *Eagles East. The Army Air Forces and the Soviet Union, 1941–1945*. Tallahassee, Fla., 1970

497) Lunderstad, G. *The American Non-Policy Toward Eastern Europe, 1943–1947*. Tromsö, 1978

498) Marienfeld, Wolfgang. *Konferenzen über Deutschland. Die alliierte Deutschlandplanung und -politik, 1941–1949*. Hanover, 1962

499) Mastny, Vajtech. *Russia's Road to the Cold War. Diplomacy, Warfare, and Politics of Communism, 1941–1945*. New York, 1979

500) Matloff, Maurice. *Strategic Planning for Coalition Warfare, 1943–1944*. Washington, DC, 1959

501) Matloff, Maurice, and Edwin M. Snell. *Strategic Planning for Coalition Warfare, 1941–1942*. Washington, DC, 1953

502) McNeill, William H. *America, Britain and Russia. Their Cooperation and Conflict, 1941–1946*. London, 1953

503) Meissner, Boris. *Rußland, die Westmächte und Deutschland. Die sowjetische Deutschlandpolitik, 1943–1953*. Hamburg, 1953

504) Neumann, William L. *Making the Peace, 1941–1945. The Diplomacy of the Wartime Conferences*. Washington, 1950

505) Nisbet, Robert. *Roosevelt and Stalin*. Munich, 1992

506) Pozdeeva, L.V. *Anglo-amerikansie otnosenija v gody vtoroj mirovoj vojny 1941–1945*. Moscow, 1969

507) *Report of the Crimea Conference, 11. Feb., 1945*. London, 1945

508) Schofield, Brian Betham. *The Russian Convoys*. London, 1964

509) Sipols, V.J., I.A. Cel'sev, and V. N. Belezki. *Jalta – Potsdam: Basis der europäischen Nachkriegsordnung*. East Berlin, 1985

510) Snell, John L., ed. *The Meaning of Yalta. Big Three Diplomacy and the New Balance of Power*. Toronto, 1956; Baton Rouge, 1958

511) ____. *Wartime Origins of the East-West Dilemma Germany*. New Orleans, 1959

512) Sosinskij, S.B. *Akcija "Argonavt" (Krymskaja konferencija i ocenka v SSA)*. Moscow, 1970
513) Stettinius, Edward R.J. *Roosevelt and the Russians. The Yalta Conference.* Edited by W. Johnson. London, 1950
514) Stoler, Mark A. *The Politics of the Second Front. American Military Planning and Diplomacy in Coalition Warfare, 1941–1943*. Westport, Conn., 1977
516) ____. "The Soviet Union and the Second Front in American Strategic Planning, 1941–1942." In *Soviet-U.S. Relations, 1933–1942*, edited by G.N. Sevost'iannov and W. F. Kimball, pp. 88–103. Moscow, 1989
517) Sulzberger, Cyrus L. *Such a Peace. The Roots and Ashes of Yalta*. New York, 1982
518) Sywottek, Arnold. "Die sowjetische Kriegszielpolitik im Zweiten Weltkrieg 1941–1945. Zum Stand der historich-politischen Analyse und Diskussion." In *"Unternehmen Barbarossa"*, edited by Gerd R. Ueberschär and Wolfram Wette, pp. 237–252. Paderborn, 1984
519) Tyrell, Albrecht. *Großbritannien und die Deutschlandpolitik der Alliierten, 1941–1945*. Dokumente zur Deutschlandpolitik, Beiheft, vol. 2. Frankfurt a.M., 1987
520) Undasynov, I.N. *Ruzvel't, Cercill i vtoroj front*. Moscow, 1965
521) Weidenfeld, Werner. *Jalta und die Teilung Deutschlands. Schicksalsfrage für Europa*. Andernach, 1969
522) Yergin, Daniel. *Shattered Peace. The Origins of the Cold War and the National Security State*. Boston, 1977

8. The End of the Eastern Empire

523) Antoni, Michael. *Das Potsdamer Abkommen – Trauma oder Chance? Geltung, Inhalt und staatsrechtliche Bedeutung*. Berlin, 1985
524) Badstübner, Rolf. *Code 'Terminal'. Die Potsdamer Konferenz.* East Berlin, 1985
525) Benz, Wolfgang. Potsdam 1945. *Besatzungsherrschaft und Neuaufbau im Vier-Zonen-Deutschland.* Munich, 1986
526) *Die Berliner Konferenz der Drei Mächte. Der Alliierte Kontrollrat für Deutschland. Die Alliierte Kommandantur der Stadt Berlin. Kommuniqués, Deklarationen, Proklomationen, Gesetze, Befehle.* East Berlin, 1946
527) Deuerlein, Ernst. *Deklamation oder Ersatzfrieden? Die Konferenz von Potsdam 1945.* Stuttgart, 1970
528) Eichwede, Wolfgang. "Die Sowjetunion und Deutschland 1945." In *Zusammenbruch oder Befreiung? Zur Aktualität des 8. Mai 1945*, edited by Ulrich Albrecht et al., pp. 120–139. Berlin, 1986
529) Feis, Herbert. *Zwischen Krieg und Frieden. Das Potsdamer Abkommen*. Frankfurt a.M., 1962
530) Hacker, Jens. *Sowjetunion und DDR zum Potsdamer Abkommen*. Cologne, 1968
531) Hansen, Reimer. *Das Ende des Dritten Reiches. Die deutsche Kapitulation 1945*. Stuttgart, 1966
532) Hillgruber, Andreas. *Zweierlei Untergang. Die Zerschlagung des Deutschen Reiches und das Ende des europäischen Judentums*. Berlin, 1986

533) Kegel, Gerhard. *Ein Vierteljahrhundert danach. Das Potsdamer Abkommen und was aus ihm geworden ist*. East Berlin, 1970

534) Kogelfranz, Siegfried. *Das Erbe von Jalta. Die Opfer und die Davongekommenen*. Reinbek, 1985

535) Longmate, Norman. *When We Won the War. The Story of Victory in Europe, 1945*. London, 1977

536) Loth, Wilfried. "Weltpolitische Zäsur 1945. Der Zweite Weltkrieg und der Untergang des alten Europa." In *Nicht nur Hitlers Krieg*, edited by Christoph Kleßmann, pp. 99–112. Düsseldorf, 1989

537) Lucas, James. *Last Days of the Reich. The Collapse of Nazi Germany, May 1945*. London, 1986

538) Luedde-Neurath, Walter. *Regierung Dönitz. Die letzten Tage des Dritten Reiches*. With an epilogue "Die Regierung Dönitz in der heutigen wissenschaftlichen Forschung" by Walter Baum. 3rd enl. edn. Göttingen, 1964

539) Müller, Rolf-Dieter, and Gerd R. Ueberschär. *Kriegsende 1945. Die Zerstörung des Deutschen Reiches*. Frankfurt a.M., 1994

540) *Potsdam und die deutsche Frage*. With contributions by Ernst Deuerlein, Alexander Fischer, Eberhard Menzel and Gerhard Wettig. Cologne, 1970

541) Rozanov, German L. *Das Ende des Dritten Reiches*. East Berlin, 1965

542) Sipols, V.J., I.A. Cel'sev, and V. N. Belezki. *Jalta – Potsdam: Basis der europäischen Nachkriegsordnung*. East Berlin, 1985

543) Steinert, Marlis G. *Die 23 Tage der Regierung Dönitz*. Düsseldorf, 1967

544) Tschuikow, Marschall W. *Das Ende des Dritten Reiches*. Munich, 1966

545) Wagner, Wolfgang. *Die Entstehung der Oder-Neiße-Linie in den diplomatischen Verhandlungen während des Zweiten Weltkrieges*. 3rd enl. edn. Marburg, 1968

Part B

THE MILITARY CAMPAIGN

Introduction

The bloodiest battles of the Second World War took place on the Eastern Front and the greatest crimes committed by the Nazis occurred along and just behind this front. After the original German attack, the Eastern Front became the scene for both sides of a vicious, ideologically driven war of opposing world views.

Hitler expected the war for "*Lebensraum* in the east" to establish Germany as a great world power. This required extreme methods of warfare and ruthless conquest, exploitation, and resettlement of Soviet territories. The Soviet leaders were prepared to defend their country just as ferociously. The "Great Patriotic War" proclaimed by Stalin led to the ultimate defeat of the German aggressor and laid the foundations for the emergence of the Soviet Union as a superpower. For over forty-five years thereafter, the story of the hard-fought victory over the powerful German army functioned as a great unifying myth, until the ultimate collapse of Communist rule and the Soviet empire.

The struggle on the Eastern Front owed its unique nature, not least of all, to what it meant for both Hitler's and Stalin's lust for power. This was not a "normal, ordinary war." The conflict was influenced by party considerations on both sides, and it soon developed into a struggle of brutal terror as each side sought total triumph over the other.

The all-out nature of the war affected not only military operations but also historical analysis after 1945. For those looking back, there were no shades of gray; there was only intense black and white. For a long time, historical accounts of the military aspects of Operation Barbarossa were dominated by these sharp contrasts. The Soviet leadership was eager to portray the war as a glorious and noble struggle to free the peoples of eastern Europe from fascism and national socialism; the Germans who wrote about the war were for the most part former participants, eager to uphold the unsullied reputation of the Wehrmacht. This attempt was prompted largely by all the revelations about the crimes of the Nazi regime emanating from the trial of the main war criminals and other ensuing trials before the International Military Tribunal in Nuremberg (Nos. 182, 189).

The first historical accounts of military operations from a German point of view were written for studies produced by the U.S. Army at the height of the Cold War, when America was particularly sensitive to the possibility of war with its erstwhile ally. (A guide to these old studies has been brought out by the U.S. Army.) Senior officers in the former Wehrmacht played an important part in these studies, producing numerous accounts for the Americans of the struggle on the Eastern Front under the direction of former general Franz Halder, who had been chief of army general staff at the time of the attack on the Soviet Union. These authors could draw on their personal experience – for instance, Walter Schwabedissen's accounts in regard to Luftwaffe activities in the East (No. 987). They emphasized both that Germany had engaged in a preventive war and that Hitler was solely responsible for the failure of the Russian campaign through his dilettantish interference in the planning and execution of military operations. At the same time, they insisted on the brave, irreproachable behavior of the Wehrmacht. All the blatant crimes that had been committed were allegedly the work of the SS, the SD, and party people in the occupied areas "to the rear of the fighting troops."

This view dominated most of the memoirs that appeared in subsequent years by Bernhard von Loßberg (No. 251), Adolf Heusinger (No. 232), Heinz Guderian (No. 228), Erich von Manstein (No. 253), Hermann Hoth (No. 403), and Walter Chales de Beaulieu (No. 376). The overviews of Kurt von Tippelskirch (No. 106), Alfred Philippi (No. 91), and Wilhelm-Ernst Paulus (No. 334) in his early dissertation at the University of Bonn also focused on strictly military events. These works were based chiefly on eyewitness accounts by former officers. They influenced the first studies undertaken in the United States, which also emphasized professional military analysis of the war on the Eastern Front – for instance, the works of Otto A.W. John

(No. 79), Wladyslaw Anders (No. 33), and George E. Blau (No. 285). On the basis of these studies Earl F. Ziemke, John Erickson, and David M. Glantz wrote remarkable overviews about the Russo-German war (Nos. 119, 53, 58–60).

General overviews of the war against the Soviet Union were likewise largely given to black-and-white approaches. This was at least partially due to the difficulty in finding source materials, since most German military records had been seized by the victorious Allies. These views were also influenced by political ambitions of the day and general attitudes in the first few years after the war.

Memories of the struggle in the East were colored primarily by events in the second half of the war: the "Russian steamroller," the revolutionary thrust of Bolshevism into the West and on to world revolution, the brutality of the partisan war, the Red Army's harsh treatment and plundering of the German civilian population, the suffering and hardship experienced in Soviet prisoner-of-war camps in the East, and the fate of refugees and expellees from Germany's eastern provinces. The issue of German war aims and activities in the early stages of Operation Barbarossa, when the invaders were still confident of victory, tended to be overlooked. This helped, at least for a time, to preserve the reputation of the traditional German military elites, who were gradually returning to important positions in West German society.

Another obstacle to an objective account of the war on the Eastern Front during the 1950s was Communist propaganda that appropriated historical events, determining in advance the outcome of Marxist-Leninist research in the Soviet Union and its satellite states. Again and again, Soviet propaganda underlined the "inevitable victory" of the Red Army and the superiority that the Bolshevik socialist system had demonstrated in the Second World War. Contemporary political considerations also prompted Communist propagandists to make blanket assertions that Hitler's generals and the monopoly capitalists and imperialists who had stood behind them under fascism were again planning to attack the "the workers' state" with the help of the Americans. Typical of the accounts of the war heavily influenced by Communist ideology were those of Soviet dictator Joseph Stalin (No. 186), S. Golikov (No. 61), and Gerhard Förster (Nos. 54, 215). Anyone in the Western occupation zones and then in the early Federal Republic of Germany who denied Hitler's sole responsibility for the conduct of the war, pointing to other social circles that also had a strong influence over the nature of the German war effort, had to face a storm of accusations about being a tool of Communist propaganda.

It was not until German war records began being released by the Allies in the 1960s that new, comprehensive interpretations of Nazi strategy and conduct of the war became possible. An excellent example of this was Andreas Hillgruber's standard work, *Hitlers Strategie*, in 1940/41 (No. 310), which was first published in 1965 but still retains its validity. It provided a convincing framework for studies of the early stages of Operation Barbarossa. The two large studies undertaken by Norman Rich on *Hitler's War Aims* (No. 92) and by Robert Cecil on *Hitler's Decision to Invade Russia* (No. 288) stood in the tradition established by Hillgruber. Lothar Gruchmann's study of the Second World War (No. 63) also took advantage of the new source materials that were then becoming available. Finally, Ernst Nolte clearly defined the true nature of the German war in the East with his well-known conclusion that it was "the most horrendous war of conquest, enslavement and annihilation that the modern world has ever seen" (No. C/16a, p. 436).

These comprehensive studies of the history of the Second World War and of the struggle against the Soviet Union were based on the publication of numerous source materials, which filled out the narrow selection of Nazi documents available and encouraged new questions and approaches. Among these source materials were Hitler's *Tischgespräche im Führerhauptquartier* (No. 181), which has now appeared in several new revised editions and is most readily accessible in the version *Aufzeichnungen Heinrich Heims: Hitler's Monologe* (No. 168). Further examples are the corresponding volumes of the *Akten zur deutschen Auswärtigen Politik* (No. A/46) with its supplementary appendices; the several volumes of the *Kriegstagebuch des Oberkommandos der Wehrmacht 1940–1945* (No. 184); *Hitler's Weisungen für die Kriegsführung 1939–1945* (No. 165); and Franz Halder's personal war diary, the *Tägliche Aufzeichnungen des Chefs des Generalstabes des Heeres 1939–1942* (No. 162).

Important information on the general course of the war in the East can be gathered from the posthumously published memoirs, letters, and reports of the former chief of the Wehrmacht high command, Field Marshal Wilhelm Keitel, which Walter Görlitz published (No. 159), as well as of the army's quartermaster general, General Eduard Wagner (No. 190); the former German military attaché in Moscow and later general of the Russian volunteer units, General Ernst Köstring (No. 148); the chief of the war economy and armaments office, General Georg Thomas (No. D/18a); and the deputy chief of the armed forces operational staff, General Walter Warlimont (No. 276).

Valuable information about the entire Soviet-German war can also be found in more recent publications of memoirs and diaries by Hitler's closest military associates, such as army adjutant Gerhard Engel (No. 171) and Luftwaffe adjutant Nicolaus von Below (No. 203), as well as such diplomats as Hans von Herwarth (No. 231).

Interest continued to remain high, however, in specifically military events in the East. Monographs of this kind were offered by former generals Alfred Philippi and Ferdinand Heim (No. 91), as well as by Hubert Lanz (No. 248), Carl Wagener (Nos. 112, 503), and Rudolf Hofmann (No. 402). For English-speaking readers, David M. Glantz has published several studies of the history of the war on the Eastern Front (Nos. 58, 59, 60).

At the same time, a new historical genre developed to provide veterans with sympathetic descriptions of their experiences on the battlefields of the East. Works of this kind – for example, those of Werner Haupt (Nos. 65–71) – provided for the most part an uncritical view of events in Russia. Beyond this historiographical subculture there emerged an extensive *Landser* literature, or popular literature for former privates, which tended to glorify war and refurbish the old view that the enemies in the Red Army were inferior. Great simplifications such as those of Erich Kerns (Erich Kernmayr) in *Der große Rausch* fed easily into works by the radical Right and neo-Nazis aimed at the popular market. Still other popular studies of the war proved very successful, especially those of the former war correspondent Paul K. Schmidt, who offered comprehensive descriptions of various campaigns under the pseudonym Paul Carell (No. 375), as well as those of Pierre Rondière (No. 433). A special overview is presented in the photo documentation of Jewgeni Chaldej on his way from Moscow to Berlin (No. 209a).

The broadcasting in Germany of the Soviet-American television series "The Unknown War" in 1981 prompted several authors to write works based largely on the series, although they failed to meet any kind of academic standards (Nos. 35, 51, 94).

A good summary of the political and military aims of both the Soviets and the Germans can be found in the recent overviews produced by a number of people at the Militärgeschichtliches Forschungsamt in Potsdam, formerly in Freiburg, in the series *Das Deutsche Reich und der Zweite Weltkrieg* (No. 371). This work attempts to cover many different aspects such as politics, economics, diplomacy, military tactics, strategy, and social developments, resulting in the end in a many-faceted depiction. The chapters on the war in the East in Gerhard L. Weinberg's *A World at Arms* also offer excellent overviews on the basis of the most recent research (No. 114).

The previously dominant conviction that the Wehrmacht had always conducted itself in exemplary fashion was challenged vehemently in a study by Hans-Adolf Jacobsen (No. C/49) and Heinrich Uhlig (No. C/54) of the horde of "criminal orders." In another work, Uhlig emphasized Hitler's virtually total responsibility for the "planning and conduct of the eastern campaign" (No. 355). In a recent work, Ernst Klee and Willi Dreßen documented the war of wanton destruction conducted against civilian populations in the East and the behavior of those Germans responsible for it (No. C/5, *Gott mit uns;* for further literature on this topic, see Part C of this book).

The memoirs and notes of a British journalist who spent the war years in Moscow, Alexander Werth, provided an overview of the war from the Soviet side from a surprising source (No. 115). Further works on the military aspects of the entire Soviet-German war appeared in the United States and Great Britain – for instance, Alan Clark's book (No. 41).

A comprehensive Soviet view of the war began to appear in 1960 with the publication of the first volume of the six-part *History of the Great Patriotic War of the Soviet Union 1941–1945* (Nos. 56, 77). It was produced by the Moscow Institute for Marxism-Leninism of the Central Committee of the Communist party of the Soviet Union, and for the first time some government information was made available. Thanks to the efforts of Andreas Hillgruber and Hans-Adolf Jacobsen, a summary volume by Boris S. Tel'puchovskij had already appeared in German translation in 1959, with many commentaries by the editors (Nos. 72, 101, 102). The Soviet journalist Lev Besymenski also aroused considerable interest with his collection of documents and analysis of events leading up to the war, which was also published in the Federal Republic (No. 38). East German and Soviet historians attempted to produce together further omnibus volumes based on a Marxist-Leninist approach and the party's official interpretation of the Soviet-German war as an act of "German imperialism." On the occasion of the twentieth anniversary of the German attack on the Soviet Union, the publication of *Juni 1941* (No. 282, as well as Nos. 287, 406) provided another opportunity to consider Hitler's aggression and examine the views of West German historians.

Beginning in 1973–74, an extensive series entitled *Geschichte des Zweiten Weltkrieges 1939–1945* in the USSR and *Deutschland im zweiten Weltkrieg* in the GDR was published in Moscow and East Berlin by the institutes for Marxism-Leninism of the respective party Central Committees (Nos. 57, 47). This series was also based on simplistic Marxist-Leninist dogma reflecting official party doctrine. It was aimed in its makeup and composition at a broad public and contained an extensive, "officially approved" description of the war with very strong ideological accents, especially in value judgments and interpretations. In the section on the military history of the war against the Soviet Union, GDR historians provided many contributions for both volumes on the "anti-Soviet course of the war" (No. 312) and on the "fiasco of anti-Soviet aggression" (Nos. 54, 89). They portrayed the failure of the German blitzkrieg strategy in the East as "inevitable" due to the laws of history and the unparalleled efforts of the Soviet state.

The "de-Stalinization" process initiated at the twentieth party congress of the Soviet Union on 24 and 25 February 1956 led to a short phase of historiographical thaw in the 1960s. Several memoirs of former Soviet generals and marshals began to offer critical comments on Stalin's conduct of the war, opening up an initial opportunity for dialogue with Western historians. Andreas Hillgruber and Hans-Adolf Jacobsen provided Western readers with an interesting overview of these developments in Soviet historiography in their introduction to Boris Tel'puchovskij's book (No. 102), entitled "The Second World War as Reflected in Soviet Communist Historiography." Klaus Reinhardt offered another overview of Communist historiography up to 1972 in his book on the Battle of Moscow, which is now also available in English (Nos. 486, 488).

Particular attention was paid to the memoirs of the most important Soviet supreme commander and later minister of defense, Marshal Georgij K. Zukov, which also appeared in German translation (No. 279). Konstantin Simonov then provided an important supplement to these memoirs (Simonov in Bonwetsch, No. 6). A tenth uncut and unrevised edition of Zukov's memoirs appeared in 1990. A good overview from a Western perspective of other writings by Soviet army leaders and Marxist-Leninist historians in the Soviet Union can be found in the collections published by Seweryn Bialer and Peter Gosztony

(Nos. 123, 225). Good overviews from a Communist perspective can be found in the publications of Gerhard Förster, Erhard Moritz, Werner Stang, Horst Giertz, P. Shilin, and Gerhart Hass and in the omnibus volume *Soviet Research into the Second World War* published in Moscow (Nos. 9, 15, 22, 30, 54, 89, 121, 122, 157, 210, 219, 220, 296, 330, 342, 467). They remind us that a central concern of most Soviet publications remained to refresh memories of the heroic deeds of the Red Army during the war. Among the important recent publications of Soviet army commanders are the memoirs of former marshals Konstantin K. Rokossovskij and Aleksandr M. Vasilevskij, Army General S.M. Stemenko, and General Sandalov, who concerned himself in particular with the battles waged by the Fourth Army at the outbreak of the war (Nos. 264, 272, 270, 63; Sandalov in No. 6). After the advent of *perestroika* in the Soviet Union, supplements to some of the older memoirs of Soviet army commanders were published in Moscow in the *Journal of Military History* containing critical additions to the earlier whitewashed versions.[1]

The most extensive criticism of the shortcomings of the Soviet leadership and of the country's past was undertaken by the former Soviet general Pjotr Grigorenko (No. 393). Together with Alexander M. Nekric (No. 425), he was especially anxious to reveal the devastating effects of the cult of personality surrounding the Soviet dictator, the impact of the Stalinist purges on the Red Army, the failure to realize that the Germans were going to attack, the resulting inadequate war preparations, and Stalin's repeated interference in the conduct of operations, all of which were responsible for the grievous defeats and heavy losses of life in the first few months after the outbreak of the war on 22 June 1941. Grigorenko directed his accusations as well at other high military and political figures, some of whom were still in power.

The Soviet leaders and bureaucracy soon found that they had many reasons to attempt to dampen these efforts to come to terms with the past. Men such as Grigorenko were silenced; even Zukov was dismissed. Nekric was accused of abandoning Communist orthodoxy and forced to emigrate. After Khrushchev was deposed, official histories under Brezhnev admitted some general errors in the conduct of the war but continued to eulogize the past under the heroic leadership of the party, employing

1. See in this regard the post-1988 volumes of the *Journal of Military History* (Voenno-Istoriceskij Zurnal, VIZ), Moscow.

the victory over the "Fascist aggressors" as one of the government's most important arguments to legitimize the dictatorial, bullying tactics of the Soviet regime.

The result was an ideological crackdown on Soviet historians, so that very little interesting information appeared in most Soviet publications. They neither employed critical historical methodologies nor had access to primary sources, since the special state archives and other party archives with war records remained closed to them, too. Least controlled and manipulated by the Communist party were volumes of photographs, such as those of Vladimir Karpov, which attempted to show the darker side of the war in Russia through pictures that had never been seen before in the West (Nos. 80, 132, 133).

Following the collapse of Communism and the dissolution of the Soviet Union itself in December 1991, severe historical judgments of Stalin as a military commander and political leader began appearing, as noted by Roy Medwedew in his three-volume work and by the Soviet colonel Robert Savuskin in his critical comments in his *Darstellung des bewaffneten Kampfes in einer künftigen Geschichte des Großen Vaterländischen Krieges des Sowjetvolkes* (Nos. 18, 19, 137). Judgments of past Soviet historical scholarship also became harsh, for there was allegedly "no place" in them for "penetrating intellectual work." The archives remained largely closed to Soviet historians as well, and their works were subject to doctrinaire controls and politically imposed dogmas. Dimitri Wolkogonow was the first Soviet historian to gain access to large numbers of records in the Soviet archives for his critical biography of Stalin that appeared in Russian in 1989 and shortly thereafter in German translation (Nos. 149, 150).

The numerous Soviet and Marxist-Leninist publications were therefore of little value. Often they were pure propaganda, whose findings were dictated by Moscow and which paid little attention to the international research. The many works that hewed closely to the dogmatic definitions of Marx, Engels, and Lenin can safely be forgotten. However, the new conditions after the collapse of the Soviet empire allowed much progress to be made in substantive research into the Soviet-German war (No. 79). Recent works on military history in the CIS have met with considerable interest, as has the new work of the Moscow Institute for Military History entitled *History of the Great Patriotic War of the Soviet People*. Work on this ten-volume series began in August 1987, originally still under the direction of the late

Dimitri Wolkogonow. Doubts about the project have arisen, however, for several reasons: the sweeping outline adopted by Wolkogonow was revised under Defense Minister Dimitry T. Yazov and chief-of-staff Marshal S.F. Achromeev; the anticipated publication of the first volume in June 1991 was postponed because of anti-Communist contents; the work has now been pared down to four volumes; and Wolkogonow was removed as project leader (Nos. 312, 367a, 391a). Furthermore, the authors once again do not have unlimited access to the state archives in Moscow.[2] Equally misguided is the more recent thesis that singles out Stalin and claims that he alone was responsible, as a dilettante in military affairs, for most of the Soviet casualties or that he should shoulder all the responsibility and opprobrium for the Communist terror. These attempts to lay all the blame at the feet of one individual smack in many ways of the apologetic memoirs written by German generals after the war. They, too, claimed that Hitler's amateurism was the reason for their military defeats. It is hoped that Soviet historians will soon abandon this oversimplified view.

Much was written in the West beginning in the 1970s about the question of Hitler's sole responsibility for military and strategic decisions and any belief he might have harbored that Stalin's policies posed a threat to Germany. The great duel between the two dictators was well described in Alan Bullock's dual biography *Hitler and Stalin* (No. 125) and also in the new biography of Hitler by Kurt Pätzold and Manfred Weißbecker (No. 142a) and in the detailed report *Double Deception* by James Barros and Richard Gregor (No. 282a). Research into military and political questions again focused on the question of a preventive war. The following works are of interest here to the extent that they include in their discussion military aspects of Hitler's war aims and Stalin's general war strategy: David Irving (Nos. 76, 404), Martin van Creveld (No. 380), Erich Helmdach (No. 307), Hartmut Schustereit (No. 340), and Joachim Hoffmann (Nos. 313, 401). However, research into the preventive-war theory falls largely under the heading of "Policies and Strategy" (see Part A of this volume). The failure of the above authors to take into account Hitler's ideological program to conquer "*Lebensraum* in the east" skews their conclusions. This criticism has often been raised in regard to recent proponents of

2. See the report in the *Süddeutsche Zeitung* of 24 June 1991, p. 8, and the comments made to the authors during a visit to the Institute for Military History in Moscow on 25 February 1993.

the preventive-war theory such as Viktor Suworow, Ernst Topitsch, Max Klüver, and Fritz Becker. This is made clear in the recent omnibus volumes of Gerd R. Ueberschär and Wolfram Wette, as well as in the works of Bernd Wegner and Wolfgang Michalka, and in Hans-Heinrich Nolte's summary of the current research (Nos. 21, 107, 113, 336, 354, 426). In the meantime, Dimitri Wolkogonow, Vladimir Karpov, and Valerij Danilov have demonstrated on the basis of recently revealed Soviet sources that General Zukov, the chief of the Soviet general staff, and Marshal Timoshenko, the People's Commissar for Defense, drew up on 15 May 1941 a plan for a preventive military strike by the Red Army in response to the deployment of the Wehrmacht on the Eastern frontiers (Nos. 133, 149, 150, 291). However, Stalin rejected the execution of this plan and adhered to his policy of appeasement. For this reason, Rainer F. Schmidt has designated Stalin's tactics and calculations before Operation Barbarossa as "a misguided strategy for all cases" (No. 339).

About the Individual Phases of the Military Struggle

An important source for the planning, preparation, and armaments of Operation Barbarossa is the publications of various private and official war diaries covering the entire eastern war – for example, those of the chief of the general staff, Franz Halder (No. 162); and those of the OKW, or high command of the armed forces (No. 184). Together with the memoirs and reports of other German planners of the operation (see, for example, No. 276), they make possible a comprehensive reconstruction of German war aims. Brigadier General Marcks' "Eastern Operations Plan" records from August 1940 are a particularly rich source of information about the early planning of the OKH, or army high command, as early as the summer of 1940 (No. 317). Before the publication of these records, the overall plans for the German operations were researched and described as part of a military study undertaken by the U.S. Department of the Army. The contributions of Robert Gibbons (No. 299) and Andreas Hillgruber (No. 309) highlight in particular the Germans' reckless underestimation during their planning of the Red Army's strength.

Some Marxist-Leninist works by Olaf Groehler, Erhard Moritz, and Hans Busse examine in particular the failure to appreciate the strength of the Red Army and the Soviet Union and their enormous military achievement in fending off the German advance on Moscow in 1941 (Nos. 157, 303, 89, 294, 330, 287, 373).

Several broad studies of Soviet-German relations in 1939–41 and about the "historical viewpoint of Operation Barbarossa" (Nos. 107, 113, 450) – as well as monographs examining the decision to attack and preparations for the attack, such as those of Heinrich Uhlig (No. 355), Gerd R. Ueberschär (Nos. 353, 354), and Andreas Hillgruber (Nos. 310, 311) – have demonstrated that the military planning was based directly on Hitler's ideologically motivated desire to conquer new *Lebensraum* in the East. Of little value are works that attempt to deny that Germany launched a surprise attack or that endeavor, like Bernd Stegemann's study (No. 346), to downplay the part played by Nazi ideology in the military decision-making and planning. These tendencies can be found in the works of Viktor Suworow (No. 349 [Viktor Rezun]), Ernst Topitsch (No. 351), Werner Maser (No. 327b), and recently Joachim Hoffmann (No. 313) and Fritz Becker (No. 283). In a more recent work, Oleg Starkow pointed out that information from Soviet deserters (such as NKVD General Lyushkov, who fled to the Japanese from Manchuria in 1938) reinforced the Germans in their conviction that the Red Army had been weakened and posed little threat (No. 345). The publication of Pawel Sudoplatow now offers information on the Soviet military secret service in the war (No. 1165). In contrast, Russel H.S. Stolfi has pointed to the possibility of tactical surprise as a basic motive for the attack and as the reason for Germany's initial successes. Also in this category are the works of Victor Suworow, Ernst Topitsch, and Fritz Becker, which point to a Soviet offensive against the West, code-named operation "Thunderstorm" (Nos. 348, 349, 351, 283).

In regard to the planning of the campaign, Silvio Furlani sketched out the particular importance of the Pripet Marshes for operational planning in the southern and central sections of the Eastern Front (No. 298). General overviews of German military preparations for the campaign are provided by Barry A. Leach (No. 325) and Albert Beer in his 1978 dissertation (No. 284), as well as by Ernst Klink in the fourth volume of *Das Deutsche Reich und der Zweite Weltkrieg* (Nos. 318, 319). Klink's study and Heinz Magenheimer's 1969 dissertation (No. 326) also cover operations until the winter of 1941–42. On the basis of his study solely of the available military records, Klink attempted to portray the operations decided upon by Hitler and leading Wehrmacht circles as "apolitical." He also concluded that Hitler had provided excellent military leadership, in contrast to the "poor decisions" of Chief of General Staff Franz Halder. However, other researchers have denied all this, and there is little evidence for Klink's views in the available records. This is true in particular for the decision to attack the Soviet Union, which was made directly by Hitler and not by the general staff. Klink's narrow military view also enticed him into sidling up to the long-disproved Nazi claim that this was a preventive war, while failing to clearly define this alleged "preventive" policy to forestall Stalin's aggressive actions as part of a European defense against Bolshevism.

Communist historians were especially interested in the failure of the Nazis' blitzkrieg strategy and the operational problems experienced by the German military from the early days of the attack until the assault on Moscow. This can be seen in the works of Wolf Stern, Ernst Stenzel, Gerhard Förster, Werner Knoll, and Helmut Göpfert (Nos. 443, 54, 296, 467, 322, 308, 391).

* * *

The outcome of the Battle of Moscow in the winter of 1941–42 has led repeatedly to questions about the turning point or the decisive battle in the Second World War (No. 488). This battle was certainly one of the determining events in the war in Europe. From the perspective of the entire war from 1939 to 1945, the debate about turning points and climaxes has time and again resulted in corrections in the accepted view of history and in controversies about the course of political and military events. It all boils down to the question of which of the great battles and operations should be seen as the turning point in the worldwide war. A number of years ago, Andreas Hillgruber examined this question of military and political "climaxes," selecting July 1941 as the "zenith of the Second World War." At this time, after the conquest of France and what appeared in the summer of 1941 to be the imminent demise of the USSR, the war seemed to have developed into a global showdown of the Third Reich and Japan versus Great Britain and the United States (No. 400).

The discussion of these climaxes and turning points produced greater or lesser emphasis on the Soviet-German front as the main focus of the entire war. The perceived military and political importance of the Soviet Union in comparison with the Western Allies varied accordingly. Marxist-Leninist historians considered it "basic" to understand that the war on the Eastern Front had a decisive influence on the course of the entire war (Nos. 10, 23, 96, 435, 490). In the view of these historians, the "great battle before Moscow" was, if not the "basic turning point in the Second World War," at least a strong beginning to this turning point (No. 10).

One must consider the strong emotional impact that the immediate danger to the nation's capital had on the Soviet people and their historians. It is understandable that Soviet historians would assess the threat as being far more serious and the Soviet victory as far more significant than would historians in other countries. The importance of the "duel to the death on the approaches to the Soviet capital" (Nos. 490, 491, 492) becomes especially apparent when one considers that Hitler and the OKH assumed that the attack on Moscow would be the decisive battle in the war on the Soviet Union. To this extent, it is true that the struggle for Moscow was "the most important battle in the early phase" of the Soviet-German war (No. 470).

The events and outcome of this battle have therefore been subjected to intense scrutiny by both Marxist-Leninist historians and historians in the Federal Republic and elsewhere in the West. This can be seen in the basic study by Klaus Reinhardt (which has also appeared in English translation); in the memoirs of Generals von Tippelskirch, Guderian, Hofmann, Philippi, and Heim (Nos. 487, 488, 106, 228, 402, 91); and in the English-language publications (partly including operational questions) of Harrison E. Salisbury, Albert Seaton, Ronald Seth, Alan Clark, Brian I. Fugate, Russel H.S. Stolfi, John Keegan, Trumbull Higgins, Barry A. Leach, James Lucas, Barton Whaley, Earl F. Ziemke, David M. Glantz, John Erickson, and George E. Blau (Nos. 489, 99, 495, 41, 389, 348, 407, 399, 325, 87, 116, 452, 58, 59, 60, 53, 602, 285), as well as in the omnibus volume of James F. Dunnigan (No. 49). The resulting differences of opinion between Western and Eastern historians were even described by GDR historians as "one of the major themes in the ideological confrontation between Marxist-Leninist historians and bourgeois historians" (No. 470).

This held true as well for historians in the Soviet Union. Publications about the Battle of Moscow were allegedly among the "most important areas of ideological conflict between socialism and capitalism," especially as Communists saw a connection with postwar problems and their ramifications into the present. Descriptions and evaluations of the struggle for the Soviet capital also often played a contemporary political role, with Soviets accusing West German historians of "strengthening present anti-Soviet policies through historical propaganda." Attempts were made to link anti-Communist policies toward the Soviet Union with "military and political problems that have continued to fester into the present." Furthermore, an "increasing reliance on the arsenal of the Cold War" was detected in East-West relations (No. 470). The Battle of Moscow therefore played a particularly key role in the Soviet leaders' sense of insecurity.

Many publications on the war with the Soviet Union showed the importance of conquering the Soviet capital in Hitler's ideologically driven war plan. The victory over Moscow was supposed to enable the Third Reich to wage a struggle with the United States for the position of "world power" on the basis of an economically self-sufficient empire in continental Europe. The preparatory work and plans for operational studies for the Eastern war began shortly after the cease-fire was signed with France in the summer of 1940. Corresponding war games were conducted in the fall of 1940, and their results presented to Hitler on 5 December 1940.

Despite the ideological motives behind the invasion, differences of opinion between Hitler and the army high command were already apparent in the preparatory phase over whether the brunt of the attack should be directed against Moscow or against the vital war industry and grain-growing areas on the two wings of the operation. There were repeated changes in the priority assigned to the conquest of the Moscow, Leningrad, and Kiev areas. After the first breakthroughs of the enemy lines, Hitler wanted the central armies to turn to the north and south. Eventually the army high command renounced carrying on a long dispute over this because it was confident that operations would be directed mainly at Moscow in accordance with Directive 21, "Case Barbarossa," and the OKH deployment orders of 31 January 1941. They set the final goal of the operations as the "Volga-Archangel Line," so that the industrial areas in the Urals would fall within range of Göring's Luftwaffe.

According to Directive 21, the capture of Moscow represented "a decisive political and economic stroke, and the elimination of the most important railroad junction." No mention was made of how the war was to be ended once the Volga (Astrakhan)-Archangel line had been reached or how victory was to be achieved if the Soviet army could not be destroyed west of the Dvina and Dnieper.

Although opinions varied about the priority of the various military targets – Leningrad, Moscow, the Ukraine with the Donets Basin, and the oil fields of the Caucasus – there was no criticism among the leading military figures in the OKW and OKH of the disdain exhibited by Directive 21 for the military might of the Red Army. The Germans were convinced that after the surprise attack on the Soviet Union on 22 June, the enemy forces west of the Dvina and Dnieper could be surrounded and destroyed by means of "bold" panzer advances. The war would end victoriously in just a few weeks. Hitler later described this war as the "greatest struggle in world history." In accordance with this feeling, a gargantuan force of 153 German divisions crossed the Soviet border between the Baltic and Black seas, including almost 3.6 million German and allied soldiers, about 3,000 tanks, and over 2,700 aircraft.

Through the failings of the leaders in Moscow, the Red Army units in the western military districts were unprepared for the German attack and suffered heavy losses, even though they numbered about 140 divisions and 40 brigades with about 2.9 million men equipped with 10,000 to 15,000 tanks (although of an older style) and 8,000 aircraft. The errors and omissions of the Russian leadership were made particularly clear in the works of A. Nekric, P. Grigorenko, and P.V. Malcev (Nos. 393, 425, 391, 392). The Soviets were certainly thunderstruck by the power of the German attack. Recent biographies of Stalin show that he did not think that Hitler would attack and expected instead to reach another political compromise with the Third Reich (Nos. 149, 150). Once Stalin recognized the mortal danger to the Soviet state and Hitler's plans for radical annihilation, and succeeded in composing himself after the personal embarrassment of the attack, he ordered a new style of total warfare. In his radio address of 3 July 1941, he proclaimed a great "patriotic war," calling for a "struggle without mercy," for "scorched earth" tactics, and for partisan attacks behind the German lines (Nos. 186, A/6, A/45).

The collapse of the Red Army in the border areas strengthened Hitler's conviction that he could afford to wage a two-front war for a short period of time and sowed great confidence in final victory in the German high command. Hitler calculated that military operations would last at most six weeks. The time to realize his great dreams for the East seemed finally at hand. In his monologues in the Führer headquarters, he confidently chose the Urals as the new border and told the Japanese ambassador, General Oshima, that the area of German domination would extend even beyond the Urals, as can be seen in source publications of these conversations (No. 168). However, in his detailed study of the "concentration of Soviet troops in the Bialystok salient" and of the battle of the "pocket of Volkovysk," Volker Detlef Heydorn has shown that the Soviets managed orderly retreats even from battles near the border (No. 308).

The German dictator went so far as to decide that Moscow and Leningrad should just be leveled. They, together with Kiev, would simply be surrounded and their supply systems then destroyed by artillery fire and the Luftwaffe. As he told Goebbels on 18 August 1941, Moscow would be totally eradicated "as a center of Bolshevik resistance." According to Hitler, "probably not much will remain" of Leningrad either. By early August the Führer had already let it be known that, after the conquest, huge pieces of equipment would be used to flood the city of Moscow, creating a mighty lake in its place. These plans to obliterate cities inhabited by millions of people had already been laid down in the first phase of the war, independent of the course of the struggle or of offers to surrender. They cannot therefore be justified by pointing to the experiences with Soviet demolition squads during the conquest of Kiev, which did not occur until the end of September 1941.

The full brutality of Hitler's plans for the military and political destruction of the Soviet Union can be seen in his infamous conference with Rosenberg, Göring, Keitel, Lammers, and Bormann on 16 July, when he distributed the booty that had still to be conquered. The Führer explained in detail his future policies for the occupied Eastern territories (see Part D in this volume): the Third Reich would "never again leave these territories." The basic task was "skillfully to divide the huge pie." The German occupation would aim "first to control, second to administer, and third to exploit."

The full extent of German confidence in imminent victory was illustrated by the actions of the senior SD leader and SS Standartenführer Dr. A.F. Six, who appeared shortly thereafter with the so-called Moscow advance squad in the headquarters of the Fourth Army, which was still fighting west of Smolensk, because he wished to proceed directly behind the front-line troops and thus enter Moscow in good time. This "special squad" was supposed to take over "security police duties" in the Soviet capital under SS-Einsatzgruppe B, as well as to secure conquered goods, archives, art, and cultural artifacts. No scholarly studies at all have been undertaken so far of these intentions.

Hitler's own overweening confidence in victory can be seen in several source volumes and studies. On 22 July 1941, he declared to the Croatian minister of defense, Marshal Kvaternik, that the Soviet armies had already been destroyed and within six weeks all serious resistance would cease to exist. Most Russian units would be liquidated in six to eight weeks (No. A/46, vol. 13, 1). Hitler could "only laugh" at the notion that the Soviet Union might be able thereafter to raise new armies in the Urals. The Führer's belief that he was on the verge of inevitable victory explains as well the candid way in which he told Kvaternik that he planned to systematically eliminate Jews, like a "source of bacteria," from all the conquered Eastern territories and even from all Europe. It should be remembered that Hitler viewed the Bolshevik political and military leaders of the Soviet Union as "leading Jewish circles" and that his struggle against the Jews would therefore also be reflected in the war against the Soviet Union (see in this regard the literature pointed out in Part C).

Hitler's conviction that the Soviet Union was already defeated is likewise evident in the orders he issued, in his discussions of the military situation, and in his conversations with diplomats. For instance, in the guidelines and supplements he issued on 14 July 1941 to OKW Order 32 concerning preparations for the period after Operation Barbarossa had been successfully completed, Hitler ordered that the brunt of war production be shifted from the army to the navy and air force. He haughtily assumed that the European part of the Soviet Union was already virtually conquered and brought under control, and he was beginning to plan substantial cuts to the army. The Führer thought that about sixty divisions and an air fleet would suffice to secure the conquered Eastern territories. In conversations with the Japanese ambassador, he spoke at the same time of their common struggle against both the Soviet Union and the United States. He envisaged Japan conducting the war in the Pacific as a kind of junior partner. Now that he alone had won the decisive victories over the Soviet Union, he toyed with the idea of having Japan enter the war against the shattered Soviet Union by way of Vladivostok.

There was a remarkable amount of agreement among Hitler and almost all the leading German military figures in their underestimation of Soviet military might. This has been pointed out in particular by Andreas Hillgruber (Nos. 309, 331, C/31, C/48). Self-delusion and overestimation of Germany's potential led these men to ignore the first warning signs of military problems on the Eastern Front – for instance, the army high command soon had almost no reserve troops left. It is surprising that most generals and senior officers shared Hitler's convictions at the time, even though some individual specialists issued warnings, as several studies have shown and as a former staff officer of the LIII army corps, Walther Lammers, has impressively documented in his self-published *Fahrtberichte aus der Zeit des deutsch-sowjetischen Krieges 1941* (Nos. 174, 416).

Berlin was not alone among Western capitals in its skeptical view of the Soviet capacity to resist, as various publications have shown. Finland participated in the war against the Soviet Union, and the Finns also assumed that the Wehrmacht would destroy the Soviet state in two or three months. British and American military and government circles were very unsure of the Soviet Union's ability to defend itself after the German attack. The U.S. Secretary of War, Henry Stimson, and his chief of staff, General Marshall, assumed that the Red Army would quickly be defeated after one or at the very most three months. Secretary of the Navy Frank Knox estimated that the Soviet Union would collapse in six to eight weeks. In Britain, the chief of the imperial general staff, General Dill, said that the Soviet army would be rounded up "like cattle" (No. 310, p. 444f., 558ff.). President Roosevelt, on the other hand, was of the opinion that the Soviet Union would hold out.

The first battles of encirclement showed that Soviet military might had been underestimated. Express admissions were soon made to this effect – for instance, in very striking form in the edited war diaries of General Halder (No. 162). By the end of July, German leaders began receiving more and more indications that they had greatly underrated the ability of the Soviet Union to defend itself in many ways and especially its military power. The notes that a German general staff officer wrote in his diary (which was later published) and studies by Andreas Hillgruber of the fierce Battle of Smolensk, a city captured by Army Group Center on 16 July 1941, illustrate the operational and strategic difficulties facing the Germans as they pushed farther toward Moscow (Nos. 420, 74), as do the descriptions by Klaus Segbers, John Barber, Mark Harrison, John and Carol Garrard, Baibakov, and Kölm of Soviet mobilization and of the movement and reestablishment of the economy and war industries in the eastern part of the country (Nos. 23, 1168a, 1173, 1173a, 1175a). Several omnibus volumes written from a Marxist perspective portray not only the Soviet political and social system but also the successful mobilization of the hinterland as the "mainsprings of victory" (No. 9; cf. Nos. 1168a, 1173).

All in all, the strengths and fighting power of the Red Army, with its huge reservoirs of manpower, were far superior to anything the German leaders had imagined. Despite the early Nazi victories, the large number of Soviets taken prisoner, and the vast expanses of land conquered, the Soviets fought on doggedly and with great skill, thereby averting the quick conquest of Leningrad, Moscow, and the industrial areas of the Donets Basin on which the Germans were counting. The assumption that the Soviet Union would rapidly crumble or disintegrate from within proved to be grossly in error. In fact, it was the German forces that were gradually worn down by the conquest of such vast expanses, and their ability to launch powerful new offensives steadily eroded. The great logistic problems the Germans had are excellently described by F. Schüler (No. 1163). In addition, after Stalin's radio appeal of 3 July for a great "patriotic war," partisan attacks began to hamper the delivery of supplies to the front-line forces.

In the meantime, however, the Wehrmacht was able to register another impressive victory in the Battle of Smolensk, which drew to a close in early August 1941. The victory at Smolensk marked the end of the first phase of operations (Nos. 400, 446). Nevertheless, while the Battle of Smolensk raged, the Soviet high command used the time to strengthen its defensive positions before Moscow and to create new units under Marshal Timoshenko as operational detachments. They succeeded in blocking a quick dash for the capital, especially as their defensive positions had been improved at a feverish pace while the German panzer units had to wait to be replenished and reorganized.

Since Army Group South was much slower in attaining its operational aims and Hitler now reverted to his old plan of positioning the brunt of the attack on the wings, violent disputes erupted in the OKW and OKH over the new strategy. Several studies, memoirs, and collections of documents have been published in regard to this strategically important discussion (Nos. 76, 165, 228, 276, 355, 373). That of Jacob W. Kipp (No. 408a) offers a good overview. Hitler finally ordered that the main German effort be concentrated on Army Group South for its advance on Kiev, the Crimea, and the Donets area and attempt to cut off Soviet oil supplies from the Caucasus.

This decision represented a signal change in the planning and conduct of operations, giving the Soviets under Timoshenko time to reinforce their defensive positions before Moscow. The conclusion of the battle in the Kiev area on 26 September 1941 (the city had already been taken on 19 September) marked another stunning victory for the Wehrmacht. Several Soviet armies were surrounded and destroyed. Once again, Hitler was convinced that the Soviet Union had exhausted its military resources. Army Group Center was directed to resume its advance on Moscow, destroying Timoshenko's units east of Smolensk before the onset of winter and seizing both Moscow and Leningrad. The attack on Moscow was given the code name "Typhoon."

Although German troops had pushed deep into the Soviet Union, advancing to around Smolensk and the gates of Leningrad and seizing much of the Ukraine, their leaders were now divided about the prospects for future success. After visiting Army Group Center, Chief of General Staff Franz Halder determined that the losses in men and matériel suffered by this army of 200,000 could no longer be made up. Even the most urgent requirements of Operation Typhoon could only be satisfied with great difficulty. Since virtually no strategic reserves were left, the power of any German offensives would steadily erode, especially as more and more troops were tied down behind the lines fending off partisan attacks. Rudolf Steiner's study of panzer tactics, using German war diaries, shows clearly how quickly the strength of German panzer units was sapped by numerous supply problems and the difficult terrain. This history of military operations is now available in English translation (No. 441).

There are many detailed studies in German, English, and Russian of the offensive against Moscow beginning on 26 September 1941, an offensive that Hitler bombastically described as the last great decisive battle of the year. They depict both the double battle of Vyazma-Bryansk and the Wehrmacht's advance to the outskirts of Moscow, some twenty-five miles (forty km) from the city center, as well as the Red Army's stunning counterattack of 5 and 6 December 1941 and the resulting crisis for the entire German front (Nos. 371, 459, 468, 470, 487, 488, 490, 495). General Zukov bears witness in his memoirs to how intensively and carefully the Soviet army organized the Battle of Moscow (No. 279). In the German literature, the Wehrmacht's failure before Moscow is often explained by the difficult winter conditions. Hitler, too, used this argument. In actual fact though, the winter was neither especially hard nor unusual. Soviet and recent Russian literature has described in particular the danger in the first half of October that the Wehrmacht would succeed in seizing the capital after German units reached the gates of Moscow at Khimki, and Stalin with his aides beginning to prepare to flee. Pavlenko reports, based on statements by Zukov, that the Soviet dictator was staggered by the appearance of the Wehrmacht before Moscow and for a time even wanted to abandon the struggle totally (see Pavlenko in No. 6).

Several works describe how the Germans constantly discovered new Red Army units turning up before their lines. General Zukov was indeed able to strengthen his front considerably through the addition of troops from Siberia and the Far East and to offset very quickly the losses of Vyazma-Bryansk. The exact number of reinforcements from Siberia and the Far East continues to be a source of some doubt in the literature. Marxist-Leninist historians have denied that the Red Army was thereby able to establish numerical superiority over the Germans (Nos. 57, 83, 459, 470, 486). In any case, the eastern divisions played an important role in the outcome of the Battle of Moscow – whether they played a deciding role will have to await comprehensive analysis of the documents in the newly opened Soviet archives.

The Soviet leaders were possibly able to transfer these units from the east and from border areas opposite Japan thanks to the information supplied by their undercover agent Richard Sorge (No. 128a), who worked in the German embassy in Tokyo and succeeded in informing Moscow, before his discovery and arrest on 18 October 1941, that the Japanese had decided to strike in the South Pacific and would thus abide by their neutrality pact with the Soviets. As a result, it is possible that Moscow therefore felt able to relocate troops to the west.

During the bitter struggle for Moscow, both sides went to ideologically motivated excess in the verbal denigration and demonizing of their opponents. Stalin used the twenty-fourth anniversary of the October Revolution to call again upon the population to wage a great "patriotic war." In his public address of 6 November 1941, which had to be made from the Mayakovskaya subway station, he promised to rain down death and destruction on the German invaders. It is here that Joachim Hoffmann in his new book sees the origin of Stalin's "war of destruction" (No. 74a). Although admitting that the Red Army had suffered heavy losses, Stalin declared nevertheless that Hitler's "blitzkrieg plan" had failed. At the traditional military parade on Red Square, he implored the units marching off directly to the front to resist the advancing tide with all their might (Nos. 115, 149, 186).

Stalin's appeal to pour death and destruction on the German invader was taken up by the German propaganda machine, which called for an all-out struggle against the "onrushing Red rabble." Field Marshal von Reichenau, who had distinguished himself in the autumn through his infamous orders for a pitiless struggle against Bolshevism, pilloried the "bloodthirstiness" of the "bestial" Soviet leadership in orders issued to Army Group South in December 1941 (No. 501, p. 157). These orders were especially appreciated by Hitler, who had spoken himself in an address on 3 October 1941 of the "cruel, bestial and animalistic opponent." They were then issued to the other army groups in the guise of special daily orders.

The fact that German commanders such as Field Marshal von Reichenau, General Hoth, and Lieutenant General von Manstein would issue such orders of their own calling for pitiless extermination reveals not only the army's embrace of Hitler's war of extermination against the Soviet Union but also its willingness to help the SS and SD in their campaigns of terror and annihilation against civilians and Jews. This has been demonstrated repeatedly in convincing fashion in recent writings (No. C/12, and other literature in Part C).

On the other hand, retired general Freiherr von Gersdorff, who served on the general staff of Army Group Center, confirmed in his memoirs that the "shooting of Jews, prisoners and even commissars was almost always refused by the officer corps" of Fourth Army units and was "viewed as an affront to the honor of the German army and especially of the German officer corps" (No. 177, p. 397f.). The "question of responsibility" for these atrocities is also mentioned, but left unanswered in the end. The last months of 1941 witnessed mounting callousness and brutality on both sides as they struggled tenaciously for Moscow.

The offhand way in which the German leaders overextended the military capability of their own troops during the attack on Moscow has been illustrated by the American historian Earl F. Ziemke in his study of the leadership conference of Orsha on 13 November 1941 (No. 452). The army chief of general staff, Franz Halder, summoned the chiefs of general staff of the army groups, armies, and panzer armies to a basic discussion in Orsha, near Smolensk. Views differed widely on the further course of operations and on the strength and battle readiness of the attacking units. The supreme commanders from various headquarters spoke out against further offensives and new goals that were, in their view, as ambitious as they were unrealistic. Hitler and the army high command, on the other hand, estimated the Germans' offensive power to be superior to the Soviets' defensive capabilities. They discussed and set such unrealistic goals as the industrial areas of Vorosilovgrad, Ivanov, Yaroslavl, and Rybinsk as well as "urgently desired" goals of Maikop, Stalingrad, Vologda, and Gorki. The supreme commander of Army Group Center, Field Marshal von Bock, and General Halder finally agreed that Moscow should be attacked in a "last burst of energy." The army high command had already had the rationale for this "uttermost undertaking" approved by Hitler on 11 November – before the discussions in Orsha even began.

Despite warnings to the contrary, the decision was therefore made to attack Moscow. It was assumed that the Red Army must be equally exhausted as the Germans and have already deployed all its reserves. The leadership knowingly bet everything on one operation. The deciding factor in their gamble would not be numerical or material superiority but the assumed superior leadership and fortitude of German soldiers. Memories from the First World War of the "miracle on the Marne" played a particular role in this decision, especially for the generals and older officers: such a "miracle" could not happen once again on the approaches to Moscow. In addition, many felt that they wished to do their absolute utmost before breaking off the advance.

It was symptomatic of the Germans' confidence in their own superiority that they utilized the most optimistic assessments of such crucial factors as their own strength, the enemy strength, and weather conditions in deciding to force at this time an ultimate decision on the approaches to Moscow. The army high command had evidently lost all ability to assess what was feasible and what was not. In the eyes of Halder and Field Marshal von Brauchitsch, the success of a further advance seemed to be mostly a "question of willpower." A few months later, the chief of general staff was still describing the entire war against the Soviet Union as a "war of willpower," as recent studies have shown (No. 501).

Several works on Soviet partisan activities and the supply problem (Nos. 1163, 1164, and see comments in Parts C and D) depict the mounting "transportation crisis" behind the German front, which was greatly aggravated by regular partisan attacks on the German supply lines, and the effects that this crisis had on the front-line troops. By early December, the German forces were short of spare parts and supplies in all areas. Some troops even went without food for extended periods of time. As a result, the offensive capability of the German divisions was rapidly dwindling. In addition, it had become apparent that the enemy would not simply collapse all along the front, as the Germans had hoped. After all their prodigious feats, the German troops before Moscow had clearly exhausted their last ounce of strength. The extent to which they suffered from problems of supply can be seen in the successful publication of combined memoirs and reports from front-line troops by Hans Meier-Welcker, who served on the Eastern Front in 1941–42 as a general staff officer (No. 420). The abandonment of offensive operations on 3 and 5 December marked the culmination of the offensive and of attempts to seize Moscow. The Wehrmacht failed therefore to conclude its operations in the East successfully.

While the Germans were still considering drawing into a strengthened shorter line the units whose forward progress had been stopped, the Red Army launched a surprise but well-prepared counteroffensive on 5 and 6 December 1941. The Soviet armies under Marshals and Generals Zukov, Konev, Cerevicenko, and Meretskov smashed through the weak German lines. Opinions vary, even in the Soviet literature, about the exact number of new divisions from the Far East and Central Asia that were re-deployed and about whether they played a decisive role in the success of the attack (Nos. 102, 459). By bringing in about ten new armies, the Red Army succeeded in breaking through the German front in several areas and penetrating deep behind the lines, so that several German armies found themselves in danger of being surrounded.

Since Leeb's army group in the north had to break off its advance on Tikhvin and evacuate the city once again on 9 December, no reserves were available from this quarter. The commander in chief of the German army, Field Marshal von Brauchitsch, gave up and asked to be released for reasons of health. Over the next few days, German commanders on the front asked repeatedly for permission to withdraw and quickly undertake evasive maneuvers. But Hitler would have none of it, issuing repeated orders not to yield a "foot of ground" and to fight on fanatically. Any substantial withdrawals were forbidden. In the next few days, several commanders in chief and generals who continued to insist on retreat were replaced, dismissed, or relieved of their command at their own request by Hitler (for instance, von Bock, von Leeb, Hoepner, Guderian, Strauß, Förster, Count von Sponeck, Baron von Gablenz, Kübler, Geyer). On 19 December, Hitler took over from Brauchitsch the duties of commander in chief of the army, which enabled him to blame Brauchitsch for the defeat. However, General Halder remained the army chief of general staff. According to new biographical research, it was typical of Halder's personality that he even hoped at this point for a better working relationship with Hitler (Nos. 130a, 148a).

Hitler refused to admit defeat. Fortunately for him, Japan attacked Pearl Harbor on 7 December, and another power entered the war on the side of the Third Reich. This enabled Hitler politically to eclipse and overshadow the catastrophe on the Eastern Front. The Führer immediately agreed to join Japan in declaring war on the United States, without demanding that Japan enter the war against the Soviet Union (see the literature in Part A).

By the end of December, the first stage in the Soviet counteroffensive was completed. The Red Army had successfully eliminated the German threat to Moscow, throwing the Wehrmacht back to between 60 and 175 miles (100 and 280 km) from its goal. In January 1942, the Soviets staged a general offensive along the entire front from the Baltic to the Sea of Asov in a bid to destroy the Eastern army and in particular to surround and obliterate Army Group Center through a vast pincers movement. As the Soviet historian Samsonov has shown, these ambitious goals could not be achieved without setting particular priorities, especially as the Soviet units soon lacked the necessary reserves, weapons, and munitions to maintain their momentum (No. 490).

In mid-January 1942, Hitler finally approved a partial retreat of Army Group Center to "winter positions." By the end of the month, this had significantly weakened the offensive capabilities of the Red Army, possibly preventing a war-deciding breakthrough by the Soviets and the entrapment of Army Group Center. The Soviet literature has attributed the Red Army's failure to take advantage of this opportunity to Stalin's scatterbrained conduct of operations and his insistence on nothing but frontal assaults (Nos. 279, 486). The high command of the German army noted with relief in February 1942 that the Soviet offensive finally seemed to have been thwarted (No. 184, vol. 1, p. 1093).

The reasons for the failure of Operation Barbarossa before the gates of Moscow were discussed not only at the time in German headquarters and command posts but also in the postwar literature, as can by seen, for instance, for English-language work in the excellent study by Alfred W. Turney (No. 500). The fortieth anniversary of the Battle of Moscow prompted a wave of interest in the Red Army's stirring defense of the capital among both

Western and Communist historians. The crucial role of the Battle of Moscow in the failure of the Germans' blitzkrieg strategy was especially emphasized in the works of Janusz Piekalkiewicz (No. 484), Lev Besymenski (No. 459), Gerhart Hass (No. 470), Aleksandr M. Samsonov (Nos. 491, 492), and Klaus Reinhardt (Nos. 487, 488).

Germans have typically pointed to the bad weather and the inexorable powers of nature in order to conceal the part played by their own hubris. Not only Hitler and his cronies but also the military leaders immediately began blaming poor weather, snowfall, rainfall, and mud for the failure of the German army (No. A/46, vol. 13, series D, pp. 697, 733; series E, vol. 1, p. 104ff. [ADAP]). Goebbels later adopted this explanation and conducted a propaganda campaign around it. In statements after the war, Field Marshal Keitel and General Jodl of the armed forces high command also stressed the impact of the winter of 1941, which was allegedly the most severe since the early nineteenth century. Both were of the opinion that it was the winter that had overcome even the most determined of wills. In the academic literature, the problems caused by the weather are not denied, but they are seen as only one factor among many in the Battle of Moscow. It is wrong to emphasize them to such an extent that they become the main reason for the German defeat, as was often the case in older studies and still is on occasion (Nos. 40, 76, 106, 444).

This view was most sharply criticized by Soviet and East German historians, because giving "General Winter" or "General Mud" credit for stopping the Wehrmacht indirectly disparaged the achievements and might of the Red Army (Nos. 459, 470). Blaming the weather for the failure leads to further speculation that the German army would have succeeded in conquering Moscow if the Balkan campaign had not delayed the launching of the attack by two months. In this, army leaders were clearly trying to explain away their own failings by blaming the weather (No. 488, p. 78). According to the data, the precipitation and cold were not nearly so extreme as Hitler claimed. Moreover, it was cold for both sides and snow fell on the Red Army as well. In general, "all the propaganda about 'General Winter' was simply stupid," said German general staff officer Von d. Leyen in his memoirs, noting further: "It was fundamental to an eastern campaign to know that it can be cold in Russia at this time of year" (No. 174a, p. 37f.).

Goebbels' diaries, which are now generally available, show that the Nazi party leaders were also eager to cast blame for the defeat on the personal failings of certain individuals, thereby finding various other scapegoats. In connection with the dismissals ordered by Hitler, the German commanders were accused at times of incompetence, cowardice, defeatism, and lack of resolve in times of crisis. Goebbels placed much of the blame on the dismissed commander in chief of the army, Field Marshal von Brauchitsch (No. 107, p. 166). In the view of the minister of propaganda, Hitler alone had managed to save the front.

These ideas have influenced the literature to the extent that it is considered ominous that differences of opinion had already arisen between Hitler and the army high command in the summer of 1941, leading to a failure to establish a main goal and to exploit the initial success with a rapid drive on Moscow. As a result, both the army high command's "detour" by way of Kiev and Hitler's direct assault on Moscow were allegedly conducted in a tentative manner. However, these arguments lose much of their impact when one considers that the Germans' further operational plans were always predicated on unrealistic expectations and that the basic differences of opinion between Hitler and the high command over the conduct of the war were therefore not so crucial. It is also not helpful to reduce the problem to a simple "Hitler-Halder duel" in order to explain the defeat, as is done in David Irving's study and in the fourth volume of the series *Das Dritte Reich und der Zweite Weltkrieg*. According to these interpretations, Hitler's insight and operational plans were better, but Halder hindered their implementation because he insisted on following his own ideas (Nos. 76, 319). In the end, Hitler was responsible for all decisions.

It is noteworthy as well that the army leaders supported Hitler in his unrealistic planning and at times even outdid him. For instance, Brauchitsch, Halder, and Bock were just as determined as Hitler in mid-November 1941 to wager everything on a final push to conquer Moscow despite the advancing winter.

It is simply erroneous to claim that espionage and treachery were the main reasons why "Preventive Blow Barbarossa" failed, as can sometimes be seen in right-wing or apologetic German publications. Continuing the apologetic line, David Irving has portrayed Hitler as the savior of the Eastern Front, who provided a shining example "in the dark months of that winter" and "with iron determination" fended off "cruel defeat" from the Eastern army (No. 76). Older works often repeat Goebbels' and Keitel's exaggerated praise for Hitler's "iron energy" and his reckless orders not to retreat, which they credit with having saved the German forces from the same fate that had befallen Napoleon's army in 1812 (Nos. 67, 159, 802,). More recent studies have pointed out that Hitler's orders to stand firm led necessarily to a war in which things were continually cobbled together, which could not ultimately be successful (Nos. 99, 488). Hitler himself was convinced that the German army survived the winter thanks only to his military genius. Seen from this perspective, the people from his inner circle who wrote memoirs, such as Field Marshal Keitel, viewed the orders to stand firm at any cost as "correct," while the front-line commanders' requests to withdraw were "narrow-minded, egotistical misconceptions dictated by the problems of the moment" (No. 159).

General Loßberg, who at the time was an expert on army operations in the OKW, confirmed in his later review of events that the German units were still under firm command at the time, so that an early, planned withdrawal would not have posed "any serious threat" to the front as a whole, while mobile operations would have kept units intact. Furthermore, General Halder stated after the war that severe losses in men and matériel "could surely have been avoided" if not for Hitler's orders to stand firm (No. 251). He further alleged that Hitler transformed an occasionally useful tactic into a doctrine to be applied to later situations, as Stalingrad was to show. As a result, a "useful idea" became "a serious error through untrammeled overuse" (No. 229). The first consequences of this error were already evident by early 1942, when substantial German units were trapped in the pockets of Demyansk and Kholm as a result of Hitler's orders to stand firm.

Among the many reasons for the German defeat before the gates of Moscow, the available studies show that the most important was the vast underestimation of the military potential of the Soviet Union and the might of the Red Army, especially as this prompted an arrogant belief that the Soviets could be quickly defeated with only barely sufficient military and economic resources. As Heinrich Uhlig and Andreas Hillgruber show, this hubris caused a "blindness to reality," arising partially out of "anti-Communist delusions" (Nos. 355, 310). However, these failings cannot be ascribed to Hitler alone, as was clearly demonstrated by the army high command's planning at the leaders' conference in Orsha.

The defeat before Moscow demolished the military plans on which Operation Barbarossa was based, namely a quick blitzkrieg. For the first time since 1939, an army grown accustomed to victory had to swallow a stinging defeat like Göring's Luftwaffe in the Battle of Britain in 1940. Losses were very high, as the literature has often shown (Nos. 99, 488, 490, 493, 503). By January 1942, the Wehrmacht had lost about 6,000 aircraft and more than 3,250 tanks and artillery pieces; almost 918,000 men were dead, wounded, missing or captured – a figure amounting to about 28.7 percent of the army's average strength of 3.2 million soldiers.

As a result of the severe setback in the winter of 1941–42, the armed forces high command discovered that it could not provide enough soldiers and war matériel to restore the Wehrmacht's strength to what it had been before the Battle of Moscow began. Although the strategic initiative had not yet passed to the Red Army, its successes freed Great Britain at least from the danger of a German invasion, for the Wehrmacht was facing a crisis of its own on the Eastern Front.

The Red Army, too, had suffered huge losses. By the end of 1941, 3.35 million Soviet soldiers had been taken prisoner. The high command of the German army calculated that more than 20,000 Soviet tanks and 2,300 aircraft had been destroyed or captured. But still the Red Army did not collapse; indeed, its success before Moscow only increased its prestige as well as its military and political standing, and the spirits of Soviet soldiers and civilians alike improved considerably.

Marxist-Leninist historians understandably emphasize the fact that the Red Army alone won the Battle of Moscow, before large amounts of Anglo-American aid began to arrive or a second front was created in the west (Nos. 279, 490). They state over and over again that the Wehrmacht suffered its first major, decisive defeat at Moscow, not at Stalingrad or Kursk. The Soviet success in this battle is ascribed in particular to the skill of the Soviet leadership or even to the enormous political and organizational work of the Soviet government and the Communist party, in its role as the inspiration and leader of the Soviet people and its armed forces (Nos. 10, 102, 392, 443).

The failure of the German invasion plan had grave effects in the economic arena as well. The Soviet victory before Moscow meant that the Germans would have to continue the war in the Soviet Union while simultaneously fighting in the west against Great Britain and their new opponent, the United States. It looked as if the war would drag on for a long time yet the economic basis to support such a war of attrition still had not been created in Germany. After formation of the great anti-Hitler coalition, the only remaining question was how long Germany and its Axis allies could hold out against the superior resources of the English-speaking powers, which after 1942 were also pouring increasing amounts of war matériel into the Soviet Union.

Berlin was forced to adapt the German economy to a lengthy war and to undertake "total mobilization" of the economic system. The defeat before Moscow brought about a clear and abrupt shift away from the blitzkrieg concept in the planning of war production, as shown in the work of Rolf-Dieter Müller (Nos. 371, A/469, 473).

For the Soviets, on the other hand, the Battle of Moscow eased the pressure on the war economy. This was due mainly to increasing production from industries that had been evacuated to the east. The successful war effort on the Soviet home front is described in particular in the work of Mark Harrison and John Barber (Nos. 394, 1168a). The deliveries of war matériel from Britain and the United States beginning in 1942 helped as well, after the U.S. Senate approved shipments to the Soviet Union on 5 November 1941 and Moscow's allies came to a new appreciation of the Soviets' military and strategic strength following their success in repelling the German invasion, as shown in a study by George C. Herring (No. A/483). Stalin could now take a more independent, self-confident approach to the Western Allies than he had been able to do at the time of their first contacts in July 1941. On the whole, the Soviet victory before Moscow consolidated the anti-fascist coalition and greatly burnished the international prestige of the Soviet Union, as Hans-Werner Schaaf has shown from a Marxist perspective (No. 493). For the rest of the war, Moscow managed cleverly to exploit the military and political independence from Western aid that it had demonstrated in the winter of 1941 before the gates of Moscow.

The Battle of Moscow was clearly a disaster for Hitler's blitzkrieg plans and for his entire improvised war plan and political aims, such as they can be discerned at the outset of Operation Barbarossa. In view of the crucial role played by the war in the East in Hitler's overall strategy to make the Third Reich the world superpower, as outlined at the outset, the defeat before Moscow was devastating. It nullified all Hitler's plans and goals for the occupied Eastern territories of the Soviet Union and thwarted his attempt to eliminate the Soviet Union as a military force before the United States entered the war. The victory of the Red Army before Moscow was certainly a watershed in the entire war. In the East, it marked the end of German blitzkrieg. Thereafter, Hitler could only attempt for as long as possible somehow to bring the Soviet Union to its knees by mounting attack after attack, while missing no opportunities to squeeze the last ounce of energy out of the German Reich.

* * *

The German advances on Moscow and on Leningrad both failed in their attempts to seize cities with millions of people. Already by the middle of September, Hitler was compelled to divert forces from the attack on Leningrad and to abandon attempts to capture the city in favor of surrounding it and "wiping it from the face of the earth" through artillery and aerial bombardment. The area north of the Neva River would then be turned over to the Finns, who had participated in the war against the Soviets. Recent studies of the ensuing siege of Leningrad have documented the horrendous impact of this largely on the civilian population, as hundreds of thousands starved to death during the many months of the blockade (No. 518).

On 14 June 1941 in the Chancellery in Berlin, Hitler had presented the gathered Wehrmacht commanders with the operational goals for the attack on the Soviet Union to be launched on 22 June 1941, in contravention of the Nazi-Soviet pact. The capture of Leningrad was one of the main goals of the new campaign, in addition to the conquest of the Ukraine, of the industrial area of the Donets, and of the Caucasian oil fields. Leningrad was, he said, the "cradle of Bolshevism," and it held a particular fascination for him as the earlier St. Petersburg of the Russian czars and a symbol of Russia's claim to great power status and dominion over the Baltic. From the very beginning, the conquest of Leningrad was a firmly established aim of the invasion. It was accordingly mentioned as early as 18 December 1940 in Directive 21 as a primary objective of Army Group North in Operation Barbarossa. The former czarist capital would not only be captured; like many other cities and areas, it would be obliterated. The planning and conduct of German operations were dominated consistently from the start by such radical plans for annihilating and extirpating the enemy. The close connections between the way in which the war was waged and Hitler's plans to eradicate Leningrad have been demonstrated beyond any doubt by recent research (No. 584). This program then influenced individual military operations in many different ways.

According to the operational plans of the army high command, Leningrad would be captured through a thrust along the coast by Army Group North under the command of Field Marshal Ritter von Leeb. This would eliminate the Soviet naval bases, secure the Baltic Sea for transportation and supplies, and provide a land connection with the Finnish army. For this reason, Finnish forces would also take part in the besieging and capturing of the city.

Following the initial attack on 22 June 1941, Army Group North pushed rapidly forward, driving the opposing Soviet Northwest Front under General Kuznetsov and his successor, General Sobennikov, far to the rear. By 26 June, German units had already reached the Dvina, and Riga was captured on 1 July. Here, too, the Red Army suffered heavy losses. In the following second part of the operation, German units captured Ostrov south of Pleskau/Pskov on 5 July, Pleskau/Pskov itself on 9 July, and Porkhov on 11 July. Here, too, Hitler counted on rapid victory. In the full flush of victory, he announced that Moscow and Leningrad would be rendered uninhabitable and wiped from the face of the earth. On 16 July, the Führer commented that he would "level Leningrad and then turn it over to the Finns". On 18 August, Hitler told Propaganda Minister Goebbels that, like Moscow, "probably not much will remain" of Leningrad. Hitler's plans to eradicate such huge cities as Leningrad, Moscow, and Kiev had nothing to do with the exigencies of the military situation and can be understood only in the context of his ideologically and racially motivated dreams of conquest and annihilation.

As the literature on military and operational aspects of the war emphasizes, the resistance offered by the Red Army stiffened after mid-July under the command of Marshal Kliment Voroshilov, so that it was no longer possible for Army Group North to carry out its plans for a quick motorized dash over Novgorod all the way to Leningrad (Nos. 319, 371, 584). Although Hitler insisted that Leningrad must be taken, it was beginning to become apparent by the end of July that Army Group North alone would not be able to conquer and secure the city.

As a result of the difficulties and problems encountered by Army Group North as the campaign wore on, its task was finally limited to "cutting off or surrounding Leningrad," since no more reservists were available. At the same time, several of Hitler's statements and orders indicate that he continued to view Leningrad as a "vital area" to the Soviet Union and a central war aim. Only after the conquest of Leningrad and Kiev would he agree to the offensive against Moscow preferred by the army high command. As a result, the course of the attack on Leningrad became especially important for the success of the entire Operation Barbarossa. The Germans failed to take Leningrad, although the towns of Narva, Kingisepp, and Tallinn were overrun and the Moscow-Leningrad railroad line was cut at Chudovo, southeast of Leningrad and Mga. A heavy armored assault on the defensive ring around Leningrad was initiated in September, with massive support from the Luftwaffe, but it met with staunch resistance from the defenders under General Zukov, who had taken over command of the Leningrad front on 13 September. Valentin Koval'cuk has described in detail the suffering and deprivations of the population as well as their extensive attempts to defend themselves against artillery bombardment and aerial attacks (Nos. 544–547).

On 8 September, the German forces took Schlüsselburg (Slisselburg) and by mid-September they had reached the outermost suburbs of Leningrad and Krasnoye Selo. With this, the city of Leningrad was cut off from its vital land connection and railroad line to Tikhvin and encircled. However, the Red Army continued to mount stubborn resistance, preventing the Wehrmacht from cracking the inner defensive line. In mid-September, Hitler ordered the attacks on the defensive ring stopped and the city sealed off from the outside in order to force it to surrender through bombardment and starvation.

The German command staffs deliberated on various occasions about how they would accept the capitulation of the city and what would be done with its inhabitants. The military commanders under Field Marshal von Leeb clearly wished to take their lead from Hitler in regard to whether to accept a capitulation, level the city by bombardment, or starve it to death. Finally the *Landesverteidigung* department of the Wehrmacht command staff in the armed forces high command put together on 21 September the infamous "Leningrad presentation notice" about the various possibilities, including the suggestion that the civilian population of the city be treated as a military target and starved to death, while the city was dynamited into oblivion. The area north of the Neva would then be given to the Finns.

Hitler's brutality and complete disregard for human life were reemphasized in his statement to the German ambassador in occupied Paris, Otto Abetz, on 16 September 1941: "The 'venomous nest Petersburg' out of which Asiatic poison had so long 'gushed' into the Baltic Sea would have to disappear from the face of the earth" (No. 181). His directive to refuse any offer to capitulate was often discussed among the staffs of the units fighting at Leningrad. The question arose of whether the German soldiers would obey orders to shoot at civilians and whether their nerves could withstand firing again and again at women, children, and defenseless old men if the population attempted to break out. German leaders were fully aware that the millions of people trapped in Leningrad could not possibly be fed from German sources.

Army administrative offices were still occupying themselves with these questions at the end of October 1941, when the capitulation of Leningrad was becoming increasingly unlikely. Field Marshal Ritter von Leeb decided that he wanted mines laid in front of the German lines so that his troops would not have to be directly involved in slaughtering civilians. If much of the population of Leningrad was to die, then this should at least not occur right under the noses of German soldiers.

In any case, once several of Army Group North's panzer units had been transferred to the Battle of Moscow, it no longer had the strength after the end of September to tighten its grip on Leningrad. The panzer units were replaced by infantry, including the 250th infantry division, the "Blue Division" composed of Spanish volunteers. These Spaniards were often mentioned but were unable to undertake any offensives (Nos. 1088, 1091, 1092, 1103, 1106, 1118, 1124). The Wehrmacht failed to advance any farther on Leningrad or to prevent supplies from reaching the city over Lake Ladoga. As a result, Leningrad's supply depots, airports, and key military posts remained outside the range of the German artillery. The attempt to starve the civilian population failed therefore to force the Soviets to surrender the city.

Army Group North succeeded temporarily in seizing Tikhvin on 8 November, but this did little to affect the situation, especially as the city was retaken by the Red Army a month later after intense struggles, with many casualties. The failure of the German offensive against Leningrad and Tikhvin affected the attitude of the Finnish high command in Helsinki, which became even less willing to attack Leningrad from the north (Nos. 352, 537, 582, 583). For it was also under pressure from the Western Allies.

The lack of offensive punch due to the shortage of manpower along the northern wing of the front was illustrated by the fact that the two German corps encircled at Kholm and Demyansk by Red Army counterattacks in January and February 1942 could not be liberated until April and May 1942, and even then with great difficulty. However, in parrying the attack of the Soviets' Second Shock Army and 54th Army on the Volkhov front, the German units succeeded in encircling the former under General Andrei A. Vlasov and capturing many Soviet soldiers, including Vlasov himself. Vlasov's experiences in his encircled and abandoned position later influenced his decision to join the Germans in their struggle against Stalin (Nos. 1071, 1085, 1097, 1101, 1127, 1130).

In late December, officials in the offices of the chief of general staff considered whether a poison gas attack could be carried out on Leningrad. As Gellermann has shown in his study, they pondered the amount of gas that would be needed to seize the city in this way (No. 55a). According to their calculations, hundreds of thousands of poison gas shells would be needed, as well as more than 330 batteries to fire them all. The plan was dropped because so much artillery was not available, thus sparing Leningraders an even more horrible fate than the blockade they had endured since September 1941.

In the spring of 1942, Hitler ordered once again that Leningrad was to be seized and land connections established with the Finns. No new forces were made available for this task, even though the Finnish government insisted that the strategic problem posed by Leningrad would have to be solved before it could participate in any further offensives against the Murman railroad and on to the White Sea. Operational planning in the north depended henceforth on the success of the advances on Stalingrad and into the Caucasus. The full encirclement of Leningrad and capture of the Ingermanland would be postponed until success had been achieved in the southern wing of the front.

When the southern offensive in the summer of 1942 seemed headed for success, Hitler ordered preparations for renewed attacks on Leningrad in early September (Operation *Feuerzauber*, or Fire Magic, which was renamed Operation *Nordlicht*, or Northern Light, on 1 August). Five new divisions from the Eleventh Army fighting in the Crimea were to be transferred north for the attack. Field Marshal von Manstein would command the offensive, using heavy artillery as had been done at Sevastopol (Nos. 536, 619). Hitler repeated his demand that Leningrad and its inhabitants be obliterated, returning to his previous formulation that Leningrad should be "leveled" (*"dem Erdboden gleichzumachen"*) after the occupation.

However, preparations for Operation *Nordlicht* could not be carried out as planned because the Leningrad and Volkhov Front under Generals Govorov and Mereckov made several dangerous advances and counterattacks on the Demyansk corridor and south of Lake Ladoga near Mga-Sinyavino. The German assault on Leningrad planned for early September was postponed and then finally canceled in mid-October as not feasible at the time. As a result, the Wehrmacht failed to complete the encirclement of Leningrad in 1942 as well, and the Soviets managed to improve the supply lines. Leningrad became the "hero city," a symbol of the unbroken will of the Red Army and the Soviet people and of their successful resistance to the German invasion. This is depicted at length in the Soviet literature above all (Nos. 544–547). Finally, the Soviet forces succeeded in Operation *Iskra* (Spark) on 18 January 1943 in breaching the German lines around Schlüsselburg (Slisselburg) and breaking the tight blockade of the city after 496 days, a blockade that had brought untold suffering to the former czarist capital and had cost hundreds of thousands of lives; according to recent Russian figures, 662,000 people died during the blockade of hunger, sickness, and exhaustion as well as from German artillery fire. Nevertheless, the city remained under siege, though at a greater distance, until the end of January 1944, when the Red Army drove the Germans forty to sixty miles (sixty to one hundred km) back from Leningrad and recaptured Novgorod. As a result, final delivery from the direct threat of German attack did not come until 900 days had passed.

* * *

In his contribution to the sixth volume of the serial *Das Deutsche Reich und der Zweite Weltkrieg*, Bernd Wegner has provided a new, comprehensive analysis of the German summer offensive of 1942 toward Stalingrad and the Caucasus, which was planned in the spring of the year following the Wehrmacht's successful stabilization of the front (No. 619). Wegner points out in summary that the German summer offensive of 1942 on the southern wing of the front, Operation *Blau* (Blue), was designed as blitzkrieg, just like the original Operation Barbarossa in 1941. It aimed to conquer by the fall of 1942 new sources of raw materials that were strategically essential for an extended war against the Allies. Since the Wehrmacht was already suffering from severe shortages of men and matériel, the offensive was limited to only one of the three army groups. Wegner's study documents the operations attempting to bring Leningrad to its knees in the north and break through to the Caucasus in the south, depriving the Soviet Union of its remaining strength there, while holding the center of the front steady. Biographies of Chief of General Staff Franz Halder have shown that he supported these operational goals, although there were warnings from within the army high command that they were "utopian" (Nos. 130a, 148a).

In order to remedy the shortage of troops in the units to engage in the summer offensive, Germany's allies were encouraged more than in the past to participate militarily in the "struggle against Bolshevism." Recent studies have shown that this "Europe propaganda" was quite successful, with Italy, Rumania, Hungary, Croatia, and Slovakia providing units and armies of their own for the new offensive on the Eastern Front (Nos. 1114, 1116, A/298, A/322, and further titles in Part A).

By the summer of 1942, the capture of the Kerch Peninsula and of the cities of Sevastopol, Voronezh, and Kharkov-Izyum had created the necessary basis for the great offensive (Nos. 91, 216, 253, 272, 601, 607, 613, 615, 622). Operation *Blau* began on 28 June 1942, aimed at capturing the oil fields of Maikop, Grozny, and Baku on the Caspian Sea. The Wehrmacht's early successes could be ascribed in part to surprise and the miscalculations of Stalin and the Stavka. Both assumed that Moscow would be the main target of the summer offensive. When the German attack surged forward in the first days of July between the Donets and Don rivers, the Soviets sought first to block the path to the bend in the Don and Stalingrad by redistributing the Red Army and then to escape being surrounded by the rapidly advancing Sixth Army under General Friedrich Paulus by skillful withdrawal.

As the German advance on Stalingrad and Rostov progressed, however, the extreme shortage of mechanized attack units was felt more and more. Equally fatal was Hitler's decision to split Army Group South into two parts, Army Groups A and B, and to divide the entire offensive into one advance toward Stalingrad and Astrakhan by Army Group B and another simultaneous but divergent advance toward the Caucasus and Baku by Army Group A. In addition, most of the Eleventh Army, which had completed its mission in capturing Sevastopol, was withdrawn from the Southern Front and sent to join Army Group North. Although Hitler wished above all to capture the oil fields of Maikop and Grozny, the two army groups did not have enough troops to achieve their goals. The resulting differences of opinion between Hitler and the army high command led finally to the dismissal of Chief of General Staff Halder and his replacement by General Zeitzler (Nos. 130a, 148a).

After its first advance, Army Group A began pushing rapidly southward from its bridgehead at Rostov after 26 July 1942 and succeeded in reaching the Caucasus. However, it soon became apparent that the success of the operations in the Caucasus would be decided at Stalingrad on the Volga, for it was there that Stalin mounted a stiff defense. Consequently, the Fourth Panzer Army was redirected and turned to attack Stalingrad from the south. Operational studies and picture histories of the war have taken a particular interest in the breathtaking mountain operation of 21 August 1942, which led to a spectacular advance to Mount Elbrus and various passes in the Caucasus. The interest was less in the military aspect of the operation than in the "Caucasian adventure" and "brilliant mountaineering achievement," as Josef M. Bauer has described it in his account of his personal experience, which is now available in paperback (Nos. 625, 626, 635, 647, 652, 655, 667, 669, 686, 719, 735). The mountain offensive succeeded in raising the Reich war flag on Europe's highest peak; however, as a tactical move it had little effect, especially since the units of Army Group A under Field Marshal List failed to achieve the very ambitious goal of the operation, namely seizing the Caucasian oil fields. They remained stalled on the northern slopes of the Caucasus and around Novorossiysk. Annoyed at this failure, Hitler dismissed Field Marshal List and assumed personal command of Army Group A.

After the attack in the Caucasus floundered, interest focused all the more on the second aim of the summer offensive: blocking the Volga by capturing Stalingrad. Enormous quantities of material have been written about the struggle for the city on the Volga bearing the name of the Soviet dictator. Over two hundred publications deal primarily with this battle, far surpassing any other (No. 745). The number and importance of these publications reflect the frequent view that the German defeat at Stalingrad marked the turning point in the Second World War – if not in the entire war, then at least in the war on the Soviet-German front.

Even people at the time saw it as a highly symbolic event when the remnants of the German Sixth Army finally laid down their arms on 2 February 1943 in the northern part of the city. The supreme commander of this army, Field Marshal Friedrich Paulus, had already surrendered with his staff two days earlier. He failed to order all the remaining pockets of German resistance in Stalingrad to capitulate at the same time in order not to contravene Hitler's command to hold out to the last man. The final capitulation on 2 February 1943 brought seventy-two days of ferocious and horrible struggle to an end. After the Soviets succeeded in breaching the German front, taking Kalach and Sovecky to the west of Stalingrad on 23 November 1942 and thereby encircling the Sixth Army, both sides fought on grimly and determinedly. Of the approximately 300,000 German soldiers who had originally been trapped, only about 108,000 survived the fighting in order to drag themselves off into Soviet captivity. Of these, only roughly 6,000 ever returned to Germany after the war. Around 30,000 to 45,000 wounded German soldiers were flown out while the battle still raged. The Soviets later counted about 146,000 dead German soldiers. The exact numbers are still in dispute in the literature (see No. 745).

The Wehrmacht's momentous defeat on the Volga has to be seen in the context of the conditions under which the Germans launched their summer offensive of 1942 on the southern wing of the front. The loss of the Sixth Army resulted in the end from the decision made by Hitler and high army commanders in the summer of 1942 to split the German advance in southern Russia into two diverging thrusts, one to the Volga and the other to the Caucasus. Neither advance was backed up with sufficient reserves. Furthermore, not enough units were available to protect the flanks of the Sixth Army advancing on Stalingrad, so that they had to be defended by inadequately equipped Rumanian and Italian troops. The attack on Stalingrad was thus launched with clearly inadequate forces.

These serious deficiencies, which would later prove crucial for the course of the war, were rashly overlooked by the German leaders, even though they realized from the outset that the Red Army would put up a very fierce struggle over Stalingrad. Panzer units did not therefore succeed in quickly snatching the city in September in a surprise onslaught. In fact, the Soviets had time to bring in fresh troops and strengthen the city's defenses with the help of the civilian population, which was not evacuated for a long time.

While the assault on Stalingrad was still under way, Hitler was already proclaiming his ruthless plans to obliterate it: the entire male population would be eliminated because "Stalingrad is particularly dangerous with its one million, thoroughly Communist inhabitants" (Nos. 745, p. 20; 162). Women and children would be deported. The people of Stalingrad therefore faced the same fate as the people of Moscow and Leningrad, where Hitler also wanted to eradicate both the population and the city itself (No. 745, p. 20).

In September and October, the eight armies of the Soviets' Stalingrad, Don, and Southwestern Front succeeded in slowing the German advance by means of large counterattacks, so that the Sixth Army ground only slowly ahead toward Stalingrad through a series of sharp battles with many casualties. The Russian armies on this front were commanded by Generals Eremenko, Rokossowksij, and Vatutin, assisted by General Zukov as the representative of the Soviet high command on the Don and Volga. On 6 October, Hitler demanded that Stalingrad be eliminated not only as a center of transportation and war production but also "fully occupied." He also claimed publicly on 30 September and 8 November that victory had already been achieved and the city bearing Stalin's name conquered (No. 745, p. 21). However, German soldiers were still engaged in heavy street fighting for every house and building, while continuing to suffer many casualties. Recent studies have shown that already by this time the Sixth Army could not be adequately supplied (No. 745, contribution of R.-D. Müller).

As Alan Bullock has demonstrated in his dual biography of Hitler and Stalin, Hitler's statements clearly show that he saw the conquest of the city that had born Stalin's name since 1925 as a matter of prestige. The struggle for Stalingrad became symbolic of the struggle between the two tyrants (No. 125). No voluntary retreats were therefore possible without one of the two dictators losing face and suffering a tremendous loss of prestige.

On 19–20 November, the Red Army launched Operation Uranus, a counterattack consisting of a huge pincer movement on both sides of Stalingrad undertaken after careful, highly secret preparations. The German-Rumanian front lines were quickly breached and the Sixth Army trapped. Although Luftwaffe commanders immediately pointed out the difficulty of adequately supplying the troops trapped in Stalingrad by air, General Paulus hesitated to break out immediately to the southwest. Instead he flew into the pocket at Hitler's command and awaited further instructions from "Führer headquarters." On 21 November, Hitler ordered the army to hold its ground and hunker down in the city. The high commands of the Sixth Army and Army Group B, together with leading Luftwaffe commanders at the front, suggested that the Sixth Army should soon be withdrawn behind the Don because it could not long be supplied from the air. In fact, it could be provided with only one-tenth of its normal daily requirement of about 950 tons.

Nevertheless, Hitler refused to listen and ordered the army to remain in Stalingrad. Göring's Luftwaffe would supply the encircled twenty-two German divisions as well as the Rumanian and Croatian units from the air. However, the former chief of staff of *Luftflotte* 4, Herhudt von Rohden, has shown in his study that the Luftwaffe was at no time able to deliver the minimum daily requirement of 500 tons of supplies for the 300,000 encircled troops (Nos. 656, 673).

While General Paulus and his chief of general staff, Brigadier General Schmidt, bowed to Hitler's instructions and halted the preparations that were already being made to break out, the officer commanding the LI army corps, General Walther von Seydlitz-Kurzbach, demanded the "immediate commencement of break-out operations" in a memorandum presented on 25 November. Seydlitz appealed in vain to the conscience of his superior, as he recalled movingly in his memoirs: "If the army high command does not immediately rescind the command to dig in and hold out, then you have a higher duty to your own conscience, the army and the German people to exercise your freedom of action, denied to you by previous orders, and seize the opportunity that still exists to attack, thereby averting ultimate disaster. The total annihilation of 200,000 soldiers and all their matériel stands in the balance. There is no other choice." (Nos. 126, 636, 729) However, Paulus and Brigadier General Schmidt refused to accede to this demand, and the Sixth Army passed up the opportunity to break out.

Hitler attempted to improve the situation through structural changes in the leadership and command. Since he could not afford to send any new units to the Volga to help stabilize the front, he sent a new command staff. On 26 November, Field Marshal Erich von Manstein was named supreme commander of the newly created Army Group Don. Manstein believed that a relief operation could restore the situation to what it had been and that the Sixth Army should remain for the time being on the banks of the Volga in order to preserve what Hitler considered to be the most important military and political achievement of the summer offensive.

In response to a "Führer order," the relief offensive *Wintergewitter* (Winter Storm) was begun in earnest on 12 December, under the supreme commander of the Fourth Panzer Army, General Hoth. Comprehensive studies of this offensive have been written by Scheibert and Manstein (Nos. 253, 619, 680, 720). However, the German forces were insufficient, particularly the air cover, and the advance stalled about twenty-five to thirty miles (forty to fifty km) away from the Sixth Army as a result of powerful Soviet counterattacks. At the same time, the Red Army succeeded in punching a large hole in the German-Italian front on the Chir near Rostov, putting the entire southern wing in danger of being cut off. It should be taken into account that army and air force units were needed in North Africa at the same time in order to set up a new army group there. Hitler refused to accept the suggestion made during Hoth's relief operation that the Sixth Army should simultaneously pull out of Stalingrad and attempt to break out to the southwest (Operation *Donnerschlag*, or Thunder Clap).

Thereafter the Sixth Army was left to its fate. It was a bitter experience for the ordinary German soldiers, abandoned in what the army high command henceforth called "Fortress Stalingrad," to see outside relief efforts gradually dry up and supplies dwindle after the failure of the relief attempt around Christmas 1942. The Sixth Army could no longer be supplied with enough food, and the soldiers were beginning to starve slowly by the end of December. Soon munitions and fuel began to run out as well (Nos. 656, 680, 745, contributions of Müller and Eckart).

By the end of the year, the German soldiers had become so physically exhausted and weakened as a result of the paucity of supplies delivered by air that all hope faded of breaking out of the Stalingrad pocket. "Senior levels" spoke of the need for the soldiers of the Sixth Army to sacrifice themselves by extending their death throes as long as possible, for a continuation of their hopeless struggle would allegedly allow the rest of the southern wing of the front to be strengthened. However, the men in Stalingrad felt themselves betrayed and written off, and they complained bitterly about the unfulfilled promises from Berlin. Hitler lied about making every effort to relieve the defenders of Stalingrad, but Paulus continued to believe him and consequently rejected the Red Army demand of 8 January to lay down arms and capitulate, even though Paulus knew that large numbers of his troops were starving, freezing, and dying when exposed to the drumfire of enemy artillery and fighter bombers without cover or defense. In his statements after the war (No. 745, p. 29), Paulus confirmed that the suffering and misery of the soldiers of the Sixth Army surpassed anything "that German soldiers had experienced since the beginning of the Second World War." Nevertheless, he commanded them to fight on to the last bullet, just as Hitler had ordered.

On 10 January 1943, the Soviet army under General Rokossowskij began an assault on the German pocket, quickly smashing deep holes in the western part of the ring. By 20 January the remnants of the Sixth Army had been driven together in the ruins of the city they had once so confidently entered, waiting for the coup de grâce. After the airfields of Besargino and Pitomnik were lost, supplies were flown into the only remaining auxiliary field of Gumrak. Nonetheless, the men of the Sixth Army fought on, dying by the thousands. Desperate scenes were played out on the airfields at this time. On 22 January, Soviet troops broke through the southwestern part of the ring, once again raising the question of whether the army high command should finally abandon the hopeless but still murderous struggle and capitulate. However, Hitler intervened once again, announcing that "capitulation is out of the question"; Paulus obeyed and commanded his troops to fight on.

After mid-January, conditions in the Stalingrad pocket were horrific. Starving, freezing soldiers, many of them wounded, sought to crawl into the city. The situation there was not much better, as 20,000 wounded sought shelter among the ruins. On the tenth anniversary of the Nazi seizure of power, Paulus sent his congratulations to Hitler: Germany would ultimately triumph if the struggle of the Sixth Army in Stalingrad was taken by Germans as inspiration never to give up, even under the most hopeless conditions. After the war, Paulus was a witness at the Nuremberg Trials, where he stated that in the end these "telegrams of devotion" to Hitler were only an attempt to give some meaning to the "horror" of what was happening in Stalingrad (No. 182, vol. 7, p. 318).

Although Hitler had long written off the soldiers of the Sixth Army, he forbade them to capitulate for reasons of prestige. The generals in the pocket continued to obey, although the mass suffering and death of their troops could no longer be justified from any military point of view. It was highly irresponsible to continue fighting after 28 January, when all supplies for treating the sick and wounded ran out. By this time, 40,000 men lay wounded amidst the ruins of the city.

After the war, some authors justified Hitler's command to stand firm by claiming that the prolonged resistance in Stalingrad prevented the entire southern wing of the front from collapsing and allowed the troops withdrawing from the Caucasus to escape. It is true that at first about five Soviet armies were tied down at Stalingrad. Thereafter, however, Chief of General Staff Zeitzler judged the situation differently, and after mid-January 1943 he urged that the Sixth Army be allowed to decide for itself whether to capitulate (No. 751a). But Hitler insisted that the army he had written off should nevertheless fight on to the last man. Accordingly, Paulus even had other officers initiate his own capitulation on 31 January in the basement of the central Univermag department store, in order to remain at least formally loyal to Hitler's orders to fight on to the last man.

For the Soviet Union, Stalingrad marked an enormous victory over the German aggressor. It demonstrated that the Red Army could actually defeat the Wehrmacht on the field of battle. It greatly boosted the morale and confidence of the Soviet armies and encouraged them to think offensively. These effects were repeatedly emphasized in Soviet postwar publications (Nos. 56, 57).

At the Teheran Conference, the western Allies publicly demonstrated their great respect for this victory. Churchill presented the Soviet dictator with an honorary sword from King George VI for the citizens of Stalingrad as a sign of "the admiration of the British people." President Roosevelt publicly praised the "courage, bravery and sacrifice" of the "brave defenders" of Stalingrad. The battle had been a "turning point in the Allied war against the forces of aggression."

The Germans, for their part, had to admit defeat. Göring attempted to explain it away in a propaganda speech by admitting that the Germans had underestimated the Red Army and had been taken in by its alleged "great bluff" of playing on its earlier weaknesses. Goebbels took personal charge of the propaganda explaining the defeat in order to mitigate the "shock effect of Stalingrad." He used this setback to call for a ruthless "total war" (Nos. 656; 754, contribution of W. Wette). Day after day it was repeated that the sacrifice of the soldiers in Stalingrad was "not in vain." According to the newly issued Wehrmacht report (No. 190a), "they died, so that Germany might live."

It is noteworthy that many of the officers taken prisoner at Stalingrad blamed Hitler primarily for the loss of 250,000 men and joined the National Committee for Free Germany or the German Officers League, providing their services for the propaganda war against the German dictator. Several studies of the National Committee for Free Germany confirmed that this movement arose from the horror of Stalingrad. Among the fifty generals who signed the appeal to the German people of 14 December 1944 to overthrow Hitler, fifteen had experienced the Stalingrad pocket (Nos. 1137, A/453).

Officers who had been flown out of Stalingrad and thus saved also hoped after the final capitulation of the Sixth Army that this would lead to dissension and rebellion against Hitler. They believed that Hitler should refrain from direct involvement in the conduct of the war. Members of the German resistance hoped that the slow agony of the Sixth Army would prompt a revolt against Hitler aimed at saving it from ultimate catastrophe. However, they had no connections with Paulus, and he had no knowledge of their aims and plans. The retired Generaloberst Beck and von Rundstedt and Manstein were urged, but to no avail, to take action against the dictator. In their final pamphlet of 18 February 1943, the students of the "White Rose" urged German youth to rise up against the Nazis in view of the frightfully "senseless and irresponsible" deaths of the men in Stalingrad. Their calls were in vain (No. 745, p. 40).

In any case, it was now too late to negotiate a political settlement of the war, for the Allies had been demanding Germany's "unconditional surrender" since 24 January 1943. The Battle of Stalingrad did not lead to a quick conclusion to the war but rather to even greater mobilization of Germany's material and human resources in order to carry on the struggle against the enemies of the Fatherland with unremitting ferocity. Total war continued.

The Battle of Stalingrad has nevertheless become a symbol both of Germany's crushing defeat in the East and of misplaced loyalty and obedience to the Führer. Stalingrad was also emblematic of the "limitations and inadequacies" of German military planning and of "a self-concept that allowed judgment to succumb to obsession and a sense of responsibility to be equated with carrying out orders," as Johannes Fischer remarked in retrospect (No. 656). The catastrophe of Stalingrad exposed for all to see the inhumanity and irresponsibility of the Nazi regime toward its own people in the pursuit of its megalomaniacal and criminal aims. Stalingrad provided a foretaste of the brutal, senseless fighting that would be continued right to the bitter end of total defeat in May 1945.

The Battle of Stalingrad has therefore been a subject of particular fascination for historians, who began researching these apocalyptic events soon after the war's end. In retrospect, the defeat of the Sixth Army became a warning sign of the ultimate military and political collapse of the Nazi regime and a signal of the approaching end of Hitler's dictatorship, whose hubris, blindness, and inhumanity were responsible for the deaths of thousands and thousands of men along the Volga.

The first German publications after 1945, still short on analysis, saw the Battle of Stalingrad as a "tragedy" or "catastrophe" inflicted by the overwhelming forces of fate. German readers were first familiarized with the Soviet view of these events in the "first authentic reports of the Russian generals Rokossowskij, Voronov, Telegin, and Malinin, as well as of Russian war correspondents," which appeared in German translation as early as 1945 (No. 745, contribution of Ueberschär). These reports had already been published by the Allied powers several times during the war. Thereafter Stalingrad, as the mass grave of the fascist invaders, came to be seen as the "funeral pyre of Hitler's war plans" and a "blazing example" of the "flame of freedom" in the struggle against fascism.

The first German reports and memoirs of the battle emphasized the experiences of many individual soldiers in the pocket and the suffering and deprivations endured by those who were taken prisoner by the Soviets (Nos. 646, 657, 725, 737). As the "height of human folly," Stalingrad even became a topic for drama, film scripts, and poetry. The first studies generally answered any questions about guilt and responsibility for the deaths of so many soldiers by pointing to Hitler.

Many reports blamed the Luftwaffe for the inadequate supplies delivered to the Sixth Army. However, this accusation was denied by Hans-Detlef Herhudt von Rohden in *Die Luftwaffe ringt um Stalingrad* (No. 673), which depicted the desperate attempts of the puny air transport units to satisfy at least some of the needs of the Sixth Army from the air. Herhudt von Rohden also pointed out the early warnings from senior Luftwaffe commanders that it was impossible to supply an entire army from the air.

The former Communist writer and later president of the National Committee for Free Germany, Erich Weinert, published a "Front Notebook" on the Battle of Stalingrad, which he wrote from behind Red Army lines (No. 742). These notes were already published during the war in magazines and brochures in London, New York, and Moscow. However, they eventually proved to be little more than a whitewashing panegyric to the Red Army when it came to describing the fate of the German prisoners of war.

The value of Heinz Schröter's work, *Stalingrad ... bis zur letzten Patrone* (No. 723), is disputed. As a former war correspondent in a propaganda company, he relied on material that was gathered after the surrender of the Sixth Army by the ministry of propaganda for the official *Heroes' Book* on Stalingrad that it had planned. In the end, however, Minister of Propaganda Goebbels forbade publication because he was taken aback by the at times critical and unvarnished eyewitness reports it contained. In any case, Schröter's work has now been reissued on the occasion of the fiftieth anniversary of the Battle of Stalingrad (No. 723, new edn.).

In 1950 and 1952, this same author published anonymously *Letzte Briefe aus Stalingrad* (Nos. 634, 631, 651), but these "last letters from Stalingrad" proved not to be authentic. In his more recent book, Schröter repeats statistics from these letters about the mood of the troops that either are incorrect or cannot be verified. On the other hand, in 1952, Walter and Hans Bähr published the letters of the physician Kurt Reuber in an authentic selection of 22,000 "war letters from students who died" (No. 153a). Most of the early German accounts were memoirs or operational studies by participants in the battle, such as the works of Hans Doerr, Joachim Wieder, Horst Scheibert, and Erich von Manstein, some of which have been reissued. Others were "Divisional Histories" of units that participated in the battle (Nos. 648, 746, 747, 720, 721, 722, 253).

It turned out, however, that sober operational histories did not provide the elemental experience of war that many contemporaries and later generations wanted. Stalingrad, as an experience of total destruction, therefore also attracted other forms of literature, as can be seen especially in the popularity of the novels written about the battle at about the same time by Theodor Plievier, Fritz Wöss (Friedrich Weiß), and Heinrich Gerlach (Nos. 664, E/288–290). They understandably tend more than cool, collected operational studies to emphasize the horror and apocalyptic outcome of the Battle of Stalingrad, as seen from the point of view of ordinary soldiers, yet they manage to avoid false pathos. Soviet novels were also very successful, as can be seen, for instance, in the works of Konstantin Simonov, Viktor Nekrassov, and Vassily Grossman, who was a correspondent on the Eastern Front for the Soviet army newspaper *Red Star* and whose works have also been translated into German (Nos. E/260, 261, 283, 299a).

On the basis of the interrogation of the chief of staff of the Sixth Army, Major General Schmidt, and the notes of Field Marshal Paulus, which were published after he died in Dresden in February 1957, Walter Görlitz made a first attempt to situate the events at Stalingrad in the strategic course of the entire war on the Eastern Front (No. 704). He concentrated above all on the operational decisions of the high command, in an attempt to justify Paulus's own decisions. The writings of the former chief of general staff of the German army, General Zeitzler, take a similar approach (No. 751a). However, more recent studies of the ability of the chiefs of general staff in the army high command, of the chief of staff of the Wehrmacht high command, and of senior Wehrmacht officers in the field to advise and influence the Führer come to quite different conclusions about the ability of these generals to influence and act independently than either Zeitzler or Paulus admitted.

The early large omnibus volumes that appeared in the GDR and the USSR about these aspects of Stalingrad were based on ideological clichés and the simplifications of Marxist-Leninist historiography. Some of these works appeared in German, as did some of the similar memoirs of famous leaders of the Soviet army. Their one-sided and heroic phrases about the glories of the Red Army served as well to justify Communist rule in the former GDR, whose founding was not infrequently seen as a legacy of the catastrophe of Stalingrad. This can be seen in the omnibus volumes *Probleme der Geschichte des zweiten Weltkrieges* and *Der zweite Weltkrieg 1939–1945*, published in 1958 and 1959, with contributions from Soviet Marshal Yeremenko and former Wehrmacht general major Otto Korfes, as well as in the memoirs that appeared soon thereafter of Marshal Vasilij Cuikov, whose army defended Stalingrad. The study by Tel'puchovskij, which also appeared in German (Nos. 1212, 91a, 114a), is marred as well by the need to follow party directions.

By the time of the twentieth anniversary of the Battle of Stalingrad, perspective on the events had improved and interest focused not only on operational questions but also on the military and political significance of the struggle. At the same time, more comments by survivors or returned soldiers were published, such as those of the former colonel and adjutant in the Sixth Army, Wilhelm Adam, who after the war became an officer in the East German People's Army (No. 623). Adam's book was very well received and was reissued on numerous occasions, a step that was extremely unusual for the state-run East German literature of the time. Also published in several editions in the GDR was the report of Helmut Welz, a former captain and later member of the National Committee for Free Germany, as well as the autobiography of Otto Rühle and the memoirs of former colonel and later local-level GDR politician Luitpold Steidle, who was also prompted by his experience at Stalingrad to join the

German Officers League and play an active role in the National Committee for Free Germany (Nos. 713, 732, 743).

In the next few years, historians in the Federal Republic of Germany likewise took a particular interest in the Battle of Stalingrad. The survey of the Forty-Fourth Infantry Division *"Hoch- und Deutschmeister,"* whose Austrian soldiers also fell at Stalingrad or were captured, belongs in the genre of "divisional histories" (No. 722a). The former war correspondent Paul K. Schmidt wrote popular works (under the pseudonym Paul Carell), as did Werner Haupt and Horst Scheibert. Carell's work on the battle was published again in 1992 in a revised version under the name *Stalingrad-Buch* (Nos. 39a, 672). Johannes Fischer, on the other hand, brought a rigorous academic approach to his study of the failed attempt to supply the Sixth Army from the air (No. 656).

In 1973, the American William E. Craig presented a comprehensive study of the battle as seen from both sides. He conducted numerous interviews with participants of various ranks and functions, although he also tarted his book up with meretricious anecdotes (No. 640). Albert Seaton's comprehensive study, *Russo-German War 1941–45*, which was also published in a German edition (No. 99), focused primarily on strategic developments in the Battle of Stalingrad. Seaton described this battle as certainly one of the greatest defeats suffered by the German army, but not at all the turning point in the war.

The military historian Manfred Kehrig then wrote the first comprehensive analysis and well-founded overview of the battle using the German war documents and personal effects and notes of dead soldiers that had been made available by 1974 (No. 680). This study is still considered a standard work on military events at Stalingrad. Shortly thereafter, Herbert Selle and Walther von Seydlitz published memoirs examining once again from their points of view the fateful decision on the part of senior Sixth Army commanders not to attempt to break out while the opportunity still existed (Nos. 725, 729). James D. Carnes' biography of General von Seydlitz examines his role at Stalingrad and also in the National Committee for Free Germany (No. 636).

In a work published first in English under the title *The Secret of Stalingrad*, Walter Kerr investigated how the Soviets succeeded in keeping largely secret from the Germans the enormous concentration of troops and supplies they had amassed to the rear of Stalingrad for the great counterattack of 18/20 November 1942. Also in 1977, Janusz Piekalkiewicz published an operational history as seen from both sides entitled *Anatomie einer Schlacht*, with vivid photographs. This book is now available in a new paperback edition (No. 706). Udo Giulini's description of his experiences and the study by the former Sixteenth Panzer-Division doctor Werner Gerlach focus on their impressions and experiences as Soviet prisoners after the Battle of Stalingrad, both for the rest of the war and for many years thereafter (Nos. 665, 664).

Geoffrey Jukes' work is basically a documentation of military operations. He describes the Battle of Stalingrad as the "bloodiest battle" of the Second World War and the "turning point" in the war (No. 678). He based much of his research on the third volume of the *History of the Great Patriotic War of the Soviet Union* published in Moscow in 1961 and on the fifth and sixth volumes of the *History of the Second World War*, which began appearing in 1975 and was edited on behalf of the party by Soviet Marshal Andrei Grechko (Nos. 56, 57). In addition, several memoirs of Soviet army commanders were also available at the time, among them the memoirs of Marshal Andrej Eremenko (1964), Pavel Batov (1965), Marshal Georgij Zukov (1969), Marshal Konstantin Rokossovskij (1973), and Marshal Aleksandr Vasilevskij (1977), as well as those of the chief of staff of the Sixty-Second Army under Cuikov, Marshal Nikolaj Krylov (1981) (Nos. 214, 201, 279, 264, 272, 690). However, these memoirs always reflected the party's political line at the time. As Horst Giertz stated in his survey of Soviet historiography, without exception these publications aimed from the outset to prove that the decisive battle in the "Great Patriotic War" was fought at Stalingrad and that the Red Army, under Stalin's "brilliant leadership," thereby engineered the turning point in the war (No. 745, contribution of Giertz). These standard, one-sided songs of praise were not based on research in the archives but on anecdotes, party reports, and stories in the press. The impulses and political directions emanating from Moscow in regard to the Red Army's heroic struggle at Stalingrad were then largely followed in the third volume of *Deutschland im zweiten Weltkrieg*, published by the GDR Academy of Sciences. As a result, it too is now dated (No. 47).

The same is true of the typically Soviet approach to history as the exploits of heroes, which is widely reflected in the memoirs of soldiers serving in the lower ranks that were published in large numbers, such as those of Vodolagin (1960), as well as collections of letters by ordinary soldiers (see Nos. 56 and E/200,

E/203). Apart from the plethora of memoirs and hero-worshipping publications, there are only two really noteworthy studies providing a well-founded analysis from a Soviet point of view: those of Konstantin K. Rokossowskij (No. 731) and Aleksandr M. Samsonov (No. 717). However, it was not until the fourth edition of Samsonov's groundbreaking work appeared in 1989 that he was able to reproduce important new documents discussing, for instance, the creation of brutal punishment units behind the front. Soviet historiography did not escape its hackneyed approaches enforced by the Communist party and begin questioning controversial issues until G.V. Kljucarev wrote his critical analysis wondering why the Soviets failed at the time of their advance to Rostov and the lower course of the Don to encircle and destroy the entire German southern wing as far as the Caucasus (Nos. 683; 745 with contribution of Giertz; No. 6, p. 186).

The inability of professional historians to exhaust fully the traumatic experiences of the men left hanging between life and death at Stalingrad and to satisfy the expectations of broad numbers of readers is shown by the great success of other approaches, especially Alexander Kluge's 1964 novel *Schlachtbeschreibung*. Kluge's moving description of the experiences of common soldiers and attempt to demythologize the events evidently filled a great need and aroused much interest. The revised and expanded version of his novel that appeared fourteen years later was also very well received (No. E/274).

The fortieth anniversary in 1982–83 of the Battle of Stalingrad prompted interest in new directions. The publication in 1987 of Wilhelm Raimund Beyer's personal experiences, *Stalingrad. Unten wo das Leben konkret war*, broke new ground in its deliberate analysis of the experiences and ordeals of common soldiers (No. 631). Beyer's project to research and portray the effects of the war on the everyday life of "little people" was taken up by several other authors, too. Alois Beck, who served in Stalingrad as a Catholic chaplain, undertook a similar approach in his 1983 study of Stalingrad entitled *Vom einfachen Landser bis zum General* (No. 627). The search for new sources that would allow ordinary soldiers, from whom little had been heard, to report directly on their own experiences led to the publication of several picture albums and documentations with letters from the front, illustrating the private lives of common soldiers.

Wilhelm Tieke, Franz Kurowski, and Ulrich Freytag stuck to the operational approach to the Battle of Stalingrad in their studies (Nos. 615, 735, 736, 694, 661a) and said little to satisfy the new interest in the experiences of ordinary soldiers. In the sixth volume of the serial *Das Deutsche Reich und der Zweite Weltkrieg*, Bernd Wegner provided a convincing, comprehensive overview of military events on the basis of a broad knowledge of the literature and extensive analysis of the available documents (No. 619).

With the end of Communist rule, the Soviet archives were opened to researchers, and captured German letters from the front that had been stored there could be analyzed and even published in part. Jürgen Reulecke and Ute Daniel handled the German edition of *Ich will raus aus diesem Wahnsinn*, which provided new sources for a history of the common soldiers and their shocking experiences at Stalingrad. This innovative volume has now been published as well in paperback (No. E/199). The particular perspective to be gained from letters from the front conveying the view "from below" could also be seen in the Stalingrad exhibition catalog put together on the occasion of the fiftieth anniversary of the German attack on the Soviet Union and in the still-unpublished dissertation of Jens Ebert, written in East Berlin in 1989 (Nos. 651a, 731a). In 1991, Wolfgang Wiesen provided an especially impressive view of the "sober, unvarnished reality of war, as seen 'from below' through the eyes of an ordinary German soldier and retold through letters from the front to his family," in his edition of the letters of his uncle, Bertold Paulus, who was among the missing in Stalingrad (No. E/207a).

The new publications at the time of the fiftieth anniversary in 1992–93 of the Battle of Stalingrad were influenced by this new emphasis on the perspective of ordinary soldiers. Apart from a few works that hewed to outmoded descriptions of the "heroic struggle" of the Sixth Army, such as those of Paul Carell and Franz Kurowski, as well as new editions of Herhudt von Rohden and Heinz Schröter (No. 673), most books focused on the extraordinary criminality of the struggle ordered by Hitler and the political significance of the battle – for instance, the updated reissue from Joachim Wieder; the omnibus volumes of Jens Ebert, Jürgen Förster, and Martin Kruse; and the memoirs of Franz Sapp, Horst Zank, and Edgar Klaus (Nos. 747, 651, 659, 689a, 718, 751, 682a). In addition, Christoph Fromm and Joseph Vilsmaier published literary supplements to a new film about Stalingrad (Nos. 662, 738).

The new omnibus volume of Gerd R. Ueberschär and Wolfram Wette lays particular emphasis on the war of the "little man" in Stalingrad. Not only German and Soviet historians but also "ordinary soldiers" from both sides speak their pieces (No. 745). The five-part television series *"Entscheidung Stalingrad"* has an accompanying volume that does much the same by drawing on many eyewitness reports. The series was televised in early 1993 in both Russia and Germany as a Russo-German coproduction (No. 684). Such recent coproductions by Russians and Germans are a hopeful sign of a trend toward joint study of this ferocious and withering battle between the two peoples.

The German catastrophe at Stalingrad has often led in the literature to the conclusion that the battle marked the "turning point in the Second World War." This is correct to the extent that after Stalingrad the Wehrmacht could not produce any more rapid strings of victories in blitzkrieg style. However, even before Stalingrad, Germany's meager remaining economic and manpower resources made ultimate victory in the East very unlikely. The defeat on the southern wing of the front merely destroyed any lingering hopes of final triumph in the East. Soviet Marxist historians have deduced from this that the Red Army's triumph at Stalingrad followed particular historical laws. While the Soviet victory cannot really be said to have followed historical laws, it did deprive the Germans of the strategic initiative once and for all. Thereafter it lay with the Soviets. Understandably, Moscow has always highlighted this military consequence on all anniversaries of the battle.[3]

As the Germans' hopes of conquering Stalingrad faded, so too did their chances of achieving their second aim of reopening the north Caucasian oil fields that had been destroyed by the Soviets. Only with great difficulty did the German units manage to escape the area between the Don and the Caucasus. Army Group A was able to elude encirclement by the Red Army and move back into the "Gotenkopf" position thanks to an admirable operative achievement by way of Rostov and the Kuban bridgehead, after Hitler finally approved a staged withdrawal on 28 December 1942. Wolfgang Birkenfeld's research has shown that it was illusory, in any case, to believe that the oil from the Caucasus would be sufficient to cover German crude-oil needs for the duration of the war (No. D/421).

* * *

3. See, for example, the newspaper article "Moskau: Der Westen verfälscht Stalingrad" about the reports of "Krasnaya Svesda," *Frankfurter Allgemeine Zeitung*, no. 262 (16 November 1972): 7

By pulling back and drawing up units from the Caucasus, the Germans succeeded by the spring of 1943 in stabilizing the new southern wing of the front on the Donets and Mius rivers and launching a counteroffensive in March 1943, under the skillful leadership of Field Marshal von Manstein, which led to the recapture of the cities of Kharkov and Byelgorod. Eberhard Schwarz has written a solid analysis of the successful stabilization of the Eastern Front after the debacle of Stalingrad (No. 777). It demonstrates impressively how the Wehrmacht once again succeeded in the spring of 1943 under Manstein's leadership in stopping the Soviet advance on the southern wing of the front and launching a very successful counterattack of its own, taking a great deal of territory and pushing the front back to the Donets. Schwarz's presentation has been considerably supplemented by Manstein's own memoirs (No. 253). On the Soviet side, Colonel W.P. Morosow undertook a quite critical examination of why the Soviet offensive in the spring of 1943 in the Donets Basin failed to achieve its objectives, pointing out weaknesses in the military leadership (No. 771).

The stabilized front in the summer of 1943 again provided the Germans with a stage from which to launch a partial offensive. After several postponements, the assault on the Kursk salient began on 5 July, in what would be the last German offensive on the Eastern Front. A pincer attack was launched to choke off the 75-mile- (120-km-) deep and 125-mile- (200-km-) wide bulge in the Soviet front line, thereby shortening the front and gaining prisoners of war and civilians to be put to work in the Reich. The failure of Operation Citadel only a few days later marked the beginning of the lengthy period of continuous retreat for the Wehrmacht. At the same time, the Germans had to weaken their forces further on the Eastern Front by drawing off more units for the new front in Italy facing the Western Allies. The Germans' final loss of the "law of activity" in the great tank battle around Kursk, in which the new "Tiger" and "Panther" tanks were used for the first time, has often been described in the literature and portrayed as the beginning of the string of victories that would carry the Red Army all the way to Berlin (Nos. 761, 776). Antonius John has now portrayed, from the point of view of the immediate participants, the ferocious course of the battle and the enormous achievement of the Wehrmacht in stabilizing the southern flank of the Eastern Front and launching the attack on Kursk, even though it failed. He intended his account as an admonition to the younger generations of both countries (No. 758). After the German attack was called off on 13 July 1943, the various fronts under the overall command of General Zukov (the Bryansk Front under Popov, the Western Front under Sokolovsky, the Steppes Front under Konev, the Central Front under Vatutin, the Voronezh Front under Rokossowskij, the Southwestern Front under Malinovsky, and the Southern Front under Tolbukhin) went over to the offensive along a 375-mile- (600-km-) long stretch and managed to liberate the Donets Basin. On 22 August, Kharkov was recaptured for the second time.

The Red Army also seized the initiative in the northern sector and, in accordance with plans devised by Marshal Vasilevskij, assailed the Army Group North front alongside both Leningrad and Novgorod. The Soviets succeeded in driving the Germans from Lake Ilmen, Novgorod, Luga, and Neval as far as Lake Peipus. Offensives to the west and south of Kiev were equally successful, retaking the industrial area in the bend of the Dnieper and the Crimean Peninsula. Andreas Hillgruber has made a separate, comprehensive study of the problems related to the Wehrmacht's withdrawal from the Crimea in April and May 1944 (Nos. 804, 814). The Soviet forces pushed rapidly ahead, reaching Chernovitz and the Carpathian Mountains by the spring of 1944 and thereby encircling several German divisions with about 55,000 soldiers in the area of Cherkassy. Despite difficult circumstances and heavy losses, portions of these divisions succeeded in breaking out to the west, as has been described in the literature on several occasions (No. 820). The battle around Cherkassy-Korsun is thus described in the Soviet literature as "Stalingrad on the Dnieper" (No. 817).

* * *

Hitler's rigid commands to hold firm pinned the German forces down in so-called fortified areas and deprived them of their ability to maneuver (No. 795). This, together with the lack of military reserves, led finally to the collapse of Army Group Center in White Russia, when the Red Army under Marshals Zukov and Vassilevsky launched a powerful offensive on 22 June 1944 with a pincer movement near Minsk and Vitebsk. The destruction of Army Group Center resulted in huge losses of men and matériel that could never be made up. The Fourth and Ninth Armies, as well as the Third Panzer Army, were almost totally demolished, and twenty-eight German divisions numbering about 350,000 men were destroyed. Hundreds of thousands were taken prisoner. Studies by Gerd Niepold, Hermann Gackenholz, Otto Heidkämper, Earl F. Ziemke, and Alexander Buchner (Nos. 812, 796, 797, 803, 821, 791) analyze German war diaries (and partially reproduce them) to provide a detailed reconstruction of the great defeats at Cherkassy, Tarnopol, Vitebsk, Bobruysk, Yassy, and Kishinev. The Soviets have also published many works about these events, although most concentrate in the usual way on unequivocal praise for the heroic struggle of the Red Army to free White Russia and the Crimea (Nos. 787, 783, 789, 790, 793, 798, 799, 800, 809).

After the collapse of the center of the German front in the summer of 1944, the Red Army was able to drive powerful spearheads into the northern and southern wings and achieve further successes. Army Group North had been pushed back ever since January 1944. For almost 900 days it had besieged Leningrad, in an attempt to starve and destroy the city in accordance with Hitler's plans. Now, after the destruction of the German armies in the center, it faced encirclement in the Baltic area through its open flank. The Wehrmacht had to abandon Pleskau and Narva. On 27 July 1944, Soviet forces under General Bagramyan reached the Baltic Sea near Tukum on the Bay of Riga, cutting off Army Group North. Instead of withdrawing the thirty battle-ready divisions (accounting for nearly one-third of the total strength of the German army in the East) to defend the East Prussian frontier, Hitler ordered them to stand firm in the Courland Peninsula (No. 875). There was no convincing military rationale for this unless Hitler accepted the position of Admiral Dönitz that it was necessary to hold Courland as a base for the German submarines in the Baltic. On the other hand, their hopeless struggle was apparently intended to keep the door ajar to the east, in case the fortunes of war shifted in Germany's favor. Another hypothesis cannot be fully excluded: Hitler felt he could afford to neglect Germany's eastern frontier because, although there was possibly some doubt about the willingness of units on the Western Front to fight, there was absolutely no doubt on the Eastern Front. Perhaps he hoped somehow to persuade the British and Americans to join him in a crusade against "Bolshevism," and he therefore left the army group in the Baltic as a stepping stone for renewed operations.

To the south, Soviet troops attacked Army Group Northern Ukraine, recapturing Lvov and the oil-producing area of Drogobych. On 1 August 1944, the secret Polish "Armija Krajowa" under General Bor-Komorowski launched the Warsaw uprising against the retreating Germans; however, it failed, in particular because Stalin failed to provide assistance to the Polish underground army on the Vistula. For two months the revolt continued, but it was finally brutally put down by Himmler's SS units. The Warsaw uprising and the futile attempts of the Western Allies to support this valiant effort have often been movingly described in the literature (see, among others, No. 978). However, only now that Moscow's archives have been opened will the despicable behavior of Stalin and the Stavka be fully exposed.

The Soviet drive toward the Balkans moved successfully ahead, after the Red Army under Marshal Timoshenko punched through the Rumanian-German defensive line on the Prut on 20 August 1944. The Red Army's victory carried it as far as the Danube and had the political effect of persuading Rumania to join the Allied side and declare war on Germany. Only with great difficulty did individual elements of the Army Group Northern Ukraine under General Frießner succeed in retreating over the Carpathian passes. In Slovakia, an uprising broke out against the government of President Josef Tiso, which was allied with the German Reich. It was put down, however, by German troops after two months (Nos. 843, 896).

Army Group North remained cut off from the Reich in the Baltic area after the loss of the city of Riga. Some twenty-six divisions were left to carry on in isolation under the new name of Army Group Courland. Some divisions defended themselves in various costly defensive actions until the end of the war. Only ten divisions could be brought back across the Baltic to German territory in early 1945. The struggle to survive in Courland has been described in several works (Nos. 532, 740, 875, 1182, 1184–1188).

* * *

Only the German navy provided military support for the cut-off units. It carried out the wounded and refugees and also brought its heavy guns to bear on land battles near the sea. The cost of these naval actions in the Baltic was very high. As a result of the lack of air cover, nearly the entire German Baltic fleet was destroyed. By the end of April 1945, only the cruisers *Prinz Eugen* and *Nürnberg* were still fit for duty. From spontaneous beginnings, a large-scale rescue operation soon developed across the Baltic under the command of Admiral Konrad Engelhardt, in which almost 800 naval, cargo, and passenger ships, as well as small cutters, took part (Nos. 1006, 1007, 1009, 1056). After the Red Army entered East Prussia in early 1945, refugees and soldiers were evacuated in this way, largely from the Bay of Danzig. By May 1945, between two and three million people had been evacuated by sea, with around one percent of them – or 20,000 to 25,000 people – losing their lives in the process.

Best known is the sinking of the *Wilhelm Gustloff* on 30 January 1945. The former cruise ship was loaded with about 6,000 refugees when it was torpedoed off the Pomeranian coast by a Soviet submarine. Heart-rending scenes were played out on board the slowly sinking ship. Only 838 people survived. These events were vividly described in a work by Heinz Schön, who has published numerous detailed studies of the flight across the Baltic (Nos. 1057–1060, 1193). Several thousand people also drowned when the hospital ship *General Steuben* and the freighter *Goya* sank. Despite such losses, the German navy continued the rescue operation until the very end. As late as 8 May 1945, 25,000 soldiers arrived in Schleswig-Holstein from the Bay of Danzig, where a few small pockets of German soldiers held out until the end of the war (No. 1178). A general overview of the battles and operations in the western part of the Baltic Sea during the last three months of the war is given by Wolfgang Müller and Reinhard Kramer (No. 1036).

The German air force had been almost totally destroyed by the Western Allies and therefore could not assist in the evacuation of the civilian population. The air war in the East was fought by the German Luftwaffe in the first half of the campaign until the defeat at Stalingrad in early 1943. Especially with regard to its tactical role providing support to army units, the transport fleet suffered heavy losses here that could no longer be made up for (Nos. 965, 973, 977).

By early 1945, the Russians had the shortest path to Berlin. Their successful summer offensive had been held up in October 1944, first at the Vistula and then on the East Prussian border. Hitler's eastern armies had been severely mauled and could scarcely mount any organized defense at the so-called East Wall, the reactivated line of fortifications along the Narew, Vistula, and San rivers. However, by late 1944 the Red Army also needed time, after its enormous leap forward, to stockpile supplies and prepare for the invasion of Germany.

On 12 and 14 January 1945, Stalin's armies moved out of their bridgeheads west of the Vistula at Baranow, Magnuszew, and Pulawy and headed for the Oder. Several army groups took part: the First, Second, and Third Belorussian Fronts and the First and Fourth Ukrainian Fronts under Marshals Zukov, Rokossowskij, and Konev. By the end of January, a huge offensive led by strong tank units was under way across the entire Eastern Front. The weakened German Army Group Center (under General Reinhardt) and Group A (under General Harpe) were unable to offer much more than token resistance, since they had no reserves left at all. Their forward line of resistance was quickly breached in several locations, and much of the German Third and Fourth Panzer Armies and of the Second Army was annihilated. After only four days, a unified German front had ceased to exist. The Wehrmacht was forced to evacuate Warsaw on 17 January and Cracow on 19 January. That same day, the Red Army reached the Silesian border. Posen, Thorn, and Graudenz were surrounded, and were immediately declared by Hitler to be "fortresses." By the end of January, the militarily important industrial areas of Upper Silesia had fallen intact into the hands of Marshal Konev's armies (No. 899).

In East Prussia as well, the powerful Soviet tank units could not be stopped by the quickly marshaled replacement and supply-line units, local defense and *Volkssturm* units, policemen, and the Hitler Youth (Nos. 850, 851, 1265). On 21 January, the Russians occupied the symbolic area of Tannenberg, monument and scene of the great German victory over the Russian army in 1914, and pushed forward toward Elbing. The old Prussian fortress and coronation city of Königsberg was surrounded on 29 January 1945 (Nos. 837, 862, 865, 866, 1196, 1233). Shortly thereafter, the Red Army reached the Oder at Küstrin, and on the last day of the month, it established a strategically important bridgehead across the river. Breslau was surrounded by mid-February, though it was stubbornly defended as a "fortress" city until 6 May 1945 (Nos. 866, 900, 902, 908, 917, 919, 933).

Despite the obvious collapse of his Eastern Front, Hitler did not send any reinforcements, just loyal generals and fanatical party leaders: General Schörner, assisted by Gauleiter Hanke, was to defend Silesia with Army Group South, while General Rendulic took over the new Army Group North (previously Army Group Center) and organized the defense of East Prussia. Gauleiter Koch, however, soon fled westward. Finally, Reichsführer SS Heinrich Himmler took over supreme command of the newly formed Army Group Weichsel (Vistula) and was charged with the defense of Pomerania. At the same time,

Himmler was responsible for "national defense on German soil behind the entire eastern front." However, such changes in personnel did nothing to stabilize the front in Silesia, East Prussia, or Pomerania. Posen capitulated on 22 February, and on 26 February the Red Army reached the Baltic Sea at Kolberg. The encircled city was declared a "fortress," but it had to surrender in any case on 18 March. Gdingen fell on 28 March, and Danzig on 30 March, after holding out since 14 March.

The battles waged in eastern Germany with grossly inadequate forces led in the harsh winter days to many civilian deaths as well. They were not the result of any fanatical people's war, which the Nazis hoped to organize. Far from strengthening the people's will to resist, Berlin's anti-Bolshevik campaign of atrocity and hate propaganda prompted the unorganized flight of millions of people. They left reluctantly, often only at the last minute, with the result that many were trapped in the thick of battle or were caught by the pursuing Russian tanks and mowed down. The British historian Christopher Duffy, of the Sandhurst Royal Military Academy, pointed out the direct connection between military operations and the deaths of millions of German civilians in the East in his recent study *Red Storm on the Reich* (No. 1217). In his book, which is now also available in German, he came to the conclusion that the racially motivated crimes committed by the Germans in the East and the Soviets' resulting thirst for revenge were not the main reason for the atrocities committed by the Red Army. Instead, traditional values had allegedly been perverted under both dictatorships well before 1939 in the period between the wars. British newspapers severely criticized this British military historian for suggesting that German soldiers, as Western Europe's representatives against Bolshevism, fought a "just defensive war" against the unimaginable acts of revenge of the Red Army and that this struggle was therefore justified. Duffy was accused of having intentionally written from a revisionist perspective.

Heavy civilian casualties were caused as well by the militarily senseless street fighting in the cities Hitler declared to be "fortresses." By the time Breslau finally capitulated on 6 May, seventy percent of the buildings had been destroyed or severely damaged by artillery fire. Königsberg had also been nearly totally devastated when the Red Army finally captured it on 9 April. Erhard Lucas-Busemann has produced a study of the fall of the two towns that goes well beyond a description of the military events (No. 866). New documents on the fate of Königsberg have been published by Eberhard Beckherrn and Alexej Dubatow (No. 1177). Silesia and Pomerania soon came to experience the wave of atrocities and murders by numbers of savage, revengeful Soviet soldiers, soon joined by Polish radicals, that had already been visited upon East Prussia in the fall of 1944, beginning with the massacre of the civilian population of the village of Nemmersdorf. Large numbers of German civilians died, and women and girls were raped, mutilated, and murdered in random acts of violence. This is documented in *Görlitzer Tagebuch* by Franz Scholz as well as in Marco P. Chiodo's publication *Sterben und Vertreibung der Deutschen im Osten* (Nos. 940, 904). A general overview is also offered in the new edition of Jürgen Thorwald's trilogy *Die Illusion – Es begann an der Weichsel – Das Ende an der Elbe* (Nos. 893, 943–94). For forty-five years, these atrocities were not openly acknowledged in the Soviet press. The Soviet historian Michail Semirjaga has provided a preliminary outline and analysis, attempting to explain the hatred for Germans inculcated in Red Army soldiers (No. 1298).

* * *

Already by the end of January 1945, Soviet troops had reached the Oder in some places and immediately established bridgeheads (No. 1207). Repeated German counterattacks failed. Of particular strategic importance for the Soviet attack on Berlin was the successful enlargement of the bridgehead at Küstrin. This threatened the entire German front along the Oder, which was supposed to be defended by the already devastated Army Group Weichsel. According to the earlier calculations of the German general staff, the Nibelungen Line along the Oder and Neisse rivers was to be the "backbone of the decisive battle for the heart of the German Reich" (No. 1213, p. 686).

However, the reinforcement of this defensive system was begun much too late, on 9 March 1945. The population was urged to dig out antitank ditches and deeply staggered positions as quickly as possible. The Seelow Heights were especially heavily fortified because they blocked the shortest path to Berlin, only forty-five miles (seventy km) away. All reserves that were still available were called up to man the defensive belt, and large mine fields were laid. In mid-April, the Führer announced that he was confident that the Battle of Berlin would end with a complete German victory (No. 1213, p. 688). In his "daily orders to the fighters on the eastern front" for 15–16 April 1945, which also appeared in all the newspapers that were still being published in the Reich, Hitler exhorted the German people to fight on (No. 1265, p. 65).

The Red Army prepared itself intensively for the final mammoth assault on the German capital, as Soviet publications show in graphic terms (No. 1280). The Elbe would be reached within two weeks. The most difficult task fell to the First Belorussian Front under Marshal Zukov, namely to capture Berlin in a frontal assault over the Seelow Heights (No. 279).

The vast Soviet offensive began on 16 April 1945 with a stupendous artillery bombardment. The British officer Tony Le Tissier has written an impressive, well-researched work on the course of military events about the "Durchbruch an der Oder" and the fighting "from the Seelow Heights to the Chancellery in Berlin," which is also available in German translation (No. 925). Le Tissier repeatedly points out the operational mistakes made by the Soviet commanders in this offensive, which resulted in very heavy Soviet casualties. The attack on Seelow advanced well at first but then bogged down in a bloody struggle with the German Ninth Army and flak units from Berlin that had been stationed there. Although the Red Army suffered heavy casualties, the Ninth Army was vastly inferior and could not hold out for long. This is documented in the new study by Richard Lakowski (No. 1254a). After a few days, the front maintained by Army Group Weichsel disintegrated under the force of the Soviet blows.

At the same time, the First Ukrainian Front under Marshal Konev launched a successful offensive to the south in the Lausitz region of the Neisse River near Muskau. The mass Soviet attacks soon decimated the weak front of the Fourth Panzer Army, which formed the left flank of Army Group Center. Thousands of Soviet tanks and several infantry armies poured into Saxony, northwestward to surround Berlin, and westward toward the Elbe. The Soviets advanced at such a rapid pace that the high command of the German army had to move its headquarters at Zossen in great haste. On 20 April – Hitler's birthday – Soviet tanks appeared by the autobahn south of Berlin, threatening the Ninth Army from the rear. Hitler forbade a plan to withdraw this army past Berlin in order to create a new front together with the Third Panzer Army east of the Elbe. On 21 April, the Ninth Army was surrounded southeast of Berlin. However, it continued its final battle until the beginning of May (No. 1211).

The Fourth Panzer Army also could not long hold its thinly defended front in southern Saxony. On 25 April 1945, troops of the 69th U.S. Infantry Division encountered the 58th Soviet

Guards Rifle Division near Torgau on the Elbe. That same day, the Soviets closed their ring around Berlin at Ketzin, northwest of Potsdam. The Fourth Panzer Army withdrew in the last week of April toward the Czech border, fending off heavy assaults.

On 20 April 1945, the Second Belorussian Front began its drive to surround Berlin on the north from the lower reaches of the Oder. Despite difficult terrain, it succeeded in warding off stiff German counterattacks and establishing a bridgehead south of Stettin. Both sides suffered heavy casualties, with the Germans losing the last of their reserves. The Third Panzer Army faced being surrounded from both sides, since the First Belorussian Front had by now broken through the German defensive system in the Seelow area. Marshal Zukov's troops mauled the flanks of the Third Panzer Army as they pushed rapidly forward toward Berlin, before passing north of the city (No. 279). Its attempt to create new lines of resistance failed. On 3 May, a spearhead of the Second Belorussian Front encountered British troops near Grabow. Greifswald was occupied on 30 April, Stralsund on 1 May, and Rostock one day later. On 3 May, Soviet and British troops again met southwest of Wismar.

After the breakthrough on the Oder, German headquarters placed its hopes in Berlin's defensive system. At the same time, efforts were made to stabilize the front outside Berlin by sending further reserves. The Germans attempted to relieve the pressure on the city and weaken the enemy by counterattacking at various places on the front. Above all, they wanted to gain time.

The German troops in Austria also came under heavy Russian attack. On 6 May, Army Group G abandoned the struggle in southern Germany in the name of all the remaining forces there, eliminating any possibility of Hitler escaping from Berlin into the Alps.

The final defeat of the Wehrmacht in March and April 1945 in the area between the Rhine and Oder deprived the dictator of his final sources of power. As he himself felt, he scarcely had any influence at all any more over the remaining pockets of Nazi dominion in the north and south. In any case, they were hardly of any military value.

The eradication of national socialism was the stated war aim of the anti-Hitler coalition. This goal had not yet been achieved, however, with the crushing of the Wehrmacht, the outward defense of the German Reich. The heart of the resistance and the continuation of the war was the German dictator himself, who insisted that the war continue until "final victory." So long as the

Führer still lived, as the conspirators of "20 July" had realized one year earlier, national socialism could not be driven from Germany. Hitler's personal power and Himmler's SS state had to be eradicated through the conquest of Berlin, in order to stamp out national socialism as a danger to humanity. The publications of Anthony Read, David Fisher, Guido Knopp, Reinhard Rürup, and Bengt von zur Mühlen contain new and extensive accounts and reports on the "fall of Berlin," depicting the *Endkampf* for the capital of the Reich from various perspectives (Nos. 1276, 1246, 1282, 1264). The works of Olaf Groehler, Ernst Günther Schenck, and Anton Joachimsthaler are devoted to the events in the Chancellery in Berlin and in the Führerbunker below ground in the Wilhemstraße (Nos. 1227, 1228, 1243, 1293).

On 20 April 1945 – Hitler's fifty-sixth birthday – the inhabitants of Berlin came under heavy bombardment by British and American aircraft, while the tank spearheads of the First Ukrainian Front were already twelve miles (twenty km) south of the city at Zossen. Joseph Goebbels, the only one of Hitler's old cronies and confidants to remain in Berlin, spoke melodramatically in his usual birthday address of the approaching "final test" (No. 1265, p. 81). Most Berliners probably hoped this was true, at least in the sense that the war would finally end. Goebbels, however, wanted Germans to enter this "most difficult trial full of hope and with deep, unshakable belief" in the "genius" of Hitler. As the Gauleiter and Commissar of Defense for Berlin, Goebbels attempted in the next few days "with fanatic obstinacy" to rally the defense of the city. It would be "defended to the very end," he announced. The "Bolshevik storm" would break on the walls of Berlin (No. 1265, p. 81). Nonetheless, Goebbels' hysterical propaganda could not staunch his own doubts, as we now know thanks to the publication of his diary, in which he had been recording for more than a year his shattering recognition that the Eastern Front was disintegrating and the soldiers' morale crumbling.

Goebbels encouraged Hitler's decision to remain in Berlin. Grand Admiral Karl Dönitz, the supreme commander of the navy, traveled to Plön in Schleswig-Holstein; Heinrich Himmler went to Hohenlychen in northern Germany; and Reichsmarshall Hermann Göring had the Luftwaffe transport him to Berchtesgaden. Minister of Armaments Albert Speer also preferred to fly out of Berlin and await the end of the war in western Germany. As the political leadership was restructured, so was the military leadership. The army high command was amalgamated with the high command of the armed forces. General Hans Krebs, the last army chief of general staff for the Eastern Front, remained as Hitler's assistant in close proximity to the dictator until the end.

At the final large discussion of the military situation, deep in the bowels of the earth at the Führerbunker on 22 April 1945, Hitler announced his decision to continue defending Berlin. The newly created Twelfth Army under General Walther Wenck was to attack the Soviet ring from the west, at the same time that "Army Group Steiner" (the Third SS Panzer Corps) under SS *Obergruppenführer* Felix Steiner attacked from the north. However, neither army was able to seriously affect the besieging forces of Soviet marshals Zukov and Konev. In a surprising move on 23 April, Hitler named the commanding general of the LVI Panzer Corps, Lieutenant General Helmuth Weidling, battle commander and "commander of the Berlin Defensive Area." Weidling had originally intended to withdraw to the west with his remaining forces. The troops from Weidling's Panzer Corps entered the city and helped to strengthen the front around Berlin, which already ran through villages on the edge of the city.

The final battle for Berlin began with a Soviet artillery barrage lasting several hours and virtually continuous fighter-bomber attacks on the inner city (Nos. 1225, 1230, 1264, 1277). The defensive forces in Berlin consisted of emergency and *Volkssturm* units, remnants of the LVI Panzer Corps, and flak units – including many Waffen-SS volunteers from France, Holland, Norway, Belgium, and Lithuania – and 4,000 Hitler Youth. For heavy armor, there were forty to fifty tanks. The preparations were insufficient for the proper defense of Berlin as a "fortress." Facing the defenders of the city were vastly superior Soviet armies consisting of approximately 2.5 million men.

Many civilians lost their lives in the struggle for Berlin. On 27 April, Hitler gave the fateful order to open the sluice gates of the Spree and to blast open the top of the S-Bahn tunnels and the bulkheads of the Landwehr Canal between the Schöneberg and Möckern bridges in order to flood the S-Bahn and subway tunnels and prevent further Soviet soldiers from entering these avenues into the city. However, this also drowned many wounded German soldiers and civilians who had sought shelter beneath the Anhalter and Potsdam train stations. Despite stubborn street battles, or at times even fighting from rooftop to rooftop, the Germans were gradually pushed back into the heart of the city. Here, around the Führerbunker, was the relatively small defensive area Citadel under the command of SS Brigadier Mohnke. In the Unter den Linden sector he had at his command the Frenchmen of the Thirty-Third Waffen Grenadier Division, SS Charlemagne, who were fighting on the German side, as well as the Latvian volunteers of the Fifteenth SS Waffen Grenadier Division. They were motivated mostly by slogans such as "the European war against Bolshevism" (Nos. 1114, 1114a, 1260).

On 27 April 1945, Potsdam and Spandau were lost, and the Red Army had already named General Berzarin to be the first Soviet commandant of Berlin. The next day, the Soviet artillery targeted the grounds of the Chancellery. Hitler wrote his personal and political testaments. The most important provision was the appointment of Grand Admiral Karl Dönitz as Hitler's successor as president and of Goebbels as chancellor. On 30 April around noon, Soviet soldiers of the light infantry regiments 380, 674, and 756 surged to the Reichstag, and at 2:25 P.M. they raised the hammer and cycle on the cupola of the devastated building. At 3:30 P.M., Hitler committed suicide. As he had previously ordered, SS adjutants burned his and Eva Braun's corpses in the garden of the Chancellery. This was to prevent them from falling into the hands of Soviet soldiers and possibly being put on public display, as had happened a few days earlier to the bodies of Mussolini and his mistress in northern Italy. Hitler's death has always been the cause of legends and speculation, although his death is clearly documented, as is shown in the recent books by Heinz Günther Schenk and Anton Joachimsthaler (Nos. 1243, 1293).

By agreement with new Reich Chancellor Goebbels, General Krebs met on 1 May with the Soviet army general Cuikov to offer him a truce (No. 1313). When the Soviets demanded unconditional surrender, the talks were broken off. In the evening of this dramatic day, the "Führer headquarters" finally issued an official announcement that Hitler was dead. However, even this report, like so many before, was a lie. It alleged that the Führer, who had not been seen with any weapons for a long time, had nevertheless fallen in the Chancellery, "fighting for Germany against Bolshevism till his last breath" (No. 1204). In the very early hours of 2 May, General Weidling finally accepted as battle commander of Berlin General Cuikov's demand for unconditional surrender. It came into effect at three o'clock that afternoon. Berlin had fallen to the enemy.

On the evening of 2 May 1945, salvos of joy were fired off in the Soviet capital. For understandable reasons, the people of Moscow were particularly elated at the capture of Berlin. Three and a half years earlier, in December 1941, German troops had reached the outskirts of Moscow, and the people of the city had barely escaped the total annihilation Hitler had planned for them.

On 4 May, when people were still fighting and dying in many places, the high command of the Wehrmacht reported from Grand Admiral Dönitz's headquarters in the usual overblown Nazi style: "The battle for the capital of the Reich has come to an end. In actions of unparalleled heroism, troops from all segments of the Wehrmacht as well as *Volkssturm* units remained faithful to their oath of allegiance and resisted to their last breath, setting an example of German soldiery at its very best" (No. 190a, p. 565). No mention was made by the generals of how Hitler had abused these soldiers to the very end out of his personal thirst for power or of how deeply they had become involved in his criminal conduct of the war. The present state of the research on the significance of the end of the war in May 1945 as a turning point in the military and political development in Europe is presented in the publication *Kriegsende 1945* by Rolf-Dieter Müller and Gerd R. Ueberschär as well as in an omnibus volume edited by Hans-Erich Volkmann (Nos. 1265, 1317a).

* * *

In the final phase of the war, the terror and horror intensified beyond all imagination. Foreign contingents and auxiliary troops as helper forces fighting alongside the Wehrmacht and SS were particularly affected. Hundreds of thousands of foreigners wore German uniforms. There are numerous publications about these "comrades in arms" from friendly or allied nations. Vancetti Safronov has even published a well-received Russian study of the fate of the Italian troops fighting with the Germans on the Eastern Front (Nos. 1114, 1114a, 1119a). Surprisingly, most of the foreign soldiers in Hitler's armies were Soviet citizens (Nos. 1090–92, 1097, 1102, 1123, 1132). Historians have often examined how this willingness of some Soviets to fight on the German side, which varied in intensity from region to region, could have been used more successfully and "more rationally" for Nazi military and political ends (Nos. 1099–1101). This aspect of the Eastern campaign received exaggerated attention at the time of the Cold War, but it is now overstated in the West only occasionally. For a long time, Communist historians totally ignored the willingness of the Soviet population to collaborate because this action contradicted the dogma of progress and high achievement under a Communist society and rule. The speculation about whether the Germans could possibly have won the war if they had employed the often described "Eastern legions" differently is based on a failure to appreciate the actual military resources of the Soviet empire.

By the fall of 1944, Slavic peoples who had earlier been disqualified as *Untermenschen* (subhumans) were allowed to form under Himmler a Russian army of liberation (*Russkaya Osvoboditelnaya Armiya,* or ROA), in a final marshaling of a few tens of thousands of "fighters against Bolshevism." Two publications by Jürgen Thorwald illustrate particularly well the shift in the assessment of the phenomenon of collaboration. In the early 1950s, he collected material on Vlasov's army for Western secret services and published it in a euphemistic presentation (Nos. 1131, 1132). Twenty years later, he returned to this topic and arrived at quite different conclusions, giving his book the revelatory title *Die Illusion* (No. 1132).

The leader of this Russian Liberation Army, General Andrei Vlasov, was captured by the Americans in northern Bohemia and turned over to the Soviets. He was executed in Moscow in August 1946. The British and Americans also delivered most of his followers into the hands of the Soviets in dramatic fashion. These prisoners disappeared into the Soviet labor camps, as Alexander Solzhenitsyn has described in *The Gulag Archipelago* (No. 1126a). The interesting connection between Vlasov's army and Russian emigré groups in the West, as well as their hopes for Russia's future, has been described in a study by Catherine Andreyev (No. 1071). Within the framework of the bitter and increasingly intense struggle between Moscow and Berlin from 1944/45 onward, helper forces recruited from other peoples and nationalities were deployed more and more frequently and fought, often won over with dubious promises, at the side of the Wehrmacht or the Red Army. This is documented in the volume *Im Bunde mit dem Feind,* edited by Stefan Doernberg, and by the most recent research on the scope of action of the *Nationalkomitee Freies Deutschland* (NKFD) and the *Band Deutscher Offiziere* in the USSR (Nos. 1084, 1137).

Staring defeat in the face, Hitler declared to Minister of Armaments Speer on 19 March 1945 that the future belonged to the "stronger eastern people" (i.e. the Russians) and not to the

Germans. This declaration, which Speer relates in his memoirs, was a final admission of the total failure of the Führer's plans for conquest in the East (No. A/90a). His disappointment and bitterness are readily understandable in view of the fact that he had always considered the East to be the central theater of the Second World War. In the end, ultimate victory or defeat for the Third Reich was indeed largely decided on the broad, rich plains of southern Russia.

* * *

Hitler and Goebbels agreed in private on the criminal nature of the war they planned to wage in the East, as can now be seen in Goebbels' diaries. Shortly before the attack of 22 June 1941, the minister of propaganda declared to the Führer: "If we emerge victorious, who will inquire as to our methods. We are already so deeply into all this that we must win; otherwise, our entire people will be eradicated, with us at the head together with everything that we value" (Nos. A/64, 64a). This policy and method of warfare had clear effects on the number of victims of the war, about which a long discussion took place after 1945.

After three years of fierce fighting marked by unimaginable brutality, the defeated units of the Wehrmacht began by 1944 to flood back over Germany's borders. They left behind a burned-out, plundered land. Millions of Soviet citizens had been killed or deported to Germany. Some Wehrmacht administrative offices even took note of the plundering, rape, willful executions, and other crimes. Today there are still no precise figures in the Soviet literature on the number of Soviet soldiers and civilians who died. For a long time, the state kept these figures secret and blocked any serious historical research. In 1946, Stalin announced that only seven million had died in total, in order to avoid admitting higher losses than the Germans themselves had suffered and to evade personal responsibility for the high Russian losses. In the 1960s, Khrushchev set total Russian casualties at twenty million or more dead (including eight to ten million soldiers). According to official information released to the press in 1990, Russian losses were about twenty-seven million dead, including almost nine million soldiers.[4] In 1992, the *Russian Journal of Military History* set the number of losses at twenty-one to twenty-two million (*Voenno-Istoriceskij Zurnal* [*VIZ*] 6

4. *Frankfurter Allgemeine Zeitung* (21 April 1990): 5

July 1992: 32). Viktor Anfilov provided new figures for the number of Soviet soldiers who were captured by the Germans in the first few months of the war, corresponding basically to the earlier German figures (No. E/313a). Still unanswered, and still a subject of considerable controversy in Russia, is the question of why the Red Army's losses for the entire war were so much higher than those of the Wehrmacht. The recent publication *No Longer Secret*, by a collective of Russian authors under General G. Krivoseev, set Red Army losses at 8.7 million and total Soviet losses at almost twenty-seven million. However, the authors leave many questions unanswered, even though they were allowed to analyze for the first time the original sources in the Russian archives (No. E/367b). There are no reliable figures in the Soviet documents for the first part of the Soviet-German war.

The Red Army's behavior once it crossed into German territory can only be understood in light of what had happened previously. It is not a matter of viewing it as retribution but of recognizing and understanding certain connections. The Wehrmacht had also suffered heavy casualties by the time it capitulated under Grand Admiral Dönitz on 8 May 1945. About 960,000 had died, 3.8 million had been wounded, and 1.2 million were missing. There were additional losses as well, of course, among the SS and among the railroad workers, postal defense workers, engineers, civil servants, and party bosses who fell victim to partisan attacks behind the lines.

Bibliography

1. General, 1941–1945

a) Bibliographies, Literature, and Research Reports

1) Alföldi, Laszlo M. *World War 2. The Eastern and Balkan Front. The Axis Forces in Europe.* Carlisle Barracks, Pa., 1978

2) Beitter, Gerda. "Die Truppengeschichten der Roten Armee im Zweiten Weltkrieg. (Literaturbericht und Bibliographie)." In *Jahresbibliographie der Bibliothek für Zeitgeschichte* vol. 46, 1974, pp. 429–572. Munich, 1975

3) _____. *Die Rote Armee im 2. Weltkrieg. Eine Bibliographie ihrer Truppengeschichten im Zweiten Weltkrieg.* Schriften der Bibliothek für Zeitgeschichte, vol. 34. Koblenz, 1984

4) Boch, Rudolf. "Der Krieg im Osten 1941–1945. Bilanz und Perspektiven der bundesdeutschen Forschung." In *Was ist Gesellschaftsgeschichte? Positionen, Themen, Analysen*, edited by Manfred Hettling et al., pp. 248–258. Munich, 1991

5) Boltin, E.A. "Über den Stand und einige Probleme der Erforschung der Geschichte des zweiten Weltkrieges in der Sowjetunion." *Zeitschrift für Geschichtswissenschaft* vol. 6 (1958): pp. 990–998

6) Bonwetsch, Bernd. "Der 'Große Vaterländische Krieg' und seine Geschichte." In *Die Umwertung der sowjetischen Geschichte*, edited by Dietrich Geyer, pp. 167–187. Göttingen, 1991

7) Borck, Karin, ed. *Sowjetische Forschungen (1917 bis 1991) zur Geschichte der deutsch-russichen Beziehungen von den Anfängen bis 1949. Bibliographie*. Berlin, 1993 (see the special chapter "1941–1945, 7. 5 Militärgeschichte, Kriegsgeschichte", pp. 261–306)

7a) Galagher, M.P. *The Soviet History of World War II. Myths, Realities and Memories*. New York, 1963

8) *Geroi Velikoj Otecestvennoj vojny 1941–1945. Straricy biografij. Rekomendatel'nyj bibliograficeskij ukazatel'*. Edited by N.P. Baranova et al. Moscow, 1981

9) Giertz, Horst. "Neuere sowjetische Literatur zum Großen Vaterländischen Krieg der UdSSR." *Militärgeschichte* vol. 25, no. 6 (1986): pp. 544–556
10) Hass, Gerhart. "Die sowjetische Geschichtsschreibung über den Großen Vaterländischen Krieg." *Militärgeschichte* vol. 3 (1982): pp. 351 ff.
11) ____. "Der deutsch-sowjetische Krieg 1941–1945. Zu einigen Legenden über seine Vorgeschichte und den Verlauf der ersten Kriegswochen." *Zeitschrift für Geschichtswissenschaft* vol. 39, no. 7 (1991): pp. 647–662
12) Jacobsen, Hans-Adolf. *Zur Konzeption einer Geschichte des Zweiten Weltkrieges 1939–1945. Disposition mit kritisch ausgewähltem Schrifttum*. Schriften der Bibliothek für Zeitgeschichte, Weltkriegsbücherei Stuttgart, N. F., vol. 2. Frankfurt, 1964
13) Kumanev, Georgij A. *Velikaja Otecestvennaja Vojna Sovetskogo Sojuza (1941–1945 gg.). Bibliografija sovetskoj istoriceskoj literatury za 1946–1959 gg*. Moscow, 1960
14) Kusnezowa, O.W., and K.I. Selesnjow. "Der politisch-moralische Zustand der faschistischen deutschen Truppen an der sowjetisch-deutschen Front in den Jahren 1941–1945. Überblick über die sowjetischen Quellen und Literatur." *Zeitschrift für Militärgeschichte* vol. 9, no. 5 (1970): pp. 598–608
15) Moritz, Erhard, and Werner Stang. "Sowjetische Publikationen über den Großen Vaterländischen Krieg der Sowjetunion." *Militärgeschichte* vol. 6 (1973): pp. 731–739
16) Parrish, Michael. *The U.S.S.R. in World War II. An Annotated Bibliography of Books Published in the Soviet Union, 1945–1975. With an Addenda for the Years 1975–1980*. 2 vols. New York, 1981–82
17) Rathkolb, Oliver. "Literatur- und Forschungsbericht über das 'Kriegsende 1945' am Beispiel ausgewählter bundesdeutscher und österreichischer Publikationen." *Zeitgeschichte* vol. 12, no. 5 (1985): pp. 176–186
18) Savuskin, Robert A. "Kakim budet desjatitomnik?" *Voenno-Istoriceskij Zurnal* no. 10 (1988): pp. 71–74
19) ____. (Sawuschin) "Zur Darstellung des bewaffneten Kampfes in einer künftigen Geschichte des Großen Vaterländischen Krieges des Sowjetvolkes." *Militärgeschichte* vol. 29, no. 2 (1990): pp. 131–140
20) ____. (Savushkin) "In the Tracks of a Tragedy. On the 50th Anniversary of the Start of the Great Patriotic War." *The Journal of Soviet Military Studies* vol. 4, no. 2 (1991): pp. 213–251
21) Schröder, Hans-Hennings. "Die Lehren von 1941. Die Diskussion um die Neubewertung des 'Großen Vaterländischen Krieges' in der Sowjetunion." In *Der Zweite Weltkrieg. Analysen, Grundzüge, Forschungsbilanzen*, edited by Wolfgang Michalka, pp. 608–625. Munich, 1989
22) Shilin, P. "Der Große Vaterländische Krieg 1941–1945. Militärhistorische Literatur." In *Die Sowjetische Geschichtswissenschaft in der gegenwärtigen Etappe. Zum XVI. Internationalen Historikerkongress, (Stuttgart, August 1985)*, edited by the Academy of Sciences of the USSR, pp. 72 ff. Moscow, 1985
Shilin P., see also Zilin, P.
23) *Sowjetische Forschungen über den zweiten Weltkrieg*. Edited by the Academy of Sciences of the USSR. Probleme der Modernen Welt, vol. 1. Moscow, 1976
24) *SSSR v gody Velikoj Otecestvennoj vojny (ijun 1941–sentjabr 1945 g.). Ukazatel' sovetskoj literatury za 1941–1967 gg*. Moscow, 1977

25) *SSSR v gody Velikoj Otecestvennoj vojny (ijun 1941–sentjabr 1945 g.). Geroi fronta i tyla. Ukazatel' sovetskoj literatury za 1941–1967 gg.* Moscow, 1981
26) *Trudy Archiva ROA v N'ju Iorke*. 2 parts. New York, 1961–1966
27) Ueberschär, Gerd R. "Hitler's Decision to Attack the Soviet Union in Recent German Historiography." In *Operation Barbarossa: The German Attack on the Soviet Union, June 22, 1941*, edited by Norman Naimark et al., pp. 297–315. Special Issue of *Soviet Union* vol. 18, nos. 1–3 (1991)
28) _____. "Hitlers Entscheidung zum Krieg gegen die Sowjetunion und die Präventivkriegsdiskussion in der neueren Literatur." In *22. Juni 1941. Der Überfall auf die Sowjetunion*, edited by Hans Schafranek and Robert Streibel, pp. 13–35. Vienna, 1991
29) *Velikaja Otecestvennaja Vojna Sovetskogo Sojuza (1941–1945 gg.). Rekomendatel'nyj ukazatel' literatury*. Edited by Biblioteka SSSR imeni V.I. Lenina. Moscow, 1965
30) Zilin, P. A., A.S. Jakusevskij, and E.N. Kuikov. *Kritika asnavnych koncapcij burzuaznoj Istoriografij vtoroj mirovoj vojny*. Moscow, 1983

b) Overviews

31) Aaken, Wolf van. *Hexenkessel Ostfront. Von Smolensk bis Breslau. (1941–1945)*. Rastatt, 1964
32) Abraham, Heinz. *1941–1945. Großer Vaterländischer Krieg der Sowjetunion*. Berlin, 1985
33) Anders, Wladyslaw. *Hitler's Defeat in Russia*. Chicago, 1953
34) Baird, Jay Warren. *German Home Propaganda, 1941–1945, and the Russian Front*. Diss., Univ. of Columbia, 1966; Ann Arbor, 1978
35) Bartsch, Michael, Hans-Frieder Schebesch, and Rainer Scheppelmann. *Der Krieg im Osten 1941–1945. Historische Einführung, Kommentare und Dokumente*. Cologne, 1981
36) *Battles Hitler Lost and the Soviet Marshalls Who Won Them*. New York, 1986
37) Benz, Wigbert. *Der Rußlandfeldzug des Dritten Reiches: Ursachen, Ziele, Wirkungen*. Frankfurt, 1986
38) Besymenski, Lew. *Sonderakte "Barbarossa". Dokumente, Darstellung, Deutung*. Stuttgart, 1968 (Russian edn: *Osobaja papka "Barbarossa"*. Moscow, 1972)
39) Carell, Paul. *Der Rußlandkrieg. Fotografiert von Soldaten. Der Bildband zum Unternehmen Barbarossa und Verbrannte Erde*. Frankfurt a.M., 1967
39a) Carell, Paul [Paul K. Schmidt]. *Unternehmen Barbarossa. Der Marsch nach Rußland*. Frankfurt, 1953
40) Cecil, Robert. *Hitlers Griff nach Rußland*. Graz, 1977
41) Clark, Alan. *Barbarossa. The Russian-German Conflict, 1941–45*. London, 1965; 2nd edn London, 1995
42) Costantini, Aime. *L'Union sovietique en guerre (1941–1945)*. Edited by Etat-Major de l'Armée de Terre, Service Historique. 3 vols. Paris, 1968–69
43) Dahms, Hellmuth G. "Der Weltanschauungskrieg gegen die Sowjetunion." In *Der 2. Weltkrieg*, pp. 303–420. Gütersloh, 1968

44) Dasicev, V. *"Soversenno sekretno! Tol'ko dlja komandovanija!" Strategija fasistskoj Germanii v voine protiv SSSR. Dokumenty i materialy.* Moscow, 1967
44a) Dear, I.C.B, and M.R.D. Foot, eds. *The Oxford Companion to the Second World War.* Oxford, 1995
45) Deborin, Grigorij A. *Vtoraja Mirovaja Vojna. Voenno-politiceskij ocerk.* Edited by I.I. Zubkova. Moscow, 1958 (German edn: *Der zweite Weltkrieg.* East Berlin, 1960)
46) Desroches, Alain. *La Campagne de Russie d'Adolf Hitler (juin 1941–mai 1945).* Paris, 1964
46a) *Das Deutsche Reich und der Zweite Weltkrieg.* Vols. 1–6. Stuttgart, 1976ff.
47) *Deutschland im zweiten Weltkrieg.* Ed. by the Academy of Sciences of the GDR, under an author collective headed by Wolfgang Schuhmann and Karl Drechsler. 5 vols. East Berlin, 1975ff.
48) Droschdow, Georgi, and Jewgeni Ryabko. *Russia at War, 1941–45.* London, 1987; New York, 1987
49) Dunnigan, James F., ed. *The Russian Front. Germany's War in the East, 1941–1945.* London, 1978
50) Dupuy, Trevor N., and Paul Martell. *Great Battles on Eastern Front. The Soviet-German War, 1941–1945.* Indianapolis, 1982
51) Eickhoff, Michael, Wilhelm Pagels, and Willy Reschl. *Der unvergessene Krieg. Hitler-Deutschland gegen die Sowjetunion 1941–1945.* Cologne, 1981
52) Elleinstein, Jean. *L'U.R.S.S. en guerre. 1939–1946.* Paris, 1974
53) Erickson, John. *Stalin's War with Germany.* 2 vols. London, 1975–83
53a) _____. *The Road to Stalingrad.* London, 1975
53b) _____. *The Road to Berlin.* Boulder, Co., 1983
53c) _____. *The Soviet High Command. A Military-Political History, 1918–1941.* London, 1962
54) Förster, Gerhard. "Das Scheitern der faschistischen Strategie im Kampf gegen die Sowjetunion." In *Das Fiasko der antisowjetischen Aggression. Studien zur Kriegführung des deutschen Imperialismus gegen die UdSSR (1941–1945),* edited by Erhard Moritz, pp. 11–44. East Berlin, 1978
55) Garder, Michel. *Une Guerre pas comme les autres. La Guerre germano-soviétique.* Paris, 1962
55a) Gellermann, Günther. *Der Krieg, der nicht stattfand. Möglichkeiten, Überlegungen und Entscheidungen der deutschen Obersten Führung zur Verwendung chemischer Kampfstoffe im Zweiten Weltkrieg.* Koblenz, 1986
56) *Geschichte des Großen Vaterländischen Krieges der Sowjetunion.* Edited by Institut für Marxismus-Leninismus beim Zentralkomittee der Kommunistischen Partei der Sowjetunion. 6 vols. Especially vol. 1, *Die Vorbereitung und Entfesselung des zweiten Weltkrieges durch die imperialistischen Mächte*; vol. 2, *Die Abwehr des wortbrüchigen Überfalls des faschistischen Deutschlands auf die Sowjetunion – Die Schaffung der Voraussetzungen für den grundlegenden Umschwung im Kriege*; vol. 3, *Der grundlegende Umschwung im Verlauf des Großen Vaterländischen Krieges.* East Berlin, 1962–1964
57) *Geschichte des zweiten Weltkrieges 1939–1945.* Edited by Institut für Militärgeschichte des Ministeriums für Verteidigung der UdSSR. 12

vols. Vol. 4, *Die faschistische Aggression gegen die UdSSR. Der Zusammenbruch der Blitzkriegsstrategie*. East Berlin 1977; vol. 5, *Das Scheitern der Aggressionspläne des faschistischen Blocks*. East Berlin 1977; vol. 6, *Der grundlegende Umschwung im Krieg*. East Berlin, 1979

58) Glantz, David M. *Soviet Military Deception in the Second World War*. London, 1989

59) ____. *The Military Strategic of the Soviet Union: a History*. London, 1992

60) ____. *Soviet Military Operational Art*. London, 1991

61) Golikov, S. *Vydajusciesja Pobedy sovetskoj armii v Velikoj Otecestvennoj Vojne*. Moscow, 1952 (German edn: *Die Sowjetarmee im Großen Vaterländischen Krieg*. East Berlin, 1954)

62) *Der Große Vaterländische Krieg des Sowjetvolkes und die Gegenwart*. Edited by "Gesellschaftswissenschaften und Gegenwart" der Akademie der Wissenschaften der UdSSR. Moscow, 1985

63) Gruchmann, Lothar. *Der Zweite Weltkrieg*. 7th edn. Munich, 1982

64) Guillaume, Augustin. *La Guerre germano-soviétique 1941–1945*. Paris, 1949

65) Haupt, Werner. *Heeresgruppe Nord 1941–1945*. Bad Nauheim, 1966

66) ____. *Der Kampf im Nordabschnitt der Ostfront. Heeresgruppe Nord 1941–1945*. Bad Nauheim, 1967

67) ____. *Heeresgruppe Mitte 1941–1945*. Dorheim, 1968

68) ____. *Bildchronik der Heeresgruppe Mitte 1941–1945*. Dorheim, 1969

69) ____. *Moskau – Rshew – Orel – Minsk. Bildbericht der Heeresgruppe Mitte, 1941–1944*. Friedberg, 1978

70) ____. *Die Schlachten der Heeresgruppe Süd. Aus der Sicht der Divisionen*. Friedberg, 1985

71) Haupt, Werner, and Carl Wagener. *Bildchronik der Heeresgruppe Süd*. Dorheim, 1969

72) Hillgruber, Andreas. "Der deutsch-sowjetische Krieg 1941–1945" In *Die sowjetische Geschichte des Großen Vaterländischen Krieges 1941–1945*, by Boris S. Telpuchowski, pp. 1E–12E. Frankfurt, 1961

73) ____. "Der Zweite Weltkrieg, 1939–1945." In *Osteuropa-Handbuch. Sowjetunion. Außenpolitik 1917–1955*, edited by Dietrich Geyer, pp. 270–342. Cologne, 1972

74) ____. *Der Zweite Weltkrieg 1939–1945. Kriegsziele und Strategie der großen Mächte*. Stuttgart, 1982

74a) Hoffmann, Joachim. *Stalins Vernichtungskrieg 1941–1945*. 2nd edn. Munich, 1995

75) Holmston, A. *Auf magischen Wegen. Der Ostfeldzug. Philosophie des Krieges*. Buenos Aires, 1948

76) Irving, David. *Hitler und seine Feldherren*. Frankfurt a.M., 1975

77) *Istorija Velikoj Otecestvennoj Vojny Sovetskogo Sojuza 1941–1945*. 6 vols. Moscow, 1960–1965 (German edn: *Geschichte des Großen Vaterländischen Krieges der Sowjetunion 1941–1945*. 6 vols. Berlin, 1962–1966)

78) *Istoriografija Velikoj Otecestvennoj vojny. Sbornik statej*. Moscow, 1980

79) John, Otto A.W. "Germany's Eastern Front, 1939–45." *The Army Quarterly* vol. 60 (July 1950): pp. 196–206

80) Karpov, Vladimir. *Rußland im Krieg. 1941–1945*. With texts by Georgi Drosdow and Jewgeni Ryabko. Edited by Carey Schofield. Zurich, 1988

81) Kern, Erich [Erich Kernmayr]. *Der große Rausch: Rußlandfeldzug 1941–1945*. Zurich, 1948; new edn Waiblingen, 1950; 2nd edn Göttingen, 1961

82) Kissel, Hans. *Gefechte in Rußland 1941–1944*. Frankfurt, 1956

83) Kjellberg, Sven Herman. *Rußland im Krieg. 1920–1945*. Zurich, 1945

84) Knopp, Guido. *Der verdammte Krieg. Das "Unternehmen Barbarossa"*. Munich, 1991

85) Lederrey, Ernest. *La défaite allemande à l'est. Les armées soviétiques en guerre de 1941 à 1945*. Paris, 1951

86) Liddell Hart, B. H. "The Russo-German Campaign." In *The Soviet Army*, by B.H. Liddell Hart, pp. 100–126. London, 1956

87) Lucas, James. *War on the Eastern Front, 1941–1945. The German Soldier in Russia*. London, 1979

87a) Magenheimer, Heinz. *Kriegswenden in Europa 1939–1945. Führungsentschlüsse, Hintergründe, Alternativen*. Munich, 1995

88) Mayer, S.L., ed. *The Russian War-Machine, 1917–1945*. London, 1977

89) Moritz, Erhard, ed. *Das Fiasko der antisowjetischen Aggression. Studien zur Kriegführung des deutschen Imperialismus gegen die UdSSR (1941–1945)*. Schriften des Militärgeschichtlichen Instituts der DDR. East Berlin, 1978

90) Mrazkowa, Daniela, and Vladimir Remes, eds. *The Russian War, 1941–1945*. New York, 1977 (German edn: *Von Moskau nach Berlin. Der Krieg im Osten 1941–1945, gesehen von russischen Fotografen*. Oldenburg, 1979)

91) Philippi, Alfred, and Ferdinand Heim. *Der Feldzug gegen Sowjetrußland 1941 bis 1945. Ein operativer Überblick*. Edited by Arbeitskreis für Wehrforschung. Stuttgart, 1962

91a) *Probleme der Geschichte des zweiten Weltkrieges*. Edited by Leo Stern. East Berlin, 1958

91b) Rauh, Manfred. *Geschichte des Zweiten Weltkriegs*. Vol. 2, *Der europäische Krieg 1939–1941*. Berlin, 1995

92) Rich, Norman. *Hitler's War Aims*. 2 vols. New York, 1973–74

93) Rusco, Pierre, and Philippe Randa. *Stoi! Quarante mois de combat sur le front russe*. Paris, 1988

94) Salisbury, Harrison E. *The Unknown War*. New York, 1978 (German edn: *Die Ostfront. Der unvergessene Krieg 1941–1945*. Vienna, 1981)

95) Samsonov, Aleksandr M. *Pages from the History of the Antifascist War*. Problems of the contemporary world, 58. Moscow, 1978

96) _____. *Krach fasistskoj agressii 1939–1945. Istoriceskij ocerk*. Moscow, 1980

97) _____. *Vtoraja mirovaja vojna 1939–1945. Ocerk vaznejsisch sobytij*. Moscow, 1985

98) Scheibert, Horst, and Ulrich Elfrath. *Panzer in Rußland. Die deutschen gepanzerten Verbände im Osten 1941–1944*. Dorheim, 1971

99) Seaton, Albert. *The Russo-German War, 1941–1945*. London, 1971 (German edn: *Der russisch-deutsche Krieg 1941–1945*. Frankfurt, 1973)

100) *SSSR v Velikoj Otecestvennoj vojne 1941–1945. Kratkaja chronika*. Moscow, 1970

101) Tel'puchovskij, Vladimir B. *Osnovnye Periody velikoj otecestvennoj vojny (1941–1945 gg.)*. Moscow, 1965

102) Tel'puchovskij, Boris S. *Velikaja Otecestvennaja Vojna Sovetskogo Sojuza 1941–1945. Kratkij ocerk*. Moscow, 1959 (German edn: *Die sowjetische*

Geschichte des Großen Vaterländischen Krieges 1941–45. Edited by Andreas Hillgruber and Hans-Adolf Jacobsen. Frankfurt, 1961)

103) ____, ed. *Velikaja Otecestvennaja Vojna Sovetskogo Sojuza 1941–1945. Kratkaja ist*. Moscow, 1984

104) Tel'puchovskij, Boris S., et al., eds. *Ocerki istorii velikoj otecestvennoj vojny 1941–1945*. Moscow, 1955

105) Thies, Jochen. *Architekt der Weltherrschaft. Die "Endziele" Hitlers*. Düsseldorf, 1976

106) Tippelskirch, Kurt von. *Geschichte des Zweiten Weltkrieges*. Bonn, 1951

107) Ueberschär, Gerd R., and Wolfram Wette, eds. *"Unternehmen Barbarossa". Der deutsche Überfall auf die Sowjetunion 1941. Berichte, Analysen, Dokumente*. Paderborn, 1984; new paperback edn: *Der deutsche Überfall auf die Sowjetunion. "Unternehmen Barbarossa" 1941*. 2nd edn Frankfurt a.M., 1991

108) *Velikaja Otecestvennaja Vojna. Kratkij naucno-popularnyj ocerk*. Moscow, 1970

109) *Velikaja Otecestvennaja Vojna Sovetskogo Sojuza 1941–1945. Kratkaja istorija*. 2nd edn. Moscow, 1970 (English edn: *Great Patriotic War of the Soviet Union, 1941–1945. A General Outline*. Moscow, 1974)

110) *Velikaja otecestvennaja ... Kratkaja, illustrirovannaja istorija vojny dlja junosestva*. Edited by N. Eronin and V. Taborko. Moscow, 1975

111) *Pogranicnye Vojska SSSR v Velikoj Otecestvennoj Vojne 1941. Sbornik dokumentov i materialov*. Edited by E.D. Solovev. Moscow, 1976

112) Wagener, Carl. *Heeresgruppe Süd. Der Kampf im Süden der Ostfront 1941–1945*. Bad Nauheim, 1967

113) Wegner, Bernd, ed. *Zwei Wege nach Moskau. Vom Hitler-Stalin-Pakt bis zum "Unternehmen Barbarossa"*. Munich, 1991

114) Weinberg, Gerhard L. *A World at Arms. A Global History of World War II*. New York, 1994 (German edn: *Eine Welt in Waffen. Die globale Geschichte des Zweiten Weltkriegs*. Stuttgart, 1995) (see the chapters about the "Ostfront")

114a) *Der Zweite Weltkrieg 1939–1945. Wirklichkeit und Fälschung*. Edited by Deutsche Sektion der Kommission der Historiker der DDR und der UdSSR. East Berlin, 1959

115) Werth, Alexander. *Russia at War, 1941–1945*. New York, 1964 (French edn: *La Russie en guerre*. Paris, 1964; German edn: *Rußland im Krieg 1941–1945*. Munich, 1965)

116) Whaley, Barton. *Codeword Barbarossa*. Cambridge, Mass., 1973

117) Zaloga, Steven J., and James Grandsen. *The Eastern Front. Armour Camouflage and Markings, 1941–1945*. London, 1983 (German edn: Zaloga, Steven J., James Grandsen, and Horst Scheibert. *Die Panzer der Ostfront*. Friedberg, 1985)

118) Zentner, Kurt. *Nur einmal konnte Stalin siegen. Lehren und Bilder aus dem Rußlandfeldzug 1941–45*. Hamburg, 1952

119) Ziemke, Earl F. *Stalingrad to Berlin: the German Defeat in the East*. Washington, DC, 1968

120) ____. *Moscow to Stalingrad: Decision in the East*. Washington, DC, 1987

121) Zilin, P.A., ed. *Velikaja Otecestvennaja vojna Sovetskogo Sojuza 1941–1945. Kratkaja istorija*. 3rd edn. Moscow, 1984

122) ____. *Velikaja Otecestvennaja Narodnaja 1941–1945. Kratkij istoriceskij ocerk*. Moscow, 1985

c) Biographies

123) Bialer, Seweryn, ed. *Stalin and His Generals. Soviet Military Memoirs of World War II*. London, 1970

124) Blank, Aleksandr, and Boris Chavkin. *Vtoraja Zizn Feldmarsala Pauljusa*. Moscow, 1990

125) Bullock, Alan. *Hitler and Stalin. Parallel Lives*. London, 1991 (German edn: *Hitler und Stalin. Parallele Leben*. Berlin, 1991)

126) Carnes, James Donald. *General zwischen Hitler und Stalin. Das Schicksal des Walther von Seydlitz*. Düsseldorf, 1980

127) Chaney, Otto P. *Zhukov*. Newton Abbot, 1972

128) Conquest, Robert. *Stalin – Breaker of Nations*. London, 1991 (German edn: *Stalin. Der totale Wille zur Macht. Biographie*. Munich, 1991)

128a) Deakin, F.W., and G.R. Storry. *Richard Sorge. Die Geschichte eines großen Doppelspiels*. Munich, 1965

129) Egorov, Petr Ja. *Marsal Mereckov*. Moscow, 1974

130) Golubovic, V.S. *Marsal R. Ja. Malinovskij*. Moscow, 1984

130a) Hartmann, Christian. *Halder*. Paderborn, 1991

131) Kardasov, Vladislav I. *Rokossovskij*. Moscow, 1984

132) Karpov, Vladimir V. *The Commander*. London, 1987

133) _____. "Zhukov." *Kommunist vooruzennych sil* no. 5 (1990): pp. 62–68

134) Keegan, John. *Guderian*. New York, 1973

135) Konecki, Tadeusz, and Ireneusz Ruszkiewicz. *Marsalek dwoch narodow*. Warsaw, 1976

136) Laqueur, Walter. *Stalin. The Glasnost Revelations*. London, 1990 (German edn: Munich, 1990)

136a) Pätzold, Kurt, and Manfred Weißbecker. *Adolf Hitler. Eine politische Biographie*. Leipzig, 1995

137) Medwedew, Roy. *Das Urteil der Geschichte. Stalin und Stalinismus*. 3 vols. Berlin, 1992

138) Mel'nikov, Semen I. *Marsal Rybalko. Vospominanija byvsego clena Voennogo soveta 3-j gvardejskoj tankovoj armii*. Kiev, 1980

139) Mitcham, Samuel W. *Hitler's Field Marshals and Their Battles*. London, 1988; US edn: Chelsea, 1990

140) Morozow, Michael. *Der Georgier. Stalins Weg und Herrschaft*. Munich, 1980

141) Ortenberg, David I. *Marsal Moskalenko*. Kiev, 1984

142) *Heerführer des Großen Vaterländischen Krieges. Zwölf Lebensbilder*. 2 vols. East Berlin, 1978

142a) Pätzold, Kurt, and Manfred Weißbecker. *Adolf Hitler*. Leipzig, 1995

143) *Polkovodcy i voenaacal'niki Velikoj Otecestvennoj. Sbornik*. 2 vols. Moscow, 1971

144) Portugal'skij, R.M. *Marsal I. S. Kanev*. Moscow, 1985

144a) Reschin, Leonid. *General zwischen den Fronten. Walter von Seydlitz in sowjetischer Gefangenschaft und Haft 1943–1955*. Berlin, 1995

144b) _____. *Feldmarschall im Kreuzverhör. Friedrich Paulus in sowjetischer Gefangenschaft 1943–1953*. Berlin, 1996

145) Seaton, Albert. *Stalin as Military Commander*. New York, 1976

146) Shukman, Harold, ed. *Stalin's Generals*. London, 1993

146a) Smelser, Ronald, and Enrico Syring, eds. *Die Militärelite des Dritten Reichs. 27 biographische Skizzen*. Berlin, 1995

147) Sperker, Karl Heinrich. *Generaloberst Erhard Raus. Ein Truppenführer im Ostfeldzug*. Osnabrück, 1988
148) Teske, Hermann, ed. *General Ernst Köstring. Der militärische Mittler zwischen dem Deutschen Reich und der Sowjetunion*. Profile bedeutender Soldaten, vol. 1. Frankfurt, 1965
148a) Ueberschär, Gerd R. *Generaloberst Franz Halder. Generalstabchef, Gegner und Gefangener Hitlers*. Göttingen, 1991
149) Wolkogonow, Dimitri A. *Stalin. Triumph und Tragödie. Ein politisches Porträt*. Düsseldorf, 1989
150) ____. "Stalin als Oberster Befehlshaber." In *Zwei Wege nach Moskau. Vom Hitler-Stalin-Pakt bis zum "Unternehmen Barbarossa"*, edited by Bernd Wegner, pp. 480–497. Munich, 1991
151) Zacharov, J.D. *General armii N. F. Vatutin*. Moscow, 1985

d) Sources and Contemporary Literature

152) *Allen Gewalten zum Trotz. Bilder vom Feldzug im Osten*. Edited by OKW. Berlin, 1942
153) *An Army of Heroes. True Stories of Soviet Fighting Men (1943)*. Moscow, 1944
153a) Bähr, Walter, and Hans Bähr, eds. *Kriegsbriefe gefallener Studenten 1939–1945*. Tübingen, 1952
154) Beinhauer, Eugen, ed. *Artillerie im Osten*. Berlin, 1944
154a) Bock, Generalfeldmarschall Fedor von. *Zwischen Pflicht und Verweigerung. Das Kriegstagebuch*. Edited by Klaus Gerbet. Munich, 1995
155) Didier, Friedrich. *Ich sah den Bolschewismus. Dokumente der Wahrheit gegen die Bolschewistische Lüge. (Thüringer schreiben an ihren Gauleiter und Reichsstatthalter)*. 2nd edn. Weimar, 1942
156) Eichholtz, Dietrich, and Wolfgang Schumann, eds. *Anatomie des Krieges. Neue Dokumente über die Rolle des deutschen Monopolkapitals bei der Vorbereitung und Durchführung des zweiten Weltkrieges*. East Berlin, 1969
157) Förster, G., and O. Groehler, eds. *Der zweite Weltkrieg. Dokumente*. East Berlin, 1974
158) Geisler, P.A. Eugen. *Unser Weg nach Sewastopol. Aus einem Tagebuch*. N.p., 1942
159) Görlitz, Walter, ed. *Generalfeldmarschall Keitel. Verbrecher oder Offizier? Erinnerungen, Briefe, Dokumente des Chefs OKW*. Göttingen, 1961
160) Greiner, Helmuth. *Die oberste Wehrmachtführung 1939–1943*. Wiesbaden, 1951
161) Haferkorn, Hans. *Ostwärts bis Sewastopol. Mit einer Infanterie-Division in Sowjet-Rußland*. Munich, 1943
162) Halder, Franz. *Kriegstagebuch. Tägliche Aufzeichnungen des Chefs des Generalstabes des Heeres 1939–1942*. 3 vols. Stuttgart, 1962–64
163) Hass, Gerhart, and Wolfgang Schumann, eds. *Anatomie der Aggression. Neue Dokumente zu den Kriegszielen des faschistischen deutschen Imperialismus im zweiten Weltkrieg*. East Berlin, 1972
164) Hohoff, Kurt. *Woina – Woina. Russisches Tagebuch*. Düsseldorf, 1951
165) Hubatsch, Walther, ed. *Hitlers Weisungen für die Kriegführung 1939–1945. Dokumente des Oberkommandos der Wehrmacht*. Frankfurt, 1962

166) Jacobsen, Hans-Adolf. *1939–1945. Der Zweite Weltkrieg in Chronik und Dokumenten*. Darmstadt, 1961

167) Jacobsen, Hans-Adolf, ed. *Mißtrauische Nachbarn. Deutsche Ostpolitik 1919/1970. Dokumentation und Analyse*. Düsseldorf, 1970

168) Jochmann, Werner, ed. *Adolf Hitler. Monologe im Führerhauptquartier 1941–1944. Die Aufzeichnungen Heinrich Heims*. Hamburg, 1980

169) *Kampf gegen die Sowjets. Berichte und Bilder vom Beginn des Ostfeldzugs bis zum Frühjahr 1942*. Edited by OKW. Berlin, 1943

170) Kohl, Paul. *"Ich wundere mich, daß ich noch lebe." Sowjetische Augenzeugen berichten*. Gütersloh, 1990

171) Kotze, Hildegard von, ed. *Heeresadjutant bei Hitler 1938–1943. Aufzeichnungen des Majors Engel*. Stuttgart, 1974

172) Krug, Hans Joachim. *Pionierzug Niederegger. Eine Geschichte aus dem Ostfeldzug*. Berlin, 1942

173) *Südlich des Ladogasees. Winter 1943*. Edited by Armee vor Leningrad. Riga, 1943

174) Lammers, Walther, ed. *"Fahrtberichte" aus der Zeit des deutsch-sowjetischen Krieges 1941. Protokolle des Begleitoffiziers des Kommandierenden Generals LIII. Armeekorps*. Boppard, 1988

174a) Leyen, Ferdinand Prinz v.d. *Rückblick zum Mauerwald. Vier Kriegsjahre im OKH*. 2nd edn. Munich, 1966

175) Lucke, Fritz, ed. *Panzerkeil im Osten. Gedenkbuch der Berlin-Märkischen Panzerdivision*. Berlin, 1942

176) Madej, Victor, ed. *Red Army Order-of-Battle. 1941–1943*. Allentown, Pa., 1983

177) Mohrmann, Wolf-Dieter, ed. *Der Krieg hier ist hart und grausam! Feldpostbriefe an den Osnabrücker Regierungspräsidenten 1941–1944*. Osnabrück, 1984

178) Müller, Norbert. "Dokumente zur Rolle der Wehrmacht bei der Deportation sowjetischer Bürger zur Zwangsarbeit in Deutschland 1941–1944." Bulletin des Arbeitskreises 2. Weltkrieg, pp. 29–62. East Berlin, 1970

179) *Nordpfeiler der Ostfront. Berichte von Günther Heysing*. Edited by Armee Lindemann, Propaganda-Kompanie. Berlin, [1943?]

180) *An der mittleren Ostfront. Ein deutsches Korps im Kampf gegen die Sowjets*. Edited by Stellvertretendes Generalkommando des XIII. Armeekorps. Nuremberg, 1942

181) Picker, Henry. *Hitlers Tischgespräche im Führerhauptquartier*. Stuttgart, 1977

182) *Der Prozeß gegen die Hauptkriegsverbrecher vor dem Internationalen Militärgerichtshof (International Military Tribunal= IMT), Nürnberg 14. Oktober 1945–1. Oktober 1946*. Nuremberg, 1947–49

183) Rürup, Reinhard, ed. *Der Krieg gegen die Sowjetunion 1941–1945. Eine Dokumentation*. Berlin, 1991

184) Schramm, Percy Ernst, ed. *Kriegstagebuch des Oberkommandos der Wehrmacht (Wehrmachtführungsstab) 1940–1945*. 4 vols. Frankfurt a.M., 1961–65

185) Slesina, Horst. *Soldaten gegen Tod und Teufel. Unser Kampf in der Sowjetunion. Eine soldat. Deutung*. Düsseldorf, 1943

186) Stalin, Iosif. *O Velikoj Otecestvennoj Vojne Sovetskogo Sojuza*. Moscow, 1946 (German edn: *Über den Großen Vaterländischen Krieg der Sowjetunion*. Moscow, 1946)

187) Strzemiaczny, von. "Der Feldzug gegen Sowjetrußland im Jahre 1941: Die Kämpfe bis Ende Oktober." *Jahrbuch des deutschen Heeres* (1942): pp. 86–118

188) *Die soldatische Tat. Berichte von Mitkämpfern des Heeres*. Edited by Oberkommando des Heeres. Vol. 3, *Der Kampf im Osten 1942/43*. Berlin, 1944

189) *Trials of War Criminals Before the Nuremberg Military Tribunals under Control Council Law No. 10, Nuremberg, October 1946 – April 1949*. Washington, DC, 1950–53

190) Wagner, Elisabeth, ed. *Der Generalquartiermeister. Briefe und Tagebuchaufzeichnungen des Generalquartiermeisters des Heeres, General der Artillerie Eduard Wagner*. Munich, 1963

190a) Wegmann, Günter, ed. *"Das Oberkommando der Wehrmacht gibt bekannt ...". Der deutsche Wehrmachtbericht*. 3 vols., Osnabrück, 1982

e) Personal Accounts and Memoirs (1941–45)

191) Albrecht, Karl I. *Sie aber werden die Welt zerstören ....* Munich, 1954

192) Aleksievic, Svetlana. *Der Krieg hat kein weibliches Gesicht*. Berlin, 1987

193) Altunin, Aleksandr T. *Zvezdy nad Visloj*. Moscow, 1984

194) Andreev, Andrej M. *Ot pervogo mgnovenija do poslednego*. Moscow, 1984

195) Antipenko, Nikolaj A. *Na glavnom Napravlenii*. Moscow, 1967 and 1971 (German edn: *In der Hauptrichtung*. East Berlin, 1973)

196) Archipov, Vasilij S. *Vremja tankovych atak*. Moscow, 1981

197) Babadzanjan, Amazasp Ch. *Dorogi pobedy*. Moscow, 1981 (German edn: Hauptmarschall der Panzertruppen A. Ch. Babadshanjan. *Hauptstoßkraft*. East Berlin, 1985)

198) Bagramjan, Ivan Ch. *Tak nacinalas vojna*. Moscow, 1977 (German edn: *So begann der Krieg*. East Berlin, 1972)

199) _____. *Tak sli my k pobede*. Moscow, 1977 (German edn: *So schritten wir zum Sieg*. East Berlin, 1984)

200) _____. *Moi vospominanija*. Erevan, 1980

201) Batov, Pavel I. *V Pochodach i bojach*. Moscow, 1962 (German edn: *Von der Wolga zur Oder*. East Berlin, 1965)

202) Beloborodov, Afanasij P. *Vsegda v boju*. Moscow, 1978

203) Below, Nicolaus von. *Als Hitlers Adjutant 1937–1945*. Mainz, 1980

204) Birjuzov, Sergej S. *Surovye Gody*. Moscow, 1966

205) Böttger, Armin. *Überstehen war alles. Stationen und Impressionen eines Lebensweges vom Soldaten im Panzer zum Professor der Zahnmedizin*. 2nd edn. Berg am See, 1993 (1st edn: *Durchkommen war alles*)

206) Bragin, Michail. *Ot Moskvy do Berlina. Staty i ocerki voennogo korrespondenta*. Moscow, 1948

207) Braznin, Il'ja Ja. *V Velikoj Otecestvennoj vojny. Zapiski voennogo korrespondenta*. Moscow, 1971

208) Bulatov, Fatych G. *Budni frontovych let. Zapiski generala*. Kazan, 1970

209) Burcev, Michail I. *Einsichten*. East Berlin, 1985

209a) Chaldej, Jewgeni. *Von Moskau nach Berlin*. Edited by Ernst Volland and Heinz Krimmer. Berlin, 1995

210) Chartschenko, V. K. *Zur besonderen Verwendung*. East Berlin, 1985

211) Cujkov, Vasilij I. *Ot Stalingrada do Berlina*. Moscow, 1980, 1985 (German edn: *Gardisten auf dem Weg nach Berlin*. 2nd edn. Berlin, 1980)

212) Degrelle, Leon. *Front de l'est 1941–1945*. Paris, 1969

213) Dragunskij, David A. *Gody v brone*. Moscow, 1973 (German edn: *Jahre im Panzer*. East Berlin, 1980)

214) Eremenko, Andrej I. *Gody vozmezdija 1943–1945*. Moscow, 1969

215) Förster, Gerhard. "Memoiren führender sowjetischer Militärs über den Großen Vaterländischen Krieg der Sowjetunion." *Jahrbuch für Geschichte der sozialistischer Länder Europas* vol. 15, no. 2 (1971): pp. 145–156

216) Fretter-Pico, Maximilian. *Mißbrauchte Infanterie. Deutsche Infanteriedivisionen im osteuropäischen Großraum 1941–1944*. Frankfurt a.M., 1957

217) _____. *"... verlassen von des Sieges Göttern"*. Wiesbaden, 1969

218) Galickij, Kuzma N. *Gody surovych ispytamij 1941–1944. Zapiski komandarma*. Moscow, 1973

219) Giertz, Horst, and S. Jäger. "Memoiren sowjetischer Militärs über den Großen Vaterländischen Krieg der Sowjetunion." *Militärgeschichte* no. 5 (1979): pp. 607ff.

220) Giertz, Horst, and P. Schramm. "Sowjetische Memoirenliteratur über den Großen Vaterländischen Krieg der Sowjetunion. Auswahlbibliographie." *Jahrbuch für Geschichte der sozialistischen Länder Europas* vol. 25, no. 1 (1981): pp. 163ff.

221) Giller, William. *Und wieder in den Kampf*. East Berlin, 1977

222) Golowko, A.A. *Zwischen Spitzbergen und Tiksibucht*. East Berlin, 1986

223) Gorcakov, Petr A. *Vremja trevog i pobed*. 2nd edn. Moscow, 1981

224) Gorjacev, Segrgej Georgievic. *Ot Volgi do Al'p*. Kiev, 1982

225) Gosztony, Peter. "Memoiren russischer Kriegsteilnehmer (1941–1945)." In *Jahresbibliogaphie der Bibliothek für Zeitgeschichte Stuttgart* vol. 44, 1972, pp. 535–558. Frankfurt a.M., 1973

226) Grossmann, Vasilij. *The Years of War (1941–1945)*. Moscow, 1946

227) Grunert, Hansheinrich. *Der zerrissene Soldat*. Berlin, 1962

228) Guderian, Heinz. *Erinnerungen eines Soldaten*. 15th edn. Stuttgart, 1996

229) Halder, Franz. *Hitler als Feldherr*. Munich, 1949

230) Hamm, Johann Anton. *Als Priester in Rußland. Ein Tagebuch (1941–1944)*. 2nd edn. Trier, 1960

231) Herwarth, Hans von. *Zwischen Hitler und Stalin. Erlebte Zeitgeschichte 1931 bis 1945*. Frankfurt, 1982

232) Heusinger, Adolf. *Befehl im Wiederstreit. Schicksalsstunden der deutschen Armee 1923–1945*. Tübingen, 1950

233) Jakubovskij, Ivan I. *Zemlja v ogne*. Moscow, 1975 (German edn: Jakubowski, Iwan. *Erde im Feuer*. East Berlin, 1977)

234) Kageneck, August von. *Lieutenant sous la Tête de Mort*. Paris, 1968

235) Kalasnik, Michail Ch. *Ispytanie ognem*. Moscow, 1978

236) Kalinow, Kyrill D. *Sowjetmarschälle haben das Wort*. Hamburg, 1950

237) Katukov, Michail E. *Na Ostrie glavnogo udara*. Moscow, 1974 (German edn: Katukow, Michail. *An der Spitze des Hauptstoßes*. East Berlin, 1979)

238) Katyskin, Ivan S. *Sluzili my v stabe armejskom*. Moscow, 1979

239) Kazakov, Konstantin P. *Artillerijskij Grom*. Moscow, 1978

240) Kernmayr, Hans G. *Wir waren keine Banditen*. Düsseldorf, 1952

241) Killian, Hans. *Im Schatten der Siege. Chirurg am Ilmenseee 1941–1942–1943*. Munich, 1964

242) Kondrat'ev, Zachar I. *Dorogi vojny*. Moscow, 1968 (German edn: *Straßen des Krieges*. East Berlin, 1981)
243) Konev, Ivan S. *Zapiski komandujuscego frontom. 1943–1944*. Moscow, 1972 (German edn: Konew, Iwan S. *Aufzeichnungen eines Frontoberbefehlshabers 1943/44*. Berlin, 1978; English edn: *Year of Victory*. Moscow, 1969)
244) Kosevoj, Petr K. *V Gody voennye*. Moscow, 1978
245) Krajnjukov, Konstantin Vasilevic. *Oruzie osobogo roda*. Moscow, 1977
246) Kuznecov, Nikolaj Gerasimovic. *Na flotach boevaja Trevoga, 1941/42*. Moscow, 1971
247) ____. *Auf Siegeskurs*. East Berlin, 1979
248) Lanz, Hubert. *Wie es zum Rußlandfeldzug kam und warum wir ihn verloren haben. Studie*. Munich, 1971
249) Leljusenko, Dimitrij D. *Moskva – Stalingrad – Berlin – Praga. Zapiski Komandarma*. Moscow, 1970; 2nd edn 1973; 3rd edn 1975; 4th edn 1985
250) Leonhard, Wolfgang. *Die Revolution entläßt ihre Kinder*. Cologne, 1955
251) Loßberg, Bernhard von. *Im Wehrmachtführungsstab. Bericht eines Generalstabsoffiziers*. 2nd edn. Hamburg, 1950
252) Erickson, John, ed. *Main Front. Soviet Leaders Look Back on World War II*. London, 1987
253) Manstein, Erich von. *Verlorene Siege*. Bonn, 1955
254) Mende, Erich. *Das verdammte Gewissen. Zeuge der Zeit 1921–1945*. 2nd edn. Munich, 1983
255) Mereckov, Kirill A. *Na Sluzbe naroda. Stranicy vospominanij*. Moscow, 1968 (German edn: *Im Dienste des Volkes*. East Berlin, 1972)
256) Metelmann, Henry. *Through Hell for Hitler. A Dramatic First-Hand Account of Fighting with the Wehrmacht*. Wellingborough, 1990
257) Miranov, W. B. *Die stählerne Garde*. East Berlin, 1986
258) Moskalenko, Kirill S. *Na jugozapadnom Napravlenii. Vospominanija komandarma*. 2 vols. Moscow, 1969–1972 (German edn: *In der Südwestrichtung*. East Berlin, 1979)
259) Pabst, Helmut. *Der Ruf der äußersten Grenze. Tagebuch eines Frontsoldaten*. Tübingen, 1953; new edn: *Der Ruf der äußersten Grenze. Aufzeichnungen aus dem Kriege. Rußland 1941–1943*. Die graue Reihe, vol. 5. Heidenheim, 1987
260) Perau, Josef. *Priester im Heere Hitlers. Erinnerungen 1940–1945*. Essen, 1962
261) Petrow, Wasilij S. *Kanoniere*. East Berlin, 1986
262) Pliev, Issa A. *Pod gvardejskim Znamenem*. Ordzonikidze, 1976
263) Remmer, A., and P. Brunkert. *Abseits der Rollbahn. Russische Impressionen 1942/43*. 2nd edn. Husum, 1987
264) Rokossovskij, Konstantin K. *Soldatskij Dolg*. Moscow, 1968 (German edn: *Soldatenpflicht. Erinnerungen eines Frontoberbefehlshabers*. East Berlin, 1971, 1973; English edn: *A Soldier's Duty*. Moscow, 1970)
265) Sausin, Fedor S. *Chleb nas soldatskij*. Moscow, 1980 (German edn: *Soldatenbrot*. East Berlin, 1984)
266) Sceglov, D. A. *Nebel über der Newa. Aufzeichnungen eines Freiwilligen*. East Berlin, 1964
267) Schramm, Peter. "Sowjetische Memoirenliteratur über den Großen Vaterländischen Krieg der Sowjetunion. Auswahlbibliographie."

Militärgeschichte vol. 20, no. 3 (1981): pp. 356–365
Schukow, see Zukov

268) Siewert, Curt. *Schuldig? Die Generale unter Hitler*. Bad Mergentheim, 1968

269) Simonow, Konstantin. *Kriegstagebücher*. 2 vols. Munich, 1979

270) Stemenko, Sergej M. *General'nyj Stab v gody vojny*. Moscow, 1968–1973 (German edn: Schtemenko, S.M. *Im Generalstab*. 2 vols. 3rd edn. East Berlin, 1971; English edn: Shtemenko, S. *The Soviet General Staff at War 1941–1945*. Moscow, 1970)

271) Talbott, Strobe, ed. *Khrushchev Remembers*. Boston, 1970 (German edn: *Chruschtschow erinnert sich. Die authentischen Memoiren*. Reinbek bei Hamburg, 1992)

272) Vasilevskij, Aleksandr M. *Delo vsej zizni*. Moscow, 1973 (German edn: Wassilewski, A. *Sache des ganzen Lebens*. East Berlin, 1977)

273) Vaupsasov, Stanislav A. *Na trevoziych Perekrestkach*. Moscow 1977 (German edn: Waupschassow, S. *Vierzig Jahre in der sowjetischen Aufklärung*. Moscow, 1978)

274) Virski, Fred. *My Life in the Red Army*. New York, 1949

275) Volosin, Maksim A. *Razvedciki vsegda vperedi*. Moscow, 1977 (German edn: Woloschin, M.A. *Aufklärer sind immer vorn*. East Berlin, 1984)

276) Warlimont, Walter. *Im Hauptquartier der deutschen Wehrmacht 1939–1945. Grundlagen, Formen, Gestalten*. Frankfurt a.M., 1964

277) Wette, Wolfram. "'Es roch nach Ungeheuerlichem.' Zeitzeugenbericht eines Panzerschützen über die Stimmung in einer Einheit des deutschen Ostheeres am Vorabend des Überfalls auf die Sowjetunion 1941." *1999* vol. 4 (1989): pp. 62–73

278) Zadov, Aleksej S. *Cetyre Goda vojny*. Moscow, 1978

279) Zukov, Georgij K. *Vospominanija i razmyslenija*. Moscow, 1969; 2nd edn in 2 vols, 1974; 3rd edn in 3 vols, 1988 (East German edn: Shukow, G.K. *Erinnerungen und Gedanken*. 2 vols. 5th edn. East Berlin, 1976; West German edn: Schukow, G.K. *Erinnerungen und Gedanken*. Stuttgart, 1969; English edn: *Reminiscences and Reflections*. 2 vols. Moscow, 1985)

280) _____, (Zhukov). *Marshal Zhukov's Greatest Battles*. New York, 1969

281) Zukov, Jurij A. *Ljudi 40-ch godov: Zapiski voennogo korrespondenta*. Moscow, 1990

2. Planning, Preparations, and Armaments for "Operation Barbarossa"

282) Anderle, Alfred. "Der Weg zum 22. Juni 1941." In *Juni 1941. Beiträge zur Geschichte des hitlerfaschistischen Überfalls auf die Sowjetunion*, edited by Alfred Anderle and Werner Basler, pp. 9–43. East Berlin, 1961

282a) Barros, James, and Richard Gregor. *Double Deception. Stalin, Hitler and the Invasion of Russia*. Dekalb, Ill., 1995

283) Becker, Fritz. *Im Kampf um Europa: Stalins Schachzüge gegen Deutschland und den Westen*. Graz, 1991

284) Beer, Albert. "Der Fall Barbarossa. Untersuchungen zur Geschichte der Vorbereitungen des deutschen Feldzuges gegen die Union der

Sozialistischen Sowjetrepubliken im Jahre 1941." Diss., Univ. Münster, 1978

285) Blau, George E. *The German Campaign in Russia. Planning and Operations 1940–42*. Department of the Army, VIII. Washington, 1955

286) Brühl, Reinhard. "Zur Vorbereitung des Überfalls des faschistischen deutschen Imperialismus auf die Sowjetunion." *Zeitschrift für Militärgeschichte* vol. 10, no. 5 (1971): pp. 531–546

287) Busse, Hans. "Die faschistische Lüge vom Präventivkrieg Hitlerdeutschlands gegen die UdSSR." In *Juni 1941. Beiträge zur Geschichte des hitlerfaschistischen Überfalls auf die Sowjetunion*, edited by Alfred Anderle and Werner Basler, pp. 83–101. East Berlin, 1961

288) Cecil, Robert. *Hitlers Decision to Invade Russia*. London, 1975 (German edn: *Hitlers Griff nach Rußland*. Graz, 1977)

289) "A Collection of Combat Documents Covering the First Three Days of the Great Patriotic War." *The Journal of Soviet Military Studies* vol. 4, no. 1 (1991): pp. 150–189

290) "A Collection of Combat Documents Covering Soviet Western Front Operation, 24–30 June 1941." *The Journal of Soviet Military Studies* vol. 4, no. 2 (1991): pp. 327–385

291) Danilow, Walerij. "Hat der Generalstab der Roten Armee einen Präventivschlag gegen Deutschland vorbereitet?" *Österreichische Militärische Zeitschrift* vol. 31, no. 1 (1993): pp. 41–51

292) Deist, Wilhelm. "Die militärische Planung des 'Unternehmens Barabarossa'." In *"Unternehmen Barbarossa". Zum historischen Ort der deutsch-sowjetischen Beziehungen von 1933 bis Herbst 1941*, edited by Roland G. Foerster, pp. 109–122. Munich, 1993

293) Erickson, John. "Kriegsvorbereitungen der Sowjetunion 1940/41." In *Probleme des Zweiten Weltkrieges*, edited by Andreas Hillgruber, pp. 75–99. Cologne, 1967

294) *Fall Barbarossa. Dokumente zur Vorbereitung der faschistischen Wehrmacht auf die Aggression gegen die Sowjetunion (1940/1941).* Compiled and introduced by Erhard Moritz. Berlin, 1970

295) Fleischhauer, Ingeborg. *Der Widerstand gegen den Rußlandfeldzug*. Berlin, 1987

296) Förster, Gerhard, et al. "Der Barbarossa-Plan in Politik und Kriegführung Hitler-Deutschlands 1939/41." *Zeitschrift für Geschichtswissenschaft* vol. 7 (1959): pp. 529–552

297) Fomin, Vasilij T. *Fasistskaja Germanija vo vtoroj mirovoj vojne. Sentjabr 1939 g.–ijun 1941 g.* Moscow, 1978

298) Furlani, Silvio. "Pripjet-Problem und Barbarossa-Planung." *Beiträge zur Zeitgeschichte*. Festschrift Ludwig Jedlicka zum 60. Geburtstag (1976): pp. 281–297

299) Gibbons, Robert Joseph. "Opposition gegen 'Barbarossa' im Herbst 1940. Eine Denkschrift aus der deutschen Botschaft in Moskau." *Vierteljahrshefte zur Zeitgeschichte* vol. 23 (1975): pp. 332–340

300) Göpfert, Helmut. "Die militärische Vorbereitung des faschistischen Überfalls auf die Sowjetunion." *Zeitschrift für Geschichtswissenschaft* vol. 14, no. 2 (1966): pp. 1092–1116

301) Gorodetsky, Gabriel. "Stalin und Hitlers Angriff auf die Sowjetunion." In *Zwei Wege nach Moskau. Vom Hitler-Stalin-Pakt bis zum*

"Unternehmen Barbarossa", edited by Bernd Wegner, pp. 347–366. Munich, 1991

302) Gorlow, S.A. "Warnungen aus dem 'Unternehmen Barbarossa'. Aus den Akten der Sowjetvertretung in Berlin 1940–1941." *Osteuropa* vol. 41 (1991): p. 545–561

303) Groehler, Olaf. "Zur Einschätzung der Roten Armee durch die faschistische Wehrmacht im ersten Halbjahr 1941, dargestellt am Beispiel AOK 4." *Zeitschrift für Militärgeschichte* vol. 7 (1968): pp. 724–738

304) ____. "Ziele und Vernunft: Hitler und die deutschen Militärs." In *Operation "Barbarossa": The German Attack on the Soviet Union, June 22, 1941*, edited by Norman Naimark et al., pp. 59–77. Special issue of *Soviet Union*, vol. 18, nos. 1–3. Salt Lake City, Utah, 1991

305) Hagen, Mark von. "Soviet Soldiers and Officers on the Eve of the German Invasion: Towards a Description of Social Psychology and Political Attitudes." In *Operation "Barbarossa": The German Attack on the Soviet Union, June 22, 1941*, edited by Norman Naimark et al., pp. 79–101. Special issue of *Soviet Union*, vol. 18, nos. 1–3. Salt Lake City, Utah, 1991

306) Hass, Gerhart. "Der deutsch-sowjetische Krieg 1941–1945. Zu einigen Legenden über seine Vorgeschichte und den Verlauf der ersten Kriegswochen." *Zeitschrift für Geschichtswissenschaft* vol. 39 (1991): pp. 647–662

307) Helmdach, Erich. *Überfall? Der sowjetisch-deutsche Aufmarsch 1941*. Neckargemünd, 1975; 2nd edn 1976

308) Heydorn, Volker Detlef. *Der sowjetische Aufmarsch in Bialystoker Balkon bis zum 22. Juni 1941 und der Kessel von Wolkowysk*. Munich, 1989

309) Hillgruber, Andreas. "Das Rußland-Bild der führenden deutschen Militärs vor Beginn des Angriffs auf die Sowjetunion." In *Rußland-Deutschland-Amerika. Festschrift für Fritz T. Epstein zum 80. Geburtstag*, edited by Alexander Fischer, Günter Moltmann and Klaus Schwabe, pp. 296–310. Wiesbaden, 1978

310) ____. *Hitlers Strategie. Politik und Kriegführung 1940–1941*. Frankfurt, 1965; 2nd edn 1982

311) ____. "Noch einmal: Hitlers Wendung gegen die Sowjetunion 1940. Nicht (Militär-) 'Strategie oder Ideologie', sondern 'Programm' und 'Weltkriegsstrategie'." *Geschichte in Wissenschaft und Unterricht* vol. 33 (1982): pp. 214–226

312) Höhn, Hans, ed. *Auf antisowjetischem Kriegskurs. Studien zur militärischen Vorbereitung des deutschen Imperialismus auf die Aggression gegen die UdSSR (1933–1941)*. Berlin, 1970

313) Hoffmann, Joachim. "Die Angriffsvorbereitungen der Sowjetunion 1941." In *Zwei Wege nach Moskau. Vom Hitler-Stalin-Pakt bis zum "Unternehmen Barbarossa"*, edited by Bernd Wegner, pp. 367–388. Munich, 1991

314) Kampe, Hans-Georg. "Die fernmeldetechnische Sicherstellung des faschistischen Überfalls auf die Sowjetunion." *Militärgeschichte* vol. 20, no. 3 (1981): pp. 295–315

315) Kirsin, Jurij J. "Die sowjetischen Streitkräfte am Vorabend des Großen Vaterländischen Krieges." In *Zwei Wege nach Moskau. Vom Hitler-Stalin-Pakt bis zum "Unternehmen Barbarossa"*, edited by Bernd Wegner, pp. 389–403. Munich, 1991

316) Klee, Karl. "Zur Vorgeschichte des Rußlandfeldzuges." *Wehrwissenschaftliche Rundschau* vol. 2, no. 12 (1952): pp. 577–587

317) Klein, Friedhelm, and Ingo Lachnit. "Der 'Operationsentwurf Ost' des Generalmajors Marcks vom 5. August 1940." *Wehrforschung* vol. 4 (1972): pp. 114–123

318) Klink, Ernst. "Die militärische Konzeption des Krieges gegen die Sowjetunion." In *Das Deutsche Reich und der Zweite Weltkrieg*. Vol. 4, *Der Angriff auf die Sowjetunion*, pp. 190–326. Stuttgart, 1983

319) _____. "Die Operationsführung." In *Das Deutsche Reich und der Zweite Weltkrieg*. Vol. 4, *Der Angriff auf die Sowjetunion*, pp. 451–652. Stuttgart, 1983

320) Klee, Karl. "Zur Vorgeschichte des Rußlandfeldzuges." *Wehrwissenschaftliche Rundschau* vol. 2 (1952): pp. 577–587

321) Kluever, Max. *Präventivschlag 1941. Zur Vorgeschichte des Rußlandfeldzuges*. Leoni am Starnberger See, 1986

322) Knoll, Werner. "Kriegsspiele der faschistischen Wehrmachtführung zur Vorbereitung des Überfalls auf die UdSSR." *Militärgeschichte* vol. 20 (1981): pp. 495–478

323) Lachnit, Ingo. "Das 'Unternehmen Barbarossa'. Die strategische Konzeption des Rußlandfeldzuges 1941." *Damals* vol. 4, no. 7 (1972): pp. 591–609

324) Lakowski, Richard. "Zwischen Professionalismus und Nazismus: die Wehrmacht des Dritten Reiches vor dem Überfall auf die UdSSR." In *Zwei Wege nach Moskau. Vom Hitler-Stalin-Pakt bis zum "Unternehmen Barbarossa"*, edited by Bernd Wegner, pp.149–166. Munich, 1991

325) Leach, Barry A. *A German Stategy against Russia. 1939–1941*. Oxford, 1973

326) Magenheimer, Heinz H. "Der deutsche Angriff auf Sowjetrußland 1941. Das operative Problem und Ablauf des Feldzuges." Diss., Univ. of Vienna, 1969

327) _____. "Der deutsche Angriff auf Sowjetrußland 1941." *Österreichische Militärische Zeitschrift* vol. 9, no. 3 (1971): pp. 157–164

328) Mercalov, Andrej N. "Der 22. Juni 1941: Anmerkungen eines sowjetischen Historikers." *Aus Politik und Zeitgeschichte. Beilage zur Wochenzeitung Das Parlament* No. 24 (1991): pp. 25–36

329) Mitrafanova, A.V., ed. *Ural – frontu*. Moscow, 1985

330) Moritz, Erhard. *Fall Barbarossa. Dokumente zur Vorbereitung der faschistischen Wehrmacht auf die Aggression gegen die Sowjetunion*. East Berlin, 1970

331) _____. "Die Einschätzung der Roten Armee durch den faschistischen Generalstab 1935 bis 1941." *Zeitschrift für Militärgeschichte* vol. 6 (1969): pp. 154–170

332) Müller, Norbert. "Zur Rolle der Wehrmachtführung bei der Planung und Vorbereitung des faschistischen Okkupationsregimes in den besetzten sowjetischen Gebieten." *Zeitschrift für Militärgeschichte* vol. 6 (1967): pp. 415–431

333) Murr, S. *Die Nacht vor Barbarossa*. Munich, 1986

334) Paulus, Wilhelm-Ernst. *Die Entwicklung der Planung des Rußlandfeldzuges 1940/41*. Phil. Diss, Univ. Bonn, 1956

335) Philippi, Alfred. "Das Pripjetproblem. Eine Studie über die operative Bedeutung des Pripjetgebietes für den Feldzug des Jahres 1941." *Wehrwissenschaftliche Rundschau* Beiheft 2 (March 1956)

336) Pietrow-Ennker, Bianka. "Deutschland im Juni 1941 – ein Opfer sowjetischer Aggression? Zur Kontroverse über die Präventivkriegsthese." In *Der Zweite Weltkrieg. Analysen, Grundzüge, Forschungsbilanzen*, edited by Wolfgang Michalka, pp. 586–607. Munich, 1989

336a) Post, Walter. *Unternehmen Barbarossa. Deutsche und sowjetische Angriffspläne 1940/41*. Hamburg, 1995

337) Rotundo, Louis. "War Plans and the 1941 Kremlin Wargame." *The Journal of Strategic Studies* vol. 10, no. 1 (1987): pp. 84–97

338) Schafranek, Hans, and Robert Streibel, eds. *22. Juni 1941. Der Überfall auf die Sowjetunion*. Vienna, 1991

339) Schmidt, Rainer F. "Eine verfehlte Strategie für alle Fälle. Stalins Taktik und Kalkül im Vorfeld des Unternehmens 'Barbarossa'." *Geschichte in Wissenschaft und Unterricht* vol. 16, no. 6 (1994): pp. 368–379

340) Schustereit, Hartmut. *Vabanque: Hitlers Angriff auf die Sowjetunion 1941 als Versuch, durch den Sieg im Osten den Westen zu bezwingen*. Herford, 1988

341) Seraphim, Hans-Günther. "Hitlers Entschluß zum Angriff auf Rußland (Eine Entgegnung)." *Vierteljahrshefte für Zeitgeschichte* vol. 2, no. 3 (1954): pp. 240–254

342) Shilin, P. A. "Die Rolle des deutschen Generalstabes bei der Vorbereitung des Krieges gegen die UdSSR." In *Der deutsche Imperialismus und der zweite Weltkrieg*. Vol. 1, pp. 87–111 vol. 2, pp. 685–707. East Berlin, 1960

343) Slutsch, Sergej. " Der 22. Juni 1941 und die Frage nach dem Eintritt der Sowjetunion in den Zweiten Weltkrieg." In *22. Juni 1941. Der Überfall auf die Sowjetunion*, edited by Hans Schafranek and Robert Streibel, pp. 53–61. Vienna, 1991

344) Solovev, Sergej P. *Zamysly i plany. Obzor voennogo planirovanija nemecko-fasistskogo generalnogo Staba*. Moscow, 1964

345) Starkow, Oleg. "Militärischer Geheimnisverrat am Vorabend von 1941 'Barbarossa'." *Österreichische Militärische Zeitschrift* vol. 29, no. 4 (1991): pp. 327–330

346) Stegemann, Bernd. "Der Entschluß zum Unternehmen Barbarossa. Strategie oder Ideologie?" *Geschichte in Wissenschaft und Unterricht* vol. 33, no. 4 (1982): pp. 205–213

347) _____. "Geschichte und Politik. Zur Diskussiion über den deutschen Angriff auf die Sowjetunion 1941." *Beiträge zur Konfliktforschung* vol. 17, no. 1 (1987): pp. 73–97

348) Stolfi, Russel. "Barbarossa. German Grand Deception and the Achievment of Strategic and Tactical Surprise against the Soviet Union, 1940–1941." In *Strategic Military Deception*, edited by Donald C. Daniel, pp. 195–223. New York, 1982

349) Suvorov (Suworow), Victor. *Ledokol. Istorija tak nazyvaemoj "Velikoj Otecestvennoj vojny". Kratkij kurs*. Paris, 1989 (German edn: *Der Eisbrecher. Hitler in Stalins Kalkül*. Stuttgart, 1989; English edn: *Icebreaker. Who Started the Second World War?* London, 1990)

349a) Suworow, Viktor. *Der Tag M*. Stuttgart, 1995

350) Tippelskirch, Kurt von. "Hitlers Kriegsführung nach dem Frankreichfeldzug im Hinblick auf 'Barbarossa'." *Wehrwissenschaftliche Rundschau* vol. 4 (1954): pp. 145–156
351) Topitsch, Ernst. *Stalins Krieg. Die sowjetische Langzeitstrategie gegen den Westen als rationale Machtpolitik*. Munich, 1985; new edn: *Stalins Krieg. Moskaus Griff nach der Weltherrschaft – Strategie und Scheitern*. Herford, 1993; English edn: *Stalin's War. A Radical New Theory of the Origins of the Second World War*. New York, 1987
352) Ueberschär, Gerd R. "Die Einbeziehung Skandinaviens in die Planung 'Barbarossa'." In *Das Deutsche Reich und der Zweite Weltkrieg*. Vol. 4, *Der Angriff auf die Sowjetunion*, pp. 365–412. Stuttgart, 1983
353) ____. "Hitlers Entschluß zum 'Lebensraum'-Krieg im Osten. Programmatisches Ziel oder militärstrategisches Kalkül?" In *Der deutsche Überfall auf die Sowjetunion 1941. Berichte, Analysen, Dokumente*, edited by Gerd R. Ueberschär and Wolfram Wette, pp. 83–110. Paderborn, 1984
354) ____. "'Der Pakt mit dem Satan, um den Teufel auszutreiben.' Der deutsch-sowjetische Nichtangiffsvertrag und Hitlers Kriegsabsicht gegen die UdSSR." In *Der Zweite Weltkrieg. Analysen, Grundzüge, Forschungsbilanzen*, edited by Wolfgang Michalka, pp. 568–585. Munich, 1989
355) Uhlig, Heinrich. "Das Einwirken Hitlers auf Planung und Führung des Ostfeldzuges." In *Vollmacht des Gewissens*, edited by Europäische Publikation e.V., vol. 2, pp. 147–286. Frankfurt a.M., 1965
356) Wegner, Bernd. ed. *Zwei Wege nach Moskau. Vom Hitler-Stalin-Pakt zum "Unternehmen Barbarossa"*. Munich, 1991
357) Weinberg, Gerhard L. "Der deutsche Entschluß zum Angriff auf die Sowjetunion." *Vierteljahrshefte für Zeitgeschichte* vol. 1, no. 4 (1955): pp. 301–318
358) Zapantis, Andrew L. *Hitler's Balkan Campaign and the Invasion of the USSR*. Irvington, 1987
359) Zhilin, P. *They Sealed Their Own Doom*. Moscow, 1970

3. The Attack and Campaign of 1941

360) Afanasev, Nikolaj M. *Pervye Zalpy*. Moscow, 1967
361) Alescenko, Nikolaj M. *Oni zasciscali Odessu*. Moscow, 1970
362) Anfilov, Viktor A. *Nacalo Velikoj Otecestvennoj Vojny (22 ijunja–seredina ijulja 1941 goda). Voenno-istoric. ocerk*. Moscow, 1962
363) ____. *Proval "blickriga"*. Moscow, 1974
364) ____. *Nezabyvaemyj Sorok pervyj*. Moscow, 1982
365) Arendt, Hans-Jürgen, and Jörg Kretschmer. "Der Überfall auf die UdSSR 1941. Aus dem Kriegstagebuch des deutschen Soldaten Hans Wolf." *Zeitschrift für Geschichtswissenschaft* vol. 39 (1991): pp. 587–597
366) Azarov, Il'ja I. *Osazdennaja Odessa*. Odessa, 1975
367) Bagramjan, Ivan Ch. *Gorod-voin na Dnepre*. Moscow, 1965
368) ____. *Tak nacinalas vojna*. Moscow, 1977 (German edn: *So begann der Krieg*. East Berlin, 1972)

369) Ben-Arie, Katriek. "La chute de Brest-Litovsk (1941)." *Guerres Mondiales et Conflits Contemporains* vol. 37, no. 146 (1987): pp. 71–96
370) Bethell, Nicholas. *Russia Besieged*. Alexandria, 1977 (German edn: *Der Angriff auf Rußland*. Amsterdam, 1980, 1981)
371) Boog, Horst, et al. *Der Angriff auf die Sowjetunion*. Vol. 4 of *Das Deutsche Reich und der Zweite Weltkrieg*. Stuttgart, 1983; new paperback edn Frankfurt a.M., 1991 (English edn: *Germany and the Second World War*. Vol. 4. Oxford, 1997)
372) *Bug v ogne*. Edited by A.A. Krupennikov et al. Minsk, 1970
373) Busse, Hans. "Das Scheitern des Operationsplanes 'Barbarossa' im Sommer 1941 und die militaristische Legende von der 'Führungskrise'." *Zeitschrift für Militärgeschichte* vol. 1 (1962): pp. 62–83
374) *Operations in 1941*. In *The German Campaign in Russsia. Planning and Operations 1940–42*, by George E. Blau, pp. 44–90. Washington, 1955
375) Carell, Paul [Paul K. Schmidt]. *Unternehmen Barbarossa. Der Marsch nach Rußland*. Frankfurt a.M., 1963
376) Chales de Beaulieu, Walter. "Sturm bis vor Moskaus Tore. Der Einsatz der Panzergruppe 4." *Wehrwissenschaftliche Rundschau* vol. 6 (1956): pp. 345–365, 432–439
377) Chor'kov, Anatolij G. "Die Rote Armee in der Anfangsperiode des Großen Vaterländischen Krieges." In *Zwei Wege nach Moskau. Vom Hitler-Stalin-Pakt bis zum "Unternehmen Barbarossa"*, edited by Bernd Wegner, pp. 425–442. Munich, 1991
378) ____. "Die Anfangsphase des Krieges – das Jahr 1941." In *"Unternehmen Barbarossa". Zum historischen Ort der deutsch-sowjetischen Beziehungen von 1933 bis Herbst 1941*, edited by Roland G. Foerster, pp. 137–150. Munich, 1993
379) Cox, Goffrey. *The Red Army Moves*. London, 1941
380) Creveld, Martin van. "The German Attack on the USSR. The Destruction of a Legend." *European Studies Review* vol. 2 (1972): pp. 69–86
381) Czollek, Roswitha, and Dietrich Eichholtz. "Die deutschen Monopole und der 22. Juni 1941. Dokumente zu Kriegszielen und Kriegsplanung führender Konzerne beim Überfall auf die Sowjetunion." *Zeitschrift für Geschichtswissenschaft* vol. 15 (1967): pp. 64–76
382) Czollek, Roswitha, and Dietrich Eichholtz. "Zur wirtschaftspolitischen Konzeption des deutschen Imperialismus beim Überfall auf die Sowjetunion. Aufbau und Zielsetzung des staatsmonopolistischen Apparats für den faschistischen Beute- und Vernichtungskrieg." *Jahrbuch für Wirtschaftsgeschichte* vol. 1 (1968): pp. 141–181
383) Dallin, Alexander. "Stalin and the German Invasion." In *Operation Barbarossa. The German Attack on the Soviet Union, June 22, 1941*, edited by Norman Naimark et al., pp. 19–37. Special Issue of *Soviet Union*, vol. 18, nos. 1–3. Salt Lake City, Utah, 1991
384) Drechsler, Karl, et al. *Deutschland im Zweiten Weltkrieg*. Vol. 2, *Vom Überfall auf die Sowjetunion bis zur sowjetischen Gegenoffensive bei Stalingrad (Juni 1941 bis November 1942)*. East Berlin, 1975
385) Dupays, Paul. *Genre nouveau de Blitzkrieg. Chronique historique URSS et autres événements imposants en août et septembre 1941*. London, 1946
386) Eremenko, Andrej I. *V Nacale vojny*. Moscow, 1964

387) Evstigneev, Vladimir N. *70 geroiceskich Dnej. Kratkij istoric. ocerk oborony Odessy*. Moscow, 1964
388) Forstmeier, Friedrich. *Odessa 1941. Der Kampf um Stadt und Hafen. 15. August–16. Oktober 1941*. Freiburg, 1967
389) Fugate, Brian I. *Operation Barbarossa. Strategy and Tactics on the Eastern Front, 1941*. Novato, 1984
390) Glantz, David M., ed. *The Initial Period of War on the Eastern Front, 22 June–August 1941*. London, 1993
391) Göpfert, Helmut. "Zur Anfangsperiode des faschistschen Überfalls auf die Sowjetunion." *Zeitschrift für Militärgeschichte* vol. 4, no. 2 (1965): pp. 161–173
392) _____. "Das Scheitern des Blitzkrieges der faschistischen Wehrmacht an der deutsch-sowjetischen Front." In *Das Fiasko der antisowjetischen Aggression. Studien zur Kriegführung gegen die UdSSR (1941–1945)*, edited by Erhard Moritz, pp. 45–73. East Berlin, 1978
393) Grigorenko, Pjotr. K. *Der sowjetische Zusammenbruch, 1941*. Frankfurt a.M., 1969
394) Harrison, Mark. "'Barbarossa': Die sowjetische Antwort, 1941." In *Zwei Wege nach Moskau. Vom Hitler-Stalin-Pakt bis zum "Unternehmen Barbarossa"*, edited by Bernd Wegner, Bernd, pp. 443–463. Munich, 1991
395) Hatzfeld, Lutz. *Vormarsch Anno 41*. Parts 1–4. Düsseldorf, 1975–78
396) Haupt, Werner. *Baltikum 1941. Die Geschichte eines ungelösten Problems*. Neckargemünd, 1963
397) _____. *Kiew – die größte Kesselschlacht der Geschichte (1941)*. Bad Nauheim, 1964, 1980
398) _____. *Die Deutschen vor Moskau 1941/1942. Bildchronik einer Schlacht der verfehlten Strategie*. Dorheim, 1972
399) Higgins, Trumbull. *Hitler and Russia. The Third Reich in a Two-Front War, 1937–1943*. New York, 1966
400) Hillgruber, Andreas. *Der Zenit des Zweiten Weltkrieges, Juli 1941*. Wiesbaden, 1977
401) Hoffmann, Joachim. "Die Kriegsführung aus der Sicht der Sowjetunion." In *Das Deutsche Reich und der Zweite Weltkrieg*. Vol. 4, *Der Angriff auf die Sowjetunion*, pp. 713–809. Stuttgart, 1983
402) Hofmann, Rudolf. "Die Schlacht von Moskau 1941." In *Entscheidungsschlachten des Zweiten Weltkrieges*, edited by Hans Adolf Jacobsen and Jürgen Rohwer, pp. 139–184. Frankfurt a.M., 1960
403) Hoth, Hermann. *Panzer-Operationen. Die Panzergruppe 3 und der operative Gedanke der deutschen Führung Sommer 1941*. Heidelberg, 1956
404) Irving, David. *Hitler's War*. London, 1977 (German edn: *Hitlers Krieg. Die Siege 1939–1942*. Munich, 1983)
405) Jackson, W. *Seven Roads to Moscow. A Study of the Military Invasions of Russia*. London, 1957
406) *Juni 1941. Beiträge zur Geschichte des hitlerfaschistischen Überfalls auf die Sowjetunion*. Editorial staff: Alfred Anderle and Werner Basler. Veröffentlichungen des Instituts für Geschichte der Völker der UdSSR, Reihe B, Abhandlungen, vol. 2. East Berlin, 1961
407) Keegan, John. *Barbarossa: Invasion of Russia, 1941*. New York, 1971
408) Kieler, Heinz J. *Noch ist es Tag. Rußland 1941/42*. Witten, 1955

408a) Kipp, Jacob W. *Barbarossa, Soviet Covering Forces and Initial Period of the War: Military History and the Airland Battle*. Fort Leavenworth, Kan., 1987

409) Klapdor, Ewald. *Der Ostfeldzug 1941 – eine vorprogrammierte Niederlage? Die Panzergruppe 1 zwischen Bug und Don*. Siek, 1989

410) Konecki, T. *Sewastopol: 1941–1942, 1944*. Warsaw, 1987

411) Korol'kov, J. *V Katakombach Odessy. Dokumental'naja povest'*. Moscow, 1968

412) *Wir erobern die Krim. Soldaten der Krim-Armee berichten*. Neustadt a.d.Weinstraße, 1943

413) Krupennikov, A.A., et al. *Brestskaja Krepost'. Putevoditel' po mestam boev*. Izd. 4., ispravl. Minsk, 1964

414) Krylov, Nikolaj I. *Ne pomerket nikogda. (Zapiski ob Odessy v avguste – oktj. 1941)*. Moscow, 1969

415) Kuznecov, Nikolaj G. *Auf Siegeskurs*. East Berlin, 1979

416) Lammers, Walther. *Zur Mentalität deutscher Generale bei Beginn des Krieges gegen die Sowjetunion (Juni bis Dezember 1941)*. Sitzungsberichte der Wissenschaftlichen Gesellschaft an der Johann Wolfgang Goethe Universität Frankfurt am Main, vol. 26, no. 2. Stuttgart, 1990

417) Mackensen, Eberhard von. *Vom Bug zum Kaukasus. Das 3. Panzerkorps im Feldzug gegen Sowjetrußland 1941/42*. Die Wehrmacht im Kampf, vol. 42. Neckargemünd, 1967

418) Magenheimer, Heinz. "Leningrad oder Moskau? Zur operativen Problematik im Ostfeldzug 1941." *Wehrforschung* no. 1 (1975): pp. 22–29

419) Melzer, Walther. *Kampf um die Baltischen Inseln 1917–1941–1944. Eine Studie zur triphibischen Kampfführung*. Neckargemünd, 1960

420) Meier-Welcker, Hans. *Aufzeichnungen eines Generalstabsoffiziers 1939–1942*. Freiburg, 1982

421) Michels, Josef. *Dreimal Orel. Ein Buch der Kameradschaft*. Recklinghausen, 1952

422) Moskalenko, Anatolij Z. *Kiev. Dok. povest v pismach, dnevnikach i vospominanijach ucastnikov istor. epopei zascity i osvobozdenija goroda v 1941–1943 gg*. Moscow, 1978

423) Munzel, Oskar. *Panzer-Taktik. Raids gepanzerter Verbände im Ostfeldzug 1941/42*. Neckargemünd, 1959

424) Nekric, Alexander M. *1941 – 22. ijunja*. Moscow, 1965 (French edn: *L'Armée rouge assassinée. 22. juin 1941*. Paris, 1968)

425) Nekric, Alexander, and Pjotr Grigorenko. *Genickschuß. Die Rote Armee am 22. Juni 1941*. Edited by Georges Haupt. Vienna, 1969

426) Nolte, Hans-Heinrich. *Der deutsche Überfall auf die Sowjetunion 1941. Text und Dokumentation*. Hanover, 1991

427) *The Onslaught. The German Drive to Stalingrad. Documentation in 150 Unpublished Colour Photographs from the German Archive for Art and History*. With an historical essay by Heinrich Graf Einsiedel. London, 1984

428) *Ostlandreiter ohne Chance. Beiträge zur Geschichte des faschistischen Überfalls auf die Sowjetunion*. Editorial staff Gerhart Hass. East Berlin, 1963

429) Pfleger, Ernst Karl. *"Ran an den Don, Kampfgruppe 482!"*. Vienna, 1958

430) Philippi, Alfred. *Das Pripjetproblem. Eine Studie über die operative Bedeutung des Pripjetgebietes für den Feldzug des Jahres 1941.* Wehrwissenschaftliche Rundschau, no. 2. Frankfurt, 1956

431) Quarrie, Bruce. *Panzer in Russia 1941–1943.* World War Two Photo Albums, no. 9. Cambridge, 1979

432) Reinhardt, Klaus. "Vor vierzig Jahren: Unternehmen Barbarossa – Anfang vom Ende." *Heere international* vol. 1, pp. 203–213

433) Rondiere, Pierre. *Et le monde retint son souffle ... Le 22 juin 1941 et Staline.* Paris, 1967 (German edn: ... *und die Welt hielt den Atem an. Der Angriff auf Sowjetrußland am 22. Juni 1941.* Rastatt, 1968)

434) Rotundo, L. "War Plans and the 1941 Kremlin Wargame." *The Journal of Strategic Studies* vol. 10, no. 1 (1987): pp. 84–97

435) Samsonov, Alexander M. *Snat'i pomnit.* Moscow, 1989

436) Schmied, Josef. *Chronik eines Frontsoldaten.* Marktredwitz, 1970

437) Segbers, Klaus. *Die Sowjetunion im Zweiten Weltkrieg. Die Mobilmachung von Verwaltung, Wirtschaft und Gesellschaft im "Großen Vaterländischen Krieg" 1941–1943.* Studien zur Zeitgeschichte, vol. 32. Munich, 1987

438) Sella, Amnon. "'Barbarossa': Surprise Attack and Communication." *Journal of Contemporary History* vol. 13, no. 3 (1978): pp. 555–583

439) Starkow, Oleg. "Militärischer Geheimsnisverrat am Vorabend von 1941 'Barbarossa'." *Österreichische Militärische Zeitschrift* vol. 29, no. 4 (1991): pp. 327–330

440) Steets, Hans. *Gebirgsjäger zwischen Dnjepr und Don. Vom Tschernigowka zum Mius Okt.–Dez. 1941.* Heidelberg, 1957

441) Steiger, Rudolf. *Armour Tactics in the Second World War. Panzer Army Campaigns of 1939–1941 in German War Diaries.* New York, 1991 (German edn: *Panzertaktik im Spiegel deutscher Kriegstagebücher 1939–1941.* Freiburg, 1973; 3rd edn 1975)

442) Stern, Leo. "Der Überfall des faschistischen Deutschlands auf die Sowjetunion und die Lehren für die Gegenwart." In *Ostlandreiter ohne Chance. Beiträge zur Geschichte des faschistischen Überfalls auf die Sowjetunion*, editorial staff Gerhart Hass, pp. 1–16. East Berlin, 1963

443) Stern, Wolf, and Ernst Stenzel. "Die Blitzkriegsstrategie des deutschen Militarismus und ihr Scheitern beim Überfall auf die Sowjetunion." *Jahrbuch für die Geschichte der UdSSR und der volksdemokratischen Länder Europas* vol. 5 (1961): pp. 23–42

444) Stolfi, Russel H.S. "Barbarossa Revisited: A Critical Reappraisal of the Opening Stages of the Russo-German Campaign (June–December 1941)." *Journal of Modern History* vol. 54 (1982): pp. 27–46

445) *Strategy and Tactics of the Soviet-German War.* By officers of the Red Army and Soviet war correspondents. London, 1941

446) Tashean, John E. "Smolensk 1941: Zum Kulminationspunkt in Theorie und Praxis." In *Die operative Idee und ihre Grundlagen. Ausgewählte Operationen des Zweiten Weltkrieges*, edited by Militärgeschichtliches Forschungsamt, pp. 39–51. Vorträge zur Militärgeschichte, vol. 10. Herford, 1989

447) Ten Kate, F. *De Duitse aanval op de Soviet-Unie in 1941. Een krijgsgeschiedkundige studie.* 2 vols. Groningen, 1968

448) *Der Überfall*. Edited by Archiv für Kunst und Geschichte, mit einem zeitgeschichtlichen Essay von Heinrich Graf von Einsiedel. Hamburg, 1984
449) *Vom Bug nach Stalingrad*. Edited by Gerhard Schmid et al. 2nd edn. Rastatt, 1979
450) Weinberg, Gerhard L. "Der Überfall auf die Sowjetunion im Zusammenhang mit Hitlers diplomatischen und militärischen Gesamtplanungen." In *"Unternehmen Barbarossa". Zum historischen Ort der deutsch-sowjetischen Beziehungen von 1933 bis Herbst 1941*, edited by Roland G. Foerster, pp. 177–185. Munich, 1993
451) Whaley, Barton. *Codeword Barbarossa*. Cambridge, 1973
452) Ziemke, Earl F. "Franz Halder at Orsha: The German General Staff Seeks a Consensus." *Military Affairs* vol. 39, no. 4 (1975): pp. 173–176

4. The Turning Point before the Gates of Moscow as a Result of the Winter Offensive, 1941–42

453) Alescenko, Nikolaj M. *Moskovskij Sovet v 1941–1945 gg*. Moscow, 1980
454) Andreev, P. P. *Razgrom gitler-fasistskich armiej pod Moskvoj*. Moscow, 1957
455) Anfilov, Viktor A. *Proval "blickriga*. Moscow, 1974
456) _____. *Krushenie pochoda Gitlera na Moskvu 1941*. Moscow, 1989
457) Bean, Bryan, ed. *Sevruk, Vladimir, Moscow, Stalingrad. 1941–1942. Recollections, Stories, Reports*. Moscow, 1970
458) Belonosov, I.I., et al. *Moskva – frontu 1941–1945. Sbornik dokumentov i materialov*. Moscow, 1966
459) Besymenski, Lev A. *Ukroscenie "Tajfuna"*. Moscow, 1978 (German edn: *Die Schlacht um Moskau*. Cologne, 1981)
460) *Bitva za Moskvu*. Moscow, 1966
461) Block, Andreas. *Du sollst nicht morden. Menschen auf den Schlachtfeldern von 1941–43 vor Moskau und in Stalingrad. Versuch einer kritischen Analyse des Unternehmens Barbarossa von einem Betroffenen*. Dortmund, 1989; 2nd edn 1990
462) Bukov, K.I. *Pobeda pod Moskvoj*. Moscow, 1962
463) Cassidy, Henry C. *Moskau 1941–1943*. Zurich, 1944
464) Conrady, Alexander. *Rückzug vor Moskau, Winter 1941–1942. Aus der Geschichte der 36. Inf. Div.* Vol. 1, *6.12.1941 – 23.1.1942*. Neckargemünd, 1974
465) Dill, Hans Joachim. *Der Feldzug im Osten vom September bis Dezember 1941*. Stuttgart, 1982
466) Einbeck, Eberhard. *Das Exempel Graf Sponeck. Ein Beitrag zum Thema: Hitler und die Generale*. Bremen, 1970
467) Förster, Gerhard, ed. *Vor Moskau und Stalingrad fiel die Entscheidung*. East Berlin, 1960
468) Fokin, N. A. "Das Scheitern des faschistischen Blitzkrieges gegen die UdSSR und das Entstehen der Voraussetzungen für den grundlegenden Umschwung im Verlauf des Großen Vaterländischen Krieges der Sowjetunion." In *Ostlandreiter ohne Chance. Beiträge zur*

Geschichte des faschistischen Überfalls auf die Sowjetunion, editorial staff Gerhart Hass. East Berlin, 1963
469) Haape, Heinrich. *Endstation Moskau. 1941/1942. Tagebuch eines Frontarztes*. Stuttgart, 1980
470) Hass, Gerhart. "Die Schlacht bei Moskau. Zu einigen militärpolitischen Schlußfolgerungen der bürgerlichen Historiographie." *Militärgeschichte* vol. 20, no. 5 (1981): pp. 517–527
471) Haupt, Werner. *Demjansk 1942. Ein Bollwerk im Osten*. Bad Nauheim, 1961; 2nd edn 1963. Reprint without Chapter 1 and Appendix, Friedberg, 1984
472) _____. *Die Deutschen vor Moskau 1941/42. Bildchronik einer Schlacht der verfehlten Strategie*. Dornheim, 1972
473) _____. *Sturm auf Moskau. Der Angriff. Die Schlacht. Der Rückschlag*. Friedberg, 1986
474) Jukes, Geoffrey. *The Defense of Moscow*. New York, 1969 (German edn: *Panzer vor Moskau*. Rastatt, 1984)
475) Kazakov, Vasilij I. *Na Perelome. O bivach pod Moskvoj i na Volge. 1941–42*. Moscow, 1962
476) Kroener, Bernhard R. "Der 'erfrorene Blitzkrieg'. Strategische Planungen der deutschen Führung gegen die Sowjetunion und die Ursachen ihres Scheiterns." In *Zwei Wege nach Moskau. Vom Hitler-Stalin-Pakt bis zum "Unternehmen Barbarossa"*, edited by Bernd Wegner, pp. 133–148. Munich, 1991
477) Lefevre, Eric, and Jean Mabire. *La LVF*. Paris, 1985
478) Lesueur, Larry. *Twelve Months That Changed the World*. New York, 1943
479) Muriev, Dado Z. *Proval operacii "Tajfun"*. Moscow, 1966 (English edn: *The Rout of "Typhoon". The Battle of Moscow, 1941–1942*. Moscow, 1979)
480) *Ot Moskvy do Berlina*. Moscow, 1966
481) *Pamjat'. Moskovskaja bitva 1941–1942 gg*. Moscow, 1986
482) Parrish, Michael, ed. *Battle for Moscow. The 1942 Soviet General Staff Study*. Washington, 1989
483) Paul, Wolfgang. *Erfrorener Sieg. Die Schlacht um Moskau 1941/42*. 2nd edn. Esslingen, 1975
484) Piekalkiewicz, Janusz. *Moscow 1941. The Frozen Offensive*. Novato, Calif., 1991 (German edn: *Die Schlacht um Moskau. Die erfrorene Offensive*. Bergisch Gladbach, 1981)
485) Porter, Cathy, and Marc Jones. *Moscow in World War II*. London, 1987
486) Reinhardt, Klaus. "Die Schlacht vor Moskau im Spiegel der sowjetischen Geschichtsschreibung." In *Jahresbibliographie der Bibliothek für Zeitgeschichte*, vol. 43, 1971, pp. 451–478. Frankfurt a.M., 1972
487) _____. "Das Scheitern der Strategie Hitlers vor Moskau im Winter 1941/42." In *Das Jahr 1941 in der europäischen Politik. Vorträge der Tagung des Collegium Carolinum in Weißach am Tegernsee vom 18. – 21. November 1971*, edited by Karl Bosl, pp. 95–119. Munich, 1972
488) _____. *Moscow – The Turning Point. The Failure of Hitler's Strategy in the Winter of 1941–42*. Oxford, 1992 (German edn: *Die Wende vor Moskau. Das Scheitern der Strategie Hitlers im Winter 1941/42*. Stuttgart, 1972)

489) Salisbury, Harrison E. "Moscow." In *Decisive Battles of the Twentieth Century. Land - Sea - Air*, edited by Noble Frankland and Christopher Dowling, pp. 127–140. London, 1976
490) Samsonov, Aleksandr M. *Velikaja Bitva pod Moskvoj. 1941–42*. Moscow, 1958 (German edn: *Die große Schlacht vor Moskau 1941–1942*. East Berlin, 1959)
491) _____. *Porazenie vermachta pod Moskvoj*. Moscow, 1981
492) _____. *Moskva, 1941 god ot tragedii prazenij k velikoj pobede*. Moscow, 1991
493) Schaaf, Hans-Werner. "Zu den Auswirkungen der Schlachten von Moskau und Stalingrad auf die Festigung der Anti-Hitler-Koalition und den Zerfall des faschistischen Blocks." In *Juni 1941. Beiträge zur Geschichte des hitlerfaschistischen Überfalls auf die Sowjetunion*, edited by Alfred Anderle and Werner Basler, pp. 207–248. East Berlin, 1961
494) Schweinberger, Hans M. *Waffenmeister Berger. Winterschlacht um Moskau 1941/42*. Schwäbisch Hall, 1976
495) Seth, Ronald. *Operation Barbarossa. The Battle for Moscow*. London, 1964
496) Shaw, John. *Red Army Resurgent*. Alexandria, 1979 (German edn: *Der russische Gegenschlag*. Amsterdam, 1982)
497) Sokolovskij, Vasilij Danilovic, ed. *Razgrom nemecko-fasistskich vojsk pod Moskvoj*. Moscow, 1964
498) Talenski, N. *Zwei mächtige Schläge. Die Zerschmetterung der deutschen Armeen bei Moskau und bei Stalingrad*. Moscow, 1943
499) Telegin, Konstantin F. *Ne otdali Moskvy!* Moscow, 1968
500) Turney, Alfred W. *Disaster at Moscow: von Bock's Campaigns, 1941–1942*. Albuquerque, 1970
501) Ueberschär, Gerd R. "Das Scheitern des 'Unternehmens Barbarossa'. Der deutsch-sowjetische Krieg vom Überfall bis zur Wende vor Moskau im Winter 1941/42." In *"Unternehmen Barbarossa". Der deutsche Überfall auf die Sowjetunion 1941*, edited by Gerd R. Ueberschär and Wolfram Wette, pp. 141–172. Paderborn, 1984; new paperback edn: *Der deutsche Überfall auf die Sowjetunion. "Unternehmen Barbarossa" 1941*, pp. 85–122. Frankfurt a.M., 1991.
502) Vasil'ev, A.V. *Razgrom nemecko-fasistskichj vojsk pod Moskvoj*. Moscow, 1964
503) Wagener, Carl. *Moskau 1941. Der Angriff auf die russische Hauptstadt*. Bad Nauheim, 1965
504) Wegner, Bernd. "Dezember 1941: die Wende zum globalen Krieg als strategisches Problem der deutschen Führung." In *Zwei Wege nach Moskau. Vom Hitler-Stalin-Pakt bis zum "Unternehmen Barbarossa"*, edited by Bernd Wegner, pp. 640–658. Munich, 1991
505) Werth, Alexander. *Moscow '41*. London, 1942
506) _____. *Moscow War Diary*. New York, 1942
507) Zuravlev, Daniil A. *Ognevoj Scit Moskvy*. Moscow, 1972

5. The War on the Northern Front, 1941–44: Leningrad, Volkhov and the Polar Sea Front

508) Adamovitsch (Adamovic), Ales, and Daniil Granin. *Das Blockadebuch*. East Berlin, 1984
509) Babin, A.I., ed. *Karel'skij Front v Velikoj Otecestvennoj voine. 1941–1945 gg. Voenno-istoriceskij ocerk*. Moscow, 1984

510) ____. *Na Volchovskom Fronte. 1941–1944*. Moscow, 1982
511) Barbasin, I.P. *Bitva za Leningrad. 1941–1944*. Moscow, 1964
512) Bardin, Stepan Mi. ... *i statskie nadeli sineli*. Moscow, 1978
513) Basovskij, M.A., ed. *Nepokorennyj Placdarm. Vospominanija ucastnikov oborony Oranienbaumskogo placdarma 1941–1944*. Leningrad, 1987
514) Bassow, A. "Das Aufbrechen der Blockade Leningrads und die Veränderung der Lage in der strategischen Nordwestrichtung." *Militärgeschichte* vol. 26, no. 1 (1987): pp. 33–40
515) *Na Beregach Volchova*. Edited by A.G. Fedoruk. Leningrad, 1967
516) Bergschicker, Heinz. *Leningrad – Stadt, die den Tod bezwang*. Frankfurt a.M., 1966
517) *Bitva za Leningrad 1941–1944*. Edited by S.P. Platonov. Moscow, 1964
518) *Blockade. Leningrad 1941–1944. Dokumente und Essays von Russen und Deutschen*. Reinbek, 1992
519) Buxa, Werner. *Der Kampf am Wolchow und um Leningrad 1941–1944. Eine Dokumentation in Bildern*. Dorheim, 1969
520) Bycevskij, Boris V. *Gorod-front. O bojach pod Leningradom v 1941–1943 gg*. Moscow, 1963
521) Chales de Beaulieu, Walter. "Der Vorstoß auf Leningrad 1941." In *Generaloberst Erich Hoepner*, edited by Walter Chales de Beaulieu, pp. 129–190. Neckargemünd, 1969
522) *Deviat'sot geroiceskich dnej. Sbornik dokumentov i materialov o geroiceskoj borbe trudjascichsja Leningrada v 1941–1944 gg*. Edited by Ch.Ch. Kamalov. Moscow, 1966
523) *Deviat'sot Dnej. Literaturno-chudozestvennyj i dokumental'nyj sbornik posvjascennyj geroiceskoj oborone Leningrada v godi velikoj otetschest vennoj voini 1941–1944*. Edited by N.G. Michajlovskij. Leningrad, 1957
524) *Na Doroge zizni. Vospominanija o frontovoj Ladoge*. Edited by P.L. Bogdanov. Moscow, 1980
525) Dudin, M., and V. Solov'ev. *Radi tvoej zizni*. 2nd edn. Leningrad, 1967
526) *Duell mit der Abwehr. Dokumentarische Skizzen über die Tschekisten der Leningrader Front 1941 bis 1945*. East Berlin, 1971
527) Dzieszynski, Ryszard. *Leningrad 1941–1944*. Warsaw, 1986
528) Gebhardt, J.F. "Petsamo-Kirkenes Operations (7–30 October 1944): A Soviet Joint and Combined Arms Operation in Arctic Terrain." *The Journal of Soviet Military Studies* vol. 2, no. 1 (1989): pp. 49–86
529) Golusko, Ivan M. *Panzer erwachen wieder*. East Berlin, 1981
530) Goure, Leon. *The Siege of Leningrad*. Stanford, Calif., 1962 (French edn: *Le Siège de Léningrad*. Paris, 1966)
531) Halsti, Wolf H. *Ratkaisu 1944*. Helsinki, 1957
532) Haupt, Werner. *Leningrad, Wolchow, Kurland. Bildbericht der Heeresgruppe Nord 1941–1945*. Friedberg, 1976
533) ____. *Leningrad. Die 900-Tage-Schlacht. 1941–1944*. Friedberg, 1980
534) Henderson, Margaret. *Dear Allies. A Story of Women in Monklands and Besieged Leningrad*. Coatbridge, 1988
535) Hess, Wilhelm. *Eismeerfront 1941. Aufmarsch und Kämpfe des Gebirgskorps Norwegen in den Tundren vor Murmansk*. Heidelberg, 1956
536) Hillgruber, Andreas. *"Nordlicht" – Die deutschen Pläne zur Eroberung Leningrads im Jahre 1942*. Wiesbaden, 1964

537) Hölter, Hermann. *Armee in der Arktis. Die Operationen der deutschen Lappland-Armee*. 2nd edn. Munich, 1977
538) Inber, Vera. *Fast drei Jahre. Aus einem Leningrader Tagebuch*. 2nd edn. Berlin, 1947
539) *Operacija "Iskra". Prorvy blokady Leningrada*. Edited by Semen Moiseevic Bojcov and Semen Nikolaevic Borscev. Leningrad, 1973
540) Karaev, Georgij N., Jurij N. Jablockin, and Tichon I. Vorob'ev. *Po Mestam boevoj slavy. Leningrad i Leningradskaja oblast'*. Leningrad, 1962
541) Karasev, Aleksandr Vasil'evic. *Leningradcy v gody blockady 1941–1943*. Moscow, 1959
542) ____. *Na Zascite goroda Lenina*. Moscow, 1961
543) Kochina, Elena. *Blockade Diary*. Ann Arbor, 1990
544) Koval'cuk, Valentin M. *Leningrad i Bol'saja zemlja. Istorija Ladozskoj kommunikacii blokirovannogo Leningrada v 1941–1943 gg*. Leningrad, 1975
545) ____. *Doroga Pobedy osazdennogo Leningrada. Zeleznodoroznaja magistral' Slissel'burg – Poljany v 1943 g*. Leningrad, 1984
546) ____. "Leningrad im Zweiten Weltkrieg." In *Städte im Zweiten Weltkrieg*, edited by Marlene P. Hiller, Eberhard Jäckel and Jürgen Rohwer, pp. 57–73. Essen, 1991
547) ____ (Kowaltschuk, Walentin). "Die Verteidigung Leningrads durch die Rote Armee." In *Blockade. Leningrad 1941–1944. Dokumente und Essays von Russen und Deutschen*. Reinbek, 1992
548) Kozlov, Georgij K. *V Lesach Karelii 1941 g*. Moscow, 1963
549) Kulagin, Georgii A. *Dnevnik i pamjat'. O perezitom v gody blockady*. Leningrad, 1978
550) *Leningrad v blokade. Plakaty 1941–1944*. Introduced by V.A. Gusev. Leningrad, 1983
551) Luknickij, Pavel N. *Na Beregach Nevy*. Moscow, 1961
552) ____. *Skvoz vsju Blokadu*. Leningrad, 1964
553) ____. *Leningrad dejstvuet. Frontovoj dnevnik*. Moscow, 1964
554) Magracev, L. *Reportaz iz blokady*. Leningrad, 1989
555) Michel'son, Vladimir I., and Michail Ivanovic Jalygin. *Vozdusnyj Most*. Moscow, 1982
556) *900 Tage Blockade – Leningrad. Leiden und Widerstand der Zivilbevölkerung im Krieg. 3 Mappen*. Edited by Pädagogisches Zentrum Berlin. Berlin, 1991
557) Nosyrev, D.P., et al., eds. *V Poedinke s abverom. Dokument. ocerk o cekistach Leningradskogo fronta 1941–1945*. 2nd edn. Leningrad, 1974
558) *Oborona Leningrada 1941–1944. Vospominanija i dnevniki ucastnikov*. Introduced by Marsal M.V. Zacharov. Leningrad, 1968
559) Oesch, K.L. *Suomen kohtaalon ratkaisu Kannaksella v. 1944*. Helsinki, 1957
560) Pavlov, Dimitrij V. *Leningrad v blokada 1941 god*. Moscow, 1958, 1961; new edn., 1967 (English edn: *Leningrad 1941. The Blockade*. Foreword by Harrison E. Salisbury. Chicago, 1965; German edn: *Die Blockade von Leningrad 1941*. Frauenfeld, 1967; French edn: *Leningrad 1941–1942*. Paris, 1967)
561) *Plamja nad Nevoj. Kollektivnaja dokumental'naja povest'*. Compiled by B.A. Markov. Leningrad, 1964

562) *Parol' – "Pobeda!". Vospominanija ucastnikov bitvy za Leningrad.* Leningrad, 1969
563) *Podvig Leningrada. Dokumental'no-chudozestvennyj sbornik.* Moscow, 1960
564) Pohlmann, Hartwig. *Wolchow. 900 Tage Kampf um Leningrad 1941–1944.* Bad Nauheim, 1962
565) Rintala, Paavo. *Leningrader Schicksalssymphonie. Bericht über die von den Deutschen und den Finnen in den Jahren 1941–1943 belagerte Stadt und ihre Einwohner.* Rostock, 1970
566) Rüf, Hans. *Gebirgsjäger vor Murmansk. Der Kampf des Gebirgskorps "Norwegen" an der Eismeerfront.* Innsbruck, 1957
567) Ruef, Karl. *Winterschlacht im Mai. Die Zerreißprobe des Gebirgskorps Norwegen (XIX. Geb. A. K.) vor Murmansk.* Graz, 1984
568) Rumjancev, Nikolaj M. *Razgrom vraga v zapoljar'e. 1941–1944 gg. Voenno-istoriceskij ocerk.* Moscow, 1963
569) Rusakov, Zinovij Grigorevic. *Nasim morem byla Ladoga. Morjaki Ladozskoj voennoj flotilii v bitve za Leningrad.* Leningrad, 1980
570) Sajanov, Vissarion. *Leningradskij Dnevnik (1941–44).* Moscow, 1963
571) Salisbury, Harrison E. *The 900 Days. The Siege of Leningrad.* New York, 1969; new edn New York, 1985 and London, 1986 (German edn: *900 Tage. Die Belagerung von Leningrad.* Frankfurt a.M., 1970)
572) *Schlacht am Wolchow (1942). Berichte von Kriegsberichtern.* Compiled by Falko Kleve. Edited by the Propaganda-Kompanie einer Armee. Riga, 1942
573) Schreiber, Franz. *Kampf unter dem Nordlicht. Deutsch-finnische Waffenbruderschaft am Polarkreis. Die Geschichte der SS-Gebirgs-Division Nord (1941–1945).* Osnabrück, 1969
574) Skrjabin, Elena. *Leningrader Tagebuch. Aufzeichnungen aus den Kriegsjahren 1941–1945.* Munich, 1972
575) ____. *Von Petersburg bis Leningrad. Eine Jugend zwischen Monarchie und Revolution.* Wiesbaden, 1986
576) Smirnov, S.A. *Murmanskaja oblast' v gody velikoj otecestvennoj vojny 1941–1945 gg.* Murmansk, 1959
577) Sumilov, Nikolaj D. *V Dni blockady.* Moscow, 1974
578) Sviridov, Vladimir P., Vjaceslav P. Jakutovic, and Vladimir E. Vasilenko. *Bitva za Leningrad. 1941–1944.* Leningrad, 1962
579) Tichonov, Nikolaj, et al., eds. *The Defence of Leningrad. Eye-Witness Accounts of the Siege (1942/43).* London, 1943
580) *Neunhundert Tage. Zeugnisse von der heldenhaften Verteidigung Leningrads im Großen Vaterländischen Krieg.* 2nd edn. East Berlin, 1960
581) Trachtenberg, David. *Nevskij Prospekt v dni vojny i mira. Reportaz fotokorrespondentaa Davida Trachtenberga.* Leningrad, 1970
582) Ueberschär, Gerd R. "Koalitionskriegführung im Zweiten Weltkrieg. Probleme der deutsch-finnischen Waffenbrüderschaft im Kampf gegen die Sowjetunion." In *Militärgeschichte. Probleme – Thesen – Wege,* edited by Militärgeschichtliches Forschungsamt, pp. 355–382. Stuttgart, 1982
583) ____. "Kriegführung und Politik in Nordeuropa." In *Das Deutsche Reich und der Zweite Weltkrieg.* Vol. 4, *Der Angriff auf die Sowjetunion,* pp. 810–882. Stuttgart, 1983

584) ____. "Der Angriff auf Leningrad und die Blockade der Stadt durch die deutsche Wehrmacht." In *Blockade. Leningrad 1941–1944. Dokumente und Essays von Russen und Deutschen*, pp. 94–105. Reinbek, 1992
585) *Veteran*. Edited by J.F. Potechin. Leningrad, 1977
586) Visnevskij, Vsevolod V. *Dnevniki voennych let. 1943, 1945 gg.* Edited by E. Jankovskaja. Moscow, 1974
587) Voronkov (Woronkow), Nikolaj N. *900 Days – the Siege of Leningrad.* Moscow, 1982
588) Werth, Alexander. *Leningrad*. London, 1944
589) Wiesbauer, Toni. *In Eis und Tundra. Drei Jahre an der Lapplandfront.* Neckargemünd, 1963
590) Wykes, Alan. *The Siege of Leningrad: Epic of Survival*. Ballantine's Illustrated History of World War II. Battle Book, no. 5. New York, 1968
591) Zacharov, Ivan Z. *Syny i doceri Sovetskoj Latvii v bojach za gorod Lenina.* Riga, 1983
592) Zdanov, Nikolaj N. *Ognevoj Scit Leningrada 1941–1943 gg.* Moscow, 1965
593) Zdanova, Tat'jana A. *Krepost' na Neve. Oborona Leningrada v velikoj otecestvennoj vojne*. Moscow, 1960
594) Ziemke, Earl F. *The German Northern Theater of Operations, 1940–1945.* Department of Army, no. 20–271. Washington, 1959
595) Zubakov, Vasilij E. *Nevskaja Tverdynja. Bitva za Leningrad v gody Velikoj Otecestvennoj Vojny 1941–1944.* Moscow, 1960
596) ____. *Proryv blokady Leningrada (janvar 1943 g.)*. Moscow, 1963
597) ____. *Leningrad – gorod-geroj*. Moscow, 1981

6. The Wehrmacht Regains the Initiative: the Summer Offensive of 1942 (Sebastopol, Crimea)

598) *V Bojach za Charkovscinu. Vospominanija ucastnikov Velikoj Otecestvennoj vojny.* 4th edn. Charkov, 1978
599) Borisov, Boris A. *Sevastopol'cy ne sdajutsja*. Moscow, 1958; new edn Moscow, 1961
600) ____. *Podvig Sevastopolja. Vospominanija (1941/42)*. Simferopol', 1959
601) Buchner, Alex. *Sewastopol. Der Angriff auf die stärkste Festung der Welt 1942*. Friedberg, 1978
602) Erickson, John. *The Road to Stalingrad. Stalin's War with Germany.* London, 1975; New York, 1983
603) Förster, Gerhard, and Wolfgang Wünsche. "Zur militärpolitischen und strategisch-operativen Planung des Sommerfeldzuges der faschistischen Wehrmacht 1942." *Zeitschrift für Militärgeschichte* vol. 6 (1967): pp. 660–675
604) ____. "Die Sommeroffensive der faschistischen Wehrmacht im Jahre 1942." *Zeitschrift für Militärgeschichte* vol. 7, no. 6 (1968): pp. 692–706 and vol. 8, no. 2 (1969): pp. 179–195
605) Grossmann, Horst. *Rshew. Eckpfeiler der Ostfront*. Bad Nauheim, 1962
606) Jatmanov, Ivan S. *Takoe ne zabyvaetsja ... Vospominanija o geroiceskoj oborone Odessy i Sevastopolja v 1941–1942 gg.* Joskar-Ola, 1971
607) Kel'ner, Efim I. *Geroiceskaja Oborona Sevastopolja 1941–1942.* Simferopol', 1958

608) Kissel, Hans. *Angriff einer Infanteriedivision. Die 101. leichte Infanteriedivision in der Frühjahrsschlacht bei Charkow, Mai 1942.* Heidelberg, 1958
609) Konecki, Tadeusz. *Sewastopol: 1941–1942, 1944.* Warsaw, 1987
610) Kulakov, Nikolaj M. *Gorod morskoj slavy. O geroiceskoj oborone Sevastopolja 1941–1942 gody.* Moscow, 1964
611) Luckij, Igor. *More i plen (1940–1945). Tragedija Sewastopolja.* New York, n.d.
612) Möller, Eberhard Wolfgang. *Russisches Tagebuch. Aufzeichnungen vom Südabschnitt der Ostfront 1941 bis 1943.* Osnabrück, 1971
613) Maksimov, Sergej N. *Oborona Sevastopolja 1941–1942.* Moscow, 1959
614) Pawlas, Karl R. *Die Erstürmung der Festung Sewastopol und die deutsche Geheimwaffe 80 cm (E) "Dora".* Nuremberg, 1969
615) Tieke, Wilhelm. *Im Südabschnitt der Ostfront. Die entscheidenden Operationen.* Gummersbach, 1984
616) Vaneev, G.I., et al. *Geroiceskaja Oborona Sevastopolja 1941–1942.* Moscow, 1969
617) Wegner, Bernd. "Hitlers zweiter Feldzug gegen die Sowjetunion. Strategische Grundlagen und historische Bedeutung." In *Der Zweite Weltkrieg. Analysen, Grundzüge, Forschungsbilanzen*, edited by Wolfgang Michalka, pp. 652–666. Munich, 1989
618) ____. "The Road to Defeat: The German Campaigns in Russia, 1941–43." *The Journal of Strategic Studies* vol. 13, no. 1 (1990): pp. 105–127
619) ____. "Der Krieg gegen die Sowjetunion 1942/43" In *Der Globale Krieg. Die Ausweitung zum Weltkrieg und der Wechsel der Initiative 1941–1943*, edited by Horst Boog et al., pp. 761–1102. Das Deutsche Reich und der Zweite Weltkrieg, vol. 6. Stuttgart, 1990
620) Winkler, Walter. *Inferno Sewastopol. Ein Gefreiter, der Karabiner 98k, und 25 Tage Sturm auf eine Festung.* Neckargemünd, 1962
621) Zidilov, Evgenij Ivanovic. *My otstaivali Sevastopol'.* Moscow, 1960
622) Ziemke, Earl F. *Moscow to Stalingrad: Decision in the East.* Washington, DC, 1987

7. The Battles of Stalingrad and the Caucasus, 1942–43

623) Adam, Wilhelm. *Der schwere Entschluß.* East Berlin, 1965
624) Badanin, Boris V. *Na boevych Rubezach Kavkaza. Ocerki po inzenernomu obespeceniju bitvy za Kavkaz v Velikoj Otecestvennoj Vojne (1942–1943 gg.).* Moscow, 1962
625) Bauer, Josef Martin. *Kaukasisches Abenteuer. Die Besteigung des Elbrus am 21. August 1942.* Esslingen, 1950
626) ____. *Unternehmen "Elbrus". Das kaukasische Abenteuer 1942.* 3rd edn. Munich, 1976; new edn Frankfurt, 1992
627) Beck, Alois, et al. *...bis Stalingrad.* Ulm, 1983
628) Bentzien, Hans. *Festung vor dem Sturm.* East Berlin, 1986
629) Berg, Werner. *Verdun, Stalingrad. Ein nachdenklicher Vergleich.* Wuppertal, 1977
630) Bergschicker, Heinz. *Stalingrad. Eine Chronik in Bildern.* East Berlin, 1961

631) Beyer, Wilhelm Raimund. *Stalingrad. Unten, wo das Leben konkret war.* Frankfurt a.M., 1987
632) *Bitva za Stalingrad.* Volgograd, 1969
633) *Letzte Briefe aus Stalingrad.* Frankfurt a.M., 1950
634) "Letzte Briefe aus Stalingrad." *Politik und Zeitgeschichte, Beilage zur Wochenzeitung Das Parlament* no. 52 (28. Dec. 1955): pp. 793–802
635) Buchner, Alex. *Der Bergkrieg im Kaukasus. Die deutsche Gebirgstruppe 1942.* Friedberg, 1977
636) Carnes, James Donald. *General zwischen Hitler und Stalin. Das Schicksal des Walther von Seydlitz.* Düsseldorf, 1980
637) Carell, Paul. *Stalingrad. Sieg und Untergang der 6. Armee.* Berlin, 1992
638) Casu, Giovannni. *Un Sardo nella steppa russa, 1941–43.* Oristano, 1985
639) Ckitisvili, Karlo Varlamovic. *Zakavkaze v gody Velikoj Otecestvennoj Vojny. 1941–1945 gg.* Tbilissi, 1969
640) Craig, William. *Enemy at the Gates. The Battle for Stalingrad.* London, 1973 (German edn: *Die Schlacht um Stalingrad. Der Untergang der 6. Armee. Kriegswende an der Wolga.* Munich, 1974)
641) Cujkov, Vasilij I. *Nacalo puti.* Moscow, 1959 (German edn: *Stalingrad – Anfang des Weges.* East Berlin, 1961; English edn: *The Battle for Stalingrad.* New York, 1964)
642) ____. *Vystojav, my pobedili. (Zapiski komandarma 62-j).* Moscow, 1960
643) ____. *180 Dnej v ogne srazenij. Iz zapisok komandanta 62-j (armii).* Moscow, 1962
644) ____. *Srazenije veka. (Stalingrad).* Moscow, 1975 (German edn: *Die Schlacht des Jahrhunderts.* East Berlin, 1980)
645) ____. ed. *Stalingrad: uroki istorii. Vospominanija ucastnikov bitvy 1.* Moscow, 1976 (German edn: *Stalingrad. Lehren der Geschichte.* Frankfurt a.M., 1979)
646) Dibold, Hans. *Arzt in Stalingrad. Passion einer Gefangenschaft.* Salzburg, 1949
647) Dimt, Peter. *Flammender Kaukasus.* Berg am See, 1984
648) Doerr, Hans. *Der Feldzug nach Stalingrad. Versuch eines operativen Überblicks. (Juni 1942 bis Januar 1943).* Darmstadt, 1955; new edn Friedberg, 1958
649) Doronin, Pavel I. *Soldaty Stalingrada.* Kisinev, 1974
650) *Dvesi ognennych dnej. (Bitva za Stalingrad 1942/43).* Moscow, 1968 (English edn: *Two hundred Days of Fire. Accounts by Participants and Witnesses of the Battle of Stalingrad.* Moscow, 1970)
651) Ebert, Jens, ed. *Stalingrad – eine deutsche Legende.* Reinbek, 1992
651a) ____. "Zwischen Mythos und Wirklichkeit. Die Schlacht um Stalingrad in deutschsprachigen authentischen und literarischen Texten." Diss., Humboldt Univ., East Berlin, 1989
652) Eichholtz, Dietrich. "Der Raubzug des faschistischen deutschen Imperialismus zu den Erdölquellen des Kaukasus 1941–1943." *Jahrbuch für Geschichte* vol. 14 (1976): pp. 445–503
653) *Stalingradskaja Epopea.* Edited by V.P. Pecorkin. With a preface by M.V. Zacharov. Moscow, 1968
654) Eremenko, Andrej I. *Stalingrad. Zapiski komandujuscego frontom.*Moscow, 1961 (German edn: *Tage der Entscheidung.* East Berlin, 1964; French edn: *Stalingrad. Notes du Commandant en chef.* Paris, 1963)

655) Ernsthausen, Adolf von. *Wende im Kaukasus (1942/1943).* Neckargemünd, 1958
656) Fischer, Johannes. "Über den Entschluss zur Luftversorgung Stalingrads. Ein Beitrag zur militärischen Führung im Dritten Reich." *Militärgeschichtliche Mitteilungen* vol. 2 (1969): pp. 7–68
657) Fischer, Kurt J. *Der Gefangene von Stalingrad. Bericht eines Heimgekehrten.* Willsbach, 1948
658) Förster, Jürgen. *Stalingrad. Risse im Bündnis 1942–43.* Freiburg, 1975
659) Förster, Jürgen, ed. *Stalingrad. Ereignis – Wirkung – Symbol.* Munich, 1992; 2nd edn. 1993
660) Forstmeier, Friedrich. *Die Räumung des Kuban-Brückenkopfes im Herbst 1943.* Darmstadt, 1964
661) Fortuna, Piero, and Raffaello Uboldi. *Il tragico Don. Cronache della campagna italiana in Russia. 1941–1943.* 2nd edn. Milan, 1980
661a) Freytag, U. *Konnte die 6. Armee vor ihrem Untergang in Stalingrad aus der Einschließung ausbrechen oder welche Faktoren verhinderten den Ausbruch?* Kassel, 1988
662) Fromm, Christoph. *Stalingrad. Der Roman.* Munich, 1993
663) Galin, Boris. *Irgendwo im Donbass.* East Berlin, 1949
664) Gerlach, Heinrich. *Die verratene Armee. Der Stalingrad-Roman.* Frankfurt a. M., 1993
665) Giulini, Udo. *Stalingrad und mein zweites Leben. Begegnungen, Erlebnisse, Eindrücke, Erfahrungen.* Neustadt, 1978
666) Görlitz, Walter. "Die Schlacht um Stalingrad 1942–1943." In *Entscheidungsschlachten des Zweiten Weltkrieges*, pp. 273–322. Frankfurt a.M., 1960
667) Grecko, Andrej A. *Bitva za Kavkaz. (1942/43).* Moscow, 1969 (German edn: *Die Schlacht um den Kaukasus.* 2nd edn. East Berlin, 1972)
668) Gucmazov, A., M. Traskunov, and K. Ckitisvili. *Zakavkazskij Front Velikoj Otecestvennoj vojny.* Tbilissi, 1971
669) Gusev, Aleksandr M. *El'brus v ogne.* Moscow, 1980
669a) Haidin, Wolfgang. *Stalingrad. Kampf und Gefangenschaft. Überlebt.* Steyr, 1995
670) Hasemann, Richard. *Südrand Armjansk (Kämpfe um die Landenge Krim).* Pfullingen, 1952
671) Haupt, Werner. *Krim, Stalingrad, Kaukasus. Bildbericht der Heeresgruppe Süd 1941–1945.* Friedberg, 1977
672) Haupt, Werner, and Horst Scheibert. *Die große Offensive 1942 – Ziel Stalingrad. Eine Bilddokumentation in Farbe.* Dorheim, 1972
673) Herhudt von Rohden, Hans-Detlef. *Die Luftwaffe ringt um Stalingrad.* Wiesbaden, 1950; new edn Frankfurt a.M., 1993
674) Hirst, Ronald M. A. *Dokumente zum Endkampf der 6. Armee in Stalingrad. Namenliste der Kommandeure und Offiziere.* Springfield, Va, 1967
675) Horváth, Miklós. *A 2.Magyar Haderseg megsemmisülese a Donnal.* Budapest, 1959
676) Inaudi, Giuseppe. *La Notte piu lunga. La battaglia del Solstizio d'Inverno sul Don.* Rome, 1979
677) Jakovlev, Nikolaj N. *19 Nojabrja 1942.* Moscow, 1972; 2nd edn 1979
678) Jukes, Geoffrey. *Stalingrad, the Turning Point.* Ballantine's Illustrated History of World War II. Battle Books, no. 3. New York, 1968 (German edn: *Stalingrad. Die Wende im Zweiten Weltkrieg.* Rastatt, 1982)

679) ____. *Hitler's Stalingrad Decisions*. International Crisis Behavior Series, vol. 5. Berkeley, Calif., 1985
680) Kehrig, Manfred. *Stalingrad. Analyse und Dokumentation einer Schlacht*. Beiträge zur Militär- und Kriegsgeschichte, vol. 15. Stuttgart, 1974
681) Kemmerich, Parzival. *Im Vorfeld von Stalingrad. Tagebuchblätter (1942/43)*. Munich, 1964
682) Kerr, Walter. *Das Geheimnis Stalingrad. Hintergründe einer Entscheidungsschlacht*. Vienna, 1977
682a) Klaus, Edgar. *Durch die Hölle des Krieges. Erinnerungen eines deutschen Unternehmers an Stalingrad, Gefangenschaft und Wiederaufbau*. Berlin, 1993
683) Kljucarev, Georgij V. "Novyj vzgljad na chod Stalingradskoj bitvy." *Voprosy istorii* no. 12 (1989): pp. 54–67
684) Knopp, Guido. *Entscheidung Stalingrad. Der verdammte Krieg*. Munich, 1992
685) Kolesnik, Aleksandr D. *Velikaja Bitva na Volge*. Moscow, 1958
686) Konrad, Rudolf. *Kampf um den Kaukasus*. Munich, 1955
687) Konsalik, Heinz G. *Stalingrad. Porträt einer Stadt. Inferno einer Schlacht, Protokoll eines Wahnsinns*. Bayreuth, 1968
688) Koroteev, V. *Stalingradskoe cudo*. Volgograd, 1967
689) Kossa, Istvan. *Dunatol a Donig*. Budapest, 1960
689a) Kruse, M. ed. *Die Stalingrad-Madonna. Das Werk Kurt Reubers als Dokument der Versöhnung*. Hanover, 1992
690) Krylov, Nikolaj I. *Stalingradskij Rubez*. Moscow, 1979 (German edn: *Die entscheidende Schlacht des 2. Weltkrieges*. Moscow, 1981)
691) *Krym v Velikoj Otecestvennoj Vojne Sovetskogo Sojuza 1941–1945 gg.* Simferopol', 1963
691a) Kumpfmüller, Michael. *Die Schlacht von Stalingrad. Metamorphosen eines deutschen Mythos*. Munich, 1995
692) Kurowski, Franz. *Luftbrücke Stalingrad. Die Tragödie der Luftfahrt und der Untergang der 6. Armee*. Berg am See, n.d.
694) ____. *Stalingrad. Die Schlacht, die Hitlers Mythos zerstörte*. Bergisch Gladbach, 1992
695) Kulis, V. M. "Fal'sifikacija istorii Stalingradskoj bitvy v reaktionnoj amerikanskoj i anglijskoj literature." *Voprosy Istorii* no. 12 (1953): pp. 137–149
696) Laskin, Ivan A. *Na Puti k perelomu*. Moscow, 1977
697) Leljusenko, D.D. *Moskva – Stalingrad – Berlin – Praga. Zapiski komandarma*. Moscow, 1975
698) Lenz, Friedrich. *Stalingrad – der "verlorene" Sieg*. Heidelberg, 1956
699) Maule, Henry. "Stalingrad." In *The Great Battles of World War II*, by Henry Maule, pp. 256–291. London, 1972
700) Michel, Karl. *Es begann am Don*. Bern, 1946
701) Milhaud, Gerard. *Stalingrad. Porte de la victoire*. Paris, 1946
702) Nemeskuerty, Istvan. *Requiem egy hadseregert*. Budapest, 1972 (German edn: *Untergang einer Armee*. Berlin, 1976)
703) *The Onslaught. The German Drive to Stalingrad. Documents in 150 Unpublished Colour Photographs from the German Archive for Art and History*. With an historical essay by Heinrich Graf Einsiedel. London, 1984

704) Paulus, Friedrich. *"Ich stehe hier auf Befehl!" Lebensweg des Generalfeldmarschalls Friedrich Paulus. Mit den Aufzeichnungen aus dem Nachlaß*. Edited by Walter Görlitz. Frankfurt a.M., 1960 (French edn: *Stalingrad. Lettres et documents ined., rassemblés par Walter Görlitz*. Paris, 1960)
705) Pickert, Wolfgang. *Vom Kuban-Brückenkopf bis Sewastopol. Flakartillerie im Verband der 17. Armee. (1943/44)*. Heidelberg, 1955
706) Piekalkiewicz, Janusz. *Stalingrad. Anatomie einer Schlacht*. Munich, 1977
707) Plotnikov, Jurij V. *Die Stalingrader Schlacht 1942–1943*. Moscow, 1982
708) Rebentisch, Ernst. *Zum Kaukasus und zu den Tauern*. Boppard, 1963
709) Ricchezza, Antonio. *L'Avanzata dell' armata italiana e le due battaglie difensive del Don*. Milan, 1971
710) Rieker, Karlheinrich. *Ein Mann [Hitler] verliert einen Weltkrieg. Die entscheidenden Monate des deutsch-russischen Krieges 1942/43*. Frankfurt a.M., 1955
711) Rotundo, Louis C. "The Road to Stalingrad Revisited." *RUSI Journal* vol. 132, no. 2 (1987): pp. 57–65
712) Rotundo, Louis C., ed. *Battle for Stalingrad. The 1943 Soviet General Staff Study*. Washington, 1989
713) Rühle, Otto. *Genesung in Jelabuga. Autobiographischer Bericht*. East Berlin, 1967
714) Russo, Mariano. *Il Don senza pace*. Brescia, 1969
715) Sadarananda, Dana V. *Beyond Stalingrad: Manstein and the Operation of Army Group Don*. New York, 1990
716) Sammis, Edward R. *Last Stand at Stalingrad. The Battle that Saved the World (1942/43)*. New York, 1966
717) Samsonov, Aleksandr M. *Stalingradskaja Bitva. Ot oborony i otstuplenij k velikoj pobede na Volge. Istoricc. ocerk*. Moscow, 1960; 2nd edn Moscow, 1968; 4th edn Moscow, 1989 (Italian edn: *Stalingrado, fronte russo*. Milan, 1961)
718) Sapp, Franz. *Gefangen in Stalingrad 1943 bis 1946*. Steyr, 1992
719) Sawjalov, A.S., and T.J. Kaljadin. *Die Schlacht um den Kaukasus 1942–1943*. East Berlin, 1959
720) Scheibert, Horst. *Nach Stalingrad – 48 Kilometer! Der Einsatzvorstoß der 6. Panzerdivision. Dezember 1942*. Heidelberg, 1956; new edn *...Bis Stalingrad 48 Kilometer. Der Versuch, die eingeschlossenen Armeen zu befreien*. Friedberg, 1979
721) _____. *Zwischen Don und Donez. Winter 1942/43*. Neckargemünd, 1961; new edn *Panzer zwischen Don und Donez. Die Winterkämpfe 1942/43*. Friedberg, 1979
722) _____. *Einsatzversuch Stalingrad. Dokumentation einer Panzerschlacht in Wort und Bild. Das LVII. Panzerkorps im Dezember 1942*. Neckargemünd, 1968
722a) Dettmer, F., K. Lamprecht, and W. Schimak. *Die 4. Infanterie-Division. Tagebuch der Hoch- und Deutschmeister*. Vienna, 1969
723) Schroeter, Heinz. *Stalingrad "...bis zur letzten Patrone"*. Osnabrück, 1953; new edn Klagenfurt, 1992; as paperback Frankfurt a.M., 1993
724) Schwarz, Andreas. *Woronesh/Donstellung 1942/1943. (Ausgewählte Dokumente)*. 2 parts. 2nd edn. Bayreuth, 1978

725) Selle, Herbert. *Wofür? Erinnerungen eines Führenden Pioniers vom Bug zur Wolga*. Neckargemünd, 1977
726) Semirjaga, Michail I. *Echo Stalingradskoj bit'y*. Volgograd, 1969
727) Seth, Ronald. *Stalingrad – Point of Return. The Story of the Battle, August 1942–February 1943*. London, 1959
728) Sevruk, Vladimir. *Moscow, Stalingrad. 1941–1942. Recollections, Stories, Reports*. Edited by Bryan Bean. Moscow, 1970
729) Seydlitz, Walther von. *Stalingrad. Konflikt und Konsequenz. Erinnerungen*. Oldenburg, 1977
730) Skipper, G.C. *Battle of Stalingrad*. Chicago, 1981
731) *Stalingrad (1942/43). Die ersten Berichte der russischen Generäle Rokossowski [u.a.] sowie russischer Kriegsberichterstatter*. Zurich, 1945
731a) *Stalingrad. Materialien zur Ausstellung "Stalingrad – Briefe aus dem Kessel" vom 20. Juni – 4. August 1991 im Kunstamt Kreuzberg-Bethanien*. Edited by DGB Landesbezirk Berlin/Brandenburg et al. Berlin, 1991
732) Steidle, Luitpold. *Entscheidung an der Wolga*. East Berlin, 1969
733) Stupov, A.D., and V.L. Kokunov. *62-ja armija v bojach za Stalingrad*. Moscow, 1949
734) Suliny, Francois. *Le Piéton de Stalingrad*. Paris, 1975
735) Tieke, Wilhelm. *Der Kaukasus und das Öl. Der deutsch-sowjetische Krieg in Kaukasien. 1942/43*. Osnabrück, 1970
736) ____. *Im Südabschnitt der Ostfront. Die entscheidenden Operationen*. Gummersbach, 1984
737) Toepke, Günter. *Stalingrad, wie es wirklich war*. Stade, 1949
Ueberschär, Gerd R., and Wolfram Wette, eds., see Wette, Wolfram
738) Vilsmaier, Joseph. *Stalingrad. Eine Armee wird geopfert*. Munich, 1992
739) *Vor Moskau und Stalingrad fiel die Entscheidung*. Editorial staff Gerhard Förster. East Berlin, 1960
740) Wanhoefer, Günter. *Pioniere nach vorn! Vom Kaukasus bis Kurland 1942–1944*. Neckargemund, 1962
741) Wegner, Bernd. "Der Krieg gegen die Sowjetunion 1942/43." In *Der Globale Krieg. Die Ausweitung zum Weltkrieg und der Wechsel der Initiative 1941–1943*, edited by Horst Boog et al, pp. 761–1102. Das Deutsche Reich und der Zweite Weltkrieg, vol. 6. Stuttgart, 1990
742) Weinert, Erich. *Memento Stalingrad. Frontnotizbuch. Worte als Partisanen. Aus dem Bericht über das Nationalkomitee "Freies Deutschland"*. Compiled by Willi Bredel. East Berlin, 1961
743) Welz, Helmut. *Verratene Grenadiere*. East Berlin, 1964, 1966, 1970
744) Werth, Alexander. *The Year of Stalingrad. An Historical Record and a Study of Russian Mentality, Methods and Policies*. London, 1946
745) Wette, Wolfram, and Gerd R. Ueberschär, eds. *Stalingrad. Mythos und Wirklichkeit einer Schlacht*. Frankfurt a.M., 1992; 2nd edn 1993
746) Wieder, Joachim. *Die Tragödie von Stalingrad. Erinnerungen eines Überlebenden*. Deggendorf, 1955
747) ____. *Stalingrad und die Verantwortung des Soldaten*. Munich, 1962; 4th renewed edn edited by Heinrich Graf von Einsiedel, Munich, 1993
748) Wilhelm, Hans-Heinrich, and Louis de Jong. *Zwei Legenden aus dem Dritten Reich*. Part 1, *Die Prognosen der Abteilung fremde Heere Ost*

1942–1945. Part 2, *Hat Felix Kersten das Niederländische Volk gerettet?* Stuttgart, 1974
749) Zakrutkin, Vitalij. *Zavkazskie Zapiski (1942–1943)*. Moscow, 1948; Moscow, 1962
750) Zamjatin, N.M. *Bitva pod Stalingradom*. Moscow, 1944
751) Zank, Horst. *Stalingrad. Kessel und Gefangenschaft*. Herford, 1993
751a) Zeitzler, Kurt. "Stalingrad." In *The Fatal Decisions*, edited by William Richardson and Seymour Freidin, pp. 115–165. London, 1956

8. From the Don to "Operation Citadel": the Battles of Charkhov and Kursk, 1943

752) Arsenin, Nikolaj D., and Valentin N. Nazarov. *49 Dnej v ogne (o gerojach Kurskoj bitvy)*. Moscow, 1961
753) *The Battle of Kursk*. Moscow, 1974
754) *Befehl des Gewissens. Charkow Winter 1943*. Edited by Bundesverband der Soldaten der ehemaligen Waffen-SS. Osnabrück, 1976
755) *Kurskaja Bitva. Vospominanija ucastnikov (1943–1968)*. Edited by Z.N. Alekseev et al. Voronez, 1968
756) Caidin, Martin. *The Tigers Are Burning*. New York, 1975
757) Chant, Christopher. *Kursk*. London, 1975
758) Conrady, Alexander. *Die Wende 1943. Charkow-Orel*. Aus der Geschichte der 36. Infanterie- und Panzer Grenadier Division, vol. 3. Neckargemünd, 1978
759) Engelmann, Joachim. *Zitadelle. Die größte Panzerschlacht im Osten 1943*. Friedberg, 1980
760) Francesconi, Manilo. *Russia 1943*. Pordenone, 1983
761) Ganze, I.S., ed. *Bojach za Charkovscinu. Vospominanija ucastnikov Velikoj Otecestvennoj vojny*. Charkov,1973; new edn 1978
762) Glantz, David M. "Soviet Operational Intelligence in the Kursk operation, July 1943." *Intelligence and National Security* vol. 5, no. 1 (1990): pp. 5–49
763) _____. *From the Don to the Dnepr: Soviet Offensive Operations, December 1942–August 1943*. London, 1991
763a) Healy, Mark. *Kursk 1943: Tide Turns in the East*. London, 1992
763b) Heidkaemper, Otto. *Witebsk. Kampf und Untergang der 3. Panzerarmee (1943/44)*. Heidelberg, 1954
763c) Heinrici, Gotthard, and Friedrich Wilhelm Hauck. "Zitadelle. Der Angriff auf den russischen Stellungsvorsprung bei Kursk." *Wehrwissenschaftliche Rundschau* vol. 15 (1965): pp. 463–486, pp. 529–544. pp. 582–604
763d) Isaev, S.I., and V.N. Levcenko. *Geroi – osvoboditeli Char'kovsciny*. Charkov, 1988
763e) John, Antonius. *Kursk '43. Szenen einer Entscheidungsschlacht*. Bonn, 1993
763f) Jukes, Goffrey. *Kursk, the Clash of Armour (July 1943)*. Ballantine's Illustrated History of World War II. Battle Book, no. 7. New York, 1969 (German edn: *Die Schlacht der 6000 Panzer. Kursk und Orel 1943*. Rastatt, 1982)

763g) Karpinski, Antoni. *Kursk 1943*. Warsaw, 1983
763h) Klink, Ernst. *Das Gesetz des Handelns. Die Operation "Zitadelle" 1943*. Stuttgart, 1966
763i) Koltunov, Grigorij A., and Boris G. Solov'ev. Moscow, 1970, 1983
763j) Konev, Ivan S. *Zapiski komandujuscego frontom 1943–1944*. Moscow, 1972 (German edn: *Aufzeichnungen eines Frontoberbefehlshabers 1943/44*. East Berlin, 1978)
764) Krieger, Evgeny. *From Moscow to the Prussian Frontier (1942–1944)*. London, 1944
765) Madeja, W. Victor. *The Russo-German War. Summer – Autumn 1943*. Allentown, Pa., 1987
766) Managarov, Ivan M. *V Srazenij za Charkov*. Charkov, 1983
767) Markin, Il'ja I. *Kurskaja Bitva*. Moscow, 1958 (German edn: *Die Kursker Schlacht (1943)*. East Berlin, 1960)
768) _____. *Na Kurskoj Duge (1943 g.)* Moscow, 1961
769) Markusenko, Ivan S. *Don v Velikoj Otecestvennoj vojne*. Rostov, 1977
770) Moiseev, Oleg V. *Velikaja Bitva na Dnepre (1943), Idejno-polit. rabota v vojskach v period boev za Dnepr i Kiev*. Kiev, 1963
771) Morosow (Morozov), V. P. *Westlich von Woronesh. Abriss der Angriffsoperationen der sowjetischen Truppen, Jan.– Febr. 1943*. East Berlin, 1959
772) Moskalenko, Kirill S. *Na jugo-zapadnom Napravleniii. Vospominanija komandarma*. Moscow, 1973
773) _____. *Kiev. Dok. poveest' v pismach istor. epopei zascity i osvobozdenija goroda v 1941–1943 gg*. Moscow, 1978
774) _____, ed. *Bitva na Kurskoj duge (1943)*. Moscow, 1975
775) Mulligan, T.P. "Spies, Ciphers and 'Zitadelle': Intelligence and the Battle of Kursk, 1943." *Journal of Contemporary History* vol. 22, no. 2 (1987): pp. 236–260
776) Piekalkiewicz, Janusz. *Unternehmen Zitadelle*. Bergisch-Gladbach, 1983
777) Schwarz, Eberhard. *Die Stabilisierung der Ostfront nach Stalingrad. Mansteins Gegenschlag zwischen Donez und Dnjepr im Frühjahr 1943*. Göttingen, 1985
778) Solov'ev, Boris G. *The Battle of the Kursk Salient, 1943*. Moscow, 1979
779) _____. *The Turning-Point of World War II. The Campaigns of Summer and Autumn 1943 on the Soviet-German Front*. Moscow, 1982
780) Stadler, Silvester. *Die Offensive gegen Kursk 1943. II. SS-Panzerkorps als Stoßkeil im Großkampf*. Osnabrück, 1980
781) Tel'puchovskij, Boris S. *Bitva za Dnepr i osvobo-zdenie Kieva (1943 g.)* Moscow, 1966
782) Utkin, Grigorij M. *Geroi Dnepra*. Moscow, 1960
783) Vorozejkin, Arsenij V. *Nad Kurskoj Dugoj*. Moscow, 1962
784) Wünsche, Wolfgang. "Kursk 1943. Die Entschlußfassung der faschistischen deutschen Führung für 'Zitadelle'." *Militärgeschichte* (1973): pp. 272–283
785) Zins, Alfred. *Die Operation Zitadelle. Die militärgeschichtliche Diskussion und ihr Niederschlag im öffentlichen Bewußtsein als didaktisches Problem*. Frankfurt a.M., 1986
786) Zukov, Jurij G. *Ukroscenije "tigrov" 1943. (Chudozestvenno-dokumental'nye ocerki)*. Moscow, 1961

9. The Collapse of the Eastern Front in 1944 ("Operation Bagration"): White Russia, the Crimea, and the Southern Front

787) Akalovic, Nikolaj M. *Osvobozdenie Belorussii: ljudi, podvigi*. Minsk, 1985
788) Akulov, Michail R. *Kerc' – gorod-geroi*. Moscow, 1980
789) Basov, A.V. *Krym v Velikoj Otecestvennoj vojne 1941–1945*. Moscow, 1987
790) Bortnjak, J.A., et al., eds. *Korsun-Sevcenkivska Bitva*. Kiev, 1968
791) Buchner, Alexander. *Ostfront 1944. Tscherkassy – Tarnopol – Krim – Witebsk – Bobruisk – Brody – Jassy – Kischinew*. Friedberg, 1988
792) Carell, Paul. *Verbrannte Erde. Schlacht zwischen Wolga und Weichsel (1943–44)*. Berlin, 1966
793) Cujkov, Vasilij I. *V Bojach za Ukrainu. Gvardejzi Stalingrada v Bojach protiv faschistskich zachvattschikov za osvoboschtschdenie Sovetskoj Ukrainij*. Kiev, 1972
794) Erlau, Peter. *Flucht aus der weißen Hölle. Erinnerungen an die große Kesselschlacht der 1. Panzerarmee Hube im Raum um Kamenez-Podolsk vom 8. März bis 9. April 1944*. Stuttgart, 1964
795) Fricke, Gert. *"Fester Platz" Tarnopol 1944*. Freiburg, 1969
796) Gackenholz, Hermann. "Dokumentation zum Zusammenbruch der Heeresgruppe Mitte im Sommer 1944." *Vierteljahrshefte für Zeitgeschichte* vol. 3, no. 3 (1955): pp. 317ff.
797) _____. "The Collapse of Army Group Centre in 1944." In *Decisive Battles of World War II*, pp. 355–382. London, 1965 (German edn: "Der Zusammenbruch der Heeresgruppe Mitte 1944." In *Entscheidungsschlachten des Zweiten Weltkrieges*, edited by Hans-Adolf Jacobsen and Jürgen Rohwer, pp. 445–474. Frankfurt a.M., 1960)
798) Garmas, Petr E. *Sevastopol' – gorod-geroi*. Moscow, 1983
799) *Geroi-osvoboditeli Cerkassciny*. Edited by Aleksandr A. Berezovskij and A.N. Zudina. Dnepropetrovsk, 1980
800) Gladkov, Teodor K. *Operation Bagration*. Moscow, 1980
801) Grylev, Anatolij N. *Dnepr – Karpaty – Krym. Ossvobozdenie pravobereznoj Ukrainy i Kryma v 1944 godu*. Moscow, 1970
802) Haupt, Werner. *Die Schlachten der Heeresgruppe Mitte. Aus der Sicht der Divisionen*. Friedberg, 1983
803) Heidkämper, Otto. *Witebsk. Kampf und Untergang der 3. Panzerarmee (1943/44)*. Heidelberg, 1954
804) Hillgruber, Andreas. *Die Räumung der Krim 1944. Eine Studie zur Entstehung der deutschen Führungsentschlüsse*. Wehrwissenschaftliche Rundschau, Beiheft 9. Berlin, 1959
805) Hinze, Rolf. *Der Zusammenbruch der Heeresgruppe Mitte im Osten 1944*. Stuttgart, 1980
806) _____. *Das Ostfront-Drama 1944*. Stuttgart, 1987
806a) _____. *Mit dem Mut der Verzweiflung. Das Schicksal der Heeresgruppen Nordukraine, Südukraine, Süd-/Ostmark 1944/45*. Meerbusch, 1993
807) Kissel, Hans. *Vom Dnjepr zum Dnjestr. Rückzugskämpfe des Grenadierregiments 683 (im Rahmen der 335. I. D.). 9. März bis 12. April 1944*. Freiburg, 1970
808) Krainjukow, Konstantin W. *Vom Dnepr zur Weichsel*. East Berlin, 1977
809) Malanin, Konstantin A. *Razgrom vraga v Belorussii (1944 god.)* Moscow, 1961

810) Mazulenko, Viktor A. *Die Zerschlagung der Heeresgruppe Südukraine August – September 1944*. East Berlin, 1959
811) Neverov, Igor M. *Sevastopol'. Stranicy geroiceskoj zascity i osvobozdenija goroda-geroja 1941–1944*. Moscow, 1983
812) Niepold, Gerd. *Mittlere Ostfront Juni '44. Darstellung, Beurteilung, Lehren*. Herford, 1985
813) *Osvobozdenie Belorussii 1944*. Edited by M.M. Malachov and V.M. Samosenko. Moscow, 1970
814) Pickert, Wolfgang. *Vom Kuban-Brückenkopf bis Sewastopol*. Heidelberg, 1955
815) Przytocki, Kazimierz. *Im Aufklärungspanzer*. East Berlin, 1979
815a) Salewski, Michael, and Guntram Schulze-Wegener, eds. *Kriegsjahr 1944. Im Großen und im Kleinen*. Stuttgart, 1995
816) Samsonov, Alexander M., ed. *Osvobozdenie Belorussii 1944*. Moscow, 1974
817) Smirnov, Sergej S. *Stalingrad na Dnepre. Ocerk Korsun-Sevcenkovskoj bitvy (1944)*. Moscow, 1954
818) ____. *Na Vojne*. Part 1, *Geroi Brestskoj Kreposti*. Part 2. *Stalingrad na Dnepre*. Part 3, *Na poljach Vengrii*. Moscow, 1961
819) Tieke, Wilhelm. *Kampf um die Krim. 1941–1944. Der deutsche Bericht über die Eroberung der Krim durch die 11. Armee (von Manstein) und die Verteidigung durch die 17. Armee (Jaenecke) bis zum bitteren Ende*. Gummersbach, 1975
820) Vormann, Nikolaus von. *Tscherkassy*. Heidelberg, 1954
821) Ziemke, Earl F. *Stalingrad to Berlin: The German Defeat in the East*. Washington, 1968
822) ____. *Der Vormarsch der Roten Armee*. Amsterdam, 1982

10. The Soviet Breakthrough to the Balkans and East Prussia

823) Baljazin, Vol'demar Nikolaevic. *Sturm Kenigsberga (6.–9. aprelja 1945 g.)* Moscow, 1964
824) Banny, L. *Schild im Osten. Der Südostwall zwischen Donau und Untersteiermark 1944/45*. Lackenbach, 1985
825) Bantea, Eugen, Constantin Nikolae, and Gheorghe Zaharia. *La Roumanie dans la guerre antihitlerienne. Août 1944 – mai 1945*. Bucharest, 1970 (German edn: *Rumänien im Antihitlerkrieg. 23. August 1944 – 12. Mai 1945*. Bucharest, 1976)
826) Birjuzov, S.S., and Rade Chamovic, eds. *Belgradskaja Operacija*. Moscow, 1964
827) *Bitva za Bokuvinu (1944 g.)* Uzgorod, 1967
828) *V Bojach za Moldaviju*. Edited by P.I. Doronin. Kisinev, 1976
829) Borth, Fred. *Nicht zu jung zum Sterben: die "Hitler-Jugend" im Kampf um Wien 1945*. Vienna, 1988
830) Casper, Willibald. *Der Krieg der Verlorenen. Ostpreußen 1945 – Erinnerungen eines Soldaten an den letzten Kampf der "Panzergrenadier-Division Großdeutschland"*. Rodgau, 1986
831) Ceaucescu, Ilie. *The Entire People's War for the Homelands Defence with the Romanians. From Times of Yore to Present Days*. Bucharest, 1980

832) Ceaucescu, Ilie, et al., eds. *Romania and the Great Victory*. Bucharest, 1985
833) Cohen, Asher. *The Halutz Resistance in Hungary, 1942–1944*. New York, 1986
834) Croy, Otto R. *Wien 1945. Ein Tagebuch in Wort und Bild*. Eisenstadt, 1975
835) Danimann, Franz, et al., eds. *Österreich im April '45. Die ersten Schritte der zweiten Republik*. Vienna, 1985
836) Dieckert, Kurt, and Horst Grossmann. *Der Kampf um Ostpreußen (1944–1945). Ein authentischer Dokumentarbericht*. Munich, 1960; new edn *Der Kampf um Ostpreußen. Der umfassende Dokumentarbericht über das Kriegsgeschehen in Ostpreußen*. Stuttgart, 1976; 11th edn 1995
837) Erhardt, Traugott. *Die Geschichte der Festung Königsberg/Pr. 1257–1945*. Ostdeutsche Beiträge, vol. 179. Würzburg, 1960
838) Farkas, Ferenc. *Tatarhago visszanez (1944)*. Buenos Aires, 1952
839) Friessner, Hans. *Verratene Schlachten. Die Tragödie der deutschen Wehrmacht in Rumänien und Ungarn*. Hamburg, 1956 (Russian edn: *Proigrannye Srazenija*. Moscow, 1966)
840) Galantai, Maria. *The Changing of the Guard. The Siege of Budapest 1944–45*. London, 1961
841) Galickij, Kuzma N. *V Bojach za Vostocnuju Prussiju. Zapiski Komandirujuscego 11-j gvardejskoj armiej*. Moscow, 1970
842) Golema, Andrej. *Oslobodzovanie juzdeho a stredneho Slovenska vojskami II ukrajinskeho frontu*. Banska Bystrica, 1965
843) Gosiorovsky, Milos. *Slovenske narodne Povstanie*. Bratislava, 1954
844) Gosztony, Peter. *Der Kampf um Budapest 1944/45*. Munich, 1964
845) _____. *Endkampf an der Donau 1944/45*. Vienna, 1969
846) _____. *A magyar Honvedseg a masodik vilaghaboruban*. Rome, 1986
847) _____. "Der Krieg zwischen Bulgarien und Deutschlend 1944/45." *Wehrwissenschaftliche Rundschau* vol. 17, no. 1 (1967): pp. 22–38; no. 2 (1967): pp. 89–99; no. 3 (1967): pp. 163–176
848) Gretschko, Andrej A. *Über die Karpaten*. East Berlin, 1972
849) Hnilicka, Karl. *Das Ende auf dem Balkan. 1944/45. Die militärische Räumung Jugoslawiens durch die deutsche Wehrmacht*. Göttingen, 1970
850) Hillgruber, Andreas. *Der Zusammenbruch im Osten 1944/45 als Problem der deutschen Nationalgeschichte und der europäischen Geschichte*. Rheinisch-Westfälische Akademie der Wissenschaften, Vorträge, G 277. Opladen, 1985
851) Hossbach, Friedrich. *Die Schlacht um Ostpreußen. Aus den Kämpfen der deutschen 4. Armee um Ostpreußen vom 19.7.1944 – 30.1.1945*. Überlingen, 1951
852) *Istorija na Otecestvenata vojna na Bulgarija 1944–1945*. Sofia, 1981
853) Jamnicky, Branislav. *Osvobozeni Moravy (1945)*. Brno, 1964
854) Jester, Werner. *Im Todessturm von Budapest 1945*. Neckargemünd, 1960
855) Kernmayr, Erich. *Die letzte Schlacht. Ungarn 1944–45*. Göttingen, 1960
856) Kissel, Hans. *Die Panzerschlachten in der Puszta im Oktober 1944*. Neckargemünd, 1960
857) _____. *Die Katastrophe in Rumänien 1944*. Beiträge zur Wehrforschung, edited by Arbeitskreis für Wehrforschung, vol. 5/6. Darmstadt, 1964

858) Konev, Ivan S., ed. *Za Osvobozdenie Cechoslovakii*. Moscow, 1965
859) Kopelew, Lew. *Aufbewahren für alle Zeit!* Hamburg, 1976
860) Krainjukow, Konstantin W. *Vom Dnepr zur Weichsel*. East Berlin, 1977
861) Lambert, Gilles. *Operation Hazalah*. Budapest 1944 (French edn: *Les jeunes sionistes face aux Nazis et aux Juifs de Hongrie*. Paris, 1972)
862) Lasch, Otto. *So fiel Königsberg. Kampf und Untergang von Ostpreußens Hauptstadt*. Munich, 1958; new edn Stuttgart, 1976
863) Lebedev, Nikolaj I. *Krach fasizma v Rumynii*. Moscow, 1976
864) Levcenko, V. S. *Srazenie v Karpatach. (Nastuplenie 1-j gvardejskoj armii sentjabr-nojabr 1944 g.)* Moscow, 1960
865) Linck, Hugo. *Königsberg 1945–1948*. Leer, 1952
866) Lucas-Busemann, Erhard. *So fielen Königsberg und Breslau. Nachdenken über eine Katastrophe ein halbes Jahrhundert danach*. Berlin, 1994
867) Maculenko, V.A. *Razgrom-t na nemskofasistkite vojski v Balkanskogo napravlenie*. Sofia, 1959
868) Maier, Georg. *Drama zwischen Budapest und Wien. Der Endkampf der 6. Panzerarmee 1945*. Osnabrück, 1985
869) Malachov, Michail M. *Ot Balatona do Veny. (Janvar–Aprel' 1945 g.)*. Moscow, 1959
870) ____. *Osvobozdenie Vengrii i vostocnoj Avstrii (Okt. 1944 – Apr. 1945 g.)*. Moscow, 1965
871) Malinovskij, R.J., ed. *Jassko-Kisinevskie Kanny*. Moscow, 1964
872) ____, ed. *Budapest, Vena, Praga. (4 apr., 13 apr., 9 maja 1945)*. Moscow, 1965
873) Maron, Karl. *Von Charkow bis Berlin. Frontberichte aus dem 2. Weltkrieg (1943–45)*. East Berlin, 1960
874) Matern, Norbert. *Ostpreußen als die Bomben fielen*. Düsseldorf, 1986
875) Niepold, Gerd. *Panzeroperationen "Doppelkopf" und "Cäsar". Kurland Sommer '44*. Herford, 1987
876) Oelvedi, Ignac. *A Budai Var es a Debreceni csata. Horthyek katasztrofa politikaja 1944 öszen*. Budapest, 1970
877) Orme, Alexandra. *Comes the Comrade!* New York, 1950
878) Peyinghaus, Marianne. *Stille Jahre in Gertlauken. Erinnerungen an Ostpreußen*. Berlin, 1985
879) Prcela, John, and Stanko Guldescu. *Operation Slaughterhouse. Eyewitness Accounts of Postwar Massacres in Yugoslavia. (The Bleiburg-Maribor Massacres)*. Philadelphia, 1970
880) Ranki, György. *Unternehmen Margarethe. Die deutsche Besetzung Ungarns*. Vienna, 1984
881) Rauchensteiner, Manfred. *Der Krieg in Österreich 1945*. Vienna, 1970; 2nd new edn 1984
882) Reinoß, Herbert, ed. *Letzte Tage in Ostpreußen. Erinnerung an Flucht und Vertreibung*. Munich, 1983
883) Rossiwall, Theo. *Die letzten Tage. Die militärische Besetzung Österreichs (28. März–9. Mai) 1945*. Vienna, 1969
884) Schaerf, Adolf. *April 1945 in Wien*. Vienna, 1948
885) Schiebold, Kurt. *Opfergang in Rumänien*. Tübingen, 1952
886) Schmidt-Richberg, Erich. *Der Endkampf auf dem Balkan. Die Operationen der Heeresgruppe E von Griechenland bis zu den Alpen*. Heidelberg, 1955

887) Schwark, Theodor. *Unter Wölfen. Versteckt auf der Flucht im Vertreibungsjahr 1945 in Ostpreußen und Pommern*. Kiel, 1985

888) Shehu, Mehmet. *La Bataille pour la libération de Tirana (25 sept.–17 nov. 1944)*. Tirana, n.d.; Paris, 1969

889) Stokoe, E.G. *Lower the Ramps. Experiences with the 43rd Royal Marine Commando in Yugoslavia*. Maidstone, 1974

890) Svoboda, Ludvik. *Z Buzukulu do Prahy*. Prague, 1974

891) Tarasov, Sergej P. *Boj u ozera Balaton (Jan. 1945 g.)*. Moscow, 1959

892) Thayer, Charles W. *Hands across the Caviar*. Philadelphia, 1952

893) Thorwald, Jürgen. *Die große Flucht*. Vol. 1, *Es begann an der Weichsel*. Vol. 2, *Das Ende an der Elbe*. Stuttgart, 1962; new edn 1965; new revised edn with *Die Illusion* in a box Munich, 1995

894) Tieke, Wilhelm. *Vom Plattensee bis Österreich. Heeresgruppe Süd 1945*. Gummersbach, 1975

895) Toth, Sandor Ö. *Budapest Felszabaditasa 1944–1945*. Budapest, 1975

896) Venohr, Wolfgang. *Aufstand für die Tschechoslowakei. Der slowakische Freiheitskampf von 1944*. Hamburg, 1969

897) Wagner, Ruth Maria, and Hans Ulrich Stamm. *Die letzten Stunden daheim. Ostpreußens Schicksal in schwerer Zeit. Nach Dokumenten und Berichten zusammengestellt*. Cologne, 1972

898) Walzl, August. *Kärnten 1945. Vom NS-Regime zur Besatzungsherrschaft im Alpen-Adria-Raum*. Klagenfurt, 1985

11. The Struggle for the Vistula and Oder and in Bohemia, Moravia, Poland, Pomerania, and Silesia

899) Ahlfen, Hans von. *Der Kampf um Schlesien. Ein authentischer Dokumentarbericht*. Munich, 1961; new edn *Der Kampf um Schlesien. 1944–1945*. Stuttgart, 1976

900) Ahlfen, Hans von, and Hermann Niehoff. *So kämpfte Breslau. Verteidigung und Untergang von Schlesiens Hauptstadt*. Munich, 1959; new edn Stuttgart, 1976

901) Amort, Cestmir. *SSSR a osvozeni Ceskoslovenska*. Prague, 1970

902) Arnhold, Paul. *Der gnadenlose Weg. Von der Weichsel nach Breslau. 12. Januar–15. Februar 1945*. Velbert, 1966

903) Bokov, F.E. *Vesna pobedy*. 2nd edn. Moscow, 1985 (German edn: *Frühjahr des Sieges und der Befreiung*. East Berlin, 1979; 2nd edn 1981)

904) Chiodo, Marco P. *Sterben und Vertreibung der Deutschen im Osten 1944–1949. Die Vorgänge aus der Sicht des Auslands*. Berlin, 1993; paperback edn Berlin, 1995

905) Dolata, Boleslaw. *Wyzwolenie Polski 1944–1945*. Edited by Woyskowy Institut Historyczny. Warsaw, 1966

906) _____. *Wyzwolenie Polski 1944–1945. (Dzialania wyzwolencze armii radzieckiej i ludowego wojska polskiego. XXX-lecie PRL)*. Warsaw, 1974

907) Freytag von Loringhoven, Hanns Baron. *Das letzte Aufgebot des Teufels. Dramatischer Einsatz des Volkssturmbataillons 7/108 Franken mit den Kompanien Rothenburg o.d.T., Ansbach, Weißenburg, Dinkelsbühl (Oderabschnitt 1945)*. Ansbach, 1965

908) Gleiss, Horst G. *Breslauer Apokalypse 1945. Dokumentarchronik vom Todeskampf und Untergang einer deutschen Stadt und Festung am Ende des 2. Weltkrieges*. Vols 1–5. Wedel, 1986

909) Granzow, Klaus, ed. *Letzte Tage in Pommern. Tagebücher, Erinnerungen und Dokumente der Vertreibung*. Munich, 1984

910) Grau, Karl F. *Schlesisches Inferno. Kriegsverbrechen der Roten Armee beim Einbruch in Schlesien 1945, eine Dokumentation*. Introduced by Ernst Deuerlein. Stuttgart, 1966

911) Gunter, Georg. *Letzter Lorbeer. Vorgeschichte. Geschichte der Kämpfe in Oberschlesien von Januar bis Mai 1945*. Darmstadt, 1974

912) Haas, Georg Ralph. *Brände an der Oder*. Für Deutschland. Kriegsberichte der Waffen-SS, vol. 1. Siegburg-Niederpleis, 1962

913) Hartung, Hugo. *Schlesien 1944/45. Aufzeichnungen und Tagebücher*. Munich, 1956

914) Helm, Rudolf. *Volkssturm-Saga, (Erlebnisse beim 1. Kurhessischen Volkssturmbataillon in Ostdeutschland 1945)*. Kassel, 1961

915) Henning, Eleonore. *Aus Deutschlands dunklen Tagen. Erlebnisse in Pommern am Ende des Zweiten Weltkrieges*. Bad Liebenzell, 1982

916) Hielscher, Alexander K. *Das Kriegsende 1945 im Westen des Warthelandes und im Osten der Kurmark*. Bielefeld, 1987

917) Hornig, Ernst. *Breslau 1945. Erlebnisse in der eingeschlossenen Stadt*. Munich, 1975

918) Hubert, H. *Do widzenia na Unter den Linden*. Warsaw, 1963

919) Kaps, Johannes. *The Tragedy of Silesia 1945–46. A Documentary Account with a Special Survey of the Archdiocese of Breslau*. Munich, 1954 (German edn: *Die Tragödie Schlesiens 1945/46 in Dokumenten. Unter besonderer Berücksichtigung des Erzbistums Breslau*. Munich, 1952)

920) ____. *The Martyrdom and Heroism of the Women of East Germany. An Excerpt from the Silesian Passion, 1945–1946*. Munich, 1955

921) Komornicki, Stanislaw. *Kolobrzeg 1945*. Warsaw, 1973

922) Kotowicz, Waldemar. *Droga ku morzu*. Warsaw, 1974

923) Krockow, C. Graf von. *Die Stunde der Frauen. Bericht aus Pommern 1944–1947, nach einer Erzählung von L. Fritz-Krockow*. Stuttgart, 1988

924) Lakowski, Richard. *Seelow 1945. Die Entscheidungsschlacht an der Oder*. 2nd edn. Berlin, 1995

925) Le Tissier, Tony. *Zhukov at the Oder*. London, 1994 (German edn: *Durchbruch an der Oder. Der Vormarsch der Roten Armee 1945*. Berlin, 1995)

926) Lindenblatt, Helmut. *Pommern 1945. Eines der letzten Kapitel in der Geschichte vom Untergang des Dritten Reiches*. Leer, 1984

927) Magenheimer, Heinz. *Abwehrschlacht an der Weichsel 1945. Vorbereitung, Ablauf, Erfahrungen*. Freiburg, 1976

928) Mai, Joachim, ed. *Vom Narew bis an die Elbe. Erinnerungen sowjetischer Kriegsteilnehmer der 2. Belorussischen Front (1945)*. East Berlin, 1965

929) Margules, Jozef. *Przyczolki warszawskie. (Analiza dzialan l AWP w rejonie Warszawy we wrzesniu 1944 r.)* Edited by Wojskowy Instytut Historyczny. Warsaw, 1962

930) ____. *Boje 1 Armii WP w obszarze Warszawy (sierpien-wrzesien 1944)*. Edited by Wojskowy Instytut Historyczny. Warsaw, 1967

931) Matronov, P.S. *Za Zlatu Pragu*. Moscow, 1965

932) Murawski, Erich. *Die Eroberung Pommerns durch die Rote Armee (1945).* Boppard am Rhein, 1969
933) Peikert, Paul. *"Festung Breslau" in den Berichten eines Pfarrers. 22. Januar – 6. Mai 1945.* Edited by Karol Jonca and Alfred Konieczny. Wroclaw, 1966; 5th edn East Berlin, 1974
934) Pless-Damm, Ursula. *Weg ins Ungewisse. Tagebuchaufzeichnungen aus Pommern und Polen 1945.* Bremen, 1964
935) Poralla, Peter. *Unvergänglicher Schmerz. Ein Protokoll der Geschichte: Danzigs Schicksalsjahr 1945.* Freiburg, 1985
936) Schäufler, Hans. *1945 – Panzer an der Weichsel. Soldaten der letzten Stunde.* Stuttgart, 1979
937) Schimmel-Falkenau, Walter. *Breslau. Vom Herzog zum Gauleiter.* Frankfurt a.M., 1965
940) Scholz, Franz. *Görlitzer Tagebuch. Chronik einer Vertreibung 1945/46.* Berlin, 1990; paperback edn 1994
941) Siegert, R. *Der Tiger von Posen. Schicksal einer Panzerbesatzung im Kriegswinter 1945.* Mülheim/Ruhr, 1986
941a) Streibel, Robert, ed. *Flucht und Vertreibung. Zwischen Aufrechnung und Verdrängung.* Vienna, 1994
942) Stukowski, Joseph. *Bis zuletzt in Schneidemühl. Ein Tatsachenbericht aus dem Jahre 1945.* 2nd edn. Hamburg, 1961
943) Thorwald, Jürgen. *Es begann an der Weichsel. Flucht und Vertreibung der Deutschen aus dem Osten.* Stuttgart, 1949; 4th edn 1951; new revised edn together with *Die Illusion* and *Das Ende an der Elbe* in a box Munich, 1995
944) ____. *Flight in the Winter. Russia Conquers, January to May 1945.* New York, 1951
Tissier, see Le Tissier, Tony
945) Voelker, Johannes. *Die letzten Tage von Kolberg (4.–18. 3. 1945).* Ostdeutsche Beiträge aus dem Göttinger Arbeitskreis, vol. 12. Würzburg, 1959
946) Zavjalov, Aleksandr S., and Tichon E. Kaljadin. *Vostocno-Pomeranskaja nastupitel`naja Operacija sovetskich vojsk, fevral`-mart 1945 g. Voenno-istoriceskij ocerk.* Moscow, 1960

12. The Air War in the Eastern Theater

947) Aniscenkov, Pantelejmon S., and Vasilij E. Surinov. *Tre`ja Vozdusnaja.* Moscow, 1984
948) Astasenkov, Petr T., and Nikolaj Nikolaevic Denisov. *Komandarm krylatych.* Moscow, 1983
949) Berezovoj, Ivan N. *Tak srazalis gvardejcy.* Moscow, 1960
950) Cottam, Kazimiera J. *Soviet Airwomen in Combat in World War II.* Manhattan, Kan., 1983
951) Drum, Karl. *Airpower and Russian Partisan Warfare.* Edited by Littleton B. Atkinson [et al.]. USAF Historical Studies, no. 177. New York, 1968
952) Efimov, Aleksandr N. *Nad Polem boja.* Moscow, 1976
953) Fedorov, Aleksej G. *Aviacija v bitve pod Moskvoj.* Moscow, 1971
954) Glantz, David M. *History of the Soviet Airborne Forces.* Ilford, 1994
955) Golley, John. *Hurricanes over Murmansk.* Wellingborough, 1987

956) Groehler, Olaf. "Der Weg in die Katastrophe. Die faschistische Luftwaffe bei Stalingrad. 1942/43." In *Flieger-Kalender der DDR*, pp. 80–98. East Berlin, 1973
957) Grecko, Stepan N. *Resenija prinimalis' na zemle*. Moscow, 1984
958) Hardesty, Von. *Red Phoenix. The Rise of Soviet Air Power, 1941–1945*. London, 1982
959) Held, Werner. *Die deutschen Jagdgeschwader im Rußlandfeldzug*. Friedberg, 1986
960) Herhudt von Rohden, Hans-Detlef. *Die Luftwaffe ringt um Stalingrad*. Wiesbaden, 1950
961) Heysing, Günther. *Adler gegen Falken. Dokumentation. Sonderdienste der deutschen Luftwaffe im Krieg gegen die Sowjetunion*. Hamburg, 1967
962) Holl, Hans. *Die Bombennacht von Poltawa. Deutsche Kampfflugzeuge gegen amerikanische Bomber in Rußland*. Munich, 1959
963) Ivanov, Petr N. *Kryl'ja nad morem. Istorija sozdanja, razbitija i voenni dejatelnosti aviacii voenno-morskogo flota SSSR (1917–1945)*. Moscow, 1973
964) Kozhevnikov, M.N. *The Command and Staff of the Soviet Army Air Force in the Great Patriotic War 1941–1945. A Soviet View*. Edited by the US Air Force. Washington, 1985
965) Kurowski, Franz. *Balkenkreuz und Roter Stern*. Friedberg, 1984
966) ____. *Luftbrücke Stalingrad. Die Tragödie der Luftfahrt und der Untergang der 6. Armee*. Berg am See, n.d.
967) Kursenkow, Sergej G. *Jagdflieger Arseni Wassiljewitsch Woroshejkin*. East Berlin, 1964; 2nd edn 1968
968) Lee, Asher. *The Soviet Air Force*. New York, 1950
969) Lipfert, Helmut. *Das Tagebuch des Hauptmann Lipfert. Erlebnisse eines Jagdfliegers während des Rückzuges im Osten 1943–45, bearbeitet von Werner Girbig*. Stuttgart, 1973
970) Lisov, Ivan I., and Anatolij F. Korol'cenko. *Desantniki atakujut s nebaa*. Moscow, 1984
971) Matern, Norbert. *Ostpreußen als die Bomben fielen*. Düsseldorf, 1986
972) Michel'son, Vladimir I., and Michail I. Jalygin. *Vozdusny Most*. Moscow, 1982
973) Muller, Richard. *The German Air War in Russia*. Baltimore, Md., 1993
974) Myles, Bruce. *Night Witches. The Untold Story of Soviet Women in Combat*. Novato, Calif., 1981
975) Novokov, Aleksandr A. *V nebe Leningrada. Zapiski komandujuscego aviaciej*. Moscow, 1970
976) *Normandie-Niemen*. Parts 1–6. Paris, 1972–74
977) Nowarra, Heinz J. *Luftwaffeneinsatz "Barbarossa"*. Friedberg, n.d.
978) Orpen, Neil. *Airlift to Warsaw. The Rising of 1944*. Norman, Okla., 1984
979) Philpott, Bryan. *German Bombers over Russia*. Cambridge, 1979
980) ____. *German Fighters over Russia*. Cambridge, 1980
981) Plocher, Hermann. *The German Air Force versus Russia, 1941, 1942, 1943*. Edited by Harry R. Fletcher. 3 vols. USAF Historical Studies, no. 153–155. New York, 1968
982) Pokryschkin, Alexander I. *Himmel des Krieges*. East Berlin, 1974
983) Poplavskij, Stanislav. *Kampfgefährten*. East Berlin, 1980
984) Pracik, I. A. *Frontovoe nebo*. Moscow, 1965
Rohden, see Herhudt von Rohden

985) Rossbach, Max. *Der Motor brennt! Fliegerabenteuer aus dem Ostfeldzug.* Im Auftrag des OKW. Berlin, 1942
986) Rudel, Hans-Ulrich. *Trotzdem*. 5th edn. Preussisch Oldendorf, 1981
987) Schwabedissen, Walter. *The Russian Air Force in the Eyes of German Commanders*. Introduction by Telford Taylor. New York, 1960
988) Semenov, A. F. *Na vziete*. Moscow, 1969
989) Sevcuk, Vasilij M. *Komandir atakuet pervym*. Moscow, 1980
990) Shores, Christopher Frances. *Luftwaffe Fighter Units. Russia, June 1941–45*. London, 1978
991) Skripko, Nikolaj S. *Po Celjam bliznim i dal'nim*. Moscow, 1981
992) "Sovetskaja Aviacija v Velikoj Otecestvennoj Vojne 1941–1945 gg." *Aviacija i kosmonavtika SSSR*, (1968): pp. 86–231
993) Tolover, Raymond F., and Trevor J. Constable. *The Blond Knight of Germany*. Blue Ridge Summit, Pa., 1985 (German edn: *Holt Hartmann vom Himmel! Die Geschichte des erfolgreichsten Jagdfliegers der Welt.* Stuttgart, 1971)
994) Tschetschewna (Cecneva), Marina P. *Der Himmel bleibt unser*. East Berlin, 1982
995) Uebe, Klaus. *Russian Reactions to German Airpower in World War II*. USAF Historical Studies, no. 176. New York, 1968
996) Vazin, Fedor A. *Vozdusnyj Taran*. Moscow, 1962
997) Vorozejkin, Arsenij V. *Poslednie Ataki. Dokumental'naja povest'*. Moscow, 1979
998) Warner, Ray, ed. *The Soviet Air Force in World War 2. The Official History*. Originally published by the Ministry of Defense of the USSR. Newton Abbot, 1974

13. The Naval War in the Eastern Theater

999) Achkasov, V.I., and N.B. Pavlovich. *Soviet Naval Operations in the Great Patriotic War 1941–1945*. Annapolis, Md., 1981
1000) Ackasov, V.I., ed. *Krasnoznamennyj Baltijskij Flot*. 2 vols. Moscow, 1973–75
1001) Ackasov, V.I., et al., eds. *Boevoj Put' Sovetskogo Voenno-Morskogo flota*. Moscow, 1974
1002) Ackasov, V.I., and B.A. Vajner. *Krasnoznamennyj Baltijskij Flot v Velikoj Otecestvennoj Vojne*. Moscow, 1957
1003) Aleksandrov, Nikolaj I. *Druzba – tovarisci*. Moscow, 1963
1004) Antier, Jean-Jacques. *La Bataille des Convois de Mourmansk*. Paris, 1981
1005) Badigin, Konstantin. *Vom Eismeer zum Pazifik*. East Berlin, 1988
1006) Bekker, Cajus [H. D. Berenbrok]. *Ostsee – deutsches Schicksal 1944/45. Der authentische Bericht vom letzten Einsatz der Kriegsmarine und der Rettung von mehr als zwei Millionen deutscher Menschen über See*. Oldenburg, 1955
1007) _____. *Flucht übers Meer. Ostsee – deutsches Schicksal 1945*. 2nd edn. Oldenburg, 1964
1008) Blond, Georges. *Convois vers l'U.R.S.S.* Paris, 1950 (German edn: *Kurs Murmansk. Die Schicksalsfahrten des alliierten Eismeerkonvois [1942–45]*. Oldenburg, 1957)

1009) Brustat-Naval, Fritz. *Unternehmen Rettung. Letztes Schiff nach Westen.* Herford, 1970
1010) Campbell, Ian, and Donald Macintyre. *The Kola Run. A Record of Arctic Convoys, 1941–1945.* London, 1958
1011) Chorkov, Gelij I. *Sovetskie nadvodnye Korabli v Velikoj Oecesvennoy vojne.* Moscow, 1981
1012) Connell, G.G. *Arctic Destroyers. The 17th Flotilla.* London, 1982
1013) Derevjanko, Konstantin I. *Na trudnych Dorogach vojny.* Leningrad, 1985
1014) Dobson, Christopher, John Miller, and Ronald Payne. *The Cruellest Night. German's Dunkirk and the Sinking of the Wilhelm Gustloff.* London, 1979 (German edn: *Die Versenkung der "Wilhelm Gustloff".* Vienna, 1979)
1015) Dubrowski, Wladimir G. *Minen vor Sewastopol.* East Berlin, 1960
1016) Edlinskij, S.F. *Severnyj transportnyj flot v Velikoj Otecestvennoj vojne Sovetskogo Sojuza 1941–1945 gg.* Moscow, 1963
1017) Enders, Gerd. *Auch kleine Igel haben Stacheln.* Herford, 1984
1018) ____. *Überlandtransport deutscher U-Boote im Jahre 1942–43 von der Ostsee zum Schwarzen Meer.* Landsberg/Lech, 1988
1019) Fredmann, Ernst. *Sie kamen übers Meer. Die gröβte Rettungsaktion der Geschichte.* Cologne, 1971
1020) Gebhardt, James F. "Soviet Naval Special Purpose Forces: Origins and Operations in the Second World War." *The Journal of Soviet Military Studies* vol. 2, no. 4 (1989): pp. 536–578
1021) Gerdau, Kurt. *Albatros. Rettung über See.* Herford, 1984
1022) ____. *Goya. Rettung über See. Die gröβte Schiffskatastrophe der Welt.* Herford, 1985
1023) ____. *Ubena. Rettung über See. Im Kielwasser des Krieges.* Herford, 1985
1024) Godlevskij, G.F., N.M. Grecanjuk, and V.M. Kononenko. *Pochody boevye. Eskadra Cernomorskogo flota v velikoj otecestvennoj vojnne (1941–43).* Moscow, 1966
1025) Golovko, Arsennij G. *Vmeste s flotom.* Moscow, 1960; new edn 1979 (English edn: *With the Red Fleet. The War Memoirs of the Late Admiral Arseni G. Golovko.* Edited by Sir Aubrey Mansergh. London, 1965; German edn: *Zwischen Spitzbergen und Tiksibucht.* East Berlin, 1986)
1026) Grecanjuk, N., et al. *Baltijskij Flot. Istoiceskij ocerk.* Moscow, 1960
1027) Huan, Claude. *L'Enigme des sous-marins soviétiques.* Paris, 1959
1028) Irving, David. *The Destruction of Convoy PQ 17.* London, 1968; new edn 1980 (German edn: *Die Vernichtung des Geleitzuges PQ 17.* Hamburg, 1982)
1029) Isakov, I.S. *The Red Fleet in the Second World War.* London, n.d.
1030) Jensen, William. *Russerne paa Bornholm (1945). Indtryk og samtaler.* Copenhagen, 1945
1031) Karweina, Günter. *Geleitzug PQ 17. Ein Tatsachenbericht aus dem Jahr 1942.* Hamburg, 1964
1032) Kusnezow (Kucnecov), Nikolaj G. *Gefechtsalarm in den Flotten.* East Berlin, 1974
1033) ____. *Auf Siegeskurs.* East Berlin, 1979
1034) Lund, Paul, and Harry Ludlam. *PQ 17 – Convoy to Hell. The Survivors' Story.* London, 1968

1035) Kirin, Iosif D. *Cernomorskij Flot v bitve za Kavkaz (1942–43)*. Moscow, 1958
1036) Kramer, Reinhard, and Wolfgang Müller. *Gesunken und verschollen. Menschen- und Schiffsschicksale Ostsee 1945*. Herford, 1994
1037) Lanitzki, Günter. *Kreuzer Edinburgh. Goldtresor und Seemannsgrab*. Berlin, 1988
1038) Meister, Jürg. *Der Seekrieg in den osteuropäischen Gewässern 1941–45*. Munich, 1958
1039) _____. *The Soviet Navy*. London, 1972
1040) _____. *Soviet Warships of the Second World War*. London, 1977
1041) Melzer, Walther. *Kampf um die Baltischen Inseln 1917 - 1941 - 1944. Eine Studie zur triphibischen Kampfführung*. Neckargemünd, 1960
1042) Moore, Donald. *All of One Company*. 2nd pr. London, 1957
1043) Mosceev, Vladimir M., et al. *V studenych Glubinach*. Moscow, 1980
1044) *Operationsgebiet östliche Ostsee und der finnisch-baltische Raum 1944*. Edited by Militärgeschichtliches Forschungsamt. Stuttgart, 1961
1045) Penzin, K.V. *Cernomorskij flot v oborone Odessy*. Moscow, 1956
1046) Petrov, A. *U vrazeskich beregov*. Murmansk, 1962
1047) Petrov, Boris F. *V bojach i pochodach. Iz vospominanij voennogo morjaka*. Leningrad, 1988
1048) Piterskij, N.A., et al., eds. *Boevoj Put' sovetskogo voenno-morskogo flota*. Moscow, 1967 (German edn: *Die Sowjetflotte im Zweiten Weltkrieg*. Edited by Jürgen Rohwer. Oldenburg, 1966)
1049) Platnikov, J.V., ed. *M. N. Kozevnikov, Komandovanie i Stab VVS Sovetskaj Armii v Veilkoj Otecestvennoj vojne 1941–1945*. 2nd revised edn. Moscow, 1985
1050) Pope, Dudley. *73 North. The Battle of the Barents Sea*. London, 1958
1051) Pukkila, Eino. *Taisteluhälytys. Suomen laivasto jatkosodassa*. Porvoo, 1961
1052) *Boevoj Put' Sovetskogo Voenno-Morskogo flota*. Moscow, 1974
1053) Puzyrev, Viktor P. *Belomorskaja Flotilija v Velikoj Otecestvennoj vojne*. Moscow, 1981
1054) Rohwer, Jürgen. *Die Versenkung der jüdischen Flüchtlingstransporter Struma und Mefkure im Schwarzen Meer (Febr. 1942, Aug. 1944). Historische Untersuchung*. Schriften der Bibliothek für Zeitgeschichte, vol. 49. Frankfurt a.M., 1965
1055) _____. "Die sowjetische Flotte im Zweiten Weltkrieg." In *Jahresbibliographie der Bibliothek für Zeitgeschichte* vol. 32, 1960, pp. 383–410. Frankfurt a.M., 1962
1056) Ruge, Friedrich. *Die Sowjetflotte als Gegner im Seekrieg 1941–1945*. Stuttgart, 1981 (English edn: *The Soviets as Naval Opponents, 1941–1945*. Annapolis, Md., 1979)
1057) Schön, Heinz. *Die letzte Fahrt der Gustloff. Tatsachenbericht eines Überlebenden*. Rastatt, 1960
1058) _____. *Ostsee '45. Menschen – Schiffe – Schicksale*. Stuttgart, 1983
1059) _____. *Die "Gustloff-Katastrophe". Bericht eines Überlebenden über die größte Schiffskatastrophe im Zweiten Weltkrieg*. Stuttgart, 1984
1060) _____. *Flucht über die Ostsee 1944/45 im Bild. Ein Foto-Report über das größte Rettungswerk der Seegeschichte*. Stuttgart, 1985; 4th edn 1995
1061) Schofield, Brian B. *The Russian Convoys (1941–1945)*. London, 1964
1062) _____. *Geleitzugschlachten in der Hölle des Nordmeeres*. Herford, 1980

1063) Schulz, Joh. *Kampf der "kleinen Fische". Die 3. Räumboot-Flottille beim Einsatz im Schwarzen Meer (1943–1944)*. Munich, 1960
1064) *Seekrieg im Osten. Der Kampf der deutschen Kriegsmarine gegen die Sowjets, mit einem Geleitwort v. Generaladmiral Carls und einem Vorwort v. Korvettenkapitän Hoefer*. Edited by the Marinepropaganda – Abt. Nord, editorial staff: Heinz Woltereck. Leipzig, 1943
1065) Stevenson, G.C. "Submarine Losses in the Eastern Baltic in World War II." *Warship International* vol. 23, no. 4 (1986): pp. 371–394
1066) Sverdlov, Arkadij V. *Na More Azovskom (1941–44)*. Moscow, 1966
1067) Vajner, Boris A. *Severnyj flot v Velikoj Otecestvennoj Vojne*. Moscow, 1964
1068) Vaneev, Gennadij I. *Cernomorcy v Velikoj Otecestvennoj Vojne*. Moscow, 1978
1069) V'junenko, Nikolaj P. *Cernomorskij Flot v Velikoj Otecestvennoj Vojne (1941–45)*. Moscow, 1957

14. The Military Use of Helper Forces and Allies by the Wehrmacht and the Red Army

1070) Adonyi-Naredy, Franz von. *Ungarns Armee im Zweiten Weltkrieg. Deutschlands letzter Verbündeter*. Neckargemünd, 1971
1071) Andreyev, Catherine. *Vlassov and the Russian Liberation Movement. Soviet Reality and Emigré Theories*. Cambridge, 1987
1072) Antonjan, Marlen O. *Truzeniki tyla v Velikoj Otecestvennoj Vojne*. Moscow, 1960
1073) *L'8a Armata italiana (AMIR) nella seconda battaglia difensiva del Don (11 Dic. 1942 – 31 Gennaio 1943)*. Rome, 1946
1074) Auria, Michele de. *La mia Russia. Cappellano – combattente – prigioniero*. Pompei, 1967
1075) Basistov, Yuri. "Un punto de vista sovietico sobre la Division Azul." *Defensa* vol. 13, no. 142 (1990): pp. 57–61
1076) Bedeschi, Giulio. *Centomila gavette di ghiaccio. (Armata italiana in Russia (AMIR) 1942/43)*. Milan, 1968
1077) Bergagnini, Giovanni. *Nie ponimaiu (non capisco)*. Udine, 1981
1078) Burzew, Michail I. "Deutsche Antifaschisten an der Seite der Roten Armee im Großen Vaterländischen Krieg der UdSSR. Gedanken und Erinnerungen." *Zeitschrift für Militärgeschichte* vol. 8, no. 4 (1969): pp. 416–431
1079) Caballero Jurado, Carlos. *Foreign Volunteers of the Wehrmacht, 1941–45*. London, 1985
1080) Cerkassov, Konstantin. *General Kononov. Otvet pered istoriej za odnu popytku*. Melbourne, 1963
1081) Chiavazza, Carlo. *Scritto sulla neve*. Reggio Emilia, 1979
1082) Dallin, Alexander. *The Kaminsky Brigade 1941–1944. A Case Study of German Exploitation of Soviet Disaffection*. Cambridge, Mass., 1956
1083) De Giorgi, Giulio. *Con la Divisione Ravenna. Tutte le sue vicende sino al rientro dalla Russsia 1939–1943*. Milan, 1973
1084) Doernberg, Stefan, et al., eds. *Im Bunde mit dem Feind. Deutsche auf alliierter Seite*. Berlin, 1995

1085) Dwinger, Edwin Erich. *General Wlassow. Eine Tragödie unserer Zeit.* Frankfurt a.M., 1951

1086) Emilian, Ion Valeriu. *Der phantastische Ritt. Rumäniens Kavallerie an der Seite der deutschen Wehrmacht im Kampf gegen den Bolschewismus.* Preußisch Oldendorf, 1977

1087) Emilian, Ion Valeriu, and Marcilly, Jean. *Les Cavaliers de l'apocalypse.* Paris, 1974

1088) Esteban-Infantes, Emilio. *"Blaue Division". Spaniens Freiwillige an der Ostfront.* Leoni, 1958; 2nd edn 1977

1087) Förster, Jürgen. "Croisade de l'Europe contre le bolchevisme. La participation d'unités de volontaires Européens à l'opération 'Barberousse' en 1941." *Revue d'Histoire de la Deuxième Guerre Mondiale* vol. 30 (1980): pp. 1–26

1088) Forell, Fritz von. *Sie ritten in die Ewigkwit … Kampf und Untergang der Donkosaken im 2. Weltkrieg.* Bielefeld, 1957

1089) Geoffre, Francois de. *Normandie – Niemen. Souvenirs d'un pilote (1943–1945).* Paris, 1952

1090) Gosztony, Peter. "Über die Entstehung des Nationalkomitees und der nationalen Militärformationen der osteuropäischen Nationen in der Sowjetunion während des Zweiten Weltkrieges." *Militärgeschichtliche Mitteilungen* no. 2 (1973): pp. 31–56 and no. 1 (1975): pp. 75–98

1091) _____. *Hitlers fremde Heere. Das Schicksal der nichtdeutschen Armeen im Ostfeldzug.* Düsseldorf, 1976

1092) _____. *Deutschlands Waffengefährten an der Ostfront, 1941–1945.* Stuttgart, 1981

1093) _____. *Stalins fremde Heere. Das Schicksal der nichtsowjetischen Truppen im Rahmen der Roten Armee 1941–1945.* Bonn, 1991

1094) Haaest, Erik. *Frostknuder. Frikorps Danmark-folk om kampene ved Welikije Luki og korpsets endeligt.* Lynge, 1975

1095) _____. *Frontsvin. Frikorps Danmark-folk om kampene ved Ilmensoen.* Lynge, 1976

1096) Hamacher, Gottfried. "Als Frontbeauftragter des Nationalkomitees 'Freies Deutschland' im Einsatz." *Zeitschrift für Militärgeschichte* vol. 77, no. 3 (1968): pp. 355–369

1097) Hecht, Günther. *General Wlassow. Millionen Russen vertrauten ihm.* Limburg, 1961

1098) Hillgruber, Andreas. "Der Einbau der verbündeten Armeen in die deutsche Ostfront 1941–1944." *Wehrwissenschaftliche Rundschau* vol. 10, no. 12 (1960): pp. 659–682

1099) Hoffmann, Joachim. *Deutsche und Kalmyken 1942 bis 1945.* Freiburg, 1974

1100) _____. *Die Ostlegionen 1941–1943. Turkotataren, Kaukasier und Wolgafinnen im deutschen Heer.* Freiburg, 1976

1101) _____. *Die Geschichte der Wlassow-Armee.* Freiburg, 1984

1102) Kern, Erich [Erich Kernmayr]. *General von Pannwitz und seine Kosaken.* Göttingen, 1963

1103) Kleinfeld, Gerald R., and Lewis A. Tambs. *Hitler's Spanish Legion. The Blue Division in Russia.* Carbondale, Ill., 1979

1104) Kügelgen, Else, and Bernd von Kügelgen, eds. *Die Front war überall. Erlebnnisse und Berichte vom Kampf des Nationalkomitees "Freies Deutschland".* 3rd edn. East Berlin, 1968

1105) Labat, Sergent. *Les Places étaient chères.* Paris, 1951

1106) Larrazabal, Ramon Salas. "La division 'AZUL'." *Guerres Mondiales et Conflits Contemporains* vol. 158 (1990): pp. 41–64

1107) Lengyel, Bela von. "Die ungarischen Truppen im Rußland-Feldzug 1941." *Allgemeine schweizerische Militär-Zeitschrift* vol. 126, no. 10 (1960): pp. 866–881 and no. 11 (1960): pp. 946–960

1108) Luoni, Vittorio. *La "Pasubio" sul fronte russo*. Rome, 1977

1109) Mabire, Jean. *La division Nordland*. Paris, 1982

1110) ____. *Die SS-Panzer-Division "Wiking". Germanische Freiwillige im Kampf für Europa*. Preußisch Oldendorf, 1983

1111) Manninen, Ohto. "Operation Barbarossa and the Nordic Countries." In *Scandinavia during the Second World War*, pp. 139–181. Oslo, 1983

1112) Mühlen, Patrick von zur. *Zwischen Hakenkreuz und Sowjetstern. Der Nationalismus der sowjetischen Orientvölker im Zweiten Weltkrieg*. Düsseldorf, 1971

1113) ____. "Die Nationalitätenfrage im Kriege: das Beispiel der sowjetischen Orientvölker." In *22. Juni 1941. Der Überfall auf die Sowjetunion*, edited by Hans Schafranek and Robert Streibel, pp. 129–139. Vienna, 1991

1114) Neulen, Hans Werner. *Eurofaschismus und der Zweite Weltkrieg. Europas verratene Söhne*. Munich, 1980

1114a) ____. *An deutscher Seite. Internationale Freiwillige von Wehrmacht und Waffen-SS*. Munich, 1985

1115) Nyvltova, Dana, and Vlastimil Koznar. *Cestou bojove slavy. Obrazova publikace o ceskoslovenskych vojenskych jednotkach v Sovetskem Svazu za Velke Vlastenecke Valky*. Prague, 1960

1116) *Le Operazioni delle unita italiane al fronte russo. 1941–1943*. Rome, 1977

1117) Pandea, Adrian, Ion Pavelescu, and Eftimie Ardeleanu. *Romani la Stalingrad. Viziunea romaneasca asupra tragediei din Cotul Donului si Stepa Calmuca*. Bucharest, 1992

1118) Proctor, Raymond Lambert. "The 'Blue Division': An Episode in German-Spanish Wartime Relations." Diss., Univ. Oregon, 1966; Ann Arbor, Mich., 1978

1119) Ricchezza, Antonio. *Editoria illustrata di tutta la campagna di Russia. Luglio 1941 – maggio 1943*. Vols. 1–4. Milan, 1971–72

119a) Safranov, V.G. *Italjanskie vojska na sovetsko-germanskom fronte 1941–1943*. Moscow, 1990

1120) Saint-Loup. *Les S.S. de la toison d'or. Flamands et Wallons au combat 1941–1945*. Paris, 1975

1121) Sajer, Guy. *Denn dieser Tage Qual war groß. Bericht eines vergessenen Soldaten*. Vienna, 1969

1122) Sauvage, Roger. *Un du Normandie-Niemen (1944–45)*. Paris, 1963

1123) Schwarz, Wolfgang. *Kosaken. Kampf und Untergang eines Reitervolkes*. Esslingen, 1976

1124) Scurr, John. *Germany's Spanish Volunteers 1941–45. The Blue Division in Russia*. London, 1980

1125) *Sie kämpften für Deutschland. Zur Geschichte des Kampfes der Bewegung "Freies Deutschland" bei der 1. Ukrainischen Front der Sowjetarmee*. East Berlin, 1959

1126) Sokorski, Wlodzimierz. *Damals. (Erinnerungen des ehemaligen stellvertretenden Kommandeurs der 1. polnischen Division und des 1. polnischen Korps 1941–1945)*. Warsaw, 1980

1126a) Solzhenitsyn, Alexander. *Der Archipel Gulag*. Vols. 1–3. Bern, 1973–1974

1127) Steenberg, Sven. *Wlassow – Verräter oder Patriot?* Cologne, 1968
1128) Stern, Mario G. *Alpini im russischen Schnee*. Heidelberg, 1954
1129) Strassner, Peter. *Europäische Freiwillige. Die Geschichte der 5. SS-Panzerdivision Wiking (1940–1945)*. Osnabrück, 1968
1130) Strik-Strikfeldt, Wilfried. *Gegen Hitler und Stalin. General Wlassow und die russische Freiheitsbewegung*. Mainz, 1970
1131) Thorwald, Jürgen. *Wen sie verderben wollen. Bericht des großen Verrats*. Stuttgart, 1952
1132) ____. *Die Illusion. Rotarmisten in Hitlers Heeren*. Munich, 1974; 2nd edn 1976; new special revised edn together with *Es begann an der Weichsel* and *Das Ende an der Elbe* in one box Munich, 1995
1133) Ueberschär, Gerd R. "Guerre de coalition ou guerre séparée. Conception et structures de la stratégie germano-finlandaise dans la guerre contre l'URSS (1941–1944)." *Revue d'Histoire de la Deuxième Guerre Mondiale* vol. 30, no. 118 (1980): pp. 27–68
1134) ____. "Koalitionskriegführung im Zweiten Weltkrieg. Probleme der deutsch-finnischen Waffenbrüderschaft im Kampf gegen die Sowjetunion." In *Militärgeschichte. Probleme – Thesen – Wege*, edited by Militärgeschichtliches Forschungsamt, pp. 355–382. Stuttgart, 1982
1135) ____. "Kriegführung und Politik in Nordeuropa." In *Das Deutsche Reich und der Zweite Weltkrieg*. Vol. 4, *Der Angriff auf die Sowjetunion*, pp. 810–822. Stuttgart, 1983
1136) ____. "Freiwilllige aus Nordeuropa zu Beginn des Krieges gegen die Sowjetunion." In *Das Deutsche Reich und der Zweite Weltkrieg*. Vol. 4, *Der Angriff auf die Sowjetunion*, pp. 926–935. Stuttgart, 1983
1137) ____, ed. *Das Nationalkomitee "Freies Deutschland" und der Bund Deutscher Offiziere*. Frankfurt a.M., 1995
1138) Vacca, G. *In Russia: tappa a Karkow (1942–1943)*. Bari, 1955
1139) *Vae Victis! ou deux ans dans la L(égion) V(oluntaires) F(rançaises). Précédé de "Mon point de vue" par Remy*. Paris, 1948
1140) Vogelsang, Henning von. *Kriegsende – in Liechtenstein. Das Schicksal der Ersten Russische Nationalarmee der Deutschen Wehrmacht*. Freiburg, 1985
1141) Wever, Bruno de. *Oostfronters. Vlamingen in het Vlaams Legioen en de Waffen SS*. Tielt en Wesp, 1985
1142) Wolff, Willy. *An der Seite der Roten Armee. Zum Wirken des Nationalkomitees "Freies Deutschland" an der sowjetisch-deutschen Front 1943 bis 1945*. 2nd edn. East Berlin, 1975; 3rd edn 1982

15. Logistics, Weapons, Intelligence, Railways, and Communications

1143) Arazi, Doron. "Horchdienst und Blitzkrieg: die deutsche militärische Funkaufklärung im Unternehmen 'Barbarossa'." In *Zwei Wege nach Moskau. Vom Hitler-Stalin-Pakt bis zum "Unternehmen Barbarossa"*, edited by Bernd Wegner, pp. 221–234. Munich, 1991
Costello, John, see Zarew, Oleg
1144) Glantz, David M. *The Role of Intelligence in Soviet Military Strategy in World War II*. Novato, Calif, 1990
1145) ____. *Soviet Military Intelligence in War*. London, 1990

1146) Grove, Eric. *Russian Armour, 1941–1943*. London, 1977
1147) Joachimsthaler, Anton. *Die Breitspurbahn. Das Projekt zur Erschließung des groß-europäischen Raumes 1942–1945*. 3rd edn. Munich, 1985
1148) Kabanov, Pavel A. *Stal'nye Peregony*. Moscow, 1973
1149) *Mify i pravda. Kritika burzuaznych izmyslenij o pricinach ekonom. pobedy SSSR*. Leningrad, 1969
1150) Kosovic, Stepan S., and Aleksandr M. Filimonov. *Sovetskie Zeleznodoroznye. Voenno-istoriceskij ocerk*. Moscow, 1984
1151) Kovalev, Ivan V. *Transport v Velikoj Otecestvennoj vojne (1941–1945 gg.)* Moscow, 1981
1152) Kreidler, Eugen. *Die Eisenbahnen im Machtbereich der Achsenmächte während des Zweiten Weltkrieges. Einsatz und Leistung für die Wehrmacht und Kriegswirtschaft*. Göttingen, 1975
1153) Kumanev, Georgij A. *Sovetskie zeleznodorozniki v gody Velikoj Otecestvennoj vojny. 1941–1945*. Moscow, 1963
1154) ____. *Na Sluzbe fronta i tyla. Zelezno-doroznyj transport SSSR nakanune i v gody Velikoj Otecestvennoj vojny 1938–1945*. Moscow, 1976
1155) ____. *Vojna i zeleznodoroznyj transport SSSR, 1941–1945*. Moscow, 1988
1156) Kurkotkina, S.K., ed. *Tyl Sovetskych Vooruzennych Sil v Velikoj Otecestvennoj Vojne 1941–1945 gg*. Moscow, 1977
1157) Pavlov, Dimitrij V. *Stojkost'*. Moscow, 1979
1158) Peressypkin, Iwan T. *Nervenstränge des Sieges*. Berlin, 1982
1159) Piekalkiewicz, Janusz. *Die deutsche Reichsbahn im Zweiten Weltkrieg*. Stuttgart, 1979
1160) Possony, Stefan T. "Hitlers Unternehmen 'Barbarossa' und die Rolle des sowjetischen Geheimdienstschefs Berija." *Beiträge zur Konfliktforschung* vol. 5, no. 3 (1975): pp. 99–114
1161) Pottgiesser, Hans. *Die deutsche Reichsbahn im Ostfeldzug 1939–1944*. Neckargemünd, 1960; 2nd edn 1975
1162) Ringsdorf, Ulrich. "Organisatorische Entwicklung und Aufgaben der Abteilung Fremde Heere Ost im Generalstab des Heeres." In *Beiträge zum Archivwesen, zur Quellenkunde und zur Geschichte. Festschrift für Hans Booms*, edited by Friedrich Kahlenberg, pp. 800–810. Boppard, 1989
1163) Schüler, Klaus A. Friedrich. *Logistik im Rußlandfeldzug. Die Rolle der Eisenbahn bei Planung, Vorbereitung und Durchführung des deutschen Angriffs auf die Sowjetunion bis zur Krise vor Moskau im Winter 1941/42*. Frankfurt, 1987
1164) ____. "Der Ostfeldzug als Transport- und Versorgungsproblem." In *Zwei Wege nach Moskau. Vom Hitler-Stalin-Pakt bis zum "Unternehmen Barbarossa"*, edited by Bernd Wegner, pp. 203–220. Munich, 1991
1165) Sudoplatow, Pawel A., and Anatolij Sudoplatow. *Special Tasks. The Memoirs of an Unwanted Witness – A Soviet Spymaster*. New York, 1994 (German edn: *Der Handlanger der Macht. Enthüllungen eines KGB-Generals*. Düsseldorf, 1994)
1166) Teske, Hermann. "Die Eisenbahn als operatives Führungsmittel im Kriege gegen Rußland." *Wehrwissenschaftliche Rundschau* vol. 1, no. 9/10 (1951): pp. 51–55
1167) Zarew, Oleg, and John Costello. *Deadly Illusions – Alexander Orlov and the Looking Glass War*. New York, 1992 (German edn: *Der Superagent. Der Mann, der Stalin erpreßte*. Vienna, 1993)

16. Daily Life of Civilians and Soldiers in the War (Homefront)

1168) Barber, John. "Popular Reactions in Moscow to the German Invasion of June 22, 1941." In *Operation Barbarossa: The German Attack on the Soviet Union, June 22, 1941*, edited by Norman Naimark et al., pp. 5–18. Special Issue of *Soviet Union*, vol. 18, nos. 1–3. Salt Lake City, Utah, 1991

1168a) Barber, John, and Mark Harrison. *The Soviet Home Front, 1941–1945: A Social and Economic History of the U.S.S.R. in World War II*. New York, 1991

1169) Bartov, Omer. "Daily Life and Motivation in War: the Wehrmacht in the Soviet Union." *The Journal of Strategic Studies* vol. 12, no. 2 (1989): pp. 200–214

1170) _____. "Von unten betrachtet: Überleben, Zusammenhalt und Brutalität an der Ostfront." In *Zwei Wege nach Moskau. Vom Hitler-Stalin-Pakt bis zum "Unternehmen Barbarossa"*, edited by Bernd Wegner, pp. 326–344. Munich, 1991

1171) Boddenberg, Werner. *Die Kriegsgefangenenpost deutscher Soldaten in sowjetischem Gewahrsam und die Post von ihren Angehörigen während des II. Weltkrieges*. Berlin, 1985

1172) Cecchi, Aldo. *L'Organisazione della posta militare italiana in Russia (1941–1943)*. Quaderni di storia postale, no. 1. Prato, 1982

1173) Garrard, John, and Carol Garrard, eds. *World War 2 and the Soviet People. Selected Papers from the Fourth World Congress for Soviet and East European Studies*. Harrogate, 1990; New York, 1993

1173a) Harrison, Mark. *Soviet Planning in Peace and War, 1938–1945*. Cambridge, 1985

1174) Henke, Klaus-Dietmar, ed. *Von Stalingrad zur Währungsreform. Zur Sozialgeschichte des Umbruchs in Deutschland*. Munich, 1988

1175) Schröder, Hans J. "Erfahrungen deutscher Mannschaftssoldaten während der ersten Phase des Rußlandkrieges." In *Zwei Wege nach Moskau. Vom Hitler-Stalin-Pakt bis zum "Unternehmen Barbarossa"*, edited by Bernd Wegner, pp. 309–325. Munich, 1991

1175a) Seghers, Klaus. *Die Sowjetunion im Zweiten Weltkrieg. Die Mobilisierung von Verwaltung, Wirtschaft und Gesellschaft im "Großen Vaterländischen Krieg"*. Munich, 1987

17. The Struggle in Courland and on the Baltic Coast, 1945

1176) *Abwehrkämpfe am Nordflügel der Ostfront 1944–1945*. Edited by Militärgeschichtliches Forschungsamt. Stuttgart, 1963

1177) Beckherrn, Eberhard, and Alexej Dubatow. *Die Köngisberg Papiere. Schicksal einer deutschen Stadt. Neue Dokumente aus russischen Archiven*. Munich, 1994

1178) Bidlingmaier, Ingrid. *Entstehung und Räumung der Ostseebrückenköpfe 1945*. Neckargemünd, 1962

1179) *Bor'ba za Sovetskuju Pribaltiku v Velikoj Otecestvennoj vojne. 1941–1945*. 3 vols. Riga, 1966

1180) Casper, W. *Der Krieg der Verlorenen. Ostpreußen 1945 – Erinnerungen eines Soldaten an den letzten Kampf der "Panzergrenadier-Division Großdeutschland"*. Rodgau, 1986
1181) Dieckert, Kurt, and Horst Großmann. *Der Kampf um Ostpreußen. Ein authentischer Dokumentarbericht*. Munich, 1980
1182) Forwick, Helmuth. "Der Rückzug der Heeresgruppe Nord nach Kurland (1944)." In *Abwehrkämpfe am Nordflügel der Ostfront 1944–1945*, edited by Militärgeschichtliches Forschungsamt, pp. 101–214. Stuttgart, 1963
1183) Goldas, M. *Tarybine Armija – Tarybu Lietuvos isvaduotoja. Bibliografine rodykle, (Gol'das: Sovetskaja Armija – osvoboditel'nica Sovetskoj Litvy. Bibliogr. ukazatel', russ.)* Vilnius, 1976
1184) Haupt, Werner. *Kurland. Die letzte Front. Schicksal für 2 Armeen*. Bad Nauheim, 1959; 4th edn 1964
1185) ____. *Kurland. Bildchronik der vergessenen Heeresgruppe 1944/1945*. Dorheim, 1970
1186) ____. *Leningrad, Wolchow, Kurland. Bildbericht der Heeresgruppe Nord 1941–1945*. Friedberg, 1976
1187) ____. *Kurland. Die vergessene Heeresgruppe 1944/45*. Friedberg, 1979
1188) ____. *Das war Kurland*. Friedberg, 1987
1189) Kieser, Egbert. *Danziger Bucht 1945. Dokumentation einer Katastrophe*. Esslingen, 1978
1190) Krüger, D. *Militärische Ereignisse im April/Mai 1945 zwischen Haff und Müritz*. Neubrandenburg, 1985
1191) Niepold, G. *Panzeroperationen "Doppelkopf" und "Cäsar". Kurland Sommer '44*. Herford, 1987
1192) Reinoß, Herbert, ed. *Letzte Tage in Ostpreußen. Erinnerungen an Flucht und Vertreibung*. 2nd edn. Munich, 1985
1193) Schön, Heinz. *Die letzten Kriegstage. Ostseehäfen 1945*. Stuttgart, 1995
1194) Schwark, T. *Unter Wölfen. Versteckt und auf der Flucht im Vertreibungsjahr 1945 in Ostpreußen und Pommern*. Kiel, 1985
1195) Solschenizyn, Alexander. *Ostpreußische Nächte*. Darmstadt-Neuwied, 1976
1196) Springenschmid, Karl. *Die letzten Tage Lützows. Wie 420 ospreußische Hitlerjungen 1945 aus Kampf und Einsatz gerettet wurden*. Offenhausener Reihe, vol. 20/21. Vaterstetten, 1977; new edn *"Raus aus Königsberg!" Wie 420 ostpreußische Jungen 1945 aus Kampf und Einsatz gerettet wurden*. Kiel, 1981
1197) Uhlich, Werner. "Aus meinem Kriegstagebuch, Spätsommer 1944 in Ostpreußen – April 1945 auf der Frischen Nehrung." *Deutsches Soldatenjahrbuch* vols 22 –31 (1974–83)

18. The Red Army Conquers Berlin and the Fighting Ends

1198) "Die Agonie der faschistischen Clique in Berlin. (Nach Aussagen des Generals Weidling, des letzten deutschen Befehlshabers)." *Voenno-Istoriceskij Zurnal* vol. 10 (1961): pp. 89–98
1199) Altner, Helmut. *Totentanz Berlin. Tagebuchblätter eines 18-jährigen*. Offenbach, 1947

1200) Ambrose, Stephen E. *Eisenhower at Berlin, 1945. The Decision to Halt at the Elbe*. New York, 1967

1201) Andreas-Friedrich, Ruth. *Schauplatz Berlin. Ein deutsches Tagebuch (1938–1948)*. Munich, 1962; new edn *Schauplatz Berlin. Ein Tagebuch [des Widerstands] aufgezeichnet 1938–1945*. Reinbek, 1964

1202) Baerwald, Horst, and Klaus Polkehn. *Bis fünf nach zwölf*. East Berlin, 1960

1203) Batov, P.I. *Operacija "Oder". Boevye dejstvija 65-j armii v Berlinskoj operacii. Aprel' – maj 1945 g*. Moscow, 1965

1204) Besymenski, Lew A. *The Death of Adolf Hitler. Unknown Documents from Soviet Archives*. New York, 1978 (German edn: *Der Tod des Adolf Hitler. Unbekannte Dokumente aus Moskauer Archiven*. Introduced by Karl-Heinz Janßen. Hamburg, 1968)

1205) Böddeker, Günter. *Der Untergang des Dritten Reiches. Mit den Berichten des Oberkommandos der Wehrmacht vom 6. Jan. – 9. Mai 1945 und Bilddokumenten*. Munich, 1985

1206) Böll, Heinrich, et al. *Das Ende. Autoren aus 9 Ländern erinnern sich an die letzten Tage des Zweiten Weltkrieges*. Cologne, 1985

1206a) Bohn, Robert, and Jürgen Elvert, eds. *Kriegsende im Norden. Vom heißen zum kalten Krieg*. Stuttgart, 1995

1206b) Bokow, Fedor E. *Frühjahr des Sieges und der Befreiung*. East Berlin, 1979

1206c) Boldt, Gerhard. *Die letzten Tage der Reichskanzlei. (Kampf um Berlin. April/Mai 1945)*. Hamburg, 1947; new edn Reinbek, 1964

1206d) _____. *Hitler – Die letzten zehn Tage*. Frankfurt a.M., 1973

1207) Boltin, E.A., and S.I. Rostschin. "Konnte die Sowjetarmee Berlin im Februar 1945 einnehmen?" *Zeitschrift für Militärgeschichte* vol. 5, no. 6 (1966): pp. 718–723

1208) Bornemann, Manfred. *Die letzten Tage der Festung Harz. Das Geschehen im April 1945*. Clausthal-Zellerfeld, 1978

1209) Brett-Smith, Richard. *Berlin '45. The Grey City*. London, 1966

1210) Burkert, Hans-Norbert, Klaus Matußek, and Doris Obschernitzki. *Zerstört, besiegt, befreit. Der Kampf um Berlin bis zur Kapitulation 1945*. Berlin, 1985

1211) Busse, Theodor. "Die letzte Schlacht der 9. Armee." *Wehrwissenschaftliche Rundschau* vol. 5, no. 4 (1955): pp. 145–168

1212) Cuikov, Vasilij I. *Ot Stalingrada do Berlina*. Moscow, 1980

Cuikov, see also Tschuikow

1213) *Deutschland im zweiten Weltkrieg*. Vol. 6, *Die Zerschlagung des Hitlerfaschismus und die Befreiung des deutschen Volkes (Juni 1944 bis zum 8. Mai 1945)*. By an author collective headed by Wolfgang Schumann and Olaf Groehler. Berlin, 1985

1214) Diem, Lieselott. *Fliehen oder bleiben? Dramatisches Kriegsende in Berlin*. Freiburg, 1982

1215) Doernberg, Stefan. *Befreiung 1945. Ein Augenzeugenbericht*. East Berlin, 1975

1216) Dollinger, Hans. *Die letzten hundert Tage. Das Ende des Zweiten Weltkrieges in Europa und Asien*. Munich, 1965

1217) Duffy, Christopher. *Red Storm on the Reich. The Soviet March on Germany 1945*. London, 1991 (German edn: *Der Sturm auf das Reich. Der Vormarsch der Roten Armee 1945*. Munich, 1994)

1218) Erickson, John. *The Road to Berlin*. Stalin's War with Germany, vol. 2. London, 1983; Boulder, Colo., 1983

1219) Filmer, Werner, et al., eds. *Mensch, der Krieg ist aus. Zeitzeugen erinnern sich*. Düsseldorf, 1985

1220) Findahl, Theo. *Letzter Akt - Berlin 1939–1945*. Hamburg, 1946

1221) Gaedke, Dieter. *Berlin 1945 (Literaturbericht und Bibliographie)*. Frankfurt a.M., 1972

1222) Gardner, Brian. *The Wasted Hour. The Tragedy of 1945*. London, 1963 (German edn: *1945 oder die versäumte Zukunft*. Vienna, 1965)

1223) Gellermann, Günther. *Die Armee Wenck. Hitlers letzte Hoffnung. Aufstellung, Einsatz und Ende der 12. deutschen Armee im Frühjahr 1945*. Koblenz, 1984

1224) Goebbels, Joseph. *Tagebücher 1945. Die letzten Aufzeichnungen*. Hamburg, 1977

1225) Gosztony, Peter, ed. *Der Kampf um Berlin 1945 in Augenzeugenberichten*. Düsseldorf, 1970; new edn 1985

1226) Grisebach, Hanna. *Davongekommen! Potsdamer Tagebuch 1945–46*. Heidelberg, 1972

1227) Groehler, Olaf. *Das Ende der Reichskanzlei (2. Mai 1945)*. East Berlin, 1976

1228) _____. *1945. Die Neue Reichskanzlei. Das Ende*. Berlin, 1995

1229) Gurev, Michail Vasil'evic. *Do Sten Rejchstaga. Zapiski voennogo korrespondenta*. Moscow, 1973

1230) Haupt, Werner. *Berlin 1945. Hitlers letzte Schlacht*. Rastatt, 1963 (Spanish edn: *Berlin 1945*. Barcelona, 1964; Italian edn: *La Caduta di Berlino*. Milan, 1965)

1231) _____. *Berlin 1945. Literaturbericht und Bibliographie*. Frankfurt a.M., 1967

1232) _____. *1945. Das Ende im Osten. Chronik vom Kampf in Ost- und Mitteldeutschland. Der Untergang der Divisionen in Ostpreußen, Danzig, Westpreußen, Mecklenburg, Pommern, Schlesien, Sachsen, Berlin und Brandenburg*. Dorheim, 1970

1233) _____. *Königsberg, Breslau, Wien, Berlin. Bildbericht vom Ende der Ostfront 1945*. Friedberg, 1978

1234) _____. *Als die Rote Armee nach Deutschland kam. Der Untergang der Divisionen in Ostpreußen, Danzig, Westpreußen, Mecklenburg, Pommern, Schlesien, Sachsen, Berlin und Brandenburg*. Friedberg, [1981?]

1235) _____. "1945: Der Endkampf um die 'Festung Berlin'. Die 17tägige Schlacht um die Reichshauptstadt." *Damals* vol. 9, no. 10 (1977): pp. 899–928

1236) Hielscher, A.K. *Das Kriegsende 1945 im Westen des Warthelandes und im Osten der Kurmark*. Bielefeld, 1987

1237) _____. "Das Kriegsende 1945 im Westteil des Warthelandes und im Osten der Neumark." *Zeitschrift für Ostforschung* vol. 34, no. 2 (1985): pp. 211–248

1238) Hillgruber, Andreas. *Zweierlei Untergang. Die Zerschlagung des Deutschen Reiches und das Ende des europäischen Judentums*. Berlin, 1986

1239) _____. "Der Zusammenbruch im Osten 1944/45 als Problem der deutschen Nationalgeschichte und der europäischen Geschichte." In

Zweierlei Untergang. Die Zerschlagung des Deutschen Reiches und das Ende des europäischen Judentums, edited by Andreas Hillgruber, pp. 11–74. Berlin, 1986

1240) Horstmann, Lali. *Nothing for Tears*. London, 1953

1241) Italiaander, Rolf, Arnold Bauer, and Herbert Krafft. *Berlins Stunde Null. Ein Bild-/Text-Band*. Düsseldorf, 1979

1242) Jerk, Wiking. *Endkampf um Berlin*. Buenos Aires, 1947

1243) Joachimsthaler, Anton. *Hitlers Ende. Legenden und Dokumente*. Munich, 1995

1244) Kardorff, Ursula von. *Berliner Aufzeichnungen 1942–1945*. Munich, 1962; new edn 1976

1245) Kempka, Erich. *Ich habe Adolf Hitler verbrannt*. Munich, 1952

1246) Knopp, Guido. *Das Ende 1945. Der verdammte Krieg*. Munich, 1995

1247) Koller, Karl. *Der letzte Monat. Tagebuchaufzeichnungen des ehemaligen Chefs des Generalstabes der deutschen Luftwaffe vom 14. April bis 27. Mai 1945*. Mannheim, 1949; new edns 1985, 1995

1248) Komornicki, Stanislaw. *Berlin – 1945*. Warsaw, 1979

1249) Konev, Ivan S. *Sorok pjatyj. Voennye memuary*. Moscow, 1966; 2nd edn 1970 (German edn: *Das Jahr fünfundvierzig*. East Berlin, 1969; 4th edn 1980; English edn: *Year of Victory*. Moscow, 1969; French edn: *L'Invasion du 3e Reich. Mémoires de guerre 1945*. Paris, 1968)

1250) Kuby, Erich. *Die Russen in Berlin 1945*. Munich, 1965

1251) Kurowski, Franz. *Armee Wenck. Die 12. Armee zwischen Elbe und Oder*. Neckargemünd, 1967

1252) _____. *Bedingungslose Kapitulation. Inferno in Deutschland 1945*. Leoni am Starnberger See, 1983

1253) _____. *Endkampf um das Reich 1944–1945. Hitlers letzte Bastionen*. Friedberg, 1987

1254) Lakowski, Richard, and Klaus Dorst. *Berlin, Frühjahr 1945*. East Berlin, 1985

1254a) _____. *Seelow 1945. Die Entscheidungsschlacht an der Oder*. Berlin, 1995

1255) Le Tissier, Tony. *The Battle of Berlin 1945*. London, 1988 (German edn: *Der Kampf um Berlin 1945. Von den Seelower Höhen zur Reichskanzlei*. Berlin, 1991; 2nd edn 1992)

1256) Longmate, Norman. *When We Won the War. The Story of Victory in Europe, 1945*. London, 1977

1257) Lucas, James. *Last Days of the Reich. The Collapse of Nazi Germany, May 1945*. London, 1986

1258) Ludwigg, Henri. *L'Assassinat de Hitler*. Paris, 1963

1259) Luedde-Neurath, Walter. *Regierung Dönitz. Die letzten Tage des Dritten Reiches*. 3rd edn. Göttingen, 1964

1260) Mabire, Jean. *Berlin im Todeskampf 1945. Französische Freiwillige der Waffen-SS als letzte Verteidiger der Reichskanzlei*. Preußisch Oldendorf, 1977

1261) Malanowski, Wolfgang, ed. *1945. Deutschland in der Stunde Null*. Hamburg, 1985

1262) Mednikov, Anatolij M. *Berlinskaja Tetrad'. Rasskazy o bojach Berline*. Moscow, 1962

1263) Mironow, W.B. *Die stählerne Garde*. East Berlin 1986

1264) Mühlen, Bengt von zur, et al., eds. *Der Todeskampf der Reichshauptstadt*. Berlin, 1994

1265) Müller, Rolf-Dieter, and Gerd R. Ueberschär. *Kriegsende 1945. Die Zerstörung des Deutschen Reiches*. Frankfurt a.M., 1994; 2nd edn 1994; 3rd edn 1995 (Italian edn: *La Fine del Terzo Reich*. Bologna, 1995)

1266) Musmanno, Michael A. *Ten Days to Die*. London, 1951 (German edn: *In zehn Tagen kommt der Tod. Augenzeugen berichten über das Ende Hitlers. Authentische Darstellung der letzten Wochen im Führerbunker der Reichskanzlei*. Munich, 1950)

1267) Nalecz, Stanislaw. *Nad Nysa i Szprewa*. Warsaw, 1953

1268) *1945. Das Jahr der endgültigen Niederlage der faschistischen Wehrmacht*. Editorial staff Gerhard Förster et al. East Berlin, 1985

1269) Neustroev, Stepan Andreevic. *Put' k Rejchstagu*. Moscow, 1961

1270) O'Donnell, James P., and Uwe Bahnsen. *Die Katakombe. Das Ende in der Reichskanzlei*. Stuttgart, 1975

1271) Paul, Wolfgang. *Der Endkampf um Deutschland. 1945*. Esslingen, 1976

1272) Pilop, M. *Die Befreiung der Lausitz. Militärhistorischer Abriß der Kämpfe im Jahre 1945*. Bautzen, 1985

1273) Poche, Klaus, and Hans Oliva. *Das OKW gibt nichts mehr bekannt*. East Berlin, 1962

1274) Pocock, Tom. *1945. The Dawn Came up Like Thunder*. London, 1983

1275) Polewoi, Boris. *Berlin 896 km. Aufzeichnungen eines Frontkorrespondenten*. Berlin, 1975

1276) Read, Anthony, and David Fisher. *The Fall of Berlin*. London, 1992 (German edn: *Der Fall von Berlin*. Berlin, 1995)

1277) Rein, Heinz. *Finale Berlin*. Berlin, 1948; Frankfurt a.M., 1980

1277a) Reymann, Hellmuth. "'Ich sollte die Reichshauptstadt verteidigen.' 6. März bis 24. Aptil 1945. Erinnerungen des Berliner Kampfkommandanten." *Damals* vol. 16, no. 5 (1984): pp. 423–446

1278) Rodemann, Karl. *Das Berliner Schloß und sein Untergang. Ein Bildbericht über die Zerstörung Berliner Kulturdenkmäler*. Berlin, 1951

1279) Rosenkranz, Maria, ed. *Gottseidank wir leben. Augenzeugen berichten aus dem Jahre 1945*. Munich, 1985

1280) Rozanov, German Leont'evic. *Poslednie dni Gitlera. Iz istorii krusenija fasistskoj Germanii*. Moscow, 1961; new edn *Krusenie fasistskoj Germanii. Dopoln. i pererabot. izd. knigi "Poslednie dni Gitlera"*. Moscow, 1963 (German edn: *Hitlers letzte Tage*. East Berlin, 1963)

1281) ____. *Das Ende des Dritten Reiches*. East Berlin, 1965

1282) Rürup, Reinhard, ed. *Berlin 1945*. Berlin, 1995 (German edn: *Berlin 1945. Eine Dokumentation*. Berlin, 1995)

1283) Ryan, Cornelius. *The Last Battle*. London, 1966 (German edn: *Der letzte Kampf*. Munich, 1966; French edn: *La dernière Bataille*. Paris, 1966)

1284) Rzevskaja, Elena M. *Berlin, maj 1945. Zapiski voennogo perevodcika*. Moscow, 1965; 2nd edn 1985 (German edn: *Hitlers Ende ohne Mythos*. East Berlin, 1965, 1967)

1285) Samsonov, Aleksandr M., ed. *9 Maja 1945 goda*. Moscow, 1970

1286) Satilov, Vasilij M. *Znamja nad Rejchstagom*. Moscow, 1966; 2nd edn 1970; 3rd edn 1975

1287) ____. *Znamenoscy sturmujot Rejchstag*. Moscow, 1975; 3rd edn 1985

1288) ____. *Poslednie Sagi k pobede. Dokumental'naja povest'*. Moscow, 1981
1289) Sbojcakov, Maksim I. *Oni brali Reichstag. Dokumental'naja povest'*. Moscow, 1968
1290) Sbojcakov, Maksim I., and Vladimir G. Cerevkov. *Znamja pobedy nad Reichstagom*. Moscow, 1960
1291) Schäfer, Hans-Dieter. *Berlin im Zweiten Weltkrieg. Der Untergang der Reichshauptstadt in Augenzeugenberichten*. Munich, 1985
1292) Scheel, Klaus, ed. *Die Befreiung Berlins. Eine Dokumentation*. East Berlin, 1975; 2nd edn Berlin, 1985
1293) Schenck, Ernst Günther. *Ich sah Berlin sterben. Als Arzt in der Reichskanzlei*. Herford, 1970; Stockach, 1983; new revised edn *Das Notlazarett unter der Reichskanzlei. Ein Arzt erlebt Hitlers Ende in Berlin, mit noch unveröffentlichten Karten*. Neuried, 1995
1294) Schramm, Percy Ernst, ed. *Die Niederlage 1945. Aus dem Kriegstagebuch des Oberkommandos der Wehrmacht*. Munich, 1962; 2nd edn 1985
1295) Schultz, Joachim. *Die letzten 30 Tage*. Stuttgart, 1951
1296) Schultz-Naumann, Joachim. *Die letzten 30 Tage. Das Kriegstagebuch des OKW April bis Mai 1945. Die Schlacht um Berlin*. Munich, 1980
1297) ____. *Mecklenburg 1945*. Munich, 1989
1298) Semirjaga, Michail. "Die Rote Armee in Deutschland im Jahre 1945." In *Erobern und Vernichten. Der Krieg gegen die Sowjetunion 1941–1945. Essays*, edited by Peter Jahn and Reinhard Rürup, pp. 200–210. Berlin, 1991
1299) Sillner, Leo. *Als alles in Scherben fiel. Das Ende des 2. Weltkrieges in Deutschland*. Munich, 1970
1300) Simons, Gerald. *Die deutsche Kapitulation*. Amsterdam, 1982
1301) Slowe, Peter, and Richard Woods. *Battlefield Berlin: Siege, Surrender and Occupation, 1945*. London, 1988
1302) Stapor, Zdzislaw. *Bitwa o Berlin. Dzialania 1 Armii WP, kwiecien – maj 1945*. Warsaw, 1973
1303) ____. *Berlin 1945*. Warsaw, 1980
1304) Strawson, John. *The Battle for Berlin*. London, 1974
1305) Studnitz, Hans-Georg von. *Als Berlin brannte. Diarium der Jahre 1943–1945*. Stuttgart, 1963
1306) Subbotin, Vassilij J. *Kak koncajutsja vojny*. Moscow, 1965 (German edn: *Wir stürmten den Reichstag. Aufzeichnungen eines Frontkorrespondenten*. East Berlin, 1969)
1307) Thorwald, Jürgen. *Das Ende an der Elbe. Die letzten Monate des Zweiten Weltkrieges im Osten*. Stuttgart, 1949; 6th edn 1954; new revised edn together with *Die Illusion* and *Es begann an der Weichsel* in a box Munich, 1995
1308) Tieke, Wilhelm. *Das Ende zwischen Oder und Elbe – Der Kampf um Berlin 1945*. Stuttgart, 1981; 2nd edn 1992
Tissier, see Le Tissier
1309) Toland, John. *The Last 100 Days*. New York, 1966 (German edn: *Das Finale. Die letzten hundert Tage*. Munich, 1968)
1310) Toupet, Armand. *Berlin 1945, 22 avril – 29 avril. Ce fut l'enfer*. Paris, 1985
1311) Trevor-Roper, Hugh R. *The Last Days of Hitler*. New York, 1947; 4th edn London, 1955 (German edn *Hitlers letzte Tage*. N.p., 1947; 3rd edn Frankfurt a.M., 1965)

1312) Trojanovskij, P.I. *Sturm Berlina. Zapiski voennogo korrespondenta.* Moscow, 1971

1313) Tschuikow (Cujkov), Wasilij. *The End of the Third Reich.* Moscow, 1978 (German edn: *Das Ende des Dritten Reiches.* Munich, 1966)

1314) Tully, Andrew. *Berlin: Story of a Battle.* New York, 1963

1315) Valentiner, Ulrik. *Braendpunkt Berlin. 20. april – 2. maj 1945.* Copenhagen, 1978

1316) Veselov, Y.S., ed. *Sturm Berlina. Vospominanija, pisma, dnevniki ucastnikov boev za Berlin.* Moscow, 1948

1317) Visnevskij, Vsevolod V. *Dnevniki voennych let. 1943, 1945 gg.* Moscow, 1974

1317a) Volkmann, Hans-Erich, ed. *Das Ende des Dritten Reiches – Ende des Zweiten Weltkrieges. Eine perspektivische Rundschau.* Munich, 1995

1318) Vorob'ev, F.D., I.V. Parot'kin, and A.N. Simanskij. *Poslednij Sturm. (Berlinskaja operacija 1945 g.)* Moscow, 1970

1319) Whiting, Charles. *The End of the War. Europe: April 15 – May 23, 1945.* New York, 1973

1320) *A Woman in Berlin (1945).* London, 1957 (German edn: *Eine Frau in Berlin. Tagebuchaufzeichnungen (20. April – 22. Juni 1945)* Geneva, 1959)

1321) Wyssozki, V.N. *Unternehmen Terminal. Zum 30. Jahrestag des Potsdamer Abkommens.* East Berlin, 1975

1322) Ziemke, Earl F. *The Battle of Berlin – End of the Third Reich.* New York, 1968 (German edn: *Die Schlacht um Berlin.* Rastatt, 1982)

1323) Zincenko, Fedor M. *Voni sturmuvali rejchstag.* Kiev, 1978

1324) ____. *Geroi sturma rejchstaga.* Moscow, 1983

Part C

THE IDEOLOGICALLY MOTIVATED WAR OF ANNIHILATION IN THE EAST

Introduction

For the Nazi leaders, the campaign against the Soviet Union was fundamentally different from the outset from any other because it was a struggle of ideologies. Several studies, overviews, omnibus volumes, and collections of documents (see, among others, Nos. A/6, A/14, A/17, A/19, A/20, B/107, B/113, B/114, B/310, 1, 2, 3) demonstrate that Hitler's ideologically motivated desire to conquer *Lebensraum* in the East strongly influenced from the beginning the planning of, preparations for, and extent of the war of annihilation in the East and in some respects was the determining factor. Hitler was no longer spurred by the usual kind of great power politics and struggle against his country's political and military rivals but rather by a desire to fully implement the "eastern program" he had laid out many years earlier. This involved the most extreme plans for the destruction and obliteration of the Soviet Union. While issuing the usual directives and orders to prepare an offensive against the Soviet Union, Hitler was at pains to add one component underlying all the rest: to effect a racist war of annihilation. He left no doubt that the forthcoming campaign, which he viewed as "more than a mere struggle of weaponry" (No. B/107, p. 40), would be a campaign of extraordinary devastation and brutality. The Soviet Union would become the Nazis' "India," a laboratory for racial politics and *Lebensraum* for the Germanic peoples (No. 47). The particular nature of the Eastern campaign, its uniqueness in comparison with the "normal war" waged in western and northern Europe, could be seen both in Hitler's statements about the impending campaign to "demolish" and "eradicate" the Soviet Union and in the detailed plans that were drawn up to control and govern the *Lebensraum* that would be conquered in the East (Nos. 1, 17).

Hitler made no attempt to hide the ideological and racist nature of this totalitarian war. Peter Longerich has collected and published compelling documents detailing plans for a racist war of annihilation (Nos. 296, 294). Volumes written from a Marxist perspective, *Eine Schuld, die nicht erlischt*, and the editions by Norbert Müller and Erhard Moritz contain exemplary documents on the war crimes committed by the Germans in the Soviet Union (No. 18). Already in *Mein Kampf,* Hitler had stated that he wanted the national socialist movement "to be openly seen and recognized by the rest of the world as a vehicle for particular political intentions." According to the Führer, "this should be immediately recognizable."[1] The ideological motivation in his plans could be clearly seen on 30 March 1941 when he called for the "eradication" of Communism "for all time" and for the "liquidation of the Bolshevik commissars and the Communist intelligentsia" in a speech about the impending "struggle of two world views" before 250 senior officers. "No direct, decisive challenges to these intentions were heard from the assembled generals." (No. B/162, vol. II, p. 335f.)

* * *

Even before the war began, its ideological slant could also be seen clearly in the commands and criminal orders that were issued, such as the "Special Areas Guidelines for Directive No. 21 (Operation Barbarossa)," issued on 13 March 1941; the edict on the "Conduct of Courts Martial in the 'Barbarossa' Area," issued on 13 May 1941; the "Guidelines on the Behavior of Troops in Russia," issued on 19 May 1941; and the "Guidelines on the Treatment of Political Commissars," issued on 6 June 1941. In addition, there was the special assignment given by Hitler to Reichsführer SS Heinrich Himmler, who was to assume responsibility for beginning the physical liquidation of "Jewish-Bolshevik" elements in the population with the help of SD *Einsatzgruppen*, or Action Groups. This would occur directly behind the front in the rear of the army areas.

Hitler's orders for annihilation and eradication make it clear that the most important part of the war for him began with the

1. Adolf Hitler, *Mein Kampf* (jubilee ed., Munich, 1935), p. 758.

offensive against the Soviet Union. This was confirmed by the judgment delivered in "Case 12" against the high command of the Wehrmacht before the American military court in Nuremberg on 28 October 1948, as well as by the early studies of Hans-Adolf Jacobsen, Gerald Reitlinger, and Heinrich Uhlig (Nos. 7, 20, 49, 54). Much research by Helmut Krausnick, Manfred Messerschmidt, Hans-Heinrich Wilhelm, Jürgen Förster, and, recently, Omar Bartov has provided further evidence of the dirty "war against the commissars," which is contrasted with the "clean" war conducted by the Wehrmacht according to the view propagated by German generals in their comments about the war (Nos. 2, 3, 23, 25, 50, 51, 52).

Finally, Hans-Heinrich Wilhelm produced a volume of documents dealing with the connection between "racial policies and the conduct of the war." It focused in particular on the Wehrmacht's complicity with the security police. Wilhelm documented in detail the notes in Goebbels' diary, which is now available, about the planned war of annihilation in the East (No. 22). Voices are still raised claiming that the German units and task forces did not carry out their orders in regard to captured commissars, or that they deliberately falsified the figures about the number of commissars shot; however, detailed research has proved that these belated claims are not true (No. 3). In most cases, the German divisions, corps, and armies on the Eastern Front carried out their criminal orders. So far, there are no research results to the contrary, although right-wing circles have long been announcing the imminent presentation of such findings.

Shortly before and on the day the offensive was launched, Hitler and Goebbels appeared very relieved that the great undertaking was under way. Goebbels noted in his diary that the Führer had been working on this campaign since the previous July. "Everything has been accomplished," he noted, and "nothing more" remained but to attack, "so that this cancer ... can be burned out." In a telling comment, Goebbels added: "What we have been fighting against our whole lives is now about to be *eradicated*."

Such thoughts found concrete expression in directives and procedures, developed in cooperation with both the OKW and OKH, that contravened international law and trampled on traditional concepts of the rules of war. These directives and procedures expose the brutal, inhuman core of the planned campaign and show that Hitler's racially based *Lebensraum* program provided the impetus for the decision to attack. The orders for the

Eastern campaign also show Hitler's desire to radicalize the war. In addition, they reveal the extent to which the OKW and OKH cooperated in planning and conducting the war of annihilation. Both command staffs helped to formulate criminal orders and then issued them, convinced that "the troops must also participate in the battle of ideologies in the eastern campaign," as General Halder noted in his diary on 6 May 1941 (No. B/162).

In mid-May and early June 1941, the general staff and enemy intelligence officers of the various units and commands were brought to special informational and instructional meetings to be informed about the technical aspects of cooperating with the police and special SD units in carrying out the "criminal orders," since some of these orders could be passed along only by word of mouth. The meetings with commanders of the SD *(Sicherheitsdienst)* and the police were jointly organized by Quartermaster-General Wagner, SD chief Heydrich, and OKW intelligence chief Canaris. Thereafter the Wehrmacht was never able to distance itself from this approach. It launched the war against the Soviet Union intent on barbarity and criminal activity and never deviated from this path.

Hitler would not have been able to carry out this special war of annihilation and liquidation as successfully as he did if he had not had direct or indirect support from many elements and elites in German military, economic, and diplomatic circles, through either what they did or what they failed to do. Only with this support were the national socialists able to mobilize anti-Communist and anti-Semitic sentiments for the purpose of criminal activities. Ernst Klee and Willi Dreßen, for instance, have provided very detailed evidence in their recent publications that many ordinary soldiers and policemen supported the war of annihilation and exhibited a propensity for brutality (No. 181). Omar Bartov has also written impressive studies of the extent to which German soldiers were willing to participate in "barbarizing" the war (Nos. 23, 24, 25).

The Nazis' plans for implementing their Eastern program, as revealed in individual orders and commands, justify calling the war against the Soviet Union "the most monstrous war of conquest, enslavement and annihilation in modern history" (No. 16a, p. 436). On the basis of this conviction, Jörg Friedrich studied the history of humanity at war, writing a lengthy book, now also available in paperback, about the "law of war," using the Eastern campaign as a prime example. Ranging all too far back into medieval times, he delved above all into the records of the

1948 Nuremberg Trials of the OKW, which had long lain dormant. Friedrich described in detail the desire of the Nazi leadership to radicalize the "ideological war" in the East after the summer of 1941. In his view, the key reason why the Wehrmacht colluded in the criminal conduct of the war and in the genocide of the Jews was not any affinity among the generals for Nazi racial convictions but rather their belief in the theory of total war. However, in attempting to write a general history of war, Friedrich's reach exceeded his grasp, and his presentation of the war between Germany and the Soviet Union remains – in view of the immense amount of source material – unfocused, impenetrable, and ultimately unsatisfying.

The most instructive analysis of the special nature of the Eastern campaign can still be found in the work of Andreas Hillgruber. According to him, the "eastern program" had four general political and economic goals that actuated the Nazi campaign against the Soviet Union and revealed the intention to annihilate and obliterate the foe (No. B/310):

1. liquidation of the "Jewish-Bolshevik" elite as well as the Jews in east-central Europe;
2. conquest of *Lebensraum* and colonies for the Third Reich;
3. slaughter and enslavement of the Slavic masses under German domination in so-called Reich Commissariats that would be created;
4. creation of a vast, self-sufficient territory in continental Europe that would be highly resistant to blockade and in which the conquered lands of the Soviet Union would complement the German economy, securing German domination of Europe and providing a springboard toward the achievement of Nazi Germany's ultimate goal of world power.

* * *

The racial element in Operation Barbarossa could be very clearly seen in the treatment to be accorded captured enemy soldiers. The various orders and edicts on the handling of Soviet prisoners before and after the first onslaught of 22 June 1941 point directly to a policy of annihilation and ruthless treatment of "Jewish Bolshevism." These orders and commands constituted a break with German military tradition. After the first border skirmishes and battles of encirclement, Soviet prisoners poured into German camps, where they were treated from the outset much worse than captured Western soldiers, as can be seen in the comparison drawn by David Rolf (No. 83). As a direct result of these orders and the ensuing brutality, between 2.5 and 3.3 million Soviet prisoners of war had died by the spring of 1945, out of a total of 5.7 million (these figures according to Ueberschär, No. B/107, p. 312). Of the more than 3.3 million Soviet soldiers taken prisoner by the Wehrmacht before the end of 1941, most were already dead by the spring of 1942.

The series of orders and directives behind the "special treatment" of Soviet prisoners of war came to light at the Nuremberg Trials (Nos. 20, B/182). The series began at the time of the preparations for the offensive, when the Wehrmacht prepared to encourage the view that Red Army soldiers were not "comrades in arms" but adversaries in a racial war of annihilation who had to be ruthlessly "liquidated." When captured, they were considered little more than "useless mouths" to feed. The Wehrmacht's totally inadequate preparations to provide food and shelter for captured enemy soldiers lead one to conclude that its commanders countenanced from the outset the widespread death that inevitably ensued.

For many years, there was no historical research into this matter. The first study was conducted by the Polish historian Szymon Datner in 1964 (No. 63). It was based mainly on records of the Nuremberg Trials. A thorough, critical analysis of the history of Soviet prisoners of war was begun after the Americans returned captured Wehrmacht records to Germany. Documents gathered for the numerous trials of individual Nazi criminals after the war proved very useful as well. The most important work in this area was done by the Heidelberg historian Christian Streit. As a member of the younger generation, he did not shy away from highlighting the culpability of the Wehrmacht in this regard (Nos. 91–95). He looked in particular at Wehrmacht cooperation with the Action Groups in murdering prisoners of war and at the policies adopted toward Soviet soldiers who survived and were eventually used for slave labor. A revised new edition of his thorough, comprehensive study was published in 1991. Here Streit provides an excellent overview of the research into prisoners of war (No. 91).

Shortly after Streit's first book appeared, Alfred Streim, who was one of the state prosecutors responsible for bringing Nazis to justice, published another overview of this question (Nos. 88, 89, 90), which basically confirmed what Streit had said. Streim used primarily source materials that had been collected for trials of former Nazis. In a later, shortened pocketbook edition of his voluminous study, he took a clearer stand than previously against any "sweeping condemnation" of the entire Wehrmacht (No. 89). Wehrmacht veterans who were still alive denied the new research results, although they were unable to provide any concrete proof for their self-justification (No. 84).

A controversy arose among historians about the exact number of Soviet prisoners of war who died in German captivity. Christian Streit set this figure at about 3.3 million, while Alfred Streim concluded that at least 2.5 million died. The Freiburg military historian Joachim Hoffmann calculated that between 2 and 2.8 million Soviet prisoners of war died, out of a total of 5.24 million (Nos. B/313, p. 730; 72). Hans Roschmann gave still lower figures in his account of his personal experiences (No. 84). Soviet calculations of the number of Red Army prisoners of war who died or were killed vary between 1.8 and 4 million (No. 68). Recently, Russian historians have set the number of Soviet armed forces personnel who were captured by the Germans at 4.059 million (No. 78). Bernd Bonwetsch has published a short overview of this entire question (No. 56).

The policy of killing captured Soviet soldiers was carried out without any regard for international law. The Nazi leaders refused any legal obligations regarding prisoners of war, although there was some discussion with the Soviets about mutual observance of the 1929 Geneva Convention on Prisoners of War and of the 1907 Hague Convention on the laws and customs of warfare on land. The Soviets made an offer to this effect in July 1941, but it was expressly rejected by Hitler on 25 August 1941. Recently, a controversy arose about whether Stalin's offer was serious or not, pitting Hoffmann on one side against Streit, Müller, and Ueberschär on the other (in No. B/371, 91). This question cannot be definitely resolved. In any case, Hitler was not interested in Moscow's offer. General obligations under international law remained in effect, although they, too, were ignored.

Already on 16 June 1941, the OKW department responsible for prisoners of war announced that "strict, energetic measures should be taken at the least sign of resistance." Several further orders emphasized and heightened demands for tough, uncompromising treatment. This went so far that shooting prisoners of war was portrayed as "generally lawful" and normally expected. After discussions with the OKW, SD chief Heydrich issued orders on 17 and 24 July 1941 concerning picking out "politically undesirable prisoners of war" and turning them over to the security police or SD Action Commandos for execution. Approximately 500,000 to 600,000 Soviet prisoners of war were selected in this way to be executed by Action Commandos. The victims were led away immediately after capture. These *Ausgesonderte* – these included "all the Jews" – were either killed at once or turned over to the SS to be shot. The relevant guidelines and orders have been reprinted and documented in many different publications (cf. No. B/107).

Many more prisoners of war died while being transported to the camps because the responsible army and armed forces officials knowingly provided far too little food, shelter, and medical treatment to the hordes of prisoners. Although senior officers in the German army knew full well that Soviet prisoners of war were receiving insufficient food, they ordered a drastic reduction in the already skimpy rations on 21 October 1941, with the result that soon two to three percent of Soviet prisoners were dying daily. This reduction was inspired by Göring's demand that food provisions for the German civilian population be improved at the expense of supplies in the conquered areas of the Soviet Union. Both Christian Streit and Rolf-Dieter Müller have published accounts of the rations provided to prisoners of war (Nos. 93; 14, p. 1195f.; B/107). Under the depressing title *Ich habe geweint vor Hunger* (I Cried from Hunger), Dieter Bach and Jochen Leyendecker compared the sorry plights of German and Soviet prisoners of war (No. 55). Their highly informative omnibus volume quickly describes many aspects of daily life in the POW camps and strategies for survival. The large number of deaths among Soviet prisoners of war can be further explained by the completely inadequate shelter provided to them and by the long trips to the POW camps. Thousands of exhausted, enervated prisoners were shot by guards as they struggled to reach the camps on foot. A particularly horrific fate awaited those Soviet prisoners of war who were carted off to concentration camps, especially Auschwitz, as slave laborers or subjects of medical experiments (No. 58).

In December 1941, it became clear as the German offensive ground to a halt before the gates of Moscow that Operation Barbarossa would not end soon in another marvelous victory for blitzkrieg and that Soviet prisoners of war would be needed as cheap labor for the German war economy and armaments plants. As a result, the food and shelter provided to captured Soviets began to improve in early 1942. By the summer, the mortality rate was declining, although it always remained higher than among captured personnel from other Allied nations. By the summer of 1944, Soviet prisoners of war were provided the same amount of food as other prisoners of war, so that they had a real chance of survival.

Typical of the inhuman regulations for handling Soviet prisoners of war were the framework commands issued on 8 September 1941 by Major General Hermann Reinecke, the chief of the general armed forces office in the OKW responsible for prisoners of war. He ordered tougher treatment of Soviet prisoners of war, commanding the guards to respond very severely and harshly. In addition, special methods were to be instituted for picking out politically undesirable prisoners, who were to be turned over to the Action Commandos and shot. Admiral Wilhelm Canaris, the head of armed forces intelligence, sought in vain, together with friends of similar views, to raise objections and concerns about Reinecke's edict. Canaris strongly opposed the deliberate murder of politically undesirable prisoners, as demanded by Reinecke. However, he failed to make any headway with his colleagues in the OKW under the command of Field Marshal Keitel. In fact, Keitel was inclined to condone the brutal treatment of prisoners of war because the essence of the Eastern campaign was, in his view, "the annihilation of a particular ideology," namely Bolshevism.

This belief, as expressed by Keitel, was widespread not only in Nazi circles but in the officer corps as well. This was the main reason for the officers' willingness to conduct the "struggle against the Bolsheviks" as a fierce war of annihilation between two opposing ideologies, in flagrant disregard of the international community and the international rules of war. Relatively few officers openly opposed this attitude and sought ways to mitigate the mass murder on the Eastern Front, as did Admiral Canaris, Colonel Oster, Major von Gersdorff, Lieutenant Colonel Stieff, Count von Moltke, and other officers who took part in the Resistance.

Not only the German conquerors despised the Red Army soldiers captured in the early phase of the campaign – so did their own leaders in Moscow. According to Soviet military doctrine, soldiers were expected to fight to the death and were forbidden to surrender under any conditions. As a result, Stalin did not make any serious attempt to protect those who were captured. To him, they were traitors who deserved their fate. They did not even exist according to Soviet propaganda. In the first part of the Eastern campaign, an unusually large number of Soviet prisoners became willing accomplices of the Germans. These numbers remained higher than the corresponding figure for the Western Allies until the end of the war. This is all the more striking in view of the especially cruel treatment meted out to Soviets, the bloody mass murders and crimes, and the Germans' intention to establish colonies, which they made no attempt to conceal. The unusual willingness to help the Germans can only be explained by the prevailing conditions under Stalin and the tensions between the various nationalities in the Soviet Union.

Considerable numbers of Soviet prisoners of war began assisting the Wehrmacht directly. It was hard to make firm distinctions between captured Soviet soldiers, partisans, forcibly recruited "voluntary helpers" of the Wehrmacht, eastern workers, and, at the end of the war, people who had been forcibly evacuated (see in this regard Part D: The Occupation). The recruitment of about onr million voluntary workers from the prison camps has to be seen in the context of the miserable conditions that prevailed and widespread death among the sick and those who could not work. It is reasonable to assume that many of the volunteers among the "eastern troops" on the one hand were trying to escape certain death in the camps on the one hand and on the other rejected the conditions of the Stalin regime. Others, however, definitely wanted to participate in the political resistance to Bolshevism and the dictator Stalin (No. 65). They assisted the Nazi assassins of their own people in the desperate hope that the Germans would eventually alter their policies in the East. Information about these people from a German point of view can be found in a book about General Ernst Köstring, "General of the Volunteer Units" (No. 96).

The vast majority of Soviet prisoners of war, if they survived the camps at all as able-bodied workers, were subjected to ruthless treatment as forced laborers. They performed very strenuous tasks under generally murderous conditions, and their position was scarcely any better than that of the Jewish slave laborers. However, as the war continued, conditions for various Soviet slave laborers and their chances of survival varied considerably. Recently, locally organized studies of individual POW camps, often undertaken by groups of concerned citizens in so-called history workshops, have produced more detailed information about the living conditions and daily events in camps such as Bergen-Belsen, Stukenbrock, Fallingbostel, Neuengamme, and Sandbostel (Nos. 73–75, 79, 82, 85–87). New source materials about the Stukenbrock camp were recently found in the State Archives of the Russian Federation in Moscow. An omnibus volume on the "Reichseinsatz," edited by Ulrich Herbert, provides a comparison with the rest of occupied Europe. It also offers a careful, differentiated account of the working conditions of civilian workers, prisoners of war, and concentration camp inmates (Nos. 69, 70).

In contrast to prisoners of war from other Allied countries, Soviets who survived Hitler's camps did not return to their homeland after the war as liberated heroes. Many underwent forced repatriation, while others succeeded in remaining in the West, including quite a few war criminals. Since Stalin distrusted members of the Red Army who had been captured, most Soviet prisoners of war passed straight from the German concentration camps to the camps of the "Gulag Archipelago," so compellingly described by Alexander Solzhenitsyn (No. E/301a).

In the past, Soviet historians engaged for the most part in a disinformation campaign about the extent of the prisoner-of-war problem in order to squelch any discussion of the share of the guilt borne by Soviet leaders. In the official works published under the title of *The Great Patriotic War of the Soviet Union* (see No. B/56), prisoners of war were not discussed. The few studies that mentioned captured Soviet soldiers at all portrayed them only as putting up heroic resistance in the Nazi camps (Nos. 59, 60). The first comprehensive study of Soviet prisoners of war, by E.A. Brodsky, was finally published in 1987, twenty-five years after it had been written (No. 61). The memoirs of four Soviet prisoners of war, published under the patronage of Alexander Solzhenitsyn, were also prevented from reaching a larger audience (No. 62). The first account of the repatriation problem available to Soviet readers was written by V.N. Zemskov (No. 100). It is unlikely that there will be much opportunity in the near future to study the full extent of the camps and the fate that befell Soviet prisoners of war caught up in the web of surrender, collaboration, and resistance.

* * *

When the Wehrmacht launched its offensive on 22 June 1941, it sliced into the most westerly part of the Soviet Union, which at the time of the czars had been "the pale of Jewish settlement." Here lived the over four million Jews of eastern Europe, the greatest concentration in Europe (Nos. 327, 120). After the desperate flight of about 800,000 to one million of these people, approximately 3 to 3.2 million were left to fall into Nazi hands (Nos. 208, 283, 330, 340). The German occupiers planned to eradicate this population in order to "make room" for German settlements and other regional development plans, in accordance with the schemes of the Nazi hierarchy. On 15 July 1941, the chief of planning in the SS Reich security headquarters, Konrad Meyer, presented the first draft of what would become the "General Plan for the East" to Heinrich Himmler, the "Reichsführer SS" and "Reich Commissar for the Consolidation of the German Nation." This draft plan called for vast, megalomaniacal deportations of more than thirty million Jews and Slavs from eastern Poland, the Baltic countries, White Russia, and the Ukraine and for resettlement of these areas by Germans and other "Germanic" peoples. Studies by Helmut Heiber, Christopher R. Browning, Rolf-Dieter Müller, Czeslaw Madajczyk, and Wolfgang Benz have shown in detail that Jews would be excluded from these areas (Nos. 15, 137, 156, 225, 300, 301; see also the further information in Part D: The Occupation). In addition, an extensive collection of sources on Nazi policy, *Vom Generalplan Ost zum Generalsiedlungsplan*, now exists, offering all documents available on this subject (No. 303). Under the heading "Jews and other victims of Nazi racial policy," the omnibus volume *Faschismus und Rassismus* delves into individual aspects of anti-Semitism in Nazi ideology and policies and provides further information. In so doing, Dietrich Eichholtz depicts the fate that befell the affected peoples of eastern Europe under the General Plan for the East (Nos. 187, 188).

The genocide of the Jews developed out of these racial goals. The first broad overview of the Holocaust by Gerald Reitlinger was reissued in 1992 for the seventh time (No. 346). It is still considered an in-depth standard work on the "Final Solution." Equally comprehensive and well informed are the studies by Leni Yahil, Gideon Hausner, Wolfgang Scheffler, Lucy S. Dawidowicz, Yehuda Bauer, Nora Levin, and Martin Gilbert (Nos. 132, 173, 205, 220, 284, 361, 415). Gerhard Schoenberner published a very successful volume of texts and pictures containing numerous photographs of the Holocaust (No. 370). Pointing the way for future research into the entire history of the Holocaust is also the monumental work of Raul Hilberg, which covers numerous events in great detail. Hilberg, an American historian who was born in Vienna, first published his study of *The Destruction of the European Jews* in Chicago in 1961. It appeared in German translation in 1982 and was published once again in a full-length, three-volume, German paperback edition in 1990 as part of the series *Die Zeit des Nationalsozialismus*, edited by Walter H. Pehle (No. 228). Hilberg provides a comprehensive picture of the entire apparatus for annihilating Jews, its structures and bureaucratic channels. Expanding on his first work, Hilberg then published another volume of documents in 1972 (Nos. 229, 230). In his much heeded autobiography *Unerbetene Erinnerung*, he describes his dedicated research on the history of the persecution of the Jews as a "revolt against silence" (No. 233). Further extensive documentations of the history of persecution of the Jews and of the Holocaust were produced by John Mendelsohn, Peter Longerich, Arad Yitzhak, Israel Gutman, Abraham Margaliot, Lucy S. Dawidowicz, and Kurt Pätzold. A report by Adalbert Rückerl contains further documentation, as does a collection of sentences imposed by German courts after 1945 for murders committed under the Nazi regime, as well as the report, now in an extended new edition, of Robert M.W. Kempner, *SS im Kreuzverhör*, on his activities as U.S. prosecutor at the trials of the SS *Einsatzgruppen-Prozeß* in Nuremberg in 1947/48 (Nos. 116, 175, 216, 294, 314, 333, 356, 357, 358). After the trial of Adolf Eichmann in Jerusalem, several studies and volumes of documents appeared about the testimony he had given. Some of them contained detailed information about how the "Final Solution" was carried out; Hannah Arendt's report has now been republished as a paperback (Nos. 118, 146, 270). New overviews of the Auschwitz and other Nazi crime trials are offered by Gerhard Werle and Thomas Wandres as well as by Jürgen Wilke, Birgit Schenk, Akiba Cohen, and Tamil Zemach (Nos. 168, 409).

The four-volume *Encyclopedia of the Holocaust* was intended as an erudite lexicographical reference work about the genocide of the Jews. It was edited by Israel Gutman, the longtime director of the Yad Vashem Holocaust Research Center in Jerusalem, and was a joint production of Yad Vashem, the Holocaust Martyrs, and the Heroes Remembrance Authority, published simultaneously in Israel and the United States (No. 218). More than 200 researchers from an array of countries provided a comprehensive overview of the current state of the research into the causes, background, and consequences of the destruction of the Jews. The original English edition served as the basis for the German edition that appeared somewhat later in three volumes; a four-volume German paperback edition is now available (No. 218). Bibliographical reference works about the Holocaust include the work compiled by Israel W. Charny and the guides compiled by Jacob Robinson and Philip Friedman, by Abraham J. Edelheit and Hershel Edelheit, and by Michael R. Marrus (Nos. 166, 185, 308, 351). Martin Broszat, Michael Marrus, and Konrad Kwiet published research reports that also provide good overviews (Nos. 152, 266, 307).

A recent study by Gerd Robel offers a detailed analysis of the number of Jews living in the areas of the Soviet Union conquered by the Germans who died in the Holocaust. This study appeared in the handbook *Dimension des Völkermordes*, edited by Wolfgang Benz, which provided an excellent overview of the discussion surrounding the assertion that nearly six million Jews died at the hands of the Nazis in all of Europe (No. 138). The magnitude of the slaughter in the Soviet Union was also discussed in a study by Yitzhak Arad (No. 114). Dov Levin undertook this same task with regard to the territories annexed by the Soviet Union at the time of the Nazi-Soviet pact (No. 281).

Soviet Jewry suffered a cruel and inhuman fate as a result of the Nazis' militant, ideologically motivated racial policies. According to the Nazis, "Jewish Bolshevism" was "world enemy number one." It symbolized the menace they subjectively perceived and led to the mad concept of a "Jewish threat." It was the looming menace of "Jewish Bolshevism" that the Nazis were determined to destroy. In his unfortunately undocumented study, *Why Did the Heavens not Darken?*, Arno Mayer described how this policy of annihilation was conceived and implemented in combination with Operation Barbarossa, the surprise attack on the Soviet Union in June 1941 (No. 310). According to Mayer, the genocide of the Jews in the conquered areas of the Soviet Union was the result of fortuitous developments after the Wehrmacht reached particular bottlenecks and moments of truth and the Nazi leaders realized that the war in the East was lost. Only then did the Nazis turn their attention to implementing fully their plans to liquidate the Jews. This interpretation, and some chronological mistakes, were heavily criticized, especially in English-speaking countries (see, among, others Nos. 317, 355). It is generally agreed that the anti-Semitism of Hitler and his acolytes was the driving force, the "primary ideology," behind the Nazi policy of war and annihilation after 1939 (No. 362).

The uniqueness of the Holocaust as the foundation of Hitler's Eastern program assumed particular importance in the "Historikerstreit" in Germany in the mid-1980s. However, the discussion ranged far beyond the destruction of the Jews in eastern Europe.

Volume 19 of the *Yad Vashem Studies* of 1988 provided an account of the historical place of questions and answers about the Holocaust. Further information can be found in works by Richard Evans, Lucy S. Dawidowicz, Israel Gutman, Otto D. Kulka, Charles Maier, Christian Meier, Saul Friedländer, and Peter Baldwin (Nos. 125, 174, 178, 192, 200, 215, 262, 304, 311, 312).

Before the Eastern campaign began, the Reich Security Headquarters established "security police and SD Action Groups" to conduct the war of annihilation as part of special security police duties outside the purview of the regular army. In the course of organizing this, a detailed arrangement was worked out in April 1941 with the high command of the army, which approved the proposed division of tasks. Information about the organization of the Action Groups, which reported solely to Reichsführer SS Heinrich Himmler, and about the mass murders they committed in the early phase of the Eastern campaign can be found in studies by Helmut Krausnick, Hans-Heinrich Wilhelm, Martin Broszat, Alfred Steim, Robert W. Kempner, Jürgen Förster, and Ronald Headland as well as in the early volumes of the proceedings of the Nuremberg Trials (Nos. 3, 12, 159, 249, 250, 297, 390, 391, B/182).

In order to carry out the genocide, four *Einsatzgruppen,* or Action Groups, were created, each between 600 and 1,000 men strong: Action Group A under SS *Gruppenführer* and Lieutenant General Walter Stahlecker, Action Group B under SS *Brigadeführer* and Major General and chief of Reich criminal police Arthur Nebe, Action Group C under SS *Oberführer* and Brigadier Otto Rasch, and Action Group D under SS *Standartenführer* and Colonel Otto Ohlendorf. Each Action Group had four or five Special Commandos *(Sonderkommandos)* or Action Commandos *(Einsatzkommandos).* As the war proceeded, reports were continually written about the activities of the Action Groups and the number of people killed. They were called "USSR Event Reports" from June 1941 to April 1942 and "Reports from the Occupied Eastern Territories" from May 1942 to May 1943. In addition, comprehensive "Activity and Position Reports of the Security Police and SD Action Groups in the USSR" were also produced from June 1941 until March 1942. The value of these sources as historical "Messages of Murder" has been described and analyzed excellently by Ronald Headland in a recent publication (Nos. 117, 222, 223). Further information about the tasks and activities of the Action Groups can also be found in a study by Alfred Streim as well as in the published judgment handed down in "Case 9," the so-called Action Groups trial (Nos. 20, 275, 392).

These publications describe the murders committed not only by the Action Commandos but also by the Special Commandos and other forces of the senior SS commanders and police chiefs in the rear of the army areas. Three further SS brigades, attached to the Reichsführer SS Operational Staff and under direct orders from Heinrich Himmler, operated as another special murder unit (Nos. 121, 160). Between June 1941 and April 1942, about 550,000 people were killed by the Action Groups and Commandos.

For a long time, controversy has swirled around a putative written or verbal "Führer directive" ordering the mass murder of Jews, since no written orders from Hitler have ever been found or proved to have existed (No. 308). The Stuttgart historian Eberhard Jäckel has repeatedly insisted that only Hitler could have initiated a campaign to make Germany and the countries it conquered "free of Jews" (No. 242). Such a "Führer directive" could have been issued after Hitler's meeting with Himmler and Heydrich on 24 September 1941. According to Helmut Krausnick and Richard Breitman, Hitler may have issued his order as early as March 1941 (Nos. 148, 259, 391). In 1985, Andreas Hillgruber published some preliminary findings in this regard in his study *War in the East and the Extermination of the Jews.* He emphasized Hitler's clearly recognizable desire both to publicly announce the physical annihilation of the Jews and to carry it out to the very end (Nos. 235, 236). David Bankier also highlighted the key role Hitler played in making decisions about the "Jewish question" (No. 126). On the other hand, the Swiss historian Philippe Burrin claimed in a study published in French and now available in German translation that Hitler was basically resolved to destroy the Jews but was only spurred into action by a "murderous wrath" in the autumn of 1941 when it became clear that blitzkrieg would likely fail in the East. The Jews would pay for the failure (No. 161). However, on 17 June 1941 in Berlin, SS Major General Reinhard Heydrich had already informed the SS and SD chiefs in detail about the mass murders they were to carry out. In addition, Göring had given Heydrich clear instructions on 31 July 1941 to make "all necessary organizational, technical and material preparations ... for a comprehensive solution to the Jewish problem in the German sphere of influence in Europe." A new and detailed overview of the history of the decision is provided by the Berlin historian Götz Aly; his study covers the period from 1 September 1939 until the Wannsee Conference on 20 January 1942. He points out that the most important conditions for the "Final Solution" were not created until the war. According to his conclusion, there was no single resolution but rather "for the Führer state [an] unusually long and complex decision-making process," which, in connection with the Nazi settlement plans for the East, led to the Holocaust (No. 103).

In response to this "Bestellung," as Heydrich called it (or "order" in the realm of commerce), the SD commander sought to reach a broad understanding among all the departments and bureaus involved in the "comprehensive solution of the Jewish problem." The original conference planned for December 1941 had to be postponed because of the military setback before the gates of Moscow and the entry of the United States into the war. However, the meeting was finally held on 20 January 1942 in a villa on the Wannsee. At this Wannsee Conference, the participants gave Heydrich their full, "joyous" support for the liquidation of eleven million Jews in Europe, in a process that had already begun. The minutes of the Wannsee Conference, taken by SS Lieutenant Colonel Adolf Eichmann, were preserved in the records of the Nuremberg Trials and have gained a certain infamy as the key written document *(Schlüsseldokument)* in Heydrich's planning and initiation of the physical extermination of European Jews in the framework of the "Final Solution" that took place with the consent of Hitler and Göring. Numerous historians, such as Wolfgang Scheffler, Götz Aly, and Susanne Heim have portrayed these minutes as a central document in the genocide of European Jews in fulfillment of Nazi racial policies (Nos. 105, 363, 365). These minutes demonstrate that the genocide was not to remain confined to Soviet Jews but was to include all eleven million Jews throughout Europe, to the extent that they could be rounded up in areas under German occupation or influence.

Recently, Kurt Pätzold, Erika Schwarz, and Johannes Tuchel have published further, careful documentation about the course of the Wannsee Conference and about the villa where it was held, which has now finally been turned into a memorial and educational center (Nos. 334, 335, 402). Tuchel succeeds in totally dispelling the absurd doubts cast on the authenticity of these minutes by right-wing extremists. Eberhard Jäckel also recently published a new interpretation of the Wannsee Conference, pointing out the differing approaches to the Jewish question taken by Hitler and Heydrich and downgrading the importance of this particular conference. No decision was made there, he says, to implement the "final solution to the Jewish question." Instead, the conference was intended primarily to enhance Heydrich's personal prestige and to provide information to the central departments that would be involved in the genocide already taking place (No. 354).

Christopher Browning and Hans-Jürgen Döscher published separate studies of the deep involvement of the German Foreign Office in the "implementation of the orders to murder" Jews. They analyze in detail the efforts that were made to provide diplomatic cover abroad for all the killing (Nos. 153, 177). In addition, Yitzhak Arad has provided a preliminary overview of the involvement of the Eastern Ministry under Alfred Rosenberg in carrying out the "Final Solution" (No. 110).

Heydrich made it clear to the senior government officials and the NSDAP leaders attending the Wannsee Conference that Hitler had put Heinrich Himmler in charge of the centrally controlled "Final Solution." Himmler's role has been described in detail in new biographies of the "Reichsführer SS" by Richard Breitman and Peter Padfield (Nos. 148, 331). Breitman describes Himmler as an obedient mastermind murderer who eagerly turned Hitler's orders into reality through the SS.

* * *

Numerous descriptions and documentary works are available on the genocide of six million Jews – the Holocaust, or Shoah – that occurred not only in the Soviet Union but throughout all of Nazi- or fascist-controlled Europe. Many were published as commemorative volumes after a myriad of international conferences, in a fitting tribute to all the innocent victims and in order to keep alive memories of this particularly barbarous aspect of the Second World War. In addition to reissues of older works are recent studies by Gerald Reitlinger, Raul Hilberg, Lea Rosh and Eberhard Jäckel; the omnibus volume *Shoah and the War*; and the brief summaries by Barbara Rogasky and Ronnie S. Landau. In *Der Tod ist ein Meister aus Deutschland*, Lea Rosh and Eberhard Jäckel gathered eyewitness reports that provide a broad overview of the genocide of the Jews in twelve of the seventeen European countries in which it occurred. This work has been reissued several times since 1992, in paperback editions as well (Nos. 170, 228, 229, 230, 346, 354). In addition, Inge Deutschkron, Debórah

Dwork, André Stein, and Alwin Meyer have published particularly moving collections of documents and reports about crimes against children and their lives of suffering in the ghettos and camps of Europe (Nos. 176, 183, 316, 385).

The Action Commandos and Special Commandos were placed under "SD and security police commanders" or "chiefs of the security police and SD (BdS)," who soon established local offices in the newly created German General Areas of the so-called Reich Commissariats. In addition to murdering Jewish civilians, these commandos also carried out tactical military operations against Soviet partisans to the rear of the army areas. Soon they were no longer mobile units but had firmly established local and regional offices.

The SS and SD units also employed foreign nationals to help carry out both parts of their job of allegedly ensuring the "internal pacification" of the conquered areas of the Soviet Union. These foreigners stemmed mostly from nationalistic non-Russian groups that also had strong anti-Semitic feelings. Himmler issued explicit orders "not to put any obstacles" in the way of the "self-cleansing efforts" of these anti-Semitic and anti-Communist groups. Furthermore, the outbreak of spontaneous, local pogroms was to be encouraged with the help of these "national self-protection groups," during which they could assume some of the burden for the SS and SD of murdering Jews. This strategy succeeded in the Baltic and the Ukraine, where many Jews were cruelly murdered by local people. These murders were facilitated by the fact that, even before the war, relations between Jews and the local population had often been tense in these areas (No. 282). The Ukrainian church likewise played a very dubious role in the anti-Semitic measures and among the anti-Semitic "helpers" in the Ukraine, as Simon Redlich has shown (No. 345).

Exact figures are still not available on the number of these local "helpers." However, the number of Estonians, Lithuanians, Latvians, and Ukrainians who participated in para-police forces and of Crimean Tartars who participated in "protection squads" was not negligible. Their basic political hope was that the Germans would support their ethnic groups and grant them autonomy and self-determination as a reward for the assistance they provided. But this was not to be: according to the Nazis' plans, both the Baltic countries and the Crimea were to become areas of "Germanic" settlement. Studies on the occupation policy by Alexander Dallin and Sepp Myllyniemi describe these matters in detail (Nos. 1, D/159). Despite local participation in the murder of Jews, ultimate responsibility still lay with the Germans. The "helpers" or "protection squads" operated on behalf of the Germans and in accordance with Nazi racial policies. In the newly created countries in the European part of the former Soviet Union, researchers are beginning only very hesitantly to study this national history of anti-Semitism.

Max Kaufmann and Bernhard Press have written two detailed accounts of anti-Semitic actions in Latvia. Like the work of Margers Vestermanis or the descriptions provided by survivors of the Holocaust, they deal with the participation of local Latvian forces (Nos. 143, 247, 342, 366, 367, 404). As far as Lithuania is concerned, Gigorijus Smoliakovas has described his own experiences as one of the few Jews to survive. By July 1944, approximately ninety-four percent of Lithuanian Jews had been murdered. Shortly before and after the Wehrmacht marched in, "Lithuanian volunteers" for the SD committed unspeakable acts against Jews in Kovno. By 1 December 1941, they had allegedly killed between 4,000 and 10,000 Lithuanian Jews (Nos. 279, 282, 380).

In northern Bukovina and Bessarabia (which after being conquered was to be reattached to Rumania), and in the occupied portions of Transnistria with the area around Odessa, Action Group D could count on the assistance of foreign nationals. In this case, Rumanian troops behaved just as brutally toward Jews as did the German SD commandos (Nos. 108, 151, 193, 289). During the deportations to Transnistria, Jews were callously allowed to starve, with the result that between 130,000 and 150,000 died. A plan to save them failed when the Germans refused to give their consent to it (No. 329). The large, well-established Jewish population of the Bukovinian capital of Chernovtsy was deported or murdered. In addition, 50,000 to 80,000 Jewish inhabitants of Odessa were murdered by the Rumanians (No. 289).

As the Action Groups went about their grim business, they occasionally came into close contact with army units and Wehrmacht bureaus that sometimes took part in the executions. Ernst Klee and Willy Dreßen have documented the "active complicity" of the Wehrmacht with SD and SS murder commandos (Nos. 179, 181). The records these researchers gathered provide relentless evidence of the deep involvement of many Wehrmacht soldiers in the murder of Jewish civilians in the occupied areas of the Soviet Union. A documentation that deals with the connection between racial policy and the conduct of the war and particularly considers the complicity between the security police and the Wehrmacht was recently produced by Hans-Heinrich Wilhelm (No. 22). He documents in detail the relevant notes on the planned war of annihilation in the East to be found in Goebbels' diaries, which are now available. The "criminal orders" mentioned above were executed mainly by the divisions, corps, and armies on the Eastern Front (No. 3). Research results to the contrary have not been presented as yet, although notification of their appearance has been given more than once by "right-wing nationalist quarters." The Secret Field Police also cooperated closely with the SS and SD, as did the security divisions to the rear of the army areas, in individual measures undertaken as part of the "Final Solution" regarding the Jewish civilian population. Helmut Krausnick, Hans-Heinrich Wilhelm, and several historians from the Militärgeschichtliches Forschungsamt, previously in Freiburg, as well as Christian Streit and the English historian Theo Schulte have presented important results on this subject (Nos. 12, 45, 395, B/107). The part played by the city commandant of Kiev, General Kurt Eberhard, and his units in rounding up and murdering 33,771 Jewish inhabitants of the Ukrainian capital on 29–30 September 1941 is well known. Erhard R. Wiehn has gathered extensive documentation about this massacre in the ravine of Babi Yar (No. 411).

It is difficult to determine the exact extent to which army units supported individual massacres or to make generalizations about the willingness of the Wehrmacht in general to participate in the "work" of the Action Groups. It is significant, though, that ideologically inglorious tainted orders have been preserved from several commanders, in which they demand "complete understanding" for the "need for tough but justified atonement on the part of Jewish *Untermenschen*" – for instance, the already mentioned framework orders issued by Field Marshal von Reichenau on 10 October 1941 (see No. B/107). The Israeli historian Yehuda L. Wallach has pointed out comparable views expressed by Field Marshal von Manstein, who issued a similar order as supreme commander of the Eleventh Army in the south and in the Crimea (No. 405). On the recommendation of Hitler and Field Marshal von Rundstedt, Reichenau's orders were reissued by several other commanders (including von Manstein, Hoth, and Busch). Manfred Messerschmidt has demonstrated in general that senior commanders of the Wehrmacht had few scruples about cooperating in the genocide (No. 315). More recent assessments assign a greater direct participation of the Wehrmacht in the war crimes and the Holocaust. This is now documented in the omnibus volume *Vernichtungskrieg*, which was presented in 1995 on the occasion of the Hamburg exhibition on the war crimes of the Wehrmacht and raised considerable interest (No. 35).

While the Action Group firing squads went about their "work," a number of Jewish ghettos were created in the Baltic countries and, most important, in the bigger cities of White Russia, Volynia (Western Ukraine), and Ukraine, in the area under Action Group B commanded by SS Major General Nebe, because large Jewish populations lived there. These ghettos could be found in, for instance, Riga, Vilna, Minsk, Byalystok, Grodno, Korets, Dubno, Kovel, Gantsevitsi, and Lida. Several informative accounts have been published of the structure and organization of these ghettos, as well as of daily life in the ghettos, which were forced to produce goods for the German war economy and armaments plants (Nos. 164, 165, 291, 366, 381, 382).

A volume of source materials by Hartmut Lenhard, "*Lebensraum im Osten. Deutsche in Belorußland 1941–1944* (No. 13), focuses on events in the Minsk ghetto, to which German Jews were sent as well, and on the murder of Jews in the "General District of White Ruthenia," as Belarus was called at the time. This publication includes an excellent folder of documents and materials for use in schools and for adult education. These describe both the horrendous effects of the war and the brutality of the SS, the SD, and the police as they went about their business of liquidating Jews in the areas of White Russia conquered by the Wehrmacht. In *The Eye of the Hurricane*, Shalom Chalovsky portrays the murder of the Jews of White Russia, carried out through the office of the "SD commander and security police chief" in Minsk, as the epicenter of these activities (No. 165). Another study of these events is being undertaken by the Institute for Social Studies in Hamburg. In addition, Paul Kohl described the German massacre in White Russia in a volume designed to be an account of his travels. Kohl followed the route taken almost four decades earlier by Army Group Center as it marched on Moscow, allowing plenty of space in his book for eyewitness accounts by Soviets whom he encountered along the way. In all, the book, now available in paperback, bears shattering witness to the German campaign of annihilation against the population of White Russia (No. 11). Kohl's book also recalls the leveling of the White Russian village of Khatyn and the murder of all its inhabitants by SS brigade "Dirlewanger." The central memorial for all of White Russia was erected in this place in 1969 (see as well No. 293).

Beginning in the fall of 1941, extensive mass executions again took place in White Russia as squads cleared the ghettos. Finally, the ghettos were destroyed in the framework of "Action Reinhard" beginning in the summer of 1942 (No. 231). On 21 June 1943, Himmler issued orders to dissolve all ghettos in the Reichskommissariat Ostland as well. By the end of the year, tens of thousands of Jews had been murdered in the cities of Ostland or transported to Treblinka or Auschwitz and murdered there. The same fate befell Jews living in ghettos in the larger cities of Lithuania (Kaunas, Vilnius, and Siauliai) and Latvia (Riga and Libau). Here they found only a short reprieve before they, too, were murdered (Nos. 111, 143, 207, 247, 342, 366, 399).

Accounts by Helmut Krausnick, Hans-Heinrich Wilhelm, Willi Dreßen, and Ernst Klee describe in detail the savage procedures followed by brutish and sometimes drunken SS and SD personnel as well as policemen in executing Jews (Nos. 5, 12). A firsthand description can be found as well in the report written on 1 December 1941 by SS Colonel Jäger, who took part as leader of Action Commando 3 in the murder of 137,000 Jews (including 55,000 women and 34,000 children). This report, which survived the war, is available in German and English (reprint in Nos. 229; 230, p. 46f; 356; 357).

In order to prevent the personal brutalization of the SS men involved, gas trucks were introduced in late 1941 and the Jews were murdered by means of the exhaust and carbon monoxide poisoning (No. 136). However, this method was not efficient enough for the Nazi murderers. In September 1941, the SS began experimenting in Auschwitz I with the use of the poisonous gas Zyklon B for the mass execution of Soviet prisoners of war, as has been described in an omnibus volume edited by Eugen Kogon, Hermann Langbein, and Adalbert Rückerl (No. 254). From October 1941 onward, deportation trains filled with Jews began rolling toward the Baltic states and the East. Soon, the concentration camps Auschwitz-Birkenau, Chelmo, Sobibor, Belzec, Treblinka, and Lublin-Majdanek were built (Nos. 113, 348, 364), which, from spring/summer 1942 until November 1943, were also used in the framework of "Operation Reinhard" for the liquidation of the Jews from the territory under German rule (Nos. 112, 231). Jean-Claude Pressac, who himself once doubted the Holocaust, has described the various procedures for liquidating inmates and how they were carried out from a technical point of view (No. 343). His detailed study is now available in German and English translation and as a German paperback and effectively disproves right-wing works such as the *Leuchter Report* that like to point to various alleged technical snags and contradictions in order to deny the Holocaust as a whole. The huge geographic sweep of the Holocaust can be seen in collections of maps and pictures by Martin Gilbert (Nos. 204, 206).

The troops assigned to carrying out the "Final Solution" were indoctrinated in the Nazi belief that Jews could be ascribed on the basis of their very race to the partisans and therefore needed to be shot. As a result, executions of Jews proceeded even when the police and security units behind the lines were more heavily engaged in fighting Soviet partisans. Heiner Lichtenstein has described the role played by the regular German police – "Himmler's green helpers" – and the role of the German *Reichsbahn* in the execution of Jews (Nos. 285, 286). Only a few Jews succeeded in joining the partisans and resistance groups in order to fight their tormentors directly. Descriptions of the desperate struggle waged by Soviet Jews who succeeded in joining the partisans can be found above all in the two-volume work *Jewish Partisans* by Jack Porter and in several monographs and in contributions to *Yad Vashem Studies* (Nos. 102, 115, 129, 184, 207, 276, 280, 341, 383). For a long time, there was no summary of the resistance put up by the Jews in Europe to national socialism. On the basis of numerous personal testimonies, accounts, leaflets, and poems published for the first time in German, Arno Lustiger, himself a survivor of the Holocaust, is now able to present an impressive survey of the "life-and-death" struggle involved in the resistance put up by threatened European Jews from 1933 to 1945. As a kind of legacy, Lustiger's richly illustrated work offers an overview, divided into countries and biographies, of the various forms resistance to the Nazi system took, including the regular military service of Jews fighting with the Allies (No. 299).

The execution of Jews during this "second phase of the killing," as Hilberg puts it, was accordingly justified by the Germans as a preventive measure and an integral part of the struggle waged by police and Wehrmacht security units against bands of partisans. Reports to superiors placed these murders of Jews under the heading of executions of plunderers and partisans. Only a few Wehrmacht officers realized, as the future General Röttinger did, that fighting these bands "ultimately had the aim of using the army to make the ruthless liquidation of Jewry and other undesirable elements possible" (cf. statement of General Röttinger, wartime head of the General Staff of the 4th Army on the Eastern Front, 1945, in the German Military Archives, Bundesarchiv – Militärarchiv, Freiburg, N 422/11, p. 4). Further tens of thousands of Jews fell victim in 1942–43 to these "police actions."

On the fiftieth anniversary of the liberation of the extermination camp Auschwitz by the Red Army on 27 January 1945, the *Schwarzbuch* of the former Jewish Anti-Fascist Committee of the Soviet Union appeared (No. 186). It documents in a shattering and in part very personal way the genocide of the Soviet Jews in the context of the German-Soviet war. The volume of documents collected by Wassilij Grossmann (died 1964) and Ilja Ehrenburg (died 1967) is an extraordinary book with an unusual history. On the basis of numerous reports by eyewitnesses and survivors, it deals with the mass murder of the Soviet Jews in the Soviet areas under German occupation. At the same time, the book has its own history, as it was censored several times and its publication prevented under Soviet tyranny. The material collected by the Jewish Anti-Fascist Committee of the Soviet Union from 1942 to 1946 bears witness to the inhumanity and racial mania of the Nazis as well as to the brutish crimes they and their collaborators perpetrated against children, women, the old, and the sick. The *Schwarzbuch* offers new evidence and information on two aspects. It testifies to the often active role of the Wehrmacht in the annihilation of the Jews and the sometimes fierce resistance of the Jews in the East. When the Jewish Anti-Fascist Committee was dissolved again by Moscow after it had been founded following the German attack in accordance with the wishes of the Soviet government with an eye to gaining the support of the free world, the intended publication of its archive material – proposed by Albert Einstein – was prevented. The manuscript prepared for publication by Ehrenburg and Grossmann was ultimately destroyed on Stalin's orders. Part of the repeatedly censored manuscript did leave the country, however, and, commissioned by Yad Vashem in Israel, was first published in Russian in 1980; in 1981, an English and a Hebrew edition followed. Since a page proof of the complete *Schwarzbuch* survived the Stalin regime in a hiding place until 1992, Arno Lustiger was then able to bring out the original *Schwarzbuch* as a unique primary source in a complete edition. The book helps substantiate the extent of the horrible crimes. Unfortunately, detailed commentary on and occasional revision of some particulars are missing. In the meantime, further material from the committee's archives not included in the first

Schwarzbuch has been published in two volumes in Jerusalem (*Das unbekannte Schwarzbuch* and *Sowjetische Juden schreiben an Ilja Ehrenburg*).

Saul Friedländer, Georg M. Kren, and Leon Rappoport attempted to come to terms with the Holocaust from psychological, moral, and historical perspectives using as an example Himmler's infamous speech to high SS officers in Posen on 4 October 1943. Similar efforts to fathom the genocide of the Jews can be found in *Grenzen des Verstehens*, a collection of individual essays edited by Hanno Loewy, and in an omnibus volume edited by Petes Hayes (Nos. 199, 221, 260, 292). An intellectual controversy erupted around the "rationality" of the "Final Solution," as described, for example, by Susanne Heim and Götz Aly in their book *Vordenker der Vernichtung* (No. 105). Aly had already set forth his position in 1987 in connection with the question of whether there was an "economy of the Final Solution" (No. 104). They claimed that the Holocaust was part of far more ambitious plans to exterminate ethnic groups in the future. Aly puts this theory at the center of his new book, making a connection between displacing the Eastern populations and the "Final Solution" (No. 103). However, Christopher Browning, Ulrich Herbert, and Dan Diner cast doubt on this in the "debate about the connection between social policy and genocide," as Wolfgang Schneider called the omnibus volume that he edited, and its detailed discussion of "annihilation policy" (No. 369). They emphasized more the irrational or racist aspects of the policy, which resulted in the capricious, unpredictable slaughtering of people.

The argument over "rationality" is closely related to the quarrel between the "intentionalists" and "structuralists" among historians. Whereas the former believe that a decision was made by Hitler, Himmler, and senior Nazi leaders to wipe out the European Jews, the structuralists, or functionalists, believe that the Final Solution was the product of an unintentional radicalization process within the chaotic Nazi state. While Uwe Adam, Martin Broszat, Arno Mayer, and Hans Mommsen view the murder of the Jews as a structuralist result of the permanent state of emergency in the Nazi state and as the Nazis' reaction to the setbacks the Wehrmacht suffered on the Eastern Front beginning in the late autumn of 1941, Christopher Browning associates the decision to eradicate the Jews with the string of German victories in September and October 1941 (Nos. 154, 155).

Andreas Hillgruber has repeatedly emphasized the importance of Hitler and his racial program to the genocide of the Jews in the conquered areas of the Soviet Union (No. 236, 237). Gerald Fleming generally shares this view as well (No. 194). In contrast to Hillgruber, who interprets the genocide of the Jews as a "separate theater of the war," Omar Bartov stresses the symbiotic relationship between the Final Solution and the Eastern campaign (Nos. 23, 24, 25, 239). In *The Path to Genocide*, the American historian Christopher R. Browning describes two phases in the Holocaust, with the Jews in the conquered Soviet Union being the first to be slaughtered, followed by Jews elsewhere in Europe (No. 157). Gunnar Heinsohn describes forty-two known models explaining the murder of the Jews (No. 226). He names Hitler's intention to annihilate Jewry in order to eradicate the Jewish ethic of the holiness of life, thus giving him a free hand for the desired *Lebensraum im Osten* and to murder at will.

More recently, several essays, anthologies, and studies have dealt both with the problem of how to come to terms with the Holocaust and describe it as a historical event and with its long-term emotional effects after 1945. Writings such as those of James E. Young, Gertrud Hardtmann, Christopher Browning, and Michael R. Marrus take a critical look as well at the surviving accounts by the victims and at the "oral history" of the genocide of the Jews (Nos. 155, 196, 202, 219, 272, 308, 417). Gaining better access to the collection of original testimonies of the approximately 150,000 survivors of the Holocaust from all over the world is one aim of the Survivors of the Shoah Visual History Foundation, set up by Steven Spielberg in Los Angeles in 1994. The Fortunoff Video Archive for Holocaust Testimonies at Yale University in Connecticut and the Moses-Mendelssohn Zentrum at the University of Potsdam have undertaken a similar attempt. The study, presentation, and interpretation of the Holocaust as a traumatic historic experience in postwar historiography is the subject of individual studies by James E. Young, and of R.J.B. Bosworth (Nos. 145, 417).

Now that fifty years have passed since the end of the war, people are beginning to think about the "historical place" of the Holocaust and its changing meaning in a changed world. Thought is given to the crisis in human behavior reflected in such an incomprehensible event, as is impressively demonstrated by the anthology published by Asher Cohen, Joav Gelber, and Charlotte Wardi following a conference in Haifa in 1986

(Nos. 131, 135, 169, see also 172, 214, 216, 217, 221, 237, 260). For Detlev Claussen, modern anti-Semitism marks the "limits of the Enlightenment" in Europe (No. 167). Helmut Schreiner and Matthias Hey have brought out two complementary anthologies on the topicality of the murder of the European Jews for the "presence of the Shoah" and on the educational aspects of remembering as a specific "echo of the Holocaust" (No. 372).

The volume presented in connection with a conference held by the Evangelische Akademie Arnoldshain in January 1992 and called *Arnoldshainer Texte* presents interesting aspects of various ways of recollecting the Holocaust in West and East Germany. Particularly the contributions of Ulrich Herbert and Olaf Groehler on historiography as well as those of Gerhard Werle and Wolfgang Bock on dealing with the Holocaust within the respective systems of criminal justice allow direct comparisons; further comparisons can be found in the volume on the work carried out in memorial centers, on coming to terms with the Holocaust psychologically, and on the literature (No. 320). An effective overview on ways of "dealing with the Holocaust after 1945" can be found in the book edited by Rolf Steininger. It is the result of a series of lectures held at the University of Innsbruck and offers a great variety of individual historical themes and reflections (No. 387). The same applies to the description of the persecution of the Jews in the books *Writing and the Holocaust* by Berel Lang and *Writing and Rewriting the Holocaust* by James E. Young, the latter now available in German (Nos. 269, 417).

The standard work of Martin S. Bergmann, Milton E. Jucovy, and Judith S. Kerstenberg, now in both English and German, is devoted to one particular aspect. In their anthology *Generations of the Holocaust*, they present investigations into the psychological results of the Holocaust in the second generation following the mass murder of the Jews (No. 139). The present-day significance and "political relevance of non-accepted guilt" is described by Gesine Schwan in the book *Tabu und Geschichte*, edited by Peter Bettelheim and Robert Streibel (No. 373a). The journalist Ian Buruma investigated the particular problem of the varying ways of "coming to terms with the past in Germany and Japan." He compares the different approaches to coming to terms with crimes committed by both countries in the past (No. 162). A brief survey of "remembering the Shoah in Israel" can be found in the recent essay by Yaacov Lozowick (No. 298). Tom

Segev takes a very critical look at the problem of how Israel and the Zionist "policy of remembering" deal with the Holocaust in his new book *The Seventh Million* (No. 375).

* * *

According to the most recent research and reports published by Gerd Robel, Raul Hilberg, Martin Gilbert, and Georges Wellers, the number of Jews killed in the parts of the Soviet Union under German occupation remains a subject of some controversy. While older figures varied between 700,000 and two million, more recent calculations – for instance, those of Gerd Robel – put the number of murdered Jews in the Soviet Union (in its expanded borders of June 1941) at about 2.8 to three million. The high number of Soviet Jews among the almost six million victims in all of Europe is therefore very striking (Nos. 120, 205, 208, 228, 330, 350, 396, 408).[2]

This conclusion is very emphatically confirmed in all the omnibus volumes of recent research and at international conferences. Convincing interim results were published by Eberhard Jäckel and Jürgen Rohwer in *Der Mord an den Juden im Zweiten Weltkrieg*, which looked in particular at the question of Hitler's decision-making and the implementation of genocide (No. 243). In 1986, Gerhard Hirschfeld published in London an omnibus volume entitled *The Policies of Genocide,* which focused on the close connection between crimes against Soviet prisoners of war and against Jews (No. 240). He also informed English-speaking readers about Hans Mommsen's interpretation in *The Realization of the Unthinkable*, which had first appeared in German in 1983 (see No. 322).

After an international conference in London in 1992, David Cesarani, the director of the Wiener Library in London, put together an omnibus volume entitled *The Final Solution – Origins and Implementation* (No. 163), which testified to the solid knowledge and advanced state of the research into the Holocaust that has now been achieved. The firmly established facts can be seen very well in the closing essay in the volume by Yehuda Bauer on the "Significance of the Final Solution." Cesarani presents interesting new questions and answers about

2. According to Raul Hilberg, 5.1 million died. In the compilation *Dimensionen des Völkermordes*, the estimates vary from 5.29 million to 6 million (of whom about 535,000 were killed by the Action Groups and more than 3 million by gas).

the unfathomable genocide of the Jews in the general context of European history. The recent contributions to the volume illuminate the responsibility for the Holocaust of non-German governments and peoples, both in Europe and elsewhere, who failed to provide substantial help to the Jews and left the Nazis virtually undisturbed in this regard as they went about their "work." Numerous ideas for further studies and more probing research can be gleaned from Shmuel Krakowski's report in the omnibus volume on "Documents on the Holocaust in the Archives of the Former Soviet Union." The fact that ideology and politics under Nazi rule were the cause and the prerequisite for the crimes of violence toward the Jews and others persecuted for reasons of race is documented in the anthology published by Helge Grabitz, Klaus Bästlein, and Johannes Tuchel on the "normality of the crime" and dedicated to Wolfgang Scheffler as the Festschrift on the occasion of his sixty-fifth birthday. With its twenty-three contributions by numerous well-known experts, the book gives an impressive survey of the research on Nazi crimes of violence (No. 212).

Several studies, especially those of David Bankier and Otto D. Kulka, have shown that the German people suspected and in some cases knew full well what was happening to the Jews who were deported to the East, even though they were altogether too willing to claim after 1945 that "no one was there and no one knew," as Jörg Wollenberg put it so fittingly in the title of his anthology. A fundamental contribution in this area is David Bankier's new study *The Germans and the Final Solution*, in which he emphasizes that the German population was well aware of the events surrounding the Holocaust and tolerated them more out of apathy than out of anti-Semitic indoctrination. This is also stressed by Otto D. Kulka and Rainer C. Baum (Nos. 127, 128, 135, 210, 261, 263, 323, 388, 413). Especially shocking is the fact that many Germans who were involved in the crimes in the East viewed the months when the murder groups were in action as "a lovely time," as Ernst Klee, Willi Dreßen, and Volker Rieß point out (No. 180).

Some research has now been published that examines the extent to which Allied and other governments were aware of what was happening to the Jews. Despite the Germans' wall of silence toward the outside world, detailed information reached Allied and neutral countries, especially governments, as has been shown by Walter Laqueur, Raul Hilberg, Richard Breitman, David S. Wyman, John F. Morley, Jonathan Steinberg, and

Bernard Wasserstein (Nos. 150, 232, 273, 325, 386, 406, 414). With the recent release of formerly secret British documents, we know that Prime Minister Winston Churchill had been informed by 1942 at the latest about the appalling number of deaths in Auschwitz and other German concentration camps. For a long time, however, the Western Allies failed to give these reports appropriate attention. The ambivalent attitude of the Allies toward Nazi persecution of the Jews and the Auschwitz complex has been described by Shlomo Aronson, Jonathan Steinberg, and Martin Gilbert (Nos. 119, 203, 386). In addition, Richard Foregger and Heiner Lichtenstein provided an analysis of the opportunities for the Western Allies to bomb the gas chambers in Auschwitz from the air, thus preventing or postponing the murdering (Nos. 195, 285). Moreover, in their anthology *The Shoah and the War*, Asher Cohen, Yehoyakim Cochavi, and Yoav Gelber attempt to show the context and the background of the Holocaust not only as far as German war policy was concerned but also with regard to the politics of the confederate and the occupied countries, the Allies and Jewish relief organizations (No. 170).

Studies by Christopher R. Browning, Hans Safrian, Ernst Klee, and Willi Dreßen provide important answers to how millions of Jews could be murdered in the Soviet Union and Europe and what groups took part in it. The "Eichmann men" (as Safrian calls them in his book *Eichmann-Männer*) as well as the police and Wehrmacht personnel who took part in the Holocaust were not beasts. These "soldiers of evil," as the Israeli historian and journalist Tom Segev says, were largely ambitious newcomers eager to rise in their careers, who were steeped in militant anti-Semitism and therefore endorsed the brutality (Nos. 158, 180, 181, 359, 374). Safrian, whose study has now been published in paperback, emphasizes that these men were quite willing to go along with the state-sanctioned violence against Jews. He demonstrates, on the basis of a solid knowledge of the facts, that there were very many upwardly mobile Austrians among them who did not need any "Führer directive" to persecute and kill Jews. Peter R. Black's biography of Heydrich's successor as head of the Reich Security Office, Ernst Kaltenbrunner, can be seen as an effective exemplary study of those Austrian national socialists who gained important Nazi posts (No. 141).

As Raul Hilberg pointed out in his recent volume, *Täter, Opfer und Zuschauer*, the perpetrators came from all social strata and occupations (No. 232). Their ranks included many academics, such as government lawyers. The large number of academics involved in planning and administering the Holocaust was pointed out by Götz Aly and Susanne Heim in *Vordenker der Vernichtung*. This key work has now been reissued in paperback (No. 105). It establishes the connection between youthful anti-Semitism and later participation in the genocide. Saul Friedländer had already written an impressive historiographic analysis of this in an overview published in 1985 (No. 198). The progression "from hostility to Jews to the Holocaust" was shown as well in an omnibus volume edited by Hubert A. Strauss and Norbert Kampe and in a volume by George L. Mosse entitled *Toward the Final Solution; A History of European Racism* (Nos. 326, 389). The inner systematics of anti-Semitic thought processes and the variety of thought patterns in anti-Semitic ideas are depicted in the anthology *Antisemitismus - Vorurteile und Mythen*, edited by Julius H. Schoeps and Joachim Schlör (No. 371). The connection of the German elites to the Holocaust has been studied in particular by Rainer C. Baum (No. 135).

Christopher R. Browning wrote an excellent description of "very normal men." He studied an action undertaken by a reserve police battalion of about 500 men, who "in the line of duty" in 1942–43 shot or beat to death more than 38,000 Jewish men, women, children, and old people (No. 158). We also know now that the two large Christian denominations in Germany did not remain innocent of all involvement or failure to take action when they discovered what was happening (Nos. 140, 213, 325). Research is just beginning into the individual German soldiers, policemen, and SS or SD men who refused to participate in executing Jews, gypsies, partisans, or Soviet prisoners of war, or who tried to prevent the executions or help the victims. Preliminary studies, biographies, or autobiographies about fellow citizens who tried to help Jews escape the Nazis can be found in works by Mordecai Paldiel, David H. Kittermann, Carol Littner, Sandra Myers, Eric Silver, Gay Block, and Malka Drucker (Nos. 142, 251, 290, 336, 337, 379). Steven Spielberg's film *Schindler's List* – Thomas Keneally's book of the same name is now also available (No. 248) – and Eric Silver's *Book of the Just* and Mordecai Paldiel's *The Path of the Righteous* have been recent memorable reminders full of feeling of the activities of individual helpers (Nos. 337, 379). Silver's book, with its biographical sketches of forty "just" helpers, has also been published in German under the title *Sie waren stille Helden*. In Yad Vashem, 276 Germans, besides the thousands of Poles, Dutch, and French, were honored as "just." Gustav Trampe has published an international volume on the "avenue of the just" in Yad Vashem (No. 400).

Holocaust memorial and research centers have existed in a number of countries – especially in the United States – for many years. The best known is Yad Vashem in Israel. Recently, the Beit Hashoah-Museum of Tolerance was established in Los Angeles. In addition, the United States Holocaust Memorial Museum, to which a research institute is attached, opened in Washington, D.C. in April 1993.[3] The omnibus volume *The Texture of Memory (Holocaust Memorials and Meaning)*, which was edited by James E. Young and published as a companion text to an exhibition shown in Germany and the United States in 1994–95, provides an account of the motives, rituals, and places of remembrance. This artistically ambitious publication documents with many illustrations the worldwide attempts to capture in artistic form the baffling genocide of the Jews. In addition, Young provides an initial survey of the history of Holocaust memorials (No. 418).

In cooperation with Yad Vashem and the American Holocaust Memorial Museum, an internationally recognized periodical entitled *Holocaust and Genocide Studies* has been published since 1986. At a rate of two volumes a year, it provides an impressive array of studies and research information. The editor in chief is now Richard D. Breitman; up until 1995, it was Yehuda Bauer from Jerusalem, who is also responsible for the new series of the periodical that began in 1993. As an outstanding expert in the Holocaust, he also has many publications of his own to his credit (Nos. 131, 132, 133). Likewise very informative is the periodical *Yad Vashem Studies*, published since 1957 by the Holocaust Martyrs' and Heroes' Remembrance Authority of the Yad Vashem memorial in Jerusalem, which studies various aspects of the "European Jewish Catastrophe and Resistance" during the Second World War, as well as *Dimensions - A Journal of Holocaust Studies*, published by the Braun Center for Holocaust Studies in New York, and the yearbooks of the Leo Baeck Institute.[4] As a German counterpart, the *Dachauer Hefte*, which are compiled according to sub-

3. An up-to-date list of the most important Holocaust memorial and research centers is published in every volume of the periodical *Holocaust and Genocide Studies*, 1986ff.

4. Cf., e.g., Konrad Kwiet, "Problems of Jewish Resistance Historiography," *Leo Baeck Institute Year Book*, vol. 24 (1979): 37–57.

ject matter, have appeared since 1985. They are edited by Barbara Distel and Wolfgang Benz and are available individually as reprints in paperback (No. 171).

For a long time, there was little interest in Germany – notwithstanding numerous local memorial centers for the victims of Nazi persecution – in creating a central counterpart to all these memorials in the homeland of the former perpetrators, despite repeated demands. Since 1991, however, concrete steps have been taken to erect a German "central Holocaust research and documentation center" in Frankfurt on Main. The aim of the Fritz Bauer Institute, founded in January 1995 as part of a foundation as a "center for the study and documentation of the history and impact of the Holocaust," is to collect extensive material on the Holocaust, national socialism, and anti-Semitism and to study the history and impact of the Nazi policy of annihilation.[5] At the same time, efforts are being made to create a central memorial in Berlin to the Jews murdered in Europe.[6] It is also noteworthy that so far Soviet historians have paid little attention to the genocide of the Jews as a unique historical phenomenon, as Zvi Gitelman has pointed out (No. 209; Gitelman in No. 418). The fact that this took place for a long time in the context of the political attitude of the leadership in Moscow is documented in a new study by Sonja Margolina, *Das Ende der Lügen*, on the Russian Jews (No. 306).

Another irritating note is struck by the strong band of Nazi apologists in the United States gathered around *The Journal of Historical Review* and the British historian David Irving, who attack the standard view of the Holocaust. In their publications, some of which sell very well, they adduce pseudo-scientific facts, as in the *Leuchter Report*, to downplay the genocide of the Jews and even to deny it in general. How distortive and untenable the evidence is that ostensibly refutes the gassings in the concentration camp Mauthausen on the basis of the alleged Lachout "document" is documented in detail in the brochure produced by the Viennese Documentation Archive of the Austrian Resistance on the anatomy of this falsification. A further informative documentation of this archive on "running wild with reality"

5. Cf. the series *Materialien*, edited by the Fritz Bauer Institute and the city of Frankfurt; in particular No. 5, containing the concept and final report of the planning group on the foundation of the institute.

6. Jakob Schulze-Rohr, "Für die ermordeten Juden Europas: Berlin bekommt das Holocaustdenkmal," *Tribüne, Zeitschrift zum Verständnis des Judentums*, vol. 33, no. 130, pp. 14–18.

reveals revisionist historiography as "pseudoscientific propaganda" (Nos. 107, 123). This instructive work appeared in 1995 in a new, expanded edition with the title *Wahrheit und Auschwitzlüge*, edited by Brigitte Bailer, Wolfgang Benz, and Wolfgang Neugebauer (No. 124). The activities of the apologists were already described by Gill Seidel and Rivkah Knoller in 1986 and 1989 (Nos. 376, 253). Till Bastian and the American historian Deborah E. Lipstadt deserve credit for again drawing attention to the distortive contents of the so-called revisionist efforts, particularly the "Auschwitz lie." They both disprove the crude theories of the soi-disant "experts" that are passed off more and more often as allegedly "interesting contributions to the scientific controversy," exposing them as untrue and untenable (Nos. 130, 288). These theories nevertheless find their way to an increasing extent into right-wing publications as well as into the writing and ideas of Germany's new "conservative revolution," as Friedbert Pflüger was able to prove recently in his noteworthy book *Deutschland driftet*, also using the example of the "Auschwitz lie" (No. 339). Ernst Nolte, with his historical-philosophical interpretations, also includes pseudoscientific and radical revisionists in respectable academic circles, classing their interpretations as "serious" and part of the "normal course of research," as he has made plain in press interviews and in his new book *Streitpunkte* (No. E/382; cf. further references in Part E).

* * *

Research into Nazi propaganda and the orders given to the Wehrmacht have demonstrated the extent to which German propaganda, indoctrination, and reporting about Operation Barbarossa were influenced by Hitler's extermination plans and how important the Nazi leadership felt "mental preparation" and indoctrination were for the Eastern campaign (Nos. 424, 427, 429, 430). Just as detrimental in its effect on the German population's view of the Soviet Union was the negative "image of Russia in the Third Reich," documented by recently published letters and diaries of soldiers on the Eastern Front about their willing murder of Jews and women soldiers in the Red Army, edited by Hannes Heer and Walter Manoschek (Nos. 9, 305). During the preparations for the launching of Operation Barbarossa on 22 June 1941, Propaganda Minister Goebbels expressed his satisfaction that he was now finally able to attack

"Jewish Bolshevism" openly without regard for the Nazi-Soviet pact. At a press conference held on the day of the attack, Goebbels stated that the anti-Bolshevik propaganda signaled a return to the old, ideological "struggle against plutocracy and Bolshevism." This notion was embroidered further until the autumn of 1941, when it culminated in an appeal to all of Europe to join in a "European crusade against Bolshevism" (see the literature pointed out in Parts A and B). However, Hitler and Goebbels neglected to mention to the European governments and friendly nations to whom they directed this appeal that a campaign had been launched at the same time to murder the Jews in every country of Europe under Hitler's sway. While the Nazis still displayed considerable reticence in front of foreigners about their ultimate ideological and political intentions in eastern Europe, their conviction that "Aryan *Herrenmenschen*" should totally destroy "Jewish Bolshevism" was made clear to the German population through propaganda and articles in the press about "Jewish and Slavic *Untermenschen.*"

Beginning in the fall of 1941, the Nazis scaled pinnacles of verbal excess in denigrating and demonizing the enemy. Stalin had utilized the twenty-fourth anniversary of the October Revolution to exhort the Soviet population to wage a mighty "Patriotic War." In his public address of 6 November 1941, which had to be delivered in the shelter of Moscow's Mayakovskaya subway station because the front was so close, he threatened to rain death and destruction on the German invaders. The Soviet forces were urged to resist the threat to the motherland with all their strength and to destroy and kill the German occupiers (Nos. B/115, B/186). Stalin's speech was taken up in turn by the Nazis in order to appeal to German soldiers to intensify their struggle against the "onslaught of the Red rabble." The historians Manfred Messerschmidt and Omar Bartov have shown that the Wehrmacht was drenched in Nazi ideology and that this played an important role in the committing of crimes (Nos. 24, 25, 315). The soldiers were constantly inured to events through Nazi propaganda, party indoctrination, and the political press. Orders issued by the military adopted a very similar tone in encouraging savageness toward the enemy. The supreme commander of Army Group South, Field Marshal von Reichenau (who had already distinguished himself in the autumn as commander of the Sixth Army by issuing infamous framework orders calling for a ruthless struggle against Bolshevism), urged upon the soldiers under his command a "lust to slaughter the animalistic" Soviet leaders, in orders issued in December 1941 (No. B/107, p. 157). This order, too, was particularly well received by the Führer. He himself had already spoken in his address of 3 October 1941 of the "cruel, bestial and animalistic opponent," and he had Reichenau's commands reissued to the other army groups in the form of special daily orders.

The willingness of German commanders, such as Field Marshal von Reichenau, General Hoth, General Busch, and Lieutenant General von Manstein, to pass such orders along and in some cases to formulate them for themselves shows that the military leaders were prepared not only to carry out Hitler's war of annihilation against the Soviet Union but also to support the slaughter of civilians and Jews by the SS and SD. This has been demonstrated repeatedly in the recent literature (Nos. B/107, p. 158; 12).

Hans-Heinrich Wilhelm has shown the particularly important role played by Heinrich Himmler's directives and the so-called instructional guidelines issued by SS Reich Security Headquarters in encouraging the equation of "Jewishness with Bolshevism" and in demonizing Slavs as *"Untermenschen"* (No. 22). It is now generally accepted that this indoctrination, the most infamous example of which was the brochure "Der Untermensch" produced by SS Headquarters in 1942 (No. 148), had its effect on German generals, soldiers, and the civilian population.

A good example is the reaction of 300 generals, admirals, and general staff officers to Himmler's speech in Posen on 26 January 1944, in which he said that he had been charged by Hitler with the "total solution of the Jewish question" and that he and the SS had successfully completed this task "in spite of all the emotional burdens." Thereupon the assembled "generals and admirals sprang to their feet and broke into thunderous applause."[7] The Reichsführer SS could only feel confirmed in his activity and encouraged to continue.

However, a few opposing voices were raised. Retired General Baron von Gersdorff, who was on the general staff of Army Group Center, stated in his memoirs that "the shooting of Jews, prisoners and even commissars was almost universally rejected by the officer corps" of the units and forces of the Fourth Army and was "viewed as an affront to the honor of the German army

7. Bodo Scheurig, "Die abgemilderte Posener Erinnerung. Himmler, das Offizierkorps und der 20. Juli 1944," *Frankfurter Allgemeine Zeitung,* no. 166 (21 July 1993): N5

and especially of the German officer corps" (No. B/107, p. 397). The "question of responsibility" for these atrocities was also allegedly discussed but was left unanswered in the end mostly because no information was available in public declarations or press reports. Those individuals who observed the atrocities were left on their own to decide what they would do, each according to his own conscience. Ultimately, both the German and Soviet forces escalated the ferocity and bitterness of the struggle in all sectors of the Eastern Front until 1945.

For several years, Soviet prisoners of war died en masse before the very eyes of German soldiers and civilians. However, the Germans accepted these crimes as a result of Nazi indoctrination and their own convictions that Red Army soldiers were Slavic *Untermenschen*. Only a few people, such as Count von Moltke, Admiral Canaris, and General Oster in the German resistance, continued to protest. The widespread reports from German companies about miserable working conditions, maltreatment, brutal punishment, and killing of prisoners of war who were unable to work clearly demonstrate that much of the general population was influenced by Nazi political propaganda and embraced its racial ideology. In the end, most Germans probably just felt indifferent to the fate of Soviet prisoners of war and Jews, whose suffering was apparent across the land. They simply closed their eyes.

The attitude of the German civilian population to prisoners and to their fellow Jewish citizens was certainly affected by the incessant hate propaganda against the Red Army and Jews, as well as by their concern about their own sons and husbands on the Eastern Front. Those who felt sympathy were dissuaded from offering assistance by the threat of severe punishment and by the mounting difficulties in their own lives as a result of the bombing. The Nazi regime also did all that it could to isolate Soviet prisoners of war and prevent contact with the civilian population or other groups of prisoners. There are very few records about what German civilians felt about their encounters with millions of prisoners of war and so-called eastern workers, mostly women and girls from the Ukraine. Little is known as well about life in the camps where these people lived and about the internal structure of the camps. It is difficult to determine the extent to which external pressure and isolation strengthened the bonds among the prisoners themselves. However, the existing evidence does not necessarily lead one to conclude that there was much sense of solidarity. Some resistance did occur, even in concentration camps such as Buchenwald.

Ideological indoctrination played an important role in the Red Army as well. Several publications and omnibus volumes about attempts to influence the attitudes of Soviet soldiers in the field appeared in 1985. They focused in particular on the political work of the Communist party of the Soviet Union (Nos. 423, 426). The party particularly emphasized Marxism-Leninism and hatred of the enemy intruders, as can be seen in the efforts of Ilya Ehrenburg (No. 421).

* * *

Among the atrocities committed by the Soviets was the mass murder of Polish officers near Katyn. In accordance with orders issued at the highest levels, more than 4,100 captured Polish officers were shot near Smolensk in the spring of 1940. Another 10,000 Polish officers were murdered in other areas and camps. When the Germans discovered what had happened at Katyn in the spring of 1943, they attempted to turn it to political advantage (No. 446). Despite the clear conclusions of an international commission of investigation organized by Berlin, the Soviets continued to insist throughout the remainder of the Second World War and the Cold War that the Germans had killed the Polish officers. Numerous international investigations, such as that conducted by a U.S. Congressional committee in 1951–52, proved that the Soviets were indeed responsible (Nos. 435, 440, 443, 482). However, Moscow continued officially to uphold its fabrications even during Gorbachev's time. This enduring Soviet "campaign of lies and concealment" has been described very well in publications by Allen Paul, Czeslaw Madajczyk, and Franz Kadell (Nos. 450, 461, 462, 466). Kadell describes how Moscow finally acknowledged the truth about NKVD "crimes under Stalinism" only after the political transformation of Eastern Europe and the collapse of the Soviet Union itself, although even then solely in response to heavy political pressure. In addition, Madajczyk refers to Polish sources, withheld for years by the Communist government in Warsaw so as not to irritate Moscow. On 14 October 1992, Russian president Boris Yeltsin made public the previously top-secret records of Beria's secret police and gave them to Polish president Lech Walesa (Nos. 441, 452, 476). The records revealed that the approximately 14,700 Polish officers who had disappeared were murdered in response to an order issued by the Politburo of the Communist party of the Soviet Union on 5 March 1940 (No. 477). More recently, a report has been published from the viewpoint of a surviving Polish officer (No. 471).

Actions such as these on the part of the Allies undermined their own claim to be fighting for a better world and made it more difficult for them to assume the mantle of humanity and justice in the struggle against Nazi barbarism. Allied claims were discredited in other ways as well. The Soviet leaders were ruthless and brutal in enforcing their internal policies and in their policies toward the Red Army.

In the meantime, Russian works have been published on the arbitrary executions, at the behest of Stalin and Beria on 22 July 1941, of the supreme commander of the Western Front, General D.G. Pavlov; generals N.A. Klich, A.T. Grigorev, A.A. Korobkov, and V.E. Klimsovskikh; and various other officers on account of alleged cowardice in the face of the German attack. These works have rehabilitated them historically, after their legal and political rehabilitation in 1957–58 by the military collegium of the Supreme Court of the Soviet Union (No. 467).

Both sides on the Eastern Front waged a vicious war of ideologies, and captured German soldiers also suffered the consequences. They, too, suffered hunger, cold, brutality, and capricious or tormenting treatment. Marxist historians such as Alexander Blank have denied this or tried to gloss it over, for understandable reasons (No. 437). Large numbers of Germans did not fall into Soviet hands until the defeat of the Sixth Army at Stalingrad in January 1943.

Red Army officers faced a serious problem because they were not expecting a flood of exhausted, sick prisoners and their preparations were also grossly inadequate. Numerous reports by former German prisoners of war in the USSR, such as the recent one by Edgar Klaus, paint a shattering picture of the hard and dangerous conditions in the Soviet prisoner-of-war camps during the war and after it up to 1955 (Nos. 449, 453). It is generally believed that of the 3.15 million German soldiers taken prisoner by the Soviets, about 1.2 million died. The Soviet military historian V.P. Galicky calculated that 2.39 million Wehrmacht personnel were taken prisoner and 352,000 died, but these figures have been shown by more recent studies to be far too low (No. 447). According to other figures, an additional 10,000 to 100,000 Japanese prisoners of war died in Siberia. A new attempt to appraise the fate and suffering of the prisoners of war on both sides was recently undertaken in the volume produced by the Haus der Geschichte der Bundesrepublik Deutschland in Bonn in connection with the exhibition *Kriegsgefangene* held in the summer of 1995 (No. 456).

Closely connected to the German discovery at Katyn of the murdered Polish officers and the disclosure of this fact in Berlin on 13 April 1943 was the edict issued by the Supreme Soviet on 19 April 1943, announcing that captured German soldiers and other soldiers allied with Germany would be tried for war crimes. This edict, known as Ukase 43, was directed against German, Italian, Rumanian, Hungarian, and Finnish fascists "who were guilty of torturing and murdering Soviet civilians and prisoners of war."[8] This was Moscow's political reaction to official allegations that it had executed thousands of Polish prisoners. The Soviet leaders hoped to prove in this way that not they but the Germans should be held responsible for the mass execution of Polish officers. It is significant that Ukase 43 was issued on the same day that the Soviet Union broke off diplomatic relations with the Polish government in exile in London, after the Sikorski government demanded that Moscow respond to the German government's disclosures about Katyn (No. 434). Ukase 43 was evidently intended to dispel the diplomatic uproar over Katyn and prove that the Germans had committed atrocities in the territories occupied by the Wehrmacht.

This ukase served not only as the basis for many trials of proven Nazi war criminals but also for many more capricious trials of German prisoners of war. It can therefore be considered part of the ideologically motivated struggle of world views between Nazism and Communism. According to international law at the time (the Hague Convention relating to the laws and customs of warfare on land, article 6, paragraph 1), countries were entitled to try prisoners of war for war crimes. As the works of Reinhart Maurach and Martin Lang have shown (Nos. 457, 463), trials of prisoners of war were permissible under international law, even though the Soviet Union had chosen not to sign the Geneva Convention of 1929. However, prisoners of war could not be indicted for activities before the war, as Moscow did in some cases.

Charges were leveled against soldiers in the Wehrmacht, members of the SD and SS, and members of the police and the administration in formerly occupied zones of the Soviet Union. Ukase

8. Cited according to Reinhart Maurach, *Die Kriegsverbrecherprozesse gegen deutsche Gefangene in der Sowjetunion* (Hamburg, 1950), p. 85. Parts of Ukase 43 are quoted in *Frankfurter Allgemeine Zeitung,* no. 263 (11 November 1993): 36.

43 provided that each accused had to be convicted personally of a crime. The Soviets prosecuted acts of violence (e.g., murder) by fascists, as well as espionage and treason by collaborators. However, on 1 November 1943 the "Moscow Declaration of German Atrocities" was proclaimed in consultation with the Western Allies (see Foreign Relations of the United States, Diplomatic Papers, vol. I, General, pp. 768–69), naming all officers, soldiers, and members of the NSDAP responsible for the acts of brutality, massacres, and executions. Thereafter the accused no longer had to be convicted of any crime in particular. In Moscow's interpretation, they could be condemned if found responsible for events or willing participants in them. Henceforth the charges and sentences were based on little more than assumptions and suspicions. The Moscow Declaration permitted collective punishment on the basis of suspicion and was therefore contrary to international law. The use of torture to obtain confessions from German prisoners of war was also illegal and unjustified.

The available Western sources provide little information about the ideological and political motivation behind the centrally directed preparations for the trials. Preliminary research by Günther Wagenlehner and Stefan Karner offers cursory and still incomplete information (Nos. 451, 478, 479). The ideological basis for the trials was probably set forth in detail by Moscow, leaving little to chance or to decisions taken in the regions. Only analysis of the records in Moscow, which have now become more accessible, will provide precise information about the preliminary investigations and interrogations. However, research is just beginning in this area.

The interrogations were generally followed by individual trials before the military courts or militia courts of the Ministry of the Interior, with ensuing sentences. During the war and until shortly after the war ended, the trials usually ended in death sentences. Around 1949–50, the sentences generally became ten to twenty-five years of imprisonment in penal labor camps. Two of the more infamous penal labor camps in the "Gulag Archipelago" for German prisoners of war were Vorkuta and "Asbestos." Recently, Horst Schüler published a detailed study of Vorkuta (No. 468). Sometimes special boards of the Ministry of the Interior passed sentence in the absence of the accused on the basis of written records, under the so-called Oso procedure (Nos. 432, B/1126a).

A number of trials were conducted during the war – for instance, in Krasnodar in February 1943, in Mariupol in September 1943, and in Kharkov in December 1943. The trials in

Kharkov were held up as model proceedings and received considerable international attention. The trial records were published in several different languages, and Radio Moscow reported in detail on the trial on a number of occasions. The Soviet political leaders were evidently very interested in gaining broad international support.

Berlin was well informed about the trials thanks to the publication of the trial records. When Hitler was advised about the trials in Kharkov, he issued orders that similar cases of war crimes should be found among British or American prisoners of war. However, little work had been done on the trials in Germany by March 1944, when Berlin learned through a Reuters report that the Soviets were planning another show trial in the recaptured city of Kiev. Hitler again demanded that "something be done immediately." Typically, he did not mean that something should be done to help the accused prisoners of war in the Soviet Union; instead he ordered that "Anglo-American war criminals should be condemned to death" as grist for Nazi propaganda. Trials of Soviet prisoners of war did not seem to be of much interest from a propaganda point of view because these prisoners had not committed any crimes on German soil. However, the end of the war arrived without any counter-trials being instituted.

Soviet trials of captured German soldiers continued after the war as well. Individual criminal acts that became known were also punished (see the information in Part E). The often tragic individual fates suffered by German prisoners as a result of capricious Soviet trials held during the war cannot be seen in isolation. They were part of the generally very poor treatment of German prisoners of war by the Soviet authorities, as shown by several studies of what awaited captured Germans in the Soviet Union (Nos. 432, 438). The differences in how the various Allied powers treated German prisoners of war is well described in a volume of memoirs by captured German soldiers about their experiences in various countries, edited by Wolfgang Benz and Angelika Schardt (No. 436).

Speculation has arisen, and continues to arise, that millions of missing German soldiers died as captives not only of the Soviets but also of the Western Allies. In 1989, the Canadian journalist James Bacque claimed that their deaths were "planned" before the end of the war by General Eisenhower and the government of the United States. This has been refuted in the most recent study by Arthur L. Smith, who teaches in Pasadena, California, and has a number of publications to his credit in this regard (No. 472). He consigns Bacque's thesis to the realm of legend. The claim that a million German prisoners of war died in the West and not in the East can thus be considered disproved. The search for the missing million must therefore continue in POW camps in the East. Moscow declared in 1947 that it held fewer than one million German prisoners of war, but the more reliable figures of the German *Bundesländer* set this figure at more than two million at the time.

Individual criminal acts by Soviet and other Allied troops can now be studied using the records of the Wehrmacht Investigation Office, published by Alfred de Zayas. This OKW office was instructed during the war to gather materials and documents about known Allied war crimes (No. 481).

The Wehrmacht Investigation Office did not collect any information about events toward the end of the war, although this was the period when Red Army crimes and breaches of international law were particularly rampant. When Soviet soldiers first reached German soil in October 1944, the years of hate propaganda against the German aggressors propagated by people like Ilya Ehrenburg bore fruit. Soviet animosity, fueled by such things as constant viewing of German atrocities in the liberated areas, was unleashed upon the entire civilian population as soon as the border was crossed. The brutality of Soviet soldiers reached terrifying proportions. The Red Army ruled by fear, and reasonable people such as Alexander Solzhenitsyn and Lev Kopelev generally failed to prevail (Nos. E/301a; 454).

Confronted with such excesses, millions of Germans fled their homes in Warthegau, East Prussia, Danzig, Pomerania, Silesia, and East Brandenburg, heading for the West. At the same time, German civilians began being arbitrarily deported for forced labor in Silesia. Many were dragged off to remote areas of the Soviet Union, and more than 100,000 deportees died in forced labor camps (No. 465).

The accounts by Lev Kopelev and many other witnesses of the crimes committed by the Red Army as it swept across eastern Germany are evidence of the egregious brutality unleashed in this war of ideologies until the very end against unarmed and helpless women, children, old people, and prisoners. Their deaths were the painful "other price" of Hitler's war (No. 20a in Conclusion).

Bibliography

1. Generalia, Overviews, and Sources

1) Dallin, Alexander. *Deutsche Herrschaft in Rußland 1941–1944. Eine Studie in Besatzungspolitik*. Düsseldorf, 1958

2) Förster, Jürgen. "Das Unternehmen 'Barbarossa' als Eroberungs- und Vernichtungskrieg." In *Das Deutsche Reich und der Zweite Weltkrieg*. Vol. 4, *Der Angriff auf die Sowjetunion*, edited by Horst Boog et al., pp. 413–347. Stuttgart, 1983; 2nd edn 1987 (English edn: *Germany and the Second World War*. Vol. 4, *The Attack on the Soviet Union*. London, 1996)

3) _____. "Die Sicherung des Lebensraumes." In *Das Deutsche Reich und der Zweite Weltkrieg*. Vol. 4, *Der Angriff auf die Sowjetunion*, pp. 1030–1078. Stuttgart, 1983

4) _____. "Fünfzig Jahre danach: Ein historischer Rückblick auf das 'Unternehmen Barbarossa'." *Aus Politik und Zeitgeschichte* vol. 24 (1991): pp. 11–24

5) Dreßen, Willi, et al., eds. *"Gott mit uns." Der deutsche Vernichtungskrieg im Osten 1939–1945*. Frankfurt a.M., 1989

6) Dwinger, Edwin E. *Wiedersehen mit Sowjetrußland. Tagebuch vom Ostfeldzug*. Jena, 1942

7) *Fall 12. Das Urteil gegen das Oberkommando der Wehrmacht gefällt am 28. Oktober 1948 in Nürnberg vom Militärgerichtshof V der Vereinigten Staaten von Amerika*. East Berlin, 1960

8) Goitsch, Heinrich, and Hanns Rahs. *Die Wahrheit über den Ostfeldzug. Dokumente englischer Lügen und Irrtümer mit einer Chronik des Ostfeldzuges*. Düsseldorf, 1942

9) Heer, Hannes, ed. *Stets zu erschießen sind Frauen, die in der Roten Armee dienen. Geständnisse deutscher Kriegsgefangener über ihren Einsatz an der Ostfront*. Hamburg, 1995

10) *"Der Kampf im Osten". Wehrmachtausstellung in Königsberg. 12. bis 26. Okt. 1941. Ein Bericht*. Königsberg, 1942

11) Kohl, Paul. *"Ich wundere mich, daß ich noch lebe". Sowjetische Augenzeugen berichten.* Gütersloh, 1990; new paperback edn *Der Krieg der deutschen Wehrmacht und der Polizei 1941–1944. Sowjetische Überlebende berichten.* Frankfurt a.M., 1994

12) Krausnick, Helmut, and Hans-Heinrich Wilhelm. *Die Truppe des Weltanschauungskrieges. Die Einsatzgruppen der Sicherheitspolizei und des SD 1938–1942.* 2 parts. Stuttgart, 1981; only part 1 as special paperback edn: Krausnick, Helmut. *Hitlers Einsatzgruppen. Die Truppe des Weltanschauungskriegs 1938–1942.* Frankfurt a.M., 1985

13) Lenhard, Hartmut. *"Lebensraum im Osten". Deutsche in Belorußland 1941–1944. Quellen- und Materialmappe für Unterricht und Erwachsenenbildungsarbeit.* Edited by Internationales Bildungs- und Begegnungswerk Dortmund. Düsseldorf, 1991

13a) Manoschek, Walter, ed. *Die Wehrmacht im Rassenkrieg. Der Vernichtungskrieg hinter der Front.* Vienna, 1996

14) Müller, Rolf-Dieter. "Das Scheitern der wirtschaftlichen 'Blitzkriegstrategie'." In *Das Deutsche Reich und der Zweite Weltkrieg.* Vol. 4, *Der Angriff auf die Sowjetunion*, edited by Horst Boog et al., pp. 936–1029. Stuttgart, 1983; 2nd edn 1987 (English edn: *Germany and the Second World War.* Vol. 4, *The Attack on the Soviet Union.* London, 1996)

15) _____. *Hitlers Ostkrieg und die deutsche Siedlungspolitik. Die Zusammenarbeit von Wehrmacht, Wirtschaft und SS.* Frankfurt a.M., 1991

16) Müller, Norbert, ed. *Die faschistische Okkupationspolitik in den zeitweilig besetzten Gebieten der Sowjetunion (1941–1944).* Berlin, 1991

16a) Nolte, Ernst. *Der Faschismus in seiner Epoche. Die Action Française. Der italienische Faschismus. Der Nationalsozialismus.* Munich, 1963; 5th edn 1979

17) Reitlinger, Gerald. *Ein Haus auf Sand gebaut. Hitlers Gewaltpolitik in Rußland, 1941–1944.* Hamburg, 1962 (English edn: *The House Built on Sand.* New York, 1960)

18) *Eine Schuld, die nicht erlischt. Dokumente über deutsche Kriegsverbrechen in der Sowjetunion.* Cologne, 1987

19) Trevor-Roper, Hugh R. "Hitlers Kriegsziele." *Vierteljahrshefte für Zeitgeschichte* vol. 8 (1960): pp. 121–133

20) *Trials of War Criminals before the Nuernberg Military Tribunals under Control Council Law No. 10.* Edited by the US. Government Printing Office Washington. 14 vols. Vol. IV, *The Einsatzgruppen Case and the RuSHACase.* Washington, DC, 1950; vol. V, *The RuSHA Case and the Pohl Case.* Washington, DC, 1950; vol. X, *The High Command Case.* Washington, DC, 1951; vol. XI, *The High Command Case.* Washington, DC, 1950

21) *Der Untermensch.* Edited by the SS-Hauptamt-Schulungsamt. Berlin, [1941?]

21a) *Vernichtungskrieg. Verbrechen der Wehrmacht 1941 bis 1944.* Edited by Hamburger Institut für Sozialforschung. Hamburg, 1996

22) Wilhelm, Hans-Heinrich. *Rassenpolitik und Kriegführung. Sicherheitspolizei und Wehrmacht in Polen und der Sowjetunion.* Passau, 1991

2. The Indoctrination of the Wehrmacht and its Participation in the War of Annihilation

23) Bartov, Omav. *The Eastern Front, 1941–1945. German Troops and the Barbarisation of Warfare.* Houndmills, 1985

24) _____. "Brutalität und Mentalität: Zum Verhalten deutscher Soldaten an der 'Ostfront'." In *Erobern und Vernichten. Der Krieg gegen die Sowjetunion 1941–1945*, edited by Peter Jahn and Reinhard Rürup, pp. 183–199. Berlin, 1991

25) _____. *Hitler's Army. Soldiers, Nazis and the War in the Third Reich.* London, 1992 (German edn: *Hitlers Wehrmacht. Soldaten, Fanatismus und die Brutalisierung des Krieges.* Reinbek, 1995)

26) Bélov, G., and E. Boltine, eds. *Le crime méthodique. Documents éclairant la politique de l'Allemagne nazie en territoire soviétique de 1941 à 1944.* Moscow, 1963

27) Benz, Wigbert. "'Präventiver Völkermord?' Zur Kontroverse um den Charakter des deutschen Vernichtungskrieges gegen die Sowjetunion." *Blätter für deutsche und internationale Politik* vol. 33, no. 10 (1988): pp. 1215–1227

28) Förster, Jürgen. "Zur Rolle der Wehrmacht im Krieg gegen die Sowjetunion." *Aus Politik und Zeitgeschichte* no. B 45/80 (1980): pp. 3–15

29) _____. "The German Army and the Ideological War against the Soviet Union." In *The Policies of Genocide: Jews and Soviet Prisoners of War in Nazi Germany*, edited by Gerhard Hirschfeld, pp. 15–29. London, 1986

30) _____. "Das andere Gesicht des Krieges: Das 'Unternehmen Barbarossa' als Eroberungs- und Vernichtungskrieg." In *"Unternehmen Barbarossa". Zum historischen Ort der deutsch-sowjetischen Beziehungen von 1933 bis Herbst 1941*, edited by Roland G. Foerster, pp. 151–161. Munich, 1993

31) "Zum Rußland-Bild der Militärs 1941–1945." In *Das Rußlandbild im Dritten Reich*, edited by Hans-Erich Volkmann, pp. 141–163. Cologne, 1994

32) Friedrich, Jörg. *Das Gesetz des Krieges. Das deutsche Heer in Rußland 1941 bis 1945. Der Prozeß gegen das Oberkommando der Wehrmacht.* Munich, 1993; new paperback edn 1995

33) Gerns, Ditte. *Hitlers Wehrmacht in der Sowjetunion. Legenden – Wahrheit – Tradition.* Frankfurt a.M., 1985

34) Geßner, Klaus. "Geheime Feldpolizei – die Gestapo der Wehrmacht." In *Vernichtungskrieg. Verbrechen der Wehrmacht 1941–1944*, edited by Hannes Heer and Klaus Naumann, pp. 343–358. Hamburg, 1995

35) Heer, Hannes, and Klaus Naumann, eds. *Vernichtungskrieg. Verbrechen der Wehrmacht 1941–1944.* Hamburg, 1995

36) Hillgruber, Andreas. "Das Rußland-Bild der führenden deutschen Militärs vor Beginn des Angriffs auf die Sowjetunion." In *Die Zerstörung Europas. Beiträge zur Weltkriegsepoche 1914 bis 1945*, by Andreas Hillgruber, pp. 256–272. Frankfurt a.M., 1988

37) Hoffmann, J.H. "German Field Marshals as War Criminals? A British Embarrassment." *Journal of Contemporary History* vol. 23, no. 1 (1988): pp. 17–35

38) Jahn, Peter, and Reinhard Rürup, eds. *Erobern und Vernichten. Der Krieg gegen die Sowjetunion 1941–1945. Essays*. Berlin, 1991
39) Messerschmidt, Manfred. *Die Wehrmacht im NS-Staat. Zeit der Indoktrination*. Hamburg, 1969
40) _____. "Harte Sühne am Judentum. Befehlslage und Wissen in der deutschen Wehrmacht." In *"Niemand war dabei und keiner hat's gewußt." Die deutsche Öffentlichkeit und die Judenverfolgung 1933–1945*, edited by Jörg Wollenberg, pp. 113–128. Munich, 1989
41) Müller, Norbert. "Massenverbrechen von Wehrmachtorganen an der sowjetischen Zivilbevölkerung im Sommer/Herbst 1941." *Zeitschrift für Militärgeschichte* vol. 8, no. 5 (1969): pp. 537–553
42) _____. "Dokumente zur Rolle der Wehrmacht bei der Deportation sowjetischer Bürger zur Zwangsarbeit in Deutschland 1941–1944." *Bulletin des Arbeitskreises Zweiter Weltkrieg* 4 (1970): pp. 29–62
43) _____. *Wehrmacht und Okkupation 1941–1944. Die Wehrmacht und ihre Führungsorgane im Okkupationsregime des faschistischen deutschen Imperialismus auf sowjetischem Territorium*. East Berlin, 1971
44) Müller, Rolf-Dieter. "Kriegsrecht oder Willkür?" *Militärgeschichtliche Mitteilungen* no. 2/42 (1987): pp. 125–152
45) Schulte, Theo J. *The German Army and Nazi Policies in Occupied Russia*. Oxford, 1989
46) Streit, Christian. "Es geschah Schlimmeres, als wir wissen wollen. Der Fall Barbarossa." *Blätter für deutsche und internationale Politik* (1987): pp. 1287–1300
47) Ueberschär, Gerd R. "'Rußland ist unser Indien'. Das 'Unternehmen Barbarossa' als Lebensraumkrieg." In *Der Mensch gegen den Menschen. Überlegungen und Forschungen zum deutschen Überfall auf die Sowjetunion 1941*, edited by Hans-Heinrich Nolte, pp. 66–77. Hanover, 1992
48) Volkmann, Hans-Erich, ed. *Das Rußlandbild im Dritten Reich*. Cologne, 1994

3. The "Criminal Orders" Issued to German Forces

49) Jacobsen, Hans-Adolf. "Kommissarbefehl und Massenexekution sowjetischer Kriegsgefangener." In *Anatomie des SS-Staates*, edited by Hans Buchheim, vol. 2, pp. 135–232. Munich, 1967
50) Krausnick, Helmut. "Kommissarbefehl und 'Kriegsgerichtsbarkeitserlaß Barbarossa' in neuer Sicht." *Vierteljahrshefte für Zeitgeschichte* vol. 25 (1977): pp. 682–738
51) Messerschmidt, Manfred. "Kommandobefehl und NS-Völkerrechtsdenken." *Revue de Droit Pénal Militaire et de Droit de la Guerre* XI–1 (1972): pp. 110–134
52) _____. "Der verbrecherische Befehl im Kontext der 'Kriegsnotwendigkeit'." In *22. Juni 1941. Der Überfall auf die Sowjetunion*, edited by Hans Schafranek and Robert Streibel, pp. 63–74. Vienna, 1991
53) Reitlinger, Gerald. "'Leaving the Courts at Home'. The Commissar Order and the 'Barbarossa' Jurisdiction Order. The Role of Himmler and Heydrich." In *The House Built on Sand*, edited by Gerald Reitlinger, pp. 66–97. London, 1960

54) Uhlig, Heinrich. "Der verbrecherische Befehl. Eine Diskussion und ihre historisch-dokumentarischen Grundlagen." In *Vollmacht des Gewissens*, edited by Europäische Publikation e.V., vol. 2, pp. 287–410. Frankfurt a.M., 1965

4. The Treatment and Fate of Soviet Prisoners of War

55) Bach, Dieter, and Jochen Leyendecker. *"Ich habe geweint vor Hunger". Deutsche und russische Gefangene in Lagern der Zweiten Weltkriegs.* Wuppertal, 1993

56) Bonwetsch, Bernd. "Die sowjetischen Kriegsgefangenen zwischen Stalin und Hitler." *Zeitschrift für Geschichtwissenschaft* vol. 41, no. 2 (1993): pp. 135–142

57) Borgsen, Werner, and Klaus Volland. *Stalag X B Sandbostel. Zur Geschichte eines Kriegsgefangenen- und KZ-Auffanglagers in Norddeutschland 1939–1945.* Bremen, 1991

58) Brandhuber, Jerzy. "Die sowjetischen Kriegsgefangenen im Konzentrationslager Auschwitz." *Hefte von Auschwitz* vol. 4 (1961): pp. 5–62

59) Brodski, J.A. *Die Lebenden kämpfen – die illegale Organisation brüderlicher Zusammenarbeit der Kriegsgefangenen.* Moscow, 1965; East Berlin, 1968

60) Brodskij, E.A. *Vo imja pobedy nad fasizmom. Antifasistskaja bor'ba sovetskich ljudej v gitlerovskoj Germanii (1941–1945 gg.).* Moscow, 1970 (German edn: *Im Kampf gegen den Faschismus.* East Berlin, 1975)

61) _____. *Oni nje propali bes wjesti. Ne slotlenije fasistskoj newolej.* Moscow, 1987

62) Ceron, F. Ja. *Nemeckij plen sovetskoe osvobozdenie.* Paris, 1987

63) Datner, Szymon. *Crimes against POW's. Responsibility of the Wehrmacht.* Warsaw, 1964

64) Davis, Gerald H. "Prisoners of War in Twentieth-Century War Economics." *Journal of Contemporary History* vol. 12 (1977): pp. 623–634

65) Fischer, George. *Soviet Opposition to Stalin. A Case Study in World War II.* Cambridge, Mass., 1952

66) Forwick, Helmuth. "Zur Behandlung alliierter Kriegsgefangener im Zweiten Weltkrieg. Anweisung des Oberkommandos der Wehrmacht über Besuche ausländischer Kommissionen in Kriegsgefangenenlagern." *Militärgeschichtliche Mitteilungen* no. 2 (1967): pp. 119–134

67) *"50 Jahre danach". Erinnerungen an das Kriegsgefangenenlager "Stalag 326".* Edited by Arbeitskreis Versöhnung durch Erinnerung e.V. Hövelhof, 1991

68) Gareev, M.A. "O mifach starych i novych." *Voenno-Istoriceskij Zurnal* no. 4 (1993): pp. 47ff.

69) Herbert, Ulrich, ed. *Europa und der "Reichseinsatz". Ausländische Zivilarbeiter, Kriegsgefangene und KZ-Häftlinge in Deutschland 1938–1945.* Essen, 1991

70) _____. "Zwangsarbeit in Deutschland. Sowjetische Zivilarbeiter und Kriegsgefangene 1941–1945." In *Erobern und Vernichten. Der Krieg*

gegen die Sowjetunion 1941–1945, edited by Peter Jahn and Reinhard Rürup, pp. 106–130. Berlin, 1991

71) Heß, Ulrich. "Quellen zum Schicksal der Kriegsgefangenen, Zwangsarbeiter und der ausländischen Zivilarbeiter im Sächsischen Staatsarchiv Leipzig." In *Der Mensch gegen den Menschen*, edited by Hans-Heinrich Nolte, pp. 137–146. Hanover, 1992

72) Hoffmann, Joachim. *Die Geschichte der Wlassow-Armee*. Freiburg, 1986

73) Hüser, Karl. "Das Stalag 326 (VI/K) Stukenbrook-Senne 1941–1945. Sowjetische Kriegsgefangene in der Senne als Opfer des nationalsozialistischen Rassekrieges, ein Zwischenbericht." In *Opfer und Täter. Zum nationalsozialistischen und antijüdischen Alltag in Ostwestfalen-Lippe*, edited by Hubert Frankemölle, pp. 165–174. Bielefeld, 1990

74) Hüser, Karl, and Reinhard Otto. *Das Stammlager 362 (VI/K) Senne 1941–1945. Sowjetische Kriegsgefangene als Opfer des Nationalsozialistischen Weltanschauungskrieges*. Bielefeld, 1992

75) Keller, Rolf. "'Russenlager'. Sowjetische Kriegsgefangene in Bergen-Belsen, Fallingbostel-Oerbke und Wietzendorf." In *Der Mensch gegen den Menschen. Überlegungen und Forschungen zum deutschen Überfall auf die Sowjetunion 1941*, edited by Hans-Heinrich Nolte, pp. 111–136. Hanover, 1992

76) Klausch, Hans-Peter. *Widerstand in Flossenbürg: Zum antifaschistischen Widerstandskampf der deutschen, österreichischen und sowjetischen Kommunisten im Konzentrationslager Flossenbürg 1940–1945*. Oldenburg, 1990

77) Kosthorst, Erich, und Bernd Walter. *Konzentrations- und Kriegsgefangenenlager im Dritten Reich. Beispiel Emsland*. Düsseldorf, 1983

78) Krivoseev, G.F., et al. *Grif sekretnostij snjat. Poterij booryzennich sil SSSR voijnach, boevich deistbijach i boennich konfliktach. Statisticeskoe isledobanije*. Moscow, 1993

79) *Das Lager 326. Augenzeugenberichte, Fotos, Dokumente*. Edited by Arbeitskreis Blumen für Stukenbrock e.V. Porta Westfalica, 1988

80) Ludewig, Ulrich. "Die historische Forschung über Kriegsgefangene und Zwangsarbeiter im Zweiten Weltkrieg." In *Die Verbrechen des Krieges erinnern*, edited by Jörg Calließ, pp. 109–118. Loccum, 1990

81) Newland, Samuel J. *Cossacks in the German Army, 1941–1945*. London, 1980

82) Reinhard, Otto. "Das Kriegsgefangenenlager Stalag 326 (VI/K) Senne-Forellkrug." In *Verdrängte Geschichte. Verfolgung und Vernichtung in Ostwestfalen 1933–1945*, edited by Joachim Meynert and Arno Klönne, pp. 201–219. Bielefeld, 1986

83) Rolf, David. *Prisoners of the Reich. Germany's Captives, 1939–1945*. London, 1988

84) Roschmann, Hans. *Gutachten zur Behandlung und zu den Verlusten sowjetischer Kriegsgefangener in deutscher Hand von 1941–1945 und zur Bewertung der Beweiskraft des sogenannten "Documents NOKW 2125" (Nachweisung des Verbleibs der sowjetischen Kriegsgefangenen nach dem Stande vom 1. 5. 1944)*. Ingolstadt, 1982

85) Schockenhoff, Volker. "'Eine Tragödie größten Ausmaßes'. Zum Schicksal der sowjetischen Kriegsgefangenen im Stalag 326 (VI/K) Senne."

Geschichte im Westen. Halbjahres-Zeitschrift für Landes-und Zeitgeschichte vol. 6 (1991): pp. 151–161

86) Siedenhans, Michael, and Volker Pieper. "Das Kriegsgefangenen-Stammlager 326 (VI/K)." In *Die Vergessenen von Stukenbrock*, pp. 18–71. Bielefeld, 1988

87) *Stalag VI/A Hemer. Kriegsgefangenenlager 1939–1945*. Edited by Bürgerinitiative für Frieden und Abrüstung Hemer. Iserlohn, 1982

88) Streim, Alfred. *Die Behandlung sowjetischer Kriegsgefangener im "Fall Barbarossa". Eine Dokumentation*. Heidelberg, 1981

89) _____. *Sowjetische Gefangene in Hitlers Vernichtungskrieg. Berichte und Dokumente 1941–1945*. Recht, Justiz, Zeitgeschehen, vol. 35. Heidelberg, 1982

90) _____. "Das Völkerrecht und die sowjetischen Kriegsgefangenen." In *Zwei Wege nach Moskau. Vom Hitler-Stalin-Pakt bis zum "Unternehmen Barbarossa"*, edited by Bernd Wegner, pp. 291–308. Munich, 1991

91) Streit, Christian. *Keine Kameraden. Die Wehrmacht und die sowjetischen Kriegsgefangenen 1941–1945*. Stuttgart, 1978; 3rd rev. edn Bonn, 1991

92) _____. "Sozialpolitische Aspekte der Behandlung der sowjetischen Kriegsgefangenen." In *Zweiter Weltkrieg und sozialer Wandel*, edited by Waclaw Dlugoborski, pp. 184–196. Göttingen, 1981

93) _____. "Die Behandlung der sowjetischen Kriegsgefangenen und völkerrechtliche Probleme des Krieges gegen die Sowjetunion." In *"Unternehmen Barbarossa". Der deutsche Überfall auf die Sowjetunion 1941. Berichte, Analysen, Dokumente*, edited by Gerd R. Ueberschär and Wolfram Wette, pp. 197–218. Paderborn, 1984; new edn *Der deutsche Überfall auf die Sowjetunion. "Unternehmen Barbarossa" 1941*, edited by Gerd R. Ueberschär and Wolfram Wette, pp. 159–183. Frankfurt a.M., 1991

94) _____ "Sowjetische Kriegsgefangene – Massendeportationen – Zwangsarbeiter." In *Der Zweite Weltkrieg. Analysen, Grundzüge, Forschungsbilanzen*, edited by Wolfgang Michalka, pp. 747–760. Munich, 1989

95) _____. "Partisans – Resistance – Prisoners of War." In *Operation Barbarossa: The German Attack on the Soviet Union, June 22, 1941*, edited by Norman Naimark et al., pp. 259–276. Special Issue of *Soviet Union*, vol. 18, nos. 1–3. Salt Lake City, 1991

96) Teske, Hermann, and General Ernst Köstring. *Der militärische Mittler zwischen dem Deutschen Reich und der Sowjetunion 1921–1941*. Frankfurt, [1965?]

97) Vasil'ev, Aleksandr. *Rückkehr nach Stukenbrock. Erinnerungen eines russischen Kriegsgefangenen*. Cologne, 1989

98) Weischer, Heinz. *Russenlager. Russische Kriegsgefangene in Hessen (Hamm) 1942–1945*. Essen, 1991

99) Wörsdorfer, Rolf. "Das Massaker von Lemberg im Lichte der italienischen Untersuchungskommission." In: *22. Juni 1941. Der Überfall auf die Sowjetunion*, edited by Hans Schafranek and Robert Streibel, pp. 147–166. Vienna, 1991

100) Zemskov, V. N. "K vorprosy repatriacii sovetskich grazdan 1944–1951 gody." *Istorija SSSR* no. 4 (1990): pp. 28 ff.

5. The Genocide of the Jews in the East

101) Adam, Uwe D. *Judenpolitik im Dritten Reich*. Düsseldorf, 1972
102) Ainsztein, Reuben. *Jewish Resistance in Nazi-Occupied Eastern Europe with a Historical Survey of the Jew as Fighter and Soldier in the Diaspora*. London, 1974
102a) Altman, Ilya. "Toward the History of 'The Black Book'." *Yad Vashem Studies* vol. 21 (1991): pp. 221–49
103) Aly, Götz. *"Endlösung". Völkerverschiebung und der Mord an den europäischen Juden*. Frankfurt a.M., 1995
104) Aly, Götz, et al. *Sozialpolitik und Judenvernichtung. Gibt es eine Ökonomie der Endlösung?* Berlin, 1987
105) Aly, Götz, and Susanne Heim. *Vordenker der Vernichtung. Auschwitz und die deutschen Pläne für eine neue europäische Ordnung*. Hamburg, 1991; new paperback edn Frankfurt a.M., 1993; 2nd edn 1994
106) Aly, Götz, and Susanne Heim. "Deutsche Herrschaft 'im Osten': Bevölkerungspolitik und Völkermord." In *Erobern und Vernichten. Der Krieg gegen die Sowjetunion 1941–1945. Essays*, edited by Peter Jahn and Reinhard Rürup, pp. 84–105. Berlin, 1991
107) *Amoklauf gegen die Wirklichkeit. NS-Verbrechen und revisionistische Geschichtsschreibung*. Edited by Dokumentationsarchiv des österreichischen Widerstandes and Bundesministerium für Unterricht und Kunst. Vienna, 1991; 2nd edn 1992
108) Ancel, Jean. "Antonescu and the Jews." *Yad Vashem Studies* vol. 23 (1993): pp. 213–280
109) Arad, Yitzhak "'The Final Solution' in Lithuania in the Light of German Documentation." *Yad Vashem Studies* vol. 11 (1976): pp. 234–272
110) ____. "Alfred Rosenberg and the 'Final Solution' in the Occupied Soviet Territories." *Yad Vashem Studies* vol. 13 (1979): pp. 263–286
111) ____. *Ghetto in Flames. The Struggle and Destruction of the Jews in Vilna in the Holocaust*. Jerusalem, 1980
112) ____. "'Operation Reinhard': Extermination Camps of Belzec, Sobibor and Treblinka." *Yad Vashem Studies* vol. 16 (1984): pp. 205–240
113) ____. *Belzec, Sobibor, Treblinka – The Operation Reinhard Death Camps*. Bloomington, 1987
114) ____. "The Holocaust of Soviet Jewry in the Occupied Territories of the Soviet Union." *Yad Vashem Studies* vol. 21 (1991): pp. 1–47
115) ____. "The Soviet Jews in the War against Nazi Germany." *Yad Vashem Studies* vol. 23 (1993): pp. 73–125
116) Arad, Yitzhak, Yisrael Gutman, and Abrahem Margaliot, eds. *Documents on the Holocaust. Selected Sources on the Destruction of the Jews of Germany and Austria, Poland and the Soviet Union*. Jerusalem, 1981
117) Arad, Yitzak, et al., eds. *The Einsatztruppen Reports*. New York, 1989
118) Arendt, Hannah. *Eichmann in Jerusalem. A Report on the Banality of Evil*. New York, 1963 (German edn: *Eichmann in Jerusalem. Ein Bericht von der Banalität des Bösen*. Reinbek, 1978 with several edns; new paperback edn Munich, 1995)
119) Aronson, Shlomo. "Die dreifache Falle. Hitlers Judenpolitik, die Alliierten und die Juden." *Vierteljahrshefte für Zeitgeschichte* vol. 32 (1984): pp. 29–65
120) Aronson, G., and J. Frumkin, eds. *Russian Jewry*. New York, 1969

121) Baade, Fritz, et al., eds. *"Unsere Ehre heißt Treue". Kriegstagebuch des Kommandostabes RFSS. Tätigkeitsberichte der 1. und 2. SS-Infanterie-Brigade, der 1. SS-Kavallerie-Brigade und von Sonderkommandos der SS*. Vienna, 1965

122) Bästlein, Klaus, Helge Grabitz, and Johannes Tuchel, eds. *Die Normalität des Verbrechens. Bilanz und Perspektiven der Forschung zu den nationalsozialistischen Gewaltverbrechen. Festschrift für Wolfgang Scheffler zum 65. Geburtstag*. Berlin, 1994

123) Bailer-Galanda, Brigitte. *Das Lachout- "Dokument". Anatomie einer Fälschung*. Vienna, 1985

124) ____. Bailer-Galanda, Brigitte, Wolfgang Benz, and Wolfgang Neugebauer, eds. *Wahrheit und "Auschwitzlüge". Zur Bekämpfung "revisionistischer" Propaganda*. Vienna, 1995

125) Baldwin, Peter, ed. *Reworking the Past. Hitler, the Holocaust and the Historians' Debate*. Boston, 1990

126) Bankier, David. "Hitler and the Policy-Making Process on the Jewish Question." *Holocaust and Genocide Studies* vol. 3 (1988): pp. 1–20 (German edn: *Die öffentliche Meinung im Hitler-Staat. Die "Endlösung" und die Deutschen. Eine Berichtigung*. Berlin, 1995)

127) ____. "The Germans and the Holocaust: What Did They Know?" *Yad Vashem Studies* vol. 20 (1990): pp. 69–98

128) ____. *The Germans and the Final Solution. Public Opinion under Nazism*. Oxford, 1992

129) Bar-On, Zvi. "The Jews in the Soviet Partisan Movement." *Yad Vashem Studies* vol. 4 (1960): pp. 167–189

130) Bastian, Till. *Auschwitz und die "Auschwitz-Lüge". Massenmord und Geschichtsfälschung*. Munich, 1994

131) Bauer, Yehuda. *The Holocaust in Historical Perspective*. London, 1978

132) ____. *A History of the Holocaust*. New York, 1982

133) ____. "Who Was Responsible and When? Some Well-Known Documents Revisited." *Holocaust and Genocide Studies* vol. 6 (1991): pp. 129–149

134) Bauer, Yehuda, et al., eds. *Remembering for the Future. Working Papers and Addenda*. 3 vols. Oxford, 1989

135) Baum, Rainer C. *The Holocaust and the German Elite. Genocide and National Suicide in Germany 1871–1945*. Ottawa, 1981

136) Beer, Matthias. "Die Entwicklung der Gaswagen beim Mord an den Juden." *Vierteljahrshefte für Zeitgeschichte* vol. 35 (1987): pp. 403–417

137) Benz, Wolfgang. "Der Generalplan Ost. Zur Germanisierungspolitik des NS-Regimes in den besetzten Ostgebieten 1939–1945." In *Die Vertreibung der Deutschen aus dem Osten. Ursache, Ereignisse, Folgen*, edited by Wolfgang Benz, pp. 39–48. Frankfurt a.M., 1985; new edn 1995

137a) ____. *Der Holocaust*. Munich, 1995

138) Benz, Wolfgang, ed. *Dimensiones des Völkermords: Die Zahl der jüdischen Opfer des Nationalsozialismus*. Munich, 1991

138a) Berenbaum, Michael, and Yisrael Gutman, eds. *Anatomy of the Auschwitz Death Camp*. Bloomington, Ind., 1995

139) Bergmann, Martin S., Milton E. Jucovy, and Judith S. Kestenberg, eds. *Generations of the Holocaust*. New York, 1982; rev. edn 1990 (German edn: *Kinder der Opfer – Kinder der Täter. Psychoanalyse und Holocaust*. Frankfurt a.M., 1995)

140) Bethge, Eberhard. "Shoah (Holocaust) und Protestantismus." In *Der Holocaust und die Protestanten. Analysen einer Verstrickung*, edited by Jochen-Christoph Kaiser and Martin Greschat, pp. 1–37. Frankfurt a.M., 1988
141) Black, Peter H. *Ernst Kaltenbrunner. Ideological Soldier of the Third Reich*. Princeton, N. J., 1984 (German edn: *Ernst Kaltenbrunner: Vasall Himmlers: Eine SS-Karriere*. Paderborn, 1991)
142) Block, Gay, and Malka Drucker. *Rescuers. Portraits of Moral Courage in the Holocaust*. New York, 1992
143) Bobe, M., et al. *The Jews in Latvia*. Tel Aviv, 1971
144) Bolchover, Richard. *British Jewry and the Holocaust*. Cambridge, 1993
145) Bosworth, Richard J. B. *Explaining Auschwitz & Hiroshima. History Writing and the Second World War 1945–1990*. London, 1993; paperback edn 1994
146) Braham, Randolph L., ed. *The Eichmann Case. A Source Book*. New York, 1969
147) ____. *The Politics of Genocide: The Holocaust in Hungary*. 2 vols. New York, 1981
148) Breitman, Richard. *The Architect of Genocide: Himmler and the Final Solution*. New York, 1991 (German edn: *Der Architekt der "Endlösung": Himmler und die Vernichtung der europäischen Juden*. Paderborn, 1996)
149) Breitman, Richard, and Shlomo Aronson. "The End of the 'Final Solution'? Nazi Plans to Ransom Jews in 1944." *Central European History* vol. 25, no. 2 (1992): pp. 177–203
150) Breitman, Richard, and Walter Laqueur. *Breaking the Silence*. New York, 1986 (German edn: *Der Mann, der das Schweigen brach. Wie die Welt vom Holocaust erfuhr*. Frankfurt, 1986)
151) Broszat, Martin. "Das Dritte Reich und die rumänische Judenpolitik." In *Gutachten des Instituts für Zeitsgeschichte*, vol. 1, pp. 102–183. Munich, 1958
152) ____. "Hitler and the Genesis of the Final Solution: an Assessment of David Irving's Theses." *Yad Vashem Studies* vol. 13 (1979): pp. 73–125 (German edn: "Hitler und die Genesis der 'Endlösung'. Aus Anlaß der Thesen von David Irving." *Vierteljahrshefte für Zeitgeschichte* vol. 25 (1977): pp. 739–775)
153) Browning, Christopher R. *The Final Solution and the German Foreign Office: A Study of Referat III D of Abteilung Deutschland*. New York, 1978
154) ____. "A Reply to Martin Broszat regarding the Origins of the Final Solution." *Simon Wiesenthal Centre Annual* vol. 1 (1984): pp. 113–132 (German edn: "Zur Genesis der 'Endlösung'. Eine Antwort an Martin Broszat." *Vierteljahrshefte für Zeitgeschichte* vol. 29 [1981]: pp. 97–109)
155) ____. *Fateful Months: Essays on the Emergence of the Final Solution*. New York, 1985; rev. edn 1991
156) ____. "Nazi Resettlement Policy and the Search for a Solution to the Jewish Question." *German Studies Review* vol. 9 (1986): pp. 497–519
157) ____. *The Path to Genocide: Essays on Launching the Final Solution*. Cambridge, 1992
158) ____. *Ordinary Men: Reserve-Police Battalion 101 and the Final Solution in Poland*. New York, 1992 (German edn: *Ganz normale Männer. Das*

Reserve-Polizeibataillon 101 und die "Endlösung" in Polen. Reinbek, 1993)

159) Buchheim, Hans, et al. *Anatomy of the SS State*. London, 1970 (German edn: *Anatomie des SS-Staates*. 2 vols. Olten, 1965; 2nd edn Munich, 1967)

160) Büchler, Yehoshua. "Kommandostab Reichsführer-SS: Himmler's Personal Murder Brigades in 1941." *Holocaust and Genocide Studies* vol. 1, no. 1 (1986): pp. 11–25

161) Burrin, Philippe. *Hitler and the Jews*. London, 1994 (French edn: *Hitler et les Juifs. Genèse d'un génocide*. Paris, 1989. German edn: *Hitler und die Juden. Die Entscheidung für den Völkermord*. Frankfurt a.M., 1993)

162) Buruma, Ian. *Die Erbschaft der Schuld. Vergangenheitsbewältigung in Deutschland und Japan*. Munich, 1994

163) Cesarini, David, ed. *The Final Solution. Origins and Implementation*. London, 1994

164) Chalovsky, Shalom. "The German Jews in the Minsk Ghetto." *Yad Vashem Studies* vol. 17 (1986): pp. 219–245

165) ____. *In the Eye of the Hurricane. The Jews in Eastern Belorussia during World War II* (in Hebrew). Tel Aviv, 1988

166) Charny, Israel W. *Genocide: A Critical Bibliographic Review*. 2 vols. New York, 1988–1991

167) Claussen, Detlev. *Grenzen der Aufklärung. Zur gesellschaftlichen Genese des modernen Antisemitismus*. Frankfurt a.M., 1987; new rev. edn 1994

168) Cohen, Akiba A., et al. *Holocaust und NS-Prozesse. Die Presseberichterstattung in Israel und Deutschland zwischen Aneignung und Abwehr*. Vienna, 1995

169) Cohen, Asher, Joav Gelber, and Charlotte Wardi, eds. *Comprehending the Holocaust. Historical and Literary Research*. Frankfurt a.M., 1988

170) ____. Cochavi, Yehoyakim, and Yoav Gelber, eds. *The Shoah and the War*. New York, 1992

170a) Crowe, David M. *A History of the Gypsies of Eastern Europe and Russia*. Tauris, 1995

171) *Dachauer Hefte*. Vols 1–7. Edited by Wolfgang Benz and Barbara Distel. Munich, 1993ff.

172) Dadrian, Vahakn N. "Towards a Theory of Genocide Incorporating the Instance of Holocaust: Comments, Criticisms and Suggestions." *Holocaust and Genocide Studies* vol. 5, no. 2 (1990): pp. 129–143

173) Dawidowicz, Lucy S. *The War against the Jews*. London, 1975 (German edn: *Der Krieg gegen die Juden 1933–1945*. Munich, 1979)

174) ____. *The Holocaust and the Historians*. Cambridge, 1981

175) ____. ed. *A Holocaust Reader*. New York, 1976

176) Deutschkron, Inge. ... *denn ihrer war die Hölle. Kinder in Ghettos und Lagern*. Cologne, 1979

177) Döscher, Hans-Jürgen. *SS und Auswärtiges Amt im Dritten Reich. Diplomatie im Schatten der "Endlösung"*. Frankfurt, 1991; first edn as *Das Auswärtige Amt im Dritten Reich*. Berlin, 1987

178) Donat, Helmut, and Lothar Wieland, eds. *"Auschwitz erst möglich gemacht?" Überlegungen zur jüngsten konservativen Geschichtsbewältigung*. Bremen, 1991

179) Dreßen, Willi. "The Role of the Wehrmacht and the Police in the Annihilation of the Jews; the Persecution and Postwar Careers of Perpetrators in the Police Force of the Federal Republic of Germany." *Yad Vashem Studies* vol. 23 (1993): pp. 295–319

180) Dreßen, Willi, Ernst Klee, and Volker Riess, eds. *"Schöne Zeiten." Judenmord aus der Sicht der Täter und Gaffer*. Frankfurt a.M., 1988

181) Dreßen, Willi, and Ernst Klee, eds. *"Gott mit uns". Der deutsche Vernichtungskrieg im Osten 1939–1945*. Frankfurt a.M., 1989

182) Dvorjetski, Marc. *Le Ghetto de Vilna. Rapport Sanitaire*. Geneva, 1946; new edn *La Victoire du Ghetto*. Paris, 1962

183) Dwork, Deborah. *Children with a Star. Jewish Youth in Nazi Europe*. London, 1991 (German edn: *Kinder mit dem gelben Stern. Europa 1933–1945*. Munich, 1994)

184) Eckman, Lester, and Chaim Lazar. *The Jewish Resistance. The History of the Jewish Partisans in Lithuania and White Russia during the Nazi Occupation, 1940–1945*. New York, 1977

185) Edelheit, Abraham, and Hershel Edelheit, eds. *Bibliography of Holocaust Literature*. Boulder, Colo., 1986

186) Ehrenburg, Ilja, and Wassilij Grossmann. *Das Schwarzbuch. Der Genozid an den sowjetischen Juden*. Edited by Ytzhak Arad and Arno Lustiger. Reinbek, 1994

187) Eichholtz, Dietrich, et al., eds. *Faschismus und Rassismus. Kontroversen um Ideologie und Opfer*. Berlin, 1992

188) Eichholtz, Dietrich. "'Generalplan Ost' und seine Opfer." In *Faschismus und Rassismus. Kontroversen um Ideologie und Opfer*, edited by Dietrich Eichholtz et al., pp. 291–299. Berlin, 1992

189) *The Einsatzgruppen or Murder Commandos*. Vol. 10 of *The Holocaust. Selected Documents in 18 Volumes*, edited by John Mendelsohn. New York, 1982

190) Engel, David. *In the Shadow of Auschwitz. The Polish Government-In-Exile and the Jews, 1939–42*. Chapel Hill, 1987

191) _____. *Facing a Holocaust. The Polish Government-In-Exile and the Jews, 1943–1945*. Chapel Hill, 1993

192) Evans, Richard. *In Hitler's Shadow: West German Historians and the Attempt to Escape from the Nazi Past*. London, 1987 (German edn: *Im Schatten Hitlers? Historikerstreit und Vergangenheitsbewältigung in der Bundesrepublik*. Frankfurt a.M., 1991)

Fall 9, see Leszczynski, Kazimierz.

193) Fisher, Julius F. "How Many Jews Died in Transnistria?" *Jewish Social Studies* vol. 20 (1958): pp. 95–101

194) Fleming, Gerald. *Hitler und die Endlösung. "Es ist des Führers Wunsch ..."* Wiesbaden, 1982 (English edn: *Hitler and the Final Solution*. Berkeley, 1984)

194a) Fogelman, Eva. *Conscience and Courage: Rescuers of Jews during the Holocaust*. New York, 1994 (German edn: *"Wir waren keine Helden". Lebensretter im Angesicht des Holocaust. Motive, Geschichten, Hintergründe*. Frankfurt a.M., 1995)

195) Foregger, Richard. "Technical Analysis of Methods to Bomb the Gas Chambers at Auschwitz." *Holocaust and Genocide Studies* vol. 4 (1990): pp. 403–421

196) Fried, Hédi. *Fragments of a Life*. London, 1992 (German edn: *Nachschlag für eine Gestorbene. Ein Leben bis Auschwitz und ein Leben danach*. Hamburg, 1995)
197) Friedländer, Saul. "From Anti-Semitism to Extermination: A Historiographical Study of Nazi Policies toward the Jews and an Essay in Interpretation." *Yad Vashem Studies* vol. 16 (1984): pp. 1–50
198) ____. "Vom Antisemitismus zur Judenvernichtung: Eine historiographische Studie zur nationalsozialistischen Judenpolitik und Versuch einer Interpretation." In *Der Mord an den Juden im Zweiten Weltkrieg*, edited by Eberhard Jäckel and Jürgen Rohwer, pp. 18–60. Stuttgart, 1985
199) ____. "Die 'Endlösung'. Über das Unbehagen in der Geschichtsdeutung." In *Der historische Ort des Nationalsozialismus*, edited by Walter H. Pehle, pp. 81–93. Frankfurt a.M., 1990
200) Friedländer, Saul, ed. *Probing the Limits of Representation. Nazism and the "Final Solution"*. Cambridge, Mass., 1992
201) Friedlander, Albert, ed. *Out of the Whirlwind: A Reader of Holocaust Literature*. Westminster, Md., 1976
202) Friedman, Philip. *Roads to Extinction: Essays on the Holocaust*. New York, 1980
203) Gilbert, Martin. *Auschwitz and the Allies*. London, 1981 (German edn: *Auschwitz und die Alliierten*. Munich, 1982)
204) ____. *Atlas of the Holocaust*. London, 1982 (German edn: *Endlösung. Die Vertreibung und Vernichtung der Juden. Ein Atlas*. Reinbek, 1982; new edn 1995)
205) ____. *The Holocaust. The Jewish Tragedy*. London, 1986
206) ____. *The Holocaust: Maps and Photographs: A Record of the Destruction of Jewish Life in Europe during the Dark Years of Nazi Rule*. 2nd rev. edn New York, 1992
207) ____. *Surviving the Holocaust. The Kovno Ghetto Diary*. Cambridge, Mass., 1989
208) Gilboa, Y. A. *The Black Years of Soviet Jewry, 1939–1953*. Boston, Mass., 1971
209) Gitelman, Zvi. "History, Memory and Politics: The Holocaust in the Soviet Union." *Holocaust and Genocide Studies* vol. 5 (1990): pp. 23–37
209a) Goldhagen, Daniel Jonah. *Hitler's Willing Executioners. Ordinary Germans and the Holocaust*. New York, 1995 (German edn: *Hitlers willige Vollstrecker. Ganz gewöhnliche Deutsche und der Holocaust*. Berlin, 1996)
210) Gordon, Sarah. *Hitler, Germans and the Jewish Question*. Princeton, 1984
211) Grabitz, Helge, and Wolfgang Scheffler. *Letzte Spuren. Ghetto Warschau. SS-Arbeitslager Trawinki. Aktion Erntefest. Fotos und Dokumente über Opfer des Endlösungswahns im Spiegel der historischen Ereignisse*. 2nd edn. Berlin, 1993
212) Grabitz, Helge, et al., eds. *Die Normalität des Verbrechens. Bilanz und Perspektiven der Forschung zu den nationalsozialistischen Gewaltverbrechen*. Berlin, 1994
213) Greschat, Martin, and Jochen-Christoph Kaiser, eds. *Der Holocaust und die Protestanten. Analysen einer Verstrickung*. Frankfurt a.M., 1988
214) Grosser, Alfred. *Ermordung der Menschheit. Der Genozid im Gedächtnis der Völker*. Munich, 1990; new edn as paperback *Verbrechen und*

Erinnerung. Munich, 1993 (French edn: *Le crime et la mémoire*. Paris, 1989)

215) Gutman, Yisrael. *The Holocaust and its Significance*. Jerusalem, 1984

216) Gutman, Yisrael, and Livia Rothkirchen, eds. *The Catastrophe of European Jewry. Antecedents – History – Reflections*. Jerusalem, 1976

217) Gutman, Yisrael, and Gideon Greif, eds. *The Historiography of the Holocaust Period. Proceedings of the Fifth Yad Vashem International Historical Conference, Jerusalem, March 1983*. Jerusalem, 1988

218) Gutman, Yisrael, et al., eds. *Encyclopedia of the Holocaust*. 4 vols. New York, 1990 (German edn: *Enzyklopädie des Holocaust. Die Verfolgung und Ermordung der europäischen Juden*. Edited by Eberhard Jäckel, Peter Longerich and Julius H. Schoeps. 3 vols. Berlin, 1993; new paperback edn in 4 vols Munich, 1995)

218a) Hackett, David A., ed. *The Buchenwald Report*. Boulder, Co., 1995 (German edn: *Der Buchenwald-Report. Bericht über das Konzentrationslager Buchenwald bei Weimar*. Munich, 1996)

219) Hardtmann, Gertrud, ed. *Spuren der Verfolgung. Seelische Auswirkungen des Holocaust auf die Opfer und ihre Kinder*. Gerlingen, 1992

220) Hausner, Gideon. *Justice in Jerusalem*. New York, 1966 (German edn: *Die Vernichtung der Juden. Das größte Verbrechen der Geschichte*. 2nd edn Munich, 1979)

221) Hayes, Peter, ed. *Lesson and Legacies: The Meaning of the Holocaust in a Changing World*. Evanston, 1991

222) Headland, Ronald. *Messages of Murder: A Study of the Reports of the Einsatzgruppen of the Security Police and the Security Service*. East Rutherford, 1992

223) _____. "The Einsatzgruppen: The Question of their Initial Operations." *Holocaust and Genocide Studies* vol. 4 (1989): pp. 401–412

224) Heer, Hannes. "Killing Fields. Die Wehrmacht und der Holocaust." *Mittelweg 36* vol. 3 (1994): pp. 7–29

225) Heiber, Helmut. "Der Generalplan Ost." *Vierteljahrshefte für Zeitgeschichte* vol. 6 (1958): pp. 281–325

225a) Heim, Susanne. "Gibt es eine Ökonomie der "Endlösung"? Wirtschaftsrationalisierung und Vernichtungspolitik im besetzten Polen 1939 bis 1945." Diss., Freie Universität Berlin, 1991

226) Heinsohn, Gunnar. *Warum Auschwitz? Hitlers Plan und die Ratlosigkeit der Nachwelt*. Reinbek, 1995

227) Herbert, Ulrich. "Der Holocaust in der Geschichtsschreibung der Bundesrepublik Deutschland." In *Erinnerung. Zur Gegenwart des Holocaust in Deutschland-West und Deutschland-Ost*, edited by Bernhard Moltmann et al., pp. 31–45. Frankfurt a.M., 1993

227a) Herbert, Ulrich. *Best. Biographische Studien über Radikalismus, Weltanschauung und Vernunft 1903–1989*. Bonn, 1996

Heyel/Schreier, see Schreier

228) Hilberg, Raul. *The Destruction of the European Jews*. 3 vols. Chicago, 1961; New York, 1985; edn with a new postscript by the author, New York, 1978; revised and definitive edn New York, 1985 (German edn: *Die Vernichtung der europäischen Juden. Die Gesamtgeschichte des Holocaust*. Berlin, 1982; revised paperback edn *Die Vernichtung der Europäischen Juden*. 3 vols. Frankfurt a.M., 1990)

229) _____, ed. *Documents of Destruction*. Chicago, 1971

230) ____, ed. *Documents of Destruction. Germany and Jewry 1933–1945.* London, 1972
231) ____. "Die Aktion Reinhard." In *Der Mord an den Juden im Zweiten Weltkrieg*, edited by Eberhard Jäckel and Jürgen Rohwer, pp. 125–136. Stuttgart, 1985
232) ____. *Perpetrators, Victims, Bystanders. The Jewish Catastrophe, 1933–1945.* New York, 1992 (German edn: *Täter, Opfer, Zuschauer. Die Vernichtung der Juden 1933 bis 1945.* 3rd edn. Frankfurt a.M., 1992)
233) ____. *Unerbetene Erinnerung. Der Weg eines Holocaust-Forschers.* Frankfurt a.M., 1994
234) Hillgruber, Andreas. "Die 'Endlösung' und das deutsche Ostimperium als Kernstück des rassenideologischen Programms des Nationsalsozialismus." *Vierteljahrshefte für Zeitgeschichte* vol. 20, no. 2 (1972): pp. 133–153
235) ____. "Die ideologisch-dogmatische Grundlage der nationalsozialistischen Politik der Ausrottung der Juden in den besetzten Gebieten der Sowjetunion und ihre Durchführung 1941–1944." *German Studies Review* vol. 2, no. 3 (1979): pp. 263–296
236) ____. "Der Ostkrieg und die Judenvernichtung." In *"Unternehmen Barbarossa". Der deutsche Überfall auf die Sowjetunion 1941*, edited by Gerd R. Ueberschär and Wolfram Wette, pp. 219–236. Paderborn, 1984; new edn *Der deutsche Überfall auf die Sowjetunion. "Unternehmen Barbarossa" 1941*, pp. 185–205. Frankfurt a.M. 1991
237) ____. "Der geschichtliche Ort der Judenvernichtung. Eine Zusammenfassung." In *Der Mord an den Juden im Zweiten Weltkrieg*, edited by Eberhard Jäckel and Jürgen Rohwer, pp. 213–224. Stuttgart, 1985
238) ____. "The Extermination of the Jews in its Historical Context – a Recapitulation." *Yad Vashem Studies* vol. 17 (1986): pp. 1–15
239) ____. *Zweierlei Untergang: Die Zerschlagung des Deutschen Reiches und das Ende des europäischen Judentums.* Berlin, 1986
240) Hirschfeld, Gerhard, ed. *The Policies of Genocide: Jews and the Soviet Prisoners of War in Nazi Germany.* London, 1986
241) Ilnytzky, Roman. *Die Ukraine und das Reich. Tatsachen europäischer Ostpolitik. Ein Vorbericht.* 2 vols. Munich, 1955
242) Jäckel, Eberhard. "Die Entschlußbildung als historisches Problem." In *Der Mord an den Juden im Zweiten Weltkrieg*, edited by Eberhard Jäckel and Jürgen Rohwer, pp. 9–17. Stuttgart, 1985
Jäckel/Rosh, see Rosh
243) Jäckel, Eberhard, and Jürgen Rohwer, eds. *Der Mord an den Juden im Zweiten Weltkrieg. Entschlußbildung und Verwirklichung.* Stuttgart, 1985; paperback edn Frankfurt a.M., 1987
244) Kahane, David. *Lvov Ghetto Diary.* Amherst, 1990
245) Kahn, Leon, and Marjorie Morris. *No Time to Mourn. A True Story of a Jewish Partisan Fighter.* Vancouver, 1978
246) Kampe, Norbert, and Herbert A. Strauss, eds. *Antisemitismus. Von der Judenfeindschaft zum Holocaust.* Schriftenreihe der Bundeszentrale für politische Bildung, vol. 213. Bonn, 1985
247) Kaufmann, Max. *Churbn Lettland. Die Vernichtung der Juden Lettlands.* Munich, 1947
248) Keneally, Thomas. *Schindler's List.* New York, 1994

249) Kempner, Robert M.W. *SS im Kreuzverhör*. Munich, 1964; new edn *SS im Kreuzverhör. Die Elite, die Europa in Scherben brach*. Nördlingen, 1987
250) ____. *Das Dritte Reich im Kreuzverhör. Aus den unveröffentlichten Vernehmungsprotokollen des Anklägers Robert M.W. Kempner*. Munich, 1969
251) Kittermann, David H. "Those Who Said 'No!': Germans Who Refused to Execute Civilians during World War II". *German Studies Review* vol. 11, no. 2 (1988): pp. 241–254
252) Klein, Cecilie. *Sentenced to Live: A Survivor's Memoir*. New York, 1988
253) Knoller, Rivkah. *Denial of Holocaust. A Bibliography of Literature Denying or Distorting the Holocaust, and of Literature about this Phenomenon*. Ramat Gan, 1989
253a) Knopp, Guido. *Hitlers Helfer*. Gütersloh, 1996
254) Kogon, Eugen, et al., eds. *Nationalsozialistische Massentötungen durch Giftgas. Eine Dokumentation*. Frankfurt a.M. 1983, 1986, 1989
255) Kolinsky, Eva. "Remembering Auschwitz: a Survey of Recent Textbooks for the Teaching of History in German Schools." *Yad Vashem Studies* vol. 22 (1992): pp. 287–307
256) Krakowski, Shmuel. *The War of the Doomed: Jewish Armed Resistance in Poland, 1942–1944*. New York, 1984
257) Krausnick, Helmut, ed. "Denkschrift Himmlers über die Behandlung der Fremdvölkischen im Osten (Mai 1940)." *Vierteljahrshefte für Zeitgeschichte* vol. 5 (1957): pp. 194–198
258) ____. "Judenverfolgung." In *Anatomie des SS-Staates*, edited by Hans Buchheim et al. Vol. 2. Munich, 1967; 2nd edn 1979, pp. 233–366
259) ____. "Hitler und die Befehle an die Einsatzgruppen im Sommer 1941." In *Der Mord an den Juden im Zweiten Weltkrieg*, edited by Eberhard Jäckel and Jürgen Rohwer, pp. 88–106. Stuttgart, 1985
260) Kren, George M., and Leon Rappoport. *The Holocaust and the Crisis of Human Behavior*. New York, 1980
261) Kulka, Otto Duv. "Public Opinion in Nazi Germany and the 'Jewish Question'." *Jerusalem Quarterly* vol. 26 (1983): pp. 34–45
262) ____. "Die deutsche Geschichtsschreibung über den Nationalsozialismus und die 'Endlösung'. Tendenzen und Entwicklungsphasen 1924–1984." *Historische Zeitschrift* vol. 240 (1985): pp. 599–640
263) Kulka, Otto Duv, and Aron Rodrigue. "The German Population and the Jews in the Third Reich: Recent Publications and Trends in Research on German Society and the 'Jewish Question'." *Yad Vashem Studies* vol. 16 (1984): pp. 421–435
264) Kulka, Otto Duv, and Aron Rodrigue. "Singularity and Its Relativation: Changing Views in German Historiography on National Socialism and the 'Final Solution'." *Yad Vashem Studies* vol. 19 (1988): pp. 151–186
265) Kushner, Tony. "Rules of the Game: Britain, America and the Holocaust in 1944." *Holocaust and Genocide Studies* vol. 5, no. 4 (1990): pp. 381–402
266) Kwiet, Konrad. "Judenverfolgung und Judenvernichtung im Dritten Reich. Ein historiographischer Überblick." In *Ist der Nationsalsozialismus Geschichte? Zu Historisierung und Historikerstreit*, edited by Dan Diner, pp. 237–264. Frankfurt a.M., 1987
267) Lamping, Dieter, ed. *Dein aschenes Haar Sulamith. Dichtung über den Holocaust*. München, 1992

268) Landau, Ronnie S. *The Nazi Holocaust*. London, 1992
269) Lang, Berel, ed. *Writing and the Holocaust*. New York, 1988
270) Lang, Jochen von, ed. *Das Eichmann-Protokoll. Tonbandaufzeichnungen der israelischen Verhöre*. Berlin, 1982
271) Langbein, Hermann. *Menschen in Auschwitz*. Vienna, 1972; new edn 1995
271a) ____. *Der Auschwitz-Prozeß. Eine Dokumentation*. 2 vols. Frankfurt a.M., 1995
272) Lanzmann, Claude. *Shoah: An Oral History of the Holocaust*. London, 1985 (German edn: *Shoah*. Düsseldorf, 1986)
273) Laqueur, Walter. *The Terrible Secret: An Investigation into the Supression of Information about Hitler's "Final Solution"*. London, 1980 (German edn: *Was niemand wissen wollte: Die Unterdrückung der Nachrichten über Hitlers "Endlösung"*. Frankfurt, 1981)
274) Laub, Dori, and Nanette C. Auerhahn. "Holocaust Testimony." *Holocaust and Genocide Studies* vol. 5, no. 4 (1990): pp. 447–462
275) Leszcynski, Kazimierz, ed. *Fall 9. Das Urteil im SS-Einsatzgruppenprozeß gefällt am 10. April 1948 in Nürnberg vom Militärgerichtshof II der Vereinigten Staaten von Amerika*. East Berlin, 1963
276) Levin, Dov. *Fighting for their Lives: The War of Lithuanian Jews against Nazis, 1941–1945* (in Hebrew). Jerusalem, 1974
277) ____. "Estonian Jews in the U.S.S.R." *Yad Vashem Studies* vol. 11 (1976): pp. 273–297
278) ____. *With the Back to the Wall: The Fight of Latvian Jews against Nazism* (in Hebrew). Jerusalem, 1978
279) ____. "July 1944 – The Crucial Month for the Remnants of Lithuanian Jewry." *Yad Vashem Studies* vol. 16 (1984): pp. 333–361
280) ____. *Fighting Back: Lithuanian Jewry's Armed Resistance to the Nazis, 1941–1945*. New York, 1985
281) ____. *The Jews in the Soviet-Annexed Territories 1939–1941* (in Hebrew). Jerusalem, 1989
282) ____. "On the Relations between the Baltic Peoples and their Jewish Neighbors before, during and after World War II." *Holocaust and Genocide Studies* vol. 5 (1990): pp. 53–66
283) ____. "The Fateful Decision: The Flight of the Jews into the Soviet Interior in the Summer of 1941." *Yad Vashem Studies* vol. 20 (1990): pp. 115–142
284) Levin, Nora. *The Holocaust. The Destruction of European Jewry, 1933–1945*. New York, 1973
285) Lichtenstein, Heiner. *Warum Auschwitz nicht bombardiert wurde*. Cologne, 1980
286) ____. *Himmlers grüne Helfer. Die Schutz- und Ordnungspolizei im "Dritten Reich"*. Cologne, 1990
287) Lichtenstein, Heiner, et al., eds. *Täter – Opfer – Folgen. Der Holocaust in Geschichte und Gegenwart*. Schriftenreihe der Bundeszentrale für politische Bildung, vol. 335. Bonn, 1995
288) Lipstadt, Deborah E. *Beyond Belief*. New York, 1986 (German edn: *Betrifft: Leugnen des Holocaust*. Zurich, 1994)
289) Litani, Dora. "The Destruction of the Jews of Odessa in the Light of Romanian Documents." *Yad Vashem Studies* vol. 6 (1967): pp. 135–154

290) Littner, Carol, and Sandra Myers. *The Courage to Care. Rescuers of Jews during the Holocaust*. New York, 1986

291) Loewenstein, Karl. "Minsk. Im Lager der deutschen Juden." *Aus Politik und Zeitgeschichte* no. B 45/56, 7.11.1956: pp. 705–718; separate edn *Minsk*. Edited by Bundeszentrale für Heimatdienst. Schriftenreihe no. 51. Bonn, 1961

292) Loewy, Hanno, ed. *Holocaust: Die Grenzen des Verstehens. Eine Debatte über die Besetzung der Geschichte*. Reinbek, 1992

293) Loftus, John. *The Belarus Secret*. Edited by Nathan Miller. New York, 1982

294) Longerich, Peter, ed. *Die Ermordung der europäischen Juden. Eine umfassende Dokumentation des Holocaust 1941–1945*. Munich, 1989; 2nd edn 1990

295) _____. "Vom Massenmord zur 'Endlösung'. Die Erschießungen von jüdischen Zivilisten in den ersten Monaten des Ostfeldzuges im Kontext des nationalsozialistischen Judenmords." In *Zwei Wege nach Moskau. Vom Hitler-Stalin-Pakt bis zum "Unternehmen Barbarossa"*, edited by Bernd Wegner, pp. 251–274. Munich, 1991

296) _____. "Der Rußlandkrieg als rassistischer Vernichtungskrieg." In *Der Mensch gegen den Menschen. Überlegungen und Forschungen zum deutschen Überfall auf die Sowjetunion 1941*, edited by Hans-Heinrich Nolte, pp. 78–94. Hanover, 1992

297) Lozowick, Yaacov "Rollbahn Mord: The Early Activities of Einsatzgruppe C." *Holocaust and Genocide Studies* vol. 2 (1987): pp. 221–241

298) _____. "Erinnerung an die Shoah in Israel." *Geschichte in Wissenschaft und Unterricht* vol. 45 (1994): pp. 380–390

299) Lustiger, Arno. *Zum Kampf auf Leben und Tod. Vom Widerstand der Juden 1933–1945*. Cologne, 1994

300) Madajczyk, Czeslaw. "Generalplan Ost." *Polish Western Affairs* vol. 3 (1963): pp. 391–442

301) _____. "Besteht ein Synchronismus zwischen dem 'Generalplan Ost' und der Endlösung der Judenfrage?" In *Der Zweite Weltkrieg. Analysen, Grundzüge, Forschungsbilanzen*, edited by Wolfgang Michalka, pp. 844–857. Munich, 1989

302) _____. "Hitler's Direct Influence on Decisions Affecting Jews during World War II." *Yad Vashem Studies* vol. 20 (1990): pp. 53–68

303) Madajczyk, Czeslaw, et al., eds. *Vom Generalplan Ost zum Generalsiedlungsplan. Dokumente*. Munich, 1994

304) Maier, Charles. *The Unmasterable Past: History, Holocaust and German National Identity*. Cambridge, Mass., 1988

305) Manoschek, Walter, ed. *"Es gibt nur eines für das Judentum: Vernichtung". Das Judenbild in deutschen Soldatenbriefen 1939–1944*. Hamburg, 1995

306) Margolina, Sonja. *Das Ende der Lügen. Rußland und die Juden im 20. Jahrhundert*. Berlin, 1992

307) Marrus, Michael R. "The History of the Holocaust. A Survey of Recent Literature." *Journal of Modern History* vol. 59, no. 1 (1987): pp. 114–160

308) _____. *The Holocaust in History*. London, 1989

309) _____. *The Nazi Holocaust. Historical Articles on the Destruction of European Jews*. Westport, Conn., 1989

310) Mayer, Arno J. *Why Did the Heavens Not Darken? The "Final Solution" in History*. New York, 1988 (German edn: *Der Krieg als Kreuzzug. Das Deutsche Reich, Hitlers Wehrmacht und die "Endlösung"*. Reinbek, 1989)

311) Meier, Christian. "To Condemn and To Understand: A Turning Point in German Historical Remembrance." *Yad Vashem Studies* vol. 19 (1989): pp. 93–105

312) ____. *Vierzig Jahre nach Auschwitz: Deutsche Geschichtserinnerung heute*. Munich, 1990

313) Mendelsohn, Ezra. *The Jews of East Central Europe between the World Wars*. Bloomington, Ind., 1983

314) Mendelsohn, John, ed. *The Holocaust: Selected Documents*. 18 vols. New York, 1982

315) Messerschmidt, Manfred. "Harte Sühne am Judentum. Befehlslage und Wissen in der deutschen Wehrmacht." In *"Niemand war dabei und keiner hat's gewußt". Die deutsche Öffentlichkeit und die Judenverfolgung 1933–1945*, edited by Jörg Wollenberg, pp. 113–128. Munich, 1989

316) Meyer, Alwin. *Die Kinder von Auschwitz*. Göttingen, 1995

317) Michman, Dan. "Review of The High Price of Audacity." *Holocaust and Genocide Studies* vol. 6, no. 3 (1991): pp. 293–305

318) Milton, Sybil. "The Context of the Holocaust." *German Studies Review* vol. 13, no. 2 (1990): pp. 269–283

319) Mishell, William W. *Kaddish for Kovno: Life and Death in a Lithuanian Ghetto, 1941–1945*. Chicago, 1988

320) Moltmann, Bernhard, et al., eds. *Erinnerung. Zur Gegenwart des Holocaust in Deutschland-West und Deutschland-Ost*. Frankfurt a.M., 1993

321) Mommsen, Hans. "Haben die Historiker versagt? Holocaust und die deutsche Geschichtswissenschaft." *Materialien zur Politischen Bildung* vol. 2 (1979): pp. 56–62

322) ____. "The Realization of the Unthinkable: the 'Final Solution of the Jewish Question' in the Third Reich." In *The Policies of Genocide: Jews and Soviet Prisoners of War in Nazi Germany*, edited by Gerhard Hirschfeld, pp. 97–144. London, 1986 (German edn: "Die Realisierung des Utopischen: Die 'Endlösung der Judenfrage' im 'Dritten Reich'." *Geschichte und Gesellschaft* vol. 9 [1983]: pp. 381–420)

323) ____. "Was haben die Deutschen vom Völkermord an den Juden gewußt?" In *Der Judenpogrom 1938. Von der "Reichskristallnacht" zum Völkermord*, edited by Walter H. Pehle. Frankfurt a.M., 1988

324) Monneray, H. *La persécution de Juifs dans les pays de l'Est*. Paris, 1949

325) Morley, John F. *Vatican Diplomacy and the Holocaust, 1939–1945*. New York, 1980

326) Mosse, George L. *Towards the Final Solution. A History of European Racism*. New York, 1978 (German edn: *Die Geschichte des Rassismus in Europa*. New edn Frankfurt a.M., 1994)

327) Mosse, George L., and Bela Vago, eds. *Jews and Non-Jews in Eastern Europe, 1918–1945*. New York, 1974

328) Mueller-Tupath, Karla. *Reichsführers gehorsamster Becher. Eine deutsche Karriere*. Hamburg, 1982

328a) Ogorreck, Ralf. *Die Einsatzgruppen und die "Genesis der Endlösung"*. Berlin, 1996
329) Ophir, Ephraim. "Was the Transnistria Rescue Plan Achievable?" *Holocaust and Genocide Studies* vol. 6 (1991): pp. 1–16
330) Orbach, Wila. "The Destruction of the Jews in the Nazi-Occupied Territories of the USSR." *Soviet Jewish Affairs* vol. 2 (1976): pp. 14–51
331) Padfield, Peter. *Himmler: Reichsführer SS*. New York, 1991
332) Pätzold, Kurt. "Rassismus und Antisemitismus in der Kriegsideologie des faschistischen Deutschen Reiches." *Zeitschrift für Geschichtswissenschaft* vol. 28 (1980): pp. 424–441
333) _____, ed. *Verfolgung, Vertreibung, Vernichtung. Dokumente des faschistischen Antisemitismus 1933 bis 1942*. Frankfurt a.M., 1984
334) _____. "Die Wannsee-Konferenz – zu ihrem Platz in der Geschichte der Judenvernichtung." In *Faschismus und Rassismus. Kontroversen um Ideologie und Opfer*, edited by Dietrich Eichholtz et al., pp. 257–290. Berlin, 1992
335) Pätzold, Kurt, and Erika Schwarz. *Tagesordnung: Judenmord. Die Wannsee-Konferenz am 20. Januar 1942. Eine Dokumentation zur Organisation der "Endlösung"*. Berlin, 1992
336) Paldiel, Mordecai. "'To the Righteous among the Nations who Risked Their Lives to Rescue Jews'." *Yad Vashem Studies* vol. 19 (1988): pp. 403–425
337) _____. *The Path of the Righteous. Gentile Rescuers of Jews during the Holocaust*. Hoboken, N J, 1992, 1993
338) Pehle, Walter H., ed. *Genocide*. New York, 1991 (German edn: *Der Judenpogrom 1938. Von der "Reichskristallnacht" zum Völkermord*. Frankfurt a.M., 1988)
339) Pflüger, Friedbert. *Deutschland driftet. Die konservative Revolution entdeckt ihre Kinder*. Düsseldorf, 1994
340) Pinchuk, Ben-Cion. "Was There a Soviet Policy for Evacuating the Jews? The Case of the Annexed Territories." *Slavic Review* vol. 39 (1980): pp. 44–55
341) Porter, Jack N., ed. *Jewish Partisans. A Documentary of Jewish Resistance in the Soviet Union during World War II*. 2 vols. Washington, DC, 1982
342) Press, Bernhard. *Judenmord in Lettland. 1941–1945*. Berlin, 1992
343) Pressac, Jean-Claude. *Auschwitz. Technique and Operation of the Gas Chambers*. New York, 1989 (French edn: *Les crématoires d'Auschwitz*. Paris, 1993; German edn: *Die Krematorien von Auschwitz. Die Technik des Massenmordes*. Munich, 1994; new paperback edn 1995)
344) Rautkailio, Hannu. *Finland and the Holocaust. The Rescue of Finland's Jews*. New York, 1987
345) Redlich, Simon. "Metropolitan Andrei Sheptyts'kyi, Ukrainians and Jews during and after the Holocaust." *Holocaust and Genocide Studies* vol. 5 (1990): pp. 39–51
346) Reitlinger, Gerald. *The Final Solution – The Attempt of Exterminate the Jews of Europe, 1939–1945*. London, 1953 (German edn: *Die Endlösung. Hitlers Versuch der Ausrottung der Juden Europas 1939–1945*. Berlin, 1956; 7th edn 1992)

347) ____ *The SS: Alibi of a Nation, 1922–1945.* 2nd rev. edn Melbourne, 1957 (German edn: *Die SS. Tragödie einer deutschen Epoche*. Vienna, 1957)

348) Renz, Werner. *Auschwitz. Annotierte Bibliographie der deutschsprachigen Auschwitzliteratur*. Verzeichnisse der Arbeitsstelle zur Vorbereitung des Frankfurter Lern- und Dokumentationszentrum des Holocaust, Fritz-Bauer-Institut. Frankfurt a.M., 1994

349) Riwash, Joseph. *Resistance and Revenge, 1939–1949*. Montreal, 1981

350) Robel, Gert. "Sowjetunion". In *Dimension des Völkermordes. Die Zahl der jüdischen Opfer des Nationalsozialismus*, edited by Wolfgang Benz, pp. 499–560. Munich, 1991

351) Robinson, Jacob, and Philip Friedman. *Guide to Jewish History under Nazi Impact*. Yad Vashem Martyr's and Heroes' Memorial Authority, Jerusalem and Yivo Institute for Jewish Research, New York, Joint Documentary Projects, Bibliographical Series no. 1. New York, 1960

352) Röder, Werner. *Sonderfahndungsliste UdSSR*. Dokumente der Zeitgeschichte, vol. 1. Erlangen, 1976

353) Rogasky, Barbara. *Smoke and Ashes: The Story of the Holocaust*. Oxford, 1991

354) Rosh, Lea, and Eberhard Jäckel. *"Der Tod ist ein Meister aus Deutschland". Deportation und Ermordung der Juden. Kollaboration und Verweigerung in Europa*. Hamburg, 1990; 5th edn 1991; paperback edn Munich, 1992; 2nd edn 1993

355) Roth, John K. "Review of *Holocaust Revision*, by Arno Mayer." *Holocaust and Genocide Studies* vol. 5 (1990): pp. 217–221

356) Rückerl, Adalbert, ed. *NS-Prozesse. Nach 25 Jahren Strafverfolgung: Möglichkeiten – Grenzen – Ergebnisse*. Karlsruhe, 1971; 2nd edn 1972

357) ____. *Die Strafverfolgung von NS-Verbrechen 1945–1978. Eine Dokumentation*. Karlsruhe, 1979

358) Rüter-Ehlermann, Adelheid L., and C.F. Rüter, eds. *Justiz und NS-Verbrechen. Sammlung deutscher Strafurteile wegen nationalsozialistischer Tötungsverbrechen 1945–1966*. 22 vols. Amsterdam, 1968–1981

359) Safrian, Hans. *Die Eichmann-Männer*. Vienna, 1993; new edn as paperback *Eichmann und seine Gehilfen*. Frankfurt a.M., 1995

360) Saint George, George. *Les Massacres de Babyi-Yar*. Paris, 1969

360a) Sandkühler, Thomas. *"Endlösung" in Galizien. Der Judenmord in Ostpolen und die Rettungsinitiativen von Berthold Beitz 1941-1944*. Bonn, 1996

361) Scheffler, Wolfgang. *Judenverfolgung im Dritten Reich*. Berlin, 1964

362) ____. "Zur Entstehungsgeschichte der Endlösung." *Aus Politik und Zeitgeschichte* no. B 43/82, 30.10.1982: pp. 3–10

363) ____. "Wege zur 'Endlösung'." In *Antisemitismus. Von der Judenfeinschaft zum Holocaust*, edited by Herbert A. Strauss and Norbert Kampe, pp. 186–214. Schriftenreihe der Bundeszentrale für politische Bildung, vol. 213. Bonn, 1984

364) ____. "Chelmno, Sobibór, Betzec und Majdanek." In *Der Mord an den Juden im Zweiten Weltkrieg*, edited by Eberhard Jäckel and Jürgen Rohwer, pp. 145–151. Stuttgart, 1985

365) ____. "Die Bedeutung der Wannsee-Konferenz im Rahmen der nationalsozialistischen Ausrottungspolitik." In *Die Organisation des*

Judenmordes auf der Wannseekonferenz 1942, edited by Hans-Jochen Barkenings and Heinz-Jürgen Joppien, pp. 7–20. Begegnungen 2/87. Mülheim/Ruhr, 1987

366) Schneider, Gertrude. *Journey into Terror. Story of the Riga Ghetto*. New York, 1979

367) _____, ed. *Muted Voices. Jewish Survivors of Latvia Remember*. New York, 1987

368) Schneider, Ulrich, ed. *Auschwitz – ein Prozeß. Geschichte, Fragen, Wirkungen*. Cologne, 1994

369) Schneider, Wolfgang, ed. *"Vernichtungspolitik". Eine Debatte über den Zusammenhang von Sozialpolitik und Genozid im nationalsozialistischen Deutschland*. Hamburg, 1991

370) Schoenberner, Gerhard. *Der gelbe Stern – Die Judenverfolgung in Europa 1933–1945*. Frankfurt a.M., 1991

371) Schoeps, Julius H, and Joachim Schlör, eds. *Antisemitismus. Vorurteile und Mythen*. Munich, 1995

372) Schreier, Helmut, and Matthias Heyl, eds. *Das Echo des Holocaust. Pädagogische Aspekte des Erinnerns*. Hamburg, 1993; 2nd edn 1994

373) Schreier, Helmut, and Matthias Heyl, eds. *Die Gegenwart der Schoah. Zur Aktualität des Mordes an den europäischen Juden*. Hamburg, 1994

373a) Schwan, Gesine. "Die politische Relevanz nicht-verarbeiteter Schuld." In *Tabu und Geschichte. Kultur des kollektiven Erinnerns*, edited by Peter Bettelheim and Robert Streibel, pp. 29–44. Vienna, 1994

374) Segev, Tom. *Soldiers of Evil. The Commandants of the Nazi Concentration Camps*. New York, 1988 (German edn: *Die Soldaten des Bösen. Zur Geschichte der KZ-Kommandanten*. Reinbek, 1992)

375) _____. *The Seventh Million. The Israelis and the Holocaust*. New York, 1993 (German edn: *Die siebte Million. Der Holocaust und Israels Politik der Erinnerung*. Reinbek, 1995)

376) Seidel, Gill. *The Holocaust Denial: Antisemitism, Racism and the New Right*. Manchester, 1986

377) Sereny, Gitta. *Into that Darkness. From Mercy Killing to Mass Murder*. London, 1974

378) Sherman-Zander, Hilde. *Zwischen Tag und Dunkel. Mädchenjahre im Ghetto*. Frankfurt a.M., 1984

379) Silver, Eric. *The Book of the Just. The Silent Heroes who Saved Jews from Hitler*. London, 1992 (German edn: *Sie waren stille Helden. Frauen und Männer, die Juden vor den Nazis retteten*. Munich, 1994)

380) Smoliakovas, Grigorijus. *Die Nacht, die Jahre dauerte. Ein jüdisches Überlebensschicksal in Litauen 1941–1945*. Konstanz, 1992

380a) Sofsky, Wolfgang. *Die Ordnung des Terrors. Das Konzentrationslager*. Frankfurt a.M., 1993

381) Spector, Shmuel. "The Jews of Volhynia and their Reaction to Extermination." *Yad Vashem Studies* vol. 15 (1983): pp. 159–186

382) _____. *The Holocaust of Volhynian Jews, 1941–1944* (in Hebrew). Jerusalem, 1986 (English edn: 1990)

383) _____. "Jews in the Resistance and Partisan Movement in the Soviet Ukraine." *Yad Vashem Studies* vol. 23 (1993): pp. 127–143

384) *Städte im Osten klagen Hitler an! Amtliche Berichte der außerordentlichen staatlichen Untersuchungskommission der*

Sowjetunion über die von den deutschen Faschisten in Lemberg und Minsk begangenen Greueltaten. Singen, 1945

385) Stein, André. *Hidden Children*. London, 1993 (German edn: *Versteckt und vergessen. Kinder des Holocaust*. Vienna, 1995)

386) Steinberg, Jonathan. *All or Nothing. The Axis and the Holocaust, 1941–43*. Cambridge, 1990

387) Steininger, Rolf, ed. *Der Umgang mit dem Holocaust. Europa - USA - Israel*. Schriften des Instituts für Zeitgeschichte der Universität Innsbruck und des Jüdischen Museums Hohenems, vol. 1. Vienna, 1994

388) Stokes, Lawrence D. "The German People and the Destruction of the European Jews." *Central European History* vol. 6 (1973): pp. 167–191

389) Strauss, Herbert A., and Norbert Kampe, eds. *Antisemitismus. Von der Judenfeindschaft zum Holocaust*. Bonn, 1985

390) Streim, Alfred. "Zum Beispiel: Die Verbrechen der Einsatzgruppen in der Sowjetunion." In *NS-Prozesse. Nach 25 Jahren Strafverfolgung: Möglichkeiten - Grenzen - Ergebnisse*, edited by Adalbert Rückerl, pp. 65–106. Karlsruhe, 1971

391) _____. "Zur Eröffnung des allgemeinen Judenvernichtungsbefehls gegenüber den Einsatzguppen." In *Der Mord an den Juden im Zweiten Weltkrieg*, edited by Eberhard Jäckel and Jürgen Rohwer, pp. 107–124. Stuttgart, 1985

392) _____. "The Tasks of the SS Einsatzgruppen." *Simon Wiesenthal Center Annual* vol. 4 (1987): pp. 309–328

393) _____. "Konzentrationslager auf dem Gebiet der Sowjetunion." *Dachauer Hefte* vol. 5 (1989): pp. 174–187

394) Streit, Christian. "The German Army and the Policies of Genocide." In *The Policies of Genocide: Jews and Soviet Prisoners of War in Nazi Germany*, edited by Gerhard Hirschfeld, pp. 1–14. London, 1986

395) _____. "Ostkrieg, Antibolschewismus und 'Endlösung'." *Geschichte und Gesellschaft* vol. 17, no. 2 (1991): pp. 242–255

396) Suzman, Arthur, and Denis Diamond. "Der Mord an sechs Millionen Juden. Die Wahrheit ist unteilbar." *Aus Politik und Zeitgeschichte* no. B 30/78, 29.7.1978: pp. 4–21

396a) Tec, Nechama. *Bewaffneter Widerstand. Jüdische Partisanen im Zweiten Weltkrieg*. Gerlingen, 1996

397) Tenenbaum, Josef. *In Search of a Lost People*. New York, 1949

398) _____. *Race and Reich. The Story of an Epoch*. New York, 1956

399) Tory, Abraham. *Surviving the Holocaust: The Kovno Ghetto Diary*. Edited by Martin Gilbert. Cambridge, Mass., 1990

400) Trampe, Gustav, ed. *Menschlichkeit in unmenschlicher Zeit. Allee der Gerechten*. Frankfurt a.M., 1995

Trials, see no. 20)

401) Trunk, Isaiah. *Judenrat. The Jewish Councils in Eastern Europe under Nazi Occupation*. New York, 1972

402) Tuchel, Johannes. *Am großen Wannsee 56–58. Von der Villa Minoux zum Haus der Wannsee-Konferenz*. Publikationen der Gedenkstätte Haus der Wannsee-Konferenz, vol. 1. Berlin, 1992

403) Ueberschär, Gerd R. "Der Mord an den Juden und der Ostkrieg. Zum Forschungsstand über den Holocaust." In *Täter - Opfer - Folgen. Der Holocaust in Geschichte und Gegenwart*, edited by Heiner Lichtenstein

and Otto R. Romberg, pp. 49–81. Bonn, 1995

404) Vestermanis, Margers. "Der lettische Anteil an der 'Endlösung'. Versuch einer Antwort." In *Die Schatten der Vergangenheit. Impulse zur Historisierung des Nationalsozialismus*, edited by Uwe Backes, Eckehard Jesse and Rainer Zitelmann, pp. 426–449. Berlin, 1990

405) Wallach, Jehuda L. "Feldmarschall Erich von Manstein und die deutsche Judenausrottung in Rußland." *Jahrbuch des Instituts für Deutsche Geschichte* vol. 4 (1975): pp. 457–472

406) Wasserstein, Bernard. *Britain and the Jews of Europe, 1939–1945.* Oxford, 1979

407) Webber, Jonathan. *Die Zukunft von Auschwitz.* 2nd edn. Frankfurt a.M., 1994

408) Wellers, Georges. "La 'solution finale de la question juive' et la mythomanie néo-nazi." *Le Monde Juif* vol. 33, no. 86 (1977): pp. 41–84 (German edn: "Die Zahl der Opfer der 'Endlösung' und der Korherr-Bericht." *Aus Politik und Zeitgeschichte* no. B 30/78, 29.7.1978: pp. 22–39)

409) Werle, Gerhard, and Thomas Wandres. *Auschwitz vor Gericht. Völkermord und bundesdeutsche Strafjustiz. Mit einer Dokumentation des Auschwitz-Urteils.* Munich, 1995

409a) Werner, Harold. *Fighting Back. A Memoir of Jewish Resistance in World War II.* Columbia, 1995

410) Wetzel, Juliane. *Trauma und Tabu. Jüdisches Leben in Deutschland nach dem Holocaust.* In *Ende des Dritten Reiches – Ende des Zweiten Weltkriegs. Eine perspektivische Rückschau*, edited by Hans-Erich Volkmann, pp. 419–456. Munich, 1995

411) Wiehn, Erhard R., ed. *Die Schoáh von Babij Jar. Das Massaker deutscher Sonderkommandos an der jüdischen Bevölkerung von Kiew 1941 fünfzig Jahre danach zum Gedenken.* Konstanz, 1991

412) Wolff, Jeanette. *Sadismus oder Wahnsinn?* Greiz, 1946

413) Wollenberg, Jörg, ed. *"Niemand war dabei und keiner hat's gewußt". Die deutsche Öffentlichkeit und die Judenverfolgung 1933–1945.* Munich, 1989

413a) Wood, E. Thomas, and Stanislaw M. Jankowski. *Karski: How One Man Tried to Stop the Holocaust.* Chichester, 1994

414) Wyman, David S. *The Abandonment of the Jews. America and the Holocaust 1941–1945.* New York, 1984 (German edn: *Das unerwünschte Volk. Amerika und die Vernichtung der europäischen Juden.* Ismaning, 1986)

415) Yahil, Leni. *The Holocaust. The Fate of the European Jewry, 1932–1945.* New York, 1990

416) ____. "Some Remarks about Hitler's Impact on the Nazis' Jewish Policy." *Yad Vashem Studies* vol. 23 (1993): pp. 281–293

417) Young, James E. *Writing and Rewriting the Holocaust: Narrative and the Consequences of Interpretation.* Bloomington, Ind., 1986 (German edn: *Beschreiben des Holocaust. Darstellung und Folgen der Interpretation.* Frankfurt a.M., 1992)

418) ____. *Texture of Memory.* New York, 1994 (German edn: *Mahnmale des Holocaust. Motive, Rituale und Stätten des Gedenkens.* Munich, 1994)

419) Zvi Bar-On, A. "The Jews in the Soviet Partisan Movement." *Yad Vashem Studies* vol. 4 (1960): pp. 167–189

6. Propaganda and Reporting for the War of Annihilation in the East

420) Buchbender, Ortwin. *Das tönende Erz. Deutsche Propaganda gegen die Rote Armee im Zweiten Weltkrieg.* Stuttgart, 1978
421) Goldberg, Anatol. *Ilya Ehrenburg. Writing, Politics and the Art of Survival.* London, 1984
422) Hesse, Erich. *Der sowjetrussische Partisanenkrieg 1941 bis 1944 im Spiegel deutscher Kampfanweisungen und Befehle.* Göttingen, 1969; 2nd rev. edn 1993
423) Kostjukovskij, B.A., ed. *Komissary na linii ognja 1941–1945.* 3 vols. Moscow, 1985
424) Messerschmidt, Manfred. *Die Wehrmacht im SS-Staat. Zeit der Indoktrination.* Hamburg, 1969
425) Skirdo, Mitrofan Pavlovic. *Moral'nyj Faktor v Velikoj Otecestvennoj Vojne.* Moscow, 1959
426) Sredin, G.V., ed. *Ideologiceskaja rabota KPSS v dejstvujuscej armii 1941–1945 gg.* Moscow, 1985
427) Stang, Werner. "Richtlinien für die Meinungsmanipulierung der deutschen Soldaten des Heeres 1939 bis 1943." *Zeitschrift für Geschichtswissenschaft* vol. 41, no. 6 (1993): pp. 513–531
428) *Der Untermensch.* Edited by Reichsführer-SS, SS-Hauptamt-Schulungsamt. Berlin, 1942
429) Wette, Wolfram. "Der 22. Juni 1941 und die NS-Propaganda." In *22. Juni 1941. Der Überfall auf die Sowjetunion*, edited by Hans Schafranek and Robert Streibel, pp. 75–85. Vienna, 1991
430) ____. "Die propagandistische Begleitmusik zum deutschen Überfall auf die Sowjetunion am 22. Juni 1941." In *Der deutsche Überfall auf die Sowjetunion. "Unternehmen Barbarossa" 1941*, edited by Gerd R. Ueberschär and Wolfram Wette, pp. 45–65. Frankfurt a.M., 1991

7. Propaganda about Communist Class Warfare, German Prisoners of War in the USSR, and Soviet War Crimes until 1945

431) Ahrens, Wilfried, ed. *Verbrechen an Deutschen. Die Opfer im Osten.* 3rd edn. Sauerlach-Arget, 1980
432) Bährens, Kurt. "Deutsche in Straflagern und Gefängnissen der Sowjetunion." In *Zur Geschichte der deutschen Kriegsgefangenen des Zweiten Weltkrieges.* Vol. V/1–3, edited by Erich Maschke. Munich, 1965
433) Bauer, Karl. *Gedächtnisprotokoll: Ein Prozess in Minsk.* Herford, 1990
434) Becker, Eberhard. *Das Rätsel des Ukas 43 und eine Erkundung des Archipel Gulag.* Hamburg, 1991

435) Beckmann, Oda. "Katyn – Moskaus Kampf gegen die historische Wahrheit. Die Verschleierung eines Kriegsverbrechens." *Beiträge zur Konfliktforschung* vol. 10, no. 4 (1980): pp. 137–163
436) Benz, Wolfgang, and Angelika Schardt, eds. *Kriegsgefangenschaft. Berichte über das Leben in Gefangenenlagern der Alliierten von Otto Engelberg, Hans Jonitz, Kurt Glaser und Heinz Pust*. Munich, 1991; in paperback *Deutsche Kriegsgefangene im Zweiten Weltkrieg*. Frankfurt a.M, 1996
437) Blank, Alexander. *Die deutschen Kriegsgefangenen in der UdSSR*. Cologne, 1979
438) Böhme, Kurt W. *Die deutschen Kriegsgefangenen in sowjetischer Hand. Eine Bilanz*. Zur Geschichte der deutschen Kriegsgefangenen des Zweiten Weltkrieges, no. 7. Munich, 1966
439) Brand, Emanuel. "Nazi Criminals on Trial in the Soviet Union (1941–1945)." *Yad Vashem Bulletin* vol. 19 (1966): pp. 36–44
440) *The Crime of Katyn. Facts and Documents*. Report of the US Congress Investigation Committee. London, 1965
441) *Decyzja. Dokumenty Katynia*. Warsaw, 1992
442) Elliott, Mark R. *Pawns of Yalta. Soviet Refugees and America's Role in their Repatriation*. Urbana, 1982
442a) Epifanow, A.E., and Hein Mayer. *Die Tragödie der deutschen Kriegsgefangenen in Stalingrad von 1942 bis 1956 nach russischen Archivunterlagen*. Osnabrück, 1996
443) FitzGibbon, Louis. *Katyn. A Crime without Parallel*. London, 1971 (German edn: *Das Grauen von Katyn. Verbrechen ohne Beispiel*. Vlotho, 1980)
444) _____. *Katyn Massacre*. London, 1979
445) Forell, Fritz von. *Sie ritten in die Ewigkeit ... Kampf und Untergang der Donkosaken im 2. Weltkrieg*. Bielefeld, 1957
446) Fox, John P. "Der Fall Katyn und die Propaganda des NS-Regime." *Vierteljahrshefte für Zeitgeschichte* vol. 30 (1982): pp. 462–499
447) Galickij, V. P. "V poiskach pravdy. Vrazeskie voennoplennye v SSSR (1941–1945 gg.)." *Voenno-Istoriceskij Zurnal* no. 9 (1990): pp. 39–46
448) Getty, J. Arch., and Roberta T. Manning, eds. *Stalinistischer Terror*. Mainz, 1995
448a) Getty, J. Arch., and Roberta T. Manning, eds. *Stalinist Terror. New Perspectives*. Cambridge, 1993
Haus der Geschichte der Bundesrepublik Deutschland, ed. *Kriegsgefangenene*, see no. 456)
449) Holl, Adelbert. *"Was geschah nach Stalingrad"? 7 1/4 Jahre als Kriegs- und Strafgefangener in Russland*. Mühlheim, 1965
450) Kadell, Franz. *Die Katynlüge. Geschichte einer Manipulation. Fakten, Dokumente und Zeugen*. Munich, 1991
451) Karner, Stefan. *Im Archipel GUPVI. Kriegsgefangenschaft und Internierung in der Sowjetunion 1941–1956*. Kriegsfolgen-Forschung, vol. 1. Vienna, 1995
452) *Katyn. Dokumenty ludobojstwa*. Warsaw, 1992
453) Klaus, Edgar. *Durch die Hölle des Krieges. Erinnerungen eines deutschen Unternehmers an Stalingrad, Gefangenschaft und Wiederaufbau*. Berlin, 1991
454) Kopelew, Lew. *Aufbewahren für alle Zeit*. Munich, 1979; 6th edn 1982

455) Krasnov, Nikolaj N. *Verborgenes Rußland. Zehn Jahre Zwangsarbeit in sowjetischen Arbeitslagern*. Berlin, 1962
456) *Kriegsgefangene – Voennoeplennyji. Sowjetische Kriegsgefangene in Deutschland. Deutsche Kriegsgefangene in der Sowjetunion*. Edited by Haus der Geschichte der Bundesrepublik Deutschland. Düsseldorf, 1995
457) Lang, Martin. *Stalins Strafjustiz gegen deutsche Soldaten. Die Massenprozesse gegen deutsche Kriegsgefangene in den Jahren 1949 und 1950 in historischer Sicht*. Herford, 1981
458) Lauck, John H. *Katyn Killings: In the Record*. Clifton, NJ, 1988
458a) Lebedeva, Nataliya. "The Katyn Tragedy." *International Affairs* no. 6 (1990): pp. 98–115
459) Lehmann, Albrecht. *Gefangenschaft und Heimkehr. Deutsche Kriegsgefangene in der Sowjetunion*. Munich, 1986
460) Lojek, Jerzy. *Dzieje sprawy Katynia*. Bialystok, 1989
461) Mackiewicz, Josef. *Katyn. Ungesühntes Verbrechen*. Zurich, 1949; Frankfurt a.M., 1983; 2nd edn 1987
462) Madajczyk, Czeslaw. *Dramat katynski*. Warsaw, 1989 (German edn: *Das Drama von Katyn*. Edited by Daniela Fuchs. Berlin, 1991)
463) Maurach, Reinhart. *Die Kriegsverbrecherprozesse gegen deutsche Gefangene in der Sowjetunion*. Hamburg, 1950
464) Messerschmidt, Manfred. "Der Minsker Prozeß 1946. Gedanken zu einem sowjetischen Kriegsverbrechertribunal." In *Vernichtungskrieg. Verbrechen der Wehrmacht 1941–1944*, edited by Hannes Heer and Klaus Naumann, pp. 551–568. Hamburg, 1995
465) Mitzka, Herbert. *Zur Geschichte der Massendeportationen von Ostdeutschen in die Sowjetunion im Jahre 1945*. 2nd edn. Einhausen, 1986
466) Paul, Allen. *Katyn. The Untold Story of Stalin's Polish Massacre*. New York, 1991
467) Samsonov, Aleksandr M. *Snat'i pomnit*. Moscow, 1989
468) Schüler, Horst. *Workuta. Erinnerung ohne Angst*. Munich, 1993
469) Selesnjow, K.L. "Zur Geschiche der Zeitung 'Das freie Wort'." *Beiträge zur Geschichte der Arbeiterbewegung* 13 (1971): pp. 951–966
470) Semirjaga, Michail. "Katyn – gemeinsamer Schmerz des sowjetischen und polnischen Volkes." In *22. Juni 1941. Der Überfall auf die Sowjetunion*, edited by Hans Schafranek and Robert Streibel, pp. 141–145. Vienna, 1991
471) Slowes, Salomon W. *The Road to Katyn. A Soldier's Story*. Oxford, 1991
472) Smith, Arthur L. *Die "vermißte Million". Zum Schicksal deutscher Kriegsgefangener nach dem Zweiten Weltkrieg*. Munich, 1992
473) Steinbach, Peter. "Deutsche Kriegsgefangene in der Sowjetunion. Ein Beitrag zur deutsch-sowjetischen Beziehungsgeschichte." *Aus Politik und Zeitgeschichte* no. 24 (1991): pp. 37–52
474) Tjulpanov, S.I. "Der ideologische Kampf gegen den Faschismus im Großen Vaterländischen Krieg." *Zeitschrift für Geschichtswissenschaften* vol. 20, no. 2 (1972): pp. 147–199
475) Tolstoy, Nikolai. *The Minister and the Massacres*. London, 1986
476) Tolz, Vera. "The Katyn Documents and the CPSU hearings." *Radio Free Europe/Radio Liberty, Research Report* no. 44, 6.11.1992
476a) Vaksberg, Arkady. *Stalin against the Jews*. New York, 1995

477) Vinton, Louisa. "The Katyn Documents: Politics and History." *Radio Liberty – Research Bulletin* no. 4, 22.1.1993: pp. 19–31

478) Wagenlehner, Günther. *Stalins Willkürjustiz gegen die deutschen Kriegsgefangenen. Dokumentation und Analyse*. Bonn, 1993

479) ____. "Urteil: '25 Jahre Arbeitslager'. Die Prozesse gegen deutsche Kriegsgefangene in der Sowjetunion." In *Kriegsgefangene – Voennoplennije. Sowjetische Kriegsgefangene in Deutschland. Deutsche Kriegsgefangene in der Sowjetunion*, edited by Haus der Geschichte der Bundesrepublik Deutschland, pp. 77–84. Düsseldorf, 1995

480) Winter, Georg. *Etappen: 3802 Tage gefangen in der SU*. Euskirchen, 1988

481) Zayas, Alfred de. *The Wehrmacht War Crimes Bureau, 1939–1945*. Lincoln, Neb., 1989, 1990 (German edn: *Die Wehrmacht-Untersuchungsstelle. Deutsche Ermittlungen über alliierte Völkerrechtsverletzungen im Zweiten Weltkrieg*. Munich, 1979; 2nd rev. edn 1980; new edn as paperback Berlin, 1987)

482) Zawodny, Janusz K. *Death in the Forest – The Story of the Katyn Massacre*. Notre Dame, Ind., 1962 (German edn: *Zum Beispiel Katyn. Klärung eines Kriegsverbrechens*. Munich, 1971)

Part D

THE OCCUPATION

Introduction

It was the most intensive encounter between Germans and Russians in the long history of both peoples. More than three million German soldiers served in the East, most of them not directly in the trenches but at least behind the lines, as well as about 30,000 functionaries, officials, officers, engineers, and entrepreneurs in the occupational administration. From 1941 to 1944 they ruled over some fifty-five million Soviets. The occupied area, in which Germans and Russians encountered one another, formed the largest territory under the Nazi boot, twice as extensive in fact as the Reich itself. It was the biggest occupied area in modern European history. In the First World War, to be sure, the Germans had occupied vast swaths of Russian territory, but this paled in comparison with the second occupation in regard to both duration and the extent of territory held.[1] An even more striking contrast was in the fundamental nature of the occupation. Wilhelmine Germany certainly harbored ambitious plans for conquest and annexation, but the actual occupation was basically in accordance with the international rules of war. Hitler's Third Reich, on the other hand, did not feel fettered by any such restraints. Between the Volga and Bug rivers, the vanquished peoples faced not only conquerors in the traditional sense but a regime bent from the outset on enslaving and

1. For German occupational practices in Russia during the First World War, see Peter Borowsky, *Deutsche Ukrainepolitik 1918 unter besonderer Berücksichtigung der Wirtschaftsfragen* (Lübeck, 1970).

annihilating the local population, a strategy that generated whirlwinds of violence and hatred that rebounded only too soon upon the conquerors themselves. Both sides eventually engaged in a war of unparalleled cruelty and violence, with no distinction between combatants and noncombatants, between the front and the hinterland – truly a "total" war without equal in the long, profuse annals of European warfare.

Not only the methods that the Germans used to control the occupied territories were unparalleled but also the ambitiousness of their political and economic aspirations for these areas. Although the war was still far from over, the invaders eschewed a traditional military occupation in order to proceed at once with their plans for a political "new order" in the conquered territories. It was a megalomaniacal attempt both to redraw borders and to turn upside down the entire economic and social life of the region. What is more, the plans called for the local population to be "sorted" according to racial and political criteria and then resettled, expelled, or murdered on the spot.

The reorganization of the political and economic administration in the occupied territories did not have any direct effect on most of the people, although it did deprive them of any input that they may have had and any ability to defend their interests. They became a totally disenfranchised mass at the mercy of the German occupational authorities, who resorted to local collaborators only at the lowest levels. Most disastrous for the local population was the immediate dismantling of the Communist command economy. The old system was certainly not efficient, but it did provide most people with a secure job and enough food to eat, at least in the last few years before the German invasion. The Nazis set about immediately dismantling this economic system and replacing it (with the exception of the agricultural sector) with a totally different system that was designed solely to serve German interests and intentionally failed to provide adequately for the local population and in particular for certain regions and branches of the economy.

The victims of this plan were not unavoidable casualties of war but martyrs of a deliberate policy on the part of the occupational authorities, who set about implementing the first phase of their plan to colonize and germanize the lands of the Soviet Union. It was the beginning of a premeditated genocide on a colossal scale. The population was divided into racial categories, with "undesirable" elements or "superfluous mouths" being left to starve or simply murdered.

These measures were taken in accordance with the so-called General Plan for the East, which provided for the expulsion or elimination of eighty million people in the European part of the Soviet Union in order to create living space for settlements of German soldiers, farmers, artisans, and entrepreneurs. "Germanic" settlers of these territories would flock from all over the world in order to become part of a new upper class. The helots and serfs over whom they ruled would live on their own reservations and would gradually be expelled or liquidated as more and more German *Wehrbauern* (armed farmers) entered the area (Nos. 57, 70, 465).

These, then, were the goals of the "Greater Germanic Empire of the German Nation" for which Hitler's Wehrmacht invaded. The conquest and recasting of the Soviet Union not only would serve as the springboard to propel Germany ultimately to a position of world dominance but was also needed in the short term to provide the Reich with the economic wherewithal it required in order to win the war. German hopes for "final victory" therefore rode on successful occupation and economic exploitation of the Soviet Union.

In view of such extravagant and multifarious aims, it is not surprising that the German occupational authorities failed to design coherent, consistent policies. From the very outset, German planners were riven by disagreements and disputes over what should be accomplished immediately and what in the medium term. The occupation rested on the four pillars of the army, the SS, business representatives, and the civilian administration, but they often worked against one other, feuding and competing for authority.

The ebbing of German fortunes in the war further exacerbated differences of opinion over compromises that should be made in Hitler's master plan and concessions that should be offered to local populations in order to attempt to gain their support for the struggle against the Red Army. Many participants claimed later that failure to act decisively here may well have cost Germany the ultimate victory, for according to the old saying, "you can only beat the Russians with other Russians." The pigheadedness with which Hitler and other staunch Nazis resisted the suggestions of self-appointed reformers of his Eastern policies encouraged a new "stab-in-the-back" legend, which survived far into the postwar period and even colored the views of some historians.

After the cessation of hostilities, the internal disputes that had raged during the war flared up anew at the Nuremberg Trials conducted by the Allied powers. Again and again, the prosecutors and defense attorneys focused attention on Nazi occupational policies in the Soviet Union. Many other areas conquered by the Nazis could have provided examples of plundering, slave labor, and mass murder, but the so-called Eastern territories were the scene of the most egregious cases.

Following the war, the Soviets were very concerned with documenting the full extent of Nazi atrocities. Numerous reports of local and regional commissions of investigation were published even before hostilities had ceased (Nos. 23, 40, 41, 48, 49, 53–56). There is no doubt that these reports had a strong propagandistic streak and were intended, at least in part, to buttress Soviet claims to reparations. They were therefore of somewhat limited reliability, and many of the figures advanced were open to question; nevertheless, the victorious powers all agreed on the basic nature of the German occupation and the magnitude of the war crimes committed. In any case, cold figures could hardly adequately express the devastation that the Nazis left in their wake.

In the mind of the general public in Germany, the brutal facts of the occupation were eclipsed very quickly and thoroughly after 1945. Outrage was aroused instead by the new Soviet occupation in eastern and central Germany, which apparently confirmed all the old stereotypes and diverted attention from the former German regime in the Soviet Union.

Historical studies of this era in German history began primarily in the United States in the early 1950s because most of the captured German documents belonging both to the Wehrmacht and to the Ministry for the Occupied Eastern Territories had ended up there. The documents were security classified and hence not accessible to private scholars until the mid-1950s when the first ones were declassified. The subjects of these studies were almost universally from the perspective of the Nazis – partly because of the origin of the source materials but also because of the interest at the height of the Cold War in gaining insight into the feasibility of destabilizing the Soviet Union by fanning the suppressed nationalism of its various peoples (No. 125).

This underlying interest colored many research programs and publications at the time. The leading authorities were therefore largely emigrants, former collaborators, and nationalist advocates of independence for the Baltic states, the Ukraine, and the Caucasus. Although the conclusions of these people about the fundamental nature of the German occupation did not differ from those reached by the Allied powers at Nuremberg, they did tend to support the attempts by former prominent Nazis to rehabilitate those comrades who had sought to "moderate" German policies in the occupied Eastern territories (Nos. 3, 192).

Constant references by these authors to the willingness of some people in the occupied territories to cooperate with the Germans against Stalin tended, whether intentionally or not, to dim memories of the Nazi war aims and crimes and to lend legitimacy to Hitler's propaganda about a "crusade" against Bolshevism. There was little concern at the time with a disinterested evaluation of the situation in the early 1940s. This served the purposes of militant anti-communism in Germany and especially in the United States, but it hindered a broad historical study of the German occupation in the western Soviet Union. Exceptions were the serious scientific studies by John Armstrong about the connection between partisan warfare and occupation policy, and the important work of George Fischer about the Soviet opposition to Stalin during the Second World War (Nos. 174, 263, 398).

The most impressive of the studies undertaken in the United States at this time was the monumental work produced by Alexander Dallin. It was published immediately in German translation and still provides the most comprehensive overview of the occupation (No. 8). Basing his work on a broad assortment of source materials, Dallin depicted the various currents of thought among the German occupational authorities, the policies adopted toward various ethnic groups, economic policies, the treatment of Soviet prisoners of war and "eastern workers," and religious and cultural policies. Finally, he portrayed the attempt to engage in political warfare, the "pamphlet war," and the adoption of reforms in connection with the Vlasov movement. This overview, which was an impressive, differentiated study, although primarily from the viewpoint of the German conquerors and their lackeys, was reprinted in Germany in 1981.

The British historian Gerald Reitlinger soon published a similar study (No. 16). These efforts of Anglo-American historians seemed to relieve Germans of the need to examine for themselves this rather discomfiting period in recent German history. Dallin's results and conclusions reinforced the predominant view of the totalitarian Nazi regime and its murderous attack on the Soviet Union, as had been originally set forth in the great Hitler biography by the British historian Alan Bullock (No. A/5).

Research into this subject tended to follow the availability of captured German records. The records of the various German headquarters tended to fall into American hands, while those of local occupation authorities, if they survived the war at all, found their way into secret archives in the Soviet Union and were not made available to Western researchers until 1991, in the Moscow "special archive" and in regional archives in Minsk, Riga, and other cities. Furthermore, certain events in the war were extremely delicate topics for Soviet historians, and so they, too, in the end did not do much digging through these records. As a result, both Soviet and German historians tended to shy away from studying these extremely dramatic events, even though they had just occurred.

Historians in the former Soviet Union focused instead on the "heroic struggle" of the Soviet people in the "Great Patriotic War." The history of the peoples in the occupied areas was of interest only insofar as they had been victims of mass German reprisals or had belonged to a widespread resistance movement. According to this view, the conquered Soviet citizens had been either victims or partisans; anything else was treasonous and highly unusual. Most important was the leading role played by the Communist party. There was no room for more probing questions, such as the fate reserved for victims of the partisan counterterror.

According to the Soviet view of the war, not only in large official volumes such as the *History of the Great Patriotic War* but also in numerous small regional and local studies, there was very little collaboration with the Nazis, as had admittedly been the case in the areas of western, northern, and southeastern Europe that had fallen under Nazi domination. The history of the occupied Soviet Union was one of unrelenting resistance (No. 18).

In accordance with the usual simplifications of Marxist ideology, the Nazi conquerors were portrayed as the lackeys of monopoly capitalism. Any political, ideological, or biographical details that ran counter to this view were swept under the rug (No. 8). There had been only victims and perpetrators. De-Stalinization in the late 1950s brought a moderate thaw in this view, with the result that the peoples who had been collectively deported by Stalin for treason were at least partially rehabilitated.

Mental blocks had also formed in the West. Despite an intensive interest in the Nazi era in the Federal Republic of Germany, the occupation and the burdens it imposed were widely ignored. Attention focused above all on military history (Part B). This was not due to any lack of source materials, for captured Nazi records had been streaming steadily back to Germany from England and the United States ever since the early 1960s. However, the interest of historians was not immediately aroused, with the exception of some East Germans. Emulating Soviet practices, they undertook regional studies and studies of economic history that advanced knowledge of the German occupation (Nos. 25, 38, 427–31). These efforts gave rise by the 1980s to a project for a six-volume edition entitled *Europa unterm Hakenkreuz* (*Europe under the Swastika*) (No. 25). By the time that the volume on the Soviet Union appeared in 1991, on the fiftieth anniversary of the Nazi attack on the Soviet Union, the German Democratic Republic – this most momentous consequence for Germany of the attack – no longer existed. Although many historians in the former GDR were politically tainted and had sacrificed their professional standards to Communist doctrine, they did perform important pioneering research in this area.

In the Federal Republic of Germany, interest in the history of the occupation was spotty and emerged only gradually. However, historians did eventually address the nationalities question, the treatment of Soviet prisoners of war, and the role played by the Wehrmacht in the Nazi attempt to annihilate much of the Soviet population (Part C).

Not until 1983 were efforts made to provide a systematic analysis of the occupation in the fourth volume of a series published by the Militärgeschichtliches Forschungsamt, *Das Deutsche Reich und der Zweite Weltkrieg* (No. 86). Emancipated at last from the apologetic memoirs of actual participants, the authors substantially extended Dallin's earlier depiction of the occupation on the basis of numerous new source materials. Although the authors did not agree about all the details, they outlined the Nazi plan for a racially motivated war of annihilation, economic policies, plans to starve much of the population, the political "new order," and the security measures adopted by the occupational authorities in the first phase of the war. The dissemination of this research was much enhanced by the publication of a revised paperback edition in 1991 and of an English translation (which will be published in 1998). Volume 5/1, appearing in 1988, set the occupied Soviet Union in the context of the system established across all of occupied Europe. It included insights of the Polish historian Czeslaw Madajczyk, who pointed out parallels between the occupation in Poland and that in the European areas of the Soviet Union (Nos. 9–11).

The American historian Timothy P. Mulligan continued these attempts to expand on Dallin's work and update it with his study of the middle phase of the war on the Eastern Front, that is, 1942–43 (No. 14). He cast doubt on the claims about "missed opportunities" and emphasized all the incongruities in the plans for the propaganda war, pointing especially to its lack of realism. Mulligan analyzed the "reforms" actually undertaken in this critical phase of the occupation, the assumptions and illusions on which they were based, and the benefits that they conferred on the German war effort. He concluded that the German authorities failed utterly to regain the confidence of local populations. It was reform "from above," unrelated to local people. The authorities largely ignored even collaborators and emigrants, and the mass of the population never had any idea that reforms were being discussed. What they did see and hear about, though, were forced deportations, requisitioning of property, and reprisals taken in reaction to partisan attacks. Mulligan allowed, however, that the reformers did manage to introduce an element of pragmatism into Hitler's planning, at least for a short time, despite all the dissension in their own ranks.

Thanks to more realistic occupation policies, production increased substantially. Large numbers of "eastern workers" were shipped to Germany, and so-called *Hilfswillige* (people willing to help) joined the Wehrmacht. Yet the reformers were badly mistaken, according to Mulligan, in assuming that national socialism, once confronted with reality, could shed its ideological convictions and radically transform itself. Hitler remained the pivotal figure in Germany, and he was not about to make any radical changes in his approach.

The final phase of the German occupation in 1943–44 has remained a largely unwritten page of history, apart from the internal goings-on in the Ministry for the Occupied Eastern Territories under Alfred Rosenberg, as described by Dallin and by former department head Otto Bräutigam in his autobiography (No. 99). However, we remain far removed from another grand overview like that provided by Dallin. A lack of source materials or interesting issues cannot possibly be the main reason for this striking gap in the otherwise extensive literature on the history of the Second World War.

* * *

Insofar as German war aims in the East were concerned, there are no major disagreements among serious historians. The Nazis themselves did not really attempt to hide their objectives during the war. Despite all the propaganda about a "crusade against Bolshevism," they made it clear that they did not wish merely to free the peoples of the Soviet Union or even to pursue purely military or strategic goals. What they wanted was to conquer new *Lebensraum* in the East, that is, to enslave and exploit the European part of the Soviet Union and to establish Eastern colonies of German settlers.

These objectives naturally affected the occupation from the outset. Recent research has demonstrated that not only Nazi ideologues but many other social elites basically supported this program and the general goals of the war in the East, despite some differences of opinion about the timing and methods of Eastern colonization. However, there are still large blanks in our knowledge of the way in which various elites in the Third Reich visualized the Soviet Union of the future (No. 81).

New approaches have brought slightly different assessments of Hitler's own views, which were always the determining factor in Eastern policies. This is especially true of the economic motivations for his program (Nos. 83, 84, A/119, 465–71). However, historians are largely agreed on the roots of Hitler's outlook: his basic war aims in the East can be traced back to the war-aim discussion in Germany during the First World War.

Controversy continues to swirl, though, around the question of whether the subjugation of Russia was intended as the final step in Hitler's plans for conquest or whether Russia was merely to provide the wherewithal for a final great campaign for world dominance or even outright rule. Regardless of whether or not Hitler's ultimate aspirations were confined to the European continent (as Aigner, Jäckel, and Stoakes contend) or encompassed the entire world (as Weinberg, Hildebrand, Thies, and Hillgruber contend), the Nazi program for eastern Europe was most clearly apparent in the General Plan for the East (Nos. 65, 66, 67, 77, 78).

These SS plans are rightly considered to be crucial for a proper understanding of the history of the Second World War. Since the initial publication in 1958 of the plans for German settlements (No. 64), more and more details of the General Plan for the East have been documented and discussed (Nos. 62, 458, 465). Population transfers that actually occurred in occupied Soviet territory have also been described (Nos. 106, 113). However, to date no comprehensive overview has been published on this topic, which is nevertheless essential for understanding the Third Reich and the Second World War. This is probably because too many questions are still to be answered. We do not yet fully understand how the various versions of the General Plan came to be prepared, nor do we know much about its origins.

Opinions differ about the significance of SS planning and the part it played in the formulation of official Nazi policy. Marxist historians even dispute the idea that racist ideology was at the heart of the General Plan, emphasizing instead the securing of power. According to them, it was only in reaction to fierce resistance from the Soviet population that the German authorities instituted such a harsh regime. Accordingly, the General Plan for the East was nothing more than a "a racially embellished disguise for extreme anti-Communism and, most importantly, anti-Sovietism" (No. 62).

But was the General Plan for the East merely an example of the SS building castles in the sand? Was it just a series of pipe dreams and fantasies, of murderous experiments undertaken by racial theorists run amok, and of scurrilous plans laid down by individual SS professors and office criminals? Himmler himself was always modifying and adjusting the plan. What did other social elites make of all this? The discussions of the plan in Rosenberg's Ministry for the Occupied Eastern Territories and in the civilian administration in the East are well documented, but less is known about the posture and influence of the Wehrmacht, the SS, and business leaders.

Fortunately, a new study of the war on the Eastern Front and of German settlement policy has analyzed and documented the role of these traditional elites in formulating German war aims and settlement policies (No. 70). What emerges more clearly from this study is that Himmler took particular interest in the planning of settlements as a method of expanding his power base within the Nazi hierarchy. However, the development and implementation of the General Plan for the East depended as well on independent initiatives and the interest of other elites. No clear chain of command existed in the at times bitter struggle for power and influence that surrounded the General Plan. Business leaders were especially successful at circumventing the claims of the SS to lead the operation. There are therefore no simple answers to the question of what the proposed "Greater Germanic Reich" would look like and the extent to which it would incorporate Nazi utopian thought.

Although Rosenberg's civilian administration has often been studied, little is known about the military administration (Nos. 19, 85). This lack of interest in the military administration is all the more surprising in that most of the occupied territories remained under military administration throughout the war, despite Hitler's express desire to have traditional military administrations replaced quickly as the front advanced. However, the failure of blitzkrieg and the development of a grinding war of attrition made it necessary to leave large areas under direct Wehrmacht administration as staging grounds for military operations. Jürgen Förster and Norbert Müller have done some initial research in this area (Nos. 86–88). Various records shed light on the ideas that were circulating among the army general staff before the war about the type of occupation that would be instituted in the East. It is now evident that the army high command was quite willing, before Hitler expressed any views of his own, to relinquish to political authorities the difficult task of securing the vast hinterland and implementing the "new order." The army wished to concentrate as much as possible on military security and exploiting the land for military purposes. It is equally evident that, as early as the spring of 1941, the army high command was not much concerned about international law and the legal niceties of the occupation (No. 89).

Recently, the British historian Theo Schulte has demonstrated in detail the responsibility of the army for war crimes, exploitation, and wanton destruction in two selected army areas well behind the lines (Nos. 91, 92). Schulte's example could well encourage other empirical studies. The final report in early 1945 of the high command's War Administration Department is a particularly rich source of materials on the subject of the military administration. However, it has not yet been published. Archives in the former Soviet Union must contain many records produced by local military administrations, city commandants, area commands, and the like containing useful information for future researchers.

Very little research has also been done into the civilian administrations in the former Reich commissariats of Ostland and the Ukraine. Numerous source materials in Minsk, Riga, Vilnius, and Kiev await study. However, some new investigations of White Russia have appeared (No. 139). Insofar as the Ukraine is concerned, only some older works by emigrants have been published. On a scientific level the very important work of John Armstrong describes this aspect of Ukrainian nationalism and collaboration, but a reliable and modern historiography about the Ukraine under German occupation is still missing. These are, surprisingly enough, the only real gaps that still exist in the history of the various countries that fell under Nazi control. It is difficult to understand this state cf affairs because the Ukraine was at the very heart of the Nazi Eastern policy, and the myth of the Ukrainian granary to the world was one of the main inspirations behind German expansionary dreams in the first half of the twentieth century. The abundance of Nazi literature produced on this topic during the Second World War provides ample evidence (No. 419).

The diplomat Otto Bräutigam, one of the leading figures in the Ministry for the Occupied Eastern Territories, wrote a lengthy autobiography that provides very interesting firsthand information (although it should be read with some skepticism) about the internal disputes between his ministry and various branches of the Reich commissariats and general commissariats. Despite Bräutigam's annoying tendency to congratulate himself as a leading light of "reform," he does provide important observations and inside information (Nos. 99, 100, 109, 110). The few specialized studies on the administration of the occupied territories focus on the churches and culture as well as on the role of the SS, which eventually succeeded in infiltrating the Ministry for the Occupied Eastern Territories (Nos. 129, 132).

While the emphasis in German and English-language literature clearly lies on political affairs under the occupation, the Soviets have emphasized the resistance. Numerous monographs have depicted, usually in heroic terms, the resistance mounted in various cities, regions, and areas as well as among various ethnic groups. This topic gave a substantial boost to the sense of identity of the Soviet people and served as well to legitimize the Communist party.

The Western studies of this aspect of the occupation focus on the military facet of the partisan war. The "Alexander Studies" have long since been declassified in the United States, and a collection of portions of them has been published in the edition of John Armstrong (No. 236). In some cases, subjects of particular current interest arise as well (Nos. 248, 263, 257). Mulligan's thorough-going analysis begins with the huge discrepancy in casualties on the Soviet and German sides in White Russia. While losing 50,000 men, the Germans managed to kill five times that many partisans and civilians. This discrepancy indicates that the Germans used the struggle against the partisans as an excuse to implement their previous plans to annihilate much of the population (Nos. 324, 333). A similar study has not yet been undertaken for the Ukraine, where conditions were much more complicated because of the presence of nationalist resistance fighters alongside the Communists, leading to a struggle on three different fronts. Very little is known as well in this regard about the Baltic states, the Crimea, and the Caucasus.

Under *glasnost*, Soviet historians have begun to correct many misleading legends that were propagated. Post-Communist historians in the newly emerging states of the former Soviet Union face enormous tasks – for instance, clarifying the actual role of the Communist party of the Soviet Union as the spearhead of the resistance and the allegedly unanimous struggle waged by the entire people against the fascist occupiers. A more differentiated view of collaboration and resistance will lead to a better understanding of the Soviet people's difficult and tragic struggle to survive between the anvil of Moscow and the hammer of Berlin.

In most eastern European countries, more about collaboration with the Axis powers has been published since 1990 than in the previous four decades. However, the post-Communist revisionists often fall prey to the temptation to cast collaboration in a somewhat positive light as an expression of repressed national identities. It is all too easy for questionable nationalist groups and Nazi lackeys who assisted in mass murder to gain a false glory in this way. The main problem lies in maintaining the distinction between outright collaboration with the Nazis and "coexistence" with them in order to survive. There is no doubt that the trauma of forced collectivization, the terror of the NKVD in the Baltic republics at the time of the Nazi-Soviet pact, and Russian chauvinism under Stalin fomented extremism among leaders of the suppressed nationalities. This enabled the Nazis to recruit large numbers of people to assist in the systematic genocide of Russians, Poles, and Jews.

The various nationalities in the Soviet Union shared, however, a common tragedy in the fates reserved for Soviet prisoners of war and "eastern workers" – the almost three million forced laborers recruited by the Germans in the occupied territories. Older Soviet historiography cautiously rehabilitated these people as supposed martyrs and resistance fighters (Nos. 244, 245). Even Western research into the subject of foreign workers, which did not begin in earnest until decades after this fateful encounter between Germans and their neighbors, tended to leave "eastern" workers in the shadows (Nos. 519, 526).

Intensive research about Eastern workers was unlikely so long as the archives in the homelands of these people remained closed and personal interviews with them were much more difficult to obtain than with workers from Western countries for linguistic, geographic, and political reasons (with the exception of the Eastern workers who remained in Germany after the war). The most brutal methods of procuring foreign workers were employed in the Soviet Union, and it is impossible to reconstruct the full extent of the massive crimes committed and what happened in various individual cases.

No reliable chroniclers of the plight and reactions of the victims of the Nazi recruitment campaigns have emerged. In contrast to other occupied countries, the Germans conquered only a small part of the huge Soviet landmass. There was no ultimate German victory and truce as in the West. The Germans operated the civilian administration almost entirely by themselves, and the local populations had no method of voicing their own concerns to the authorities. All disputes over worker recruitment took place solely between various factions in the Nazi regime, while the population itself remained a mute mass caught between Berlin and Moscow. This situation is reflected even in the accounts of historians who tend to see these workers entirely from the German or the Soviet point of view, depending on the origin of their source materials.

Consideration was certainly given in the older Western literature on the occupation to the conditions under which millions of Soviet citizens were either hired to work or dragooned into working in Germany, but almost always from the viewpoint of the Germans and the problems that they faced (No. 8).

The ongoing disputes among the various factions administering the occupation revolved to a large extent around the question of forced labor – the "slave hunts" instituted by Fritz Sauckel, Hitler's "Agent General for Labor." However, viewing this question solely from the perspective of the occupying power means largely adopting the viewpoint of the perpetrators and entering the unreal world of the Nazi bureaucracy and its dominant ideology, which contrasted ever more sharply with the brutality of real events.

This problem could not be resolved so long as only German sources were available. Nazi files contained, to be sure, many reports about the reactions of the Soviet population, to which various bodies and individual officials often pointed when attempting to modify German policies. Despite all the reservations one has, these records contain very useful information that provides a certain overview of the entire question. The German documents even contain some comments by Soviet workers themselves, obtained when letters sent home by Eastern workers through the German mail system were secretly opened.

We still await a thorough overview of the recruitment of Soviet workers as a pivotal issue not only for the occupational authorities but for Germany's entire wartime economy as well. Some work has already been done, including a recent analysis of forced labor in Germany and a summary of the issues involved from the viewpoint of all the occupied countries in Europe (Nos. 518, 523). In addition, an extensive collection of experiences described by former prisoners of war and Eastern workers has been begun with the support of the Russian memorial movement. Furthermore, the biographical information in the formerly secret KGB archives and the "special archive" in Moscow is now open to researchers.

New studies being written in Russia seem likely to provide fresh insights into this question. Conservative and revisionist historians disagree even on the number of the victims. A General Staff study of Soviet losses in the Second World War arrived at a rather low figure, while other historians hit upon considerably higher figures (Part B). The records of the People's Commissariat for Repatriation, created in 1944, have just been opened and will likely provide important new information.

Russian research into this final chapter in the history of the Soviet prisoners of war and Eastern workers is still in its infancy. According to figures produced in Moscow, around 4.8 million Soviet citizens were deported by the Germans. Ninety percent of them were repatriated at the end of the war, while the rest remained in the West as immigrants. Studies by the British historian N. Tolstoy have already revealed the extent of the betrayal and brutality that followed this repatriation (Nos. 414, 506). Current Russian research is also focusing on the fate that awaited these people after they returned home, where they were often victims of reprisals and discrimination.

* * *

The economic motivations for the German assault on the Soviet Union and the ensuing occupation have aroused increased interest in recent years, after having been long overshadowed by the ideological and strategic aspects of the war. At the Nuremberg Trials, Hermann Göring assumed full responsibility for all economic policies in the East, and as a result the part played by German industry was never adequately investigated.

For many years, the final 1944–45 report of the Eastern Economic Staff was believed lost, but it has now been recovered and a comprehensive edition has appeared (No. 473). In cool figures and sober factual accounts, it summarizes a unique experiment in modern military and economic history. Under army orchestration, almost 20,000 German farmers, business executives, miners, engineers, merchants, civil servants, and officers attempted to assume complete control of the portion of the Soviet economy that fell into German hands and administer it in accordance with directives issued from Berlin. In contrast to their policy in other occupied countries, the Germans completely disregarded the local economic administration, whose leading officials had in any case either fled or been murdered. While the western portion of the Soviet Union was still not nearly as industrialized as Germany, it posed an unparalleled challenge to the Third Reich in terms of its contrasting economic and political-social structures, the size of its population, its geographic sweep, the climatic extremes, and the extent of its raw materials and agricultural possibilities.

Although Hitler's decision to invade the Soviet Union was profoundly influenced by economic considerations, he did not seek any advice from his economic experts. The high command of the Wehrmacht had given some preliminary consideration to an invasion – consideration that included economic factors – but Hitler ultimately decided on his own to attack, largely in response to his ideological aspirations. He left the details of the economic war aims and the organization of the Eastern Economic Staff to his experts. Göring assumed overall command, assigning his Four Year Plan staff and the OKW office of Armaments and the Defense Economy to the task. He also ordered that representatives of heavy industry should be involved from the outset (No. 468, p. 131).

Almost one year after the startling events of August 1939, economic leaders were accordingly informed in secret that the Wehrmacht was making plans to conquer the Eastern "treasure chest." There are no indications that these captains of industry raised any objections. They, too, were apparently convinced that victory was assured. The only doubts that were raised came from government bureaucrats. Leading economic circles in Germany were therefore privy from the outset to the Nazis' political and military plans and took advantage of the opportunity to influence the planning of the Eastern Economic Staff through the know-how they could provide and the support of company experts. The infamous directives about future economic policies in the East were spawned from the desks of these company experts and the bureaucrats in the economic ministries.

At first, their economic objectives could be easily harmonized with the Nazis' political aims and the slaughters that the SS was planning. In fact, the economic objectives even seemed to provide some rationale for mass murder. What friction arose was mostly between the agricultural policies, with their radical plans for exploiting and annihilating rural populations, and the policies of the newly created Ministry for the Occupied Eastern Territories under Alfred Rosenberg. However, this did not change the paramountcy of economic concerns in determining occupation policy, even at the expense, in case of conflict, of political and ideological beliefs (No. 108). Although it may have seemed advisable from a political point of view to treat the various nationalities differently, the economic planners initially viewed the European part of the Soviet Union as a single unit that should be treated identically in order to be efficient and achieve the greatest possible benefit for the German conquerors.

Little consideration was given to differences in the land, its resources, and the local inhabitants. This held true both for short-term plans to generate immediate benefits for the war effort and for longer-term plans for an economic "new order." Gustav Schlotterer played a key role. In the 1930s, he had been in charge of promoting exports within the Ministry of Economics, including to the Soviet Union. In 1940 he became coordinator of government and private economic planning for the "new order" in Europe, and in 1941 he assumed the positions of both chief of economic policy in Alfred Rosenberg's Ministry for the Occupied Eastern Territories and chief of the army's Eastern Economic Staff.

Schlotterer advocated a radical restructuring of the Soviet economy. He spoke openly of a "colonial economy" in which local people would be excluded from all positions of leadership. The living standards of local people would be reduced to a minimum in order to produce surpluses to help pay for the German war effort. In addition, Schlotterer wanted to eliminate completely the manufacture of finished goods. The East would become an appendage of the industrial heartland in central Europe and would satisfy its needs by trading raw materials for German industrial goods. Since the occupied Eastern territories would run a "negative balance" at first, he hoped to attract foreign capital to participate in the reconstruction. However, all settlers would have to be *"Rassegut,"* or of good race (No. 38, p. 236).

When Operation Barbarossa was launched, leading German economic circles were primarily concerned, as might be expected, with staking out the interests of their firms and branches of the economy and protecting them as much as possible from state regulation. They concentrated on how best to carve up the Soviet Union and to extract and cart off the raw materials, especially oil, coal, and ore, that were essential to the German war effort. In accordance with their traditional views of the "natural" division of labor between Germany and Russia, they did not intend to rebuild a rounded economy, especially in regard to processing. Broad swathes of Soviet industry would simply be cannibalized. The people who worked in these industries were "superfluous mouths" and would simply be allowed to starve to death (No. 471). In short, the industrialization of Russia would be reversed. In the eyes of those captains of German industry, the industrialization of Russia had been in any case unnecessary, unnatural, and even harmful and dangerous. In this way, the primacy of German industry would be secured in a future *"Großraumwirtschaft,"* or large-zone economy in Europe. Numerous economists and economic journalists worked on corresponding plans and ideas during the war.[2]

Younger members of the economic elite were especially prone to being utterly smitten by the prospect of a great victory and "staggering" economic opportunities for Germany as it assumed the mantle of a great world power. Fabulous career opportunities seemed to beckon, until all the illusions were buried beneath the snows of the Russian winter. When Hitler was presented, after the launch of the Eastern campaign, with the economic plans that had been devised, he could only express his satisfaction. In the general euphoria over the impending triumph, any moral or political scruples were extremely rare in either leading economic circles or the Wehrmacht.

German industry managed to secure a decisive role within the economic administration of the occupation. There was little competition among companies at first as they set about simply shipping seized machinery and raw materials back to Germany for use in the war effort (No. 466). The way in which the mines and industries would be apportioned remained a political decision. Hitler and Göring provided assurances that the industrial

2. See, for instance, the article by the chief of the IG Farben Economic Division, Anton Reithinger, "Voraussetzungen und Größenordnungen der kontinentaleuropäischen Großraumwirtschaft," in *Probleme des europäischen Großraumwirtschaft* (Berlin, 1942): 9–31.

booty would be privatized and would not remain in state hands; however, the Führer also declared that the soldiers fighting at the front should have first crack at the spoils once the war was over. In addition, numerous party officials were avidly awaiting the day when they could establish their own little realms in the East. Finally, Himmler was convinced that the East should become the domain of the SS. He secretly ordered a "General Plan for the East" to be drawn up, providing for German settlements in the Soviet Union as far as the Urals. He intended to present this plan to the Führer after the final victory and establish himself as the overlord of the East (Nos. 57, 70).

In the eyes of private industrialists, actual ownership therefore became the crucial question. As a result of the widespread destruction in the areas under German occupation, it seemed prudent to delay any investment in reconstruction until everyone's rights had been clarified. A provisional solution was found in the form of "sponsorships" and so-called Eastern companies, or provisional state monopolies, with some participation by private industry. In this way, industry gained an opportunity to cannibalize Soviet equipment while awaiting privileged treatment in the division of spoils once the war was over. The costs and risks of sending machinery and experts were left to the government.

Hitler, for his part, hoped to pay off the huge government debts accumulated during the war by selling off booty once the fighting had ended. He also counted, in the meantime, on earning windfall profits for the state coffers, since the costs of production in Russia would be held as low as possible and far below selling prices in Germany. However, this plan held little appeal for private companies. In addition, substantial elements within the Nazi party were hostile to capitalist profits and hoped instead to raise the general living standards of the "master race." This was what Goebbels had in mind when he proclaimed publicly that the war was not being waged in the East primarily for political or philosophical reasons but rather for gain and bread, for homes, vacations, and Volkswagens.[3] Many issues thus remained to be settled in discussions with the party, the Wehrmacht, the SS, and the government bureaucracy.

German industrialists had only a vague idea of conditions in the Soviet Union before the invasion, and the reports that reached them thereafter about the captured Soviet industries and mines only served to convince them that they should delay

3 . Joseph Goebbels, "Wofür?" in *Das Reich,* no. 22 (31. May 1942).

any massive investments as long as possible while awaiting clarification of the military and political situation. Business leaders reached these conclusions on the basis of cool economic calculation, although they were clever enough to couch their conclusions in racial and ideological terms. An important memorandum of September 1941 from *Reichsgruppe* Industry hardly varies at all from the official party line in its analysis of the future of eastern Europe under German domination. However, it clearly rejects the demands of the SS, and even of the party and policymakers in general, to play a leading role in planning the movement of German industry to the East. According to the memorandum, there was general agreement about the need for and urgency of economic activity in the East. "The basic aims of the settlement process include, in equal measure, the restoration and development of a productive economy and the ethnic Germanification of the areas to be incorporated into the Reich and creation of a racially pure human rampart against the rest of the east. Neither of these aims can be said to take priority over the other, for that would be disruptive. The overall aim is: a racially healthy people on an economically healthy footing." (No. 70, p. 156)

In early November 1941, Göring arranged a series of conferences to establish new directions for the German war economy after the failure of blitzkrieg (Nos. 9, 447). Economic exploitation of the occupied part of the Soviet Union played a major role in these plans. Not only would "eastern workers" be recruited, but the millions of Soviet prisoners of war, who had previously been considered little more than superfluous and left to starve (No. C/91), would be viewed as desirable slave workers for German mines and munition plants. Once again, Göring confirmed the Nazis' intent to operate a ruthless colonial economy. Human beings would still be treated as masses to be handled in totally arbitrary fashion. Food of the lowest quality would suffice for these workers, and rewards of "glass beads" would be all that was necessary to motivate them to work hard for their new masters.

Consequently, the destruction and plunder phase had to be halted and rudimentary methods established to operate the economy. Industries had to begin producing in order to extract raw materials, build up the transportation system, put agriculture back on its feet, and thereby help meet the soaring demands of the Wehrmacht. No one in leading political and economic circles was prepared to realize yet that it was impossible for the Germans acting alone to control and organize this vast new realm, which was twice as large as the Reich itself, contained more than fifty million people, had suffered enormous damage as a result of the war, and was subject to climatic extremes. The Nazis' original plan to destroy what was here and replace it with German colonies prevented them from making a pragmatic effort to take advantage of the political opportunity to win over the conquered peoples and gain their cooperation in rebuilding the country. The Nazis were still not prepared to offer Russians, Ukrainians and various other peoples some hope of survival, let alone to extend the hand of friendship.

A report from IG Farben's *Ostverbindungsstelle* written in early 1942 noted that Russia was "considered purely a land of agriculture and raw materials" and that "any industrial planning is basically unnecessary for the foreseeable future and any activities of this kind are not likely to be of much use" (No. 465, p. 126). Shortly thereafter, the chairman of the firm's board, Carl Krauch, produced a "Comprehensive Plan for the Ukraine" in his capacity as chief of the *Reichsamt für Wirtschaftsausbau* (Office of Economic Development). This ten-year program outlined how the Ukraine could be developed economically in accordance with German interests, treating it solely from the point of view of maximum industrial efficiency (No. 469, p. 191). The people who lived there were considered only as factors of production, although they would need "good nutrition" in order to ensure "good productivity." Particular attention was paid to the Ukraine because it produced an agricultural surplus and was also an important source of raw materials. The concentration on areas that produced a surplus and disinterest in areas that consumed more than they produced were typical of traditional colonialism. This was the essence of the matter for the captains of industry, for whom all racial considerations emanating from Rosenberg's ministry were only trimmings that might or might not be of much use.

The first anniversary of the German attack on the Soviet Union, in the summer of 1942, provided an opportunity for interim analysis of the economic effects. The assault had succeeded, even though fighting continued along the eastern fringes of the area Hitler wanted as *Lebensraum*. Most of the zones the Germans coveted for economic reasons were successfully occupied, with the exception of the oil-rich Caucasus. The spoils of war had been seized and partially carted off, and the effects of preliminary reconstruction were already being felt. However, even though the figures produced by the Eastern Economic Staff[4] were encouraging, the overall position was far from satisfying.

Enough food was produced in the occupied area, to be sure, to cover about eighty percent of the needs of the three million German soldiers on the Eastern Front. In addition, substantial quantities of grain, livestock, oilseeds, and other products were syphoned off to Germany, with the result that the rations of the German people had already been increased. Considerable amounts of oil and manganese, essential to the war effort, were already being produced. Many other raw materials had been at least located and seized. Production of goods for the Wehrmacht had already reached one billion reichsmarks, and plans for 1943 foresaw steady growth in all areas.

Nevertheless, the war was still far from over, and the German authorities administering the occupation faced mounting difficulties, including the increased resistance on the part of the population and the inability of the colonial regime to establish normal administrational and organizational procedures. As a result, the consensus surrounding the general political approach started to crumble. Changes began to appear imminent, even in the tactic of exploiting the occupied territories to the hilt. The Germans wondered whether some crucial errors had been made. How, for instance, could a policy of clearing the land of its population and launching a thirty-year program to settle it with Germanic *Wehrbauern* (armed farmers) be implemented when, at the same time, all the local inhabitants who were still alive were urgently needed as workers or even as "helper" troops for the Wehrmacht? In view of the general economic straits in which Germany found itself, every available worker was needed. Why did economic reality not carry the day? Numerous memoranda and undertakings pointed out that the Germans' economic strategy was failing, especially because of the way in which the conquered peoples were treated.

Initiatives were therefore launched in many areas to change the way in which things were done, using arguments focusing on practical matters (No. 14). No attempt was made to call the Nazis' basic racial ideology into question; however, the "necessities of war" were invoked as a reason for eliminating the most vicious aspects of the occupation. Advocates of this change in

4. Position of the OKW defense branch on the advantages of occupying Russian territory, 17 September 1942, Bundesarchiv - Militärarchiv Freiburg, RW 31/151.

direction could be found both in the Ministry for the Occupied Eastern Territories and in leading Wehrmacht circles. In addition, a group within the staff of the Four Year Plan began advancing new political initiatives based on their analysis of the economic situation. The new creed of the economic experts was: "The most important and valuable 'raw material' is people."[5]

Friedrich Richter, the specialist for Eastern questions, was of the view that the "colonial option" would have been a real possibility if the Germans had had sufficient forces available in the occupied portions of the Soviet Union. However, he was persuaded that this was not the case. "The short-term needs of the war economy have won out over the political need for judicious treatment of the eastern peoples. These objective pressures have been aggravated by the all too extensive human inadequacies of many Germans in the East, which find expression not only in financial excesses but in behavior of the most revolting kind. The crux of the entire situation is, however, the constantly fluctuating political line that emerges as a result of the arbitrary decisions taken by many local authorities or experts and the inaction of many central offices."[6]

These deliberations about how the economic output of the occupied Soviet territories could be maximized led to a proposal for a new Eastern council under Göring. It would gather support from all the important government ministries and departments for a new, modified economic policy in the East. The principles enunciated by Göring on 8 November 1941 would allegedly be "basically" upheld, although the planned "amendments" to them would have far-reaching political consequences. The land would finally be exploited in a "planned" fashion. That meant not only an end to arbitrary interventions by the Wehrmacht and SS but also, for instance, the reconstruction of the processing industry, something that had previously been ideologically taboo. Extensive changes were required in particular in the use of labor.

The most important change in this regard was in the handling of workers in the occupied zone. It was now proposed that they should be provided sufficient food and humane treatment. This same was true of the Eastern workers and prisoners of war

5. Papers by these experts were first collected in two blue folders on 10 October 1942 and given to Secretary of State Körner. They continued until the spring of 1943. They can be found in the Central State Archives in Moscow, 700/1/49.

6. Excerpt from a letter written by Richter from the front on 26 May 1943 after he was sent there, Bundesarchiv Koblenz R 6/60a.

in Germany itself. An immediate halt to resettlement programs and extensive reprivatization of the land would eliminate the local inhabitants' fear of germanization. The reformers wanted to obtain "a decision by the Führer, binding on all, that puts an end to the slave theory."[7] Without abandoning the basic political belief in German expansion to the east, the participants in this "memoranda war," whether in government ministries and offices or in the Wehrmacht, called for an about-face in policy. Russians should no longer be considered subhuman *Untermenschen*, and an attempt should be made to win them over to the struggle against the Stalinist regime. Furthermore, all public discussion of future "colonies" in the East should be dropped (No. 70, p. 198).

However, Göring failed to assume leadership of the reform movement. His dislike of Rosenberg and rivalry with Goebbels and Himmler played a role in this decision, as well as the fact that he knew that Hitler was still opposed to any deviation from the hard-line position; moreover, Göring could point out with some justification that the "mild approach" would initially reduce the flow of goods from the east and result in increased hardship for the German civilian population (No. 518, p. 256). In any case, Hitler avoided any contact with Göring for several weeks in early 1943 after the Luftwaffe failed to prevent the Stalingrad disaster. Consequently, Göring proved to be of little help to those trying to bring about a reform in Eastern policies.

The initiatives undertaken by Rosenberg and Goebbels failed in the end because Hitler was convinced that any political announcements to the Russian people would now have to await some German military successes. In this way, the concessions would not be seen as a sign of weakness.

By this time, Göring had long lost his role as "economic dictator," while Albert Speer, Hitler's architect who had been appointed Minister of Armaments in February 1942, was constantly extending his influence. Speer was not particularly committed to the East, but he was interested in practical measures to rebuild the infrastructure. Hitler issued a special mandate for the construction of munitions plants in eastern Ukraine – the so-called Ivan Program – to Paul Pleiger, Göring's energetic industrial manager. However, negotiations dragged on for months over the appointment of an official to be in charge of the Eastern economy. Rapid reconstruction seemed to take a back

7 . Notes for Göring from 20 February 1943 (see note 4).

seat to demarcating the areas of competence of various officials and ministries. In the course of the negotiations, Speer's ministry proved particularly eager to ensure that the war economy in Germany did not suffer as a result of the transfer of investment to the East, where it would fall under stronger SS influence. It had already been difficult enough trying to reduce the spread of SS influence within the economy (No. 70, p. 58).

For the most part, leading economic circles adopted a very cautious attitude to the East in 1942–43. This was quite understandable in view of the worsening military situation. Even though they were willing, in response to pressure from the Wehrmacht and economic officials, to send various experts to the occupied territories and agreed to do the technical work on some plants, the economic elite continued to hesitate over any major commitments in the occupied Soviet Union. The Gutehoffnungshütte, one of Germany's largest machinery manufacturers, which had been a leading exporter to the Soviet Union before the war, issued a report suggesting that conquered smelting works in the Ukraine should not be rebuilt but rather stripped of their components, which would be shipped back to Germany. It was purportedly wiser to resist the understandable eagerness of economic officials in the Wehrmacht, who were responding to the mounting demands from the front. The "key role" played by steel production meant that it was best not concentrated in the "Slavic areas of the far east," but rather "between the Maas and Memel," accounting to the report (No. 465, p. 128).

Private companies believed that property rights in Russia posed a major obstacle. Conquered land and facilities of economic value were considered to belong to the German government. Since the Nazis wanted to give soldiers who had fought at the front preference in the final allotment of the spoils of victory, semigovernmental "eastern societies," trusteeships, and sponsorships were created on a provisional basis until ultimate distribution and privatization could be undertaken after the war. At the height of the war, the economic elite therefore viewed Russia as no more than a possible zone of colonial expansion after "final victory," which they wanted in the meantime to cost them as little as possible. There was no great interest in the land itself or the people who lived there. Most of the experts who traveled to the occupied territories on exploratory missions apparently examined only the industrial plants and the fields. As a result, there was no change in attitudes toward Russia.

This could be seen most clearly in the treatment afforded the millions of Russians laboring as "eastern workers" or prisoners of war in German war industries. They were the most valuable "spoils of war" and were highly prized as cheap slave labor, especially in mining and on assembly lines. Although company managers and presidents were prepared to engage in internecine struggles to obtain the services of these workers, they rarely sought to obtain "humane" treatment for them. So long as the flow of fresh workers from the Soviet Union continued, forced laborers were generally viewed as little more than raw materials to be consumed. This attitude changed slightly after the reversal in the fortunes of war in 1942–43, when the Germans decided to attempt to make better use of the surprising diligence of these workers, thereby avoiding the need to draw more German women into the workforce. However, it proved difficult to procure sufficient food as well as social and medical care for these laborers in the face of the entrenched political and ideological prejudices about Russians in government and society (No. 518).

As the tides of war turned increasingly against the Wehrmacht and the Soviets demonstrated their economic might, thus disproving the prejudices about them, leading industrialists also began rethinking Germany's approach to its Eastern neighbors. Various manufacturers and economic bureaucrats, especially in Bohemia and eastern Germany, encouraged and disseminated critical memoranda about Nazi policies in the East (No. 412). At IG Farben headquarters, an old trade expert from the time of the Austrian Empire, Richard Riedl, produced an extensive memorandum for the Chancellery on the "Russian question" (No. 444). Here Riedl advocated a return to the approach Germany had hoped to follow at the time of the First World War. Through a policy of encouraging the "national disintegration of Russia" and cooperation with the various remaining nationalities, Germany could assure its ascendancy. The Reich could dominate the economy and carve out a position for itself as a great world power. The tenor of his advice could be summed up in the phrase "the way to ensure success, here as in everything, is to be satisfied with what is achievable." The Nazi leadership ultimately heeded Riedl's recommendations, although reluctantly.

German occupation policies and economic strategy changed, therefore, only in reaction to reversals in the fortunes of war. After much hesitation and despite considerable resistance, the Nazi leadership finally undertook sweeping economic reconstruction and began to take the interests of the occupied peoples more into consideration. In this way, they hoped to stabilize the hinterland and supply the front with urgently needed materials. However, the steps that were finally taken in this direction were soon negated by the advances of the Red Army after the summer of 1943 (No. 496). As the Wehrmacht entered the retreat phase of the campaign, destruction and pillage again returned to the fore as a result of the "scorched earth" strategy (No. 473). Although at the height of the Wehrmacht's advance nearly half the economic capacity of the Soviet Union was in German hands, economic exploitation of the occupied territories never proved to be the decisive factor that the Germans had hoped it would be. More than fifty-five million people fell, for good or ill, under German domination. About twenty million of them were forced into slave labor and almost three million were deported to the Reich as "eastern workers," while the first settlement commissions set to work in the homeland (No. 524).

It is estimated that the occupation authorities succeeded in restoring about ten percent of the previous level of commercial and industrial production and about fifty percent of the agricultural production. By early 1943, 5,680 industries with almost 600,000 workers had returned to production. The Germans gained a net return from this activity of at least 7.5 billion reichsmarks, according to the final report of the Eastern Economic Staff. In addition, more than five million tons of captured raw materials were shipped to the Reich along with 250,000 railroad cars full of "evacuated goods" in 1943–44. The unpaid labor of Eastern workers and prisoners of war in Germany has been estimated to have been worth about thirty billion reichsmarks (No. 473).

As a result of all this, the German war economy was able to maintain high production levels until close to the end despite heavy bombing. Already by 1942, the Wehrmacht would not have been able to continue the war in the East without the forced deliveries from the occupied territories of clothing, weapons, food, and equipment.

In the final phase of the war, the economic elites apparently lost all interest in the Soviet Union. By then they were concentrating on how to survive, and cooperation with the Soviets, who were poised to invade the Reich, was out of the question. In the extensive plans that the economic elites produced in 1944–45 for the postwar period, the Soviet Union was not mentioned at all. This was not only a result of psychological repression but also a clear choice in favor of economic orientation toward the West and hope for cooperation with the great world power, the United States. Only with American help, it was thought, could Germany be rebuilt.

The Soviet Union was one of the victorious powers, to be sure, and in fact deserved most of the credit for defeating the Third Reich, but it also had suffered terribly from war and devastation. The Soviet Union was an unlikely market or even source of raw materials for many years to come and also posed little threat as an economic competitor. While the Wehrmacht left "scorched earth" in its wake as it retreated across eastern Europe, the industries in western Germany had largely survived, keeping alive hopes for a rapid recovery (No. E/160).

The economic administration established by the military had to adjust to ever-changing priorities and was never able fully to meet the constantly rising demands. Its chief task was to feed and support the German army in the East. When the original blitzkrieg stalled, it had to reconstruct the devastated transportation system and means of production under its control. In the final phase of the war, it struggled to maintain production behind the retreating front as long as possible before evacuating the various facilities in the nick of time, leaving the enemy with nothing but scorched earth. The work of the Eastern Economic Staff was usually far removed from the spectacular military operations along the front, but it was hardly inconspicuous. Nevertheless, there has never been a full historical account of its activities. Studies of the occupation repeatedly reveal the crucial importance of economic issues but treat them nonetheless as mere aspects of political issues and decisions, as in Dallin, for example. Some older publications of source materials include only excerpts and individual points (Nos. 24, 26). However, the publication of the final report of the Eastern Economic Staff has now provided a strong basis for historical research into this area.

Reliable specialized information about such key industries as coal, iron, and, above all, oil has been available for some time, thanks to a dissertation by Robert Joseph Gibbons, even though it was based on relatively meager source materials (No. 454). Using a different methodology, Wolfgang Birkenfeld and Dietrich Eichholtz provided a more comprehensive, although still not exhaustive, analysis of the German sources in these areas (Nos. 421, 446). They also emphasized regional aspects. The only analysis of the key textile industry is in the autobiography of Hans Kehrl, who oversaw this sector during the war (No. 460a).

Comprehensive studies of other industrial and commercial sectors as well as of banking and currency issues have appeared for only the early part of the occupation in 1941 (No. 467). Werpup's recent dissertation on industrial policy does not extend beyond the facts and figures provided by the Eastern Economic Staff, but it does uncover surprising success in the reconstruction of industrial facilities in 1942–43. In Werpup's view, if the Red Army had not succeeded in pushing back the Wehrmacht in the nick of time, this industrial production would have made a decisive contribution to the German war effort (No. 496).

Agriculture was clearly the most significant sector in regard to both economic questions and the political questions facing the occupational authorities. They had to deal with the problem of whether enough could be produced and delivered to supply (in order) the Wehrmacht, Germany, and the local population. Furthermore, whether to reprivatize agriculture or to maintain the collectives was a key political issue from the outset. The clash between ideological and economic goals was more blatant in this regard than in almost any other. The German authorities were consumed from the first to the final days of the occupation with the search for compromises and temporary solutions. Sufficient attention has not been paid in the research either to the entire agricultural issue or to important related issues such as food policy, social policy, and wage policy.

Views of German economic policy have differed as widely as views of the entire occupation. Soviet historians were unanimous in their conviction that the Germans failed utterly in all ways, while Westerners usually conceded that there were some successful economic initiatives, which usually failed in the end because of Hitler's doctrinaire attitude or the ebbing of German fortunes in the war. On the basis of the final report of the Eastern Economic Staff, one would conclude that the outcome of the economic experiment in the East was far more important to the German war effort than many histories of the Second World War seem to imply. Much work remains for the researchers of the future.

Table 1 Production of Important Industrial Raw Materials in the Occupied Eastern Territories (from the occupation until the end of April 1943; in tons)

Bituminous coal	2,878,750
Brown coal	417,697
Peat	2,600,000
Shale oil	1,208,513
Mineral oil	331,000
Manganese	1,008,359
Mercury	342
Steel ingots	31,000
Cotton	8,500
Flax	110,000
Cellulose	27,935
Cement	434,000
Finished leather	5,518
Window glass (m2)	1,367,500
Bricks (no. of individual bricks)	134,000,000
Furs (no. of individual furs)	996,300
Electricity (millions of kwh)	1,050

Source: No. 473, p. 476

Table 2 Deliveries from the Occupied Eastern Territories from the Beginning of the Occupation (July 1941) until 31 December 1943 (in tons)

	For Wehrmacht	**For Reich**	**Total**
Grain	4,710,000	1,610,000	6,320,000
Legumes	83,600	53,900	137,500
Hay	1,914,000	—	1,914,000
Straw	1,404,000	—	1,404,000
Oilseeds	26,100	695,100	721,200
Lubricants	107,600	23,600	131,200
Cooking oils	7,380	6,568	13,948
Machine oils	—	2,605	2,605
Meat	537,208	63,356	600,564
Poultry	10,737	6,272	17,009
Eggs (individual eggs)	760,300,000	118,100,000	878,400,000
Fish	27,650	1,663	29,313
Potatoes	2,677,100	15,900	2,693,000
Sugar	133,000	46,440	179,440
Jam	32,779	43	32,822
Raw Gasoline (in hl)	230,000	90,000	320,000
Vegetables	330,900	6,505	377,405
Fruit	14,225	1,504	15,729

Source: No. 473, p. 449

Table 3 Industrial Workers in the Occupied Eastern Territories (early 1943)

Industrial Sector	**Number of firms**	**Number of workers**
Mining	784	188,541
Iron and metals	843	103,132
Chemicals	452	21,116
Leather	341	16,412
Textiles and clothing	742	62,997
Lumber	649	38,606
Earth, stone, construction, glass, and ceramics	974	50,786
Other industries	318	18,698
Energy	446	26,094
Defense industries	52	54,100
Total	5,680	589,369

Source: No. 473, p. 477

Bibliography

1. General

a) Bibliographies

1) Dallin, Alexander. *The German Occupation of the USSR in World War II. A Bibliography*. Compiled by Alexander Dallin with the assistance of Conrad F. Latour. War Documentation Project under contract to the Bureau of Applied Social Research, Columbia Univ. External Research Paper, 122. New York, 1955
2) Romanchuk, Bohdan. *Bibliohrafiia ukrainsk'oi knyhy v Velykonimechchyni za chas viiny*. Edited by E. Pelens'kyi. L'viv-Krakiv, 1942
3) Satov, Michajl V. *Bibliografija osvoboditel'nogo dvizenija narodov Rossii v gody Vtoroj Mirovoj Vojny (1941–1945)*. Works of the Russian Liberation Army Archive, vol. 1. New York, 1961
4) Sokolyszyn, A. *Ukrainian Selected and Classified Bibliography in English*. New York, 1972
5) Weres, R. *The Ukraine. Selected References in the English Language*. Kalamazoo, Mich., 1961

b) Overviews

6) Anders, Wladyslaw. *Hitler's Defeat in Russia*. Chicago, 1953
7) Boltin, E.A. "Obscie voprosy nemecko-fasistskoj okkupacionnoj politiki." In *Nemecko-fasistskij okkupacionnyj rezim*, pp. 15–36
8) Dallin, Alexander. *German Rule in Russia, 1941–1945*. 2nd edn. London, 1981
9) Kroener, Bernhard, Rolf-Dieter Müller, and Hans Umbreit. *Organisation und Mobilisierung des deutschen Machtbereichs*. Vol. 1, *Kriegsverwaltung, Wirtschaft und personelle Ressourcen 1939–1941*. Das Deutsche Reich und der Zweite Weltkrieg, vol. 5/1. Stuttgart, 1988

10) Madajczyk, Czeslaw. "Die Besatzungssysteme der Achsenmächte. Versuch einer komparatistischen Analyse." *Studia Historiae Oeconomicae* vol. 14 (1980): pp. 105–122

11) ____. "Deutsche Besatzungspolitik in Polen, in der UdSSR und in den Ländern Südosteuropas." In *Deutschland 1933–1945. Neue Studien zur nationalsozialistischen Herrschaft*, edited by Karl Dietrich Bracher, Manfred Funke and Hans-Adolf Jacobsen, pp. 426–439. Bonn, 1992

13) ____. *Faszyzm i okupacje 1938–1945. Wykonywanie okupacij przez panstwa Osi w Europie*. Poznan, 1983

14) Mulligan, Timothy P. *The Politics of Illusion and Empire. German Occupation Policy in the Soviet Union, 1942–1943*. New York, 1988

15) *Nemecko-fasistskij okkupacionnyj rezim*. Edited by Institut für Marxismus-Leninismus beim ZK der KPdSU, Abteilung für die Geschichte des Großen Vaterländischen Krieges. Moscow, 1965

16) Reitlinger, Gerald. *The House Built on Sand. The Conflicts of German Policy in Russia, 1939–1945*. London, 1960

17) Semirjaga, M. I. "Fasistskij okkupacionnyj rezim na vremenno zachvacennoj sovetskoj territorii." *Voprosy istorii* no. 3 (1985): pp. 3–15

18) *Nemecko-fasistkij okkupacionnyj Rezim (1941–1944 gg.)* Moscow, 1965

18a) Thomas, Georg. *Geschichte der deutschen Wehr- und Rüstungswirtschaft (1918–1943/45)*. Edited by Wolfgang Birkenfeld. Boppard, 1966.

19) Umbreit, Hans. "Auf dem Weg zur Kontinentalherrschaft." In *Das Deutsche Reich und der Zweite Weltkrieg*, vol. 5/1, pp. 3–345. Stuttgart, 1988

20) *Vozrozdenie prifrontovych i osvobozdennych rajonov SSR v gody Velikoj Otecestvennoj vojny 1941–1945*. Moscow, 1986

21) Werth, Alexander. *Russia at War, 1941–1945*. New York, 1964 (German edn: *Rußland im Krieg 1941-1945; mit 21 Karten*. Munich, 1965)

c) Sources

22) *Documents Accuse*. Compiled and annotated by B. Baranauskas and K. Ruksenas. Vilnius, 1970

23) *Dokumenty obviniaiut*. Moscow, 1945

24) Eichholtz, Dietrich and Wolfgang Schumann, eds. *Anatomie des Krieges. Neue Dokumente über die Rolle des deutschen Monopolkapitals bei der Vorbereitung und Durchführung des zweiten Weltkrieges*. East Berlin, 1969

25) *Die faschistische Okkupationspolitik in den zeitweilig besetzten Gebieten der Sowjetunion (1941–1944)*. Edited by Norbert Müller et al. Europa unterm Hakenkreuz. Die Okkupationspolitik des deutschen Faschismus 1938–1945, vol. 5. Berlin, 1991

26) Hass, Gerhart and Wolfgang Schumann, eds. *Anatomie der Aggression. Neue Dokumente zu den Kriegszielen des faschistischen deutschen Imperialismus im zweiten Weltkrieg*. East Berlin, 1972

27) *Hitlers Zweites Buch. Ein Dokument aus dem Jahre 1928*. Introduced and annotated by G.L. Weinberg. Quellen und Darstellungen zur Zeitgeschichte, vol. 7. Stuttgart, 1961

28) Inter-Allied Information Committee (later United Nations Informations Organization), ed. *Conditions in Occupied Territories: A Series of Reports*. Nos. 1–8. London, 1942–1944

29) International Military Tribunal. *Documents*. Document series PS, F, L, R, C. D, EC. Mimeographed text, partly in English translation

30) ____. *Nazi Conspiracy and Agression, Opinion and Judgement*. 8 vols. and supplements A and B. (Red Series). Washington, 1947

31) *Trial of the Major War Criminals before the International Military Tribunal*. 42 vols. (Blue Series). Nuremberg, 1947–1949

32) Jochmann, Werner, ed. *Monologe im Führerhauptquartier, 1941-1944. Die Aufzeichnungen Heinrich Heims*. Hamburg, 1980

33) Kosyk, Wolodymyr, ed. *Das Dritte Reich und die ukrainische Frage. Dokumente 1934–1944*. Munich, 1985

34) *Masinés Zudynés Lietuvoje (1941–1944). Dokumentu rinkinys*. Vilnius, 1965

35) Meyer, Alfred, ed. *Das Recht der besetzten Ostgebiete. Estland, Lettland, Litauen, Weißruthenien und Ukraine. Sammlung der Verordnungen, Erlasse und sonstigen Vorschriften über Verwaltung, Rechtspflege, Wirtschaft, Finanzwesen und Verkehr mit Erläuterungen der Referenten*. Munich, 1943

36) Michalka, Wolfgang, ed. *Das Dritte Reich. Dokumente zur Innen- und Außenpolitik*. Vol. 2, *Weltmachtanspruch und nationaler Zusammenbruch 1939–1945*. Munich, 1985

37) Moritz, E., ed. *Fall Barbarossa. Dokumente zur Vorbereitung der faschistischen Wehrmacht auf die Aggression gegen die Sowjetunion (1940/41)*. East Berlin, 1970

38) Müller, Norbert, ed. *Deutsche Besatzungspolitik in der UdSSR 1941–1944. Dokumente*. Kleine Bibliothek no. 194. Cologne, 1980

39) ____. *Okkupation, Raub, Vernichtung. Dokumente zur Besatzungspolitik der faschistischen Wehrmacht auf sowjetischem Territorium 1941 bis 1944*. East Berlin, 1980

40) *Prestuplenija nemecko-fasistskich okkupantov v Belorussii, 1941–1944. Sbornik dokumentov i materialov*. Minsk, 1963; 2nd edn 1965

41) *Prestupnye Celi – prestupnye sredstva. Dokumenty ob okkupacionnoj politike fasistskoj Germanii na territorii SSSR (1941–1944 gg.)*. Moscow, 1968

42) *Records of the Reich Ministry for the Occupied Eastern Territories, 1941–45*. Guides to German Records Microfilmed at Alexandria, Va., No. 28. Washington, 1961

43) *Records of the Office of the Reich Commissioner for the Baltic States, 1941–45*. Guides to German Records Microfilmed at Alexandria, Va., no. 31. Washington, 1961

44) Satov, Michajl V. *Materialy i dokumenty osvoboditel'nogo dvizenija narodov Rossii v gody Vtoroj Mirojoj Vojny (1941–1965)*. Works of the Russian Liberation Army Archive, vol. 2. New York, 1966

45) *Eine Schuld, die nicht erlischt. Dokumente über deutsche Kriegsverbrechen in der Sowjetunion*. Kleine Bibliothek no. 389. Cologne, 1987 (first published under the title *Verbrecherische Ziele – verbrecherische Mittel*. Moscow, 1963)

46) Smith, Bradley F., and Agnes F. Peterson, eds. *Heinrich Himmler. Geheimreden 1933 bis 1945 und andere Ansprachen*. Frankfurt, 1974

47) *Sovetskaja Ukraina v gody Velikoj Otecestvennoj vojny 1941–1945*. 3 vols. Kiev, 1980

48) SSSR. Chrezvychainaia gos. kommissia. po ustanovleniiu i rassledovaniiu zlodeianii nemets-fashist zakvatchikov. Sbornik. Moscow, 1945

49) *Städte im Osten klagen Hitler an! Amtliche Berichte der außerordentlichen staatlichen Untersuchungskommission der Sowjetunion über die von den deutschen Faschisten in Lemberg und Minsk begangenen Greueltaten*. Singen, 1945
50) United States Military Tribunals, Nuremberg. *Documents and Staff Evidence Analysis*. Mimeographed Series. Nuremberg, 1947–1948
51) _____. Cases I–XII. Mimeographed, with document series NG, NI, NO, NOKW. Nuremberg, 1946–1949
52) *Trials of War Criminals before the Nuremburg Military Tribunals under Control Council Law No. 10, Nuremberg, October, 1946 – April, 1949*. (Green Series) 15 vols. Washington, 1949–1954
53) U.S.S.R. Embassy (London), ed. *New Soviet Documents on Nazi Atrocities*. London, 1943
54) _____. *Soviet Government Statements on Nazi Atrocities*. London, 1946
55) _____. *We Shall Not Forgive! The Horrors of the German Invasion in Documents and Photographs*. Moscow, 1942
56) *Verbrecherische Ziele – verbrecherische Mittel! Dokumente der Okkupationspolitik des faschistischen Deutschlands auf dem Territorium der UdSSR (1941–1944)*. Moscow, 1963

2. War Aims

57) Aly, Götz, and Susanne Heim. *Vordenker der Vernichtung. Auschwitz und die deutschen Pläne für eine neue europäische Ordnung*. Hamburg, 1990; paperback edn Frankfurt a.M., 1993
58) Bezymenskij. L. A. "General'nyj plan 'Ost': zamysel, celi, rezul'taty." *Voprosy Istorii* no. 5 (1978): pp. 74–94
59) Bay, Achim. "Der nationalsozialistische Gedanke der Großraumwirtschaft und seine ideologischen Grundlagen. Darstellung und Kritik." Phil. diss., Univ. Erlangen-Nuremberg, 1962
60) Daitz, Werner. "Autarkie als Lebens- und Wirtschaftsordnung." In *Der Weg zur völkischen Wirtschaft, europäischen Großraumwirtschaft und gerechten Weltordnung*. Part III, *Der Weg zur gerechten Ordnung*, pp. 112–123. Dresden, 1943
61) Hass, Gerhart. "Weltmachtziele – Europastrategie – Besatzungspolitik. Aspekte einer vergleichenden Okkupationsforschung." *1999, Zeitschrift für Sozialgeschichte des 20. und 21. Jahrhunderts* no. 2 (1992): pp. 12–30
62) Eichholtz, Dietrich. "Der 'Generalplan Ost'. Über eine Ausgeburt imperialistischer Denkart und Politik (mit Dokumenten)." *Jahrbuch für Geschichte* 26 (1982): pp. 217–274
63) Gruchmann, Lothar. *Nationalsozialistische Großraumordnung. Die Konstruktion einer "deutschen Monroe-Doktrin"*. Schriftenreihe der Vierteljahrshefte für Zeitgeschichte, vol. 4. Stuttgart, 1962
64) Heiber, Helmut. "Der Generalplan Ost. Mit Dokumenten aus dem Jahr 1942." *Vierteljahrshefte für Zeitgeschichte* vol. 6, no. 3 (1958): pp. 281–325
65) Hildebrand, Klaus. "Hitlers 'Programm' und seine Realisierung 1939–1942." In *Hitler, Deutschland und die Mächte. Materialien zur*

Außenpolitik des Dritten Reiches, edited by Manfred Funke, pp. 63–93. Düsseldorf, 1976

66) Hillgruber, Andreas. “Die ‘Endlösung’ und das deutsche Ostimperium als Kernstück des rassenideologischen Programms des Nationalsozialismus.” In *Hitler, Deutschland und die Mächte. Materialien zur Außenpolitik des Dritten Reiches*, edited by Manfred Funke, pp. 94–114. Düsseldorf, 1976

67) Jäckel, Eberhard. *Hitlers Weltanschauung. Enwurf einer Herrschaft*. Rev. and enl. edn. Stuttgart, 1981

68) Kamenetsky, Ihor. *Secret Nazi Plans for Eastern Europe. A Study of Lebensraum Policies*. New York, 1961

69) Madajczyk, Czeslaw. “Generalplan Ost.” *Polish Western Affairs* vol. 3, no. 1–2 (1962): pp. 391–442

70) Müller, Rolf-Dieter. *Hitlers Ostkrieg und die deutsche Siedlungspolitik. Die Zusammenarbeit von Wehrmacht, Wirtschaft und SS*. Frankfurt a.M., 1991

71) Nedorezov, A.I. “Fasistskie plany germanizacii slavjanskich stran v gody Vtoroj mirovoj vojny.” *Nemecko-fasistskij okkupacionnyj rezim* pp. 129–148

72) Nestler, Ludwig. “Über den Zeitpunkt und die Ursachen erster Ansätze zur Modifikation der Kriegszielplanung und der Okkupationspolitik Hitlerdeutschlands (Herbst 1942 bis Frühjahr 1943).” *Studia Historiae Oeconomicae* vol. 14 (1980): pp. 123–139

73) “Zu Hitlers Ostpolitik im Sommer 1943 (Dokumentation.” *Vierteljahrshefte für Zeitgeschichte* vol. 2, no. 3 (1954): pp. 305–309

74) Rich, Norman. *Hitler’s War Aims*. Vol. II, *The Establishment of the New Order*. New York, 1974

75) Sanders, A. *Osteuropa in kontinentaleuropäischer Sicht*. Munich, 1942

76) Schumann, Wolfgang, ed. *Konzept für die “Neuordnung” der Welt. Die Kriegsziele des faschistischen deutschen Imperialismus im zweiten Weltkrieg*. East Berlin, 1977

77) Stoakes, Geoffrey. *Hitler and the Quest for World Dominion. Nazi Ideology and Foreign Policy in the 1920s*. Leamington Spa, 1986

78) Thies, Jochen. *Architekt der Weltherrschaft. Die “Endziele” Hitlers*. Düsseldorf, 1976

79) Trevor-Roper, H.R. “Hitlers Kriegsziele.” *Vierteljahrshefte für Zeitgeschichte* 8 (1960): pp. 121–133

80) Vogt, Martin. “Selbstbespiegelung im Erwartung des Sieges. Bemerkungen zu den Tischgesprächen Hitlers im Herbst 1941.” In *Der Zweite Weltkrieg*, edited by Wolfgang Michalka, pp. 641–651. Munich, 1989

81) Volkmann, Hans-Erich, ed. *Das Rußlandbild im Dritten Reich*. Cologne, 1994

82) Wippermann, Wolfgang. *Der “Deutsche Drang nach Osten”. Ideologie und Wirklichkeit eines politischen Schlagworts*. Impulse der Forschung, vol. 35. Darmstadt, 1981

83) Zitelmann, Rainer. *Hitler. Selbstverständnis eines Revolutionärs*. Stuttgart, 1989

84) _____. “Zur Begründung des ‘Lebensraum’-Motivs in Hitlers Weltanschauung.” In *Der Zweite Weltkrieg*, edited by Wolfgang Michalka, pp. 551–567. Munich, 1989

3. Military Administration

85) Bußmann, Walter. "'Notizen' aus der Abteilung Kriegsverwaltung beim Generalquartiermeister (1941/42)." In *Deutsche Frage und europäisches Gleichgewicht. Festschrift für Andreas Hillgruber zum 60. Geburtstag*, edited by Klaus Hildebrand and Reiner Pommerin, pp. 229–240. Cologne, 1985

86) Förster, Jürgen. "Die Sicherung des 'Lebensraumes'." In *Das Deutsche Reich und der Zweite Weltkrieg*, vol. 4, pp. 1030–1078. Stuttgart, 1983

87) Müller, Norbert. "Zur Rolle der Wehrmachtführung bei der Planung und Vorbereitung des faschistischen Okkupationsregimes in den besetzten sowjetischen Gebieten 1940/41." *Zeitschrift für Militärgeschichte* vol. 6, no. 4 (1967): pp. 415–431

88) _____. *Wehrmacht und Okkupation. 1941–1944. Zur Rolle der Wehrmacht und ihrer Führungsorgane im Okkupationsregime des faschistischen deutschen Imperialismus auf sowjetischem Territorium*. East Berlin, 1971

89) Müller, Rolf-Dieter. "Kriegsrecht oder Willkür? Helmuth James Graf von Moltke und die Auffassungen im Generalstab des Heeres über die Aufgaben der Militärverwaltung vor Beginn des Rußlandkrieges." *Militärgeschichtliche Mitteilungen* 35 (1987): pp. 125–151

90) Salewski, Michael. "Grundzüge der Militärverwaltung." In *Deutsche Verwaltungsgeschichte*, edited by Kurt G.A. Jeserich et al. Vol. 4, *Das Reich als Republik und in der Zeit des Nationalsozialismus*, pp. 888–911. Stuttgart, 1985

91) Schulte, Theo. *The German Army and Nazi Policies in Occupied Russia*. Oxford, 1989

92) _____. "Die Wehrmacht und die nationalsozialistische Besatzungspolitik in der Sowjetunion." In *"Unternehmen Barbarossa"*, edited by Roland G. Foerster, pp. 163–176. Munich, 1993

93) Simpson, Keith. "The German Experience of Rear Area Security on the Eastern Front, 1941–45." *Journal of the Royal United Services Institute for Defence Studies* 121 (1976): pp. 39–46

94) Umbreit, Hans. "Die deutsche Besatzungsverwaltung: Konzept und Typisierung." In *Der Zweite Weltkrieg*, edited by Wolfgang Michalka, pp. 710–727. Munich, 1989

95) _____. "Nationalsozialistische Expansion 1938–1941. Strukturen der deutschen Besatzungsverwaltungen im Zweiten Weltkrieg." In *Dienst für die Geschichte. Gedenkschrift für Walther Hubatsch, 17. Mai 1915 - 29. Dezember 1984*, edited by Michael Salewski and Josef Schröder, pp. 163–186. Göttingen, 1985

96) _____. "Die Kriegsverwaltung 1940 bis 1945 (Dokumentation)." *Militärgeschichtliche Mitteilungen* 2 (1968): pp. 105–134

4. Civilian Administration

97) Alexiev, Alex. "Soviet Nationalities in German Wartime Strategy, 1941–1945." *Conflict* vol. 4, no. 2–4 (1983): pp. 181–238

98) Aslanov, A.S. "Nacistskie vraci – soucastniki prestupllenij germanskogo fasisma." In *Nemecko-fasistskij okkupacionnyj rezim*, pp. 361–378. Moscow, 1965

99) Braeutigam, Otto. *So hat es sich zugetragen. Ein Leben als Soldat und Diplomat*. Würzburg, 1968

100) _____. *Überblick über die besetzten Ostgebiete während des 2. Weltkrieges*. Studien des Instituts für Besatzungsfragen, no. 3. Tübingen, 1954

101) Cecil, Robert. *The Myth of the Master Race: Alfred Rosenberg and Nazi Ideology*. London, 1972

102) Eichholtz, Dietrich. "'Großgermanisches Reich' und 'Generalplan Ost'. Einheitlichkeit und Unterschiedlichkeit im faschistischen Okkupationssystem." *Zeitschrift für Geschichtswissenschaft* 28 (1980): pp. 835–841

103) Farvars, Kurt. *Zeitenwende im Osten. Schicksal und Gestalt des Ostraums*. Düsseldorf, 1942

104) Fireside, H. *Icon and Swastika. The Russian Orthodox Church under Nazi and Soviet Control*. Cambridge, Mass., 1971

106) Fleischhauer, Ingeborg. *Das Dritte Reich und die Deutschen in der Sowjetunion*. Schriftenreihe der Vierteljahrshefte für Zeitgeschichte, vol. 46. Stuttgart, 1983

107) Gadolin, Carl A.J. von. *Der Norden, der Ostraum und das neue Europa*. Munich, 1943

108) Gibbons, Robert J. "Allgemeine Richtlinien für die politische und wirtschaftliche Verwaltung der besetzten Ostgebiete." *Vierteljahrshefte für Zeitgeschichte* 29 (1977): pp. 252–261

109) Herzog, Robert. *Grundzüge der deutschen Besatzungsverwaltung in den ost- und südosteuropäischen Ländern während des 2. Weltkrieges*. Studien des Instituts für Besatzungsfragen, no. 4. Tübingen, 1955

110) _____. *Besatzungsverwaltung in den besetzten Ostgebieten – Abteilung Jugend. Insbesondere: Heuaktion u. SS-Helfer-Aktion*. Tübingen, 1960

111) Klante, M., ed. *Völkerkarte der Sowjetunion*. Berlin, 1941

112) Kleist, Peter. *European Tragedy*. Isle of Man, 1965

113) Koehl, Robert L. *RKFDV, German Resettlement and Population Policy 1939–1945. A History of the Reich Commission for the Strengthening of Germandom*. Harvard Historical Monographs, no. 31. Cambridge, Mass., 1957

114) Labs, Walter. "Die Verwaltung der besetzten Ostgebiete." In *Reich, Volksordnung, Lebensraum*, vol. 5, pp. 132–166. Darmstadt, 1943

115) Lang, Serge, and Ernst von Schenk, eds. *Memoirs of Alfred Rosenberg*. Chicago, 1949

116) Lenkin, Rafael. *Axis Rule in Occupied Europe: Laws of Occupation, Analysis of Government, Proposals for Redress*. Washington, DC, 1944

117) Majer, Dietmut. *"Fremdvölkische" im Dritten Reich*. Schriften des Bundesarchivs, 28. Boppard a. Rh., 1981

118) _____. "Führerunmittelbare Sondergewalten in den besetzten Ostgebieten. Entstehung und Wirksamkeit." In *Verwaltung contra Menschenführung im Staat Hitlers. Studien zum politisch-administrativen System*, edited by Dieter Rebentisch and Karl Teppe, pp. 374–395. Göttingen, 1986

119) Mende, Gerhard von. "Die besetzten Ostgebiete." *Jahrbuch der Weltpolitik* (1943): pp. 229–236.

120) _____. "Die besetzten Ostgebiete (im Jahr 1943)." *Jahrbuch der Weltpolitik* (1944): pp. 197–201

121) _____. *Die Völker der Sowjetunion*. Reichenau, 1939

122) ____. *Die Völker des Ostraums*. Berlin, 1942
123) Meyer, Heinz. "Der Aufbau der Rechtspflege in den besetzten Ostgebieten." *Jahrbuch des Osteuropa-Instituts zu Breslau* 3, (1942): pp. 270–279
124) Nikolai, Metropolitan of Kiev and Galicia. *The Russian Orthodox Church and the War against Fascism*. Moscow, 1943
125) Samarin, Vladimir D. *Civilian Life under the German Occupation, 1942–1944*. Mimeographed Series, no. 58. New York, 1954
126) Stamati, Constantin Graf. "Zur 'Kulturpolitik' des Ostministeriums." *Vierteljahrshefte für Zeitgeschichte* vol. 6, no. 1 (1958): pp. 78–85
127) Werner, Paul. *Ein Schweizer Journalist sieht Russland*. Olten, 1942
128) Wheeler, Leonie J. "The SS and the Administration of Nazi Occupied Eastern Europe, 1939–1945." Phil. diss., Univ. of Oxford, 1981
129) Wilhelm, Hans-Heinrich. "Der SD und die Kirchen in den besetzten Ostgebieten 1941/42." *Militärgeschichtliche Mitteilungen* vol. 29 (1981): pp. 55–99
130) Zastavenko, G.F. "O roli germanskogo ministerstva vostocnych okkupirovannych oblastej'." In *Nemecko-fasistskij okkupacionyj rezim*, pp. 115–128. Moscow, 1965
131) zur Mühlen, Patrik von. *Zwischen Hakenkreuz und Sowjetstern. Der Nationalismus der sowjetischen Orientvölker im Zweiten Weltkrieg*. Bonner Schriften zur Politik und Zeitgeschichte, 5. Düsseldorf, 1971

5. Individual Regions

a) Reichskommissariat Ostland

132) Angelus, Oskar. "Die Einsetzung der deutschen Zivilverwaltung in Estland 1941." *Baltische Hefte* vol. 19 (1973): pp. 35–60
133) ____. *Tuhande Valitseja maa. Mälestusi Saksa okupatsiooni afast 1943–1944*. Stockholm, 1956
134) Anisimov, Oleg. *The German Occupation in Northern Russia during World War II: Political and Administrative Aspects*. Mimeographed Series, no. 54. New York, 1954
135) Arens, Ilmar. "Eine estnische Umsiedlung im Jahre 1943." *Baltische Hefte* vol. 12 (1966): pp. 28–32
136) Balevic, Zigmund V. *Pravoslavnaja Cerkov Latvii pod senju svastiki (1941–1944)*. Riga, 1967
137) Blank, Margot. "Theorie und Praxis nationalsozialistischer Hochschulpolitik in Riga 1941–1944." *Zeitschrift für Ostforschung* vol. 38 (1989): pp. 541–557
138) Bliumfeld, E.A. *Gitlerovskii okkupatsionnyi rezhim v Latvii (1941–1945)*. Riga, 1967
139) Chiari, Bernhard. "Deutsche Zivilverwaltung in Weißrußland 1941–1944. Die lokale Perspektive der Besatzungsgeschichte." *Militärgeschichtliche Mitteilungen* vol. 52 (1993): pp. 67–89
140) Dobrovol'skas, I.V. "Gitlervoskij okkupacionnyj rezim na territorii Sovetskoj Litvy." In *Nemecko-fasistskij okkupacionyj recim*, pp. 75–83
141) Drizul, A.A. "Latvija pod igom faszima." Diss., Riga, 1961
142) Engelhardt, Eugen. *Weißruthenien, Volk und Land*. Berlin, 1943

143) "Estland und Lettland im Kriegswinter 1942/43." *Deutsche Studien* vol. 5, no. 19 (1967): pp. 291–298
144) *Estonskii narod v Vel. Otech. voine Sovetskogo Soiuza 1941–1945*. Vol. 1. Tallin, 1971
145) *Führer durch Riga*. Riga, 1943
146) Frotscher, E. *Ostland kehrt nach Europa zurück. Notizen von einer Reise des Reichskommissars Hinrich Lohse*. Riga, 1941
147) Gerutis, Albertas. "Occupied Lithuania." In *Lithuania 700 Years*, pp. 257–312. New York, 1969
148) *Gitlerovskaia okkupatsiia v Litve*. Vilnius, 1966
149) Grishenko, P.D., et al., eds. *Bor'ba za Sovetskuiu Pribaltiku v Vel. Otech. voine 1941–1945*. 3 vols. Riga, 1966–1969
150) Handrack, Hans-Dieter. *Das Reichskommissariat Ostland. Die Kulturpolitik der deutschen Verwaltung zwischen Autonomie und Gleichschaltung 1941–1944*. Hann. Münden, 1981
151) Krastyn', I. *Bor'ba latyshskogo naroda protiv nemetskikh zakhvatchikov i porabotitelei*. Moscow, 1946
152) Kravcenko, I.S. "Nemecko-fasistskij okkupacionyj rezim v Belorussii." In *Nemecko-fasistskij okkupacionyj rezim*, pp. 49–64. Moscow, 1965
153) Kravcenko, I.S., and A.I. Zalesskij. *Belorusskij narod v gody Velikoj Otecest vennoj vojny*. Minsk, 1959
154) Larin, P.A. *Estonskii narod v Vel. Otech. voiny* Tallin, 1964
155) *Latvia in 1939–1942*. Washington, 1942
156) *Latvia Under German Occupation, 1941–1943*. Washington, 1943
157) Martinson, E. *Slugi svastiki*. Tallin, 1962
158) *Maski sorvany*. Tallin, 1961
159) Myllyniemi, Seppo. *Die Neuordnung der baltischen Länder 1941–1944. Zum nationalsozialistischen Inhalt der deutschen Besatzungspolitik*. Dissertationes historicae, 2. Historiallisia Tutkimuksia, 90. Helsinki, 1973
160) *Na dorogakh voiny. 1941–1945*. Tallin, 1970
161) *Ne zabyvai Audrini*. Riga, 1968
162) *Nemecko-fasistkaja okkupacija Estonii*. Tallin, 1963
163) *Hitlerine Okupacija Lietuvoje (Gitlerovskaja Okkupacija v Litve)*. Vilnius, 1961
164) *Gitlerovskaja Okkupacija v Litve. Sbornik Statej*. Vilnius, 1966
165) Pankseev, Aleksandr K. *Estonskij Narod v Velikoj Otecest-vennoj Vojne*. Tallin, 1980
166) Peisakovich, A.I. *Bor'ba trudiashchikhsia Beloruss SSR za vosstanovlenie nar. khoziaistva i kul'tury v gody Vel. Otech. voiny*. Minsk, 1959
167) *Nacistskaja Politka genocida i "vyzzennof zemli" v Belorussii. 1941–1944*. Edited by V. E. Lobanok. Minsk, 1984
168) *Eesti Rahvas Noukogude Liidu Suures Isamaasojas 1941–1945, Estonskij Narod v Velikoj Otecestvennoj vojne Sovetskogo Sojuza 1941–1945*. 2 vols. Tallin, 1973–1980
169) Rastikis, Stasys. "The Relations of the Provisional Government of Lithania with the German Authorities." *Lituanus* vol. 8, no. 1/2 (1962): pp. 16–22

170) Slavenas, Julius P. "Nazi Ideology and Policy in the Baltic States." *Lituanus* vol. 2, no. 1 (1965): pp. 34–47
171) Stegmann, Kurt. *Die Hochschulen in Ostland zwischen gestern und morgen*. Riga, 1943
172) Turonek, Jerzy. *Bialorus pod okupacja niemiicka*. Warsaw, 1989
173) Zimmermann, Walter, ed. *Auf Informationsfahrt im Ostland: Reiseeindrücke deutscher Schriftleiter*. Riga, 1944

b) Reichskommissariat Ukraine

174) Armstrong, John A. *Ukrainian Nationalism, 1939–1945*. New York, 1955; 2nd edn New York
175) Aytugan, M. "World War II and the National Question." *Ukrainian Quarterly* vol. 8 (1952): pp. 35–43
176) Basov, Aleksej V. *Krym v Velikoj Otecestvennoj vojne 1941–1945*. Moscow, 1987
177) Boldyrev, V. "Mestnye sudy na Ukraine v gody nemeckoj okkupacii." *Vestnik Instituta po izuceniju SSSR* no. 21 (1956): pp. 66–72
178) Buchsweiler, M. *Volksdeutsche in der Ukraine am Vorabend und Beginn des Zweiten Weltkrieges – ein Fall doppelter Loyalität?* Schriftenreihe des Instituts für Deutsche Geschichte, Universität Tel Aviv, vol. 7. Gerlingen, 1984
179) Butsko, Olexander M. *Never to be Forgotten*. Kiev, 1986
180) Child, Clifton J. "The Ukraine under German Occupation, 1941–1944." In *Hitler's Europe*, edited by A. Toynbee, pp. 632–647. London, 1954
181) Dallin, Alexander. *Odessa, 1941–1944: A Case Study of Soviet Territory under Foreign Rule*. U.S. Air Force Project RAND Research Memorandum, 1875. Santa Monica, Calif., 1957
182) Frauenfeld, Alfred E. *Und trage keine Reu'. Vom Wiener Gauleiter zum Generalkommissar der Krim. Erinnerungen und Aufzeichnungen*. Leoni am Starnberger See, 1978
183) _____. *Die Krim*. Berlin, 1942
184) _____. *Ursache und Sinn unseres Kampfes: Bolschewismus-Kapitalismus: das apokalyptische Tier mit zwei Köpfen*. Vienna, 1944
185) Geilke, Georg. "Nationalisierung in der Westukraine (Ostgalizien 1939–1944)." *Monatshefte für osteuropäisches Recht* vol. 18, no. 4 (1976): pp. 215–220
186) Ginsburg, Lev. "Beyond the Legend." *Sputnik* no. 5 (1967): pp. 88–115
187) Grigorovic, Dmitrij F. *Kiev – gorod-geroj*. Moscow, 1978
188) Grimsted, Patricia K. "The Fate of Ukrainian Cultural Treasures During World War II: The Plunder of Archives, Libraries, and Museums under the Third Reich." *Jahrbücher für Geschichte Osteuropas* vol. 39, no. 1 (1991): pp. 53–80
189) Heyer, Friedrich. *Die orthodoxe Kirche in der Ukraine von 1917 bis 1945*. Cologne, 1953
190) Horak, Stephan M. "L'Ukraine entre les Nazis et les Communistes." *Revue d'Histoire de la Deuxième Guerre Mondiale* A.33, no. 130 (1983): pp. 65–75
191) Illnytzki, Roman. *Deutschland und die Ukraine 1934–1945. Tatsachen europäischer Ostpolitik. Ein Vorbericht*. 2 vols. Munich, 1958

192) Kamenetsky, Ihor. *Hitler's Occupation of Ukraine (1941–1944). A Study of Totalitarian Imperialism*. Marquette Slavic Studies, 2. Milwaukee, Wis., 1956
193) *Kievshchina v gody Vel. Otech. voiny 1941–1945*. Kiev, 1963
194) Kondratiuk, I.I. "Rol' promyshlennosti Ukrainy v razgrome gitlerovskoi G kmanii." In *Tezisy nauchnoi konferentsii (8–10.IX.1965)*, pp. 46–78. Odessa, 1965
195) Korcek, Fero. *Obrazky z Ukrajiny. Dojmy vojenskeho dopisovatela*. Bratislava, 1941
196) Kosyk, Wolodymyr. *L'Allemagne national-socialiste et l'Ukraine*. Paris, 1986
197) ____. "Le mouvement national ukrainien de résistance." *Revue d'Histoire de la Deuxième Guerre Mondiale et des Conflits Contemporains* A.36, no. 141 (1986): pp. 59–75
198) Koval, V. S. "O politisceskom krizise okkupacionnogo rezima na Ukraine." In *Nemecko-fasistskij okkupacionnyj rezim*, pp. 65–74. Moscow, 1965
199) Laskovsky, Nikolas. "Practicing Law in the Occupied Ukraine." *The American Slavic and East European Review (New York)* XI (April 1952): pp. 123–37
200) Leibbrandt, Georg, ed. *Ukraine*. Berlin, 1942
201) Leitgeb, Josef. *Am Rande des Krieges. Aufzeichnungen in der Ukraine*. Berlin, 1942
202) Litvinov, I.D. *Proval agrarnoi politiki nemetsko-fashistskikh okkupantov na Ukraine v 1941–1943 gg*. Poltava, 1950
203) Luther, Michel. "Die Krim unter deutscher Besatzung im Zweiten Weltkrieg." *Forschungen zur osteuropäischen Geschichte*, vol. 3 (1956): pp. 28–98
204) Mirchuk, Ivan, ed. *Handbuch der Ukraine*. Leipzig, 1941
205) *Nemecko-fasitskij okkupacionnyj rezim na Ukraine*. Kiev, 1951
206) Obermaier, Franz. *Ukraine, Land der schwarzen Erde*. Vienna, 1942
207) Pauser, Franz. *Die Ukraine*. Berlin, 1943
208) Persina, Tamara S. *Fasistskij Genocid na Ukraine 1941–1944*. Kiev, 1985
209) Pulle, Giorgio. *L'Ucraina*. Rome, 1942
210) Remer, Claus. "Über die Genesis der Ukrainepolitik des deutschen Imperialismus." In *Zur Ukraine-Politik des deutschen Imperialismus. Protokoll einer Arbeitstagung am 23.9.1967 in Berlin*, edited by C. Remer. Jena, 1969
211) ____. "Die faschistischen Ukraine-Pläne und ihr Scheitern am Ende des zweiten Weltkrieges." *Jahrbuch für Geschichte der sozialistischen Länder Europas* 19 (1975): pp. 185–200
212) Sevcenko, F.P. "Nemecko-fasistskij okkupacionnyj rezim na Ukraine." In *Nemecko-fasistskij okkupacionnyj rezim*, pp. 36–49. Moscow, 1965
213) *Ukrainskaja SSR v gody Velikoj Otecestvennoj vojny Sovetskogo Sojuza. Chronika sobytij*. Edited by V.I. Klokov. Kiev, 1985
214) Stehle, Hansjakob. "Der Lemberger Metropolit Septydkyj und die Nationalsozialistische Politik in der Ukraine." *Vierteljahrshefte für Zeitgeschichte* vol. 34, no. 3 (1986): pp. 407–425
215) Stupperich, Robert. *Die Ukraine und das Baltenland*. Berlin, 1941
216) Torzecki, R. *Kwestia ukrainska w polityce III Rzeszy 1933–1945*. Warsaw, 1972

217) *Ukraine during World War II. History and its Aftermath. A Symposium.* Edited by Yuri Boshyk with the assistance of Roman Waschuk and Andriy Wynnyckij. Edmonton, 1986
218) Volodymyrovytch, B. *L'Ukraine sous l'occupation allemande.* Paris, 1948.
219) Weerd, Hans de. "Gauleiter Erich Koch in der Ukraine." *Ukraine* vol. 4, no. 2/3 (1955): pp. 41–45

c) Other Areas and Regions

220) Aftenjuk, S., et al. *Moldavskaja SSR v Velikoj Otecestvennoj Vojne Sovetskogo Sojuza 1941–1945 gg.* Kisinev, 1970
221) Bensing, Johannes. *Turkestan.* Berlin, 1943
222) Engelhardt, Walter. *Klinzy. Bildnis einer russischen Stadt nach ihrer Befreiung vom Bolschewismus.* Berlin, 1943
223) Erhorn, Irmgard. *Kaukasien.* Berlin, 1942
224) Kentmann, Paul. *Der Kaukasus; hundertfünfzig Jahre russische Herrschaft.* Leipzig, 1943
225) *Kogda busujut grozy. Kaluzskaja oblast v Velikoj Otecestvennoj Vojne.* Tula, 1968
226) Markusenko, Ivan Semenovic. *Don v Velikoj Otecestvennoj vojne.* Rostov, 1977
227) *Smolenshchina v dni voiny i v dni vosstanovleniia.* Smolensk, 1946
228) *Sovetskii Pridunaiskii krai. 1940–1945 gg.* Odessa, 1968
229) SS Wannsee Institut. *Kaukasus.* Berlin, 1942
230) *Vozorozdennyj iz ruin. Sbornik dokumentov i materialov o vosstanovlenii i razvitii g. Smolenska 1943–1962 godov.* Smolensk, 1963
231) Zaitsev, V. P. *Don v gody Vel. Otech. Voiny.* Zaporozh'e, 1959

6. Partisan War, Resistance, and Suppression

a) General Overviews

232) Abramovitch, Aaron. "La contribution des juifs soviétiques a l'écrasement du nazisme." *Le Monde Juif* no. 62, vol. 27 (1971): pp. 6–14
233) Absaljamov, M., and V. Andrianov. "Taktika sovetskich Partisan." *Voenno-Istoriceskij Zurnal* vol. 10, no. 1 (1968): pp. 42–55
234) Andrianov. "La Lutte armée des partisans soviétiques dans la Grande Guerre nationale." *Revue Historique de l'Armée* vol. 29, no. 4 (1973): pp. 88–106
235) Adrianow, Wladimir Nikolajewitsch. "Die Partisanenbewegung im Großen Vaterländischen Krieg." *Militärgeschichte* vol. 16, no. 2 (1977): pp. 158–169
236) Armstrong, John A., ed. *Soviet Partisans in World War II.* Madison, Wis., 1964
237) Artemev, Ivan Nikolajewitsch. *Pozyvnye Moskvy.* Minsk, 1978
238) Asmolov, Aleksej Nikitowitsch. *Front v tylu vermachta.* Moscow, 1977 (German edn: *Die Front im Hinterland.* East Berlin, 1987)
239) Auerbach, Hellmuth. "Die Einheit Dirlewanger." *Vierteljahrshefte für Zeitgeschichte* 10 (1962): pp. 250–263

240) Augur [pseud.]. “Die rote Partisanenbewegung.” *Allgemeine schweizerische Militärzeitung* 115 (1949): pp. 441–450, 501–516

241) Barbakov, A.A. “Partisan Movement in the Great Patriotic War of the Soviet Union.” *Revue Internationale d'Histoire Militaire* no. 44 (1979): pp. 172–180

242) Birn, Bettina. *Die höheren SS- und Polizeiführer. Himmlers Vertreter im Reich und in den besetzten Gebieten*. Düsseldorf, 1986

243) Bonwetsch, Bernd. “Sowjetische Partisanen 1941–1944. Legende und Wirklichkeit des ‘allgemeinen Volkskrieges’.” In *Partisanen und Volkskrieg. Zur Revolutionierung des Krieges im 20. Jahrhundert*, edited by Gerhard Schulz, pp. 92–124. Göttingen, 1985

244) Brodski, Josef A. “Timor und andere – Sowjetische Zwangsarbeiter im Widerstand und ihr Schicksal nach der Befreiung.” In *Europa und der “Reichseinsatz”. Ausländische Zivilarbeiter, Kriegsgefangene und KZ-Häftlinge in Deutschland 1938–1945*, edited by Ulrich Herbert, pp. 215–269. Essen, 1991

245) ____. *Vo imja pobedy nad fasizmom. Antifasitskaja bor'ba sovetskich ljudej v gitlerovskoj Germanii (1941–1945gg.)*. Moscow, 1970

246) Byckov, Lev Nikolajevic. *Partizanskoe Dvizenie v gody Velikoj Otecestvennoj Vojny 1941–1945. Kratkij ocerk*. Moscow, 1965

247) Bystrov, V. E. *Geroi Podpol'ja. O podpol'noj bor'be sovetskich patriotov v tylu nemecko-fasistskich zachvatcikov v gody Velikoj Otecestvennoj vojny*. 2 vols. Moscow, 1963; 3rd edn 1972

248) Cooper, Matthew. *The Phantom War. The German Struggle against Soviet Partisans, 1941–1944*. London, 1979

249) ____. *The Nazi War against Soviet Partisans, 1941–1944*. New York, 1979

250) De Witt, Kurt, et al. *A Survey of German Agencies Dealing with Partisan Warfare in the USSR*. Maxwell Air Force Base, 1952

251) Didvik, Praskovja. *V tylu vraga*. Kisinev, 1960

252) Dixon, Cecil Aubrey, and Otto Heilbrunn. *Communist Guerilla Warfare*. New York, 1954; London, 1954

253) Dohnanyi, Ernst von. “Combating Soviet Guerillas. (World War II).” In *The Guerilla – and How to Fight Him*, edited by T.N. Greene, pp. 201–217. New York, 1962

254) Drum, Karl. “Airpower and Russian Partisan Warfare.” In *USAF Historical Studies*, no. 117, edited by Littleton B. Atkinson et al. New York, 1968

255) “Erlebnisse mit Partisanen.” *Schweizer Militärzeitschrift* 114, vol. 12 (1948): pp. 859–872

256) Fischer, Herbert. “Probleme des militärischen Einsatzes der faschistischen Wehrmacht im Kampf gegen Partisanen.” *Zeitschrift für Militärgeschichte* 7, vol. 4 (1968): pp. 467–476

257) Gordon, Gay H. “Soviet Partisan Warfare, 1941–1944: The German Perspective.” Phil. diss., Univ. of Iowa, 1972

258) Galay, N. “The Partisan Forces.” In *The Soviet Army*, edited by Basil Henry Liddell Hart, pp. 153–171. London, 1956

259) Gridnev, Viktor Michailovic. *Borba krest'janstva okkupirovannych oblastej RSFSR protiv nemecko-fasistskoj okkupacionnoj politiki 1941–1944*. Moscow, 1976

260) *Guerilla Warfare in the Occupied Parts of the Soviet Union.* Popular Lecture Series. Moscow, 1943
261) Hawemann, Walter. *Achtung, Partisanen! Der Kampf hinter der Ostfront.* Hanover, 1953
262) Heiman, Leo. "Guerilla Warfare: An Analysis." *Military Review* vol. 43, no. 7 (1963): pp. 26–36
263) Hesse, Erich. *Der sowjetische Partisanenkrieg 1941–1944 im Spiegel deutscher Kampfanweisungen und Befehle.* Göttingen, 1969; 2nd rev. edn 1993
264) Howell, Edgar M. *The Soviet Partisan Movement, 1941–1944.* Department of the Army Pamphlet 20–244. Washington, DC, 1956
265) Jabs, Gustav. *Auf der richtigen Seite. Als Deutscher bei sowjetischen Partisanen.* East Berlin, 1960
266) *Jarost' blagorodnaja. Sbornik vospominanij partizan.* Edited by I.F. Zolotar and D.A. Sidorov. Moscow, 1963
267) Karov, D. [pseud.]. *Partisankoe dvishenie v SSSR v 1941–1945 gg.* Munich, 1954
268) Kelmsee, Peter. *Der Partisanenkampf in der Sowjetunion. Über Charakter, Inhalt und Formen des Partisanenkampfes in der UdSSR 1941–1944.* East Berlin, 1963
269) Kreidel, Hellmuth. "Über die Kampfführung im Partisanenkrieg." *Revue Militaire Generale* no. 10 (1969): pp. 696–709
270) Kuehnrich, Heinz. *Der Partisanenkrieg in Europa 1939–1945.* East Berlin, 1965
271) ____. "Zum Zusammenwirken der sowjetischen Partisanenbewegungen mit der Roten Armee, 1941–1943." *Zeitschrift für Militärgeschichte* 7, vol. 4 (1968): pp. 454–466
272) Kumanyev, G.A. "On the Soviet People's Partisan Movement in the Hitlerite Invaders' Rear, 1941–1944." *Revue Internationale d'Histoire* no. 47, pp. 180–188
273) Kurnosov, A.A. *Bor'ba sovetskich ljudej v tylu nemecko-fasistskich okkupantov (Istoriografija voprosa).* In *Istorija i istoriki. Istoriografija istorii SSSR*, pp. 169–193. Moscow 1965
274) Kusin, Il'ia. *Notes of a Guerilla Fighter.* With a Biographical Sketch by Elena Kononenko. Moscow, 1942
275) *Modern Guerilla Warfare. Fighting Communist Guerilla Movements, 1941–1961.* Edited by Franklin Mark Osanka. New York, 1962
276) Neuhaus, Wolfgang. *Kampf gegen "Sternlauf". Der Weg des deutschen Partisanen Fritz Schmenkel.* East Berlin, 1970
277) Oseraner, Michail. "Zur Teilnahme deutscher Antifaschisten an der sowjetischen Partisanenbewegung im Großen Vaterländischen Krieg." *Zeitschrift für Militärgeschichte* 8, vol. 4 (1969): pp. 469–481
278) Petrov, J.P. "Sostajanine i zadaci razrabotki istorii partizanakogo dvizenija v gody Velikoj Otcestvennoj Vojny." *Voprosy Istorii* no. 5 (1971): pp. 13–33
279) *Partijnoe Podpol'e. Dejatel'nost' podpol'nych partijnych organov i organizacij na okkupirovannoj sovetskoj territorii v gody Velikoj Otcestvennoj vojny.* Moscow, 1983
280) Ponomarenko, P., et al. *Behind the Front Lines.* London, 1945
281) Ponomarenko, P. "Soviet Partisans in the Great Patriotic War." *Soviet Military Review* no. 5 (1966): pp. 14–18; no. 6 (1966): pp. 43–46

282) Pozdniakov, Vladimir. "German Counterintelligence in Occupied Soviet Union." *Foreign Military Studies Manuscript No. P-122*, US Army Historical Division, Europe, 1952

283) Pretorius, Phil. "The Guerillas of the Soviets." *Kommando* vol. 14, no. 4 (1963): pp. 16–25

284) Pronin, Alexander. *Guerilla Warfare in the German-Occupied Soviet Territories, 1941–1944*. Ann Arbor, 1978

285) *Rear Area Security in Russia. The Soviet Second Front behind the German Lines*. Department of the Army Pamphlet no. 20-240. Washington, 1951

286) Richter, Hans. *Ordnungspolizei auf den Rollbahnen des Ostens. Bildbericht von den Einsätzen der Ordnungspolizei im Sommer 1941 im Osten, ergänzt durch kurze Erlebnisberichte*. Berlin, 1943

287) Rings, Werner. *Life with the Enemy*. London, 1982

288) Riwash, Joseph. *Resistance and Revenge, 1939–1949*. Montreal, 1981

289) Schwarz, Solomon. "Inside Occupied Russia." *New Republic* (New York), 22 February 1943

290) ____. "The Soviet Partisans and the Jews." *Modern Review* (New York), January 1949, pp. 387–400

291) Seidler, Franz W. "SS-Sondereinheit Dirlewanger. Ein Sträflingsbataillon zum Einsatz im Kampf gegen Partisanen." *Damals* 9, vol. 7 (1977): pp. 599–620

292) *Selected Soviet Sources in World War II Partisan Movement*. Maxwell Air Force Base, 1954

293) Umbreit, Hans. "Das unbewältigte Problem. Der Partisanenkrieg im Rücken der Ostfront." In *Stalingrad*, edited by Jürgen Förster, pp. 130–150. Munich, 1992

294) *We Are Guerillas. An Account of the Work of Soviet Guerillas behind the Nazi Lines*. "Soviet War News" Books, no. 3. London, 1943

295) Whittier, Henry S. "Soviet Special Operations/Partisan Warfare: Implications for Today." *Military Review* vol. 59, no. 1 (1979): pp. 48–58

296) Ziemke, Earl. *Composition and Morale of the Partisan Movement*. Maxwell Air Force Base, 1954

297) ____. *The Soviet Partisan Movement in 1941*. Maxwell Air Force Base, 1954

b) Baltic States

298) *Borba latysskogo naroda v gody Velikoj Otcestvennoj vojny 1941–1945*. Riga, 1970

299) Broszat, Martin. "Die nationale Widerstandsbewegung in Litauen 1941–1944." In *Gutachten des Instituts für Zeitgeschichte*, vol. 2, pp. 311–327. Stuttgart 1966

300) *Latviesu Tautas Cina lielaja tevijas kara (1941–1945) (Borba latysskogo naroda v gody velikoj otecestvennoj vojny 1941–1945)*. Riga, 1966

301) Gureckas, Algimantas P. "The National Resistance during the German Occupation of Lithuania." *Lituanus* vol. 8, no. 1/2 (1962): pp. 23–28

302) Levin, Dov. *Fighting Back. Lithuanian Jewry's Armed Resistance to the Nazis, 1941–1945*. New York, 1985

303) Lusys, Stasys. "The Emergence of Unified Lithuanian Resistance Movement against Occupants, 1940–1945." *Lituanus* vol. 9, no. 4 (1963)

304) Martinson, E. Ja. "Fasistskij terror v Estonii (1941–1944)." In *Nemecko-fasistskij okkupacionnyj rezim*, pp. 84–94. Moscow, 1965

305) *Na pravyi boi, na smertnyi boi*. 2 vols. Riga, 1968–1972

306) Raskevic, A.K. "Terror i prestuplenija nacistov v Latvii (1941–1944)." In *Nemecko-fasistskij okkupacionnyj rezim*, pp. 340–351. Moscow, 1965

307) Staras, P.F. *Partizanskoe dvizenie v Litve v gody Velikoj Otecestvennoj vojny*. Vilnius, 1966

c) Northern Russia

308) Abramov, M. *Bol'shevistskie gazety v tylu vraga; sbornik materialov iz podpol'nykh gazet leningradskoi oblasti v period nemetskoi okkupatsii*. Leningrad, 1946

309) _____. *Na zemle opalennoi*. Leningrad, 1968

310) Masolov, N.V., ed. *Chrabrejsie iz chrabrych. Ocerki o leningradskich partizanach - gerojach Sovetskogo Sojuza*. Leningrad, 1964

311) Nikitin, M.N., and P.I. Vagin. *The Crimes of the German Fascists in the Leningrad Region*. London, 1946

312) Petrov, Jurij Pavlovic. *Partizanskoe Dvizenie v Leningradskoj oblasti 1941–1944*. Leningrad, 1973

313) Valk, S.N., ed. Akademija Nauk SSSR, *Gorod Lenina v dni oktjabrja (1917 g.) i Velikoj Otecestvennoj Vojny 1941–1945 gg. Sbornik statej*. Moscow, 1964

314) Vinogradov, Ivan Vasil'evic. *Doroga cerez front. Zapiski partizana*. Leningrad, 1964

315) *Nepokorennaja Zemlja Pskovskaja. 1941–1944. Dokumenty i materialy*. Pskov, 1964

d) White Russia

316) Akssenov, F.V. *V ognennom koridore*. Tula, 1969

317) "Attack on a Partisan Headquarter, Lepel-Borisov, June 1943." *Infantry* vol. 53, no. 3 (1963): pp. 29–32

318) Bacilo, Fedor Afsanasevic. *Ostajus zit'. Zapiski komandira diversionnoj gruppy*. Minsk, 1981

319) Brjuchanov, Aleksej Ivanovic. *V Stabe partizanskogo dvizenija*. Minsk, 1980

320) Burke, William A. "Guerillas without Morale - The White Russian Partisans (1941–44)." *Military Review* vol. 61, no. 9 (1961): pp. 64–71

321) Chackevic, Aleksandr Fedorovic, and Roman Romanovic Krjucok. *Stanovlenie partizanskogo dvizenija v Belorussii i druzba narodov SSSR*. Minsk, 1980

322) Cholawski, Shalom. *Soldiers from the Ghetto*. San Diego, 1980

323) Dahms, Hellmuth G. "1943: Mord in Minsk. Das Attentat auf den Generalkommissar für Weißruthenien Wilhelm Kube." *Damals* 12, vol. 5 (1980): pp. 437–451; vol. 6, pp. 463–478

324) *Vsenarodnoe partizanskoe Dvizenie v Belorussii v gody Velikoj Otecestvennoj Vojny 1941–44. Dokumenty i materialy*. Minsk, 1982

325) Gora, Wladislaw, Mieczyskaw Juchniewicz, and Julian Tobiasz. *Udzial Polakow w radzieckim ruchu oporu*. Warsaw, 1972
326) Ignatenko, I.M., ed. *Vsenarodnaja Bor'ba v Belorussii protiv nemecko-fasistskich zachvatcikov v gody Velikoj Otecestvennoj vojny*. Vol. 1. Minsk, 1983
327) Institut Istorii Akad. Nauk Belorusskoj SSR. *Iz Istorii partizanskogo dvizenija v Belorussii (1941–1944 gg.) Sbornik vospominanij*. Minsk, 1961
328) Juchniewicz, Mieczislaw. *Na Wschod od Bugu. Polacy w walce antyhitlerowskiej na ziemiach ZSSR 1941–1945*. Warsaw, 1985
329) Kalinin, Petr Zacharovic. *Die Partisanenrepublik*. East Berlin, 1968
330) Kazakov, N. *Kogda gnev obzigaret serdca*. 2nd edn. Moscow, 1965
331) Manaenkov, A.L., ed. *Partizanskie Formirovanija Belorussii v gody Velikoj Otecestvennoj vojny .ijn'1941–ijl'1944*. Minsk, 1983
332) Matukovskij, Nikolaj Egorovic. *Minsk. Dokumental'naja povest'*. Moscow, 1982
333) Mulligan, Timothy P. "Reckoning the Cost of People's War: The German Experience in the Central USSR." *Russian History* vol. 9 (1982): pp. 27–48
334) *Prestupleniia nemetsko-fashiskikh okkupantov v Belorusii 1941–1944*. Compiled by Institut Istorii Akademii nauk BSSR. Minsk, 1965
335) Romanovskij, V.F. "Nacistskij terror i bezzakonija v Belorusskoj SSR." In *Nemecko-fasistskij okkupacionnyj rezim*, pp. 300–318
336) Semenova, A.V. "Istreblenie fasistskimi zachvatcikami naselenija Belorussii pod predlogom bor'by s partizanami". In *Nemecko-fasistskij okkupacionnyj rezim*, pp. 379–386. Moscow, 1965
337) Tobiasz, Julian. *Na Tylach wroga. Z dziejow wspolnej walki partyzantow polskich i radzieckich*]. Warsaw, 1966
338) Vakar, Nicholas P. *Belorussia: The Making of a Nation*. Cambridge, Mass., 1956
339) I*n den Wäldern Belorusslands. Erinnerungen sowjetischer Partisanen und deutscher Antifaschisten*. East Berlin, 1976
340) Wilenchik, Witalij. "Die Partisanenbewegung in Weißrussland, 1941–1944." In *Forschungen zur osteuropäischen Geschichte* vol. 34 (1984): pp. 129–297

e) Central Russia

341) Aleksandrovskii, P.I., and A.N. Egorev. *Partizan Frits*. Moscow, 1965
342) Gridnev, V.M. *Bor'ba krest'janstva okkupirovannych oblastei RSFSR protiv nemecko-fasistskoj okkupacionnoj politik 1941–1944*. Moscow, 1976
343) Kasatkin, Michail Andreevic. *V Tylu nemecko-fasistskich armij "Centr". Vsenarodnaja borba na okkupirovannoj territorii zapadnych oblastej RSFSR 1941–1943 gg*. Moscow, 1980
344) *Kliatvu vernosti sderzali. Partizanskoe Podmoskove v dokumentach i materialach*. Moscow, 1982
345) Kreidel, Hellmuth. "Partisanenkampf in Mittelrußland." *Revue Militaire Générale* no. 7 (1957): pp. 250–270
346) ____. "Partisanenjagd in Mittelrußland." *Revue Militaire Générale* no. 4 (1967): pp. 473–482

347) Weinberg, Gerhard L. *The Partisan Movement in the Yelnya-Dorogobuzh Area of the Smolensk Oblast*. Maxwell Air Force Base, 1954

f) Southern Russia

348) Ignatov, Petr Karpovic. *Partisanen*. East Berlin, 1953
349) ____. *Partisans of the Kuban*. London, 1946
350) Kladov, et al. *The Trial in the Case of the Atrocities Committed by the German Fascist Invaders and their Accomplices in Krasnodar, July 14–17, 1943*. Moscow, 1943
351) *The People's Verdict. A Full Report of the Proceedings at the Krasnodar and Kharkov German Atrocity Trials*. London, [ca. 1944]

g) Ukraine

352) Agurenko, B. *Dvenadtsat'*. Rostov, 1965
353) Aleksandrov, N.I. *Sevastopol'skii bronepoezd*. Simferopol', 1968
354) Bakradzde, David Il'ic. *Karpatskij Rejd*. Moscow, 1968
355) Beljavec, Vlas Fedorovic. *Doneckie Mstitell. Zapiski partizana*. Kiev, 1978
356) Bugrov, Nikolaj Nikolaevic. *Rejd v Zadneprove*. Moscow, 1964
357) Dancenkov, Fedor Semenovic. *Osoboe Porucenie*. Kiev, 1988
358) Dolzenkova, A.N., ed., *Odesskie Katakomby*. Odessa, 1973
359) Domank, A. "Vzaimodejstvie ukrainskich partizan s sovetskimi vojskami v bitve za Dnepr." *Voenno-istoriceskij zurnal* no. 9 (1983): pp. 37–41
360) Grigorovic, Dimitrij Filippovic, Vladimir Aleksandrovic Zamlinskij, and Vasilij Nikolaevic Nemajatyj. *Kommunisticeskaja Partija Ukrainy v gody Velikoj Otecestvennoj vojny*. Kiev, 1980
361) Horak, Stephan M. "L'Ukraine entre les nazis et les communistes." *Revue d'Histoire de la Deuxième Guerre Mondiale et des Conflits Contemporains* 130 (1983): pp. 65–75
362) Kanjuka, Michail. *Povest' ognennych let*. Moscow, 1981
363) Kovpak, Sidor Artemevic. *Vid Putivlja do Karpat*. Kiev, 1979
364) Kizia, L. "La lutte du peuple ukrainien." *Revue d'Histoire de la Deuxième Guerre Mondiale* 11, no. 43 (1961): pp. 21–33
365) Klokov, Vsevolod Ivanovic. *Dejstvija partizan Ukrainy na zeleznodoroznych kommunikacijach v tylu fasistskich vojsk 1941–1944*. Kiev, 1984
366) ____. *Vsenarodnaja Borba v tylu nemecko-fasistskich okkupantov na Ukraine 1941–1944. Istoriograf. ocerk 1*. Kiev, 1978
367) Koval', Michail Vasil'evic. *Borba naselenija Ukrainy protiv fasistskogo rabstva*. Kiev, 1979
368) Lebed, Mykola. *UPA: Ukrains'ka Povstans'ka Armija*. Part I, *Nimets'ka okupatsia Ukraiiny*. Vydannia Presovoho Biura UHVR, 1946
369) Makarov, Pavel Vasil'evic. *Partizany Tavrii*. Moscow, 1960
370) Makedonskij, Michail Andreevic. *Plamja nad Krymom. Vospominsnijs komandira juznogo soedinenija partizanssskich otrjadov Kryma (1941–1944)*. Simferopol', 1963
371) Martinez Codo, Henrique. "La guerilla en Ukraine." *Revue Militaire Générale* no. 5 (1963): pp. 570–592
372) Medvedev, Dimitrij. *Stout Hearts. This Happened near Rovno*. Moscow, n.d.

373) Naumov, Michail Ivanovic. *Zapadnyj Rejd. Dnevnik partizanskogo komandira*. Kiev, 1980
374) Pavliuk, E. [Evhen Stakhiv]. *Borot'ba ukrains'koho narodu na skhi dno-ukr. semiakh, 1941–1944*. Philadelphia, 1946
375) Retzlaff, Reinhard, et al. *The Trial in the Case of the Atrocities Committed by the German Fascist Invaders in the City of Kharkov and in the Kharkov Region*. Translated from the report published in Pravda, December 16–20, 1943. Moscow, 1944
376) Saburov, A.N. *Sily neiscislimye*. Moscow, 1967
377) Serman, Boris, ed. *V Katakombach Adzimuskkaja. (Dokumenty, vospominanija, stat'i)*. 2nd edn. Simferopol', 1970
378) Supreunenko, N.I. *Ukraina v Vel. Otech. voine Sovetskogo Soiuza*. Kiev, 1956
379) Zincenko, Jurij Ivanovic. *Boevoe Vzaimodejstvie partizan s castjami Krasnoj Armii na Ukraine 1941–1944*. Kiev, 1982

h) Other Areas and Regions

380) *Bojova Soivdruznist'. Zbirnik spogadiv radjanskich i chechoslovakich partizaniv*. Kiev, 1960
381) Dzuraev, Turab Dzuraevic. *Uzbekistancy – ucastniki partizanskoj vojny (1941–1945)*. Tashkent, 1975
382) Elin, Dimitrij Dimitrievic. *Partizany Moldavii. (Iz istorii partizanskogo dvizanija Moldavskogo naroda v gody Velikoj Otecestvennoj Vojny Sovetskogo Sojuza)*. Kisinev, 1974
383) Gratinic, S.A. *Fasistskij okkupacionnyj rezim i bor'ba trudjascichsja Levobereznoj Moldavii i smeznych rajonov Ukrainy protiv nemecko-rumynskich zachvatcikov (avg. 1941 – nac. 1944)*. Kisinev, 1981
384) Kazak, Vladimir Nikolaevic. *Pobratimy. Sovetskie ljudi v anti-fasistskoj borbe narodov balkanskich stran 1941–1945*. Moscow, 1975
385) Zalesskij, S., and P. Suchorukov. *Obagrennyj kovyl'*. 2nd edn. Elista, 1962

7. The Recruitment of "Hilfswillige" and Eastern Legions

386) Amirov, T. *Krakh legiona*. Alma-Ata, 1970
387) Andreyer, Catherine. *Vlasov and the Russian Liberation Movement, 1941–1945*. New York, 1987
388) Artemiev, Vyacheslav P. "Soviet Volunteers in the German Army." *Military Review* vol. 47, no. 11 (1967): pp. 56–64
389) Carnier, Pier Arrigo. *L'Armata cosacca in Italia 1944–1945*. Milan, 1990
390) Deeter, Richard E. "'Treu, tapfer, gehorsam!' The Schutzmannschaft." *Militaria* vol. 1, no. 1 (1970): pp. 11–13
391) Dwinger, Edwin Erich. *General Wlassow. Eine Tragödie unserer Zeit*. Frankfurt, 1951
392) _____. *Sie suchten die Freiheit: Schicksalsweg eines Reitervolkes*. Frankfurt, 1952
393) Elliot, Mark R. *Pawns of Yalta. Soviet Refugees and America's Role in their Repatriation*. Urbana, Ill., 1982

394) Fatalibeyli, Abo. "Azerbaidzhanskii legion v bor'be za nezavisimost'." *Svobognyi Kavkas* no. 273 (November 1951): pp. 5–10
395) Fischer, George. "General Vlasov's Official Biography." *The Russian Review* VIII (October 1949): pp. 284–301
396) ____. "Der Fall Wlassow." *Der Monat* nos. 33–35 (1951): pp. 263–279, 393–409, 519–525; also published in pamphlet form: Sonderdruck, 1951
397) ____. "Vlasov and Hitler." *Journal of Modern History* vol. 23, no. 1 (March 1951): pp. 58–71
398) ____. *Soviet Opposition to Stalin: A Case Study in World War II*. Cambridge, Mass., 1952
399) Froehlich, Sergej. *General Wlassow. Russen und Deutsche zwischen Hitler und Stalin*. Edited by Edel von Freier. Cologne, 1987
400) Hoffmann, Joachim. *Deutsche und Kalmyken 1943–1945*. Einzelschriften zur militärischen Geschichte des Zweiten Weltkrieges, vol. 14. Freiburg, 1974
401) ____. *Die Ostlegionen 1941–1943. Turkotataren, Kaukasier und Wolgafinnen im deutschen Heer*. Einzelschriften zur militärischen Geschichte des Zweiten Weltkrieges, vol. 19. Freiburg, 1981
402) ____. *Die Geschichte der Wlassow-Armee*. Einzelschriften zur militärischen Geschichte des Zweiten Weltkrieges, vol. 27. Freiburg, 1986
403) Junin, Andre. "La Defaite psychologique allemande sur le front de l'Est vue à travers le mouvement Vlassow (1942–1945)." *Revue d'Histoire de la Deuxième Guerre Mondiale* 12, no. 46 (1962): pp. 1–12
404) Kasantsev, Aleksandr. *Tret'ia sila: istoriia odnoi popytki*. Frankfurt, 1952
405) Katusev, A.F., and V.G. Oppokov. "Iudy." (Vlasovcy na sluzbe u fasizma.) *Voenno-Istoriceskij Zurnal* no. 6 (1990): pp. 68–81
406) Knight, R. "Harold Macmillan and the Cossacks: Was there a Klagenfurt Conspiracy?" *Intelligence and National Security* vol. 1, no. 2 (1986): pp. 234–254
407) Landry, Roland. "Le mouvement Vlassov." *Miroir de l'Histoire* no. 271 (1972): pp. 18–27
408) Newland, Samuel J. *Cossacks in the German Army, 1941–1945*. London, 1990
409) Parrish, Michael. "Soviet Generals in German Captivity: A Biographical Inquiry." *Survey* vol. 30, no. 4 (1989): pp. 66–86
410) Silabriedis, J., and H. Arklans. *"Political Refugees" Unmasked!* Riga, 1965
411) Steenberg, Sven. *Wlassow – Verräter oder Patriot?* Cologne, 1968
412) Strik-Strikfeldt, Wilfried. *Gegen Stalin und Hitler. General Wlassow und die russische Freiheitsbewegung*. Mainz, 1970
413) Thorwald, Jürgen. *The Illusion: Soviet Soldiers in Hitler's Armies*. New York, 1975
414) Tolstoy, Nikolai. *Victims of Yalta*. London, 1977
415) ____. *The Minister and the Massacres*. London, 1986
416) Wladimirow, W., ed. *Komitet Osvobozhdeniia Narodov Rossii*. Berlin, 1944

8. Economic Exploitation

417) Angelus, Oskar. "Wirtschaftsfragen im deutschbesetzten Estland." *Acta Baltica* vol. 16 (1976): pp. 147–171

418) Anikeev, A.A. "Die marxistische Historiographie über die Agrarpolitik des deutschen Faschismus im Zweiten Weltkrieg." *Zeitschrift für Geschichtswissenschaft* vol. 26 (1978): pp. 629–634
419) Backe, Herbert. *Die russische Getreidewirtschaft als Grundlage der Land- und Volkswirtschaft Rußlands*. Berlin, 1941
420) Bernick, Hermann. "Deutsche Pionierleistungen im Osten." In *Die Front gegen den Hunger*, pp. 82–113. Berlin, 1944
421) Birkenfeld, Wolfgang. "Illusionen am Kaukasus." In *Wissenschaft, Wirtschaft und Technik. Studien zur Geschichte*, edited by Karl-Heinz Manegold, pp. 85–91. Munich, 1969
422) Bondioli, Riccardo. *Ukraina, terra del pane*. Milan, 1941
423) Bräutigam, Otto. *Die Landwirtschaft in der Sowjetunion*. Berlin, 1942
424) Brandt, Karl, et al. *Management of Agriculture and Food in the German-Occupied and Other Areas of Fortress Europe*. Stanford, 1953
425) Buchheim, Christoph. "Die besetzten Länder im Dienste der deutschen Kriegswirtschaft. Ein Bericht der Forschungsstelle für Wehrwirtschaft." *Vierteljahrshefte für Zeitgeschichte* vol. 34 (1986): pp. 117–145
426) Buchholz, Erwin. *Die Wald- und Holzwirtschaft des Ostraumes*. Berlin, 1943
427) Czollek, Roswitha. "Estnische Phosphate im Griff der IG Farbenindustrie AG." *Jahrbuch für Wirtschaftsgeschichte* vol. 4 (1966): pp. 201–214
428) _____. "Zum Raub estnischer Ölschiefervorkommen für die deutsche Kriegswirtschaft 1941–1944." *Jahrbuch für Wirtschaftsgeschichte*, vol. 2 (1969): pp. 107–116
429) _____. *Faschismus und Okkupation. Wirtschaftspolitische Zielsetzung und Praxis des faschistischeen deutschen Besatzungsregimes in den baltischen Sowjetrepubliken während des zweiten Weltkrieges*. Akademie der Wissenschaften der DDR: Schriften des Zentralinstituts für Geschichte, vol. 39. East Berlin, 1974
430) Czollek, Roswitha, and Dietrich Eichholtz. "Die deutschen Monopole und der 22. Juni 1941. Dokumente zu Kriegszielen und Kriegsplanung führender Konzerne beim Überfall auf die Sowjetunion." *Zeitschrift für Geschichtswissenschaft* vol. 1 (1967): pp. 64–76
431) _____. "Zur wirtschaftspolitischen Konzeption des deutschen Imperialismus beim Überfall auf die Sowjetunion. Aufbau und Zielsetzung des staatsmonopolistischen Apparats für den faschistischen Beute- und Vernichtungskrieg." *Jahrbuch für Wirtschaftsgeschichte* vol. 1 (1968): pp. 141–181
432) Deutsche Arbeitsfront. Arbeitswissenschaftliches Institut. *Die Durchdringung des Ostens in Rohstoff und Landwirtschaft*. Berlin, Dezember 1941
433) _____. *Erwägungen zur Nutzung der eroberten Gebiete*. Berlin, Dezember 1941
434) _____. *Die wirtschaftlichen Möglichkeiten der Sowjetunion*. Berlin, 1941
435) _____. *Die wirtschaftsgeographische Struktur des europäischen Teiles der Sowjetunion*. Berlin, 1941
436) _____. "Der Osten als Rohstoffkammer (Bodenschätze)." Reprint in *DAF Rohstoff-Dienst* nos. 39–41 (March 1943): pp. 1415–1488
437) Deutsches Institut für Wirtschaftsforschung, ed. *Materialien zur sowjetrussischen Wirtschaftsplanung*. Die Wirtschaft der UdSSR, no. 9–10. Berlin, 1943

438) ____. *Grundzüge der sowjetischen Agrarpolitik*. Die Wirtschaft der UdSSR, no. 8. Berlin, 1944

439) Dlugoborski, Waclaw. "Economic Policy of the Third Reich in Occupied and Dependent Countries 1938–1945. An Attempt at a Typology." *Studia Historiae Oeconomicae* vol. 15 (1980): pp. 179–212

440) ____. "Die Landwirtschaft in der Sowjetunion 1941–1944. Ein Vergleich der Situation in den besetzten und unbesetzten Gebieten." In *Agriculture and Food Supply in the Second World War. Landwirtschaft und Versorgung im Zweiten Weltkrieg*, edited by Bernd Martin and Alan S. Milward, pp. 143–160. Ostfildern, 1985

441) Dlugoborski, Waclaw, and Czeslaw Madajczyk. "Ausbeutungssysteme in den besetzten Gebieten Polens und der UdSSR." In *Kriegswirtschaft und Rüstung 1939–1945*, edited by Friedrich Forstmeier and Hans-Erich Volkmann (eds.), pp. 375–416. Düsseldorf, 1977

442) Domanyts'kyi, Viktor, ed. *Sil'ske hospodarstvo Ukrainy: die Landwirtschaft in der Ukraine*. Prague, 1942

443) Dworok, Eckehard. "Konventionelle Kriegführung und kriegswirtschaftliche Zwänge. Eine Analyse ökonomischer Aspekte der deutschen Kriegführung im Zweiten Weltkrieg; insbesondere gegen die Sowjetunion." Diss., Univ. of Kassel, 1986

444) Eichholtz, Dietrich. "Wege zur Entbolschewisierung und Ent-Russung des Ostraumes. Empfehlungen des IG-Farben-Konzerns für Hitler im Frühjahr 1943, (Denkschrift von Richard Riedl)." *Jahrbuch für Wirtschaftsgeschichte* vol. 2 (1970): pp. 13–44

445) ____. *Geschichte der deutschen Kriegswirtschaft 1939–1945*. Vol. 1, *1939–1941*; vol. 2, *1941–1943*. With a chapter by Joachim Lehmann. Forschungen zur Wirtschaftsgeschichte, vol. 1. East Berlin, 1971, 1985

446) ____. "Der Raubzug des faschistischen deutschen Imperialismus zu den Erdölquellen des Kaukasus 1941–1943." *Jahrbuch für Geschichte* vol. 14 (1976): pp. 445–502

447) ____. "Die Richtlinien Görings für die Wirtschaftspolitik auf dem besetzten sowjetischen Territorium vom 8. November 1941." *Bulletin des Arbeitskreises "Zweiter Weltkrieg"* no. 1–2 (1977): pp. 73–111

448) ____. "Kriegswirtschaftliche Resultate der Okkupationspolitik des faschstischen deutschen Imperialismus 1939–1944." *Militärgeschichte* vol. 17 (1978): pp. 133–151

449) ____. "Wirtschaftspolitik und Strategie des faschistischen deutschen Imperialismus im Dnepr-Donez-Industriegebiet 1941–1943." *Militärgeschichte* vol. 18, no. 3 (1979): pp. 218–296

450) Faktorovic, Aleksandr Aleksandrovic. *Krach agrarnoj politiki nemecko-fasistskich okkupantov v Belorussii*. Minsk, 1979

451) Fröbe, Rainer. "Deutsche Wirtschaft und 'Unternehmen Barbarossa'." In *Der Mensch gegen den Menschen*, edited by Hans-Heinrich Nolte, pp. 95–110. Hanover, 1992

452) Georg, Enno. *Die wirtschaftlichen Unternehmungen der SS*. Schriftenreihe der Vierteljahrshefte für Zeitgeschichte, vol. 7. Stuttgart, 1962

453) Gerber, Berthold. *Staatliche Wirtschaftslenkung in den besetzten und annektierten Ostgebieten während des Zweiten Weltkrieges unter besonderer Berücksichtigung der treuhänderischen Verwaltung von Unternehmungen und Ostgesellschaften*. Studien des Instituts für

Besatzungsfragen in Tübingen zu den deutschen Besetzungen im Zweiten Weltkrieg, no. 17. Stuttgart, 1959

454) Gibbons, Robert Joseph. "Soviet Industry and the German War Effort, 1939–1945." Phil. diss., Yale University, 1972

455) ____. "Allgemeine Richtlinien für die politische und wirtschaftliche Verwaltung der besetzten Ostgebiete." *Vierteljahrshefte für Zeitgeschichte* vol. 25 (1977): pp. 252–261

456) Gladkov, I.A., ed. *Sovetskaja ekonomika v period Velikoj Otecestvennoj Vojny 1941–1945 gg.* Moscow, 1970

457) Greska, E.B. "Ograblenie i razorenie trudjascichsja Litovskoj SSR v period gitlerovskoj okkupacii (1941–1944)". In *Nemecko-fasistskij okkupacionnyj rezim*, pp. 249–256. Moscow, 1965

458) Hepp, Michael, ed. "Die Durchdringung des Ostens in Rohstoff- und Landwirtschaft. Vorschläge des Arbeitswissenschaftlichen Instituts der Deutschen Arbeitsfront zur Ausbeutung der UdSSR aus dem Jahre 1941." *1999. Zeitschrift für Sozialgeschichte des 20. und 21. Jahrhunderts* vol. 4 (1987): pp. 96–134

459) Herbert, Ulrich., ed. *Europa und der "Reichseinsatz". Ausländische Zivilarbeiter, Kriegsgefangene und KZ-Häftlinge in Deutschland 1938–1945*. Essen, 1991

460) Kasper, Hanns-Heinz. "Die Ausplünderung polnischer und sowjetischer Erdöllagerstätten im Gebiet der Vorkarpaten durch den deutschen Imperialismus im 2. Weltkrieg." *Jahrbuch für Wirtschaftsgeschichte* vol. 2 (1978): pp. 41–64

460a) Kehrl, Hans. *Krisenmanager im Dritten Reich. Sechs Jahre Frieden, sechs Jahre Krieg. Erinnerungen*. Düsseldorf, 1973

461) Köller, Vera. "Zur Rolle der Zentralhandelsgesellschaft Ost für landwirtschaftlichen Absatz und Bedarf mbH bei der Ausplünderung der besetzten sowjetischen Gebiete durch den deutschen Faschismus während des Zweiten Weltkrieges." In *Der deutsche Imperialismus und der Zweite Weltkrieg*, edited by Leo Stern et al., vol. 4, pp. 23–42. East Berlin, 1961

462) Kondraatenko, Ljudmila Viktorovna. *Krach ekonomiceskich planov nemecko-fasistskich zachvatcikov na Ukraine. Istoriograf. ocerk*. Kiev, 1980

463) Kotschi, Bernd. "Treuhandverwaltung in den besetzten Ostgebieten." *Ost-Europa-Markt* 24, no. 1–3 (1944): pp. 1–11

464) Looks, Hans. *Arbeitsmänner zwischen Bug und Wolga. Erlebnisberichte und Bilder vom Einsatz des jüngsten Jahrgangs an der Ostfront*. Compiled and edited by Hans Looks und Hans Fischer. Berlin, 1942

465) Müller, Rolf-Dieter. "Industrielle Interessenpolitik im Rahmen des 'Generalplans Ost'. Dokumente zum Einfluß von Wehrmacht, Industrie und SS auf die wirtschaftspolitische Zielsetzung für Hitlers Ostimperium." *Militärgeschichtliche Mitteilungen* vol. 1 (1981): pp. 101–141

466) ____. "Die Rolle der Industrie in Hitlers Ostimperium." In *Militärgeschichte. Probleme – Thesen – Wege*, edited by Manfred Messerschmidt et al., pp. 383–406. Stuttgart, 1982

467) ____. "Das Scheitern der wirtschaftlichen 'Blitzkriegsstrategie'." In *Das Deutsche Reich und der Zweite Weltkrieg*, vol. 4, pp. 936–1029. Stuttgart, 1983

468) _____. "Von der Wirtschaftsallianz zum kolonialen Ausbeutungskrieg." In *Das Deutsche Reich und der Zweite Weltkrieg*, vol. 4, pp. 98–189. Stuttgart, 1983
469) _____. "Das 'Unternehmen Barbarossa' als wirtschaftlicher Raubkrieg." In *"Unternehmen Barbarossa". Der deutsche Überfall auf die Sowjetunion 1941*, edited by Gerd R. Ueberschär and Wolfram Wette, pp. 173–196. Paderborn, 1984
470) _____. "Die Konsequenzen der 'Volksgemeinschaft': Ernährung, Ausbeutung und Vernichtung." In *Der Zweite Weltkrieg. Analysen, Grundzüge, Forschungsbilanz*, edited by Wolfgang Michalka, pp. 240–248. Munich, 1989
471) _____. "Raub, Vernichtung, Kolonisierung: Die deutsche Wirtschaftspolitik in den besetzten sowjetischen Gebieten 1941–1944." In *22. Juni 1941. Der Überfall auf die Sowjetunion*, edited by Hans Schafranek and Robert Streibel, pp. 99–111. Vienna, 1991
472) _____. "Grundzüge der deutschen Kriegswirtschaft 1939 bis 1945." In *Deutschland 1933–1945. Neue Studien zur nationalsozialistischen Herrschaft*, edited by Karl Dietrich Bracher, Manfred Funke and Hans-Adolf Jacobsen, pp. 357–376. Bonn, 1992,
473) _____, ed. *Die deutsche Wirtschaftspolitik in den besetzten sowjetischen Gebieten 1941–1943. Der Abschlußbericht des Wirtschaftsstabes Ost und Aufzeichnungen eines Angehörigen des Wirtschaftskommandos Kiew*. Deutsche Geschichtsquellen des 19. und 20. Jahrhunderts, vol. 50. Boppard, 1991
474) Oertel, Manfred. "Zur Beteiligung der Deutschen Reichsbank an der faschistischen Aggression gegen die Sowjetunion." *Militärgeschichte* vol. 5 (1981): pp. 579–586
475) Olechnovic, Galina Ivanovna. *Ekonomika Belorussii v uslovijach Velikoj Otecestvennoj vojny (1941–1945)*. Minsk, 1982
476) Pasicev, V. "K voprosy o voenno-ekonomiceskom planirovanii vojny gitlerovskim kommandovaniem." *Voenno-istoriceskij Zurnal* no. 7 (1967): pp. 66–79
477) Radandt, Hans, Lotte Zumpe, and Berthold Puchert. "Zur Rolle des deutschen Monopolkapitals bei der Okkupation im Zweiten Weltkrieg." *Bulletin des Arbeitskreises Zweiter Weltkrieg* no. 3 (1967): pp. 1–26
478) Riecke, Joachim. "Ernährung und Landwirtschaft im Kriege." In *Bilanz des Zweiten Weltkrieges. Erkenntnisse sind Verpflichtungen für die Zukunft*, pp. 329–346. Oldenburg, 1953
479) Riedel, Matthias. "Bergbau und Eisenhüttenindustrie in der Ukraine unter deutscher Besatzung 1941–1944." *Vierteljahrshefte für Zeitgeschichte* vol. 3 (1973): pp. 245–284
480) Rodewald, Hans. "Wirtschaftsbanken in der Ukraine." *Ost-Europa-Markt* 22, no. 1/2, (1942): pp. 6–10
481) Schiller, Otto. *Ziele und Ergebnisse der Agrarordnung in den besetzten Ostgebieten*. Berlin, November 1943
482) Schustereit, Hartmut. "Planung und Aufbau der Wirtschaftsorganisation Ost vor dem Rußlandfeldzug-Unternehmen 'Barbarossa' 1940/41." *Vierteljahrsschrift für Sozial- und Wirtschaftsgeschichte* 70 (1983): pp. 50–70

483) Seraphim, Hans-Jürgen. "Die Eingliederung der Landwirtschaft des Donau- und Schwarzmeerraumes in die werdende kontinentaleuropäische Wirtschaftsgemeinschaft." *Donaueuropa. Zeitschrift für die Probleme des europäischen Südostens* 2 (1942): pp. 403–418
484) Shovheniv, Ivan. *Die Wasserwirtschaft in der Ukraine*. Berlin, 1942
485) Sinicyna, N.I. "Proval gitlerovskoj agrarnoj politiki na okkupirovannoj territorii Sovetskogo Sojuza (1941–1944 gg.)" Diss. phil., Moscow, 1972
486) ____. Tomin, V.R. "Proval agrarnoj politiki gitlerovcev na okkupirovannoj territorii SSSR, 1941–1944 gg." *Voprosy Istorii* vol. 40, no. 6 (1965): pp. 32–44
487) Sorokin, G.M. "Obscie voprosy nemecko-fasistskoj ekonomiceskoj politiki." In *Nemecko-fasistskij okkupacionnyj rezim*, pp. 151–168. Moscow 1965
488) Stock, Jürgen. "Der deutsche Landwirtschaftsführer als Pionier des Fortschritts." *Deutsche Agrarpolitik* 1, no. 7/8 (1943): pp. 234–236
489) *Taschenfahrplan für die östliche Ukraine nebst Anschlußstrecken und den wichtigsten Fernverbindungen*. Dokumente zur Eisenbahngeschichte, vol. 13. Reprint of August 1942 edn. Mainz, 1980
490) Telegin, F. N. "Ispol'zovanie fasistskoj Germaniej ekonomiceskogo potenciala okkupirovannych i zavisimych gosudarstv Evropy vo troroj mirovoj vojne." Diss. phil., Moscow, 1972
491) Verein deutscher Wirtschaftswissenschaftler. *Osteuropäische Wirtschaftsfragen. Vorträge gehalten auf der Tagung zu Weimar vom 1.–3. Oktober 1942*. Leipzig, 1944
492) Virnyk, D. F. "Razrusenie i razgrablenie nemecko-fasistskimi zachvatcikami nacional'nych bogatstv Ukrainskoj SSR." In *Nemecko-fasistskij okkupacionnyj rezim*, pp. 168–186
493) Volin, Lazar. "The 'New Agrarian Order' in Nazi-Invaded Russia." *Foreign Agriculture*, vol. 7 (April 1943): pp. 75–84
494) Volkmann, Hans-Erich. "Die Sowjetunion im ökonomischen Kalkül des Dritten Reiches 1933–1941." In *"Unternehmen Barbarossa"*, edited by Roland G. Foerster, pp. 89–107. Munich, 1993
495) Voznesenskii, Nikolai. *The Economy of the U.S.S.R. during World War II*. Washington, DC, 1948
496) Werpup, Josef. "Ziele und Praxis der deutschen Kriegswirtschaft in der Sowjetunion, 1941 bis 1944, dargestellt an einzelnen Industriezweigen." Diss. phil., Bremen, 1992
497) Wiedemeyer, Gerhard. *Ukraine – Brot für Europa*. Berlin, 1942
498) Zagorul'ko, Maksim Matveevic, and Andrej Fedorovic Judenkov. *Krach ekonomiceskich planov fasistskoj Germanii na vremenno okkupirovannoj territorii SSSR*. Moscow, 1970
499) ____. *Krach plana "Ol'denburg". O sryve ekonomiceskich planov fasistskoj Germanii na okkupirovannoj territorii SSSR*. Moscow, 1974, 1980
500) Zalesskij, A.I. "Byt krest'janstva v uslovijach nemecko-fasistskoj okkupacii Belorussii." In *Nemecko-fasistskij okkupacionnyj rezim*, pp. 240–248. Moscow, 1965
501) ____. *Sovetskii patriotizm krest'ianstva v usloviiakh nemetsko-fashistskoi okkupatsii Belorussii. (1941–1944)*. Minsk, 1963

9. The Recruitment of "Ostarbeiter" and their Fate

502) Ansbacher, Heinz L. "The Problems of Interpreting Attitude Survey Data: A Case Study of the Attitude of Russian Workers in Wartime Germany." *Public Opion Quarterly* XIV (1950): pp. 126–136

503) *Arbeitseignung und Leistungsfähigkeit der Ostarbeiter in Deutschland.* Arbeitswissenschaftliches Institut der Deutschen Arbeitsfront, Berlin, 1944

504) *Arbeitseinsatz der Ostarbeiter in Deutschland. Vorläufiger Bericht zur Untersuchung des Arbeitswissenschaftlichen Instituts über Arbeitseignung und Leistungsfähigkeit der Ostarbeiter.* Berlin, 1943

505) "Der Arbeitseinsatz der Ostvölker in Deutschland." In *Arbeit und Wirtschaft*, edited by Schulungsamt der Deutschen Arbeitsfront, vol. 5–9 (1942): pp. 43–72

506) Bethell, Nicholas. *Das letzte Geheimnis. Die Auslieferung russischer Flüchtlinge an die Sowjets durch die Alliierten 1944–1947.* Frankfurt, 1980

507) Brodski, Josef A. "Die Teilnahme sowjetischer Patrioten an der antifaschistischen Widerstandsbewegung in Süddeutschland 1943–1945." In *Der deutsche Imperialismus und der zweite Weltkrieg*, edited by Leo Stern et al., vol 4, pp. 67–100. East Berlin, 1960

508) ____. *Die Lebenden kämpfen. Die illegale Organisation Brüderliche Zusammenarbeit der Kriegsgefangenen, BSW.* East Berlin, 1968

509) ____. *Im Kampf gegen den Faschismus. Sowjetische Widerstandskämpfer in Hitlerdeutschland 1941–1945.* East Berlin, 1975

510) Czollek, Roswitha. "Zwangsarbeit und Deportationen für die Kriegsmaschine in den baltischen Sowjetrepubliken (WK II)." *Jahrbuch für Wirtschaftsgeschichte* vol. 2 (1970): pp. 45–68

511) Demps, Laurenz. "Zahlen über den Einsatz ausländischer Zwangsarbeiter in Deutschland im Jahre 1943." *Zeitschrift für Geschichtswissenschaft* vol. 21 (1973): pp. 830–843

512) Ewerth, Lutz. "Der Arbeitseinsatz von Landbewohnern besetzter Gebiete des Ostens und Südostens im Zweiten Weltkrieg." Diss. phil., Tübingen, 1954

513) Fried, John E. *The Exploitation of Foreign Labor by Germany.* Montreal, 1945

514) Gawenus, Fritz. "Die Ausbeutung ausländischer Arbeitskräfte unter besonderer Berücksichtigung deportierter Sowjetbürger durch die deutschen Monopolisten. Vorwiegend dargestellt am Beispiel der Bayerischen Stickstoffwerke AG Werk Piesteritz und der Gummi-Werke 'Elbe' AG Piesteritz von 1939 bis 1945." Diss. phil., Halle-Wittenberg, 1973

515) Gestwa, Klaus. "'Es lebe Stalin' – Sowjetische Zwangsarbeiter nach Ende des Zweiten Weltkrieges. Das Beispiel der Stadt Hamm in Westfalen." *Geschichte in Wissenschaft und Unterricht* vol. 44 (1993): pp. 71–86

516) Grossmann, Anton. "Polen und Sowjetrussen als Arbeiter in Bayern 1939–1945." *Archiv für Sozialgeschichte* vol. XXIV (1984): pp. 335–398

517) Haas, Ludwig. *Auswahl und Einsatz der Ostarbeiter. Psychologische Betrachtungen, Leistung und Leistungssteigerung.* Saarbrücken, 1944

518) Herbert, Ulrich. *Fremdarbeiter. Politik und Praxis des "Ausländer-Einsatzes" in der Kriegswirtschaft des Dritten Reisches.* Berlin, 1985

519) Homze, Edward L. *Foreign Labor in Nazi Germany*. Princeton, 1967
520) Jacobmeyer, Wolfgang. *Vom Zwangsarbeiter zum Heimatlosen Ausländer. Die Displaced Persons in Westdeutschland 1945–1951*. Göttingen, 1985
521) Kannapin, Hans-Eckhardt. *Wirtschaft unter Zwang. Anmerkungen und Analysen zur rechtlichen und politischen Verantwortung der Deutschen Wirtschaft unter der Herrschaft des Nationalsozialismus, besonders im Hinblick auf den Einsatz und die Behandlung von ausländischen Arbeitskräften und Konzentrationslagerhäftlingen in deutschen Industrie- und Rüstungsbetrieben*. Cologne, 1966
522) Lindemann, Erika. "Die Arbeitsbedingungen der nichtdeutschen Arbeitskräfte im Reichsgebiet." Diss. phil., Berlin, 1944
523) Müller, Rolf-Dieter. "Die Zwangsrekrutierung von 'Ostarbeitern' 1941–1944." In *Der Zweite Weltkrieg. Analysen, Grundzüge, Forschungsbilanz*, edited by Wolfgang Michalka, pp. 772–783. Munich, 1989
524) ____. "Die Rekrutierung sowjetischer Zwangsarbeiter für die deutsche Kriegswirtschaft." In *Europa und der "Reichseinsatz". Ausländische Zivilarbeiter, Kriegsgefangene und KZ-Häftlinge in Deutschland 1938–1945*, edited by Ulrich Herbert, pp. 234–250. Essen, 1991
525) Oermann, Josef. *Die arbeitsrechtliche und steuerrechtliche Behandlung der Ostarbeiter*. Berlin, 1944
526) Pfahlmann, Hans. *Fremdarbeiter und Kriegsgefangene in der deutschen Kriegswirtschaft 1939–1945*. Darmstadt, 1968
527) Poljan, Pavel, and Zanna A. Zajonckovskaja. "Ostarbeiter in Deutschland und daheim. Ergebnisse einer Fragebogenanalyse." *Jahrbuch für Geschichte Osteuropas* vol. 41, no. 4 (1993): pp. 547–561
528) Rode, Fritz. *Der Arbeitseinsatz der Ostvölker in Deutschland*. Berlin, 1943
529) Slin'ko, I.I. "Ugon naselenija Ukrainy v fasistskoe rabstvo." In *Nemecko-fasistskij okkupacionnyj rezim*, pp. 219–230. Moscow, 1965
530) United States Office of Strategic Services. *Foreign Labor in Germany*. Research and Analysis Report, no. 1923. Washington, 24 October 1944
531) Weidner, Marcus. *Nur Gräber als Spuren. Das Leben und Sterben von Kriegsgefangenen und Fremdarbeitern in Münster während der Kriegszeit 1939–1945*. Münster, 1984
532) Zemskov, V. N. "K voprosu o repatriacii sovetskich grazdan 1944–1951 gody." *Istorija SSSR*, no. 4 (1990): pp. 26–41

Part E

THE RESULTS OF THE WAR AND COMING TO TERMS WITH THEM

1. The Results of the War

(Rolf-Dieter Müller)

Hitler's Eastern campaign brought down infinite suffering on both sides, while consuming vast amounts of strength and energy. The immense consequences of the war proved a heavy burden for both Germans and Soviets to bear for many years to come. In terms of life and health, material goods, job opportunities, and life opportunities, the Soviets suffered far more than the Germans. The Soviet Union did acquire new territories and extracted reparations, but these benefits soon proved of doubtful value. Moscow assumed a new role on the world political stage, but the burdens it imposed led, forty years later, to the collapse of the Soviet Union, especially as a result of the arms race and the Cold War.

It was apparent from the beginning of the Soviet campaign on 22 June 1941 that this war could only end in the annihilation of one of the two combatants. Hitler's dark foreboding that defeat for the Wehrmacht would spell the destruction of the German people was shared by the political elite and much of the general population. It was therefore easy for Nazi propagandists to persuade their countrymen that a victory for Bolshevism meant the enslavement and extermination of the German nation.

As the Red Army ground closer, Goebbels painted ever more excruciating scenes of horror. This propaganda was directed not only at his own people but at the Western Allies, whom he hoped to persuade that Germany was essential to them as a "bulwark against Bolshevism." The gloomy conviction among Nazi leaders that Stalin would show himself merciless in victory was occasionally pierced by glimmers of hope. This occurred for the first time after the Battle of Stalingrad, when Moscow adopted a conservative, nationalistic policy and apparently signaled that an arrangement could be reached. Hitler himself always resisted any feelers in this direction, for he knew that any weakening of the "inner front" could lead to a quick collapse, which he personally could not possibly survive. It may be that Hitler's principal motivation was his fear of being paraded before a victorious Stalin.

The fanatic continuation of the senseless war in the East, allegedly in defense of the German civilian population, only exacerbated the conditions that prevailed once the Soviets began their inexorable sweep through the Reich. The ferocious struggle, with all its deprivations and losses, inevitably rebounded on German civilians in loss of life, health, and property. The Soviets intended to ideologically transform any parts of Germany that fell under their control. Even if Germans were placed in positions of authority, as Poles were in Poland, there would be no reduction in the hardships to bear. If the western part of Germany fell into the hands of Western Allies, with their contrasting social and political system, Germany would inevitably be torn asunder and become the chief venue for future conflicts between the victorious Allied nations.

At first, however, the Allies remained true during their wartime conferences to their goal of joint administration of the conquered Reich. Stalin was therefore bound by his agreements with the Western Allies and did not have a totally free hand toward Germany and the occupation. The Allies' official commitment to preserving German unity encouraged him, however, to move quickly to establish a Communist regime in the Soviet zone in the hope of working toward a revolution in the rest of Germany. The "Ulbricht Group" of leading German Communists was accordingly dispatched very soon to East Berlin (Nos. 42, 49, 70).

In their studies of the transitional phase from the war to the postwar period, or from the spring of 1945 to the establishment of two German states, historians are virtually unanimous in seeing Hitler's Eastern campaign as the genesis of the upheavals in central Europe. Controversies erupted, however, over responsibility for the breakup of the anti-Hitler coalition and for the division of Germany. These controversies simmered for more than four decades, as part and parcel of the political and ideological struggle between the two great postwar blocs (Nos. 23, 32, 53).

Western historians were convinced that Stalin intended from the outset, in accordance with his hopes for world revolution, to sovietize eastern Germany and that these ambitions did not end on the banks of the Elbe. The Western powers were compelled, therefore, to resist this expansionism and protect their occupation zones. West German historians and experts on eastern Europe, who had earned their academic reputations under the Third Reich, soon assumed a leading role in the elaboration of this view. Typical of this was Boris Meissner and his book on Soviet policy toward Germany from 1943 to 1953, which became a standard work in the 1950s and 1960s (No. 56). Although he attempted to provide an accurate description based on documentary evidence, Meissner did not, of course, have access to reliable Soviet sources. Other leading studies also relied heavily on Western publications, especially those of the State Department in Washington, as the basis for their analysis of Soviet policy toward Germany (Nos. 23, 67).

Meanwhile, Communist historians blamed Western imperialism for the division of Germany, the creation of a "reactionary" West German state, and the betrayal of the wartime coalition. For decades they praised to the skies the political changes wrought in the Soviet zone and the inclusion of the GDR in the Soviet orbit. The Communists presented themselves as the real champions of German unity until the late 1960s, when Bonn's détente policies seemed to lead to the final establishment of two separate German states (No. 8).

As the propaganda battle continued, the Soviets published a number of records from their archives – for instance, the minutes of the wartime conferences, key German Communist party documents on German-unity policy, and documents and materials of the German Communist émigrés in the Ulbricht Group in Moscow.

On the basis of these still inadequate sources, the West German political scientist Hans-Peter Schwarz attempted in 1966 a new, comprehensive analysis of Allied and Soviet policy toward Germany (No. 71). He showed that between the initial Nazi attack on the Soviet Union and the final capitulation, the Soviet leaders wavered between their commitment to eradicate German fascism hand in hand with the English-speaking countries and the temptation to reach an arrangement with a German government that did not include Hitler, though without abandoning the ideological struggle. This ambivalence opened a window of opportunity for the Germans to seek Stalin's protection or enter into an alliance with him in order to limit the consequences of the war and possibly escape collective responsibility for the events of the campaign. Schwarz's research convinced him of the influence that German Communists held over Stalin's plans for Germany in 1944 and over their implementation after the war. Massive publications of U.S. and British documents led to the publication of cut versions of the Soviet documents, so that endless secondary literature resulted. The pioneer study of the relations between the USSR and the Western powers in the Second World War by William H. MacNeill, first edited in 1953, was reprinted in 1970 and is still valuable (No. A/502). The most important memoirs are those of James R. Deane, formerly head of the U.S. military mission in Moscow (No. A/469a). Special efforts were made to describe the aid to Russia during the war (Nos. A/487, 483) and the military cooperation (Nos. A/496, A/466) and on the other side the "unfriendly" policy of Stalin, in regard to not only the German question and the partition of Europe but also the repatriation of Soviet refugees (No. A/470) and particularly the Polish question (No. A/469).

The discussion of Stalin's policy toward Germany was given renewed impetus by the *Ostpolitik* pursued by the Federal Republic after the mid-1960s. Alexander Fischer, an expert on Eastern Europe, published another overview of the entire question in 1972, at the height of the domestic political debate over Bonn's *Ostverträge*, or treaties with the Eastern countries (No. 32). He continued Schwarz's approach, using more sources. It became clear, in the course of this research, that the Soviet leaders had never viewed Germany during the war as solely a military problem but rather as a leading political problem as well. Fischer claimed that Soviet policy toward Germany was certainly permanently affected by the attack of 22 June 1941, but not transformed. Though driven by Hitler's "betrayal" into an alliance with the Western powers, Moscow was always on the lookout for alternatives in order to reach a separate peace. Fischer distinguished five phases: first, a mixture of ideology and political calculation in 1941–42; second, toying with a possible separate peace in 1942–43; third, a nationalistic, conservative approach with the founding of the National Committee for Free Germany in 1943; fourth, the anti-German alliance of 1943–44; and, finally, the development and implementation of an antifascist program in 1944–45.

At the end of the war, the victorious Allies agreed on the need for fundamental change in Germany, but no concrete agreements had been reached on how to carry this out. The air of uncertainty spread to the German population and led to feelings of deep despondency. Soviet occupation officers reported in late May 1945 widespread "fear of the Russians," resulting from years of propaganda and a surreptitious scorn for Slavs. The horrors inflicted upon many German civilians as the Red Army ground westward galvanized these feelings and stirred fear of "sovietization" and the dictatorship of the Communist party.

Alexander Fischer emphasized that by the late summer of 1945 a certain clarification had begun to set in, which determined the further course of history. Despite all Stalin's public affirmations of German unity and "anti-Fascist, democratic" reconstruction, Soviet officers together with German Communists and "so-called anti-Fascists" had already initiated some Marxist-Leninist experiments that threatened the unity of the country and risked a cold war.

Apart from its academic value, Fischer's standard work can also be seen as a reaction to the internal debate in the Federal Republic of Germany in the early 1970s and to the intense controversies at universities over fascism theories. This is also true of the great study by the Berlin historian Ernst Nolte, in which he highlighted the role of the Cold War in the division of Germany (No. 67). Neither of these historians seemed much influenced by the revisionist school in the United States, which was already causing a considerable stir and which, in reaction to the American involvement in Vietnam, claimed that American political strategy during the Second World War was largely responsible for the outbreak of the Cold War and the division of Germany.[1] A more moderate position was articulated by Wilfried Loth in his comprehensive and much republished analysis of the processes that led to the division of the world into two blocs (No. A/495).

The mounting research since the 1970s into the postwar period has clearly shown that the Western powers were also interested in "taming" and dividing Germany. By now, the reasons for the collapse of the anti-Nazi coalition and its disagreements over Germany were seen in a much more differentiated light. In his well-documented overview of German postwar history, intended for a wider audience, Christoph Kleßmann claimed

1. See, for instance, Gabriel Kolko, *The Politics of War* (London, 1969), and David Horowitz, *Kalter Krieg: Hintergründe der US-Außenpolitik von Jalta bis Vietnam,* 2 vols. (Berlin, 1969), and the overview by Werner Link, "Die amerikanische Außenpolitik aus revisionistischer Sicht," *Neue Politische Literatur* 16 (1971): 205–20.

that further cooperation among the wartime Allies was not doomed to failure from the outset, despite all the differences and contradictions among them (No. 45). All the Allied powers were prepared to pursue a "positive policy toward Germany." However, while Great Britain and the United States had barely developed any concrete ideas before the Potsdam Conference, Stalin already had firm concepts and political personnel in place in the Soviet zone. The interpretation of Loth was criticized by many other experts but recently confirmed by the memoirs of Wladimir S. Semjonow, the political adviser to the high command of the Soviet occupation army in Germany in 1945 and later one of the most important men in Soviet foreign policy. Semjonow stated that Stalin had wanted a consensus with the Western powers in the German question, and a transfer of the Soviet system had not been on the timetable, nor was it systematically prepared (No. 73). This was the main reason why deep cleavages soon developed between the Allies. Most historians felt that it was not "objective" differences between the Allies that led to the Cold War so much as false perceptions on both sides and reactions to the measures taken by the other side. One of the key reasons for the ensuing forty years of Cold War might well have been the Soviet attitude toward Germany and the occupation at the end of the war, which was itself not only a reaction to the Eastern campaign waged by the Nazis but also a result of the influence and willfulness of the German Communists.

The collapse of the Communist realm in 1989–90 has done nothing to change this assessment. Apart from details, only a few important new sources and insights have been gained from opening the archives in the former GDR and from the still-difficult access to Russian archives. These sources enabled Wilfried Loth to buttress his assertions in a new, much acclaimed work (Nos. 8a, 51a).

According to Loth, Stalin never intended to install a Socialist state on German soil but rather a parliamentary democracy along the lines of the Weimar Republic. He hoped that this would give the Soviet Union access to the resources of the Ruhr. It would also have afforded him an attractive opportunity to gain influence over the political and economic potential of all Germany and bring it to bear against the Western powers. Stalin's efforts in this direction were frustrated partly because of Western attempts to curtain off their zones and partly because of "Walter Ulbricht's revolutionary fervour." In Loth's view, Soviet policy toward Germany in the first few years after the war was riven with contradictions, which enabled the first president of the GDR to succeed in imposing a Communist rump state in a "frenzy of class warfare." Individual representatives of the Soviet military administration obviously played a crucial role in this, especially the chief of Information Administration, Colonel Sergei Tjulpanov. He worked very closely with Ulbricht and probably had the support of influential circles in Moscow. Final conclusions about the way in which decisions were made in the Kremlin will probably have to await the disclosure of new sources.

Many studies have been published about the effects of the war on Germany, but little is known so far about the immediate effects of the war on the people of the Soviet Union and about its influence on Soviet policy in the postwar period.

The most enduring effect of the Eastern campaign and Hitler's megalomania was the division of Germany. On the other hand, the reconstruction and political transformation of the two German states that emerged were virtually complete within a decade. Another consequence of the war struck the Germans like a whiplash – an act of revenge carried out and encouraged by the Russians and tolerated by the Western powers, although they never legitimized it: the expulsion of more than eleven million inhabitants from the German lands east of the Oder and Neisse as well as of the ethnic German minorities who had lived in the countries of eastern Europe for centuries (Nos. 119a, b). The expulsions hit the Germans harder than any other consequences of the war and had an extensive impact on German society, including on relations with its neighbors. However, even this drama was over in a relatively short time. The social consequences were dealt with quickly and the political consequences kept in check. The annexation of Germany's Eastern territories by Poland and the Soviet Union and the expulsion of its German inhabitants have remained enduring consequences of the war, even after the restoration of German unity in 1990, and have apparently been accepted by Germans as the price of national unity.

The flight and expulsion of Germans from eastern Europe at the end of the Second World War or in its immediate aftermath are part of the great migrations in Europe that prompted profound social and political change in the 1940s (No. 114). In their historical studies of these events, Germans devoted themselves with much fanfare to their role as victims, with little said for decades about their role as agents in the flight and expulsion of other peoples. A recent bibliography on the expulsion of the Germans contained nearly 5,000 titles in the German language (No. 104). On the other hand, in other countries the fate visited upon millions of Germans at the end of the war was for many years of less interest. The topic was obscured for many by the fact that the expellees chose as their spokespersons men who had been, during the war, expellers themselves. Individual works that did appear, such as that of the Italian Marco Picone Chiodo, were based for the most part on West German studies (No. 99). In the formerly Communist countries of Eastern Europe, a willingness to acknowledge the injustice done to thousands upon thousands of German-speaking fellow citizens is only now beginning to crystallize. The willingness to take a fresh look at national history has progressed furthest in the Czech Republic and Hungary but is still rudimentary in Poland and even less developed in the new states of the former Soviet Union (No. 119a).

The first period of intensive German research into the expulsions lasted until about the end of the 1950s. In addition to basic statistical work and the securing of sources, which can be found in the extensive collections of the *Bundesarchiv* in Koblenz, the emphasis was on the publication of individual memoirs. The most important result of this activity was the large, government-published *Dokumentation der Vertreibung der Deutschen aus Ost-Mitteleuropa* (No. 100a). When the social integration of the refugees was completed in the 1960s, academic interest died down, leaving a largely isolated stream of so-called *Vertriebenenliteratur*, or expellee literature, that was often all too focused on individual fates and marred by politically distorted memories and polemics. This genre of literature swung between bitter laments over the injustice that had been suffered (and that was generally seen in isolation from the historical context) and justified pride over the successful integration of the expellees into West German society (No. 104).

Since the mid-1980s, a more even-handed, academic approach to the expulsions has emerged against a backdrop of changed political circumstances and improved access to records (Nos. 97, 101, 113). Even in the GDR, people began to study the formerly taboo topic of the expulsions and to boast about the successful integration (No. 109). The intensified research at the same time into the Nazi policies of destruction and annihilation placed the fate of the German expellees in the context of Hitler's aggressive war for *Lebensraum* in the USSR. In addition, the focus of the research was broadened to include all German population movements over the last 200 years, and the German expellees were put in the context of other large, often violent expulsions and migrations in the twentieth century. A leading example of this was the omnibus volume published by Klaus J. Bade in 1992 entitled *Migration in Geschichte und Gegenwart* (No. 96).

Not only does the study examine German migration into eastern Europe since the Middle Ages and overseas during the last century, but it also looks at various waves of immigrants coming into Germany. This places the flight and expulsion of Germans after 1945 in a new light. In addition, some interdisciplinary research had begun. For example, the ethnologist Albrecht Lehmann succeeded, using new methodological approaches and methods of presentation, in clarifying the difficult problems faced by expellees in integrating into West German society (No. 106). This achievement was historically unique in the number of people involved and the extent of the success, although it entailed enormous human suffering as well, as can be seen in Lehmann's sensitive analysis of the interviews carried out. Literary critics have also taken a new-found interest in the phenomenon of lost homelands and their portrait in fiction (No. 103a).

The British historian Walter Laqueur pointed out that as many as fifty million people were driven from their homelands in Europe as a result of the Second World War, either temporarily or permanently. This amounted, he said, to the greatest population movement since the Great Migrations more than one and a half millennia ago (No. 105a). Obviously, eastern and central Europe were more deeply affected by these new Great Migrations prompted by Hitler's war in the East. These migrations included the resettlement of 600,000 Germans in 1939–41, the expulsion of seven million Poles to the East, the deportation of 8 million foreign forced laborers and prisoners of war, and the genocide of the Jews. Finally, more than eleven million Germans fled or were deported at the end of the war, while 6.5 million "Displaced Persons," mostly east Europeans, waited in occupied Germany to return home.

All these people were part of the swirls of humanity churned up in eastern Europe during the Second World War for a variety of reasons, ranging from voluntary or involuntary flight or evacuation in the face of approaching enemy armies to population transfers carried out by their own or foreign governments. These enormous population movements, which remain unique in the world in their extent, were already nearing their zenith in 1941 when Stalin ordered the evacuation and more than fifteen million people had left the western parts of the Soviet Union

(No. D/473, p. 519). These evacuations included not only mass murder, especially in the Baltic states, but also forced expulsions, especially the deportations of 650,000 ethnic Germans living in the Soviet Union.

The reversal in the fortunes of war on the Eastern Front created a new situation. As the German columns retreated westward, they were preceded or accompanied by waves of people who had left their homes. These waves were a motley mixture of deportees, deserters, collaborators, and ethnic Germans, in addition to prisoners of war and concentration camp inmates. When they reached the German border in the summer of 1944, the authorities had considerable difficulty trying to stop them and bring some order to their ranks. The authorities adopted a new approach: the evacuees and refugees would join the local population in eastern and southeastern Europe in forming an anti-Bolshevik "human barricade" to stabilize the front. If these people should consequently become caught up in the Soviet war machinery or in the bowels of Stalinist policy, their fates would serve as a warning and as propaganda directed at the Western Allies.

What happened on the roads of eastern Europe in the last few months of the war? As the Red Army advanced, millions of people struggled westward on foot or in peasant carts: soldiers, stragglers, refugees, deportees. Behind the Red Army, the swarms moved in the opposite direction as evacuees and resistance fighters returned home or as population groups were deported or expelled for political reasons. The German refugees and expellees should be seen as part of these mass movements.

However, in the postwar German literature on expulsions, the fate of foreign expellees and refugees was largely overlooked. Nothing had changed in this by the mid-1980s, when the renowned Cologne historian Andreas Hillgruber (who had himself lost his East Prussian homeland as a twenty-year-old) laid out plans for a full overview of the "Catastrophe in the German East in the Winter of 1944–45." However, his insistence that the phenomenon of flight and expulsion should be seen in the entire context of German and European history in order to overcome a narrow focus of the reams of specialized literature soon gave way to the perspective of the German victims. One of his conclusions was much contested in the so-called *Historikerstreit*, or historians' dispute, namely:

> When historians look at the winter catastrophe of 1944–45, there is only one position they can adopt, even though it may be difficult in

> individual cases. They must identify with what was actually happening to the German population in the east and with the desperate, self-sacrificing efforts of the German navy and eastern army to save the population from orgies of revenge at the hands of the Red Army – mass rape, wanton murder, and arbitrary deportations – and to hold open in the final phase of the war an escape route to the west for eastern Germans, either by land or by sea. (No. A/532, p. 24f.)

It is time to abandon linear views (German eastward expansion on one hand, Soviet westward expansion on the other) and a narrow, national focus. An emphasis on the common tragedy of being uprooted from one's home can contribute to political reconciliation and to broadening our academic horizons. Eastern Europe could then be seen as a part of the European continent whose underdevelopment, in comparison with central and Western Europe, was exacerbated by the Second World War, which left it torn and scattered.

The main reason for this was the war unleashed by the Germans, although the whirlwind they sowed helped precipitate other storms as well. It is important to remember that for every German refugee or expellee there were two eastern Europeans who suffered a similar fate. They fled their homes or were driven from them by Stalinistic or nationalistic forces. The suffering of the Germans must therefore be seen in the context of the enormous upheavals in eastern and southeastern Europe, which were tamed for decades by the "Iron Curtain" but have again begun to make themselves felt. More studies need to be done of the deeper reasons for the political, social, religious, and national volatility of eastern and southeastern Europe, which may be an effect of their delayed development in comparison with central and Western Europe.

Insofar as Germans were concerned, these events have been well documented. However, in contrast to the innumerable publications about eastern Germans, very little attention has been paid to the suffering of other peoples, even of the ethnic Germans in the Soviet Union (No. D/106). There is very little in the German records about the fate of other refugees and deportees. One eyewitness account from Moravia states that after the Red Army arrived, "former Russian prisoners-of-war and forced laborers were promptly seized and subjected to very severe military drill" (No. 119b, p. 284), but such descriptions are few and far between.

Apparently, very little was written down about these events. Until the collapse of the USSR, they were taboo in the Soviet sphere of influence. Any historical documents or reports remained locked away. This is beginning to change now, but it will take many years before historians in the countries of the former Soviet Union and in the former East Bloc produce reliable accounts of these aspects of their national histories.

After the war, more than 400,000 Germans were deported to the East as "reparations deportees" or "contractual re-settlers." The fate of the forced evacuees and refugees from eastern Europe whom the Wehrmacht abandoned behind the "eastern barricade" remains largely unknown. As it surged westward, the Red Army overran more than three million of these people, mostly women and children. For the most part, those who could work had been admitted to Germany as Eastern laborers or prisoners of war (No. D/520). In order to deal with these people and investigate them, a "People's Repatriation Commissariat" was established in Moscow in the fall of 1944. Its records have only recently become available (No. D/527). After the war, 4.3 million of these people passed through "filtering camps." Of these, about 1.8 million were former prisoners of war.[2] One-third of them were drafted into the army, and twenty percent were placed in "worker battalions" for forced labor. Older people were sent home, but younger people had to spend six years in so-called special settlements. Some one to two percent were punished as war criminals or traitors. This fate was suffered both by men who had been forcibly recruited by the Germans and by many of the 750,000 volunteers and collaborators. Women were spared the ultimate punishment, but they were subjected to stiff discrimination for decades on end.

After this eastward flow of millions of people ended, the pause in the westward flow lasted only a few years. Today, hundreds of thousands are again moving westward every year, with no end in sight. This is apparently a "natural" coming together of the highly developed industrial societies in Western and central Europe and the societies of eastern Europe, an exchange of ideas and people that breaks down national barriers and sparks developments from which everyone can benefit. The Nazi attempt to join East and West under the banner of inhuman racism, with Germanic lords ruling over Slavic helots, collapsed in 1945 in an

2. According to the most recent figures of the Russian general staff, 1,836,000 prisoners of war were repatriated after the war. See *Nicht mehr geheim: Verluste der sowjetischen Streitkräfte in Kriegen, Kampfhandlungen und militärischen Konflikten* (Russ.). Author collective under G.F. Krivoseev (Moscow, 1993).

orgy of violence and destruction. Perhaps we will succeed fifty years later in developing new political and economic structures that will bring Eastern and Western Europe together in a new home for the twenty-first century, stretching from the Atlantic to the Urals, that is no longer divided into a luxurious "upstairs" and an impoverished "downstairs."

After the division of Germany and the expulsion of Germans living in the East, the heaviest burden that remained was the concern for many years after the war about the fate of German prisoners of war in the Soviet Union. There was hardly a German family anywhere that did not fear for captured or missing members. In the first decade after the war, this became a key issue in domestic politics in Germany, prompting, of course, much research and documentation. The result was the largest historiographic project undertaken in the Federal Republic in the 1950s (No. 146).

About thirty-five million combatants were taken prisoner during the Second World War, with Germans the largest single group. A smaller group of Germans was taken while the fighting still continued, but once the capitulation had been signed, everyone in the Wehrmacht, including in the Volkssturm units mobilized in the last days of the war or in its organizational and administrative offices, was taken prisoner. Some eleven million Germans were seized and shipped to prisoner-of-war camps in more than twenty countries. In the end, Germans were prisoners of war over a total of seventeen years, from the outbreak of hostilities until the final captives returned home in early 1956.

There were enormous differences between the Western Allies and the Soviet Union together with eastern European countries in the treatment accorded prisoners of war and in the number of prisoners of war held. The differences in treatment were largely due to the reaction of eastern Europeans to Hitler's pitiless war of annihilation, in addition to cultural traditions and political considerations. The distribution of German prisoners seems astonishing at first. Although more than two-thirds of the Wehrmacht served on the Eastern Front, the Red Army captured only one-third of the Wehrmacht soldiers taken prisoner, or 3.2 million people. The reason was that many units on the Eastern Front at the end of the war in 1945 fled westward to be taken captive by the Western Allies. They were motivated by years of indoctrination, their hate and scorn of Russians, and Goebbels' atrocity propaganda, as well as by their awareness in many cases of their own guilt and the crimes committed by the Wehrmacht in the East.

Apart from what German perceptions may have been, there is no doubt that conditions in Soviet camps were much harder than in Western camps. The main problem was not degradation, maltreatment, and executions, as had been the case in Nazi camps for Soviet prisoners of war, but rather hunger and heavy physical labor in climates to which the German prisoners were not accustomed. One-third of the German prisoners of war in the Soviet Union died. This is certainly a much smaller proportion than the number of the Soviet prisoners of war who died in German camps, but it is still very high in comparison with the Western camps.

In general, German prisoners of war did not concern themselves with the reasons and background for their suffering. They had their own standards by which they measured the behavior of the victorious Soviets. They generally overlooked the fact that the Soviet government did not treat its own people much better than German prisoners. It was impossible, in the burned-out, exhausted hulk of the Soviet Union, to produce enough food and quickly raise living standards. The value of individual human life and basic humanitarian standards were clearly different in the Soviet Union than in the Western democracies.

In total, there were about 2,500 Soviet prisoner-of-war camps, and the chances of survival varied considerably from one to another. Chances of survival also depended on when the soldiers were taken prisoner. Those captured in the early phase of the war, in 1941–42, had the slimmest chances of survival. About ninety percent apparently died. The men captured at Stalingrad in 1942–43 also suffered a horrible fate. Of the 90,000 emaciated and wounded men taken prisoner, no more than 6,000 survived. The next large group of soldiers to be captured were the 150,000 men taken prisoner when Army Group Center collapsed in the summer of 1944. Their death rate was also very high. On the other hand, the two million soldiers taken prisoner after the Wehrmacht finally capitulated had much better chances of survival.

All those who survived and began returning home in mounting numbers after 1946 were scarred by traumatic experiences in the camps that marked them for the rest of their lives. Those who returned home somewhat later, between 1950 and 1956, had the good fortune of meeting with an outpouring of sympathy on the part of the German populace and benefited from generous assistance and integration programs. Many individuals experienced difficult personal problems, but at least they were encouraged to talk about the ordeals they had endured – something that was denied to the Red Army soldiers who had been taken prisoner by the Germans and were "liberated" to return to their victorious homeland.

Little attention has been paid outside the Federal Republic to the fate of German prisoners of war in the East, probably because it was feared that the Germans would cultivate their role as victims in order to avoid facing what they themselves had done. German prisoners of war were only mentioned by historians in the Soviet Union and the GDR insofar as they were apparently converted to socialism in the camps by the National Committee for Free Germany (see Part A, 7b). Most of those who returned preferred not to remain in the Soviet occupation zone. The bitterness they felt was understandably exacerbated by the fact that Communist authorities flatly denied the horrific conditions in the camps and the high death rates.

The treatment accorded German prisoners of war in Soviet camps soon became a bone of contention in the political and ideological struggles of the Cold War, and the grip on the facts began to waver. For a number of years before 1955, the number of German prisoners still held in Soviet camps was vastly exaggerated in the Federal Republic. There were rumors about secret camps where prisoners of war worked as slaves. The reason for many of these overestimates was the large number of soldiers who had simply been reported missing on the Eastern Front and the reluctance of relatives to accept that they were dead. Feelings were further rankled by the numerous condemnations of German prisoners of war by courts in the Soviet Union and later in the GDR (Nos. 120, 121, 141).

These events tended, in the eyes of West Germans, to draw the finger of guilt more toward Stalin than toward Hitler. The controversy over "the justice of the victors" flared anew when the GDR collapsed in 1990 and access to the archives and hidden graveyards revealed the true extent of the deaths in the internment and prison camps in the former Soviet zone. Some sweeping generalizations ended up painting as victims of Stalinism both war criminals, who were justly condemned, and people who were arbitrarily condemned or persecuted for political reasons.

When Chancellor Konrad Adenauer traveled to Moscow in 1955 in order to initiate diplomatic relations with the Soviet Union and achieve the release of the last German prisoners of war, his trip was celebrated at home as a great triumph. The final return of the prisoners seemed for many Germans to represent a delayed triumph over Bolshevism, against which, at just that time, a new German army was being established. It was forgotten in all the hoopla that the Soviets had released most prisoners of war by 1949 and all that remained were about 30,000 former soldiers who had been condemned by Soviet courts to lengthy sentences for alleged war crimes or other transgressions.

In view of the extreme politicization of the fate of German prisoners of war in the East, the emergence of serious, academic literature on this topic is all the more remarkable. In 1957, the German Bundestag provided funds to establish a scientific commission to study the prisoner-of-war issue, headed by the respected social historian Erich Maschke in Heidelberg. Maschke maintained high academic standards in this task and sought international participation. The impressive twenty-two volumes of results have been available since 1974 (Nos. 146, 147). They contain far more than just a numerical count of German prisoners of war in the various countries where they were held. Thanks to many interviews with former prisoners and memoirs written by them, it was possible to describe the conditions under which they were captured, their survival in the camps, the forced labor, cultural life, and political discussions.

Conditions in the Soviet Union were handled appropriately in the framework of the entire work. A number of specialized studies on such factors as hunger and labor were included (No. 130). Some very recent works on prisoners of war have focused on repatriation (No. 156) or have analyzed new interviews with survivors. The Hamburg ethnologist Albrecht Lehmann wrote a vivid description of life as a prisoner of war in the Soviet Union by combining different sources ranging from personal accounts to fiction and academic studies (No. 142).

The twenty-two volumes of the Maschke commission finally came to the fore as well. When this project was completed in 1974, the SPD-FDP coalition government in Bonn decided to make it available to academic researchers only, in order to avoid pouring oil on the already heated discussion over the *Ostverträge*. The government feared an emotional reaction to a history of intense suffering, which would only hinder its policies of reconciliation. Accordingly, only a short summary of the research was published at first (No. 147). Now, however, the study and its voluminous interviews are open to anyone.

The emphasis on the suffering of German prisoners of war in the Soviet Union results in little attention being paid to the objective contribution they made to Soviet reconstruction. Many towns in the western part of the former Soviet Union still contain numerous buildings and factories that were built by German prisoners of war. It is difficult to calculate their share of total Soviet domestic product after the war. The older Communist literature says virtually nothing about this contribution. It remains to be seen whether the opening of the Russian archives will add anything to our knowledge.

Stalin had good reason not to say much about this facet of Soviet reconstruction. Together with the occupation and division of Germany, and the expellees and prisoners of war, the issue of German war reparations was one of the most ticklish results of the war. In view of the massive plundering and destruction of Soviet territory by the Germans, Stalin's potential claims for restitution were unpayable from the outset. If the standard used in the Versailles Treaty of 1919 had been applied, Germany would probably still be paying off its debts in the third millennium.

In late 1944, the books of the Wehrmacht's Eastern Economic Staff showed a preliminary net profit of 7.5 billion reichsmarks from the occupied Soviet territories. However, this was only a partial figure. The total economic benefit that Germany derived can actually be estimated at as much as fifty billion reichsmarks, and Stalin's demands could be expected to be at least in this range. At the first Allied war conference in Teheran in late 1943, the matter of reparations was left open and turned over to the newly founded European Advisory Commission headquartered in London for further study. This commission eventually came up with total reparations bill of $20 billion. At the Yalta conference in early 1945, Stalin claimed half of this amount, although his demands were rejected by the Western Allies. In the end, they agreed to establish an Allied Reparations Commission headquartered in Moscow.

When the wartime leaders met again in Potsdam six months later, reparations became closely associated with the question of the Polish border. Stalin wanted to exempt from reparations the broad expanses of eastern Germany – the traditional breadbasket of the Reich – that would be ceded to Poland. The British and American delegations recognized the danger that Stalin could use his reparation claims to weaken the Western occupation zones, with all the attendant consequences for their survival and economic health and for the continuation of Western influence in Germany. The American delegation then made a proposal that would benefit both sides: the Western Allies would recognize the Polish administrative zone east of the Oder and

Neisse as separate from the Soviet occupation zone, and in return Moscow would yield in the reparations issue and satisfy its claims from its own zone. In addition, the Soviet Union would receive fifteen percent of the reparations from the Western zones in exchange for deliveries of food, wood, and coal from its zone, and would receive ten percent of the industrial equipment, without having to provide any counterbenefits. With this deal, Moscow took advantage of the fact that the highly industrialized western part of Germany could scarcely produce anything at first without supplies of raw materials from the East, and the Western Allies accepted that the USSR should be compensated for differences in the economic capacity of the various occupation zones. The abandonment of a fixed amount of reparations and the establishment of the principle that each occupying power would satisfy its claims basically from its own occupation zone imposed a particularly heavy burden on the people in the Soviet zone.

Reparations emerged again and again at postwar conferences as a central issue, and they played an important role in the collapse of the joint military administration and the increasing division of Germany. Because of the refusal of the USSR to deliver food to the Western zones as promised, the Western powers soon put a halt to the exploitation of their zones for the benefit of the Soviet Union, which became all the more reliant on its own zone. The Soviets also benefited from the annexation of the northern slice of East Prussia. In actual practice, the unrestrained Soviet thirst for reparations made it impossible to continue the balance of imports and exports that had been agreed upon as well as the interzonal reparations settlement on the basis of a unified economy. As Moscow experienced less and less success asserting its influence over all of Germany, it grew increasingly concerned about reparations. In addition, no further compromises were possible on issues of political structure or German unity.

During the war, industry in eastern Germany had suffered far less damage than that in western Germany. However, this was more than offset after the war by the dismantling of installations and reparations from current production. It is still impossible to obtain reliable statistics on this. It remains to be seen whether the observations and estimates of Western military authorities, preserved in archives in Koblenz, London, and Washington, can be confirmed in the future by new research in the archives of the former GDR and USSR.

Table 4 Losses from Dismantlement in the Soviet Occupation Zone to the End of 1946

	As a percentage of capacity in 1936
Iron foundries and smelting	50–55%
Heavy engineering	55–63%
Automobile industry	55–63%
Electrical industry	55–63%
Precision engineering and optics	55–63%
Pulp and paper	40–50%
Nitrogen industry	50–55%
Textile industry	20–30%

Source: No. 45, p. 107

At first, the dismantling program was chaotic. Valuable goods were loaded improperly or only partially. Often they corroded during the long trip to the USSR or after failing to work properly when installed. A new approach was adopted in 1946 with the founding of Soviet Corporations. The most important companies became Soviet property and worked directly for the Soviet Union, although using a German workforce. Taking factories over was certainly a more efficient way to ensure that reparations were paid, but it cast a pall over the Soviets' relationship with, of all people, the German working class.

There have been numerous studies of economic development in the Western zones, but the first thorough regional studies of the Eastern zone were completed only a few years ago. Despite the difficulties encountered in gaining access to sources, these West German studies (Nos. 181, 194) managed to provide a realistic picture of the extent of the dismantling and the reparations. While Werner Matschke focused on political aspects of the developments in industry, Wolfgang Zank concentrated on problems with the labor force in the Eastern zone. He pointed out that the Soviets were saying already in 1943 that German reparations should be primarily in the form of labor.

This went far beyond the workers that every occupying power employed to satisfy the immediate needs of its forces, although there were 170,000 of them in the Soviet zone by late 1946. More than one-third of construction workers were employed at Soviet sites. In addition, thousands of experts moved to the Allied nations to provide them with their knowledge, involuntarily for the most part in the Eastern zone and in exchange for lucrative contracts in the Western zones. Through Soviet Corporations, the Soviets employed a large portion of the East German labor force in directly fulfilling their own Five-Year Plan. The largest and most important industry soon became uranium ore mining. This was the basis of the Soviet atomic bomb, and it is still, fifty years later, the most serious ecological vestige of the Soviet occupation.

The floods of expellees and released prisoners of war created a considerable labor surplus that was absorbed in this way. According to Zank, the shortages that constantly appeared resulted mainly from sudden, unforeseeable leaps in Soviet demand and from the general scarcity of supplies. Although the economic reconstruction of the Soviet zone got off to an impressive start in many ways, it soon bogged down, and the Soviet zone always remained behind the Western zones. By 1950, production in the Soviet zone had reached only seventy-five percent of prewar levels.

Much attention has been paid in the recent discussion of defense-plant conversion problems in modern industrial societies to the historic example of the demilitarization of Germany and the dismantlement of factories after 1945. Several research projects in the Federal Republic should provide more information about this (Nos. 180, 181, 183). This research also covers the approximately 3,000 German military scientists and technicians who were sent to the USSR between May 1945 and January 1947, only few of them voluntarily (No. 192). It is remarkable that many of these experts apparently did not perceive this move as a revolution in their professional lives, despite their new living circumstances and the fact that they were serving a contrasting political system. All the victorious Allied powers courted German arms researchers and provided them with interesting new challenges. Even though the Reich went down to defeat, these experts might well have felt that they emerged personally as "winners." In contrast to this small group, the vast majority of German prisoners of war were forced to perform heavy labor under far more difficult conditions as they reconstructed the devastated regions of eastern Europe.

For almost half a century, very little was said or written about another form of restitution for war damage or of booty and reparations. As the Wehrmacht advanced, eastern Europe was plundered of its cultural artifacts in a greater haul than in occupied Western countries. Cultural treasures of all kinds were seized by

Table 5 Overview of Major Payments and Deliveries from the Soviet Zone for Reparations and Costs of Occupation from 1945 to 1953

Payments	**In millions of marks**
Payments from public funds	
1946 to 1950	27,800
1951 to 1953	10,080
Additional cash payments	
1945–46	4,200
Surrender of profits from Soviet Corporations	
1947 to 1950	1,750
1951 to 1953	1,800
Purchase price for returned Soviet Corporations	
1951 to 1953	2,560
	48,190
Deliveries	
Deliveries of goods	
1945 to 1950	24,517
1951 to 1953	10,215
Additional expenditures and subsidies	
1945 to 1950	2,625
1951 to 1953	1,000
Costs of uranium ore mining	
1947 to 1950	3,000
1951 to 1953	4,750
Supplying Soviet Corporations with currency (before 1950) or capital withdrawals (1952–53)	1,000
Remaining assets	1,083
	48,190

From this total amount, occupation costs of about DM 16 billion should be deducted. Actual reparations were therefore about DM 32 billion in the form of deliveries from production, to which should be added the DM 5 billion estimated value of the dismantled factories, for a total of about DM 37 billion. This is approximately $12 billion, which is $2 billion more than the reparations agreed upon at the Moscow Conference in 1947 for the Soviet Union and Poland.

Source: Federal Ministry for All-German Questions, Bonn, 1953

the Germans from museums, archives, and libraries. Much of this booty was recovered by special Red Army units in 1945. In addition, more than 500,000 artifacts were turned over to the Soviets from "Collecting Points" in the American zone. However, even this did not come close to repairing Soviet losses. About 200,000 objects are still missing from museums in the former Soviet Union.

As the Red Army then advanced through Germany, it likewise requisitioned large numbers of cultural artifacts. A "Trophy Commission" was established to administer this war booty in dozens of secret depots. Between 1955 and 1958, about 1.5 million cultural artifacts were returned to their original museums in the GDR. However, experts estimated that this was only about seventy-five percent of what had been removed. Only after the recent political transformations did Moscow finally admit in 1992 that depots of war booty still existed and agree to discuss the conditions under which it might eventually be returned. Celebrated artifacts from German museums, such as "Priam's Treasure," that were long considered lost have now become the object of protracted political and economic negotiations, with no end in sight. In contrast to the silence of the past, historians and journalists have now published a plethora of sometimes sensationalistic articles about this topic (Nos. 168, 172, 177).

The end of the postwar period raised the question of whether the debts incurred through Hitler's Eastern campaign have now been paid off. When the two German states reunited in 1990, the people who lived in the former Soviet occupation zone pointed out that they had borne the brunt of the reparations. It was therefore thought to be only fair that West Germans, who had obviously had an easier time, should now contribute through transfer payments to the reconstruction of the East. Final acknowledgment of the loss in 1945 of the easternmost parts of Germany through annexation by Poland and the Soviet Union, payment of more than DM 80 billion to help resettle the Russian troops evacuating Germany, and support for Yeltsin could be seen as the final payments on this debt. However, leading politicians in the Federal Republic have also recognized an enduring German responsibility, in the light of history, for the political and economic reconstruction of Eastern Europe. For historians, this can only mean new tasks and fields of research.

2. Avoiding and Coming to Terms with the Past

(Gerd R. Ueberschär)

Fifty years after the end of the Second World War, it is time to address, not only in material terms but also in mental terms, the rifts that remain in Soviet-German or Russo-German relations as a result of Hitler's war of annihilation in the East. This was not yet possible in the years immediately after the war, when memories were still raw. Even in the years following the establishment of the Federal Republic of Germany, the view of the Eastern war adopted by the public and popular press in Germany was characterized by avoidance and denial of the true intentions of this campaign and the devastation that it wrought (No. 398). At the same time, in the Soviet Union the government imposed an uncritical, heroic view of the "Great Patriotic War," which left little opportunity for Soviets to take a clear-eyed look at their own history (Nos. 330, 354, 359, 360, 366, 384, 387, 390, 393, 408, 409). Historians in the GDR were also required to parrot this line uncritically (Nos. 313, 346, 347). It was always essential for Soviet historians to underline the leading role played by the Communist party of the Soviet Union as the organizer and historically inevitable source of the great victory (Nos. 364, 367, 391). The personal accounts and memoirs of participants, touched upon in the previous chapters on various topics, provide an eloquent example of this (cf. Nos. 198, 378, and, above all, the memoirs and eyewitness accounts listed in Parts A, B, C, and D under "Sources").

Another special genre of "war history" to be found in numerous publications was also directly concerned with the results and lessons of the Eastern campaign. However, this genre focused on the tactics and lessons of the art of war as practiced by both sides, in various weapons categories and under various geographic, climatic, and time conditions. Mounting numbers of government publications in both the United States and the Soviet Union fell into this category. Understandably, the Soviets concentrated on successful operations of their own in order to derive lessons for the future, and, for Anglo-American readers, David M. Glantz has published special studies (Nos. 210, 212–21, 229). A number of German studies and memoirs pointed out how German military operations and the occupation of the Soviet Union could have been handled "better." The authors of these works certainly distanced themselves from the Nazis, but they were still generally filled with anti-Communist sentiment. They therefore tended to pass over the criminal German attack of June 1941 in order to focus on how the Eastern campaign could have been waged more effectively (Nos. 230, D/99, D/100).

Individual themes and battles were depicted in a number of powerful literary works, including those by Peter Bamm, Gerhard Kramer, Alexander Kluge, Wassilij Grossman, Viktor Nekrassov, and Theodor Plievier (see *inter alia* Nos. 202, 239, 249, 260, 261, 262, 274, 283, 288, 289, 290). Ulrich Baron and Rolf G. Renner wrote critical surveys of this literature about the Battle of Stalingrad (Nos. 240, 293; see in this regard the information in Part B). Once more on the fiftieth anniversary of the Battle of Stalingrad, Christoph Fromm, in a new novel, described the fighting in this battle as an example of the inhumanity and insanity of the war (No. 257); his novel is based on the draft version of Josef Vilsmaier's movie "Stalingrad." Christoph Heubner provided a short summary of the Soviet literature (No. 264). However, even literary treatments hewed to a one-sided approach during the Cold War, viewing military history and battles from a particular national perspective. This was done by each side ostensibly in order to impart lessons to its own people, although also partly for commercial and traditional reasons. As a result, it was impossible or at least much more difficult for people on the opposing sides to reach a meeting of minds on the issues.

Certain circles in both countries were only too eager to use the Eastern war in order to write apologias and similar works in defense of their own dictatorship (see the information under Nos. 379, 401). However, the occasional attempts in Germany to dismiss Hitler's original war aims, rooted in his basic program, as playing only a minor role in the attack on the Soviet Union and to point to the allegedly confused strategic situation or to the Soviets' "aggressive" foreign policy in the summer of 1940 as the main reason for the Eastern campaign (Nos. 399, 402, 403) were always quickly disproved by historians using sources and key records about Hitler's intentions (Nos. 353, 414). As a result, these works found only a few supporters on the fringes of history faculties, although they were quite popular with people who had experienced the war.

Despite the counterevidence that Hitler's decision to invade the Soviet Union was not prompted by fear of what the Red Army might do, as was demonstrated in particular by historians in the GDR (No. 422), the preventive-war theory gained support in the aura of extreme right-wing groups (Nos. 349, 350, 361). There have been repeated attempts over the last few decades in publications of the extreme Right or neo-Nazi groups in Germany to justify Hitler's war against Bolshevism as a defense of Europe and to deny its barbarous intentions in contravention of international law. Sometimes these misguided views appeared in letters to the editor in technical journals with close government connections. This occurred, for instance, in 1985 in the semiofficial magazine *Europäische Wehrkunde/Wehrwissenschaftliche Rundschau*, which is published in close collaboration with the Staff College of the Bundeswehr.[3] Contrary to all established fact, a letter to the editor claimed that it was "thanks alone to the German fighting men in Russia that the Communist threat to western Europe was staved off until the arrival of the British and Americans." The letter concludes with the usual cliché that this was the greatest achievement of German soldiers in the Second World War. No mention is made of the fact that it was the Wehrmacht that attacked the Soviet Union in the first place in 1941.

We should not fail to acknowledge that the war was a devastating experience, not only for conquered Germany but also for the victorious Soviet Union, and that it left behind many traumatic memories on both sides (Nos. 392, 400). The horrible effects of the war on the Soviet Union were consciously ignored

3 . See letters to the editor in *Europäische Wehrkunde/Wehrwissenschaftliche Rundschau* 34 (1985): 306, 408, 520f., also for the following quotation.

in Germany for many years and omitted from the history textbooks used in schools (Nos. 323, 324, 325, 340, 383, 396, 397, 404). In addition, the Eastern war posed a problem of traditions for the armed forces in both the Federal Republic and the Soviet Union. Manfred Messerschmidt in particular has discussed in a number of critical studies the burdensome problem of traditions in the German military, as has Jakob Knab (Nos. 362, 377). On the other hand, Nina Tumarkin has addressed the exaggerated myth-making that went on in the Soviet Union (No. 411). How important free access to the sources in Soviet archives is for this insight is shown by the book *The Secret Becomes Clear* by Michael Voslensky, (No. 417) which is a successful report on the archives of Moscow in the period 1917 to 1991.

Shortly before the political transformation of Eastern Europe, which led to a cautious revision of Soviet historiography as well (No. 375), the so-called *Historikerstreit*, or historians' dispute, erupted in Germany in the mid-1980s, producing controversial ideas about the historical place of the Soviet-German war in the larger context of the "European civil war" from 1917 to 1945 (No. 380). The following ideas and initiatives were developed for putting the political relationship with the peoples and citizens of the Soviet Union on a new basis.

It was claimed in the German *Historikerstreit* that the Soviet dictatorship and the policies pursued by Moscow provided a particularly appropriate yardstick for comparing and assessing the German dictatorship and its crimes (No. 413). As the Berlin historian Ernst Nolte stated – in admittedly somewhat oversimplified fashion – the question is the extent to which the crimes committed by the Nazis against Jews, gypsies, Slavs, and other "inferior peoples" were a reaction to the "Asiatic barbarities" that could allegedly be expected from Stalin and the Soviet Communists in the future and that had been seen in the past in the Russian civil war and in the annihilation of the kulaks (No. 381).

Drawing a parallel between Auschwitz and the Gulag Archipelago made it possible to portray the Holocaust as a reaction and the result of psychological "compulsion" and not the result of peculiarly German developments within European culture. This approach, which "relativized" the Nazi state and its crimes and cast doubt on the unique nature of the atrocities it committed in the East, was heatedly opposed in many quarters, as was the assertion that the attack on the Soviet Union could be seen as a preventive strike (Nos. 336, 337, 345, 355, 368, 374).

It was no accident that further attempts to justify the German assault on the Soviet Union in 1941 arose at the time of the *Historikerstreit* (No. 419). It was awkward for the Federal Republic, as it tried to carve out a stronger national identity to go with its expanded, more important role in the world, that the Soviet-German war from 1941 to 1945 cannot really be portrayed as a righteous war of self-defense against Communism, as is done continually in Germany in popular war literature and *Landserheftchen*, especially in regard to the 1944–45 period. Equally awkward for the development of a national sense of identity is the plain historical truth that the war in the East was a crucial part of Hitler's plans for the so-called Final Solution of the Jewish Question in Europe.

The attempt undertaken in the wake of the *Historikerstreit* to interpret the German attack on the Soviet Union on 22 June 1941 as a preventive strike was based both on new speculation about Stalin's war policy, which was first aired in 1985 by the Graz philosopher Ernst Topitsch in his book *Stalin's War* (which was published in a revised edition in 1993) and on the questionable technical claims of military historian Joachim Hoffmann and Soviet emigrant and former Red Army general staff officer Victor Suworow (Viktor Rezun) that the Soviet Union was engaged in an offensive military buildup aimed at the German Reich (Nos. 356, 357, 405, 406, 407, 410). However, neither Topitsch's speculations nor Suworow's unproved hypotheses have contributed anything to what historians actually know.

Their theories were nevertheless widely reported in the West German press and again in Russia after 1992. In Germany, they were both supported and sharply contradicted. New sources were sought in vain to support their "preventive war" theory. Andreas Hillgruber then qualified their claims as a "relapse into early stages of the discussion that were considered closed almost twenty years ago." He pointed out "false individual statements that should be criticized" and that were based on insufficient sources and spoke even of "intentional mystification" (No. 353, pp. 214, 224). The Nazi propaganda about the preventive nature of the German attack on the Soviet Union in 1941 was reconsidered, and Hitler's program for an Eastern war was comprehensively reexamined in the context of his ideology. These efforts, as well as new research by Wigbert Benz into the cataclysmic nature of the Eastern war and by Bianka Pietrow into Soviet foreign policy in 1940–41, clearly demonstrated that the views propagated by Ernst Topitsch, Joachim Hoffmann, and Victor

Suworow were untenable (Nos. 321, 386, 412, 415). In contrast, Fritz Becker and Werner Maser have again proposed the theory that the Soviet leadership had been preparing itself for a war of aggression against Germany since the summer of 1940 and that Stalin had made a magnificent ploy to hush this up. Hitler's "preventive attack" was thus undertaken for strategic and security reasons to ward off a serious threat (Nos. 319, 373).

Recent studies by Dimitrij Wolkogonow, Walerij Danilow, and further Russian historians have furnished proof on the basis of newly discovered Russian sources that General Zukov, as head of the Soviet General Staff, and Marshal Timoshenko, at that time Volkskommissar of Defence, drew up their own plan of attack on 15 May 1941 for military reasons (Nos. 420, 335, 376). It contained the preventive strike of the Red Army against the deployment of the Wehrmacht. The significance of this document is often overrated, because Stalin strictly forbade the execution of this plan, as he wanted to avoid any provocation against Berlin. In a more recent analysis, Rainer F. Schmid defined the political calculation of Stalin in the spring and early summer of 1941 as a "misguided strategy for all cases" (No. 395). He assumes that the dictator held on "unswervingly to the maxim of avoiding a conflict" despite a general hectic actionism. Stalin therefore categorically checked Zukov and Timoshenko and rejected the preventive plan set up by them. He wanted to continue his policy of appeasement toward Hitler.

Nevertheless, in his book *Stalin's War of Extermination 1941–1945*, Joachim Hoffmann adheres to the theory about Hitler's preventive attack against the massive deployment on the part of the USSR (No. 357). In the main part of his study, Hoffmann turns his attention to Stalin's conception of a war of extermination and conquest against Germany, a conception he even announced publicly on 6 November 1941. He also describes the crimes and atrocities committed by the Red Army against the German civilian population at the end of 1944.

Typical for the recent claims that the German attack was a preventive strike to counter an alleged offensive buildup by the Red Army, these authors failed totally to investigate whether German politicians and military leaders felt any need at the time to beat Stalin to the punch – in other words, whether the idea of a preventive war had any actual bearing on German planning. Since this is demonstrably not the case, the authors relied more and more on vague speculation about Stalin's secret intentions and sought to minimize all the reasons for attacking the Soviet Union that Hitler had set forth in his basic program. The conclusions these authors draw are most peculiar. When Hitler ordered the Wehrmacht to invade the Soviet Union, he was allegedly engaging in a preventive war without realizing it and without taking this fact into account – even though he later did put Propaganda Minister Goebbels to work busily spreading the news that it had been a preventive strike. Although the Austrian military historian Heinz Magenheimer generally looks upon the theory of a preventive war with sympathy, he recently emphasized that the "preventive aspect" cannot be seen as the main reason for Hitler's decision to attack (Nos. 371, 372).

On the whole, the new, "modified theory of a preventive strike" that emerged during the *Historikerstreit* has been without lasting effect (Nos. 342, 343, 413, 414). It has found no support among leading historians of the Second World War. The theory of a preventive war or strike is without any substance and was relatively unimportant even in the context of the *Historikerstreit* in the narrow sense.

However, the theory of a preventive war, taken over from old Nazi propaganda, is part of a tendency that continually resurfaces in Germany to twist the historical facts about the Second World War in order to escape responsibility for the Soviet-German war of 1941 to 1945 and present a nationalistic, anti-Communist view of German history. The historic responsibility for the attack on the Soviet Union, in contravention of a signed treaty, cannot be shirked through speculation about Stalin's possible long-term intentions and the claims, for which no substantial proof has yet been advanced, that Hitler barely beat Stalin to the punch in 1941. To insist that Hitler and the Third Reich were responsible for the war does not mean ignoring Stalin's deeds and unscrupulous policies or minimizing his reign of terror, as opponents of the preventive-war theory are often accused of doing. What they wish is to warn against attempts to deny or justify what happened and to insist that it should not be ignored or forgotten.

Germany's President Richard von Weizsäcker pointed clearly in this direction in his address marking the fortieth anniversary of the end of the war on 8 May 1945 when he alluded in his commemoration to the suffering inflicted by the Germans on the peoples of eastern Europe: "We remember all the peoples who suffered in the war, especially the countless citizens of the Soviet Union and Poland who lost their lives .... When we recall what our eastern neighbors suffered in the war, we understand more fully that compensation, détente and friendly relations with these countries must remain features of German foreign policy, whatever the party in power."[4] In view of Weizsäcker's words (No. 418), we should not to try to elude with veiled words a particular German responsibility for reconciliation and peace. We should not avert our eyes from the realities of the German attack on the Soviet Union on 22 June 1941 and from the strong connection between Operation Barbarossa and the Holocaust, or strive desperately in every new *Historikerstreit* to prove that the attack was a justifiable "preventive strike" by the Wehrmacht against Moscow (No. 412).

It is therefore totally absurd to speak of a "takeover" by earlier Soviet historiography (No. 402), if we recognize the grievous historic burden of the war against the Soviet Union, which suffered the heaviest losses. This was plainly acknowledged in 1991 in several side projects and in the entire concept of the Berlin exhibition "The War Against the Soviet Union 1941–1945" on the fiftieth anniversary of the German attack (No. 389).

4. Richard von Weizsäcker, *Zum 40. Jahrestag der Beendigung des Krieges in Europa und der nationalsozialistischen Gewaltherrschaft* (Bonn, 1985): 2, 13.

Bibliography

1. The Results of the War

a) Soviet Policy toward Germany and the Occupation

1) Agde, Günter. *Sachsenhausen bei Berlin. Speziallager Nr. 7 1945–1950. Kassiber, Dokumente und Studien.* Berlin, 1994

2) Antipenko, N.A. "Ot kapituljacii Germanii do Potsdama. (Iz zapisok nacal'nika tyla fronta)." *Voprosy Istorii* no. 9 (1966): pp. 106–117

3) Arlt, Kurt. "Das Wirken der Sowjetischen Militäradministration in Deutschland (SMAD) im Spannungsfeld zwischen den Entschlüssen von Potsdam und den sicherheitspolitischen Interessen Moskaus 1945–1949." In *"Volksarmee schaffen – ohne Geschrei!" Studien zu den Anfängen einer "verdeckten Aufrüstung" in der SBZ/DDR 1947–1952*, edited by Bruno Thoß, pp. 91–139. Munich, 1994

4) _____. "Die militärische und ökonomische Entwaffnung in Sachsen 1945 bis 1948. Aus einem zusammenfassenden Bericht der sowjetischen Militärverwaltung vom Oktober 1948." *Militärgeschichtliche Mitteilungen* vol. 52, no. 2 (1993): pp. 371–409

5) Ash, Timothy Garton. *Im Namen Europas. Deutschland und der geteilte Kontinent*. Munich, 1993

6) Badstübner, Rolf. *Code "Terminal". Die Potsdamer Konferenz*. East Berlin, 1985

7) _____. "Die Deutschlandpolitik von KPdSU und SED und das Problem historischer Alternativen" In *Die deutsche Frage in der Nachkriegszeit*, edited by Wilfried Loth. Berlin, 1994

8) Badstübner, Rolf, and Siegfied Thomas. *Die Spaltung Deutschlands 1945–1949*. East Berlin, 1966

8a) Badstübner, Rolf, and Wilfried Loth, eds. *Wilhelm Pieck. Aufzeichnungen zur Deutschlandpolitik 1945–1953*. Berlin, 1994

9) Balfour, Michael, and John Mair. *Four-Power Control in Germany and Austria, 1945–1946*. London, 1956

10) *Befreiung und Neubeginn. Zur Stellung des 8. Mai 1945 in der deutschen Geschichte*. Wissenschaftliche Redaktion: Bernhard Weißel. East Berlin, 1968
11) Beleckij, Viktor Nikolaevic. "Pomosc' Sovetskoj Armii naseleniju osvobozdennogo Berlina." *Voenno-Istoriceskij Zurnal* no. 6 (1970): pp. 102–107
12) ____. *Die Politik der Sowjetunion in den deutschen Angelegenheiten in der Nachkriegszeit, 1945–1976*. East Berlin, 1977
13) ____. *Za stolom peregovorov. Obsuzdenie germanskich del na poslevoennych mezdunarodnych sovescanijach i vstrecach*. Moscow, 1979
14) ____. *Vstreca v Potsdame*. Moscow, 1980
15) Benz, Wolfgang. *Potsdam 1945. Besatzungsherrschaft und Neuaufbau im Vier-Zonen-Deutschland*. Munich, 1986
16) *Die Berliner Konferenz der Drei Mächte*. Der Alliierte Kontrollrat für Deutschland. Die Alliierte Kommandantur der Stadt Berlin. Komuniqués, Deklarationen, Proklamationen, Gesetze, Befehle. East Berlin, 1946
17) Bokov, F. "Pervye mirnye dni Berlina (Vospominanija. Maj – ijun' 1945 g.)." *Voenno-Istoriceskij Zurnal* no. 7 (1976): pp. 62–69
18) Boveri, Margret. *Tage des Überlebens. Berlin 1945*. Munich, 1968
19) Braas, Gerhard. *Die Entstehung der Länderverfassungen in der Sowjetischen Besatzungszone Deutschlands 1946/47*. Cologne, 1987
20) Burke, James Wakefield. *The Big Rape*. Frankfurt a.M., 1951
21) Buttlar, Walrab von. *Ziele und Zielkonflikte der Sowjetischen Deutschlandpolitik 1945–1947*. Stuttgart, 1980
22) Davidovic, D.S. "SVAG i predposylki antifasistsko-demokraticeskich preobrazivanij v Vostocnoj Germaniiv (1945–1949 gg.)." *Ezegodnik Germanskoj Istorii* (1980), pp. 21–38. Moscow, 1982
23) Deuerlein, Ernst. *Die Einheit Deutschlands*. Vol. 1, *Die Erörterungen und Entscheidungen der Kriegs- und Nachkriegskonferenzen 1941–1949*. 2nd edn. Frankfurt a.M., 1961
24) Deuerlein, Ernst, ed. *Potsdam 1945. Quellen zur Konferenz der "Großen Drei"*. Munich, 1963
25) ____. *Potsdam 1945. Ende und Anfang*. Cologne, 1970
26) Dietrich, Gerd. *Politik und Kultur in der Sowjetischen Besatzungszone Deutschlands (SBZ) 1945–1949*. Bern, 1993
27) Doernberg, Stefan. *Die Geburt eines neuen Deutschland 1945–1949. Die antifaschistisch-demokratische Umwälzung und die Entstehung der DDR*. East Berlin, 1959
28) Duhnke, Horst. *Stalinismus in Deutschland. Die Geschichte der Sowjetischen Besatzungszone*. Cologne, 1955
29) Erler, Peter, Horst Laude, and Manfred Wilke, eds. *"Nach Hitler kommen wir." Dokumente zur Programmatik der Moskauer KPD-Führung 1944/45 für Nachkriegsdeutschland*. Berlin, 1994
30) Erusalimskij, A.S. *Likvidacija Prusskogo gosudarstva*. Moscow, 1947
31) Feis, Herbert. *Zwischen Krieg und Frieden. Das Potsdamer Abkommen*. Frankfurt a.M., 1962
32) Fischer, Alexander. *Sowjetische Deutschlandpolitik im Zweiten Weltkrieg 1941–1945*. Stuttgart, 1975

33) Friedmann, Wolfgang. *The Allied Military Government of Germany.* London, 1947
34) Fritsch-Bournazel, Renata. *Die Sowjetunion und die deutsche Teilung. Die sowjetische Deutschlandpolitik 1945–1979.* Opladen, 1979
35) Galkin, A.A., and D.E. Mel'nikov. *SSSR, zapadnye derzavy i germanskij vopros. 1945–1965.* Moscow, 1966
36) Graml, Hermann. *Die Alliierten und die Teilung Deutschlands. Konflikte und Entscheidungen.* Frankfurt a.M., 1985
37) Hacker, Jens. *Sowjetunion und DDR zum Potsdamer Abkommen.* Cologne, 1968
38) Hocker, Karla. *Die letzten und die ersten Tage: Berliner Aufzeichnungen 1945 mit Berichten von Boleslaw Barlog et al.* Berlin, 1966
39) Jastrebcov, V. I. "Sotrudnicestvo Sovetskoj voennoj administracii i nemeckich demokraticeskich sil v poslevoennom pereustrojstve Vostocnoj Germanii (1945–1949 gg.)." Diss., Kiev, 1977
40) Kanzig, Helga. "Die Anwendung sowjetischer Erfahrungen und die Zusammenarbeit mit der UdSSR beim Aufbau des Sozialismus in der DDR." *Jahrbuch für Wirtschaftsgeschichte* 1 (1977): pp. 9–25
41) Kegel, Gerhard. *Ein Vierteljahrhundert danach. Das Potsdamer Abkommen und was aus ihm geworden ist.* East Berlin, 1970
42) Keiderling, Gerhard, ed. *"Gruppe Ulbricht in Berlin" April bis Juni 1945: Von den Vorbereitungen im Sommer 1944 bis zur Wiedergründung der KPD im Juni 1945.* Berlin, 1993
43) Keiderling, Gerhard, and Percy Stulz. *Berlin 1945–1968. Zur Geschichte der Hauptstadt der DDR und der selbständigen politischen Einheit Westberlin.* East Berlin, 1970
44) Kientopf, Anna. *Das friedensfeindliche Trauma. Die Rote Armee in Deutschland 1945.* Lindhorst, 1984
45) Kleßmann, Christoph. *Die doppelte Staatsgründung. Deutsche Geschichte 1945–1955.* Göttingen, 1991
46) Kleßmann, Christoph, and Georg Wagner, eds. *Das gespaltene Land. Leben in Deutschland 1945 bis 1990. Texte und Dokumente.* Munich, 1993
47) Kul'bakin, V. D. "Rol' SVAG v stanovlenii i ukreplenii druzby i sotrudnicestva mezdu sovetskim i nemeckim narodami (1945–vesna 1946 gg.)." In *Voprosy germanskogo rabocego dvizenija v sovremennuju epochu: Materialy naucnoj konferencii, posvjascennoj 30letiju sozdanija Socialisticeskoj edinoj partii Germanii (20–22 aprelja 1976 g.).* Volgograd, 1977
48) Korol', A.S. *Pomosc' Sovetskogo Sojuza v vozrozdenii i konsolidacii antifasistsko-demokraticeskich sil Vostocnoj Germanii (1945–1947 gg.).* Diss., Minsk, 1977
49) Leonhard, Wolfgang. *Die Revolution entläßt ihre Kinder.* Cologne, 1957
50) Löwenthal, Fritz. *News from Soviet Germany.* London, 1950
51) Loth, Wilfried, ed. *Die deutsche Frage in der Nachkriegszeit.* Berlin, 1994
51a) ____. *Stalins ungeliebtes Kind. Warum Moskau die DDR nicht wollte.* Berlin, 1994
52) Malinowski, L.W. "Aus den Erfahrungen eines Referenten der SMAD, 1947/1948. Mit einigen Protokollen im Anhang." *Beiträge zur Geschichte der Arbeiterbewegung* no. 22 (1980): pp. 394–401
53) Marienfeld, Wolfgang. *Konferenzen über Deutschland. Die alliierte Deutschlandplanung und -politik 1941–1949.* Hanover, 1962

54) Mattedi, Norbert. *Gründung und Entwicklung der Parteien in der Sowjetischen Besatzungszone Deutschlands 1945–1949*. Bonn, 1966
55) Meinicke, Wolfgang. "Die Entnazifizierung in der sowjetischen Besatzungszone 1945 bis 1948." *Zeitschrift für Geschichtswissenschaft* no. 32 (1984): pp. 968–979
56) Meissner, Boris. *Rußland, die Westmächte und Deutschland. Die sowjetische Deutschlandpolitik 1943–1953*. Abhandlungen der Forschungsstelle für Völkerrecht und ausländisches Recht der Universität Hamburg, vol. 5. Hamburg, 1953
57) Merzanov, M.I. *Tak eto bylo: Poslednie dni fasistskogo Berlina*. Moscow, 1983
58) *Mezdunarodnye otnosenija posle vtoroj mirovoj vojny*. 3 vols. Edited by N.N. Inozemcev et al. Vol. 1, *1945–1949*. Moscow, 1962; vol. 2, *1950–1955*. Moscow, 1963; vol. 3, *1956–1964*. Moscow, 1965
59) *Mezdunarodnye otnosenija i vnesnjaja politika Sovetskogo Sojuza 1945–1949*. Edited by G. A. Deborin et al. Moscow, 1958
60) Molotov, V. M. *Voprosy vnesnej politiki. Reci i zajavlenija. Aprel' 1945 g.–ijun' 1948 g.* Moscow, 1948
61) _____. *Reci na Parizskoj Mirnoj Konferencii. Ijul'–oktjabr' 1946g.* Moscow, 1946
62) Nettl, J. Peter. *The Eastern Zone and Soviet Policy in Germany 1945–1950*. New York, 1957
63) Niedbalski, Bernd. "Deutsche Zentralverwaltungen und deutsche Wirtschaftskommission (DWK). Ansätze zur Zentralen Wirtschaftsplanung in der SBZ 1945–1948." *Vierteljahrshefte für Zeitgeschichte* vol. 33 (1985): pp. 456–476
64) Nikitin, A.P. *Dejatel'nost' sovetskoj voennoj administracii po demokratizacii vyssego obrazovanija v Vostocnoj Germanii (1945–1949 gg.)*. Diss., Moscow, 1986
65) Nikolaev, P.A. *Politika SSA, Anglii i Francii v germanskom voprose. 1945–1954*. Moscow, 1964
66) _____. *Politika Sovetskogo Sojuza v germanskom voprose. 1945–1964*. Moscow, 1966
67) Nolte, Ernst. *Deutschland und der Kalte Krieg*. Munich, 1974; 2nd edn 1985
68) *Obrazovanie Germanskoj Demokraticeskoj Republiki. Dokumenty iv materialy*. Moscow, 1950
69) Raginskij, M.Ju. *Njurnberg: pered sudom istorii. Vospominanija ucastnika Njurnbergskogo processa*. Moscow, 1986
70) Sandford, Gregory W. *From Hitler to Ulbricht. The Communist Reconstruction of East Germany 1945–1949*. Princeton, N J., 1983
71) Schwarz, Hans-Peter. *Vom Reich zur Bundesrepublik. Deutschland im Widerstreit der außenpolitischen Konzeptionen in den Jahren der Besatzungsherrschaft 1945–1949*. Neuwied, 1966
72) Segbers, Klaus. "Die Folgen des Krieges: Die Sowjetunion seit 1945". In *Erobern und Vernichten. Der Krieg gegen die Sowjetunion 1941–1945. Essays*, edited by Peter Jahn and Reinhard Rürup, pp. 231–248. Berlin, 1991
73) Semjonow, Wladimir S. *Von Stalin bis Gorbatschow. Ein halbes Jahrhundert in diplomatischer Mission 1939–1991*. Berlin, 1995

74) Solkovic, Z.B. *Dejatel'nost sovetskich voennych komendatur na territorii Vostocnoj Germanii v 1945–1949 gg.* Diss., Moscow, 1981

75) ____. "Dokumenty o dejatel'nosti sovetskich voennych komendatur v Vostocnoj Germanii (1945–1949)." *Sovetskie Archivy* no. 4 (1978): pp. 73–79

76) Staritz, Dietrich. *Die Gründung der DDR. Von der sowjetischen Besatzungszone zum sozialistischen Staat*. Munich, 1984

77) Steininger, Rolf. *Deutsche Geschichte 1945–1961. Darstellungen und Dokumente*. 2 vols. Frankfurt a.M., 1983

78) Stolper, Wolfgang E. *The Structure of the East German Economy*. Cambridge, Mass., 1960

79) ____. "The Labor Force and Industrial Development in Soviet Germany." *The Quarterly Journal of Economics* (1957): pp. 518–545

80) Studnitz, Hans-Georg von. *Als Berlin brannte. Diarium der Jahre 1943–1945*. Stuttgart, 1963

81) Taege, H., ed. *Die Gefesselten. Deutsche Frauen in sowjetischen Konzentrationslagern in Deutschland*. Munich, 1987

82) Thomas, Siegfried. *Entscheidung in Berlin. Zur Entstehungsgeschichte der SED in der deutschen Hauptstadt 1945/46*. East Berlin, 1967

83) Thoß, Bruno. "Die Sicherheitsproblematik im Kontext der sowjetischen West- und Deutschlandpolitik 1941–1952." In *"Volksarmee schaffen – ohne Geschrei!". Studien zu den Anfängen einer "verdeckten Aufrüstung" in der SBZ/DDR 1947–1952*, edited by Bruno Thoß, pp. 23–89. Munich, 1994

84) Tjulpanov, Sergej Ivanovic. *Deutschland nach dem Kriege (1945–1949). Erinnerungen eines Offiziers der Sowjetarmee*. Edited by Stefan Doernberg. East Berlin, 1986

85) *Vnesnjaja politika Sovetskogo Sojuza. Dokumenty i materialy*. 1945: 4. September–31. December 1945, Moscow, 1949; 1946: January–December 1946, Moscow, 1952; 1947: part 1: January–June 1947, part 2: July–December 1947, Moscow, 1952; 1948: part 1: January–June 1948, Moscow, 1950, part 2: July–December 1948, Moscow, 1951, 1949: January–December 1949, Moscow, 1953

86) "Vnesnjaja politika SSSR i germanskij vopros v pervye poslevoennye gody (1945–1949 gg.)." In *Istorija vnesnej politiki SSSR (1917–1976 gg.)*. Part 2: 1945–1976 gg. Moscow, 1977

87) Weber, Hermann. *Kleine Geschichte der DDR*. Cologne, 1980; 2nd edn 1988

88) Wehner, Helfried. "Die Unterstützung der sowjetischen Militärorgane für die deutschen Antifaschisten im Mai 1945 in Sachsen." *Zeitschrift für Geschichtswissenschaft* no. 4, (1970): pp. 513–526

89) Welsh, Helga A. *Revolutionärer Wandel auf Befehl? Entnazifizierungs- und Personalpolitik in Thüringen und Sachsen (1945–1948)*. Schriftenreihe der Vierteljahrshefte für Zeitgeschichte, vol. 58. Munich, 1989

90) Wettig, Gerhard. *Die Parole der nationalen Einheit in der sowjetischen Deutschlandpolitik 1942–1967*. Berichte des BBI, no. 33/67. Cologne, 1967

91) ____. *Entmilitarisierung und Wiederbewaffnung in Deutschland 1943–1955. Internationale Auseinandersetzungen um die Rolle der Deutschen in Europa*. Schriften des Forschungsinstituts der Deutschen Gesellschaft für Auswärtige Politik, vol. 25. Munich, 1967

92) ____. "Neue Erkenntnisse aus sowjetischen Geheimdokumenten über den militärischen Aufbau in der SBZ/DDR 1947–1952." *Militärgeschichtliche Mitteilungen* vol. 53, no. 2 (1994): pp. 399–419
93) Wille, Manfred. *Entnazifizierung in der Sowjetischen Besatzungszone Deutschlands 1945–48*. Magdeburg, 1993
94) Wyssozki, V. N. *Unternehmen Terminal. Zum 30. Jahrestag des Potsdamer Abkommens*. East Berlin, 1975

b) The Expulsion of the East German Population

95) Ackermann, Volker. *Der "echte" Flüchtling. Deutsche Vertriebene und Flüchtlinge aus der DDR (1945–1961)*. Studien zur historischen Migrationsforschung, vol. 1. Essen, 1994
96) Bade, Klaus J., ed. *Deutsche im Ausland – Fremde in Deutschland. Migration in Geschichte und Gegenwart*. Munich, 1992
97) Benz, Wolfgang, ed. *Die Vertreibung der Deutschen aus dem Osten. Ursachen, Ereignisse, Folgen*. Frankfurt a.M., 1985
98) Böddecker, Günter. *Die Flüchtlinge. Die Vertreibung der Deutschen im Osten*. 4th edn. Munich, 1985
99) Chiodo, Marco P. *Sie werden die Stunde verfluchen … Sterben und Vertreibung der Deutschen im Osten 1944–1949*. Munich, 1990
100) ____. *Sterben und Vertreibung der Deutschen im Osten 1944–1949. Die Vorgänge aus der Sicht des Auslands*. Frankfurt a.M., 1993
100a) *Dokumentation der Vertreibung der Deutschen aus Ost-Mitteleuropa*. Edited by Theodor Schieder. 3 vols. Groß Denkte, Bonn 1953–196; reprint in 8 vols., München, 1984
101) Franzjoch, Marion. *Die Vertriebenen. Hemmnisse, Antriebskräfte und Wege ihrer Integration in die Bundesrepublik Deutschland*. Berlin, 1987
102) George, Bernard. *Les Russes arrivent. La plus grande migration des temps modernes*. Paris, 1966
103) Grube, Frank, and Gerhard Richter. *Flucht und Vertreibung. Deutschland zwischen 1944 und 1947*. Hamburg, 1980
103a) Helbig, Louis Ferdinand. *Der ungeheure Verlust. Flucht und Verteibung in der deutschsprachigen Belletristik*. Wiesbaden, 1988
104) Krallert-Sattler, Gertrud. *Kommentierte Bibliographie zum Flüchtlings- und Vertriebenenproblem in der Bundesrepublik Deutschland, in Österreich und in der Schweiz*. Abhandlungen zu Flüchtlingsfragen, vol. 20. Munich, 1989
105) Krockow, Christian Graf von. *Die Stunde der Frauen. Bericht aus Pommern 1944 bis 1947*. Stuttgart, 1988
105a) Laqueur, Walter. *Europe in Our Time*. New York, 1992
106) Lehmann, Albrecht. *Im Fremden ungewollt zuhaus. Flüchtlinge und Vertriebene in Westdeutschland 1945–1990*. Munich, 1991
107) Lehndorff, Hans Graf von. *East Prussian Diary. A Journal of Faith, 1945–1947*. London, 1963
108) Lemberg, Eugen, and Friedrich Edding, eds. *Die Vertriebenen in Westdeutschlend. Ihre Eingliederung und ihr Einfluß auf die Gesellschaft, Wirtschaft, Politik und Geistesleben*. Kiel, 1959
109) Meinicke, Wolfgang. "Zur Integration der Umsiedler in die Gesellschaft 1945–1952." *Zeitschrift für Geschichtswissenschaft* 36 (1988): pp. 867–878

110) Mitzka, Herbert. *Zur Geschichte der Massendeportationen von Ostdeutschen in die Sowjetunion im Jahre 1945. Ein historisch-politischer Beitrag*. Einhausen, 1985

111) Nawratil, Heinz. *Die deutschen Nachkriegsverluste unter Vertriebenen, Gefangenen und Verschleppten*. Munich, 1986

112) Nuscheler, Franz. "Historische Einordnung und Forschungsstand, statistische Grundlagen und terminologische Probleme." In *Flüchtlinge und Vertriebene in der Westdeutschen Nachkriegsgeschichte: Bilanzierung der Forschung und Perspektiven für die künftige Forschungsarbeit*, edited by Rainer Schulze et al., pp. 6–23. Hildesheim, 1987

113) Plato, Alexander von, and Wolfgang Meinicke. *Alte Heimat – neue Zeit. Flüchtlinge, Umgesiedelte, Vertriebene in der Sowjetischen Besatzungszone und in der DDR*. Berlin, 1991

114) Proudfoot, M.J. *European Refugees 1939–1952. A Study in Forced Population Movement*. London, 1957

115) Reichling, Gerhard. *Die deutschen Vertriebenen in Zahlen*. Part 1, *Umsiedler, Verschleppte, Vertriebene, Aussiedler 1940–1985*. Bonn, 1986

116) Schulze, Rainer, Doris von der Brelie-Lewien, and Helga Grebing, eds. *Flüchtlinge und Vertriebene in der westdeutschen Nachkriegsgeschichte. Bilanzierung der Forschung und Perspektiven für die künftige Forschungsarbeit*. Veröffentlichungen der Historischen Kommission für Niedersachsen und Bremen, 38: Quellen und Unterlagen zur Geschichte Niedersachsens nach 1945, vol. 4. Hildesheim, 1987

117) Seraphim, Peter-Heinz. *Die Heimatvertriebenen in der Sowjetzone*. Berlin, 1954

118) Statistisches Bundesamt. *Die deutschen Vertreibungsverluste – Bevölkerungsbilanzen dür die deutschen Vertreibungsgebiete 1939/1950*. Wiesbaden, 1958

119) Steinert, Johannes-Dieter. "Die große Flucht und die Jahre danach. Flüchtlinge und Vertriebene in den vier Besatzungszonen." In *Ende des Dritten Reiches – Ende des Zweiten Weltkrieges*, edited by Hans-Erich Volkmann, pp. 557–579. Munich, 1995

119a) Ueberschär, Gerd R. "Die Vertreibung der deutschen Bevölkerung aus dem Osten und die alliierten Grundsätze von der 'besseren Welt'." In *Flucht und Vertreibung: zwischen Aufrechnung und Verdrängung*, edited by Robert Streibel, pp. 21–41. Vienna, 1994

119b) *Vertreibung und Vertreibungsverbrechen 1945–1948. Bericht des Bundesarchivs vom 28. Mai 1974. Archivalien und ausgewählte Erlebnisberichte*. Edited by Kulturstiftung der deutschen Vertriebenen. Bonn, 1989

119c) Zayas, Alfred M. de. *Die Anglo-Amerikaner und die Vertreibung der Deutschen. Vorgeschichte, Verlauf, Folgen*. Munich, 1980

c) The Fate and Eventual Return Home of German Prisoners of War after the End of the War

120) Bährens, Kurt. *Deutsche in Straflagern und Gefängnissen der Sowjetunion*. Zur Geschichte der deutschen Kriegsgefangenen des Zweiten Weltkrieges, vol. V, 1–3. Munich, 1965

121) Bauer, Karl. *Gedächtnisprotokoll. Ein Prozeß in Minsk*. Herford, 1990
122) Benz, Wolfgang, and Angelika Schardt, eds. *Deutsche Kriegsgefangene im Zweiten Weltkrieg. Erinnerungen*. Frankfurt a.M., 1994
123) Berthold, Eva. *Kriegsgefangene im Osten*. Königstein/Taunus, 1981
124) Berthold, Willi. *Parole Heimat. Deutsche Kriegsgefangene in Ost und West*. Bayreuth, 1979
125) Blank, Alexander. *Die deutschen Kriegsgefangenen in der UdSSR*. Cologne, 1979
126) Böhme, Kurt W. *Gesucht wird ... Die dramatische Geschichte des Suchdienstes*. Munich, 1965
127) ____. *Die deutschen Kriegsgefangenen in sowjetischen Hand – eine Bilanz*. Zur Geschichte der deutschen Kriegsgefangenen des Zweiten Weltkrieges, vol. VII. Munich, 1966
128) Cartellieri, Dieter. *Die deutschen Kriegsgefangenen in der Sowjetunion – die Lagergesellschaft*. Munich, 1967
129) Einsiedel, Heinrich Graf von. *Tagebuch der Versuchung (1942–1950)*. Berlin, 1950
130) Fleischhacker, Hedwig. *Die deutschen Kriegsgefangenen in sowjetischer Hand. Der Faktor Hunger*. Zur Geschichte der deutschen Kriegsgefangenen des Zweiten Weltkrieges, vol. III. Munich, 1965
131) Galieckij, Wladimir. "Kriegsgefangene im Arbeitseinsatz." *Moskau News* no. 1 (1993)
132) Gollwitzer, Helmut. *... und führen wohin du nicht willst. Bericht einer Gefangenschaft*. 3rd edn. Gütersloh, 1977
133) Gollwitzer, Helmut, Josef Krahe, and Karl Rauch. *Und bringen ihre Garben. Aus russischer Gefangenschaft*. Stuttgart, 1956
134) Guilini, Udo. *Stalingrad und mein zweites Leben. Begegnungen – Erlebnisse – Eindrücke – Erfahrungen*. Neustadt/Weinstraße, 1978
135) Hasenclever, Wolfgang. "Freilassung und Heimschaffung der Kriegsgefangenen bei Beendigung der Feindseligkeit." Diss., Bonn, 1957
136) Ihme-Tuchel, Beate. "Die Entlassung der deutschen Kriegsgefangenen im Herbst 1955 im Spiegel der Diskussion zwischen SED und KPdSU." *Militärgeschichtliche Mitteilungen* vol. 53, no. 2 (1994): pp. 449–465
137) Karner, Stefan. "POW's in the Economy of the Former Soviet Union." In *International Conference "The System of Centrally Planned Economies in Central-East and South-East Europe after World War II and the Causes of Decay"*, edited by Vaclav Prucha et al. Prague, 1994
138) ____. "Die sowjetische Hauptverwaltung für Kriegsgefangene und Internierte. Ein Zwischenbericht." *Vierteljahrshefte für Zeitgeschichte* 42 (1994): pp. 447–471
139) Keller, Günther. "Kriegsgefangenschaft und Heimkehr. Kriminalität und strafrechtliche Behandlung der Heimkehrer." Diss., Freiburg, 1953
140) Klein, Johannes Kurt. *Stacheldraht, Hunger, Heimweh*. Düsseldorf, 1955
141) Lang, Martin. *Stalins Strafjustiz gegen deutsche Soldaten. Die Massenprozesse gegen deutsche Kriegsgefangene in den Jahren 1949 und 1950 in historischer Sicht*. Herford, 1981
142) Lehmann, Albrecht. *Gefangenschaft und Heimkehr. Deutsche Kriegsgefangene in der Sowjetunion*. Munich, 1986
143) ____. "In sowjetischer Kriegsgefangenschaft." In *Der Krieg des kleinen Mannes. Eine Militärgeschichte von unten*, edited by Wolfram Wette, pp. 295–310. Munich, 1992

144) Levie, Howard. *POWs in International Armed Conflict*. Newport, 1978

145) Lummert, Günther. *Die Strafverfahren gegen Deutsche im Ausland wegen "Kriegsverbrechen"*. Hamburg, 1949

146) Maschke, Erich, ed. *Zur Geschichte der deutschen Kriegsgefangenen des Zweiten Weltkrieges*. 22 vols. Munich, 1962–1974

147) Maschke, Erich, ed. *Die deutschen Kriegsgefangenen des Zweiten Weltkrieges. Eine Zusammenfassung*. Vol. XV of *Zur Geschichte der deutschen Kriegsgefangenen des Zweiten Weltkrieges*. Munich, 1974

148) Maurach, Herbert. *Die Kriegsverbrecherprozesse gegen deutsche Gefangene in der Sowjetunion*. Hamburg, 1950

149) Oglesby, Samuel C. *Communist Treatment of Prisoners of War*. Washington, 1972

150) Ratza, Werner. *Die deutschen Kriegsgefangenen in der Sowjetunion – Der Faktor Arbeit*. Vol. IV of *Zur Geschichte der deutschen Kriegsgefangenen des Zweiten Weltkrieges*, edited by Erich Maschke. Munich, 1973

151) Riesenberger, Dieter, ed. *Das Deutsche Rote Kreuz, Konrad Adenauer und das Kriegsgefangenenproblem. Die Rückführung der deutschen Kriegsgefangenen aus der Sowjetunion (1952–1955)*. Bremen, 1994

152) Robel, Gert. *Die deutschen Kriegsgefangenen in der Sowjetunion – Antifa*. Vol. VIII of *Zur Geschichte der deutschen Kriegsgefangenen des Zweiten Weltkrieges*, edited by Erich Maschke. Munich, 1974

153) Sapp, Franz. *Gefangen in Stalingrad 1943 bis 1946*. Steyr, 1992

154) Schenck, E.G. *Vojna Plenni*, Stockach, 1985

155) Schwarz, Wolfgang. *Die deutschen Kriegsgefangenen in der Sowjetunion. Aus dem kulturellen Leben*. Vol. VI of *Zur Geschichte der deutschen Kriegsgefangenen des Zweiten Weltkrieges*, edited by Erich Maschke. Munich, 1969

156) Smith, Arthur L. *Heimkehr aus dem Zweiten Weltkrieg. Die Entlassung der deutschen Kriegsgefangenen*. Stuttgart, 1985

157) Steinbach, Peter. "Deutsche Kriegsgefangene in der Sowjetunion. Ein Beitrag zur deutsch-sowjetischen Beziehungsgeschichte." *Aus Politik und Zeitgeschichte. Beilage zur Wochenzeitung Das Parlament* B 24/91 (7.6.1991): pp. 37–52

158) _____. "Zur Sozialgeschichte der deutschen Kriegsgefangenen in der Sowjetunion im 2. Weltkrieg und in der Frühgeschichte der BRD. Ein Beitrag zur historischen Kontinuität." *Zeitgeschichte* no. 1 (1989): pp. 1–18

159) Strasser, C. *Im Schatten des Elbrus. Autobiographische Erinnerungen eines Tiroler Bergbauern an seine russische Gefangenschaft*. Cologne, 1987

d) Reparations and Spoils of War

160) Abelshauser, Werner. "Arm, aber nicht unterentwickelt: Eine wirtschaftliche Bilanz der Stunde 'Null'." In *Zusammenbruch oder Befreiung?*, edited by Ulrich Albrecht et al., pp. 84–98. Berlin, 1986

161) Barthel, Horst. *Die wirtschaftlichen Ausgangsbedingungen der DDR. Zur Wirtschaftsentwicklung auf dem Gebiet der DDR 1945–1949/50*. East Berlin, 1979

162) Boelcke, Willi A. "Der wirtschaftliche Wiederaufbau Nachkriegsdeutschlands. Pläne, Konzeptionen, Probleme." In *Ende des Dritten Reiches – Ende des Zweiten Weltkriegs*, edited by Hans-Erich Volkmann, pp. 439–523. München, 1995
163) Bower, Tom. *The Paperclip Conspiracy. The Hunt for Nazi Scientists.* Boston, 1987
164) Deutsches Institut für Wirtschaftsforschung, ed. *Die Deutsche Wirtschaft zwei Jahre nach dem Zusammenbruch.* Berlin, 1947
165) Bundesminister für Vertriebene, Flüchtlinge und Kriegsgeschädigte, ed. *Dokumente deutscher Kriegsschäden.* 5 vols. Bonn, 1958–1964
166) Evgen'ev, V. V. *Mezdunarodno-pravovoe regulirovanie reparacij posle vtoroj mirovoj vojny.* Moscow, 1950
167) Gimbel, John. *Science, Technology, and Reparations. Exploitation and Plunder in Postwar Germany.* Stanford, 1990
168) Goldmann, Klaus, and Günter Wermusch. *Vernichtet, Verschollen, Vermarktet. Kunstschätze im Visier von Politik und Geschäft.* Asendorf, 1992
169) Gröttrup, Irmgard. *Die Besessenen und die Mächtigen. Im Schatten der Roten Rakete.* Stuttgart, 1958
170) Harmssen, Gustav Wilhelm. *Reparationen, Sozialprodukt, Lebensstandard. Versuch einer Wirtschaftsbilanz.* Bremen, 1947
171) Hofmeier, Klaus. *Die Entwicklung der Wirtschaft Mitteldeutschlands im Vergleich zur Bundesrepublik Deutschland.* Cologne-Sülz, 1968
172) Howe jr., Thomas Carr. *Salt Mines and Castles: the Discovery and Restitution of Looted European Art.* New York, 1946
173) Jerchow, Friedrich. *Deutschland in der Weltwirtschaft 1944–1947. Alliierte Deutschland- und Reparationspolitik und die Anfänge der westdeutschen Außenwirtschaft.* Düsseldorf, 1978
174) Karlsch, Rainer. *Allein bezahlt? Die Reparationsleistungen der SBZ/DDR 1945–1953.* Berlin, 1993
175) _____. "Kriegszerstörungen und Reparationslasten." In *Ende des Dritten Reiches – Ende des Zweiten Weltkriegs*, edited by Hans-Erich Volkmann, p. 525–556. Münich, 1995
176) Köhler, H. *Economic Integration in the Soviet Bloc, with an East German Case Study.* New York, 1965
177) Kurtz, Michael J. *Nazi Contraband: American Policy on the Return of the European Cultural Treasures, 1945–1955.* New York, 1985
178) Lasby, Clarence G. *Project Paperclip. German Scientists and the Cold War.* New York, 1971
179) Leptin, Gerd. *Die deutsche Wirtschaft nach 1945. Ein Ost-West-Vergleich.* Opladen, 1970
180) Mai, Gunther. "Die Alliierten und die industrielle Abrüstung Deutschlands 1945–1948." In *Rüstungsbestimmte Geschichte und das Problem der Konversion in Deutschland im 20. Jahrhundert*, edited by Detlev Bald, pp. 68–88. Münster, 1993
181) Matschke, Werner. *Die industrielle Entwicklung in der Sowjetischen Besatzungszone Deutschlands (SBZ) von 1945 bis 1948.* Berlin, 1988
182) Melzer, Manfred. *Anlagevermögen, Produktion und Beschäftigung der Industrie im Gebiet der DDR von 1936 bis 1978 sowie Schätzung des künftigen Angebotspotentials.* East Berlin, 1980

183) Mühlfriedel, Wolfgang. "Zur industriellen Konversion in der sowjetischen Besatzungszone." In *Rüstungsbestimmte Geschichte und das Problem der Konversion in Deutschland im 20. Jahrhundert*, edited by Detlev Bald, pp. 89–100. Münster, 1993

184) Pollard, Robert A. *Economic Security and the Origins of the Cold War, 1945–1950*. New York, 1985

185) Pritzel, Konstantin. *Die wirtschaftliche Integration der Sowjetischen Besatzungszone Deutschlands in den Ostblock und ihre politischen Aspekte*. Bonn, 1965; 2nd edn 1966

186) Ratchford, Benjamin Ulysses, and William D. Ross. *Berlin Reparations Assignment. Round One of the German Peace Settlement*. Chapel Hill, 1947

187) *Die Reparationen der sowjetischen Besatzungszone in den Jahren 1945 bis Ende 1953. Eine Fortführung der Untersuchungen von Franz Rupp*. Edited by Bundesministerium für gesamtdeutsche Fragen. Bonn, 1953

188) Riehl, Nikolaus. *Zehn Jahre im goldenen Käfig. Erlebnisse beim Aufbau der sowjetischen Uran-Industrie*. Stuttgart, 1988

189) Rupp, Franz. *Die Reparationsbelastung der Sowjetischen Besatzungszone*. Bonn, 1951

190) Slusser, Robert, ed. *Soviet Economic Policy in Postwar Germany. A Collection of Papers by Former Soviet Officials*. New York, 1953

191) Vogler, Johannes. *Von der Rüstungsfirma zum volkseigenen Betrieb: Aufzeichnungen eines Unternehmers der sowjetischen Besatzungszone Deutschlands von 1945–1948*. Edited by Burghard Ciesla. Munich, 1992

192) Wellmann, Arend. "Zur Emigration deutscher Wissenschaftler in die UdSSR um und nach 1945." In *Rüstungsbestimmte Geschichte und das Problem der Konversion in Deutschland im 20. Jahrhundert*, edited by Detlev Bald, pp. 101–112. Münster, 1993

193) Winkel, Harald. *Die Wirtschaft im geteilten Deutschland, 1945–1970*. Wiesbaden, 1974

194) Zank, Wolfgang. *Wirtschaft und Arbeit in Ostdeutschland 1945–1949. Probleme des Wiederaufbaus in der sowjetischen Besatzungszone Deutschlands*. Munich, 1987

195) _____. "Wirtschaftsplanung und Bewirtschaftung in der Sowjetischen Besatzungszone – Besonderheiten und Parallelen im Vergleich zum westlichen Besatzungsgebiet, 1945–1949." *Vierteljahrsschrift für Sozial- und Wirtschaftsgeschichte* 71 (1984): pp. 485–504

195a) Akinscha, Konstantin, and Grigori Koslow. *Beutekunst. Auf Schatzsuche in russischen Geheimdepots*. München, 1995

195b) Goldmann, Klaus, and Wolfgang Schneider. *Das Gold des Priamos. Geschichte einer Odyssee*. Leipzig, 1995

195c) Goldmann, Klaus, and Günter Wermusch. *Vernichtet, verschollen, vermarktet. Kunstschätze im Visier von Politik und Geschäft*. Asendorf, 1992

195d) Haase, Günther. *Kunstraub und Kunstschutz. Eine Dokumentation*. Hamburg, 1991

2. Avoiding and Coming to Terms with the Past

a) Eye-witness Accounts, Letters, and Documentary Stories

196) Bucher, Rudolf. *Zwischen Verrat und Menschlichkeit. Erlebnisse eines Schweizer Arztes an der deutsch-russischen Front 1941/42.* 2nd edn. Frauenfeld, 1967

197) Burov, Abram V. *Tvoi Geroi, Leningrad (1941–1944).* Leningrad, 1965; 2nd edn 1970

198) Erickson, John. *Main Front. Soviet Leaders Look back on World War II.* London, 1987

199) Golovchansky, A.V., et al., eds. *"Ich will raus aus diesem Wahnsinn." Deutsche Briefe von der Ostfront 1941–1945.* Foreword by W. Brandt. Wuppertal, 1991; new paperback edn Reinbek, 1993

200) *Govorjat pogibsie geroi. Predsmertnye pisma sovetskich borcov … 1941–1945 gg.* Edited by V.A. Kondrat'ev and Z.N. Politov. Moscow, 1961; 2nd edn 1963; 3rd edn 1966; 6th edn 1979; new edn 1982

201) Hupka, Herbert. *Unruhiges Gewissen. Ein deutscher Lebenslauf. Erinnerungen.* Munich, 1994

201a) John, Antonius. *Begegnungen in Orel. Vom Kriege, dem Rußland-Trauma und der Versöhnung.* Bonn, 1991

202) Kramer, Gerhard. *We Shall March Again.* New York, 1955

203) *Letters from the Dead. Last Letters from Soviet Men and Women Who Died Fighting the Nazis (1941–1945).* Moscow, 1965

204) Mielert, Harry. *Russische Erde. Kriegsbriefe aus Rußland (1941–1943).* Stuttgart, 1950

205) Pabst, Helmut. *Der Ruf der äußersten Grenze. Aufzeichnungen aus dem Kriege Rußland 1941–1943.* New revised edn. Heidenheim, 1987

206) Schwarz, Urs. "Als Schweizer Journalist in Berlin und an der Ostfront." In *1.9.1939. Europäer erinnern sich an den Zweiten Weltkrieg*, edited by Walter Leimgruber, pp. 187–198. Zurich, 1990

207) Werner, Paul. *Ein Schweizer Journalist sieht Rußland. Auf den Spuren der deutschen Armee zwischen San und Dnjepr.* 5th edn. Olten, 1942

207a) Wiesen, Wolfgang, ed. *Es grüßt Euch alle, Bertold. Die Feldpostbriefe von Bertold Paulus aus Kastel.* Nonnweiler-Otzenhausen, 1991

b) Works on Tactical Military Experience of the Soviet-German War

208) Anan'ev, I.M. *Tankovye armii v nastuplenil. Po opytu Velikoj Otecestvennoj vojny 1941–1945 gg.* Moscow, 1988

209) *Bilanz des 2. Weltkrieges.* Oldenburg, 1953

210) Deborin, Grigorij A., and Boris S. Tel'puchovskij. *Itogi i uroki Velikoj Otecestvennoj Vojny.* 2nd edn. Moscow, 1975

211) *Der Durchbruch der Schützenverbände durch eine vorbereitete Verteidigung. Nach Erfahrungen des Großen Vaterländischen Krieges der Sowjetunion 1941–1945.* Berlin, 1959

212) Glantz, David M. "August Storm. Soviet Tactical and Operational Combat in Manchuria, 1945." Combat Studies Institute, Leavenworth Papers, no. 8. Fort Leavenworth, 1983

213) _____. "The Soviet Airborne Experience." Combat Studies Institute, Research Survey, no. 4. Fort Leavenworth, 1984

214) ____. *Soviet Military Operational Art*. London,1991
215) *Russian Combat Methods in World War II*. Department of the Army Pamphlet, no. 20–230. Washington, 1950
216) *German Defense Tactics against Russian Break-throughs*. Department of the Army Pamphlet, no. 20-233. Washington, 1951
217) *Operations of Encircled Forces. German Experiences in Russia*. Department of the Army Pamphlet, no. 20-234. Washington, 1952
218) *Boevye Dejstvija strelkovogo polka. Sbornik boevych primerov*. Moscow, 1958 (German edn: *Gefechtshandlungen der Schützeneinheiten. Eine Sammlung taktischer Beispiele aus dem Großen Vaterländischen Krieg*. East Berlin, 1958)
219) *Boevye Dejstvija strelkovoj roty. Sbornik boevych primerov iz opyta Velikoj Otecestvennoy Vojny*. Moscow, 1957 (German edn: *Gefechtshandlungen der Schützenkompanie. Eine Sammlung taktischer Beispiele aus dem Großen Vaterländischen Krieg*. East Berlin, 1960)
220) *Boevye Dejstvija strelkovogo batal'ona. Sbornik boevych primerov iz Velikoj Otecestvennoj Vojny*.Moscow, 1957 (German edn: *Gefechtshandlungen des Schützenbataillons. Eine Sammlung taktischer Beispiele aus dem Großen Vaterländischen Krieg*. East Berlin, 1961)
221) Gesterding, Joachim. *Probleme der Naht. Eine Studie über die Koordinierung benachbarter Verbände*. Wehrwissenschaftliche Rundschau, Beiheft 10. Berlin, 1959
222) Golubovitsch, V. S., and M.B. Presnjakow. *Kampfhandlungen des Zuges bei Nacht. Eine Sammlung taktischer Beispiele aus dem Großen Vaterländischen Krieg*. Berlin, 1959
223) Guderian, Heinz. "Erfahrungen im Rußlandkrieg." In *Bilanz des 2. Weltkrieges*, pp. 81–98. Oldenburg, 1953
224) ____. "Über die russische Strategie im Kriege." In *Die Rote Armee*, edited by Basil Liddell Hart, Bonn, 1956 (English edn: "Russian Strategy in the War." In *The Soviet Army*, edited by Liddell Hart. London, 1956)
225) Guillaume, Augustin. *Warum siegte die Rote Armee?* Baden-Baden, 1950
226) *Military Improvisations during the Russian Campaign*. Department of the Army Pamphlet no. 20-201. Washington, 1951
227) Kurotchkin, P. A. "Der Sieg der sowjetischen Kriegskunst im Großen Vaterländischen Krieg." In *Die wichtigsten Operationen des Großen Vaterländischen Krieges 1941–1945*, edited by P.A. Shilin, pp. 683–704. East Berlin, 1958
228) Liddell Hart, Basil. *The Soviet Army*. London, 1956 (German edn: *Die Rote Armee*. Bonn, 1956)
229) Middeldorf, Eike. *Taktik im Russlandfeldzug. Erfahrungen und Folgerungen*. Darmstadt, 1956
230) Oberlaender, Theodor. *Der Osten und die Deutsche Wehrmacht. Sechs Denkschriften aus den Jahren 1941–1943 gegen die NS-Kolonialthese*. Asendorf, 1987
231) Radzievskij, Aleksej I. *Taktika v boevych primerach. (Divizija)*. Moscow, 1976
232) ____. *Tankovyj Udar. Tankovaja armija v nastupatel'noj operacii fronta po opytu Velikoj Otecestvennoj vojny*. Moscow, 1977
233) ____. *Armejskie Operacii. (Primery iz opyta Velikoj Otecestvennoy vojny)*. Moscow, 1977

234) ____. *Proryv. (Po opytu Velikoj Otecestvennoj vojny 1941–1945gg.).* Moscow, 1979
235) Shilin, P.A., ed. *Die wichtigsten Operationen des Großen Vaterländischen Krieges 1941–1945*. East Berlin, 1958 (Russian edn: Zilin, P. A., ed. *Vaznejsie Operacii Velikoj Otecestvennoj Vojny 1941–1945 gg. Sbornik statej*. Moscow, 1956)
236) Sokolov, B.V. "O sootnosenii poter' v ljudjach i boevoj technike na sovetskogo-germanskom fronte v chode Velikoj Otecestvennoj vojny." *Voprosy istorii* no. 9 (1988): pp. 116–126
237) *Terrain Factors in the Russian Campaign*. Department of the Army Pamphlet, no. 20-290. Washington, 1951
238) *Der Umschwung im Zweiten Weltkrieg*. Vorlesungen zu den Hauptproblemen der Geschichte des zweiten Weltkrieges, no. 3. East Berlin, 1961
Zilin, P. A. see Shilin. P. A.

c) Literary Accounts of the War in Poetry and Novels

239) Bamm, Peter [Curt Emmrich]. *Die unsichtbare Flagge. Ein Bericht*. 3rd edn. Munich, 1952; 9th edn 1958; new edn.: Frankfurt a.M., 1958 (English edn: *Invisible Flag*. London, 1956)
240) Baron, Ulrich. "Stalingrad als Thema der deutschsprachigen Literatur." In *Stalingrad. Mythos und Wirklichkeit einer Schlacht*, edited by Wolfram Wette and Gerd R. Ueberschär, pp. 226–232. Frankfurt a.M., 1992; 2nd edn 1993
241) Bek, Aleksandr. *La Réserve du Général Panfilov*. Paris, 1963 (German edn: *General Panfilows Reserve*. East Berlin, 1965)
242) Ber, H. W. *Kosaken-Saga. Kampf und Untergang der deutschen Kosaken-Division im Zweiten Weltkrieg*. Rastatt, 1966
243) Berg, Werner. *Der General. Ein Gang in das Gleichnis*. Wuppertal, 1968
244) *Bitva za Dnepr. Stichi, chudozestvennaja proza, publicistika*. Dnepropetrovsk, 1975
245) Bosper, Albert. *Der Hiwi Borchowitsch*. Stuttgart, 1958
246) Braun, Ernst. *Der verlorene Haufe*. Munich, 1988
247) Cakovskij, Aleksandr B. *Eto bylo v Leningrade. Trilogija*. Moscow, 1962
248) ____. *Blokada*. Moscow, 1973 (German edn: *Die Blockade*. 2 vols. Frankfurt a.M., 1975)
249) Clappier, Louis. *Festung Königsberg*. Cologne, 1952
250) Dwinger, Edwin Erich. *Wenn die Dämme brechen ... Untergang Ostpreußens*. Freiburg, 1950
251) ____. *Sie suchten die Freiheit ... Schicksalsweg eines Reitervolkes*. Freiburg, 1952
252) Eisen, Heinrich. *Bahnhof Russkinaja meldet sich nicht ...* . Frankfurt a.M., 1954
253) ____. *Der Schienenwolf*. Darmstadt, 1957
254) Fernau, Joachim. *Bericht von der Furchtbarkeit und Größe der Männer*. Oldenburg, 1954
255) Frank, Claus J. *Der Engel von Kolyma*. Gütersloh, 1970
256) Franken, Bert. *Du Doktor – Du operieren. Roman nach Tatsachen*. Bayreuth, 1976
257) Fromm, Christoph. *Stalingrad. Der Roman*. Munich, 1993

258) Gerlach, Heinrich. *Die verratene Armee. Ein Stalingrad-Roman*. Munich, 1957; new edn Munich, 1962 (English edn: *The Forsaken Army*. New York, 1959)
259) Grazioli, Edwin, and Gerhard Hofmann. *Weißt Du noch, Kamerad? Die Geschichte einer Infanterie-Kompanie im Osten*. Frankfurt a.M., 1952
260) Grossmann, Wassilij. *Stalingrad*. Moscow, 1946
261) ____. *Wende an der Wolga*. 3rd edn. East Berlin, 1959
262) Hassel, Sven. *Général S. S.* Paris, 1970
263) Hauschild, Reinhard. *Plus minus null? Das Buch der Armee, die in Ostpreußen unterging*. Darmstadt, 1952
264) Heubner, Christoph. "'Todesvögel stehen in der Luft' – Die Verarbeitung des Grauens in ausgewählten Texten sowjetischer Literatur." In *Frieden mit der Sowjetunion – eine unerledigte Aufgabe*, edited by Dietrich Goldschmidt et al., pp. 388–401. Gütersloh, 1989
265) Hubalek, Klaus. *Stalingrad. Schauspiel nach dem Roman von Theodor Plivier*. Munich, 1963
266) Imhoff, Christoph von. *Die Festung Sewastopol*. Stuttgart, 1953
267) Kaps, Paul. *Und kannten kein Erbarmen. So fiel Schlesien*. Rastatt, 1965
268) Karschkes, Helmut. *Eiswind aus Kasakstan. Roman um Stalingrad*. Rastatt, 1966
269) Katajew, Valentin. *In den Katakomben von Odessa*. Berlin, 1963
270) Kernmayr, Erich. *Kampf in der Ukraine 1941–1944*. N.p., n.d.
271) Kessler, Leo. *Claws of steel*. London, 1974
272) ____. *Death's Head*. London, 1975
273) Ketlinskaja, Vera K. *V osade*. Leningrad, 1967
274) Kluge, Alexander. *The Battle (Stalingrad 1942/43)*. New York, 1967 (German edn: *Schlachtbeschreibung, [Stalingrad 1942/43]*. Olten, 1964; new edn as: *Der Untergang der Sechsten Armee [Schlachtbeschreibung Stalingrad 1942/43]*. Munich, 1969)
275) Konsalik, Heinz. *Die Rollbahn. Roman einer geopferten Generation*. Bad Wörishofen, 1959
276) Kuehner, Otto H. *Nikolskoje*. Munich, 1954
277) Kuznecov, Anatolij Vasil'evic. *Babij Jar*. Munich, 1970
278) Leckband, Helmut. *Krigsfange. Gennem russiske lejre – Ternopol, Donbas, Stalino*. Copenhagen, 1977
279) Ledig, Gert. *Die Stalinorgel*. Hamburg, 1955
280) Moellenkamp, Werner. *Die letzte Nacht muß man wachen*. Berlin, 1957
281) Monod, Martine. *Normandie-Njemen*. East Berlin, 1962
282) Murr, Stefan. *Die Nacht vor Barbarossa*. Munich, 1986
283) Nekrassov, Viktor. *In den Schützengräben von Stalingrad*. East Berlin, 1961
284) Ostry, Anton. *Sturm in der Polarnacht*. Rastatt, 1966
285) ____. *Rollbahn in die Hölle. Der wandernde Kessel von Tscherkassy-Korsun*. Rastatt, 1967
286) Parth, Wolfgang. *Vorwärts Kameraden, wir müssen zurück*. Munich, 1958
287) Piljusin, Iosif I. *U sten Leningrada. Zapiski soldata*. Moscow, 1965
288) Plievier, Theodor. *Stalingrad*. New York, 1948 (German edn: *Stalingrad*. 6th edn. Berlin, 1946; Überlingen, 1948; Munich, 1958)
289) ____. *Moscow*. Garden City, N.Y., 1954; London, 1956 (German edn: *Moskau*. Munich, 1952)
290) ____. *Berlin*. Munich, 1954

291) Pump, Hans W. *Vor dem großen Schnee*. Hamburg, 1956
292) Reinirkens, Leonhard. *Nach Westen. Erinnerungen über einem Tagebuch*. Karlsruhe, 1948
293) Renner, Rolf Günter. "Hirn und Herz. Stalingrad als Gegenstand ideologischer und literarischer Diskurse." In *Stalingrad. Ereignis. Wirkung. Symbol*, edited by Jürgen Förster, pp. 472–492. Munich, 1992
294) Renteln, Johann Reinhold von. *Tamara*. Hamburg, 1961
295) Rimpau, Cornelia. *Zenit*. Reinbek, 1995
296) Saint-Loup. *Les Hérétiques (Divisions SS "Charlemagne")*. Paris, 1965
297) Saint-Paulien. *La Bataille de Berlin*. Paris, 1958
298) Sceglov, Dmitrij. *Ruf über die Front*. Moscow, 1963
299) Schwarz, Wolfgang. *Die unsichtbare Brücke*. Berlin, 1958
299a) Simonov, Konstantin. *Tage und Nächte*. Roman mit einem Epilog. Berlin, 1947
300) Smeth, Maria de. *Partisanen-Anna. Eine Frau zwischen den Fronten*. Rastatt, 1971
301) Solochov, Michail. *Sie kämpften für die Heimat*. East Berlin, 1960
301a) Solzhenitsyn, Alexander. *Der Archipel Gulag*. 3 vols. Bern, 1973–76
302) Stadnjuk, Ivan. *Krieg*. 2 vols. East Berlin, 1983
303) Steinberg, Werner. *Als die Uhren stehenblieben*. Halle, 1957; 2nd edn Hamburg, 1957
304) Stym, Karl J. *Wir standen schon vor Moskau*. Vienna, 1958
305) Taut, Franz. *Roter Stern am Schwarzen Meer. Vom Kuban zur Krim*. 2nd edn. Rosenheim, 1959
306) _____. *Ohne Panzer – ohne Straßen (Rußland 1941)*. Rosenheim, 1968
307) _____. *Abendmeldung. Roman einer Schlacht im Schatten Stalingrads*. Rosenheim, 1968
306) Thun, Nyota, ed. *Gesichter des Krieges. Der Große Vaterländische Krieg im Spiegel sowjetischer Prosa*. East Berlin, 1970
308) Vrba, Leopold. *Die Schlacht vor Moskau. Roman mit Dokumentation*. Rastatt, 1966
309) Wartenberg, Hermann. *Spähtrupp*. Göttingen, 1954
310) Wolf-Fried. *Tragödie Stalingrad. Drama in 3 Akten*. Basle, 1948
311) Wurm, Franz F. *Der Leutnant und sein General*. Kevelaer, 1955
For further titles of novels, see Part B (especially Stalingrad)

d) Coming to Terms with the Past: Apologias, Reception of Research Results, Struggles over Tradition, and the German "Historikerstreit"

312) Achromeev, S.F. "Vopreki istoriceskoj pravde." *Voenno-istoriceskij Zurnal* no. 4 (1991): pp. 29–35
313) Anderle, Alfred, ed. *Der Sieg der Sowjetunion über den Hitlerfaschismus. Beginn einer neuen Etappe im revolutionären Weltprozeß*. Halle, 1976
313a) Anfilov, Viktor. "Stalin und der 'Große Vaterländische Krieg' – die Diskussion geht weiter," *Osteuropa* 39 (1989): pp. A 451–59
314) Arnold, Sabine R. "Der Gedenkkomplex Wolgograd. Gedanken zum sowjetischen Totenkult." *Geschichtswerkstatt* vol. 16 (1988): pp. 46–51
315) Bach, Dieter, ed. *Kriege enden nicht im Frieden. Ein Arbeitsbuch zum deutschen Überfall auf die Sowjetunion 1941 und die Folgen*. Wuppertal, 1991

316) Backes, Uwe, Eckhard Jesse, und Rainer Zitelmann, eds. *Die Schatten der Vergangenheit. Impulse zur Historisierung des Nationalsozialismus*. Frankfurt a.M., 1990

317) Bartov, Omar. "Historians on the Eastern Front. Andreas Hillgruber and Germany's Tragedy." *Tel Aviver Jahrbuch für deutsche Geschichte* vol. 16 (1987): pp. 325–345

318) Bauriedl, Thea. "Versöhnung mit einem unbekannten Feind? – Über die Funktion von Feindbildern und über die Chancen, sie aufzulösen." In *Frieden mit der Sowjetunion – eine unerledigte Aufgabe*, edited by Dietrich Goldschmidt et al., pp. 344–357. Gütersloh, 1989

319) Becker, Fritz. *Im Kampf um Europa: Stalins Schachzüge gegen Deutschland und den Westen*. Stuttgart, 1991

320) Becker, Sophinette. "Der Umgang der Deutschen in der Bundesrepublik mit Krieg und Verbrechen in der Sowjetunion." In *Frieden mit der Sowjetunion – eine unerledigte Aufgabe*, edited by Dietrich Goldschmidt et al., pp. 358–374. Gütersloh, 1989

321) Benz, Wigbert. *Der Rußlandfeldzug des Dritten Reiches. Ursachen, Ziele, Wirkungen. Zur Bewältigung des Völkermordes unter Berücksichtigung des Geschichtsunterrichts*. Frankfurt a.M., 1986; 2nd edn 1988

322) _____. "NS-Vernichtungskrieg in der UdSSR – Quellen für den Geschichtsunterricht." *Geschichtsdidaktik* no. 4 (1987): pp. 395–400

323) _____. "Zur Rezeption des 'Unternehmens Barbarossa' in Geschichtsbüchern: Fakten und Tendenzen." *Internationale Schulbuchforschung. Zeitschrift des Georg-Eckert-Instituts* vol. 10 (1988): pp. 379–391

324) _____. "Der deutsche Vernichtungskrieg gegen die Sowjetunion in Schulgeschichtsbüchern." In *22. Juni 1941. Der Überfall auf die Sowjetunion*, edited by Hans Schafranek and Robert Streibel, pp. 167–184. Vienna, 1991

325) Benz, Wolfgang. "Verdrängen oder Erinnern? Der Krieg gegen die Sowjetunion im Bewußtsein der Deutschen." In *Erobern und Vernichten. Der Krieg gegen die Sowjetunion 1941–1945. Essays*, edited by Peter Jahn and Reinhard Rürup, pp. 211–230. Berlin, 1991

326) Bettelheim, Peter, and Robert Streibel, eds. *Tabu und Geschichte. Zur Kultur des kollektiven Erinnerns*. Vienna, 1994

327) Bismarck, Klaus von. "Offizier der deutschen Wehrmacht in der Sowjetunion 1941–1945. Begegnungen in der Sowjetunion nach 1945." In *Frieden mit der Sowjetunion – eine unerledigte Aufgabe*, edited by Dietrich Goldschmidt et al., pp. 314–330. Gütersloh, 1989

328) Boltin, E.A. "Der Große Vaterländische Krieg der Sowjetunion gegen den deutschen Faschismus – ein gerechter Volkskrieg zur Verteidigung der sozialistischen Sowjetunion und der gesamten Menschheit." In *Ostlandreiter ohne Chance. Beiträge zur Geschichte des faschistischen Überfalls auf die Sowjetunion*, edited by Gerhart Hass et al., pp. 17–43. East Berlin, 1963

329) Bonwetsch, Bernd. "Was wollte Stalin am 22. Juni 1941? Bemerkungen um "Kurzen Lehrgang" von Viktor Suworow." *Blätter für deutsche und internationale Politik* no. 5 (1989): pp. 687–695

330) _____. "Der 'Große Vaterländische Krieg' und seine Geschichte." In *Die Umwertung der sowjetischen Geschichte*, edited by Dietrich Geyer, pp.

167–188. Geschichte und Gesellschaft. Zeitschrift für Historische Sozialwissenschaft, Sonderheft 14. Göttingen, 1991

330a) ____. "Vom Hitler-Stalin-Pakt zum 'Unternehmen Barbarossa'. Die deutsch-sowjetischen Beziehungen 1939–1941 in der Kontroverse." *Osteuropa* 41 (1991): pp. 562–79

330b) Bordjugov, Gennadij, and V.A. Nevezhin, eds. *Gotovil li Stalin nastupatel'nuju vojnu protiv Gitlera?* Moscow, 1995

Borisov/Sumichin, see: Sumichin

331) Boroznjak, Aleksandr I. "Progressivnye istoriki FRG o probleme 'preodolenija proslogo' v 1945–1949 gg." *Voprosy metodologii istorii i istoriografii* no. 3 (1974): pp. 47–51

332) ____. "22. ijunja 1941 goda: Vzgljad s 'toj' storony." *Otecestvennaja istorija* no. 1 (1994): pp. 148–156

333) Boyse, Robert, ed. *Paths to War. New Essays on the Origins of the Second World War*. London, 1989

334) Brennecke, Gerhard. "Die Ursachen des deutsch-sowjetischen Krieges." In *Die Nürnberger Geschichtsentstellung*, edited by Gerhard Brennecke, pp. 301–325. Tübingen, 1970

335) Danilow, Walerij. "Hat der Generalstab der Roten Armee einen Präventivkrieg gegen Deutschland vorbereitet?" *Österreichische Militärische Zeitschrift* vol. 31, no. 1 (1993): pp. 41–51

336) Diner, Dan, ed. *Ist der Nationalsozialismus Geschichte? Zur Historisierung und Historikerstreit*. Frankfurt a.M., 1987

337) Erler, Gernot, et al. *Geschichtswende? Entsorgungsversuche zur deutschen Vergangenheit*. Freiburg, 1987

338) Evans, Richard J. *Im Schatten Hitlers? Historikerstreit und Vergangenheitsbewältigung in der Bundesrepublik*. Frankfurt a.M., 1991

339) Friedländer, Saul. "Some Reflections on the Historisation of National Socialism." *Tel Aviver Jahrbuch für deutsche Geschichte* vol. 16 (1987): pp. 310–324

340) Füllberg-Stolberg, Claus. *Die Darstellung der UdSSR nach 1945 in Geschichtsbüchern der BRD. Eine empirische Inhaltsanalyse*. Göttingen, 1981

341) Glantz, David M., and Jonathan House. *When Titans Clashed: How the Red Army Stopped Hitler*. Lawrence, Kan., 1995

342) Gorodetsky, Gabriel. "Was Stalin Planning to Attack Hitler in June 1941?" *Rusi. Journal of the Royal United Services Institute for Defence Studies* vol. 131, no. 2 (1986): pp. 69–72

343) ____. "Stalin und Hitlers Angriff auf die Sowjetunion. Eine Auseinandersetzung mit der Legende vom deutschen Präventivschlag." *Vierteljahrshefte zur Zeitgeschichte* vol. 37 (1989): pp. 645–672

344) Greschat, Martin. "Schulderklärungen der Kirchen nach dem Kriege." In *Frieden mit der Sowjetunion – eine unerledigte Aufgabe*, edited by Dietrich Goldschmidt et al., pp. 263–279. Gütersloh, 1989

345) Habermas, Jürgen. *Eine Art Schadensabwicklung*. Frankfurt a.M., 1987

346) Hass, Gerhart, ed. *Ostlandreiter ohne Chance. Beiträge zur Geschichte des faschistischen Überfalls auf die Sowjetunion*. Berlin, 1963

347) ____. "Die sowjetische Geschichtsschreibung über den Großen Vaterländischen Krieg." *Militärgeschichte* vol. 21, no. 3 (1982): pp. 351–363

348) ____. "Der deutsch-sowjetische Krieg 1941–1945. Zu einigen Legenden über seine Vorgeschichte und den Verlauf der ersten Kriegswochen." *Zeitschrift für Geschichtswissenschaft* vol. 39, no. 7 (1991): pp. 647–662

349) Helmdach, Erich. *Überfall? Der sowjetisch-deutsche Aufmarsch 1941*. Neckargmünd, 1975; 7th edn Berg am See, 1983

350) ____. *Täuschungen und Versäumnisse. Kriegsausbruch 1939/1941*. Berg am See, 1979

351) Heydorn, Volker D. *Der sowjetische Aufmarsch im Bialystoker Balkon bis zum 22. Juni 1941 und der Kessel von Wolkowysk*. Munich, 1989

352) Hillgruber, Andreas. "Der historische Ort des Unternehmens 'Barbarossa'." In *Hitlers Strategie*, by Andreas Hillgruber, pp. 564–580. Frankfurt a.M., 1965

353) ____. "Noch einmal: Hitlers Wendung gegen die Sowjetunion 1940." *Geschichte in Wissenschaft und Unterricht* vol. 33 (1982): pp. 214–226

354) Hillgruber, Andreas, and Hans-Adolf Jacobsen. "Der Zweite Weltkrieg im Spiegel der sowjetkommunistischen Geschichtsschreibung (1945–1961)." In *Die sowjetische Geschichte des Großen Vaterländischen Krieges 1941–1945*, edited by Boris S. Telpuchovskij, pp. 13E–94E. Frankfurt a.M., 1961

355) *"Historikerstreit". Die Dokumentation der Kontroverse um die Einzigartigkeit der nationalsozialistischen Judenvernichtung*. Munich, 1987

356) Hoffmann, Joachim. "Die Angriffsvorbereitungen der Sowjetunion 1941." In *Zwei Wege nach Moskau. Vom Hitler-Stalin-Pakt bis zum "Unternehmen Barbarossa"*, edited by Bernd Wegner, pp. 367–388. Munich, 1991

357) Hoffmann, Joachim. *Stalins Vernichtungskrieg 1941–1945*. Munich, 1995

358) Jepischev, Alexej A. "Der welthistorische Sieg der Sowjetarmee von 1945 und seine Bedeutung für die patriotische und internationalistische Erziehung der Armeeangehörigen." *Militärgeschichte* no. 1 (1976): pp. 16–27

359) Kim, M.P., et al., eds. *Istoriografija Velikoj Otecestvennoj vojny. Sbornik statej*. Moscow, 1980

360) Kljuev, Sergej V. *Mify i pravda. Kritika burzuaznych izmyslenij o pricinach ekonom. Pobedy SSSR* ... Leningrad, 1969

361) Klüver, Max. *Präventivschlag 1941. Zur Vorgeschichte des Rußlandfeldzuges*. Leoni/Starnberger See, 1986

362) Knab, Jakob. *Falsche Glorie. Das Traditonsverständnis der Bundeswehr*. Berlin, 1995

363) Kohl, Paul. "'Warum haben sie das getan?' – Auf der Spur der Heeresgruppe Mitte. Sowjetische Augenzeugen berichten." In *Frieden mit der Sowjetunion – eine unerledigte Aufgabe*, edited by Dietrich Goldschmidt et al., pp. 375–387. Gütersloh, 1989

364) Kondakova, Nina I. *Ideologiceskaja Pobeda nad fasizmom 1941–1945 gg*. Moscow, 1982

365) Kopelev, Lev Z. *Chranit' vecno*. Memoirs in 3 vols, vol. 2. Ann Arbor, Mich., 1975 (German edn: *Aufbewahren für alle Zeit!* Hamburg, 1976; new Russian edn: Moscow, 1990)

366) Kovalevskij, Dmitrij Ivanovic. *Velikaja Otecestvennaja Vojna Sovetskogo Sojuza 1941–1945*. Moscow, 1959

367) Kozlov, N., and A. Zajcev. *Nas partija k pobede priveela*. Moscow, 1970

367a) Krivoseev, G.F., et al. *Grif sekretnosti snjat. Poterí vooruvennich sil SSSR v Voinach, boevich deistvijach i voennich konfliktach. Statistitcheskoje issledovanje*. Moscow, 1993

367b) Krochmaljuk, V.G. "Velikaje Otecestvennaja ... " *Voenno-Istoriceskij Zurnal* 9 (1988): pp. 9–17

368) Kühnl, Reinhard, ed. *Streit ums Geschichtsbild. Die "Historiker-Debatte". Darstellung, Dokumentation, Kritik*. Cologne, 1987

369) Kumayev, Georgij. "Some Issues in Soviet Historiography concerning World War II." *Yad Vashem Studies* vol. 11 (1991): pp. 251–262

370) Lucas-Busemann, Erhard. *So fielen Königsberg und Breslau. Nachdenken über eine Katastrophe ein halbes Jahrhundert danach*. Berlin, 1994

371) Magenheimer, Heinz. "Neue Erkenntnisse zum 'Unternehmen Barbarossa'." *Österreichische Militärische Zeitschrift* vol. 29, no. 5 (1991): pp. 441–445

371a) _____. *Kriegswenden in Europa 1939–1945. Führungsentschlüsse, Hintergründe, Alternativen*. Munich, 1995

372) _____. "Zum deutsch-sowjetischen Krieg 1941. Neue Quellen und Erkenntnisse." *Österreichische Militärische Zeitschrift* vol. 32, no. 1 (1994): pp. 51–60

372a) Malanowski, Wolfgang. "Rücken an Rücken oder Brust an Brust?" *Der Spiegel* (6.3.1989): pp. 148–164

373) Maser, Werner. *Der Wortbruch. Hitler, Stalin und der Zweite Weltkrieg*. Munich, 1994

374) Meier, Christian. *Vierzig Jahre nach Auschwitz. Deutsche Geschichtserinnerung heute*. Munich, 1987

375) Medwedew, Roy. *Let History Judge. The Origins and Consequences of Stalinism*. New York, 1989 (German edn: *Das Urteil der Geschichte. Stalin und Stalinismus*. Edited by Helmut Ettinger. 3 vols. Berlin, 1992)

376) Mercalov, Andrej N. "Der 22. Juni 1941: Anmerkungen eines sowjetischen Historikers." *Aus Politik und Zeitgeschichte. Beilage zur Wochenzeitung Das Parlament* no. 24/1991 (7.6.1991): pp. 25–36

377) Messerschmidt, Manfred. "Der Kampf der Wehrmacht im Osten als Traditionsproblem." In *"Unternehmen Barbarossa". Der deutsche Überfall auf die Sowjetunion 1941. Berichte, Analysen, Dokumente*, edited by Gerd R. Ueberschär and Wolfram Wette, pp. 253–263. Paderborn, 1984; new edn: *Der deutsche Überfall auf die Sowjetunion. "Unternehmen Barbarossa" 1941*, pp. 225–237. Frankfurt a.M., 1991

378) _____. "June 1941 Seen through German Memoirs and Diaries." In *Operation Barbarossa. The German Attack on the Soviet Union, June 22, 1941*, edited by Norman Naimark et al. Salt Lake City, Utah, 1991. Special issue of *Soviet Union* vol. 18, nos. 1–3 (1991): pp. 205–219

378a) Meyer, Klaus, and Wolfgang Wippermann, eds. *Gegen das Vergessen. Der Vernichtungskrieg gegen die Sowjetunion 1941–1945*. Frankfurt a.M., 1992

379) Nekritsch, Aleksandr. "The Dynamism of the Past." In *Operation Barbarossa. The German Attack on the Soviet Union, June 22, 1941*, edited by Norman Naimark et al. Salt Lake City, Utah, 1991. Special Issue of *Soviet Union* vol. 18, nos. 1–3 (1991): pp. 221–235

380) Nolte, Ernst. *Der europäische Bürgerkrieg 1917–1945. Nationalsozialismus und Bolschewismus*. Frankfurt a.M., 1987
381) ____. *Das Vergehen der Vergangenheit. Antworten an meine Kritiker im sogenannten Historikerstreit*. Berlin, 1987
382) ____. *Streitpunkte. Heutige und künftige Kontroversen um den Nationalsozialismus*. Berlin, 1993
383) Nolte, Hans-Heinrich. *Deutsche Geschichte im sowjetischen Schulbuch*. Göttingen, 1972
384) Pavlenko, N.G. "Die entscheidende Rolle der Sowjetunion und ihrer Streitkräfte bei der Zerschlagung des deutschen Imperialismus." *Der deutsche Imperialismus und der Zweite Weltkrieg*, pp. 111–144. East Berlin, 1960
385) Pflüger, Friedbert. *Deutschland driftet. Die Konservative Revolution entdeckt ihre Kinder*. Düsseldorf, 1994
386) Pietrow-Ennker, Bianca. "Deutschland im Juni 1941 – ein Opfer sowjetischer Aggression? Zur Kontroverse über die Präventivkriegsthese." *Geschichte und Gesellschaft* vol. 14 (1988): pp. 116–135
386a) Post, Walter. *Unternehmen Barbarossa. Deutsche und sowjetische Angriffspläne 1940/41*. Hamburg, 1995; 2nd edn 1996
386b) Reichel, Peter. *Politik mit der Erinnerung. Gedächtnisorte im Streit um die nationalsozialistische Vergangenheit*. Munich, 1995
387) Rjabov, Vasilij S. *Velikij Podvig. Popularnyj ocerk o velikoj Otecestvennoj vojne*. Moscow, 1970; 2nd edn 1975
388) Robertson, Esmondo M. "Hitler Turns from the West to Russia." In *Paths to War. New Essays on the Origin of the Second World War*, edited by Robert Boyse, pp. 367–382. London 1989
389) Rürup, Reinhard, ed. *Der Krieg gegen die Sowjetunion 1941–1945. Eine Dokumentation*. Exhibition catalogue. Berlin, 1991
390) Samsonov, A. *Pages from the History of the Antifascist War*. Problems of the contemporary world, 58. Moscow, 1978
391) Savel'ev, Vasilij M., *KPSS – vdochnovitel' i organizator pobedy sovetskogo naroda v Velikoj Otecestvennoj vojne (ijun 1941–1945 gg.)*. Moscow, 1973
391a) Savuskin, R.A. "Kakim budet desjatitomnik?" *Voenno-Istoriceskij Zurnal* 10 (1988): pp. 71–74
392) Schäfer, Gert. "Die Bedeutung des deutschen Überfalls für die sowjetische Gesellschaft." In *Der Mensch gegen den Menschen. Überlegungen und Forschungen zum deutschen Überfall auf die Sowjetunion 1941*, edited by Hans-Heinrich Nolte, pp. 192–205. Hanover, 1992
393) Schapirov, Akram. *War Heroes. Stories about the Heroism of Soviet Soldiers 1941–1945*. Moscow, 1984
394) "Das Scheitern der Blitzkriegsstrategie des faschistischen deutschen Generalstabes beim Überfall auf die Sowjetunion." In *Der Umschwung im Zweiten Weltkrieg*, edited by Institut für deutsche Militärgeschichte, pp. 5–40. East Berlin, 1961
395) Schmidt, Rainer F. "Eine verfehlte Strategie für alle Fälle. Stalins Taktik und Kalkül im Vorfeld des Unternehmens 'Barbarossa'." *Geschichte in Wissenschaft und Unterricht* vol. 45 (1994): pp. 368–379
396) Schneider, Michael. *Das "Unternehmen Barbarossa". Die verdrängte Erblast für das deutsch-sowjetische Verhältnis*. Frankfurt a.M., 1989

397) ____. "Leningrad und die verdrängte Erblast von 1941." In *Blockade. Leningrad 1941–1944. Dokumente und Essays von Russen und Deutschen*, editorial by Antje Leetz and Barbara Wenner, pp. 218–225. Reinbek, 1992

398) Schreiber, Gerhard. "Zur Perzeption des Unternehmens 'Barbarossa' in der deutschen Presse." In *"Unternehmen Barbarossa". Der deutsche Überfall auf die Sowjetunion 1941*, edited by Gerd R. Ueberschär and Wolfram Wette, pp. 27–42. Paderborn, 1984

399) Schustereit, Hartmut. *Vabanque: Hitlers Angriff auf die Sowjetunion 1941 als Versuch durch den Sieg im Osten den Westen zu bezwingen*. Herford, 1988

400) Segbers, Klaus. "Die Folgen des Krieges: Die Sowjetunion seit 1945." In *Erobern und Vernichten. Der Krieg gegen die Sowjetunion 1941–1945. Essays*, edited by Peter Jahn and Reinhard Rürup, pp. 231–248. Berlin, 1991

401) Semjowa, A., et al., eds. *Der große Vaterländische Krieg des Sowjetvolkes und die Gegenwart*. Moscow, 1985

402) Stegemann, Bernd. "Der Entschluß zum Unternehmen Barbarossa. Strategie oder Ideologie?" *Geschichte in Wissenschaft und Unterricht* vol. 33 (1982): pp. 205–213

403) ____. "Geschichte und Politik. Zur Diskussion über den deutschen Angriff auf die Sowjetunion 1941." *Beiträge zur Konfliktforschung* vol. 17, no. 1 (1987): pp. 73–97

404) Streit, Christian. "Es geschah Schlimmeres, als wir wissen wollen. Der Fall Barbarossa." *Blätter für deutsche und internationale Politik* vol. 32, no. 10 (1987): pp. 1287–1300

405) Suworow, Victor. "Who Was Planning to Attack Whom in June 1941, Hitler or Stalin?" *Rusi. Journal of the Royal United Services Institute for Defence Studies* vol. 130, no. 2 (1985): pp. 50–55

406) ____. "Yes, Stalin Was Planning to Attack Hitler in June 1941." *Rusi. Journal of the Royal United Services Institute for Defence Studies* vol. 131 (1986): pp. 73ff

407) ____. *Ledokol. Istorija tak nazyvaemoj "Velikoj Otecestvennoj vojny". Kratkij kurs*. Paris, 1989 (German edn: *Der Eisbrecher. Hitler in Stalins Kalkül*. Stuttgart, 1989; English edn: *Icebreaker. Who Started the Second World War?* London, 1990

407a) ____. *Der Tag M*. Stuttgart, 1995

408) Sumichin, Viktor S., and Nikolaj V. Borisov. *Nemerknuscij Podvig. Geroizim sovetskich voinov v gody Velikoj Otecestvennoj vojny*. Moscow, 1985

409) Tel'puchovskij, Boris S. *Velikaja Otecestvennaja Vojna Sovetskogo Sojuza (1941–1945). Lekcii, procitannye na Istoriceskom fakul'tete Moskovskogo universiteta*. Moscow, 1952

410) Topitsch, Ernst. *Stalin's War. A Radical New Theory of the Origins of the Second World War*. New York, 1987 (German edn: *Stalins Krieg. Die sowjetische Langzeitstrategie gegen den Westen als rationale Machtpolitik*. Munich, 1985; new edn: *Stalins Krieg. Moskaus Griff nach der Weltherrschaft – Strategie und Scheitern*. Herford, 1993)

411) Tumarkin, Nina. "The Invasion and War as Myth and Memory." In *Operation Barbarossa: The German Attack on the Soviet Union, June*

22, 1941, edited by Norman Naimark et al. Salt Lake City, Utah, 1991. Special issue of *Soviet Union* vol. 18, nos. 1–3 (1991): pp. 277–296

412) Ueberschär, Gerd R. "Zur Wiederbelebung der 'Präventivkriegsthese'. Die neuen Rechtfertigungsversuche des deutschen Überfalls auf die UdSSR 1941 im Dienste 'psycho-politischer Aspekte' und 'psychologischer Kriegführung'." *Geschichtsdidaktik* vol. 12, no. 4 (1987): pp. 331–342

413) ____. "'Historikerstreit' und 'Präventivkriegsthese'. Zu den Rechtfertigungsversuchen des deutschen Überfalls auf die Sowjetunion 1941." *Tribüne. Zeitschrift zum Verständnis des Judentums* vol. 26, no. 103 (1987): pp. 108–116

414) ____. "Hitler's Decision to Attack the Soviet Union in Recent German Historiography." In *Operation Barbarossa. The German Attack on the Soviet Union, June 22, 1941*. Salt Lake City, Utah, 1991. Special Issue of *Soviet Union*, vol. 18, nos. 1–3 (1991): pp. 297–315

415) ____. "Das 'Unternehmen Barbarossa' gegen die Sowjetunion – ein Präventivkrieg? Zur Wiederbelebung der alten Rechtfertigungsversuche des deutschen Überfalls auf die UdSSR 1941." In *Wahrheit und "Auschwitzlüge". Zur Bekämpfung "revisionistischer" Propaganda*, edited by Brigitte Bailer-Galanda, Wolfgang Benz and Wolfgang Neugebauer, pp. 163–192. Vienna, 1995

416) Volkmann, Hans-Erich, ed. *Ende des Dritten Reiches – Ende des Zweiten Weltkriegs. Eine perspektivische Rückschau*. Munich, 1995

417) Voslensky, Michael S. *Das Geheime wird offenbar. Moskauer Archive erzählen 1917–1991*. Munich, 1995

418) Weizsäcker, Richard von. *Zum 40. Jahrestag der Beendigung des Krieges in Europa und der nationalsozialistischen Gewaltherrschaft*. Bonn, 1985

419) Wette, Wolfram. "Über die Wiederbelebung des Antibolschewismus mit historischen Mitteln. Oder: Was steckt hinter der Präventivkriegsthese." In *Geschichtswende?*, edited by Gernot Erler et al., pp. 86–115. Freiburg, 1987

420) Wolkogonow, Dimitri. *Stalin. Triumph und Tragödie. Ein politisches Porträt*. Düsseldorf, 1989

421) Zjuzyn, E.J. "Gotovil li SSSR preventivnyj udar?" *Voenno-Istoriceskij Zurnal* no. 1 (1992): pp. 7–29

422) Zukertort, Johannes. "Der deutsche Militarismus und die Legende vom Präventivkrieg Hitlerdeutschlands gegen die Sowjetunion." In *Der deutsche Imperialismus und der Zweite Weltkrieg*, vol. 1, pp. 145–154. East Berlin, 1960

CONCLUSION

From Historical Memories to "Bridges of Understanding" and Reconciliation

The importance of seeking reconciliation and building "bridges of understanding", despite the past, was pointed out in a number of works by Wigbert Benz and essays published by the Protestant Churches of Germany in 1986–87. It is crucial to discuss war in general and the war with the Soviet Union in particular in order to eliminate the widespread anti-Soviet and anti-Russian feeling that has existed in Germany for many years and to educate with proper teaching materials in a spirit of "peace and international friendship" (Nos. 3, 10, 13, E/321–24). This important task is best served by providing accurate information about Hitler's preparations for war and about the war of annihilation waged in the East, as well as about its ideological and social roots, especially as large segments of the German elites became involved. The demand for the truth must be satisfied by both sides in the war in order for reconciliation to be possible (No. 16). In a promising development, Russian historians are making a great effort to read and digest Western research quickly and to analyze sources on the Second World War that are now available in many central and regional archives, as can be seen in the undertaking of the international conference on the fiftieth anniversary of the Battle of Stalingrad held in early March 1993 in Volgograd, in the reception of this congress, and in the recent research of Aleksandr Boroznjak (Nos. 21, E/331, E/332).

The Protestant Churches also highly recommended studies of the "repressed history of the guilt of the German people *vis-à-vis* the peoples of the Soviet Union" in their deliberations prior to the publication of their new "Eastern Memoir of the Protestant Churches in Germany" (Nos. 2, 10, 13). This publication pointed out that the "Eastern Memoir" published by the churches in 1965 openly discussed the historic guilt of the German people for the suffering inflicted upon Poland and other eastern European countries and again openly admitted the fact that the war against the Soviet Union was "planned and carried out as a war of aggression and total annihilation" (Nos. 8, 13).

The signing of the Soviet-German treaty in Moscow on 12 August 1970 gave a strong new impetus to the attempts at reconciliation that were already under way. Pursuant to the signing of this treaty, numerous "Societies for the Encouragement of Relations between the Federal Republic of Germany and the Soviet Union" sprung up in the old Federal Republic, and many cities established partnerships with Soviet cities to contribute to creating a friendly basis for bilateral relations between the two peoples. Several personal accounts and reports have been published about recent meetings of Germans and Russians, including, among other things, joint "trips into the past" of the war years. These initiatives have shown, especially since the 1980s, that it is possible for Germans and Russians to meet in friendly reconciliation without having to suppress – as earlier – the dreadful experiences of the eastern war (Nos. 1, 4, 7, 12, 14, 19).

In the end, the Protestant Churches of Germany did not publish a "second eastern memoir" because most of their leading bodies were opposed in 1987, largely on political grounds. However, sixteen theses of the Protestant Churches of the Rhineland in 1988 (No. 2) and the memorandum "Peace with the Soviet Union – an Unfulfilled Task," which was published in 1989 as part of a voluminous Soviet-German omnibus volume, portrayed reconciliation as a key feature of future Russo-German relations. The latter, a splendid large handbook on the historical and political impediments to "peace with the Soviet Union" and conditions for it, was received with great interest and considerable sympathy. Thirty-seven German and Russian specialists contributed to the work, which was edited by Dietrich Goldschmidt. The authors clearly state: "Without an admission of guilt and hope for reconciliation, responsibility for maintaining the peace cannot be credibly undertaken. A new chapter in the relationship of Germans with the Soviet Union requires three things: the courage to illuminate the past, an unprejudiced study of the political and ideological conflicts of the present, and a willingness to work together on the shared tasks of the future" (No. 8).

Although the ideological conflicts mentioned here have now largely evaporated, as a result of the political transformation of the Soviet Union and its dissolution, the remaining recommendations are as valid now as they were when the work was published. Dieter Bach's *Kriege enden nicht in Frieden*, published in 1990, and Jörg Calließ's omnibus volume *Erinnerungs- und Gedenkstättenarbeit* both emphasize reconciliation as the foundation of the joint measures they recommend for the historical education of students and the general public and the basis of a commitment to peace to be sown "in the hearts and minds" of both peoples (Nos. 5, E/315). The task of furthering reconciliation has not become easier in the last five years, since the reestablishment of German unity and the dissolution of the USSR as a state have apparently produced a new winner and loser in the postwar development. This is also shown in the omnibus volume *Deutsch-russische Zeitenwende*, edited in ambitious teamwork in 1995 (No. 11). It deals with German-Russian relations from 1941 to 1995. Incomprehensibly, the role (and significance) of the *Nationalkomitee Freies Deutschland* (NKFD, National Committee for Free Germany) founded in Moscow and the *Bund Deutscher Offiziere* (Union of German Officers) from 1943 to 1945 is omitted in this book. Is this to remain unexplored territory in the two countries' efforts to come to terms with the past? We hope not, because, as examples of the particular relations between Germany and the Soviet Union during the Second World War, they deserve careful analysis.

The peoples of the former Soviet Union who experienced the eastern war are now going through enormous political changes – for instance, in the Baltic countries, White Russia, Ukraine, the states of the Caucasus, and the Russian Federation. It is difficult to foresee the extent to which their historians and teachers of history will emphasize this commitment to peace and reconciliation as a key element in relations with Germany over the next few years (Nos. 6, 20), especially as economic problems and internal political difficulties are of much more immediate concern. Their historians have enormous quantities of material to digest, including the Soviet-German war of 1941 to 1945.

BIBLIOGRAPHY

1) Aslanow, A. *Von der Wolga an die Ruhr. Begegnungen mit Deutschen in Krieg und Frieden.* Cologne, 1987

2) Bach, Dieter, ed. *Erinnern und Versöhnen. Die Sowjetunion als Thema in der Gemeinde, Gruppe, Schule.* Mülheim/Ruhr, 1988

3) Benz, Wigbert. "NS-Völkermord in der UdSSR und Friedenserziehung im Geschichtsunterricht." *Karlsruher pädagogische Beiträge* vol. 7, no. 13/14 (1986): pp. 57–69

4) Böll, Heinrich, and Lew Kopelew. *Warum haben wir aufeinander geschossen?* Bornheim-Merten, 1981

5) Calließ, Jörg, ed. *Die Verbrechen des Krieges erinnern. Erinnerungs- und Gedenkstättenarbeit für Versöhnung und Frieden.* Loccum, 1990

6) Davies, Robert W. *Soviet History in the Gorbachev Revolution.* Bloomington, Ind., 1989 (German edn: *Perestroika und Geschichte. Die Wende in der sowjetischen Historiographie.* Münich, 1991)

7) Fish, Rady, and Michael Schneider. *Iwan der Deutsche. Eine deutsch-sowjetische Reise aus der Vergangenheit in die Gegenwart.* Frankfurt a.M., 1989

8) Goldschmidt, Dietrich, et al., eds. *Frieden mit der Sowjetunion – eine unerledigte Aufgabe.* Gütersloh, 1989

9) Henke, Klaus-Dietmar, and Hans Woller, eds. *Politische Säuberung in Europa. Die Abrechnung mit Faschismus und Kollaboration nach dem Zweiten Weltkrieg.* Munich, 1991

10) Homeyer, Burkhard, Elisabeth Raiser, and Hartmut Lenhard, eds. *Brücken der Verständigung. Für ein neues Verhältnis zur Sowjetunion.* Gütersloh, 1986

11) Jacobsen, Hans-Adolf, et al., eds. *Deutsch-russische Zeitenwende. Krieg und Frieden 1941–1995.* Baden-Baden, 1995

11a) Kruse, Martin, ed. *Die Stalingrad-Madonna. Das Werk Kurt Reubers als Dokument der Versöhnung.* Hanover, 1992

12) Lahme, Walter. *Die Weisung zum Frieden.* Percha, 1982

13) Lenhard, Hartmut, ed. *Versöhnung und Frieden mit den Völkern der Sowjetunion. Herausforderungen zur Umkehr*. Gütersloh, 1987

14) ____. *Unterwegs nach Minsk. Spuren suchen – Menschen begegnen – Brücken bauen*. With contributions by Klaus von Bismarck, Friedrich Bohla, Rudi Damme, and Elisabeth Raiser. Gütersloh, 1989

15) Lilienfeld, Fairy von. "Versöhnung aus der Sicht der Kirchen in der Sowjetunion." In *Frieden mit der Sowjetunion – eine unerledigte Aufgabe*, edited by Dietrich Goldschmidt et al., pp. 301–312. Gütersloh, 1989

16) Meyer, Gert, ed. *Wir brauchen die Wahrheit. Geschichtsdiskussion in der Sowjetunion*. Cologne, 1989

17) Nolte, Hans-Heinrich, ed. *Der Mensch gegen den Menschen.Überlegungen und Forschungen zum deutschen Überfall auf die Sowjetunion 1941*. Hanover, 1992

18) Portugalow, Nikolai. "Versöhnung mit den Völkern der Sowjetunion." In *Frieden mit der Sowjetunion – eine unerledigte Aufgabe*, edited by Dietrich Goldschmidt et al., pp. 402–481. Gütersloh, 1989

19) Raffert, Joachim. "Erfahrungen bei Begegnungen in der Sowjetunion. Rückblick und Ausblick nach einem halben Jahrhundert." In *Der Mensch gegen den Menschen. Überlegungen und Forschungen zum deutschen Überfall auf die Sowjetunion 1941*, edited by Hans-Heinrich Nolte, pp. 227–236. Hanover, 1992,

20) Semirjaga, Michail. "Der Große Vaterländische Krieg im Bewußtsein des Sowjetvolkes in der Zeit von Perestrojka und Glasnost." In *1.9.39. Europäer erinnern sich an den Zweiten Weltkrieg*, edited by Walter Leimgruber, pp. 171–186. Zurich, 1990

20a) Sorge, M.K. *The Other Price of Hitler's War. German Military and Civilian Losses Resulting from World War II*. New York, 1986

21) "Stalingrad: Erinnerung und Identitätssuche." *Sozialwissenschaftliche Informationen* no. 1 (1993)

22) Tödt, Heinz Eduard. "Gefangenschaftserfahrungen und Versöhnungsbereitschaft." In *Frieden mit der Sowjetunion – eine unerledigte Aufgabe*, edited by Dietrich Goldschmidt et al., pp. 331–343. Gütersloh, 1989

23) *40. Jahrestag des Überfalls auf die Sowjetunion – Der Krieg trifft jeden ins Herz!* Berlin, 1981